PREACHING GOD'S TRANSFORMING JUSTICE

Also available in this series

Preaching God's Transforming Justice: A Lectionary Commentary, Year B

PREACHING GOD'S TRANSFORMING JUSTICE

A Lectionary Commentary, Year C

Edited by
Ronald J. Allen
Dale P. Andrews
Dawn Ottoni-Wilhelm

WJK WESTMINSTER JOHN KNOX PRESS LOUISVILLE • KENTUCKY

© 2012 Westminster John Knox Press

First edition
Published by Westminster John Knox Press
Louisville, Kentucky

12 13 14 15 16 17 18 19 20 21—10 9 8 7 6 5 4 3 2 1

Scripture quotations from the New Revised Standard Version of the Bible are copyright © 1989 by the Division of Christian Education of the National Council of the Churches of Christ in the U.S.A. and are used by permission.

Book design by Sharon Adams
Cover design by Eric Walljasper, Minneapolis, MN
Cover artwork by Yisehak F-Sellassie titled Spirit Being, *www.yisehakfinearts.com*

Library of Congress Cataloging-in-Publication Data

Preaching God's transforming justice : a lectionary commentary, year C / edited by Ronald J. Allen, Dale P. Andrews, Dawn Ottoni-Wilhelm. — 1st ed.
    p. cm.
  Includes index.
  ISBN 978-0-664-23455-3 (alk. paper)
  1. Social justice--Sermons. 2. Social justice--Biblical teaching. 3. Church year sermons. 4. Common lectionary (1992). Year C. I. Allen, Ronald J. (Ronald James), 1949– II. Andrews, Dale P., 1961– III. Wilhelm, Dawn Ottoni.
  BS680.J8P742 2012
  251'.6—dc23

2012010948

PRINTED IN THE UNITED STATES OF AMERICA

♾ The paper used in this publication meets the minimum requirements of the American National Standard for Information Sciences—Permanence of Paper for Printed Library Materials, ANSI Z39.48–1992.

Westminster John Knox Press advocates the responsible use of our natural resources. The text paper of this book is made from 30 percent postconsumer waste.

Most Westminster John Knox Press books are available at special quantity discounts when purchased in bulk by corporations, organizations, and special-interest groups. For more information, please e-mail SpecialSales@wjkbooks.com.

Contents

Note: Readings from the Revised Common Lectionary, Year C, are in regular type; Holy Days for Justice are in boldface.

Preface

The editors are grateful to the members of our households—spouses and children—not only for love and understanding during the preparation of these volumes but also for conversation, child care, and running to the store for necessary supplies of chocolate, coffee, and other things important to editorial work. We recognize our presidents, deans, and colleagues for encouragement, questions, and suggestions. The editors particularly thank the ninety persons who wrote for this series. To their already overflowing lives as activists, ministers, and scholars, they added responsibility for preparing the articles for these volumes. We honor Jon Berquist for his formative role in this project and for multiple forms of support. The editors express appreciation to J. B. Blue and Song Bok Jon, graduate students at Boston University School of Theology, who sacrificed time from their own academic responsibilities to engage in research on the Holy Days for Justice; to Vanderbilt University graduate students Casey Sigmon and Nathan Dannison for their editing gifts down the homestretch; as well as to Matthew Charles, a student research assistant also at Vanderbilt University. The editors and contributors are responsible for the limitations that result from not following the suggestions of these learned colleagues.

We send this book forward with the prayer that God will use it to help re-create the world as a community of love, peace, freedom, mutuality, respect, security, and abundance. May it be a resource for preaching that, under the influence of the Holy Spirit, empowers social transformation.

Introduction

Many people today yearn to live in a world of love, peace, freedom, mutuality, respect, security, and abundance for all. The Bible calls this combination of qualities justice. The best of the Bible and Christian tradition envision the heart of God's own mission as re-creating the world as a realm of love and justice. Joining God in this mission is at the heart of the calling of the preacher and the congregation. The aim of this three-volume series is to empower sermons as active agents in God's mission.

Ninety preachers and scholars contribute to this work. These writers are known for their insight into social dimensions of the divine purposes as well as for their capacity to interpret the social vision boldly and sensitively. Approximately half of the writers are women and half are men; about 40 percent of them African American, Hispanic, Asian American, or Native American.

Preaching for Justice: A World of Love, Peace, Freedom, Mutuality, Respect, Security, and Abundance

This commentary is a resource for preaching for a world of justice from the deepest theological convictions of biblical texts. *Preaching God's Transforming Justice* is distinctive in two ways. First, while other aids for preaching from the lectionary sometimes discuss matters of social justice, this series is the first commentary on the Revised Common Lectionary to highlight God's life-giving intentions for the social world from start to finish.[1] *Preaching God's Transforming Justice* is not simply a mirror of other lectionary commentaries (such as the impressive *Feasting on the Word: Preaching the Revised Common Lectionary*) but concentrates on how the lectionary readings can help the preacher identify and reflect theologically and ethically on the social implications of the biblical readings. Second, this series introduces twenty-two Holy Days for Justice. Explained further below, these days are intended to enlarge the church's awareness of the depth and insistence of God's call for justice and of the many ways that call comes to the church and world today.

The comments on the biblical texts are intended to be more than notes on contemporary social issues. The comments are designed to help preachers and congregations develop a deep and broad theological vision out of which to interpret the social world. Furthermore, this book aims to provide practical guidance for living more justly as individuals and communities.

Special Feature: Twenty-Two Holy Days for Justice

This commentary augments the traditional liturgical calendar by providing resources for twenty-two special Holy Days for Justice. The title for these noteworthy days, suggested by Professor Amy-Jill Levine of Vanderbilt University, requires explanation. God's mission for justice is holy. Consequently, the church's commitment to justice is holy. Some of the events, however, that call forth these special days are not holy. Indeed, some days—such as Yom haShoah (which remembers the murder of six million Jewish people by the Nazis)—are occasions for mourning. However, at the same time these days also call the church to take bold and powerful actions to join the holy work

---

1. The Revised Common Lectionary (RCL) was developed by the Consultation on Common Texts, an ecumenical consultation of liturgical scholars and denominational representatives from the United States and Canada. The RCL provides a collection of readings from Scripture to be used during worship in a schedule that follows the seasons of the church year: Advent, Christmas, Epiphany Day, Lent, Easter, Day of Pentecost, Ordinary Time. In addition, the RCL provides for a uniform set of readings to be used across denominations or other church bodies.

The RCL provides a reading from the Hebrew Bible, a Psalm response to that reading, a Gospel, and an Epistle for each preaching occasion of the year. It is presented in a three-year cycle, with each year centered around one of the Synoptic Gospels. Year A largely follows the Gospel of Matthew, Year B largely follows Mark, and Year C largely follows Luke. Selections from John are also read each year, especially during Advent, Lent, and Easter.

The RCL offers two tracks of Hebrew Bible texts for the Season after Pentecost or Ordinary Time: a semicontinuous track, which moves through stories and characters in the Hebrew Bible, and a complementary track, which ties the Hebrew Bible texts to the theme of the Gospel texts for that day. Both tracks are included in this volume.

For more information about the Revised Common Lectionary, visit the official RCL Web site at http://lectionary.library.vanderbilt.edu/ or see *The Revised Common Lectionary: The Consultation on Common Texts* (Nashville: Abingdon Press, 1992).

of God in attempting to transform the circumstances that led to lamentation. We can never undo pain and suffering, but we can try to reshape the world to minimize the danger of such things recurring, and to encourage possibilities for people and nature to live together in justice.

Each Holy Day for Justice derives from either a person or an event that helps the contemporary community become aware of arenas in the world that cry for justice. These Holy Days bridge significant phenomena in our history and present culture that do not receive adequate attention in the church's liturgical calendar or may not otherwise be noted in the congregation. They draw our attention to circumstances in need of social transformation.

Each Holy Day for Justice has a different focus. In *Preaching God's Transforming Justice* these days are placed close to the Sunday on which they occur in the Christian year and the ordinary calendar. When reaching a Holy Day for Justice in the lectionary, the preacher can choose whether to follow the readings from the Revised Common Lectionary or to work instead with the readings and themes of the Holy Day for Justice.[2] The concerns highlighted in these special days may also inspire preachers to bring those concerns to the fore in sermons prepared in conversation with the traditional lectionary readings.

In the list of Holy Days for Justice below, the editors place in parentheses a date or season when the congregation might naturally observe a Holy Day for Justice. The dates for many of the Holy Days for Justice are already widely accepted, such as the dates for World AIDS Day, the Universal Declaration of Human Rights, Martin Luther King Jr. Day, Salt March, Earth Day, Yom haShoah, and the Fourth of July. The editors assigned the dates for other Holy Days for Justice in conversation with scholars who work closely with the concerns of those days and with communities closely related to the origin of the person or concern at the center of the day. Of course, preachers and worship planners are free to observe the Holy Days for Justice on other dates that fit more naturally into the congregation's local calendar.

The Holy Days for Justice are:

1. World AIDS Day (December 1)
2. Universal Declaration of Human Rights (December 10)
3. Martin Luther King Jr. Day (January 15)
4. Asian American Heritage Day (February 19)
5. International Women's Day (March 8)

---

2. In addition, the Revised Common Lectionary already sets aside possible readings for All Saints' Day and Thanksgiving. The specific dates of some of the Holy Days for Justice change from year to year. These days are placed in the commentary in the season of the lectionary year when they typically occur.

6. Salt March Day: Marching with the Poor (March 12)
7. Oscar Romero of the Americas Day (March 24)
8. César Chávez Day (March 31)
9. Earth Day (April 22)
10. Holocaust Remembrance Day: Yom haShoah (27th of Nissan, usually from early April to early May)
11. Peace in the Home: Shalom Bayit (second Sunday in May)
12. Juneteenth: Let Freedom Ring (June 19)
13. Gifts of Sexuality and Gender (June 29)
14. Fourth of July: Seeking Liberty and Justice for All
15. Sojourner Truth Day (August 18)
16. Simchat Torah: Joy of the Torah (mid-September to early October)
17. International Day of Prayer and Witness for Peace (September 21)
18. Peoples Native to the Americas Day (fourth Friday in September)
19. World Communion Sunday (first Sunday in October)
20. Night of Power (27th Night of Ramadan: From 2011 through 2020 the date moves from September to August, July, June, May, and April)
21. World Food Day (October 16)
22. Children's Sabbaths (third weekend in October or another date that works for the congregation)

The discussions of these days in the commentary are distinctive in three ways. (1) In the case of almost every special day (with the exception of Simchat Torah: The Joy of the Torah), the editors selected four biblical texts that relate to these special emphases, including a reading from the Torah, Prophets and Writings, a reading from a Psalm, a reading from a Gospel, and another from an Epistle. The editors chose the texts for each day in the hope that the passages can become good conversation partners in helping the congregation reflect on how the day enlarges the congregation's vision and practice of justice. Most of the texts were chosen because they support potential emphases in the day, but some were chosen because they give the preacher the opportunity to enter into critical dialogue with the text or with the way the biblical text has been used in the church or the culture. While a few of the biblical texts for the Holy Days for Justice duplicate passages in the Revised Common Lectionary, most of the texts for the Holy Days for Justice are not found in the lectionary. (2) Each day is introduced by a brief paragraph offering a perspective on why that day is included. We repeat the same introductory paragraph in all three volumes. (3) Each day also includes a quote from a figure or document in the past or the present that voices a provocative perspective on the concerns represented by that day. For example, in Year A on Martin Luther King Jr. Day, the preacher is presented with an excerpt from the "Letter from Birmingham City Jail."

Some readers may initially be put off by some of these selections, especially days that also appear in the civic calendar in the United States, such as Fourth of July: Seeking Liberty and Justice for All. These days are not intended to promote uncritical celebration of present culture. On the contrary, the appearance of these days can become the occasion for the preacher to reflect critically with the congregation on the themes of those days. Some of the motifs associated in popular culture with Fourth of July, for instance, run against the grain of God's best hopes for the human family. In the name of being faithful, some preachers studiously avoid speaking about days suggested by the civic calendar. However, the congregation may too easily construe such silence as the preacher's consent to the culture's prevailing mind-set. The sermon can attempt to redress the prevailing cultural mind-set that either neglects attention to questions of justice or actively promotes injustice.

The Holy Days for Justice address the criticism that the Revised Common Lectionary does not adequately represent biblical texts that deal with matters of justice as fully as those texts are represented in the Bible. Such special days might also enlarge the vision of the preacher and the congregation while offering preachers a venue for addressing matters that are sometimes hard to reach when following the lectionary. For the congregation that may be hesitant to consider such matters, the appearance of these emphases in a formal lectionary commentary might add to the preacher's authority for speaking about them.

God's Vision for the Social World

The purposes of this commentary series are rooted in the core of God's vision for the social world. To be sure, the Bible is a diverse document in the sense that its parts were written at different times and places, in different cultural settings, and from different theological and ethical points of view—for example, Priestly, Deuteronomic, Wisdom, and apocalyptic. Nevertheless, the different materials in the Bible share the common perspective that God intends for all individuals and communities (including the world of nature) to live together in justice.

The Priestly theologians begin the Bible with the vision in Genesis 1 by picturing God creating a world in which each and every entity has a particular place and purpose and in which all entities—the ecosphere, animals, and human beings—live together in covenantal community. The role of the human being is to help the different entities live together in the mutual support that God envisions. The aim of the Ten Commandments and Israel's other laws is to create a social community that embodies how God wants people to live together in blessing. The Priestly theologians show special concern for ensuring that the poor and marginalized experience providence through care practiced by the community. Israel is to model how God wants all peoples to live together in blessing (Gen. 12:1–3). Israel is to be a light to the nations in these regards (Isa. 42:6). The church later understands its message to be grafted onto that of Israel (e.g., the church shares in the mission of being a light in the world, Matt. 5:13–14).

The Deuteronomic thinkers envisioned Israel as a community not only in covenant with God, but also as a community whose members were in covenant with one another so that all could live in love, peace, and security. Deuteronomy 15:7–8 epitomizes this attitude. "If there is among you anyone in need . . . do not be hard-hearted or tight-fisted toward your needy neighbor. You should rather open your hand, willingly lending enough to meet the need, whatever it may be." The Deuteronomic monarch is to rule with a copy of the Torah present at all times and is not to be "above other members of the community nor turning aside from the commandment" (Deut. 17:19–20). The monarch is responsible to God and to the community for seeing that justice is enacted in all aspects of Jewish life. The covenant includes nature such that when the people are faithful, nature blesses them, but when they are unfaithful, nature itself curses them (Deut. 28:1–45).

The Wisdom literature encourages practices that not only provide for individual and household prosperity but also build up the community. The wise life shows respect for the poor as full members of the community (Sir. 4:1–10). The Wisdom literature cautions the prosperous not to become self-absorbed by their possessions but to use their resources to strengthen the community. Indeed, the wise are to "speak out for those who cannot speak, for the rights of all the destitute . . . [to] defend the rights of the poor and needy" (Prov. 31:8–9). Moreover, the sages thought that God charged the natural order with wisdom so that by paying attention to the way in which the elements of nature work together, human beings can learn how God wants human beings to live as individuals and in community, as we can see in the case of the ant modeling wisdom (Prov. 6:6).

The apocalyptic theologians believed that the present world—both the social sphere and nature—is so broken, unjust, and violent that God must replace it with a new world, often called the realm of God. The apocalyptic book of 4 Ezra (2 Esdras) vividly expresses this hope:

> It is for you that Paradise is opened, the tree of life is planted, the age to come is revealed, plenty is provided, a city is built, rest is appointed, goodness is established and wisdom perfected beforehand. The root of evil is sealed up from you, illness is banished from you, and death is hidden; hell has fled and corruption has been forgotten; sorrows

have passed away, and in the end the treasure of immortality is made manifest.[3] (4 Ezra 8:52–56)

In this new world all relationships and situations manifest God's purpose. Those who defy God's desires through idolatry, exploitation of the poor, and violence are condemned.

Paul, Mark, Matthew, Luke, and most other early Christian writers share this general viewpoint (e.g., Rom. 8:18–25; Mark 13:24–27). These first-century theologians believed that the life, ministry, death, and resurrection of Jesus signaled that the final and complete manifestation of the realm of God had begun in a limited way in the ministry of Jesus and would come in its fullness with the return of Jesus. The ministry of Jesus both points to that realm and embodies it. Jesus' disciples are to alert others to the presence and coming of the realm and to live in the present as if the realm is fully here. The church is to embody the transformed world.

From the perspective of the Bible, God's vision for the interrelated communities of humankind and nature is, through and through, a social vision. It involves the intertwining relationships of God with humankind and nature, of human communities with one another, and of human communities with nature. Marjorie Suchocki, a major contemporary theologian, uses the evocative phrase "inclusive well-being" to sum up God's desire for every created entity to live in love, peace, justice, dignity, freedom, and abundance in a framework of mutually supportive community.[4] Anything that threatens the well-being of any entity in the created world goes against the purposes of God.

Individual Bible Readings and Implications for Social Justice and Transformation

Every passage in the Bible has social implications. In connection with each text in the lectionary, the commentators in this series help the congregation envision God's purposes for human community. Some texts are quite direct in this way. For example, Amos exhorts, "Let justice roll down like waters, and righteousness like an ever-flowing stream" (Amos 5:24). The prophet wants the people to practice justice. Other texts are less direct but are still potent in their implications. According to the book of Acts, Priscilla was a teacher of the gospel alongside her spouse, Aquila (Acts 18:24–28). From this and many

---

3. "The Fourth Book of Ezra," trans. Bruce M. Metzger, in *The Old Testament Pseudepigrapha: Apocalyptic Literature and Testaments*, ed. James H. Charlesworth (Garden City, NY: Doubleday & Co., 1983), 1:544. Fourth Ezra was written in the late first century CE and is sometimes known as 2 Esdras.

4. Marjorie Suchocki, *The Fall to Violence: Original Sin in Relational Theology* (New York: Continuum, 1994), 66.

other texts, we glimpse the vital role of women in the leadership of the earliest churches (e.g., Mark 16:8; Luke 8:1–3; Acts 9:36–42; 16:11–15; Rom. 16:1–3, 6, 7, 12; 1 Cor. 1:11; Phil. 4:2–4).

The contributors to these volumes articulate what the biblical writers hoped would happen in the social world of those who heard these texts in their original settings and point to ways in which interaction with the biblical texts helps today's congregations more fully embrace and enact God's intent for all to experience inclusive well-being. The following are among the questions the writers consider:

- What are God's life-giving intentions in each text?
- What does a particular text (in the context of its larger theological world) envision as a community that embodies God's social vision, a vision in which all live in inclusive well-being?
- What are the benefits of that vision for humankind and (as appropriate) nature?
- How do human beings and nature fall short of God's possibilities when they do not follow or sustain that vision?
- Do individuals or communities get hurt in the world of the text or in the way that text has been interpreted?
- What needs to happen for justice, healing, re-creation, and inclusive well-being?

At the same time, writers sometimes criticize aspects of the occasional biblical text whose social vision does not measure up to the fullness of God's intentions. For example, according to Ezekiel, God ordered marks placed on faithful people who lamented abominations that took place in Israel. God then commanded some of the faithful to murder the unfaithful. "Pass through the city . . . and kill; your eye shall not spare, and you shall show no pity. Cut down old men, young men and young women, little children and women, but touch no one who has the mark" (Ezek. 9:5–6). This passage invites the reader to believe that God commanded murder. The first letter of Peter asserts, "Slaves, accept the authority of your masters with all deference, not only those who are kind and gentle but also those who are harsh. For it is a credit to you if, being aware of God, you endure pain while suffering unjustly" (1 Pet. 2:18–19). This passage assumes the validity of slavery and encourages recipients to accept being abused.

Texts such as these do not measure up to the Bible's highest vision of God's desire for a just world; hence, many preachers cannot commend such barbed texts as positive guidance for today's community. Instead, such a preacher critiques the passage. However, even when the preacher cannot fully endorse what a text invites the congregation to believe and do, the appearance of theologically and ethically problematic texts in the lectionary can open an important door for a conversation among preacher and congregation regarding what they most truly believe concerning God's social vision. The text may not be directly instructive, but the congregation's encounter with the text can be an important occasion of theological and ethical reflection.

Naming and Confronting Systems that Frustrate God's Purposes

Individuals acting alone and with others can defy God's purposes for humankind and nature. But beyond individual and small-group actions, a key insight to emerge in recent generations is that systemic forces distort God's purposes for humankind and the larger created world. Ethicists often refer to such phenomena as systemic evil.

A system is a transpersonal network of attitudes, values, and behaviors that shape the lives of individuals and communities. Systemic evil creates force fields that push individuals and communities to distort God's purposes in the social world. Systems can affect communities as small as the Wednesday night prayer group and as large as nations and transnational associations. Examples of systemic evils that subvert God's life-giving purposes are racism, sexism, neocolonialism, ageism, nationalism, classism, heterosexism, and ecological destruction.

Preachers need to recognize and name systemic distortions of God's purposes for the social community. While this analysis is important, it sometimes leaves individuals and congregations feeling impotent in the face of massive structural forces. When possible, the writers in this series urge preachers to give these concerns a human face and to offer specific insights and stories that help congregations envision practical steps that they can take to join God in seeking to transform the social world. What attitudes and actions can individuals and congregations take to become agents of transformation? These writers want congregations to feel empowered to make a difference. We hope that each comment will offer a horizon of hope for the preacher and the congregation.

The Preacher Speaks from, to, and beyond the Local Context

The importance of taking account of the context of the congregation is a permeating emphasis today in preaching and more broadly in theological scholarship. The preacher is called to understand the congregation as a culture in its own right. The preacher should conduct an exegesis of the congregation that reveals the events, memories, values, practices, attitudes, feelings, patterns of relationship (especially power relationships), physical spaces, and larger systems that combine to make the congregation a distinct culture.

This commentary does not intend to provide the minister with prepackaged ideas for sermons but urges ministers to begin their approach to preaching on matters of justice from inside the culture of the congregation. The local pastor who has a thick understanding of the local community knows much better than a scholar in a far-off city how the life of that congregation needs to develop in order to witness more fully to God's purposes.

The preacher should typically speak *from* and *to* the local context. Rather than impose a social vision that the preacher has found in a book of theological ethics, on the Internet, or at the latest clergy network for peace and justice, the preacher can approach matters of social justice from inside the worldview of the congregation. Hence, one can usually identify points of contact between the world of the congregation and the need for transformation. The preacher can then use the base of identification and trust between the pulpit and the pew to speak *to* the congregation. To help the congregation participate more fully in God's transformative movement, the preacher will typically need to help the congregation think beyond itself.

From this point of view, the contributors to *Preaching God's Transforming Justice* intend to be conversation partners in helping preachers identify particular areas in which the congregation might reinforce patterns of thought and behavior that manifest their deepest theological convictions. We hope the book will help congregations to grow in the direction of God's social vision and to find steps they can take to become agents of justice.

Recent literature in preaching leads preachers to think of the congregation not just as a collection of individuals but as a *community*, the *body* of Christ. While sermons should help individuals imagine their particular social witnesses, sermons should also be addressed to the congregation as community and its corporate social witness.

Moreover, the congregation is itself a social world. While the larger goal of the book is to help preachers move the congregation toward reflection and mission in the larger social arena, some texts may lead the preacher to help the listeners reflect on how the internal life of the congregation can more fully witness to God's life-giving purposes.

Prophetic Preaching with a Pastoral Goal

In the broad sense, this book calls for prophetic preaching. We think of prophetic preaching in contrast to two popular notions. From one popular perspective, prophetic preaching predicts specific future events, especially those that point to the return of Jesus. This way of thinking does not catch the fullness of prophetic preaching in the Bible itself. A second popular viewpoint associates prophetic preaching with condemnation. This prophetic preacher identifies what the text is against and what is wrong in the social world, sometimes denouncing the congregation and others. These sermons can chastise the congregation without providing a word of grace and empowerment. This perspective is also incomplete.

The editors of *Preaching God's Transforming Justice* regard the purpose of all preaching as helping the congregation and others interpret the world from the standpoint of God's life-giving purposes. Preaching seeks to build up the congregation as a community of witness and to help the world embody the divine realm. The goal of all preaching is pastoral in the root sense of building up the flock so that the congregation can fulfill God's purposes. The word "pastoral" derives from the world of flocks and shepherds in which the shepherd (the pastor) did whatever was necessary to maintain the health of the flock.

From the perspective of the Bible, the prophet is a kind of ombudsperson who compares the actual behavior of the community with God's purposes of inclusive blessing. The special call of the prophet is to help the community recognize where it falls short of those purposes and what the community needs to do to return to them. On the one hand, a prophet such as Amos concentrated on how the community had departed from God's purposes by exploiting the poor and, consequently, faced judgment. On the other hand, a prophet such as Second Isaiah called attention to the fact that the community in exile did not trust in the promise of God to return them to their homeland. In both cases, the community is not living up to the fullness of God's purposes. While the prophet may need to confront the congregation, the prophet's goal is to prompt the congregation to take steps toward transformation. Prophetic preaching ultimately aims at helping the congregation to identify what needs transformation and how to take part.

Representative Social Phenomena

Preaching God's Transforming Justice urges preachers and communities toward conscious and critical theological reflection on things that are happening in the contemporary social world from the perspective of God's purpose to recreate the world as a realm of love, peace, freedom, mutuality, abundance, and respect for all. Nevertheless, some preachers refer to a limited number of social phenomena in their sermons. A preacher's hermeneutical imagination is sometimes enlarged by pondering a panorama of representative social phenomena that call for theological and ethical interpretation, such as the following:

Abortion
Absent fathers
Addictions
Affirmative action
Aging
Animal rights
Anti-Semitism
Arms sales
Church and nation
Civil religion
Classism
Colonialism
Consumerism
Death penalty
Disability perspectives
Diversity
Domestic violence
Drugs
Ecological issues
Economic exploitation
Education
Empire
Energy
Eurocentrism
Exclusivism
Flight to the suburbs
Foster care
Gambling

Gender orientation
    LGBTQA
Geneva Convention
Genocide
Gentrification
Glass ceiling
Greed
Gun control
Health care
Homelessness
Housing
Human rights
Hunger
Idols (contemporary)
Immigration
Islam and Christianity
Islamophobia
Judaism and
    Christianity
Language (inclusive,
    repressive)
Margins of society
Militarism
Multiculturalism
Nationalism
Native American rights
Neocolonialism
Peace movements
Pluralism

Police brutality
Pollution
Pornography
Postcolonialism
Poverty
Prisons
Public schools/private
    schools
Racism
Repression
Reproductive rights
Sexism
Socialism
Stranger
Systemic perspectives
Terrorism
Torture
Transnational
    corporations
Tribalism
Unemployment
Uninsured people
U.S. having no single
    racial/ethnic major-
    ity by 2040
Violence
White privilege
Xenophobia

This catalog is not suggested as a checklist of social issues that a preacher should cover in a given preaching cycle. Returning to an earlier theme, the minister who is in touch with the local culture can have a sense of where God's vision for justice interacts with particular social phenomena. Nonetheless, such a list may help some ministers think more broadly about possible points of contact between the core theological convictions of the church and the social world.[5]

---

5. A preacher might find it useful to review regularly the social forces that are current in the sphere of the congregation and in the larger world. Preachers can easily slip into thinking about social perspectives from limited and dated points of view. Preachers may find it helpful

Index of Passages in the Order of Books of the Bible

For preachers who do not regularly preach from the lectionary, and for preachers who want to look up a particular passage but do not know where it is in the lectionary, an index of passages discussed in the commentary is at the end of the volume. This index lists biblical texts in the order in which they are found in the Bible.

The contributors typically discuss the biblical texts in the following order: first lesson(s) from the Torah, Prophets and Writings; the Psalm(s); the Epistle; and the Gospel. However, a writer will occasionally take up the texts in a different sequence as part of his or her interpretive strategy for the day.

Inclusive Language, Expansive Language

This series uses inclusive language when referring to humankind. In other words, when contributors refer to people in general, they use language that includes all of their intended audience (e.g., humankind, humanity, people). When a writer refers to a particular gender (female or male), the gender-specific referent is used.

We seek to use expansive language when referring to God. In other words, the contributors draw on various names, attributes, and images of God known to us in Scripture and in our individual and corporate encounter of God in worship. We avoid using exclusively masculine references to God. When a Scripture passage repeatedly uses language for God that is male, we have sought more gender-inclusive emendations that are consistent with the intent of the original. Readers searching for an entire inclusive-language translation might try *The Inclusive Bible: The First Egalitarian Translation*.[6]

The Bible and Christian tradition use the term "Lord" to speak of both God and Jesus. The word "lord" is masculine. The English word "Lord" derives from a time when much of the European social world was hierarchical, with the lord and lady at the top and with human beings arranged in a pyramid of descending social power with the upper classes at the top and with males having authority over women. People in the upper reaches of the pyramid are authorized to dominate those below them. While we try to minimize the occurrence of the title "Lord," occasional writers in this book use "Lord" for God to call attention to God's absolute sovereignty; these writers do not

---

to interview members of the congregation regarding the social phenomena that are most in the consciousness of the congregation.

6. Priests for Equality, *The Inclusive Bible: The First Egalitarian Translation* (Lanham, MD: Rowman & Littlefield, 2007).

intend for the use of the expression "Lord" to authorize masculine superiority or the detailed social pyramid implied in the history of the word. Indeed, this book sees the purposes of God pointing toward a human community in which hierarchical domination is dismantled and power is shared.

Although the historical Jesus was a male, he announced the coming of the realm of God, a social world that is egalitarian with respect to gender and social power. In the hope of evoking these latter associations (and minimizing the pyramidal associations with "Lord"), we have shifted the designations of some historic days in the Christian Year that highlight aspects of the ministry of Jesus from lordship language to the language of "Jesus" and "Christ": Nativity of Jesus, Baptism of Jesus, Resurrection of Jesus, and Reign of Christ (in place of Nativity of the Lord, Baptism of the Lord, Resurrection of the Lord, and Christ the King).

We have also tried to speak expansively of the realm of God (NRSV: kingdom of God) by using terms such as realm, reign, rule, dominion, kin-dom, and holy commonwealth. The word "kingdom" appears where the author has specifically requested it.

Language for the Parts of the Bible

The contemporary world is a time of experimentation and critical reflection regarding how to refer to the parts of the Bible that many Christian generations referred to as the Old and New Testaments. The discussion arises because in much contemporary usage, the word "old" suggests worn-out and outdated, while "new" often implies "better" and "improved." Many Christians believe that the unexplained use of the phrases Old Testament and New Testament can contribute to supersessionism: the conviction that new and improved Christianity has taken the place of old and outdated Judaism. The old covenant is no longer in force, but has been replaced by the new covenant. When used without interpretation, this way of speaking contributes to injustice by supporting anti-Judaism and anti-Semitism. In an attempt to use language that is more just, many people today are exploring several ways forward.

As a part of the contemporary exploration, the writers in this series use a variety of expressions for these parts of the Bible. There is no fully satisfactory way of speaking. We note now the most common expressions in this series and invite the reader to remember the strengths and weaknesses of each approach.

Some leaders think that today's community can use the expressions Old and New Testaments if the church explains what that language does and does not mean.[7] In antiquity old things were often valued and honored. Moreover, the words "old" and "new" can imply nothing more than chronology: The literature of the Old Testament is older than that of the New. The church would then use the terms Old and New Testaments without casting aspersion on Judaism and without suggesting that God has made Christianity a much purer and truer religion. Occasional writers in the series use the phrases Old Testament and New Testament in this way. However, a growing number of speakers and writers think that the words Old Testament and New Testament are so deeply associated with negative pictures of Jewish people, writings, institutions, and practices that, even when carefully defined, the language feeds negative perceptions.

"Hebrew Bible" and "Hebrew Scriptures" are popular ways of referring to the first part of the Bible. These titles came about because English versions are not based primarily on the Septuagint (the translation of the Hebrew Scriptures into Greek in the third and second centuries BCE) but are translated from Hebrew (and Aramaic) manuscripts in consultation with the Septuagint. However, the designation "Hebrew Bible" raises the question of what to call the twenty-seven books that make up the other part of the Bible. We cannot call the other books the "Greek Scriptures" or the "Greek Bible" because the Septuagint is also in Greek. We cannot call them the "Christian Scriptures" or the "Christian Bible" since the church honors the entire Bible.

Occasionally Christians refer to the Old Testament as the "Jewish Bible." This nomenclature is unsatisfactory because people could understand it to mean that the first part of the Bible belongs only to the Jewish community and is not constitutive for the church. Furthermore, the Christian version differs from the Jewish Tanakh in the way that some of the books are ordered, named, and divided.

The designations "First and Second Testaments" are increasingly popular because many people see them as setting out a chronological relationship between the two bodies of literature—the First Testament came prior to the Second. However, in competitive North American culture, especially in the United States, "first" can imply first in value while "second" can imply something not as good as the first. The winner receives first place. Second place is often a disappointment. Moreover, "second" can imply second best or secondhand.

Seeking a way of referring to the Bible that respects its diversity but suggests its continuities, and that promotes respect for Judaism, writers in this

---

7. On this discussion, see further Ronald J. Allen, "Torah, Prophets, Writings, Gospels, Letters: A New Name for the Old Book," *Encounter* 68 (2007): 53–63.

series sometimes refer to the parts of the Bible as Torah, Prophets, Writings, Gospels, and Letters. This latter practice adapts a Jewish way of speaking of the scriptures as TANAKH, an acronym derived from the Hebrew for Torah, Prophets, and Writings (*torah, neviim, ketuviim*) and adds the categories of Gospels and Letters.[8] To be sure, the books in Tanakh are divided and arranged differently than in the Christian Bible. Furthermore, while some may object that the books of Acts, Hebrews, and Revelation do not fall into these categories, we note that Acts is less a separate genre and more a continuation of the Gospel of Luke. In the strict sense, Revelation has the form of a letter. Although scholars today recognize that Hebrews is an early Christian sermon, it likely circulated much like a letter.

All designations for the parts of the Bible are vexed by the fact that different churches include different books. We should really speak of a Roman Catholic canon, several Orthodox canons, and a Protestant canon. As a concession to our inability to distinguish every permutation, we ask the reader to receive these designations with a generous but critical elasticity of mind and usage.

The designation "son of man" is challenging in a different way, especially when it is used of or by Jesus. Interpreters disagree as to whether the phrase "son of man" is simply a way of saying "child of a human being" or "son of humanity" (or, more colloquially, simply "human being") or whether the phrase has a specialized theological content, such as "apocalyptic redeemer" (as in Dan. 7:13–14). Since individual contributors interpret this phrase in different ways, we sometimes leave the expression "son of man" in the text of the commentary, with individual contributors explaining how they use it.

Diverse Points of View in the Commentary

The many writers in this commentary series are diverse not only in gender, race, and ethnicity, but also in exegetical, theological, and ethical viewpoints. Turning the page from one entry to the next, the reader may encounter a liberation theologian, a neo-orthodox thinker, an ethnic theologian, a process thinker, a socialist, or a postliberal. Moreover, the writers are often individually creative in the ways in which they see the forward movement of their texts in calling for social transformation today. While all authors share the deep conviction that God is even now seeking to lead the world toward more inclusive, just community, the nuances with which they approach the biblical material and even the social world can be quite different.

---

8. For further discussion, see Allen, "Torah, Prophets, Writings, Gospels, Letters."

Rather than enforce a party line with respect to matters of exegesis, theology, and ethical vision, the individual writers bring their own voices to clear expression. The editors' hope is that each week the preacher can have a significant conversation with a writer who is an other and that the preacher's social vision will be broadened and deepened by such exposure.

Diversity also characterizes the process by which this book came into being. The editorial team itself is diverse, as it includes an African American man in the AME Zion Church, a woman of European origin from the Church of the Brethren, a historic peace church, and a man of European origin from the Christian Church (Disciples of Christ). While the editors share many convictions, their vision has been impacted deeply by insights from preachers and scholars from many other churches, movements, communities, and cultures. Dawn took the lead in editing Year A, Ron for Year B, and Dale for Year C. While the editors regarded one of their core tasks as helping the individual writers bring out their own voices forcefully, each has inevitably edited in light of her or his theological and ethical commitments.

Ultimately the goal of *Preaching God's Transforming Justice* is not simply to give preachers resources for talking about social issues, but to empower congregations to develop a theological life perspective that issues in practices of justice and to participate with God in working toward a time when all created entities—every human being and every animal and plant and element of nature—can live together as a community of love through mutual support with abundance for all.

First Sunday of Advent

Leonora Tubbs Tisdale

JEREMIAH 33:14–16
PSALM 25:1–10
1 THESSALONIANS 3:9–13
LUKE 21:25–36

The texts for this first Sunday in Advent are at times hopeful, at times prayerful, and at times foreboding. Yet they all seem to center around justice and the righteousness and holiness of God that will soon be made manifest in our midst, and how we as believers might thereby live more faithfully.

The Jeremiah lection starts the day on a hopeful note. Although people living in exile may believe God has forsaken and abandoned them, such is not the case. God promises that a "branch" will spring up from the seemingly dead stump of the Davidic line, a ruler who will govern the nations with justice and righteousness. Those living under oppression and subjugation can have hope that their situation will not last forever, but that God will redeem and save them.

Psalm 25 places us in the prayerful position of people who have known God's salvation, and who now trust in God so that God might show us how to live with justice and righteousness. How might our lives more ethically reflect God's own?

In his First Letter to the Thessalonians, the apostle Paul also sounds a prayerful note. Here he asks God to cultivate this beloved church in "holiness" to become all God intends it to be.

And finally, lest we think we have all the time in the world to get our lives in shape before that second coming of Christ with the saints, the Gospel lesson from Luke reminds us in foreboding apocalyptic language that we do not. Therefore, we had best busy ourselves with things that matter, such as caring for God's created order.

Jeremiah 33:14–16

The portion of the book of Jeremiah in which this lection appears is called the Book of Consolation. After twenty-five initial chapters in which Jeremiah pronounces oracles of judgment upon God's people, and five chapters in which the prophet recounts incidents from his own life, the tone in chapters 30–33 shifts to one of comfort and consolation. The historical context has changed, with the people of Judah now in exile in Babylon. So, in a heartening tone reminiscent of those words from Handel's *Messiah* that we so often hear sung during the Advent season—"Comfort ye, comfort ye my people" (Isa. 40:1 KJV)—Jeremiah brings his own brand of comfort and hope to those who long for an end to their reproof, separation from their homeland, and subjugation to a foreign enemy.

Earlier in this same chapter, Jeremiah proclaims that Judah's time of exile is coming to an end, and that God envisions a new future of hope, promise, and restoration. "I will restore the fortunes of Judah and the fortunes of Israel, and rebuild them as they were at first. I will cleanse them from all the guilt of their sin against me, and I will forgive all the guilt of their sin and rebellion against me. And this city shall be to me a name of joy, a praise and a glory before all the nations of the earth" (vv. 7–9a).

In today's lection, Jeremiah envisions the promise of God as a "shoot" or a "righteous branch" that will "spring up" from the seemingly dead stump in the line of Davidic rulers. Though the people of Israel and Judah may feel that the landscape of their nation is as desolate and devoid of life as Mount St. Helens was after a volcanic eruption covered its hillsides with molten lava and ash, the prophet proclaims that all is not as it seems. Even now God is at work, bringing life out of what the world considers to be dead. For a ruler will come forth from the stump of Jesse's tree—a ruler who will "execute justice [*mishpat*] and righteousness [*tsedeqah*] in the land" (v. 15). The time of oppression, persecution, and separation for God's people will come to an end, and God will establish a new day of restoration, healing, and safety.

Advent is a time for acknowledging the exilic conditions of life for those persons in our world who live in situations of injustice, who experience unrighteous hands of power over them. Whether we are talking about victims of war, domestic violence, or human trafficking, whether we are envisioning people who feel the heel of the economic oppressor on their backs or those who bear the weight of political oppression on their heads, Advent is a time for proclaiming the promises of God. The tree stump that looks to be dead and incapable of any new growth will, under the miraculous workings of God, send forth a new shoot—a tiny baby—who will continue the Davidic line.

Under his rule there will be no more oppression or subjugation, for God will inaugurate a new day and a new reign in which the peoples of the earth will live in freedom and safety and peace.

Psalm 25:1–10

Psalm 25 is fitting to begin a new liturgical year because it places us (with the psalmist) in the position of offering ourselves anew to God for God's guidance, deliverance, and instruction. "O my God, in you I trust" (v. 2). "Make me to know your ways" (v. 4a). "Lead me in your truth, and teach me" (v. 5a).

The psalm is structured as an acrostic poem in which each line begins with a successive letter of the Hebrew alphabet. The result is a sense of wholeness or completeness as the psalmist reminds us both of the goodness of God and of God's forgiveness and guidance for those who put their trust in God. The theological culmination for today's passage occurs in verse 10, where the psalmist proclaims: "All the paths of the LORD are steadfast love and faithfulness, for those who keep his covenant and his decrees."

Advent, like Lent, is a time of preparation for receiving Christ anew. This psalm reminds us that trust in God and ethical living are closely aligned. Because we trust in a God whose ways are "steadfast love" and "faithfulness," we also seek instruction and guidance from God for our right living. Our lives—both as individuals and as communities of faith—ought to reflect God's own steadfast and faithful love. Implied here is a fidelity in relationships that runs counter to much of our "instant gratification" or "I'm here for you as long as it's good for me" culture. Conversely, this passage calls to mind those people and groups who, in their own care for others—especially the sick, the hurting, and the marginalized—mirror the steadfast love of God and inspire us to be more steadfast as well.

1 Thessalonians 3:9–13

That the apostle Paul loves the people of Thessalonica is readily apparent in our reading for this first Sunday of Advent. Paul not only loves them, but also he is concerned about them; so he has sent Timothy to check up on this young church on his behalf. Timothy's reports are good ones, and they fill Paul's heart with joy. The church is staying faithful to Christ; the people are standing firm in their faith. And so Paul spends the first three chapters of this letter (thought to be his earliest) expressing his love, gratitude, and concern for the Thessalonians. His joy in the Thessalonians culminates in the opening verse of our reading for today (v. 9): "How can we thank God enough for you in return for all the joy that we feel before our God because of you?"

But this church, like any church, is not a perfect one. Therefore this passage also forms a bridge between Paul's expressions of thanksgiving for this church and his ethical encouragement to them. The bridge begins when Paul acknowledges that he longs to see the Thessalonians "face to face" in order that he might "restore whatever is lacking in [their] faith" (v. 10). Then, rather than immediately launching into a litany of all the ways the Thessalonians are falling short of what God desires of them, Paul prays for them. He prays that God will help him find his way to see them (v. 11). He prays that their love for one another might abound, just as Paul's love for them abounds (v. 12). And he prays that God will "strengthen [their] hearts in holiness" so that they might "be blameless" before God at the coming of Jesus with all the saints (v. 13).

The first Sunday of Advent, the first Sunday of a new church year, is an appropriate time for the church to look back over its past year, acknowledging both the ways in which it has done what is pleasing in the sight of God and the ways in which it has failed to do so. All of us—like the church in Thessalonica—are a mix of sinners and saints. We need those occasions in the life of faith where we take stock of where we have been and look to where and who we would like to be. For the church to do so corporately is to acknowledge those places where we have failed to promote God's justice and righteousness and peace in the world, as well as those places where we have reflected Christ's goodness in our common life together. What better way for a pastor or church leader to begin a new church year than with prayer that we might all grow in faith, abound in love, and be strengthened in holiness, so that when Christ comes again with all the saints, we might be found blameless before him?

Luke 21:25–36

The Gospel text for this first Sunday of Advent shakes us up. It is not about joyous anticipation or eager expectation—the things we usually associate with this season. Rather it is about end times, horrific natural disasters, and cosmic upheaval. With the heavy gloom and doom of its apocalyptic language, it seems about as fitting for a church decorated with an Advent wreath as Picasso's *Guernica* (his troubling portrayal of war) would be. It is unsettling, gruesome, and frightening.

Even worse, the disturbance appears to be intended. This text is meant to shake us up. Indeed, it is particularly written for people like us who are going about our business as usual, acting as if no cosmic event is about to occur that will change the whole future of the created order. God is about to break into history. And because of that action, the whole created order will never be the same.

Yes, this text intends to shake us up because God's redemption is not—as we are often inclined to think—simply about us and our individual relationships with Jesus. Redemption affects the whole created order. The sun and moon and stars, the seas and their waves, the very powers of the heavens will stand up and take notice when the Son of Humanity comes in his glory. And if we know what's good for us, we will be standing and watching, too, so that we don't miss the cosmic re-creation God will bring to pass at the second coming of Christ.

Consequently, we are called to "be on guard," lest this day catches us "unexpectedly, like a trap" (vv. 34–35). What that fully means for us, I do not pretend to know. But I suspect that in part it means we commit ourselves, here and now, to caring for the whole created order. So, when Christ comes in glory, we will not be found to be "weighed down with . . . the worries of this life" but instead will be found caring for those things that are pleasing to the Savior of the cosmos.

World AIDS Day (December 1)

Chris Glaser

ECCLESIASTES 4:1–12
PSALM 131
PHILIPPIANS 2:1–11
JOHN 13:1–20

World Aids Day began in 1988 to heighten awareness of the ways the HIV/AIDS pandemic ravages the human family and to take steps to deal with this disease.[1] This day opens the door for the preacher to learn how many people are affected by this disease and to provide reliable information about it in order to reduce the mystery and fear that still surround it in some corners. The preacher can help the congregation claim what they can do to end HIV/AIDS and to ease the suffering of those directly afflicted by HIV/AIDS and their families and friends.

I have always believed that the HIV/AIDS epidemic would end someday, but I never thought I would be around to witness it. Now I believe it's possible that I will live to see the end of AIDS. After all we have the tools to end the AIDS epidemic today. The question is, do we have the political and moral will to use those tools effectively and compassionately?

Phill Wilson[2]

Dr. Cecile de Sweemer, a Belgian medical missionary in Africa, observed the many challenges in addressing AIDS on the continent while keynoting an AIDS consultation in Toronto sponsored by the World Council of Churches. There are so many concerns in Africa—poverty, hunger, other diseases—that

1. Visit http://www.worldaidsday.org for the theme of World AIDS Day for the current year.
2. Phill Wilson, "The Way Forward," in *Not in My Family: AIDS in the African American Community*, ed. Gil L. Robertson IV (Chicago: Agate Press, 2006), 71.

AIDS must take its place as one more vital issue to be addressed. AIDS has spread widely within developing nations, including those on the African continent.

She described an incident that suggests the church is sometimes part of the problem. During a health crisis, she needed to visit a tribe known to be fearful of outsiders and hostile to whites. She asked to be left in a clearing near the village, and she stood in its center until she heard singing. Noticing the women from the village peeping at her from the trees and shrubs on the edge of the clearing, she began swaying to their song's rhythm and clapping to its beat. Hesitantly the women came forward and, one by one, joined her in the dance as they continued to sing. A woman handed her baby to her to hold as she danced, a sign of building trust. Finally the eldest woman of the village danced with her until they collapsed into one another's arms. Now the doctor was able to begin her work, sharing the medical information and materials the women needed to avert and address the crisis.

This is a model for reaching the world about AIDS. We must learn how to build trust, the best ways to enter others' worlds, in order to communicate and be of assistance. The interesting postscript to the story is that, when the doctor returned to the missionary with whom she was staying and proudly told how she had opened a line of communication with the villagers, the man's visage grew dark and angry, until he finally complained, "We teach them *not* to dance!" Indeed, sticks were used on the posteriors of any women who swayed too much as they brought their offering up the aisle to this new god. This serves as a metaphor of the way Christian influence has prevented honest talk about sexuality in Africa as well as worldwide.

Ecclesiastes 4:1–12

> Look, the tears of the oppressed—with no one to comfort them! On the side of their oppressors there was power—with no one to comfort them. And I thought the dead, who have already died, more fortunate than the living, who are still alive; but better than both is the one who has not yet been, and has not seen the evil deeds that are done under the sun. (vv. 1b–3)

Unless you have sat with someone who suffers chronic pain and discomfort, continual prejudice and discrimination, and terminal despair and hopelessness, these opening verses of chapter 4 of Ecclesiastes seem over the top. But they can become the reality for those who suffer the opportunistic infections related to AIDS, who endure those who blame the victim, and who witness the ignorance and avoidance of those who will not even raise funds in an AIDS walk, let alone bring meals or comfort them simply by sitting beside them. Nowadays in the United States, at least, it is as if AIDS work has fallen out of fashion, bringing us back to the old days before it became the au courant cause. Perhaps it is "AIDS burnout," as some have asserted, which only underscores Ecclesiastes' repeated declaration that all is vanity, a chasing after wind and dissipating vapors. But when power is coupled to inaction, oppression is born—as the Rev. Martin Luther King Jr. maintained, those who are not part of the solution are part of the problem.

Yet "two are better than one, . . . for if they fall, one will lift up the other" (vv. 9–10), and "if two lie together, they keep warm" (v. 11), while "a three-fold cord is not quickly broken" (v. 12). Though Ecclesiastes asserts work and idleness alike are vanities (v. 4), solidarity means something, even to this cynic. And wisdom: "Better is a poor but wise youth than an old but foolish king. . . . One can indeed come out of prison to reign, even though born poor in the kingdom" (vv. 13–14). The United States and the nations of Africa and the rest of the world have had more than our share of foolish kings, some of whom ignored AIDS or proclaimed lies about AIDS. But one wise king did come out of prison in South Africa: Nelson Mandela, "born poor in the kingdom" of apartheid, who championed nondiscrimination in the country's constitution and had an enlightened AIDS policy.

Psalm 131

We often neglect contemplation in our spiritual tradition, but saying this psalm over and over may provide a powerful meditation. *Theologia* once meant an active communing with God, but it has become a systematic way of distinguishing ourselves and our beliefs—a practice of division among ourselves rather than communion with God. We spend too much time discussing theological "issues," giving rise to *diabolos*, an adversarial spirit that gives the devil its name. I believe it is more vital to be a church of common prayer than one of common belief, as writer Barbara Brown Taylor has suggested.

Anyone who wants to know where the ecumenical and interfaith movements have gone only need look at the ways traditions and denominations have come together around AIDS. AIDS is a humbling experience, not just for individuals with the syndrome, but for all of us. "O LORD, my heart is not lifted up, my eyes are not raised too high" (v. 1a) may characterize us as we witness the agony of the AIDS crisis. Though there were those who contemplated its theological dimensions, mindful of the theodicy of Job, for instance, most of us cleaning up the vomit or the excrement or the sores of people with AIDS in distress did not occupy ourselves with things "too great and too marvelous" (v. 1b).

No, if we were blessed, we "calmed and quieted" our souls, and thought of being held fast by our mothers in all innocence as the chaos of AIDS enwrapped the world—from the challenges of the disease itself to the obstacles posed by those who refuse to recognize the need those challenges pose. And, if we truly lived Teresa of Avila's prayer that God has no body but our own, no hands, no feet, no face but our own, we were God the Mother to those who suffered AIDS, holding the ones having the disease or the ones who loved them, as they died or as they cried. Or we were Francis, hugging the leper of our time and finding Christ himself.

John 13:1–20

Washing one another's feet at Pendle Hill, a Quaker retreat center near Philadelphia, a man and I bonded as friends and fellow ministers. I had never experienced such tenderness and humility and sensuality in a spiritual act. Decades later, I found a way to incorporate footwashing on occasion in retreats I led. A couple married thirty years told me it was the most intimate encounter of their life together. During another retreat, a pair of strangers became lovers as a result of the exercise. At a Christian men's retreat in which we reenacted a number of sacramental acts, the evaluations revealed that footwashing was the one participants found most meaningful.

But I cannot read this story of Jesus washing the disciples' feet without thinking of a man with AIDS who refused to remove his shoes and socks for a similar exercise during a retreat in Chicago. His feet were infected with an unsightly fungus. Years later I took a friend with AIDS to the doctor and saw such infected feet for myself. His feet hurt too much to drive, and when I saw them in the doctor's office I was horrified, wondering how he could possibly recover from the swelling, discoloration, and flaking skin. It was as close to leprosy as I could imagine. At the same time, his vulnerability endeared him to me.

This prompts me to see something different in this story. Not only was Jesus demonstrating the humility we as Christians should practice, but also the disciples' vulnerability as their removing of their sandals further endeared them to him. It was a practice in intimacy as much as in humility. "Unless I wash you, you have no share with me," Jesus tells Simon Peter (v. 8). Unless Jesus is allowed to touch us where we are most vulnerable, we miss the intimacy Jesus offers.

A friend with HIV said that if he were to get sick, he would go away from his family and friends to die, not wanting to burden them. "You don't understand," I said, rather bluntly. "Allowing us to care for you would be a very great gift." Anyone who has cared for a sick child, an ailing parent, a beloved pet, a dear friend, or a dying partner knows this. While not wanting to romanticize the experience—for there are times you hate it and just want to get away—when true love is present, God is there in the giving and receiving of tender loving care. *Ubi caritas et amor, deus ibi est.*

Philippians 2:1–11

In my view, these verses are a perfect benediction on "all who, while unable to be saints but refusing to bow down to pestilences, strive their utmost to be healers."[3] Blending sound Christian theology, uplifting liturgy, and compassionate charity, these verses are truly an "encouragement in Christ," a "consolation from love," a "sharing in the Spirit," and the "compassion and sympathy" that would make the joy of any Christian teacher like Paul "complete" (vv. 1–2). Though written from prison, its boundless self-sacrificing theme comes from a poetic liturgical formula celebrating Christ Jesus' own kenotic—self-emptying—love, not regarding "equality with God as something to be exploited" (v. 6) but "taking the form of a slave" (v. 7), causing God to exalt him (vv. 9–11). It was this unifying (v. 2b) and unselfish (vv. 3–4) love practiced by early Christians that attracted new converts.

Christians and churches too often concerned with what's in it for them, from self-preservation to church growth, should listen to Paul's "encouragement in Christ" to lose their life to gain it: "Let each of you look not to your own interests, but to the interests of others" (v. 4). Ministry in the AIDS crisis means responding to the immediate needs of the nearest neighbor, tending to the fallen traveler by the roadside, rather than passing by to accomplish some ritual obligation. It was our failure to practice such urgency as well as our religious fastidiousness, ignorance, and self-preoccupation that facilitated the AIDS pandemic worldwide. May God forgive us! And may God give us the grace to do everything in our power to obliterate this modern plague as well as to stand beside those who still suffer.

"On the side of their oppressors there was power—with no one to comfort" the oppressed, Ecclesiastes 4:1 reminds us. The psalmist recommends a contemplative and humble quieting and calming of our souls, like a child in its mother's arms. In John, Jesus washes his disciples' feet, demonstrating both humility and intimacy. And Paul writes to the church at Philippi that they should follow Christ's lead and treat others as more important than themselves. In the AIDS crisis, the oppressed have been faulted, as we have so often blamed the victim. The church has been more concerned with theological divisions than the hospitality of resting in God, the gift of contemplative spirituality. Intimacy and humility are lacking. And we have thought our church institutions and ourselves more important than the world's needs. Let the same mind be in us that was in Christ Jesus, who did not regard his association with God as something to be exploited, but as an opportunity to serve (vv. 5–6).

---

3. Albert Camus, *The Plague* (New York: Vintage Books, 1972), 287.

Second Sunday of Advent

Marvin A. McMickle

MALACHI 3:1–4
LUKE 1:68–79
PHILIPPIANS 1:3–11
LUKE 3:1–6

The four texts designated for the Second Sunday of Advent remind the church that God is a God of justice. How God eventually will judge people depends in large measure on the ways in which they work for justice, especially justice for the least influential and the lowest in society in terms of economic or political power. Malachi warns us that a day of judgment will surely come. Luke 1 offers God's grace for those who repent of their sins. Philippians reminds us that what God desires is a level of righteousness that is revealed in those actions that Aristotle would refer to as being virtuous. Finally, in Luke 3 we learn that where people of great power and wealth are present in abundance, God works among the poor and powerless. God has enough power already; what God needs are people willing to serve God's purposes.

Malachi 3:1–4

An old adage says, "Be careful what you ask for, because you just might get it." It seemed clear to Israel that God's judgment would and should fall on the other nations of the earth who were acting cruelly or unjustly. It never occurred to the Israelites that the judgment of God might fall on them.

The depth and severity of God's judgment is caught by the analogies of a refiner's fire and a fuller's soap. Fullers bleached and washed garments, often with lye. The garments were scrubbed and even stomped on to remove all stains. Bleaching by stretching out the garment under the sun was the final step in the work of the fuller. The thorough cleansing done to cloth by the fuller is matched by the thorough cleansing done to metal objects by the refiner's fire. The item placed in the fire was melted into liquid in a blast

11

furnace in an attempt to remove all impurities. In both instances, the objective was to purge the object of all dirt, stain, or impurity.

What God has in mind is not the purging or purifying of cloth or metal, but the thorough purging and purifying of the very people who had been complaining about injustice, both the people of Israel in general and the descendants of Levi or the priests in particular. God was most concerned about the injustice wrought by the priests, and so the very judgment these priests wanted God to visit on others was about to become their own horrific encounter with divine judgment. Something similar was predicted in Amos 5:18—9:10.

These passages offer a clear warning to the American church in all of its forms: God's harshest judgment will be reserved not for the sinners out there in the world but for the sinners right here inside the church. We are the ones whom God will treat with a fuller's soap and a refiner's fire. We are the ones who have been exposed for engaging in one sexual scandal after another. We are the ones who engage in praise and worship inside our churches while remaining silent about the drug addiction, alcoholism, malnutrition, and failing public schools just outside the walls of our sanctuaries. Conservative political activists, most of whom undoubtedly have a church affiliation, condemn the "wasteful" spending of "big government," especially when it comes to spending on health care for all Americans, but say nothing about the human and economic costs of war.

Many in the church limit their justice agenda to the issues of abortion and human sexuality. Those same people have nothing to say about racism, sexism, prison overcrowding, cruel immigration policies, or the persistent poverty in the United States driven in part by the fact that 80 percent of the nation's wealth is controlled by less than 10 percent of the population. These Christians are quick to condemn the injustices they perceive elsewhere, but as Jesus noted in Matthew 7:3, they see the speck of sawdust in the eye of others but do not notice the plank in their own eye.

The day of judgment will surely come, but the church will be surprised by whom God chooses to judge most harshly. God speaks to the people of God with words of despair and judgment (Matt. 25:41–43): "Depart from me . . . for I was hungry and you gave me no food, I was thirsty and you gave me nothing to drink, I was a stranger and you did not welcome me."

Luke 1:68–79

If Malachi 3:1–4 tells us that God will send a messenger who will prepare the way and cleanse the temple, then Luke 1:68–79 tells us that messenger is John the Baptist. If Malachi warns Israel about the certainty of God's wrath in response to the sins of Israel, this passage reminds us about the certainty of

God's grace and forgiveness for those who are willing to repent of their sins. That is the message of Advent and of Jesus Christ; there is hope for the sinner. This Song of Zechariah (the Benedictus) is a parallel to the Song of Mary (the Magnificat), because both songs celebrate God's gracious intervention in history on behalf of the poor and the repentant.

The words spoken by Zechariah concerning the impact of John the Baptist's birth should inform our preaching today. We, too, should give God's people the knowledge of salvation through the forgiveness of their sins (v. 77). At a time when we give so much attention to the prosperity gospel which suggests that God's chief concern is to make people wealthy and healthy, this verse points us back to our true mission and calling as Christian preachers—the salvation of God's people through the forgiveness of their sins. Gardner Taylor wondered whether most preaching these days could rightly be defined as Christian, because so much of it excludes what he calls the "Jesus Presence."[1] Those who give attention to this passage in their preaching will not be guilty of such a breakdown.

God is surely a God of wrath where injustice is concerned, but Zechariah points to "the tender mercy of our God" (v. 78). John's message would announce the coming of the Messiah who will establish God's realm on earth, a realm that will be marked by a time when God will "guide our feet into the way of peace" (v. 79). That will be a time of wholeness, well-being, security, happiness, and contentment that will extend to all people. This is the message that we must preach. Someone has come into the world to redeem the people from sin. The covenant God once made with Israel has been reworked to include all those who put their faith in Jesus Christ. Those who, having repented of their own sins first, then commit to preaching a gospel of repentance and the forgiveness of sin can reverse the cruelty and injustice that surround us.

Philippians 1:3–11

This passage points us ahead to a future day of judgment, now referred to as the day of Christ Jesus. The image drawn here involves the second coming of Christ and the judgment of God's people that will take place at that time. While the Great Judgment scene in Matthew 25:31–44 points to specific acts of care and compassion that God's people should show, this passage speaks about discipleship and faithfulness in other ways. Paul gives thanks for the continued faithfulness and support the Philippian church has given him over

1. Gardner C. Taylor, "Is Our Preaching CHRISTIAN?" *The African American Pulpit*, Summer 2009, 40.

the years of his ministry (vv. 4–5). Paul then prays that the good work God has begun in those people and in that church will continue unabated until the day of Christ Jesus (v. 6).

That good work obviously begins with the prayers and the financial support that church offered to Paul. It would be good if Christians would support their churches with their prayers and with their finances. How sad it is that in so many churches, fewer than 20 percent of the people provide more than 80 percent of the money and the ministry effort. However, that is not all that Paul has in mind. Paul prays that those who have been supportive of him in the past will "determine what is best" and remain "pure and blameless" until the day of Christ Jesus (vv. 9–10). This points back to the Malachi passage and God's desire for a people purged of all sin. It also points to Ephesians 5:27, where Christ sought to offer the church up to God "without a spot or wrinkle," or 2 Peter 3:14, where believers are encouraged to "strive to be found by him at peace, without spot or blemish."

Not only should Christians seek to be personally pure and blameless, but Paul also says they should be filled with "the harvest of righteousness that comes through Jesus Christ" (v. 11). The word is not "justice," which points to the acts we should do by law or duty. The word is "righteousness," which points to those acts of kindness and concern we should freely display out of hearts filled with compassion and concern for others. Aristotle talks about being a "virtuous person," which involves three things: (1) making right choices, (2) making those right choices on a voluntary basis, (3) making right choices on a voluntary basis over a continuing period of time.[2] This is a good equivalent to being righteous, and people who live this way will have nothing to fear on the day of Christ Jesus.

Luke 3:1–6

In a world where power and influence were exercised by Tiberius Caesar, Pontius Pilate, Herod, Philip, Annas, and Caiaphas, the word of the Lord came to John the son of Zechariah in the desert. Our world is fascinated with the rich and famous and powerful, but among them we will not necessarily find persons at work with God. In 1 Corinthians 1:26–27, Paul mentions that God intentionally chose not to work only through the wise, the influential, or those of noble birth. Instead, God chose to go to work radically among the weak, the lowly, and the despised. The church has a message that will not be heard from the White House or on CNN—that is, to repent. The just society that we desire cannot be achieved by an act of Congress or a ruling by the

---

2. Wyndy Corbin Reuschling, *Reviving Evangelical Ethics: The Promises and Pitfalls of Classic Models of Morality* (Grand Rapids: Brazos Press, 2008), 56.

U.S. Supreme Court. The church must declare its message of repentance for the forgiveness of sins and the call to transformation.

Christianity in America has had a love affair with the idea of "silk stocking churches," urban and suburban congregations, black and white, composed of people who are rich and influential. The challenge for such churches has always been to engage in the gritty urban issues that are usually present in multiple forms right outside the doors of their sanctuaries. Like the rich man in Luke 16:19–31 who went to hell because he refused to see or respond to the needs of poor Lazarus who was sitting right outside the rich man's gate, many members along with the pastors of prominent churches may end up in hell for the very same reason. Harry Emerson Fosdick long ago referred to such Christians and their churches as being "rich in things and poor in soul."[3]

People long "to see the salvation of God" (v. 6). They eagerly wait for the day when crooked things will be made straight and rough ways made smooth (v. 5). Sadly, all that most churchgoers do is wait for God to do this work alone. Rather than using its resources and influence to help shape a just society, the church merely waits for the day to come. John calls upon the church to repent of its sins and then to challenge the world to do the same. Israel had been waiting for the Messiah for seven hundred years before Christ appeared. Most of Israel rejected the idea that he was the Messiah. However, those who believed in Christ's message of repentance shared that good news with the world. Today we must declare that same message of repentance as a first step on the road to becoming a just society, the beloved community, and to God's reign in our midst! In the words of Zechariah 4:6, the future we desire will come "not by might, nor by power, but by my spirit, says the LORD of hosts."

3. Harry Emerson Fosdick, "God of Grace and God of Glory," in *The Worshipping Church*, ed. Donald P. Hustad (Carol Stream, IL: Hope Publishing Co., 1990), 669.

Universal Declaration
of Human Rights (December 10)

Christine Marie Smith

LEVITICUS 25:1–17
PSALM 33:10–22
JAMES 2:1–7
MATTHEW 20:1–16

In the shadow of World War II, the United Nations set forth the Universal Declaration of Human Rights on December 10, 1948. This document asserts that all human beings are free, equal, and entitled to dignity, safety, peace, and security regardless of nationality, gender, race, ethnicity, or religion. It prohibits actions that deny these values (such as slavery, torture, or discrimination). Commemorating it in Advent, the preacher could help the congregation to repent of violations of these rights and to recognize that living by them can be an important component in preparing for the Advent of Christ.

Disregard and contempt for human rights have resulted in barbarous acts . . . and [call for] the advent of a world in which human beings shall enjoy freedom of speech and belief and freedom from fear and want (Preamble). All are born free and equal in dignity and rights. They are endowed with reason and conscience and should act towards one another in a spirit of [mutuality] (Article 1). Everyone has the right to a standard of living adequate for health and well-being (Article 16).
United Nations Universal Declaration of Human Rights

Any preacher who decides to preach about the Universal Declaration of Human Rights during Advent will not find it difficult to connect the great human vision and hope that the creators of this declaration had for a more just and humane world with the eschatological visions and hopes of this season. During Advent we actively await the transformation of our world, and we give

16

voice to the kind of visions of repentance, hope, and justice that just might help the global human community create such a world.

This Sunday is an important time to remind our religious communities that we do indeed have a global agreement, a global declaration, that affirms the inherent worth and dignity of every human being, and that there is still so much work to be done to make this declaration of human rights a reality for all God's people. In this blessed Advent season, preachers are called to proclaim a word of truth and indictment for our human failures to uphold and ensure the basic human rights of all people. If Advent is a season of waiting, then let us have the courage to remind ourselves that millions of people around the globe live in unbearable cycles of waiting: waiting for water and food, waiting for shelter and a place to call home, waiting for an end to daily emotional and physical violence, waiting for just a taste of God's promise of justice. Speaking the truth about the horrible, crushing waiting that the majority of human beings spend a lifetime experiencing could be our humble, heartfelt Advent confession.

Also, it is our responsibility to proclaim words of hope and promise. It is never too late to take action on behalf of most of the human community, who suffer from extreme oppression and injustice and who die unnecessary, heinous deaths while we who are privileged lead lives in which many articles of the Universal Declaration of Human Rights have come to fruition. We need to work for and defend the kind of basic human rights that all people need in order to survive and have some measure of safety, freedom, and dignity. This might be our heartfelt Advent vision.

Leviticus 25:1–17

This section of Leviticus confronts us with a profound vision of how human beings are to live in just relationship with one another and with the land that nourishes and sustains us. The land and all of creation are gifts from God, and human beings are custodians, stewards, temporary residents—no more, no less. God is portrayed so clearly as the ultimate landowner and holder that in verse 23 human beings are declared to be tenants and aliens. Prophetic preaching on this Sunday will surely involve lifting up this wonderfully shocking vision that every Israelite, every human being, has a right to a portion of the land in order to survive and feed one's self and one's family. This proclamation in Leviticus is its own universal declaration of human rights about land, the just ordering of creation, and the survival of all. No one really owns any part of God's creation, nor are those who have economic means entitled to a large portion of the land while others have none. All people, no matter what their circumstances, have a basic right to fairness and restoration in returning to their original and rightful portion of the land.

There is no hard evidence to suggest that the Israelites ever followed the demanding vision of jubilee described so clearly in this passage, and it is not difficult to imagine why it may never have been accomplished. It would be like every single displaced Guatemalan family returning to their rightful portion of Guatemalan land regardless of whether it is owned by a wealthy landowner or an international corporation. It would look like every family living under temporary tents in Haiti returning to a portion of their own land on which they could survive. It would be like returning to Mexico every single portion of land in the United States that was a part of the original country of Mexico. It would be like the United States erasing massive foreign debt that poor countries have accumulated to benefit the interests of the landed elite of those countries, while that debt enslaves the poor in a poverty cycle that is growing more massive with each and every year. There have been jubilee moments in the history of our global economy, but Leviticus reminds us that the social and economic realities of the Sabbath and of the years of jubilee should be the constant and repeated ordering of God's creation.

Psalm 33:10–22

This psalm is one of praise and gratitude for the steadfast love of God in our individual lives and for God's loving and enduring presence in all of creation. This is the powerful hope that we name and proclaim during the season of Advent. Our Advent hope is that God and human beings together might be able to create a more just world where the Universal Declaration of Human Rights is more than a vision for the future, but is a vision that we can realize in small and great ways in our daily lives and in the lives of people around the globe.

The words of the psalmist remind us that kings and armies, warriors and war horses "cannot save" (vv. 16–17). Only God's redemptive work in the world, incarnated through individuals, communities, and nations, is the kind of power strong enough to stop the endless violation of human rights that surrounds us, and it is God's power and steadfast love that will not let us go until all people have the basic life necessities included in the Universal Declaration of Human Rights. God is watching humankind (vv. 13–14)! And as abstract as this may seem, God holds us accountable for our sisters and brothers and their well-being if we take it seriously. With the metaphor of God's eye upon us in our hearts and minds (v. 18), let our preaching give an account of our deeds and our actions to the one who fashioned the hearts of us all (v. 15).

Matthew 20:1–16

This parable about the laborers in the vineyard confounds and challenges people of privilege and proclaims a rare word of compassion and justice for those who are poor and without work. It is most often interpreted as a parable of grace or a parable about God's surprising generosity. Perhaps it is a parable about human dignity as well. In the Universal Declaration of Human Rights, there are no "ifs" before any of the thirty articles that articulate the rights of all people. If you do certain things, then you "earn" the right to employment or education. If you are a particular kind of person, or you have certain economic resources, you "earn" your right to freedom of expression and the right to an adequate standard of living that includes housing, medical care, clothing, and food. All you have to be is a human person to be seen as worthy of the same rights as every other person. In this parable there are no "ifs" either. The workers do not have to work the same length of time to be paid a day's living wage. The workers do not have to be lucky enough to be hired early in the day to be paid a day's living wage. All the workers who come to the marketplace looking and hoping for work have the same right to a day's living wage. Many preachers so quickly make the landowner God and the laborers human beings in need of God's grace that we seldom are challenged to consider the economic realities at the heart of this parable. Those of us who are Euro-Americans are so accustomed to competition and a hierarchy of things that make one worthy of being employed, worthy of being paid a living wage, worthy of being treated with dignity, that this parable seems unfair and outrageous. People of privilege assume that they will receive what is greater and of more worth because they are entitled to it. It should shock us as religious people that we are more concerned about what is earned and fair than what is grace-filled and generous.

It would be in the spirit of the Universal Declaration of Human Rights to preach a sermon about the dignity of a day's living wage. Human rights are about material, social, and economic rights and privileges, but human rights are also about preserving the inherent dignity of the human person. Perhaps it is past time for preachers to linger on the fact that each worker went home that night with enough money to feed a family for another day.

James 2:1–7

One of the tenets of Latin American liberation theology is God's preferential option for the poor. For people of privilege, this theological assertion seems nearly unbearable, for God surely loves and cares for all of us with fierce and absolute equality. For the poor, this theological assertion must feel unbelievably hope-filled and honoring. Until the poor in our world have adequate resources to sustain their lives and restore dignity to their humanity, then God surely is urging and calling all of us in the human family to eradicate injustice, violence, and genocide that bring daily death to the poor. Has this call become one of our primary and deepest religious commitments? A similar principle applies to the Universal Declaration of Human Rights. Surely God is calling us to struggle for the basic rights of those who have no food, shelter, education, or medical care as our primary and deepest social and economic commitment before we struggle for the right to rest and leisure.

In this passage from James, the writer confronts us with the biases that cause us to give preferential treatment to those who are rich. In the highly stratified social context of the ancient world, James is boldly calling people to be unabashedly biased, all right, but to be biased on the side of those human beings who are poor. The writer of James, like the Latin American liberation theologians of our time, believes in a God who seeks after and chooses the poor as those who deserve and need our human advocacy and activism the most. As preachers, how can we join with members of the religious communities we serve to begin honestly to deconstruct and critique our privileged biases and prejudices that keep us affirming and advocating for the universal rights of the elite at the expense of God's larger family who do not possess even the most basic human rights?

Third Sunday of Advent

Monica A. Coleman

ZEPHANIAH 3:14–20
ISAIAH 12:2–6
PHILIPPIANS 4:4–7
LUKE 3:7–18

This week's lectionary readings invite us to remember that positive change is difficult, but necessary and worthwhile. John the Baptist's call to repentance, Paul's reminder that God offers presence and peace, and the praises of the prophets Isaiah and Zephaniah take us on a journey through the challenges of deep creative transformation through the God who sustains and supports us in our pursuits of justice. These texts remind us that the road to justice requires sacrifice, but the labor will pay off in the end.

Luke 3:7–18

Luke's portrayal of John the Baptist differs from the other Gospels that focus on his apocalyptic preaching (Matthew and Mark) or on his visionary ability to recognize Jesus as Savior before others. Luke's discussion of John the Baptist is more grounded in how the world in which he lives can be transformed. While using harsh language to describe the differences between those who truly repent and those who do not, this passage exhorts us to remember the challenging task of change.

The verses prior to this selection indicate that John the Baptist is in the wilderness, baptizing people and calling them to repentance. As this selection begins, John is chastising the crowds by calling them vipers—a poisonous snake common to the region. There are people who want to be baptized but have no intention of changing their lives or living ethically. The phrase "We have Abraham as our ancestor" implies that the Jewish people whom John baptized believed that their heritage and the ritual of baptism were sufficient for forgiveness and new life. John is clear that more is required. In essence, people have to change their lives for the better. Those working in justice movements can relate to John's admonition. When a new cause comes to the fore, large numbers of people are often excited and willing to be a part of the movement. But movements for a more just society require more than passion and excitement; they need a level of commitment that alters one's life. Only then can we change the world.

John's language is harsh: "the ax is lying at the root of the trees; every tree therefore that does not bear good fruit is cut down and thrown into the fire" (v. 9). Perhaps John is stating that the world most needs individuals who are willing to commit to justice with their actions as well as their words. Perhaps John's biting tongue serves to more deeply motivate the crowds to change. It seems to have the desired effect. Here, unlike in Matthew and Mark, the crowds ask, "What should we do?"

John's response gives three examples of how the community might create a more ethical and just world. Share with those who do not have. Since this query comes from "the crowds," we can presume that this is advice for ordinary people. If you have two coats, share with those who have none; if you have more food than you need, share with those who have none. As simple as a kindergarten lesson, the edict to share is a reminder that there might truly be enough for everyone if resources were more equitably distributed. First-world countries continue to live in ways of excess that literally impoverish two-thirds of the world's population. A basic ethic of sharing is a step toward justice that all can take. It rings of the environmental slogan "Live simply so others can simply live."

The tax collectors ask again, "What should we do?" The soldiers ask again, "What should we do?" The repeated asking suggests that simply following rules is not sufficient; we need to ask again and again for each context of our lives. The requirements for one group of people may not be the same for another group. Some communities may need to be more empowered; other communities may need to relinquish power. John's response to the tax collectors and soldiers offers a second lesson that is as relevant to contemporary society as it was to the text's historical audience: do not abuse power. It is clear from the passage that people expected tax collectors and soldiers to exact more from people than their jobs demanded. For these reasons, they were feared and despised. The request not to abuse power should be a simple one, yet in a society where it has become commonplace, a healthy use of power is an important move toward justice.

John does not state that radical change is necessary for individuals and communities to experience God's justice. These are actually small, everyday things that can be done. This is seemingly modest transformation—share; don't abuse power. Yet these acts can help to issue justice in the world.

Again, John deflects the attention from himself and onto the greater good that is to come. John's reference is to Jesus, but also to the new relationship between God and God's people that Jesus manifests. Luke reminds us that the Holy Spirit (the reference to fire will be even more prominent in Acts) is far more powerful than the ritual of baptism. Likewise, the more just society for which we work is more important than the individual acts of today's prophets and preachers. There is something larger than the words and activities in which we engage, and the Spirit of God undergirds it.

Philippians 4:4–7

In Philippians, Paul continues the message from the Lukan text that addresses the way to God, righteousness, and justice. The verses before this selection indicate that Euodia and Syntyche disagree over the way to Christ. Here Paul provides a response.

The prescription to rejoice is no small one for populations who continue to experience oppression and persecution. We are called to rejoice even when things seem dismal and desperate, even in the face of destruction. We can do this because "the Lord is near." While these words may signal the ways in which early churches expected the immediate return of Jesus, they may also be interpreted as a reassurance of God's presence. We can rejoice because God is near to us. We should not be worried, but we should remain in prayer with God.

What an important word of solace to those who may be weary of the struggle for justice! Rejoice! God supports and undergirds the work. Rejoice! We can continue to nurture our relationship with God, trusting that God knows about us and hears us. Rejoice! The way to righteousness and justice is paved with a joy that is grounded in assurance of God's presence and prayer. The reward for this is a peace that is illogical in the face of what is apparent to those around us. Prayer and presence can grant an internal peace to those who are working for outward peace in areas of war and violence.

Zephaniah 3:14–20

The words from the prophets Zephaniah and Isaiah are words of renewal to the exiled Israelites that follow words of condemnation. There is destruction and exile around them. The selection from Zephaniah follows charges made against Israel. They have failed to listen to God; they have strayed; they have not trusted God. They are warned of the disaster that will come if they do not repent. And the words "gather together" (2:1) call them to repent.

We can hear these words as a relevant strategy for us today. Wars and acts of terrorism splinter people within and between religions. One of the most highly developed countries, the United States of America, has one of the world's largest rates of imprisonment. As public education fails its students, many turn to private institutions and charter schools. In big ways and small, we become separated from one another. This passage need not imply that our current situations result from disobeying God or lack the faith of our traditions; rather, this passage suggests that crises are best addressed in community. It is easy for justice workers to focus on the individual tasks and causes to which they are called, but the inherent challenges should not cause us to work in isolation from or against one another. Zephaniah reminds us to stay in communication with others who are fighting for justice, and to build coalitions. Such ingathering can help address the destruction in our midst.

Then the tone of the passage shifts. The God of judgment is a God who consoles. Three themes emerge that give cause for rejoicing. The first message is that God is in the midst of the people. Despite the challenges and the distressing conditions in our midst, God has not abandoned God's people. This is an important message for those striving for creative transformation in today's world. God has not left the world to its own devices. God is active in the world. God is with us. This is the joy of the Advent message.

Second, God is in active relationship with us. Not only is Israel called to rejoice, but God is moved by the Israelites as well: "[God] will rejoice over you with gladness, [God] will renew you in [God's] love; [God] will exult over you with loud singing" (v. 17b). Our interaction with God is not a one-way street. God desires to be in relationship with the world. God desires to see justice in the world.

Third, God will help to facilitate justice in the world. The Scripture ends by indicating that God will gather. As an echo of the strategy for repentance, we see that we will have help. God does not leave us on our own to enact justice in the world. We are not strictly punished. We are not abandoned. God will help create the community that we need to see justice. This is cause for celebration!

Isaiah 12:2–6

Probably written only sixty years before the Zephaniah passage, the words from Isaiah echo the same themes of idolatry, threat, and restoration. Only a remnant remains—a remnant that has been faithful, that has turned back toward God.

This Scripture presents a psalm found outside of the book of Psalms. Some scholars even suggest that there are two psalms, and both offer thanksgiving. The refrain in verse 2 indicates thanksgiving for God's deliverance. The remaining verses introduce the metaphor of water in the wells of salvation.

This language not only indicates that we need God's salvation for life, it also draws our attention to how we must foster this life. In today's world, clean water is becoming more and more scarce, despite our technology. The richest corporations and nations claim water rights over rivers and parts of oceans. The poorest people must travel miles with buckets to find water for cooking, bathing, and drinking. Although there is enough water for everyone, structures of injustice inhibit access for all. As we recall that the root word for "salvation" is "salve," or healing, this text reminds us that health and water are basic needs for all living creatures. We all need to be able to draw water from the well; we all must be saved.

While individuals and organizations work toward justice for all, this passage provides assurance in God. We can rejoice in the midst of the work for justice because we are undergirded by trust in God. We do not have to do the work on our own. This is cause for thanks!

Fourth Sunday of Advent

John M. Buchanan

MICAH 5:2–5A
PSALM 80:1–7
HEBREWS 10:5–10
LUKE 1:39–45 (46–55)

The preacher is challenged to get all this material into a sermon and must make thoughtful choices or maybe shorten the sermon for the Fourth Sunday of Advent, Christmas Sunday, and simply read all of the texts. A reason not do that, as tempting as it seems, is that the dramatic birth of the child is for a purpose, and that purpose has everything in the world to do with the way human life is lived in the world, which is to say with complex and often controversial matters like justice and peace. The preacher should not jerk the congregation away from Bethlehem, and all it entails, too abruptly. Nor should the congregation be left thinking that the story ends there, that having celebrated Christmas there is nothing more to be said and done until next year.

Micah 5:2–5a

The beloved reference to Bethlehem and the leader who will come from there to rule Israel and "stand and feed his flock" is preceded by four chapters of strenuous and provocative prose. The prophet is angry at what he sees in Samaria and Judah. No less so today, idolatry and injustice describe the days in which we live, when Wall Street executives enjoy extravagant bonuses while hundreds of thousands of people lose their homes through foreclosure. Micah saw fields coveted and seized, houses taken away, inheritances lost, and householders oppressed. His vision of a ruler from Bethlehem who will be a shepherd and "the one of peace" is not a sentimental abstraction suitable for a Christmas card greeting, but an affirmation that God's gift of this ruler has to do with ending injustice and violent warfare, and with producing security and

26

peace, a time when people will be free to enjoy the fruit of their labor, sitting beneath their own vines and fig trees, no longer living in fear.

If the sermon is built on the extended Gospel reading, which also may take the place of the psalm, the preacher might remember that it was Micah who anticipated the radical ideas in Mary's Magnificat: "and what does the LORD require of you, but to do justice, and to love kindness, and to walk humbly with your God?" (Mic. 6:8).

Psalm 80:1–7

The preacher can also choose Luke 1:46–55, the Magnificat—"Mary's little revolutionary song," Will Willimon called it once—in place of the psalm this Sunday.[1] In Psalm 80 the holy, righteous God of antiquity is called the "Shepherd of Israel," surely one of the most beloved and theologically important ideas in Judaism and Christianity. The image of shepherd nurtures as well as assures us: "The LORD is my shepherd, I shall not want" (Ps. 23); "I am the good shepherd. The good shepherd lays down his life for the sheep" (John 10:11). God's grieving, oppressed people, eating the bread of tears, turn to the shepherd for hope and salvation and peace.

Today's psalm voices the cry of every oppressed people. From slavery in Egypt to becoming the international doormat of the Middle East, with one after another of the great military powers in the region invading, subjugating, exiling, and extracting tribute, God's people are scorned, humiliated, and ridiculed. The words of lament resonate down through the ages and speak for every suffering, oppressed people: African slaves in the United States, prisoners in Nazi concentration camps, marginalized people in our society today. "Restore us, O God [of hosts]; let your face shine, that we may be saved" (vv. 3 and 7).

There is no triumphalism here. The God of incarnation, whom Advent anticipates, will come to redeem and save. It will be in a manner nobody expects and few recognize; old political and military scores will not be settled on the battlefield or by revolution that reverses the established social order. Some of that may happen, but the divine intervention Psalm 80 pleads for will happen modestly, quietly, in a stable behind a crowded Bethlehem inn as a child is born. Wonder of wonders! The shining face of God for which we hope and long and pray will come in the tiny face of a newborn.

---

1. William H. Willimon, *On a Wild and Windy Mountain and 25 Other Meditations for the Christian Year* (Nashville: Abingdon Press, 1984), 21.

Hebrews 10:5–10

The passage is complicated; it is not always clear who is speaking. In one sentence, Christ is speaking to God, "Sacrifices and offerings you have not desired" (v. 5). In the next sentence, it appears that the author of Hebrews takes over: "Then I said, 'See, God, I have come to do your will, O God'" (v. 7). Then it is "he said" (v. 8), which refers back to Christ. The pericope as a whole is a reminder that the life of the man Jesus, born in Bethlehem of Judea, was a reflection of his people's religion at its highest and best. The author imagines Jesus saying, "Sacrifices and offerings you have not desired, . . . in burnt offerings and sin offerings you have taken no pleasure" (vv. 5–6). It is a clear reflection of another watershed moment in the religion of God's people when the prophet Amos, angry at what he was seeing in the social, political, economic, and personal life of the nation and its neighbors, thundered, "Let justice roll down like waters, and righteousness like an ever-flowing stream" (Amos 5:24).

The preacher might risk reminding the Christmas Sunday congregation that the child, whose birth will be celebrated with lovely custom, beautiful music, and a general tenor of generosity and good cheer, grew up and became a man whose words and deeds were not always celebrated. The preacher might risk a gentle reminder to the holiday congregation that Jesus was a faithful, observant Jew, who knew and quoted from Hebrew Scriptures, who certainly knew the words of Amos about justice flowing down, and Micah's famous summary of true religion (Mic. 6:6–8):

> With what shall I come before the LORD?
> . . . .
> Shall I come before him with burnt offerings,
> . . . .
> . . . with thousands of rams,
>   with ten thousands of rivers of oil?
> . . . .
> [The Lord] has told you, O mortal, what is good;
>   and what does the LORD require of you
> but to do justice, and to love kindness,
>   and to walk humbly with your God?

The preacher might suggest that the efficacy and authenticity of any celebration of the birth of the Christ child, the coming of God incarnate into human history, is in the humble walk with God, the kindness shared, and the real justice established in the world.

Luke 1:39–45 (46–55)

Luke begins his "orderly account" of the life of Jesus and the events surrounding him with a lengthy and formal prologue. His goal in writing is to impart the truth, the good news, to Theophilus, whose name appears here and also in the introduction to volume 2 of Luke's description of the beginning of Christianity, the Acts of the Apostles. Scholars suspect that Theophilus is a literary device Luke employs to frame his extraordinary tale, to ground it in life. He prepares his readers with a series of brief incidents that are beautifully written and elegant speeches by fascinating characters—Zechariah and Elizabeth and their newborn son John, the angel Gabriel, Mary of Nazareth, and, later, two wonderful elderly bit players, Simeon and Anna. Simeon's speech on the occasion of Mary's purification is a high point of Scripture as literature and a beloved liturgical prayer in the church down across the centuries, the Nunc Dimittis: "Master, now you are dismissing your servant in peace, . . . for my eyes have seen your salvation" (vv. 29–30). The prophet Anna also recognized the baby as God's redeemer.

Once again the preacher must decide how much of this beautiful story to include. Mary's visit to her older relative Elizabeth, also surprisingly pregnant, is preceded by the annunciation, in which the angel Gabriel startles young Mary of Nazareth with news that she will have a child even though she is not married and has not had sexual intercourse. Can the sermon deal with this event without becoming bogged down in a tedious discussion of the virgin birth? A good full sermon on the fascinating character of Mary in a series on these compelling characters in Luke's nativity may be better than interrupting the energy of the sermon to discuss what we mean and do not mean by Mary's virginity.

Italian Renaissance artists were fascinated with that moment when the angel appeared to Mary, and they painted it gorgeously. Frederick Buechner captures it beautifully in words:

> The pastel blues and pinks and purples, the angel's shimmering wings. Mary's look of quiet wonder, her head tilted toward the angel as his head tilted toward hers. He tells her not to be afraid but he is quaking in fear at the thought that the history of humankind now depends on the answer of a young girl.[2]

---

2. Frederick Buechner, *Peculiar Treasures: A Biblical Who's Who* (New York: Harper & Row, 1979), 39.

One of the best images of this scene, by Fra Angelico, hangs on the wall of the monastery of San Marcos in Florence, at the head of the stairs where the monks could see it every night before retiring.

"Do not be afraid," the angel tells Mary. Of course she is deeply afraid, perplexed, and anxious. "How can this be?" she asks him, but the real questions in her heart are, "What am I going to tell my parents, and what will the neighbors think?" Most frightening of all, what is she going to tell her fiancé? So she visits Elizabeth, an older relative, her aunt perhaps, who is six months along in her own unlikely and unexpected pregnancy. Elizabeth opens her home and her arms and her heart. She thinks Mary's embarrassing, awkward, and morally questionable condition is just wonderful. "Blessed are you among women," Elizabeth says to the frightened, marginalized adolescent. Every teenager needs an aunt like that, or a caring, responsible adult like Elizabeth.

That's the moment when Mary finally speaks, and what words they are! "My soul magnifies the Lord, . . . for [God] has looked with favor on the lowliness of [God's] servant." Then Mary describes what God has done and will do, a list that does not appear in Christmas cards. God has "scattered the proud . . . , brought down the powerful from their thrones, . . . filled the hungry . . . , and sent the rich away empty" (Luke 1:51–53).

The preacher can get in trouble for saying things like that. There are places in the world where the Magnificat is not translated from Latin because of its troublesome political and economic ideas. Mary's song, and before that her unlikely vocation to give birth to God's son, tell us something important about God, the true meaning of Christmas, and the believers' 365-day-a-year vocation. Young, poor, vulnerable, morally marginalized Mary means that God comes into the world in unexpected ways, through the lives of humble, unlikely, and often excluded, marginalized people. As this young woman avers, God cares deeply and passionately about people and how they live. God cares particularly about those who are shut out, people who are hungry in this abundant economy. The Magnificat ought to make us uncomfortable with the reality of homelessness in this land of plenty, the reality that millions of our children go to bed hungry every night, the reality that our economy and tax structure exacerbate the gap between rich and poor. God cares a lot about injustice and inequality and poverty and unnecessary human suffering.

A sermon on these texts ought not to scold but merely proclaim what the Bible says here about God and Mary. Her story could inspire us all to loosen our grips, upset our value system, and come to terms with our own vulnerability and dependence on others: those deepest needs the Christ child comes to meet.

Christmas Day

Elizabeth Conde-Frazier

ISAIAH 52:7–10
PSALM 98
HEBREWS 1:1–4 (5–12)
JOHN 1:1–14

How do we create alternative realities for the advent of hope in the future? Reflecting on our Christology and the many dimensions of the person of Jesus leads us to ask who he is to us and how that relationship changes who we are to others. Christ's birth is our own beginning as children of light. The Scriptures guide us in these reflections today.

Isaiah 52:7–10

The central message of this passage from Second Isaiah concerns the sovereignty of God. The people of Israel have been in exile and have lost a sense of identity, including religious identity. Away from all that is familiar to them, living in the land of their enemies, has been a suffering and disorienting experience. This affliction does not make it easy to see God, much less to see God as sovereign. God is absent, and God's arm, a symbol of strength and victory for the people, is not evident. Other powers are more visibly in control—other rulers (Nebuchadnezzar) and other gods (Baal and Molech). Among the powers in control are the people's own fears and lethargy. During this exile their consciousness has been fashioned by their oppression. However, transformation is about to take place. In this pericope the watchmen can see the redemption of God in plain sight (v. 8). The watchmen sing for joy because they see the return of God to Zion. "How beautiful upon the mountains are the feet of the messenger who announces peace, who brings good news" (v. 7). This is Advent! There will be peace and salvation. God will comfort and redeem Jerusalem (v. 9). God now bares God's holy arm, and all the nations of the earth see the salvation of God.

31

Today we can surmise that a God whose reign is sovereign comes to liberate all who, like Israel in the exile, are oppressed and in need of justice. Advent is their reminder that God comes to bring salvation.

I work in a community in which the public school system does not adequately prepare students for higher education. This results in perpetuating the oppression and consciousness of poverty. The vast majority of students believe that college is not for them, that they will fail. From that community there is no direct transportation to the financial and political district of the city, a subtle message that those residents should not set their eyes on working in places of upward mobility and of decision making for their communities.

The presence of a college where they can redeem their educational path is the advent of hope for a future. Students affirm this at every graduation when they tell their stories of hardship and the transformation that education affords them. Many colleges and universities have their roots in a time when the church had a defined sense of education as mission. How might we renew and revive this mission as part of a vision for social justice?

Psalm 98

This psalm is a response to God's deliverance. The God to be praised is a cosmic God, and therefore human beings and all creation praise God. The reason for their praise is that "all the ends of the earth have seen the victory of our God" (v. 3). The one who praises sees God's victory although it has not yet come. Perceiving it in the present moment evokes an invitation to celebrate the future and coming victory as a present hope. The psalm is both eschatological and cosmic.

The first to praise are those who believe in God's steadfast love and faithfulness (v. 3). They praise as a natural response to God's greatness and marvelous deeds by singing with their musical instruments and exclamations of acclaim and tribute (vv. 1, 4–6). This is praise not in good times but in times when the people have experienced the "disasters of sin and the terrors of history."[1] The praise is not an expression of a doctrinal belief but of a faith in the God who is sovereign and who comes to "judge the world with righteousness, and the peoples with equity" (v. 9). In other words, God comes to make right the relationships that have been disconnected and distorted.

This psalm contains themes similar to those of the psalms of enthronement, which were public celebrations of new monarchs. In this case the monarch is God, which signals that this may have been an exilic psalm. This is

1. Raymond C. Van Leeuwen, "Psalm 98," in *Psalms for Preaching and Worship: A Lectionary Commentary*, ed. Roger E. Van Harn and Brent A. Strawn (Grand Rapids: Eerdmans, 2009), 258.

anticipatory praise that creates an image of an alternative reality, the marvelous salvific acts of a righteous God.

When oppression is so strong that it seems that all efforts, all strategies, are defeated, when our voices are silenced, the liturgy becomes a moment of enacting the coming righteousness and judgment of God. To sing a new song defies and resists the oppressing hand of an abuser who wants to create the image of being the only and final option for its victim. Instead of paralyzing silence, a new song breaks out. In the midst of the most pressing cruelty, those abused and those working with them to create new realities can sing a new song as they continue to work toward a break to the violence. It is a celebration of a coming justice for those broken by mistreatment. This was the testimony of a woman who during a panel discussion on vocation spoke of how she attended college despite beatings because she believed in a different future for herself. She spoke of how God's right hand and holy arm had gotten her victory (v. 1). This determined belief in a new reality sustained her and led her to break with her isolation to find the support systems she needed.

Hebrews 1:1–4 (5–12)

This passage is prologue to an epistle about the Christology of the church. It affirms that God speaks and urges us to not refuse the one speaking (vv. 1–2).

The passage names the more recent form of God's self-disclosure. God has chosen a Son. What follows are statements that describe the Son and how God reveals Godself through the Son. The Son is heir of all, and through him the worlds were made (v. 2). The statement implies the preexistence of the Son who at the beginning of all things participates in the act of creation. He is the owner and ruler of all. Heirs inherited not only land, but cities and nations. Jesus as heir is ruler, administrator, and possessor.

Verse 3 declares the Son to be "the reflection of God's glory and the exact imprint of God's very being." This refers to the very distinct form and character of God. To know Jesus is to know and see God's glory.

The creation brought into existence by God's powerful word is sustained by the Son. The creation is an intimate part of God's expression of revelation to us. How does God speak through the creation, through every living organism and being? When we disregard or destroy the creation, what happens to the expression of God in it? As God offers this self-revelation, what is our response to God? We are not used to including this word of God in our lives in the same way as other forms of God's speaking to us. We can conclude that God speaks to us through creation. When we distance ourselves from creation, destroying it for reasons of gain, neglect, or selfishness, we shut down the voice of God to us and have gone astray in our hearts. How can we redeem this?

Verse 3 continues speaking of the Son's purification for sins and his sitting down at the right hand of the majesty in exaltation. Traditionally this is interpreted as the letter's theology of the cross, in which the sustainer of creation becomes the sin-bearer, the priestly nature of Christ. Because the Son now sits at the right hand of majesty, the Son-priest is also king.

After four verses we are left gazing at a Son who is an imprint of God, who acts on God's behalf and authority. King Jesus has a place of honor with God that is greater than that of the angels. This is Jesus, whose semblance on earth was that of a poor carpenter. He died because of his stance with the lowly.

How do the images of the son in the manger, the exalted king, and the crucified carpenter come together, and what significance do they have for us? When we struggle against injustices on behalf of the poor or with the oppressed, our faith often struggles in the midst of the hostility, and we feel all we can do is resist. When we gaze at a suffering Jesus who also sustains all things as Son-priest-king, we have the strength to sustain *la lucha* (the struggle). In Jesus we have authority, perseverance, and sustenance in the work of social justice.

John 1:1–14

This passage of the Gospel is a prologue. The purpose is to set the tone for the work by introducing characters and themes that appear in it. The themes of light, darkness, truth, life, and the Son of the Father are repeated throughout the Gospel. The name of Jesus is not explicitly used in the prologue. Instead the author allows us to see Jesus as the enfleshed "Word" as he emerges in the narrative.[2]

The prologue also introduces the uniqueness of the community and the birth of many from God, the origin of a new humanity that comes from this birth of the divine in our midst. The birth of Jesus is our own sense of becoming a new being, a collective new human race.

The Son who is born always existed from the beginning, living in intimate communion with the Father. He came to bring light to the earth by becoming a man, a human among humans, though he was not recognized when he appeared and was not accepted.

Jesus comes as the Word that fully reveals God. He is the Logos, the Greek and Hebrew conception of the idea of new beginning and wisdom,

---

2. Bruce J. Malina and Richard L. Rohrbaugh, *Social-Science Commentary on the Gospel of John* (Minneapolis: Fortress Press, 1998), 30.

the personification of God (Prov. 8). "Word" is John's term for God's self-revelation. It is God's utterance that has resulted in everything created.[3]

The Mediterranean world had what anthropologists term "zones of inter-action," each interacting with the world around him or herself and thereby revealing a bit of who he or she is to one another. For example, the zone of self-expressive speech includes communication that not only reveals one's view of another, but also is self-revealing. It is more than an appearing, a snapshot; it is a self-giving in relationship. This poetic image of intimacy is repeated in how the Word dwelt with us (v. 14). The word chosen is "pitched his tent," which reminds one of how God dwelt with the people in the desert by means of a cloud and a pillar of fire (Exod. 40:38).[4] Verse 14 ends with "we have seen his glory, the glory as of a father's only son." This is advent in the Gospel of John.

We must pause at this place and ask ourselves: which Jesus do we see? John's Jesus is the revelation of God and our light so that we may be born into the fullness of our humanity. He appears to us in a way that may not be recognizable. When we see him in the Gospel we see the son of a carpenter, a "faithful poor" who believes even while enduring injustices.[5] To see this incarnated word is to receive light. Which Jesus do we see? We could be professing to be children of light but actually remain closed to the light of God's truth, thereby enclosing ourselves in darkness. As we celebrate God enfleshed in Jesus in our midst, the advent of our own new beginning, do we truly see it? Have we accepted it by offering hospitality to the poor and the oppressed? Is the tent of our tabernacle where he chose to pitch his, or have we pitched our tent too far from the desert and desolation of poverty and struggle?

---

3. Ibid., 35.
4. Gerard S. Sloyan, *John*, Interpretation series (Atlanta: John Knox Press, 1988), 19.
5. Ibid., 18.

First Sunday after Christmas

Ruthanna B. Hooke

1 SAMUEL 2:18–20, 26
PSALM 148
COLOSSIANS 3:12–17
LUKE 2:41–52

Each year, the lectionary Gospel reading for the First Sunday after Christmas focuses on Jesus' infancy and childhood. Not much is known about this period, the "hidden years" of Jesus. In Year C, we have the only account in the canonical Gospels of his childhood, the story of his visit to the temple. Countless books for children recount the childhoods of famous or important people; these books, like 1 Samuel, seek to show that the destinies of these children were already apparent in their childhoods. Both today's Gospel passage and the text from 1 Samuel demonstrate God's radical call on our lives from childhood. Our transformation from childhood into adult discipleship involves the virtues illumined in the Colossians text and is fueled by the song of praise reverberating in the psalm.

1 Samuel 2:18–20, 26

The story of the boy Jesus in the temple parallels in certain ways the childhood of Samuel. First Samuel 2:18–20, 26 portray the hidden childhood years of one of Israel's most important leaders, the man who not only was the first prophet in Israel but also inaugurated its institution of kingship. Samuel's childhood points to the greatness of his destiny. He was born miraculously to Hannah, who dedicates him to the service of God in early childhood. In today's reading we learn that he serves faithfully in his priestly role, growing in wisdom as he grows in years. His exemplary conduct contrasts with the immorality of the sons of Eli, the chief priest, who use their power to abuse and steal from the people. Samuel's just and faithful behavior as a child prefigures his efforts in adulthood to call Israel back into just and faithful covenant with God. When the people demand that Samuel appoint a king over them, Samuel warns them against doing this, because this means rejecting God as king and voluntarily submitting to a leader who will exploit them. Samuel becomes a moral voice in the establishment of Israel as a kingdom, always holding forth the vision of an alternate reign, ruled by God. He champions a vision of a just, equitable, nonhierarchical society, in which the wealth of the nation will be used to supply the people's needs, rather than enriching those in power.

Preaching social justice from this text entails pointing out the ways that Samuel's vision is still relevant for our societies today. A society organized according to this vision would prioritize equitable distribution of wealth so that the needs of all would be met, rather than wealth and power accumulating in the hands of a few. One could point out, as Samuel did, that such hierarchically ordered societies are not only unjust but idolatrous, since they replace God's rule with human rule.

Luke 2:41–52

One important similarity between Samuel's and Jesus' childhoods is that they both face separation from their birth families in order to pursue their callings from God. Samuel is given to the service of the temple as a young child, and in the story of the boy Jesus in the temple, it is evident that Jesus' sense of vocation distances him from his birth family. From a psychological perspective, this story shows artfully the experience of parents and adolescent children: the pain of parents in recognizing that they can no longer control their child, their admonishing him, his sharp reply, the tension between his relationship to them and his need to separate from them to fulfill his life's calling. From a social justice perspective, this passage encourages us to think about what our priorities need to be, and which relationships need to be most central, in order to fulfill our calling as God's people.

Jesus' first recorded words (v. 49), "Did you not know that I must be in my Father's house?" are difficult to translate. The original Greek is literally, "Did you not know that I must be in the things of my Father?" To what "things" is Jesus referring? He could mean "my Father's house" but also "my Father's affairs" or even "my Father's associates." However we choose to translate this phrase, it is clear that Jesus is saying that he must be about the things that God is about, in the places where God is, doing what God is doing. This statement therefore points us to the programmatic "mission statements" at the beginning of Luke's Gospel, which announce what God is doing in the world, this work in which Jesus is participating. Mary's Magnificat describes this mission as bringing down the powerful from their thrones and lifting up the lowly, filling the hungry with good things and sending the rich away empty. Jesus' first proclamation, in Luke 4:14–21, uses the words of Isaiah to claim his mission as bringing good news to the poor and release to the captives, and proclaiming the year of jubilee. These are the "things" or "affairs" of God that Jesus is going to be about.

Even as a child, Jesus recognizes that to be about God's affairs is to separate from his earthly parents. So strong is his compulsion to be in the temple with the teachers of the law that he leaves his parents without even telling them where he is going. When, in extremes of anguish and worry, his parents finally find him three days later, he seems surprised by their anxiety, and his response to them is perhaps a bit unfeeling. He even seems to be breaking one of the Ten Commandments: "Honor your father and your mother" (Exod. 20:12). Jesus' seemingly uncaring reply to his parents presages a more complete rebuff of them in his adulthood: when his mother and brothers come looking for him, he says, "My mother and my brothers are those who hear the word of God and do it" (Luke 8:19–21).

Jesus' treatment of his family, in both childhood and adulthood, reminds us that the power of his mission would radically reorder his own life and the lives of those who would follow him. To proclaim the inbreaking reign of God, to teach and heal in God's name, to confront the powers that be, and to bring good news to the poor and oppressed are missions of such cosmic and divine importance that they reshape all of our relationships. Our most important relationships become the ones with those who, like us, are "about our Father's affairs." Even blood ties become secondary to those ties within the community of Jesus' disciples; these people become our new family.

This is indeed a radical and unsettling gospel, especially in American culture, where the nuclear family tends to be idealized as the fundamental building block of society and the location of goodness, morality, and self-sacrifice: the site of "family values." However, nuclear families can often become insular, self-absorbed, and self-serving—parents, for instance, can so focus on providing the best of everything to their children that they lose all concern for those outside their immediate circle. The nuclear family risks becoming an institution that merely supports the status quo and seeks to prosper under its terms, rather than challenging it in any meaningful way. To bring about social justice, Christians need to form communities that are broader than the nuclear family, that include greater racial and economic diversity than families usually do, and that have wider horizons of concern than merely promoting the well-being of their own members. Jesus' comment, "Do you not know that I must be about my Father's affairs?" relativizes families of birth in favor of communities united around the mission of God in the world. This need not translate into a call to abandon our own families, but rather it calls us to connect them in meaningful ways to communities of faith that are involved in Christ's work—preaching good news to the poor, seeking the release of captives, working for more just distribution of wealth. It would be lovely if our children could grow up not so much focused on having the fanciest education, the newest gadgets, and participating in all the right extracurricular activities, but rather that they might learn about Christ's work in the world and become involved in it.

Colossians 3:12–17

The lordship of Christ described in this letter illumines the list of virtues in Colossians 3:12–17. Christ is the one in whom, through whom, and for whom all things were created (Col. 1:16). In Christ, as head of the body, the church, all things are reconciled. Thus the writer admonishes the hearers to live their lives "holding fast to the head, from whom the whole body . . . grows with a growth that is from God" (2:19). Not only are the Colossians' lives "rooted and built up in him," but with him they have died and been raised, such that their lives are "hidden with Christ in God" (2:7; 3:3). All of these images point to the radical transformation that Christ's lordship and the Colossians' membership in his body have made to their lives. This radical change needs to be evident in the ways they live with each other: they are to show kindness, compassion, forgiveness, and, above all, love, for this is what "binds together" the whole body to Jesus the head.

This list reminds us that, even as we seek to enact the egalitarian vision of Samuel, and as we pursue the radical mission of Jesus, it is important that we go about this work in a certain way. If indeed "Christ is all and in all" (3:11), then our actions must manifest his lordship. If we abide with him, then his way of being and acting must become our own. This suggests that the means of bringing about social transformation are as important as the ends, and those means must be marked by compassion, love, forgiveness, and a willingness to live in the peace of Christ, even with those with whom we disagree. At a time when public life in the United States is coarsened by partisanship and angry, intemperate rhetoric, Christians are called to demonstrate that it is possible to hold strong convictions without demonizing or denigrating others. Colossians reminds us that the tenor of our public (and private) lives is as important as the social justice goals we seek.

Above all, it is in worship that this way of being is established and nourished. The writer of Colossians stresses the importance of letting the word of God dwell in believers richly, of teaching each other, of singing together with gratitude (v. 16).

Psalm 148

Psalm 148 is a particularly lovely text for such grateful song, as it contains one of the most expansive and inclusive calls to praise God in the Psalter. The psalmist calls for praise of God "from the heavens," from sun, moon, stars, and "highest heavens," and "from the earth"—not only from humans, animals, and plants, but even from inanimate objects such as mountains and hills. Although the final line of the Psalter (Ps. 150:6) calls for "everything that breathes" to praise the Lord, Psalm 148 goes further, for it invites praise of God from everything that exists, both animate and inanimate. As we sing or pray this psalm on the First Sunday after Christmas, we are reminded that through the worship of God, our priorities are reordered around the lordship of Christ and his mission. Through this worship, moreover, our ways of being with each other are also transformed, so that they manifest the love, kindness, forgiveness, and peace of Christ, whose body we are. The worship of God to which this psalm calls us orients us toward a realm of justice, ruled by God alone, that Samuel envisioned and defended. The worship of God focuses us once more on the work of God in the world, inviting us once again to be "about God's business," as the child Jesus was. The worship of God, such as this psalm joyfully calls forth in us, is the starting and ending point for all the transformations that living as Christ's people in the world demands of us. As we undergo each transformation, we are further equipped to live Christ's way in the world, heralding and working toward the fullness of God's reign.

Holy Name of Jesus

Dianne Bergant, CSA

NUMBERS 6:22–27
PSALM 8
GALATIANS 4:4–7
LUKE 2:15–21

As was the case with many people who played important roles in the drama of salvation (Abraham, Gen. 17:5; Jacob/Israel, Gen. 35:10; John, Luke 1:13), God chose the name of Jesus. Mary was instructed "and you will name him Jesus" (Luke 1:31). In turn, Matthew's Gospel gives the meaning of that name: "You are to name him Jesus, for he will save his people from their sins" (Matt. 1:21).

Luke 2:15–21

This passage is rich in theological themes from the experiences of the shepherds: response to divine revelation, theological insight, evangelization, praise of God, contemplative reflection, and the promise of salvation. To begin, the shepherds were not highly regarded as spiritual leaders. Actually their contemporaries considered them somewhat irreligious. One of the reasons that persons often held shepherds in some contempt was the shepherds' failure to participate in regular ritual observance. The self-righteousness behind such scorn is almost palpable and alarming! Shepherding required them to be with the flocks, supervising their grazing and growth and protecting them from harm. These responsibilities prevented them from being part of the worshiping community. It is somewhat astonishing that the Gospel narrative begins to reveal the possible responses to Jesus' birth through the supposed irreligious. These persons abandoned their vital economic posts of care for their source of sustenance to pursue the vision (2:9–15). Strikingly, the "irreligious" respond without hesitation to divine revelation. Why does the text not dwell on doubts of the vision, questions of their sanity? Would not the pronouncement of the long-awaited Messiah go to those who would know intimately the child's holy name already? These humble shepherds were the first to respond to a divine invitation to leave all for the sake of this child. While it is true that they did return to their flocks, their initial willingness to leave them has religious significance.

The angels' miraculous pronouncement could not possibly prepare the shepherds for their encounter with the actual "irreligious" scene of the family birth. And yet they do not question the religious revelation of the child. This family was in no way unusual. How were they able to see the extraordinary in the very ordinary? Does it take miraculous visions to empower our own vision and responses? What enables any of us to see traces of the divine in the very ordinary of life? Might it be the openness to God and the willingness to accept the unexpected that provide eyes of faith, which can see beyond appearances? Can justice be found in the ordinary? How can the ordinary become miraculous sources of meaning and transformation of our world? However this happened for the shepherds, upon seeing the child, they were convinced of this message about the arrival of the long-anticipated Messiah. It reoriented their priorities and their pursuit to see how God is working in the ordinary. They then went out and proclaimed this revelation to all they met. Their response to seek out God's work in the ordinary makes incredible claims on our lives no less.

The covenant ritual of circumcision after eight days is the naming ritual for Jesus both in the gift of life and to the people of faith. Year B's essay for this day underscored the meaning of Jesus' name as "God saves." Another inter-pretation of his name stresses how God "delivers." Naming Jesus announces deliverance by God. But whom does God deliver? The juxtaposition of this naming ritual for Jesus and the account of the shepherds suggests that these two stories are somehow interrelated. The shepherds represent those who are forced to live on the margins of society, those who suffer the disdain of oth-ers. Such disdain might stem from the indignity of their lives and occupation, or perhaps they do not worship in an acceptable way, as was the case with the shepherds. However, people are marginalized by others for many reasons. It could be because of their gender, their racial or ethnic origin, or their immi-grant status. It could be because of their age or physical or mental condition. The reasons could be economic or religious. Whatever the circumstances, they are marginalized. And we must ask, "From what might God deliver them?"

If we take our clue from the story of the shepherds, they are probably not delivered from what makes them unacceptable in society. This would simply confirm society's discriminatory judgment. In the case of the shepherds, with-out changing their lives, God raised them in the eyes of society, thus affirming the merit of their lives. God certainly delivers, but not as we might expect.

Again and again the Bible recounts how those who were relegated to the margins of society are placed at the heart of the drama of deliverance. The story of the shepherds and the meaning of Jesus' name reveal the character of God's loving relationship with those who have been marginalized and the manner in which deliverance transforms.

Numbers 6:22–27

With this poetic piece, Moses stands to pass along the charge of blessing from God to the priestly office, as represented by Aaron and his sons (vv. 22–23). These are examples of the mediating roles we sometimes bear before the people of God to name God's blessing.

What does it mean to name God's blessing? God instructs Moses and Moses charges the priests to bless God's people. Somehow the blessing places the name of God on the people, which in effect carries God's inbreaking promise or act to bless (v. 27). How does the benediction place God's "name" on them? Disturbingly, human history evokes images of placing one's name on property to certify ownership. Placing one's name on something or someone else earmarks ownership—hardly an intrinsic blessing! To be owned is to lose one's name, even to lose one's humanity, if we pay attention to the historical and cultural practices of conquest or domination. This form of naming mocks God with our injustice. Instead, God bestows a name to signify transformation or relationship, not ownership. How much more when God confers God's name in blessing! To be God's people is to be transformed by covenant relationship. The transformation is God's blessing or the effect of God's blessing.

As moving as this blessing might be, still present are the challenges of our exclusionary practices, even in the name of God's blessings. For example, the gender bias of its context is quite obvious. Moses is told, "Speak to Aaron and his sons" (v. 23). While the blessing itself can certainly be seen as intended for all of the people, women as well as men, those who bestow the blessing are men. Ancient Israel's priesthood was reserved for men alone. In fact, it was even more restricted. One had to be born into a priestly family to function as a legitimate priest. However, this cultural bias does not invalidate the strength of the blessing that God intended for all. The blessing was pronounced over all the Israelites, women as well as men, ordinary folk as well as priests and Levites, farmers as well as rulers. All Israelites were promised the blessing of being named with God. Read with today's Gospel, one might say that the blessing in Numbers bears God's inbreaking; and in kind, the name of Jesus is a sign of deliverance that once again promises God's inbreaking transformation.

God blesses with care and sustaining grace, and grants us peace (vv. 24–26). Actually there is very little difference in the terms of these verses. They all point to the blessings of God's care, grace, and peace that make life worth living. These blessings could mean different things to different people at different times. But basically care, grace, and peace are the fundamental characteristics of blessing. We offer benediction as we depart worship. If that blessing is also a charge to bless, how we live into God's care, grace, and peace is critically conditioned in both the transformation and the charge to transform. One could say that the ultimate response to any kind of deliverance is responding to God's care, grace, and peace—that is, responding to God's name.

Psalm 8

The image of the world depicted in this psalm is one of peace and natural harmony. One might even say that it mirrors the paradisiacal garden in Eden (Gen. 2:9). All creatures have their place, and they are under the governance and care of God's appointed representatives. However, this idyllic condition did not last, and so the blessing found in Numbers takes on importance and the promise present in the name of Jesus becomes our hope. The psalmist is overwhelmed that God would even pause to take notice of the plight of humanity. How are we to view creation in the range of God's sight?

Creation itself evidences God's splendor. We frequently locate evidence of God's wonder in the miracle of our uniqueness as the excellence of God's creation; however, the psalmist locates God's glory in the splendor of creation all around us. Too often we focus the psalm's claims of glory and honor primarily in the divine stature of humanity (v. 5). Human dominion in nature and creation only establishes divine favor (v. 6). Hence it is understandable how often the tide of God's power in creation and the grandeur of our inherited dominance sweep us away. Yet this psalm locates the wonder of God's glory in God's unmerited attention and care for humanity amid the splendor of creation that radiates divine glory so much more effectively than we do. As with the blessing in the Numbers text for this day, God's care for us is the source of life and perhaps also God's charge to humanity. We may need to preach on how the luster of God's care for humanity might radiate through our own lives. If God's wonder is evidenced in God's care for us, how then does that divine care define the character of God's charge to humanity?

Galatians 4:4–7

According to Paul, the goal of Christ's mission was to transform the Galatians from the state of slavery under the law into the adopted children of God.

Here Paul sets up the contrast between servitude under the law and freedom in Christ. In order to do this, he employs a social custom of his day. If an heir was too young to claim inheritance, a legal guardian was appointed until the heir came of age. Paul compares the believers to underage minors who, until "the fullness of time had come" (v. 4), could not claim what might be rightfully theirs. The law acted as legal guardian. All of this changed with the coming of Christ. Christians are no longer minors bound to the tutelage of the law. They are legal heirs, "adopted" children of God, since Christ is the only true Son.

Does anyone need proof of this? In answer, Paul argues that the fact that they are filled with the Spirit of Christ and dare to call God "Abba" is evidence of this new relationship with God (v. 6). Though "Abba" is not a divine title, as a term of endearment it signifies the intimate relationship between God and the people. This new relationship with God, a relationship of adoption, is the fruit of the blessing found in the passage from Numbers, and it refers to the transformed manner of living that is promised in the name of Jesus as described by Luke. All of these passages speak of something new, created by God out of love for us. Our freedom in Christ is in the name of God's relationship to humanity and God's reclaiming adoption through Christ.

Second Sunday after Christmas

Alyce M. McKenzie

JEREMIAH 31:7–14
PSALM 147:12–20
EPHESIANS 1:3–14
JOHN 1:(1–9) 10–18

I tend to approach exegesis through a narrative lens. Every text, whether it is a story or not, has a backstory, a cover story, and a sequel story. Every story has a main character who wants something and who acts to get it. What he or she wants is often called "the object of desire." Obstacles to that object of desire often come from events or the actions of other characters. And, finally, life is transformed from obtaining that object of desire, or perhaps from the struggle itself.

These four texts, from John, Ephesians, Jeremiah, and Psalms, show up this Second Sunday after Christmas in Years A, B, and C. Taking our cue from the narrative lens, we have a different conversation with them each year. In Year A our focus is on the gifts God wants to give us in these texts. In Year B we explore the obstacles to receiving those gifts. In Year C we turn our attention to the kind of life that results when we overcome these obstacles and accept the gift God offers to us.

John 1:(1–9) 10–18

The prologue to John's Gospel reveals to us Jesus' identity as the Word made flesh, Wisdom-in-Person.[1] While some scholars seek gnostic parallels for the prologue, its primary precedents are in the personification of wisdom in the book of Proverbs.[2]

---

1. Ben Witherington III, *Jesus the Sage: The Pilgrimage of Wisdom* (Minneapolis: Fortress Press, 1994).
2. Martin Scott, *Sophia and the Johannine Jesus*, Journal for the Study of the New Testament Supplement Series 71 (Sheffield: University of Sheffield Press, 1992).

Proverbs characterizes Wisdom and her gifts as light, way, food, gate, life, and fountain. This is reminiscent of Jesus' I AM sayings in John's Gospel. John has seven metaphorical soliloquies depicting Jesus: I am bread (6:35, 51), light (8:12; 9:5), sheep gate (10:7, 9), good shepherd (10:11, 14), resurrection and life (11:25), way, truth, and life (14:6), and the true vine (15:1, 5).

The prologue sets the stage for the rest of John's Gospel in equating Jesus' identity and mission with light. "What has come into being in him was life, and the life was the light of all people" (v. 4). Throughout the Gospel this image shines forth (1:9; 3:19; 8:12; 9:5; 12:46). Other strands of tradition beyond the book of Proverbs add their wattage to the light metaphor for Jesus' identity. The Messiah was expected to be the "light of the nations" (Isa. 42:6; 49:6). In calling himself the light of the world, Jesus is claiming to be the Messiah and a prophet like Moses, but one whose saving power encompasses the whole world.

The connection between Jesus and light makes a statement not just about his identity, but about ours when our lives are shaped by his. When Jesus says, in John 8:12, "I am the light of the world. Whoever follows me will never walk in darkness but will have the light of life," he is describing the path of discipleship. In Proverbs, something similar is said regarding those who follow Wisdom: "The path of the righteous is like the light of dawn . . . [but] the way of the wicked is like deep darkness" (Prov. 4:18–19). By following Jesus we become "children of light" (John 12:36).

There is plenty of reason to curse the darkness, but we have a Savior, the Word of God made flesh, Wisdom in person, who teaches us not to hide our light under a bushel, but to set it on a lamp stand so that it may give light to all in the house. "The light shines in the darkness, and the darkness did not overcome it" (v. 5). May our lives be spent reflecting the light of Christ to dwelling places well beyond our own homes.

Ephesians 1:3–14

Verses 3–14 of the opening chapter of Ephesians are "an exclamation of prayer and praise resembling those pronounced in Jewish synagogues and homes."[3] The rhythmic diction and theme of praise are reminiscent of praise psalms from the Psalter. The verses are not attributed to the word of the Lord or a dream or vision. They have come to Paul from the liturgical stream of oral tradition and are intended for use in worship. The contents of this prayerful praise reflect the extravagant generosity of God. God is the subject of most sentences. The whole passage resounds with the praise of God's glory. This praise is the purpose of God's work.[4]

3. Markus Barth, *Ephesians 1–3*, Anchor Bible (New York: Doubleday, 1986), 97.
4. Ibid., 98.

When I enter into a dialogue with a text, one question I ask myself is: What would my life look like if I lived by the good news of this text? The first fourteen verses of Ephesians suggest that our lives would be lived with confidence in the gracious actions of God, that our purpose in living would be to praise and glorify God. Not the sort of praise wherein we thank God for all blessings and pray that God does not call on us to share them with anyone else. Each act of praise to God for a certain gift should be paired with an act of sharing that gift with others.

If we lived by the good news of Ephesians 1:3–14, we would be confident in our having been forgiven and redeemed through Christ. And we would share that forgiveness with others.

We would be confident that our lives are part of a redemptive, joyful plan God has for us. And we would share that joy with others.

We would realize that God's love is for everyone, not just us. The letter includes the Jews (those who were "first to set our hope in Christ," v. 12) as well as the Gentiles (those who later heard and believed, v. 13). And we would share that inclusive love with others.

We would be confident in our spiritual inheritance (vv. 11, 14). Like other ancient practices that sealed or branded followers with some mark of their leader on their foreheads, we would live in the awareness that the Holy Spirit has set a seal on our hearts (v. 13).[5] And we would share that Spirit with others.

The danger the author of Ephesians fears is that factions in the church will seek to hoard the inheritance and begrudge others' share. I saw a bumper sticker that read, "God loves everyone, but I'm his favorite." But nothing is said in jest! Basil once said,

> The bread in your cupboard belongs to the hungry person; the coat hanging unused in your closet belongs to the one who needs it; the shoes rotting in your closet belong to the person with no shoes; the money which you put in the bank belongs to the poor. You do wrong to everyone you could help, but fail to help.[6]

Jeremiah 31:7–14

Carol Dempsey describes Jeremiah as one who persisted in hope though circumstances denied that there was any reason for hope. His life "became a

---

5. J. H. P. Thompson, *The Letters of Paul to the Ephesians, to the Colossians and to Philemon*, Cambridge Bible Commentary (New York: Cambridge University Press, 1967), 27.

6. Mary Lou Kownacki, *A Monk in the Inner City* (Maryknoll, NY: Orbis Press, 2008), 124.

living testimony to the enduring and sustaining presence of God whose work of redemption and transformation is never-ending."[7]

Jeremiah (627–581 BCE) was born into a priestly family in the town of Anathoth in the southern kingdom of Judah in a period of religious and political turbulence. The northern kingdom of Israel had fallen to the Assyrians seventy-five years before, and Judah was now flirting with destruction at the same hands. She was following in the same practices of idolatry and decadence that had left Israel easy prey to the ravenous appetite of Assyria (Jer. 7:9–10).

Jeremiah's life was shaped by perseverance in hope. He was called by God to go to people and places where he would rather not have gone to proclaim a persistently offensive message. On the surface harsh and unwelcome, the message he faithfully proclaimed contained good news: the opportunity for people to change, if they chose. Hence Dempsey describes Jeremiah as "the first to confront" and "the first to console."[8]

Jeremiah's persistence in offering hope shaped a people of hope. For more than forty years he reiterated his message. His tenacity saved Judah from its worst self and eventually enabled it to return from exile, purified from idolatry.[9]

I am reminded of the lyrics to the 1960s Civil Rights Movement anthem "A Change is Gonna Come," written in 1964 by singer-songwriter Sam Cooke. At the time, Cooke had become known for his polished persona and lighthearted songs like "You Send Me" and "Twistin' the Night Away." He felt a need to address racial discrimination, but feared the loss of his largely white fan base. Then Bob Dylan's song "Blowin' in the Wind" came out in 1963, and Cooke marveled that a white man could write such a moving song about racism. Cooke's "A Change is Gonna Come" sounds like something Jeremiah might have sung in the long years when he preached change to hard hearts and held onto persistent hope while foreign powers sought to crush his people's hope.[10]

Psalm 147:12–20

Psalm 147 is a psalm of restoration, providence and prosperity. It praises God's power as creator (v. 4) and restorer (v. 2). It praises God's compassion and provision. God "lifts up the downtrodden" (v. 6) and provides for the animals (v. 9). Verses 12–20 praise God as the one who grants the people protection and who has chosen Jacob. This psalm acknowledges that God has done something for us that God did not have to do, and something we could not do

7. Carol Dempsey, *Jeremiah: Preacher of Grace, Poet of Truth* (Collegeville, MN: Liturgical Press, 2007), xvii.
8. Ibid., 37.
9. R. E. O. White, *The Indomitable Prophet: A Biographical Commentary on Jeremiah* (Grand Rapids: Eerdmans, 1992), 7.
10. "A Change Is Gonna Come," www.songfacts.com (accessed March 29, 2010).

ourselves: call and empower us to repentance and provide for us a restoration and a joyful homecoming.

Psalm 147 is one of four praise psalms that form a joyful exclamation point at the end of the Psalter. As a hymn of praise, its tone is not the deep emotion of a lament or the desperate gratitude of thanksgiving for specific deliverance. Its purpose is to conform us to the praiseworthy character of God—a God who is creative, compassionate, and constant in divine care. This praise psalm shapes us as people who are attentive to the laments that lie beyond the praise. It shapes us as a community who celebrates who God is, but also who God wants us to be in community.

If we were to pray this psalm daily in the context of the whole Psalter, we would be more attentive to the laments of others. Old Testament scholar Renita Weems says that "not enough has been written about long dry seasons. What about those of us who . . . feel as if we have hit a brick wall and our prayers have been met with silence?"[11] She says that if the laments were absent from the Bible, "my spirit might have withered away long ago." This psalm does not seek to shape a life in which we voice our praises while our neighbor's spirit is withering away.

This psalm shapes a life that praises God in the company of others. When my friend Lucy Rose—preacher, pastor, homiletics professor, and author— was in the last stages of cancer several years ago, she asked her friends to pray through the Psalms with her in mind, to pray them for her on the days she didn't have the energy to pray them herself.

This praise psalm is not just a psalm of personal comfort. It is a psalm of communal resistance. It offers a picture of how God is, but also of how God wants things to be.

Hebrew Bible scholar Claus Westermann was imprisoned in a Russian prison camp during the Second World War. He had a copy of Luther's translation of the New Testament and the Psalms. He later wrote what the Psalms, particularly the praise psalms, meant to him and others in their time of trial:

> Whenever one in his enforced separation praised God in song or speech, or silence, he was conscious of himself not as an individual, but as a member of the congregation. When in hunger and cold, between interrogations, or as one sentenced to death, he was privileged to praise God, he knew that in all his ways he was borne up by the church's praise of God.[12]

11. Renita J. Weems, *Listening for God: A Minister's Journey through Silence and Doubt* (New York: Simon & Schuster, 1999), 18–19.

12. Claus Westermann, *The Praise of God in the Psalms*, trans. Keith R. Crim (Richmond: John Knox Press, 1965), 10.

Epiphany of Jesus

Terriel R. Byrd

ISAIAH 60:1–6
PSALM 72:1–7, 10–14
EPHESIANS 3:1–12
MATTHEW 2:1–12

This week's lectionary invites us to gather as God continually sets a table of hope before us. The prophet Isaiah invites all to stand up, indeed to arise, and experience the radiant glory of God's deliverance. The psalmist sings and celebrates the King's past, present, and future vision of justice and righteousness for all, where the poor feast at the table of sisterhood and brotherhood and find help in the time of need and freedom from their oppressors. Paul, in apostolic tradition, reminds us that God's unity is vast enough for Jew and Gentile, those who have much, those who have little, and those who have nothing. But most important for Paul, this mystery of Christ and our unity is revealed at the Lord's Table. The poor and oppressed can find hope and we all find mercy in the fruit of God's renewal and grace. And so too Matthew's Gospel reveals that God draws us from the ends of the earth to gather and unite around Christ even from his very birth. Paul's Table is filled with the promise of Christ's birth. Let us come to this renewal and unity and feast together!

Isaiah 60:1–6

The prophet Isaiah gives a spectacular view of untarnished hope after the dark season of Persian rule. God's glory is revealed. God's light bursts through and dispels the prevailing darkness. The prophet begins by telling the people to "arise" and "shine" because hope and light now radiate from God Almighty for all who wish to see. Isaiah, the eagled-eyed prophet, unreservedly proclaims the liberating power of the Almighty. His passionate proclamation comes from his soul, full of exultant praise and uninhibited joy for God after

51

Israel's deliverance. To understand Isaiah's proclamations, we must first understand the ironies of his passion. Isaiah prophesied during a time of deep despair and disillusionment. In his time, not unlike contemporary times, Isaiah despaired of untimely wars fought, corruption and oppression that led to complete social failures, and pervasive sin and rebellion against God.

In the midst of and directly after this dark despair, Isaiah by faith looked forward to the ages of light, with hope gathering around the coming messiah. "For darkness shall cover the earth, and thick darkness the peoples; but the LORD will arise upon you, and his glory will appear over you" (v. 2). God's glory shines not only on individuals but on the communities as well: "Nations shall come to your light" (v. 3). We observe in Isaiah 60 a strong and enduring faith that tomorrow is filled with promise and great reason to have hope.

Isaiah empathically challenges the faithful. He engages our hopes by inviting us into a world of those once forsaken, those who have known the heavy burden of social and economic oppression and injustices. As we reflect more deeply on their stories, we also see and experience similar stories of bewildered people in the twenty-first century yearning for humanity and liberation from the heavy load of economic and social injustice. For instance, today as many as 15 million Americans are without employment or adequate resources or economic recourse of any kind! This is the worst economic devastation to trouble the country in a generation. One need only imagine the solid wall of despair of those caught in this dilemma. In this instance, God is their only resource, if they will accept that alternative.

The prophet's words still bring hope, invite salvation, declare righteousness—they speak to peace and deliverance in the present as they did in centuries past. The prophet Isaiah highlights future blessings and subsequent fulfillment of God's covenant promise made to Abraham in Genesis 12:1–3. All of the prophecies reveal in mission and ministry the life of hope bequeathed to those who see and accept the glory and radiant light of the revealed Lord. However, the specific emphasis of the covenant includes the poor, the oppressed, those who often find themselves seemingly forsaken and forgotten. It is refreshing to hear the prophet proclaim the kind of society where justice and fairness are more than ideas, but are realized in full social context where all enjoy the abundance of the earth's resources, when we can rejoice in the thrill of call and grace (v. 5).

Today the church, Christ's body, has been called to be the radiant light "in order that you may proclaim the mighty acts of him who called you out of darkness into his marvelous light" (1 Pet. 2:9b). The church of which Christ is head is, in essence, a holy nation, in the light of Isaiah's prophecy, and a vision of hope for those now downtrodden, rejected, and despised, the poor who daily cry out to God for justice. Only God can institute the changes in the intricate and deep-rooted structures of power and influence among the nations that would enable the poor to prosper and enjoy the earth that God created for all to enjoy.

When Martin Luther King Jr. spoke his most inspiring words in the "I Have a Dream" speech in 1963, he reminded all of us of an earlier vision and hope given to inspire a nation to live up to its noble ideas of freedom and democracy. Isaiah, too, was reminding the people of his day to repent and return to the God of their salvation. In so doing, Isaiah spoke to *all* ages.

Psalm 72:1–7, 10–14

Psalm 72 is attributed to Solomon, a son of David. Solomon chose wisdom over wealth and chose prudence above the power of fame (1 Kgs. 3:10–12). It appears that one of the most profound acts of Solomon was his humble request that God grant him "an understanding mind to govern your people, able to discern between good and evil" (1 Kgs. 3:9). How wise it is to pray for prudent judgment! How wise it is for the orator in Psalm 72 to pray that the royal family extend justice by governing in a way that treats all fairly! Indeed, none would be more profoundly moved with hope and appreciate this prayer more deeply than the poor and oppressed. The orator in this psalm advocates directly for the poor when he says, "May he judge your people with righteousness, and your poor with justice" (v. 2). Certainly this prayer made the poor, those persons so often crushed under the heavy bondage of social and economic oppression, feel that someone in power understood and cared about their plight.

The major theme of this psalm is social justice. The psalmist's prayer asks God to give the king power, not only to speak but also to act in just ways concerning the poor. Leaders today who have been given similar authority to govern the poor might refine their governance toward the poor and pray similar prayers. Many injustices have been corrected and the waters of hope have run swiftly as a result of the civil and human rights gains made in our society and around the world. These gains occurred through valiant and persistent leaders who committed themselves to addressing the injustices of poverty, gender, race, and class.

The psalmist's prayer and its resultant blessings go well beyond the king's own time and boundaries. Friends take up his banner and follow him (vv. 10–11). Just leaders inspire others. Clear moral and spiritual voices are few and far between; however, one excellent exemplar of moral clarity and leadership was Dietrich Bonhoeffer, who returned to Germany to stand in opposition against Hitler and became a martyr. The psalmist is a reflection of the Abrahamic covenant to be a blessing to all people (Gen. 12:1–3).

The psalmist demonstrates the abundance of blessings that extend even through God's natural creation. When justice and righteousness abound, blessings flow! "May the mountains yield prosperity for the people, and the hills, in righteousness" (v. 3). This is referenced, too, in the book of Leviticus, "If you walk in my statutes and keep my commandments and observe them faithfully, I will give you your rains in their season, and the land shall yield its produce, and the trees of the field shall yield their fruit" (Lev. 26:3–4).

Yet in Psalm 72:12–14, the orator of the festival returns to an emphasis on the poor and their liberation from oppressors. Samuel D. Proctor reminds us that "those who serve congregations of persons victimized by racism, chronic economic depression, social ostracism, and stubborn stereotypes face a task hardly known to other preachers. They will find a hunger for identity, a thirst for freedom, and a zeal for liberation that cannot be quenched with palliatives and mild bromides."[1] Selfless acts, like those of Mother Teresa to the hopeless children in Calcutta, India, also support this hope that comes with the soothing balm of just acts.

Ephesians 3:1–12

The apostle Paul invites us to feast at the table of God's grace and mercy, to behold the mystery of faith. The apostle identifies himself as a prisoner or slave of Christ on behalf of the Gentiles. Paul writes this letter while in prison in Rome awaiting trial before Nero. Paul speaks of the revelation given to him from God; this great mystery revealed that the grace and mercy of God was extended to not only the Jew but the Gentile as well. For Paul, this revelation was reason for celebration because it marked a living hope, a new fellowship for unity within the body of Christ. What an amazing thing it is to witness unity built on a foundation of justice and righteousness. Such unity is not to be taken for granted; it must at all times be vigorously pursued.

The hope for and the realization of unity do not just happen. Around the world we have seen the devastation that is the result of disunity. In the late 1980s, the now-famous six words about the Berlin Wall ("Mr. Gorbachev, tear down this wall") spoken by President Ronald Reagan to the president of the Soviet Union, Mikhail Gorbachev, represented more than the beginning of the end of the cold war. The Berlin Wall was a barrier of hopelessness between people of Western and Eastern Europe. The destruction of the wall eradicated this hopelessness.

The senseless genocide in Rwanda in 1994 in the war between Hutus and Tutsis resulted in a million people being massacred without mercy. We know

1. Samuel D. Proctor, *How Shall They Hear: Effective Preaching for Vital Faith* (Valley Forge, PA: Judson Press, 1992), 23.

of the horrific killings in the Darfur region of the Sudan and of the violent conflicts that also divide Christians and Muslims in other parts of the globe. All of these acts are without the light of God's unity; they demonstrate the darkness of injustice and disunity. Paul's challenge is that we might see one another in the context of God's covenantal plan—a plan that unites us in beloved community.

Matthew 2:1–12

From Christ's birth, God calls us together even as God seeks out each of us! We have not always grasped how Jesus unites us between being called and being found. This mystery of Christ extends from the birth of Jesus and his parents' bringing him to the temple with an offering, to be dedicated according to the law of Moses. Simeon expressed what the Holy Spirit had revealed to him: "For my eyes have seen your salvation, which you have prepared in the presence of all peoples, a light for revelation to the Gentiles and for glory to your people Israel" (Luke 2:30–32). Like the royal birth narrative of Matthew 2, Christ draws, even invites, humanity to God. This is the mystery of Christ between being called together and being sought. As revealed in Luke 14:15–23, God has liberally set a banquet for anyone who would lay aside their own activities to come. Not only did God plan and set the banquet, but God also sent a servant into the highways and byways to seek and bid guests to come together. Even when all those invited may refuse the invitation, God gathers the least of us as cherished guests to a cherished Table. The good news is that the invitation to the banquet remains open to this day. The mystery of Jesus' birth is revealed in the mystery of Christ's own calling and his calling to us. During this season of Epiphany, may we all be reminded of the revelatory light shone by Christ's appearance and the great sacrifices needed to preserve the spirit of hope as we work for unity and just causes around the world.

First Sunday after the Epiphany (Baptism of Jesus)

Joseph Evans

ISAIAH 43:1–7
PSALM 29
ACTS 8:14–17
LUKE 3:15–17, 21–22

Sacred prophets are biblical storytellers and holistic commentators on human conditions. Jazz prophets seek to create sociospiritual awareness, a kind of epiphany. John Coltrane, the jazz saxophonist, was once called a seer, a term that is associated with biblical prophets.[1] For me, his music may be a kind of epiphany of sociospiritual awareness. It is identified in democratic processes, protest, and changes sought in systemic hegemonic and homogeneous establishments that may work knowingly or unknowingly against democracy and, by implication, the word of God. Preachers will see this as they rethink the role that jazz plays in democracy, Scripture, and social justice.

According to Ben Ratliff, a jazz critic, Coltrane "has discovered how to concentrate and to reconcile speed with melody and how to exult—in the way that a preacher . . . [is] not merely a passive dandelion in the congregation, [but] learns to exult."[2] Ratliff explains anecdotally that both of Coltrane's grandfathers, who were ministers in the African Methodist Episcopal Zion Church, had likely influenced the saxophonist's style and message.[3] Most observers of Coltrane's life and musical career would agree that he was on a religious pilgrimage.

Isaiah 43:1–7

The writer creates a word picture in verses 2–5 and briefly summarizes Israel's historical journey. Like a jazz prophet, the writer fills the riff with speed,

---

1. Ben Ratliff, *Coltrane: The Story of a Sound* (New York: Picador, 2007), xvi.
2. Ibid., xix.
3. Ibid.

intensity, and rhetorical symbols that take his audience on an emotional journey with Israel. The audience members experience Israel's fear; and like Israel, they need to hear God say, "Do not fear" (v. 1), "I will be with you" (v. 2), and the intense refrain, "Do not fear, for I am with you; I will bring your offspring from the east, and from the west I will gather you" (v. 5). The writer reflects Coltrane's modal language and offers a reason why God redeems and protects God's people: simply because God loves them (v. 4). The poet closes the previous propositions and offers as a transitory statement an expanded idea that completes the picture of the journey in verses 5–7. The journey is a democratic process.

Verses 6–7 creatively express that the democratic journey is an integrative process with social and political mutations. A close reading of these verses suggests that God's people evolve into something diverse and democratic: "I will say to the north, 'Give them up,' and to the south, 'Do not withhold; bring my sons from far away and my daughters from the end of the earth— everyone who is called by my name, whom I created for my glory, whom I formed and made.'" Those who preach sense that God is glorified when God's people respond to God's own democratic call. It is not necessarily a compromise of personal values and beliefs; instead, it is building a consensus around something greater than its parts. That is, for Christians to survive marginalization, Christians are to work together and form a body under the banner of God.

Psalm 29

In the introduction (vv. 1–2), the writer ascribes to God's glory, strength, and holiness. For the psalmist, these attributes alone are cause for people to worship God. These attributes—glory and strength—are disclosed through the holy beauty of heaven's storms.

Verses 3–11 describe natural phenomena that God alone can create. In verses 3–9, the psalmist repeats, "the voice of the LORD." God's presence is recognized in natural events. Theoretically Coltrane's music also reflects these observations in kind; they are existential democratic musings and strivings about God. The psalmist is not investigating scientific motifs. Instead, the writer chooses poetry to disclose deep feelings about the nature of God and how people are shaped by the Sovereign Actor's existence.

The psalmist describes a God of history and a Sovereign Actor who reveals God's self to God's people. He bears self-witness to the Hebrews' sociospiritual consciousness, making them aware of God's presence in human struggles and conditions. For the psalmist, God creates beauty in the middle of harshness, and Coltrane follows a similar pattern. "Coltrane's music has some extraordinary properties—the power to make you change your consciousness a little bit."[4] A way to interpret this psalm is by listening to Coltrane's *A Love Supreme*. It was written for a nine-piece group to intensify our awareness or "Acknowledgment," in which "Coltrane plays an ascending pattern in the key of E-major, then develops related melodic cells that he runs up and down for the major part of his improvisation."[5] Similarly, the psalmist changes our consciousness a little bit.

The psalm follows a similar syntactical pattern, arranged as an ascending melody. This pattern creates awareness of a powerful voice, an otherness, or epiphany's awareness. This is significant. Those who have led social change or organized social adaptations to a dominating order know that form precedes function. Their efforts may have begun with a few believers or admirers, but for those who are faithful to their causes, symbolically the music or the voice of God intensifies. In this way, those who hope to create social change must first create epiphany as social awareness of the possibilities of change.

A contemporary example of this is Wynton Marsalis's return to his native New Orleans to perform *Congo Square*, the album he had most recently released. He did this as a protest of the mistreatment of the city's citizens after Hurricane Katrina. The performance was in Congo Square, renamed Louis Armstrong Park. Marsalis prophetically sought to change our consciousness a little bit by reminding us that democratic values for blacks began in protest in Congo Square nearly two hundred years before. This is an example of sociospiritual epiphany. I suggest preaching the word of God in this way is an act of epiphany, rhetorically framing the listener's consciousness even "a little bit" each time in context.

Acts 8:14–17

Luke describes this Samaritan event as an awareness of the Holy Spirit. In a real sense, Luke writes as a coauthor with the Holy Spirit; he shares with the Holy Spirit the role of narrator and announcer of these events associated with the acts of the Spirit of Christ. As Coltrane does in "Spiritual," Luke creates space for his audience to follow the different manifestations of the Trinity.[6]

In this passage, however, the Jesus of Nazareth narrative becomes something new and different: the Christ of faith narrative. Readers and listeners can appreciate the significance of Luke's Samaritan narrative because the epiphany or sociospiritual awareness is associated with the Christ of faith.

---

4. Ibid., xi.
5. Ibid., 90–91.
6. See George Smeaton, *The Doctrine of the Holy Spirit* (Great Britain: Cromwell Press, 1997), 122–145; cf. "Vanguard" in Ratliff, *Coltrane*, 72.

This manifestation takes place in what I refer to as the Samaritan Gospel.[7] Verse 14 begins with "now when" to indicate a time sequence, something new and different. In short, something related to the narrative's new sequence happened prior to what Luke describes here. He is rhetorically strategic so that his audience is aware that these events are providentially connected, each involving the Holy Spirit's function.[8]

George Smeaton's insightful commentary defines further the function of the Holy Spirit: "The Father and Son come before us as two contracting parties, the sender and the sent; while the Holy Spirit is a concurring party in the entire provisions of the covenant (v. 14)."[9] According to Smeaton, the Holy Spirit is both the "sent" and the sender. In this instance, the Holy Spirit sends the apostles and not the Jerusalem church officials to Samaria in response to prior events (see Acts 8:9–13).

The apostles pray for the Holy Spirit (v. 15). Smeaton cautions that Christians should not neglect to pray for the presence and purpose of the Holy Spirit. "That rash and presumptuous position, by whomever it is held, is discredited by the fact that the apostles who had received the Holy Ghost on the first resurrection day continued with one accord in prayer and supplication for the promise of the father (Acts 1:14). They prayed for the Spirit though they had received the Spirit."[10] Those who preach create a climate for social change and justice, and must sense the presence of the Holy Spirit in their organization and community. Our sermons must have power manifested in activism (for example, demonstrations or boardroom negotiations), but to be effective those who preach social justice must pray for perseverance toward the fulfillment of God's promises.

John Polhill suggests that the Samaritans waited for the Holy Spirit, and how they received the Spirit differs from previous manifestations: "That the Samaritans had not yet received the Holy Spirit (v. 16) is certainly not the usual pattern of Acts. Normally the receipt of the Spirit was closely joined to baptism as part of the normative experience of conversion and commitment to Christ (cf. 2:38)."[11] Christians are recognized participants in God's narrative as both senders and the "sent." Christians share the gospel in response to events that happen in and around our present social conditions and contexts. In his last years, Coltrane adapted and changed. He prophesied that a new era for humanity would emerge that could only be identified as multiculturalism.

---

7. See Acts 1:8. This verse serves as an outline for the Acts of the Apostles (or as it might better be called, the Acts of the Spirit of Christ).

8. John B. Polhill, *Acts*, New American Commentary 26, ed. David S. Dockery et al. (Nashville: Broadman Press, 1992), 213.

9. Smeaton, *Doctrine of the Holy Spirit*, 122.

10. Ibid., 52.

11. Polhill, *Acts*, 217.

In this way, Coltrane's musical genius transcends social classes and constructs, which was not always easily embraced.[12] Still, this is epiphany. Preachers who preach this passage must take their people on a journey of evolution, adaptation, and mutations in the face of fear. Rhetorically, preachers may need to risk that they will be misunderstood in order to be understood by some.

Christians walk by faith, as they sometimes may discern only the tone of voice of the Holy Spirit. Oftentimes, the Spirit's voice is barely audible, often a whisper. Prayer intensifies the power to hear the Holy Spirit, and when the Spirit manifests Jesus as the Christ of faith, Christians must celebrate this Trinitarian manifestation in rituals and worship. Believers pray for the guidance of the Holy Spirit just as, Smeaton says, the apostles continued to do.

Luke 3:15–17, 21–22

A New Testament commentator states that "Luke's presentation of John the Baptist combines materials like that in Matthew 3:1–12 and Mark 1:2–8 with material unique to Luke (Luke 3:10–14)."[13] In the same way, Coltrane's intensity and rapid syntactical pattern is used to condense a historical, thematic, and theological journey, as we have noticed in Luke's syntactical pattern in Acts 8:14–17.

Thematically, Luke intensifies immersion in a symbolic function; it goes beyond a ritual act. Indeed, it is a spiritual journey of sociospiritual discovery. Immersion into faith draws some people into discipleship; on the other hand, immersion drives some people away. Ironically, however, by way of epiphany, both kinds of people discover Jesus. When verse 15 is read in this way, this point is clear: "People were filled with expectation, and all were questioning in their hearts concerning John, whether he might be the Messiah." If your social justice message is refined, then every believer or unbeliever will encounter the spiritual question and challenge of social justice, even if not everyone is gifted with social consciousness.[14]

Luke, however, contends that John's baptism differs from that of Jesus. "John answered all of them by saying, 'I baptize you with water; but one who is more powerful than I is coming; . . . He will baptize you with the Holy Spirit and fire'" (v. 16). This indicates that John's baptism is a ritual and preparation for an experience through Jesus with the Holy Spirit. John's baptism looks forward; Jesus' baptism is a provision of the Spirit (v. 17). John's baptism is physical act, but its function is to point toward something other. It

---

12. Ratliff, *Coltrane*, xvii.
13. Darrell L. Bock, "Luke," IVP New Testament Commentaries, http://www.biblegateway.com/resources/commentaries/?action=getChapterSections&source=1&cid=3&schap=3 (accessed August 14, 2010).
14. Ibid.

is a metaphor for a social process of separation. Notice Jesus' winnowing fork (Matt. 3:12); it is a tool used for tossing wheat or grain into the air to separate it from chaff. Epiphany recognizes that Jesus' winnowing is to identify people who will participate in the social evolution at different levels and places where they understand the process.

John the Baptist admitted that he was not the promised messiah. However, his Coltrane-like intensity and harsh tones did indicate the coming of Jesus, the Messiah. In this way, we sense epiphany. As preachers, then, we must understand our message and to whom the message is appointed. John the Baptist as a preacher knew that he was not to compromise his effective ministry by attempting to be or preach something he was not called or gifted to perform; nor could he restrain it!

Second Sunday after the Epiphany

Lincoln E. Galloway

ISAIAH 62:1–5
PSALM 36:5–10
1 CORINTHIANS 12:1–11
JOHN 2:1–11

In our texts for today, we encounter God's delighting and rejoicing in God's people through the offering of abundance, encompassing love, and gifts from the fountain of all life. We learn also that even when expressed in an individual, all of God's gifts are for the people of God and the common good of all creation.

Isaiah 62:1–5

As one hears the promise of renewal in this story, one also hears the forlorn cry of despair. The pledge not to keep silent or rest (v. 1) is a reminder of the tragic realities associated with the voiceless, with neglect and indifference. The picture is of forsaken people in circumstances of despair and perhaps paralysis. Since in the case of Zion this affliction was an international scandal, then her vindication has to be public "like the dawn and her salvation like a burning torch" (v. 1); and it has to be witnessed by "the nations" and "all the kings" (v. 2). Before such witnesses, the people will be liberated, delivered, and established as treasure, "a crown of beauty" and "a royal diadem" in the hand of a divine sovereign (v. 3).

The word of hope and restoration comes to those who have been named "Forsaken" and "Desolate" (v. 4). The first assignment is to break the silence without fear of the consequences. Roman Catholic Archbishop Dom Helder Camara, a champion of Brazil's poor, is remembered for his words: "When I give food to the poor, they call me a saint. When I ask why the poor have no

62

food, they call me a communist."[1] The "Forsaken" and "Desolate" question the silence as they live in utter poverty or endure the ravages of war as their loved ones are renamed "Collateral Damage." The message of restoration begins with a new name for those abandoned throughout the apartheid of South Africa, the genocide of Rwanda, the Shoah in Europe, and the years of slavery, lynching, racial segregation, and discrimination in the United States. The silence must also be broken for those whose sexual orientation is the source of their suffering and abandonment.

The promise of marital bliss reminds us that in the background is the suffering woman who has been cast off and rejected. Women bear the burden of abandonment, sexual violence, and domestic abuse. In the text, a call goes forth from the paralysis of desperation and the prison of silence to all who have been called forsaken or desolate, a call that the past horrors have been recognized and acknowledged. A message goes forth to the enslaved, the poor and downtrodden, the afflicted and oppressed, that God is their liberator, and God delights in them and shall rejoice over them (vv. 4–5). God's work must be our work, and the good news is that God's hand is extended to the most vulnerable of society. Therefore, we cannot be silent and we cannot rest.

Psalm 36:5–10

The selected verses fall between two sections that deal with the actions of the wicked (Ps. 36:1–4) and a petition for deliverance from evildoers (36:11–12). In the midst of these two glimpses of evil is a contrasting hymnic section that directs our attention to God's steadfast love (*hesed*). The section begins with a description of God's steadfast love as all-encompassing, then moves to celebrate steadfast love as precious, and ends with a plea for God's steadfast love to continue (vv. 5–10). Just as under the heavens, the clouds, the mighty mountains, and the great deep establish certain parameters for the cosmos, so also faithfulness, righteousness, justice, and salvation are the foundational pillars of God's *hesed*, which extends to all living creatures (vv. 5–6).

First, we are invited to recognize the interrelatedness of the created order in which we find not only our place but also the context for understanding our relationship to God and all that God has created. Ours is a place of accountability as we learn how to care for the earth and see God's handiwork from the heavens above to the great deep below. Ours is a place of action as we participate in God's work of caring, saving, and preserving "humans and animals

1. Francis McDonagh, ed., *Don Helder Camara: Essential Writings* (Maryknoll, NY: Orbis Books), 11.

alike" (v. 6). Ours is a place of worship as we stand in awe of the interconnect-edness of the universe and develop deeper reverence for all of God's creation.

Second, we celebrate *hesed* as refuge for all of God's children: "All people may take refuge in the shadow of your wings" (v. 7). People who need protection or shelter in the time of danger or distress seek refuge. We accept the challenge to testify to God's *hesed* when we offer the peoples of the world love that works toward security rather than violence and warfare, love that reduces arms sales, drug trafficking, militarism, and terrorism.

Third, we envision God's *hesed* through the lens of abundance and economic prosperity. Here also God's steadfast love is all-encompassing and all may "feast on the abundance of your house" and "drink from the river of your delights" (v. 8). We speak of God's *hesed* through acts of compassion that put food on the tables of those who live in poverty or suffer from hunger and malnutrition. The love of God does not condone economic exploitation; rather it seeks to have all of God's children around the banquet table.

The psalm extols the love of God who is the fountain of life. It brings into view a world without pollution, from the heavens above to the great deep below. It sets forth God's *hesed* that extends to all and calls forth a world of *shalom*, economic security, refuge, and fullness of life. As such it offers a call to account-ability, sustainability, and compassion, and invites deeper reverence as we participate in God's work for all living creatures in our interconnected world.

1 Corinthians 12:1–11

The central message in Paul's appeal to the church at Corinth is that God is the source of all good gifts, and all of God's gifts are for the common good. For the Christian life, God gives spiritual gifts (*charismata*) for the good of the faith community, and God's gifts are not to be appropriated exclusively for personal gain, prestige, or power. "To each is given the manifestation of the Spirit for the common good" (v. 7). This was a difficult message to hear in a context of divisiveness that may have been based on philosophical differences, socioeconomic status, cultural markers, and competing constructions of the Christian faith.

God has given diverse gifts for a diverse community, and this diversity is a source of strength to be honored and celebrated. "There are varieties of gifts, but the same Spirit; and there are varieties of services, but the same Lord; and there are varieties of activities, but it is the same God who activates all of them in everyone" (vv. 4–6). Paul makes the case that more important than ecstatic speech is, for example, a true and authentic confession that Jesus is Lord (v. 3); more important than individual rights and freedom is the common good and the advantage of others (1 Cor. 6:12; 10:23–24).

Faith communities have a long history of making difference an insurmountable barrier to faithful living, leaving behind a tarnished record of religious intolerance, racial discrimination and bigotry, gender oppression, cultural superiority and imperialism, and even indifference in the face of ethnic conflicts and genocide. Today, as our communities reflect greater multiculturalism and religious pluralism, our text invites us to recognize that God is the source of diversity. The same God gives to one and to another (vv. 8–10). Just as all of our different spiritual gifts (*charismata*) are from God, so also all of our genetic differences of the physical body or differences of gender or sexual orientation are gifts from God.

Our differences, which may be rooted in ethnicity or culture, socioeconomic status, philosophical or political ideology, are not to be sources of negative discrimination or reasons to treat each other with contempt (1 Cor. 8:9; 11:22). In writing to the church at Corinth, Paul invited them to focus on the communal nature of their faith. Today, in the same way, faith communities can model for the world how to honor diversity and heal schisms. Above all, we invite praise of God, the source of all good gifts, all *charismata*, all service and work among us. Finally, we learn that our gifts, our ministries and services that we render, and all the works that we are empowered to do are not ours but the Spirit's work among us allotting, activating, and directing all toward the glory of God and the common good.

John 2:1–11

The Gospel reading has some commonality with the Psalm reading (36:8), which painted a picture of all people feasting on the abundance of God's house and drinking from the river of God's delight. Here in the Fourth Gospel we encounter extravagant abundance as the hallmark of this first sign of Jesus. In their response to Jesus, the servants fill to the brim with water six stone water jars, each holding twenty or thirty gallons (vv. 6–8). The wine created from the water is clearly superior in quality. Yet the key to this story is that this transformation is of God and points to God. Transforming the water into wine is not just delightfully mysterious or an act of extravagant abundance; it declares the glory of God. So by the same token, at the wedding in Cana of Galilee something more than miraculous is witnessed. Indeed, this sign, on the third day, reveals Jesus' glory.

This first sign of Jesus calls forth faith within his disciples and ushers in a new era. The prophet Joel speaks metaphorically of a day when "the mountains shall drip sweet wine" and "the hills shall flow with milk" (Joel 3:18). Is this extravagant abundance of water becoming wine a symbol of this new day? Did the disciples believe that Jesus was pointing them to a day in the future, or did they believe that in Jesus they had witnessed the arrival of a new age?

The Gospel witness is emphatic that in Jesus, there is always the promise of superabundance (John 1:16). But is this promise meaningful only within an exclusively spiritual paradigm? Does this promise speak also to the world's poor, hungry, and impoverished? Is the extravagant abundance of wine or the feeding of the multitudes only symbolic, or is there a promise and a testimony or witness of hope for a new day for those who are malnourished and have very little to rely on for their daily sustenance?

This sign that Jesus performed challenges our faith communities to engage in everyday living and practice that will make a bold witness to the world that the resources given to us through God's awesome abundance must serve those who have very little. Perhaps then, every occasion of giving water may be both revealing and transformative. This is to suggest that "grace upon grace" involves giving and receiving. Further, for such a witness to reveal God and to transform, it cannot be patronizing or imperialistic.

Indeed, whenever a faith community gathers with Jesus in its midst, transformation happens, and the signs point to God's presence and glory. Such transformative encounters empower us to affirm those persons for whom the chant once lifted up in cities in the United States and continues to resonate: "I am somebody!"[2] Every gathering provides an opportunity to be transformed into a March on Washington, to give voice through a Poor People's Campaign to the humanity of all of God's children in the light of the superabundance of God's grace. Our faith communities are transformed as they participate, give and receive grace, and witness to Christ revealed, now and in the age to come.

---

2. James Haskins, *Jesse Jackson: Civil Rights Activist* (Berkeley Heights, NJ: Enslow Publishers, 2000), 7. See also, James M. Washington, ed., *A Testament of Hope: The Essential Writings and Speeches of Martin Luther King, Jr.* (San Francisco: HarperSanFrancisco, 1991), 108, 255.

Martin Luther King Jr. Day
(January 15)

Dale P. Andrews

MALACHI 2:10–12
PSALM 133
1 PETER 3:8–22
LUKE 12:4–12

Racism is the one of the most pernicious and permeating realities of life in North America. If left unchecked, racism will destroy both people of color and people of European origin. The Gospel insists that the church be anti-racist and pro-reconciling. The birthday of Martin Luther King Jr. (1929–1968) offers to preachers the opportunity not only to honor the life of this prophetic leader, not only to name the abiding oppression of marginalized racial/ethnic communities and the duplicitous dominating effects on European communities, but also to help congregations recognize practical ways that the community can join the struggle for justice.

> We have inherited a large house, a great "world house" in which we have to live together—black and white, Easterner and Westerner, Gentile and Jew, Catholic and Protestant, Moslem and Hindu—a family unduly separated in ideas, culture and interest, who, because we can never again live apart, must learn somehow to live together with each other in peace.
>
> *Martin Luther King Jr.*[1]

The texts selected for this year's observance of Martin Luther King Jr. Day focus on both the strife and blessing of unity in community. Faithfulness and fear can obviously be at odds in community, yet in divine covenant they may well become convicted resources to a just peace and to joy in the life of faith.

---

1. Martin Luther King Jr., *Where Do We Go from Here: Chaos or Community?* (Boston: Beacon Press, 1967), 167.

Psalm 133

The palmist knew something about division! From Mount Hermon to Mount Zion (v. 3), between the northern and the southern kingdoms, pilgrims would come together to sing praises and worship God, even while divided. This divine inheritance in spite of the divisions was cause to celebrate (v. 1). They were not quite enemies and not quite knowing how to be intimate friends. They might be considered "frenemies," not at war, but not at peace with one another. They could see their conquerors from outside but could not easily see past their divisions and destruction from inside, living with divided courts of covenant, disparate courts of call, split courts of community. Frenemies, they were bound together by chains but united by cause and call, an odd lot of community even while divided.

But gathering to seek God is itself an anointing with "deliciously scented"[2] oil, plentiful and overflowing with God's grace to bathe and saturate us (v. 2). The reference to the "beard of Aaron" signifies a lavish anointing, which they rejoice in still claiming as God's people. This cherished unity of their ascent this day blankets them with joy as dew blankets the earth in the breaking of dawn—dew that replenishes fragile life (v. 3). From Mount Hermon in the divided north, to Mount Zion in the divided south, God's anointing flows and falls upon God's people, calling even us into Psalms of Ascent. How very good indeed! How pleasant it is when kindred live together in unity that can be mutually supportive but are engaged in working through difference. How very good indeed to need one another even to praise and give thanks to God. May our common worship be a resource for living the faith justly and in grace with one another!

Malachi 2:10–12 and Luke 12:4–12

This brief passage in Malachi offers up one of six oracles from the prophet. Here we find strict reproach for breaking covenant, or perhaps more deeply to the point, for violating covenantal relationship with God and covenantal relationships with one another (Mal. 2:10). The violation of each reflects back on the integrity and worth of the other covenantal relationship.[3] Conviction runs deep in this text. The prophet is deeply convicted; he is convicted of his call to hold together the call of God's people to place their relationship with God before all else. Yet in a twisted turn, the people of God face criminalized conviction (judgment) for their unfaithful relationships. One wonders

2. Artur Weiser, *The Psalms: A Commentary* (Philadelphia: Westminster Press, 1962), 784.
3. George W. Harrison, "Covenant Unfaithfulness in Malachi 2:1–16," *Criswell Theological Review* 2, no. 1 (1987): 63–72.

how "hook'n up" with others outside one's community is a criminal offense; but the unfaithfulness behind even these possible survival acts, perhaps lost visions, distrust of one another, or even distrust of God's leading, are strong currents in the undertow. Are we convicted into relationship or do our relationships convict us?

In the novel and movie *O Brother, Where Art Thou?* we are not quite sure what kind of conviction holds together this tale of wayward pilgrims, which many regard as a satiric *Sullivan's Travels* version of Homer's *Odyssey*, set in Mississippi during the Great Depression. Three chain-gang convicts escape from prison work detail to search for a supposed treasure from an armored truck heist. On the run, chained by the ankles, they try to leap onto a moving train. The leader, Ulysses, so excited by his successful leap, is suddenly slammed to the floor of the car and dragged out to roll in the gravel; his partners in chains could not make the leap! They go to one of the men's cousins for help to break free from their chains. The cousin turns them in because he needs the money to survive. Through incredible turns of events, the ensemble becomes a bluegrass phenomenon. As the group is forming, they pick up a musician, Tommy, who has sold his soul to the devil at the crossroads for the charmed talent of music. The Soggy Bottom Boys are chained at the heart in "Constant Sorrow," as their one-hit-wonder bluegrass song would echo.

When we find ourselves driven or lured into faith community or ministry, we often use the term "conviction." Why does call or even covenant feel like a conviction of constant sorrow? Surely we are convicted to seek or to fulfill something. But we cannot escape the feeling that we are being convicted by, as much as feeling conviction of, some covenantal call. Does our call to faith community or even community with creation convict us, or are we convicted to fill a call under some obedience-punishment model of faithfulness? Either way, it sometimes feels like a sentence. Too often we interpret narrowly passages like the one from Malachi to mean that covenantal conviction places us at odds with difference. We then engage difference with the world or with one another in the faith community as a deadly threat. Can covenantal conviction empower an embrace of difference without losing faith in God as the source of covenantal life? This question is the challenge of preaching this text.

Martin Luther King Jr. argued for both urgency and joy in open community. This urgency and joy could be felt palpably in King's resistance to the Vietnam War. He explains that the road from resisting southern racist segregation to resisting international warfare is not so obscure. King explains that "a genuine revolution of values" calling for "a worldwide fellowship that lifts neighborly concern beyond one's tribe, race, class, and nation is in reality a call for an all-embracing and un-conditional love for all [humankind]. . . . We can no longer afford to worship the god of hate or bow before the altar of retaliation. The oceans of history are made turbulent by the ever-rising tides of hate. As Arnold Toynbee says: 'Love is the ultimate force that makes for the saving choice of life and good against the damning choice of death and evil.' "[4]

What happened to the joy of serving God, what happened to the joy of working to serve all of creation alongside and with the very convicted people of God? King saw community living with one another not in seclusion or triumphalism, but empowered to embrace the very worlds from which we come and into which we move daily, while not needing to shed one another. Is ministry, even discipleship, a sentence to confinement with a bunch of ill-mannered people? It feels like half the time we are trying to escape ministry, escape discipleship, escape the confinement of church prison, trying to shed the black-and-white stripes of a convict or the bright orange jumper of the jailhouse roadside cleaning crew. When joy and justice are reduced to obedience and compliance, they feel like jail terms of hard labor from which we need to escape.

Is escaping unfaithful? Is it a transgression to find more companionship, more trustworthiness, more safety, more familiarity with those never so blessed to be so convicted? Is there supposed to be a bond beyond the very conviction? Perhaps we are always staring beyond the fence, always feeling that conviction builds walls over which we strain to peer again and again, longing for that "keeping it real" world. Is it really supposed to be "us" against "them"? Why would anyone sign on to that gig? Is it really "us" avoiding "us"? What kind of covenantal life do we have? Are we unfaithful?

Malachi calls this kind of freedom unfaithfulness. We misinterpret the prophet when we pit the world against the faith community or vice versa. The faith community need not shed its faith to embrace difference. Much of Scripture sees the world as the feared one. We fear our enemies, we fear our neighbors, or we fear our judges. Today's Gospel of Luke passage teaches us to fear our Judge indeed, more so than those who can harm us now (Luke 12:4–5). Fear of the other leads us often to avoid our convictions. Our convictions betray, expose, and mark us. Our avoidance becomes our unfaithfulness. But Malachi sees our unfaithfulness in the lure to be like others with a lack of fear, lack of reverence, or lack of honor deep enough to take joy in our convictions alone. Arrogance is not the evidence of joy, nor does persecution evidence righteousness! Luke teaches us that our trust in God is our source of life and our courage to love. The lure and the fear of God that produces conviction (call) become resources to our faithful freedom. The chains that

---

4. Martin Luther King Jr., "Beyond Vietnam," in *A Call to Conscience: The Landmark Speeches of Dr. Martin Luther King Jr.*, ed. Clayborne Carson and Kris Shepard (New York: Warner Books, 2001), 160–61.

bind us might be the source and substance of our conviction and our freedom from frenzied fear and freedom from destructive lure.

In speaking to our chained escape, Archbishop Tutu would sometimes turn to a particular scene in yet another convict movie, *The Defiant Ones* (1958), with Sidney Poitier and Tony Curtis. They are chained prisoners on the run, black and white brothers in arms with common conviction. But the enmity between them is part of their culture, part of their being, which remains so hard to separate from their struggle together. In one scene, in sudden fear of being spotted on the run in pouring rain, they hurtle into a fifteen-foot pit to hide. But the rain-slicked mud would be both their barrier and their teacher. If they are to climb to their freedom, they have to climb together. They fail again and again at climbing alongside one another, sliding back into the pit with fists full of mud. Not until they struggle to climb with and for one another do they make it back to the road. Like the escaped prisoners, Archbishop Tutu discovers just how indispensable living in covenant becomes. Tutu even postulates that God shackles us to one another beyond our immediate vision so that in the strife for survival, we discover the life of covenantal relationship.[5]

1 Peter 3:8–22

First Peter raises good questions for us. Is our fellowship the cause of our suffering or the resource of our spiritual unity and love (v. 8)? Or is it just freeing to avoid one another? More difficult yet, over what or with whom in our community of faith do we contend in strife? What constitutes evil or abuse (v. 9) against one another? How do we live with the chains that bind us, and how do we break them; or why do we break them? Verses 10–12 recall the appeal from Psalm 34:12–16 to unity preserved by how we seek peace and goodness. We might grasp why we feel the struggles of a life of faith in the so-called freedom of the world around us. But why do we feel such suffering in the so-called freedom of the faith community? Are we really suffering for righteousness (v. 14) or for the sake of distorted "self-righteousness"?

Sometimes we feel more persecuted by one another than by anyone else. Is this suffering for the faith? Is this suffering for our convictions? Does our culture lack trust in God, or in us? Do we trust God enough to live "trustworthily" with one another? Do we trust reconciliation and restoration? Are we called to hope? Or are we just called "to suffer one another" for Christ? Christ sought life with and for us, in the face of suffering (vv. 18–19). Too often we seek life in breaking free from one another. We suffer in being chained to one

---

5. Desmond Mpilo Tutu, *No Future Without Forgiveness* (New York: Doubleday, 1999), 8.

another, but God calls us to one another. For another! With one another! Will the suffering chains be our demise or our resource to freedom?

Is our fellowship our prison? Although prison is a dangerous place to our souls, some ex-convicts long for the belonging they grew to know in prison. It is an odd belonging. But they might understand more about their covenantal relationship to survive than we do. Conviction is an odd prison; it is an odd sentence. How is hope or justice a sentence and not a freedom (v. 15)? Either one is a sentence when our conviction does not rehabilitate us, when it does not restore, when we live in prison harder than before our conviction.

King wrestled often over how to understand the unjustifiable suffering of oppression itself and suffering in the faithful work of justice making. He even worried over expressing his evolving interpretation of suffering for fear of distorting suffering into a self-glorifying sacrifice. Too often we hear scriptural texts like this passage on enduring suffering defiled to perpetuate abuse, as in domestic violence and racial oppression. But the grace of God that King professed would speak in the midst of suffering to teach him, since "there were two ways in which he could respond to [any] situation—either to react with bitterness or seek to transform the suffering into a creative force. . . . There are some who still find the cross a stumbling block, others consider it foolishness, but . . . it is the power of God unto social and individual salvation."[6] Here King struggled to navigate nonviolence, but still saw its divine sway.

When we are convicted, when we enter prison, we are doused, cleaned up to be bound up; we spend much of our time trying to rinse off the stench of guilt or even unrighteousness, but more so we try to shower again and again to rinse off the grime of living so closely with one another. However, 1 Peter expects that our baptism actually places us in the midst of the grime to live yet still (v. 21). The significance of baptism is not in washing, but a uniting with God.[7] Our relationships inside and outside the community, or "prison," are at risk without this divine assurance. What does it truly mean to be apprehended, convicted, imprisoned, or chained by faith?

---

6. Martin Luther King Jr., *Strength to Love* (1963; repr., Philadelphia: Fortress Press, 1981), 153–54.
7. Mary Schertz, "Radical Trust in the Just Judge: The Easter Texts of 1 Peter," *Word & World* 24, no. 4 (Fall 2004): 430–41.

Third Sunday after the Epiphany

Melinda A. Quivik

NEHEMIAH 8:1–3, 5–6, 8–10
PSALM 19
1 CORINTHIANS 12:12–31A
LUKE 4:14–21

Powerful underlying threads run through the lections for this day, all relating to the identity of God's people and, in a sense, culminating in the Corinthian assertions about the body of Christ. In three texts, the assembly is the focus. The assembly is the location of attentiveness to the word of the Lord. This posture of the people gathered offers a challenging image of the way in which commitments to social justice and transformation take root in human community.

Nehemiah 8:1–3, 5–6, 8–10

From exile and degradation, the people gather together and notably do not wait for Ezra, the priest, to offer them something. Instead, they tell Ezra what they already know they need: "the book of the law of Moses." We learn in the beginning of Nehemiah that the people of Israel are mourning the ruin of Jerusalem. Its walls have been breached and the gates burned. Nehemiah manages to journey to Jerusalem to see about the damage, and he arranges the rebuilding.

Stunningly, all through the book, the names of those who do the building are listed. More prominent in the book than the storyteller, whose memoir is recorded in it, are the people themselves. Not only are the builders named, but the parts of the wall and the gates on which they worked are named as well. Slowly the walls are healed. Piece by piece the gates are put into order even in the face of ridicule from others. The danger increases until the workers must carry weapons to guard the rebuilding against enemies who have threatened to tear down what they have reconstructed.

73

Yet even more trouble comes upon the people. Some Israelites are found to be charging exorbitant interest rates to their own kin, so that even while doing the rebuilding, the people are hungry and impoverished. Nehemiah, the governor, puts a stop to the exploitation by bringing charges against the offenders, who promise, at last, to mend their ways. "And all the assembly said, 'Amen,' and praised the LORD" (Neh. 5:13b). To punish Nehemiah, neighboring powers seek to trick and kill him. He recognizes their treachery and does not meet with them.

Such hardships in similar forms are the stuff of every age. We recognize betrayal, greed, and revenge as all-too-familiar sins of our own time. And even today, we marvel at the perseverance of people who continue to struggle to strengthen institutions and communities in the face of daunting opposition. In fact, the people Israel make the walls of Jerusalem solid in record time. Seeing this, their treacherous neighbors become afraid, because it seems to them impossible that such work could have been accomplished unless the God of the Israelites had a hand in it. Against all the forces that might have stopped the repairs, the work went on and was completed in a time period indicating spectacular achievement. The people then gather. The scene is a sea of people, listed by family and tribe, occupation, and relationship with Solomon. Even the animals that accompany them are listed. It is a mighty impressive lot.

In all this building, defending, protecting the work and the workers, and then the ingathering of the people, there is a sense that despite Nehemiah's inspiring leadership, the work is truly the people's. The work has become a project that seems to have embodied its own purpose: not only to build the walls of Jerusalem but in so doing to build the people too. When they finish the work, even the culminating action maintains the strength of the gathering and the power of the assembly to know its own heart and mind, to assert its own deep need, and to do so as an organic whole. We do not readily expect such behavior of crowds. For that reason, the assembly gathered before Nehemiah stands for us as an ideal image of a coalescence of separate tribes and families and individuals now transformed into one body. We know the single-mindedness of this body because the story shows a people gathering before the priest Ezra, asking him to read the book of the law before them.

This is a remarkable depiction. The assembly does not celebrate the accomplished repair until YHWH's word has been spoken in the mouth of the priest, "and the ears of all the people were attentive to the book of the law" (v. 3). Not until the governor Nehemiah, the priest Ezra, and the Levites together insist that the people stop weeping over "the words of the law" and go away to feast do the people rejoice. The governor, the priest, and the

Levites declare the day holy. Out of that holiness come the fat foods and sweet wines and, in addition, the sending of food and drink to those who had none.

Why is the day holy? We can look at what has taken place. This sanctified feasting shows us the structure of liturgical movement: the people assemble, they hear the word of the Lord, and then they celebrate with a meal. The marvel of this passage is the conjunction of completing a great work while simultaneously defending it, turning immediately to gather before YHWH's law in the midst of the city, weeping over the experience of hearing the words, and then rejoicing. Understanding the words of the law is occasion for weeping, because in the heart of the law is the promise that YHWH's power is the strength of joy. Where there is justice, there is joy. In the image of separate tribes coming together before the word of the Lord, we receive the image of justice. All people together stand equal before YHWH, who blesses each person with the holy word.

Psalm 19

Responding to the words of the Nehemiah reading, assemblies today might sing the appointed Psalm 19 and consider how the psalm is itself an enactment of the people Israel who hear the words of the law from Ezra:

> The precepts of the LORD are right,
>   rejoicing the heart;
> the commandment of the LORD is clear,
>   enlightening the eyes;
> the fear of the LORD is pure,
>   enduring forever;
> the ordinances of the LORD are true
>   and righteous altogether.
> More to be desired are they than gold,
>   even much fine gold;
> sweeter also than honey,
>   and drippings of the honeycomb.
>   (Ps. 19:8–10)

In the psalm for this day, we hear why the people of Israel would be weeping. The statutes of the law rejoice the heart because they give wisdom and light. These people are not weeping out of sorrow but out of gratitude. The assembly is filled with a cleanliness that comes from the fear of the Lord and has turned to the word of YHWH before anything else because the sweetest joy is found in the law. This is what the Lord brings upon the people: a strength that comes from the joy of the LORD.

Luke 4:14–21

We must hasten here to point out that the Gospel reading in Luke refers to the Spirit filling Jesus with power. Power comes to those who are visited by the Spirit of the Lord. We have no reason to distinguish between the joy of the Israelites and the joy that is in Jesus. It is, in both cases, an attribute *of* the Lord (joy, Spirit) that infuses.

In both stories, we see a peculiarly alert posture in the people. The people are full of strength in Nehemiah. Luke shows the people to be powerfully attentive: "The eyes of all in the synagogue were fixed on him" (v. 20). It is as if breath is being held. Expectation fills the room.

In Luke's account, Jesus has just come from the wilderness encounters with the tempter and is "filled with the power of the Spirit" (v. 14). This experience has so altered him that he exudes a palpable affect. He rouses interest. People talk. In Nazareth, in the synagogue, he reads from Isaiah and tells the people that a new reality has just been born in their presence, literally "in your hearing" (v. 21). In your ears—in the words that come to your ears—the healing and liberation promised in Isaiah have been accomplished.

Two threads run between these stories connecting Ezra and Jesus with the people in Nehemiah and in Luke. Both Ezra and Jesus bring before the people the word of the Lord: Ezra as he reads from the law, and Jesus as he proclaims the fulfillment of the law. The people in Nehemiah have gathered before the Water Gate to honor "the book of the law" (Neh. 8:1). They stand to hear the reading, respond to Ezra's blessing by saying, "Amen, Amen" (Neh. 8:6), and bow to the ground. They are united in their relationship to the word of YHWH. Likewise, in the temple when Jesus reads from the prophet Isaiah, people have gathered because "a report about him spread through all the surrounding country" (v. 14). People praise him. They stand before the word of YHWH ready to hear.

In the same way in our own time, the word of God brings together the people of every assembly. We gather as did the people who heard God's word through Ezra and Jesus. God's word unites us with our ancestors in this way. Like them, we are brought to the "Amen" of worship and ultimately to the rejoicing and fulfillment that becomes a present reality wherever the holy book is opened in the midst of God's people.

1 Corinthians 12:12–31a

The word of YHWH in Nehemiah and in Luke, opened before the assembly of the people in the twenty-first century, gathered in watchfulness and need, comes home in a sharp, tangible, welcome way in the Epistle text. The power of the Spirit offers yet another gift: to hear that in the composition of our own corporate body, each of us is integrally necessary.

It is a joyful word for those who are weak, less respected than others, and least honored to hear that the body needs each member, and that we need especially those who are without power. This is also a word of hope for those who are strong, honored, and respected. Even the mighty encounter their own weaknesses, disrespect, loss, and self-doubt. No one is immune. Anyone can be brought low and falter at any time, so all of us need to hear that we are vital to the body. Even more, the passage insists in no uncertain terms that "God has appointed" the diversity among us and empowers us to help one another with these different and vitally needed gifts. We cannot all rebuild the same gate at the same time. None of us in the body is required to be all things to all people. This is the "excellent way" that has been prepared for everyone. It is a word of hope for each person. Each has a place, an offering, and a reason to belong.

When we set out to "preach social justice," we set out (1) to hold a mirror up to the assembly; (2) to remind ourselves that each of us is special, while no one is more special than another; and (3) to assert that those who reside outside our walls can only enter through the broken surfaces, the doors, the walls that do not stand in their way. Together we secure these walls in such a way that others may come in and go out. Walls are necessary for safety and clarity, for guarding the precious members who work under pressure or threat as they seek restoration. But the walls are never impermeable. Never! They differentiate in order to offer a home and a sanctuary, but the door is always open.

These texts offer images of broken walls and mended walls, broken people and healed community, varied gifts and yet a time when everyone together turns to the giver of all gifts. When we see ourselves as a body assembled by the one who stands always outside our walls—on the side of those who do not yet belong, who have not yet been welcomed, who are not easily accepted—then we become a grateful people who only want to open wider the doors, wherever they may be flung.

Fourth Sunday after the Epiphany

Kenyatta R. Gilbert

JEREMIAH 1:4–10
PSALM 71:1–6
1 CORINTHIANS 13:1–13
LUKE 4:21–30

How does one remain devoted to a God who fashioned our existence, when soul-nourishing options seem to vanish in an age of disregard? How does one trust God's security in times when men, for sport, impregnate women and abandon their children, or when individuals cannot retire because then there is nothing to draw down to pay for their children's college tuition? How can one preach the power of love when wickedness is hardly exposed for what it is and justice too difficult to find in our hypercapitalistic American society? How is the word of Christ fulfilled in our hearing? The preacher faces deep challenges between these texts and church initiatives that often have little to do with God's intimate care or with social justice initiatives meant to build up the lives of the "least of these" who populate church pews.

Jeremiah 1:4–10

The Hebrew word *nabi'* is translated as "prophet," meaning "one who is called," in the First Testament Scripture. In the opening verses of Jeremiah we encounter the initiation of God's call and commission of the prophet Jeremiah. In this scriptural passage the prophetic call is his destiny, one divinely set before the prophet's birth. God says to Jeremiah, "Before I formed you in the womb I knew you, and before you were born I consecrated you; I appointed you a prophet to the nations" (v. 5). Though Jeremiah is appointed prophet over the nations, no reference in the narrative suggests that the prophet was called to a ceremonial office to sit and adjudicate the daily affairs of the people. Rather, the call of the prophet is accompanied by a message-bearing license to go and speak to a world that has rejected God.

Jeremiah is one called to the task of what Walter Brueggemann calls evoking an alternative community. Jeremiah will speak God's judgment and relentless hope for Israel. This task requires that prophets offer an alternative view of reality within their contextualized history, but do so in the light of divine freedom and justice.[1] The prophetic call commissions Jeremiah to speak judgingly, plucking up and pulling down, destroying and overthrowing, building and planting (v. 10). With the call comes the expectation that the social order will be reset.

Like other recipients of the prophetic call, such as Moses, Amos, and Jonah, Jeremiah laments and protests. His fears about the assignment clearly overwhelm him. But the good news for the prophet, and for the contemporary Christian, is that God's promissory word accompanies prophetic appointments and prophetic tasks. Verses 6–8 depict a reluctant and agonizing prophet receiving a divine pep talk. The purpose of the pep talk is to confirm for the prophet that the size of the assignment is always greater than that which fits into the human imagination or can be handled solely by human capability.

A preacher-expositor may raise several questions surrounding Jeremiah's call narrative. What does it mean to carry out faithfully divine instruction? Death? Since Jeremiah's call narrative seems highly personal, does this mean that prophetic revelation comes only to each individual, regarding human welfare in community as a secondary concern to divine interests? Can prophetic appeals for transformation truly come without tangible evidence about where and how this transformation manifests itself? The preacher must struggle with such questions to identify within her or his particularity what it means to fulfill certain ministry obligations. Vision and message coherency notwithstanding, unlike Jeremiah and other First Testament prophets, today's preacher prophetically proclaims through the promise and fulfillment lens of Jesus Christ, the incarnate Word as revealed in Scripture, and often she or he does this with a Bible in hand. This means that God's sustaining grace to authorize and enable one to preach prophetically should be acknowledged as an inbuilt safeguard. The preacher need not be excessively burdened or overwhelmed by the prophetic charge, but witness to an active Sovereign who is alive in the world, revealed in Scripture, and continually reframing the preacher's perception of reality while calling the messenger to a very specific agenda: to pluck up, pull down, destroy, and overthrow forces that frustrate or impinge on God's life-giving plan for creation. God preveniently calls for would-be prophets who will work to help (re)build lives in a broken world.

---

1. Walter Brueggemann, *The Prophetic Imagination* (Philadelphia: Fortress Press, 1978), 110.

Psalm 71:1–6

Prayers are sometimes prayed in anguish, at other times in anger or desperation. These emotional states are common throughout the psalms. Here we find honest talk with God. A faith traveler who returns to the well once again raises an earnest prayer in hope that God will answer this petition to save a life. The preacher who comes to this text in preparation to see how it might speak to a listening congregation might discover an assuring word when asking the following questions: Does anything happen when we pray? Does God answer prayer? If we pray for help, does help come?

The psalmist pleads for deliverance and security in a social world hostile to those who trust in God. This personal prayer demonstrates the power of hope and what it means to journey with a trustworthy God. The psalmist does not ask to be made righteous but understands that righteousness is connected to God's agency. Only through God's holy nature is true salvation made possible. In other words, the psalmist appeals to the righteousness of God.

This petition reveals the psalmist's humanity. The psalmist speaks as one naked before the Creator. Fearfulness and faithfulness are twin realities here. This is the stuff of dramatic appeal! God is rock and fortress, a mighty Sovereign who gives ear to the victimized who are unable to resist the grasp of the wicked and those persons who pervert justice. "Rescue me . . . from the hand of the wicked, from the grasp of the unjust and cruel. For you, O Lord, are my hope" (vv. 4–5). These words are intentional communication from a person who bares a heart to God in trust. The psalmist declares devotion to God, whose providential character is concretely named (v. 6). Womb imagery appears in this pericope, as it does in several other places in Scripture (for example, "Before I formed you in the womb I knew you," Jer. 1:5; "For it was you who formed my inward parts; you knit me together in my mother's womb," Ps. 139:13). History matters to this psalmist, who acknowledges God's involvement in life since birth. This means that God has delivered the psalmist before and thus there is no reason now to think that God can no longer be relied on to rescue again.

1 Corinthians 13:1–13

This scriptural passage affirms the redemptive power of unconditional love. By nature, love is inherently creative and in its full reach ingathers both good acts and "agapic praxis" to transform community. Agapic praxis is self-transcending love that is genuinely concerned about human solidarity and the work of dismantling spiritual and social forces.[2] Martin Luther King Jr. suggested that love is creative because it resists aiming arrows at any

---

2. Matthew Lamb, *Solidarity with Victims: Toward a Theology of Social Transformation* (New York: Crossroads Publishing, 1982), 1.

individual. Evil systems are the enemy love seeks to defeat. In other words, love's goal is to find some element of good in the human person, because human redemption is always love's highest ideal.[3]

On the heels of a heated debate in chapter 12 within the Corinthian church about social and religious standing in the church on the basis of spiritual gifts, Paul underlines the importance of unity among believers and valuing one another's particular gifts as needed contributions for holistic ministry. Paul's emphasis on love as essential to unity redirects the Corinthians from being preoccupied with the distribution and use of spiritual gifts. In other words, the "eternalness of love" is to be prized over temporal gifts.[4] "Love never ends. But as for prophecies, they will come to an end; as for tongues, they will cease; as for knowledge, it will come to an end" (v. 8).

To read and preach from this passage requires paying close attention to the literary features of the text and the logic Paul uses to describe the gift of love. Using if-then logic, Paul accents love's positive attributes by relating to the reader what love is not. Love does not make noise; is not taken by flattery; never boasts; and is neither arrogant nor pushy. Differently, love is patient, kind, truth seeking, and unending (vv. 4–8). Similar to Paul's literary style and rhetoric in describing the fruit of the Spirit in Galatians 5:22, Corinthians 13 attributes high significance to the character of the gifts shaping the text.

Proclamation may focus on the other-centeredness of love (v. 4a–b), its hopefulness (vv. 7, 12b), or its unbroken and boundless nature (v. 8). Though this passage is often used for preaching the wedding homily, its use should not be restricted in this way. Perhaps the most notable feature is that in the original context of this discourse, the foremost communal concern is disunity among Christians and not the institution of marriage. Such a text may invite preachers to interpret for splintered congregations the consequences of turning a blind eye to the HIV/AIDS crisis afflicting the communities where their churches are. Sermons that focus on the other-centeredness of love and its boundless nature must be a word of spiritual and psychological rescue for persons and their families who live with and die from this incurable disease. This passage puts the redemptive power of unconditional love in the forefront of a preacher's sacred imagination.

Luke 4:21–30

Luke 4 is often narrowly interpreted and invested with prophetic meaning alone, but this passage beckons us to see more. Verses 16–20 provide an

3. Martin Luther King Jr., "Love Your Enemies," in *A Knock at Midnight*, ed. Clayborne Carson (New York: Warner Books), 46–47.
4. Boykin Sanders, "1 Corinthians," in *True to Our Native Land*, ed. Brian K. Blount et al. (Minneapolis: Fortress Press, 2007), 297.

important backdrop to the focal passage. In these preceding verses Jesus out-lines the specifics of God's plan for world restoration. In a synagogue com-munity in ancient Palestine—Nazareth, to be specific—Jesus addresses those who are evidently the cultural gatekeepers of tradition. Jesus reads Isaiah's oracle and declares the nature and purpose of his anticipated earthly ministry.

Ironically, what is spoken is a vexing reminder about the community's obli-gation to God and society. Under the mantle of God's Spirit and through the provision of God's anointing, Jesus declares the anointed work to be accom-plished. That work consists of bringing good news to the disinherited ones, lighting the way for those who sit in prisons of darkness, guiding the lives of individuals in spite of their shadowy existence, and liberating the mul-titudes whose dignity-robbing wounds of spiritual and bodily enslavement require more than Band-Aid dressing. The kerygma is captured here in Jesus' announcement, "*[The Lord] has sent me to proclaim release to the captives and recovery of sight to the blind, to let the oppressed go free*" (Luke 4:18).

Jesus' inaugural vision, though well known, is blurred today. But in this earthy setting one notices God's free disclosure of Godself in the person of Jesus, and in this synagogue, Jesus interprets both Scripture (Isa. 61:1–2) and the community's religious traditions to help all to perceive God's embodied vision revealed in their midst.[5] It is here, in the direction of this vision, that the preacher's authentic self and the nature of his or her calling must be estab-lished and taken up.

In verses 21–28 that heralding is met with discussion. The hearers query Jesus' pedigree with the seemingly benign question from the crowd, "Is not this Joseph's son?" Why are they so amazed? Why does amazement turn to rage so quickly? With eyes fixed on Jesus, did they not speak well of him or applaud his graciousness? Why does the hometown crowd turn sour?

The preacher must ask these sorts of questions of the text. But also he or she must examine the text for its contemporary application. Elijah's narra-tive is cited here with references to widespread famine and poverty. Why not address world hunger? The Syrian commander Naaman is another person highlighted. He is an outcast redeemed. What might this illustration in the text say about the gospel breaking down cultural barriers? Are there poten-tial analogues between Naaman's leprous condition and those today suffering from HIV/AIDS? Jesus' inaugural vision saying, "Today this scripture has been fulfilled in your hearing," is not to be interpreted as a project completed. Rather, it is to say that persons now, like those in the synagogue, are invited to participate in a world restoration that is under way.

---

5. Ronald Allen, *Preaching Luke–Acts*, Preaching Classic Texts (St. Louis: Chalice Press, 2000), 43.

Fifth Sunday after the Epiphany

Chandra Taylor Smith

ISAIAH 6:1–8 (9–13)
PSALM 138
1 CORINTHIANS 15:1–11
LUKE 5:1–11

The provocative message from this week's lectionary fundamentally illustrates how God boldly inspires and commissions us to become agents of social justice. In Isaiah's encounter with God, we perceive—through God's fear-provoking presence as well as God's awesome grace and loving mercy—how dominating power can be both abusive, in the context of injustice, and merciful, in the context of God's justice and righteousness. The gracious poem in Psalm 138 portrays how only the continuous expressions of gratitude and praise by people from all walks of life will manifest and sustain God's vision of a just society. Moreover, in 1 Corinthians, the apostle Paul urges us through a powerful personal testimony to understand that our deep and personal belief in the good news of the death and physical resurrection of Jesus undergirds our commitment to a just society. Finally, in Luke's illustrative literary style, he paints a vivid picture of how Jesus approaches a fishing community and demonstrates his loving mercy and grace in order that the people begin to believe in God's bountiful social vision and become active agents of justice for God. Each of these Scriptures powerfully envisions God's social justice and how God anoints us through divine grace to work daily toward the dynamic just society God righteously prepares for us.

Isaiah 6:1–8 (9–13)

We can only imagine how frightened Isaiah must be as he gazes up at the tremendous vision of God hovering above him (v. 1). Isaiah cowers as he is enveloped by the celestial cloud and as the fantastic extraterrestrial beings flanking the Lord announce God's majesty. The temple doors tremble in their pivots as the strange angels bellow, "Holy, holy, holy is the LORD of hosts; the whole earth is full of [God's] glory" (vv. 2–4). Facing God's dominating presence, Isaiah is overtaken by his unworthiness, and with sincere self-deprecation declares, "Woe is me! I am lost, . . . and live among a people of unclean lips" (v. 5a). Isaiah's observations of the growing threat of Assyrian imperialism and the flagrant sinfulness and faithlessness of Jerusalem during this time (Isa. 5:1–25) drive his confession that human actions, including his own, do not merit the privilege of viewing and experiencing the power of the Lord face to face (v. 5b).

Ironically, however, Isaiah's encounter with God exposes him to a type of fear that is also intrinsic to the human experience of subjugation and injustice. Perceptive about the terror of power that is unjust, Isaiah also perceives God's righteous intentions and the human responses required for the restoration of justice. An example of the terrorizing context of injustice and human domination is the systemic abuse of millions of women around the world who cower before a force that hovers over them and strikes fear in them in personal or professional relationships. These women can attest to their feelings of unworthiness that the injustice of the abusive power inflicts on them. A similar fear or shameful resignation is also prevalent today among the people who have lost their jobs and face home foreclosures. Glimpses of such terror are in the disconcerting glares of many homeless people we pass by daily, begging along busy intersections or lingering on street corners, waving tattered signs scribbled with terse supplications for help. But there is a stark difference between the abusive powers of injustice and the righteous powers of God.

Being in the presence of God means being in the presence of the force of justice. For while Isaiah at one moment feels completely inadequate before the force of God's power and presence, in the next moment he is also liberated from his unworthiness by this same force; his sins are blotted out and his feelings of guilt disappear. God's forgiveness of Isaiah is an ultimate act of justice. He receives God's grace and loving mercy from the touch of hot coal removed from the altar and applied by one of the mercy-bearing angels (vv. 6–8). Isaiah observes how God relies on the seraphs as dynamic agents for communicating and enacting God's social vision of justice. When God seeks to commission Isaiah to break the bonds of injustice for others and asks him, "Whom shall I send, and who will go for us?" Isaiah volunteers with exclamation, "Here am I; send me!" (v. 8). He responds without hesitation because he is radically shaped by his original state of woefulness and knows the fear imposed by power that can be both abusive, in the context of injustice, as well as merciful, in the context of God's justice.

Ultimately, God commissions Isaiah to be a divine messenger because his encounter with God prepares him to have faith in the radical approach God deems necessary to establish a just society among all people. Given the binding capacity of injustice in human experience, God forewarns Isaiah that the majority of humanity will reject his righteous message (vv. 9–10). In the face of rejection, Isaiah must have faith and maintain his efforts as God's agent of justice even if only a small remnant of God's people does not yield utterly to injustice (Isa. 6:11–13). Thus agents of justice today must also be discerning about the power of injustice and maintain their faith in God's just vision.

Psalm 138

In this hymn, the dynamic and principled acts of gratitude and praise by the Davidic psalmist resolutely acknowledge the divine, loving grace and mercy that sustain God's social vision for humankind. The many occasions and expressions of thankfulness that the psalmist presents in these eight verses bring to mind the insistence that our previous generations placed on blessing the food before every meal and kneeling at the bedside in prayer before crawling under the covers every night. However, the psalmist's actions are not mere perfunctory or ritualistic expressions of gratitude and worship. He declares that he adores the Lord with his "whole heart" (v. 1a). Moreover, the psalmist acts with a certain defiance as he deliberately venerates God in the presence of presumed gods and challenges their pretense of divinity or authority (v. 1b).

As they go about their day laboring to clean and cook for other people's families, to scrub and straighten other people's offices, or to refresh other people's hotel rooms, many brown and black women today can often be heard humming a favorite worship hymn just beneath their breath in a similar spirit of praise as the psalmist. They quietly sing these praises from the depths of their "whole heart," and their melodic prayers sustain them in the face of many daily trials and tribulations. These are women who then kneel before the altars in their churches and temples, in the same manner that the psalmist boldly faced the holy temple to acknowledge that God's name, word, steadfast love, and faithfulness are exalted above everything (v. 2). Indeed, these women have powerful testimonies about how God "answered" when they called on the Lord and increased their "strength of soul" (v. 3). However, it is not just the economically and socially disadvantaged, like so many brown and black women today, who are strengthened by God and offer up regular words of gratitude. The psalmist emphasizes that even the kings of the earth must know God's words and praise the Lord (v. 4).

Essentially, the psalmist paints a vision of a just society in which everyone, including kings, lifts up God's ways because of the greatness of God's glory (v. 5). In God's righteous social order, grace and mercy endure for the "lowly," such as poor, faithful, brown and black women, but God's justice is tenuous for those who are "haughty" or overconfident in their earthly authority (v. 6). Thus the psalmist's portrayal of walking "in the midst of trouble" depicts the daily walk of poor women who are persistently challenged by injustices (v. 7a). However, God's right hand stretches out to intercede in their lives and deliver them from the wrath of injustices (v. 7b). In a final note of faithful adulation, the psalmist acknowledges that God's purpose for our life is rooted in God's "steadfast love" for humankind. In a just social order, we all must continuously reciprocate our love for God through our thankfulness and praise so that God never abandons God's merciful love for us (v. 8).

1 Corinthians 15:1–11

The apostle Paul reminds us that the dynamic manifestation of a just society requires our deeply personal belief in and acknowledgment of the "good news" of the death and physical resurrection of the body of Jesus (vv. 1–3). In other words, the possibility of living in a just society in which humanity is completely transformed, our sins reconciled, whereof we are saved and made righteous, is as radical a possibility as Jesus dying, being buried, and then coming back to life again (v. 4). The impossibility of Jesus coming back to life after death is a part of God's plan for the possibility of humanity to experience fully the transformative power of Jesus' love for the world.

Cephas, the more than five hundred brothers and sisters, the Twelve, and the apostles who witnessed Jesus' resurrected appearance all give witness to the impossible being made physically possible. Their testaments even today inspire the belief of others in the veracity of the "good news" (vv. 5–7). The contemporary witness, for example, of many single mothers who struggle with meager means but manage to keep their children off the drug- and gang-infested streets of their economically ravaged neighborhoods and to get them through high school and college is no less a witness to the impossible being made possible. Many women, men, and children who struggle under the daily injustice of poverty today are forthright about how only their belief in Jesus sustains them through the most trying times. Indeed, their testaments themselves give witness to profound faith in the good news, which assures them that their impossible predicaments of injustice can be transformed through Christ.

It is vital for people from all walks of life to believe in the death and physical resurrection of the body of Jesus. Clearly, this possibility of what seems to be impossible transforms our lives and ushers social justice into our lives no matter what our personal predicaments. Paul encountered the resurrected Jesus himself at a time when he actively "persecuted the church of God" (vv. 8–9). And yet the good news prevailed; God's grace made it possible for Paul to see the impossible and anointed him to work harder than anyone to spread that same good news, to serve and to expand God's just and righteous social order (v. 10).

Luke 5:1–11

Luke captures in this picturesque narrative how Jesus rallies a fishing community to experience his transformative mercy and begin to believe in God's bountiful social vision for them. Getting into Simon's boat and anchoring "a little way from the shore," Jesus is able to address the individuals who were crowding in on him "to hear the word of God" collectively, and he is able to manifest the vision of God's just society communally (vv. 1–3). Yet despite his teachings from the boat before the crowd, Simon is still skeptical about Jesus and questions his order to take the boat back "out into the deep water and let down [the] nets for a catch" (vv. 4–7).

To counter Simon's skepticism, Jesus reinforces his teachings by vividly demonstrating the bounty of God's righteousness. After they end up netting enough fish to swamp two boats, Simon knows that he has underestimated Jesus' vision and power. The impact of Jesus' love and mercy on the daily provisions for the community is awesome and humbling. Simon drops to his knees before Jesus in amazement and declares that he is unworthy of his blessing (vv. 8–9). However, Jesus' words of grace to Simon, James, and John are, "Do not be afraid; from now on you will be catching people" (v. 10). Thus, the encounter with Jesus' awe-inspiring generosity compels Simon and his partners to leave everything and follow him (v. 11). Just like Isaiah and Paul, they became active agents of justice for God; for it is impossible to live out passively the transformative vision of God's just social order. Everyone is an active advocate for social justice in a truly just society.

Asian American Heritage Day
(February 19)

Fumitaka Matsuoka

JEREMIAH 29:1–9
PSALM 108
ACTS 12:1–19
LUKE 9:49–50

This Day of Remembrance is honored on a Sunday near February 19, the day in 1942 on which Japanese American citizens were locked into U.S. concentration camps for the duration of World War II. Asian American Heritage Day celebrates the distinctive qualities of Asian cultures and provides a venue for non-Asians to become more acquainted with those cultures. The preacher can lift up the contributions that people of Asia have made to North America and the world at large and call the congregation to repent of the injustices inflicted upon people of Asian origin in the United States (e.g., exploitation during the building of the first transcontinental railway, Japanese internment following the Pearl Harbor attack). Preachers may also celebrate Asian Pacific American Heritage Month in May, which was recognized by a congressional and presidential act in 1979.

Back in 1969, Manzanar was a barren patch of land, no different from the rest of the high desert. Worse yet, the memory of the Internment was fading just as thoroughly. "The Camps" were an awful nightmare that those who had to endure them wanted to forget. The Perpetrators also wanted to sweep it under the rug. They didn't want to be held accountable. And if the ones it happened to don't seem to mind, what's the big deal?

The Pilgrimage was our answer to that. The shadow can be ignored, but then it never goes away. The only way to drive it out is with the Light. . . . Light brings clarity. We see things around us better, and we deal with them. "Wartime hysteria" isn't an excuse.

88

"Civil Liberties" are more than a catchphrase. "Racism" is evil.
We know that in our guts.
   And that's why we come back.

Statement from Fortieth Annual Manzanar
Pilgrimage, 2009[1]

The themes to be treated in today's biblical passages include the culturally liminal perspective of people in exile, seeing life from the divine perspective, or what Jewish theologian Abraham Heschel calls God's search for people, the organic scholarship of being accountable to community. We discover in these texts Dietrich Bonhoeffer's idea of "costly grace," grace that may cost one's life and yet gives a person the only true life.

Jeremiah 29:1–9

"But seek the welfare of the city where I have sent you into exile, and pray to the Lord on its behalf, for in its welfare you will find your welfare," says Jeremiah (v. 7). Werner Sollors, professor of Afro-American studies at Harvard University, asks, "Is there something in the transnational character of the works [of non-English-language literature] that may make their authors bolder than those situated firmly in culture and language?"[2] Novelist Yoshiko Uchida takes these bold steps with Japanese language and the cultural formation of Japanese Americans by introducing their experiences and worldviews into American literature.[3] In her writings Uchida reveals a world that is culturally liminal and a hybrid of values—in a word, an exilic existence.

   This exilic perspective was formed in the convergence of quite distinctive streams of experience in the new horizons of Asian immigration between the stark exclusion they faced daily and the American culture's self-perception of generous hospitality.[4] For our purposes here, it is important to understand that the Japanese American church community nurtured the human and divine worth of Japanese immigrants, their new generations in America, and their cultural formation in the midst of profound prejudice and marginalization. We discover through Uchida that their Christian faith empowered them

---

   1. Commemorative Program for the Fortieth Annual Manzanar Pilgrimage, April 25, 2009, 3.
   2. Robert Scholes and Robert Kellogg, *The Nature of Narrative* (New York: Oxford University Press, 1966), 6.
   3. Grice, Helena. "Yoshiko Uchida" in *Dictionary of Literary Biography, Volume 312: Asian American Writers* (Columbia, SC: Bruccoli Clark Layman; Thomson Gale, 2005), 304-309.
   4. Uchida wrote on the experience of Japanese Americans in such works as *Journey to Topaz, A Jar of Dreams* (1981), *The Best Bad Thing* (1983), *The Happiest Ending* (1985), *Samurai of God Hill* (1972) and *Desert Exile: The Uprooting of a Japanese-American Family* (1987).

to engage a racialized society with re-humanizing communal investment even in the midst of the imposed hardship. The gift we receive has been to peer into the actual worldview of a people's own narration through the transformation of new life and a new future. Writing about Japanese American women losing the very means to communicate with one another amid the trauma endured by families and communities—silenced voices, Uchida "speaks silence."[5] In other words, she testifies or gives voice to the hollow cries, dust-dried tears, and suppressed rage claiming their own humanity before God and seeking transformation of a society that is not very interested or invested.

We learn that speaking from "the silenced" requires truth-telling testimonies of visions lost and sought still again for the transformation of life. The power of domination seeks to silence even memories and demands assimilation through forgetting.[6] Jeremiah speaks to the power of silencing. How will we voice the cries of humanity claiming their divine gifts of life; how will we proclaim transformation? Can we hear the silenced pray for the ears of those dominating to open?

Uchida's voice is not merely the matter of regaining silenced voices of Asian American women. She provides us a prophetic understanding of silenced voices and speaks silence simultaneously into powerful means of proclamation. Silence, a distinctive Asian exilic experience of life, is transformed into a post-exilic voice by speaking from our memories of exile, by resounding from the margins still, by exclaiming the divine gift of life, by proclaiming the transformation of the silenced and the silencers.

Psalm 108

Two psalms put together actually comprise Psalm 108. The first five verses come from Psalm 57 and the last eight verses from Psalm 60. Psalm 108 thanks God for the end of the exile. The first part of the psalm praises the extensiveness of God's *hesed*—God's steadfast covenantal love and mercy. Abraham Joshua Heschel, a Jewish theologian, talks about *hesed* as the "displacement of subjectivity." According to Heschel, the Hebrew Bible helps us to see life from a divine perspective and not from our own. Faith is as much a result of God's search for humanity as humanity's search for God.[7] *Hesed*, God's covenantal loving-kindness, is the texture of a faith community. "Many are the facilities that help us to acquire the important worldly virtues, skills

5 Yoshiko Uchida, *Picture Bride* (1987; repr., Seattle: University of Washington Press, 1997).
6. The theme of "silence" is also treated by Japanese Canadian writer Joy Kogawa in her book *Obasan*, published first by Lester & Orpen Dennys, 1981.
7. Abraham Joshua Heschel, *Man Is Not Alone; A Philosophy of Religion* (1951; repr., New York: Farrar, Straus & Giroux, 1976).

and techniques. But where should one learn about the insights of the spirit [God's loving-kindness]? . . . It is in the synagogue where we must try to acquire such inwardness, such sensitivity."[8] *Hesed* is an umbrella of the faith community to coordinate and improve the ways in which people relate with each other and to reach out to those who are in need. Leaders of faith communities are the conduits for God's loving-kindness to become embodied in those faith communities. Leaders help the faith community and its people to "learn about the insights of the spirit of God's loving-kindness" by displacing people's perspectives with that of God.

Asian American Christian leaders say that "Asian American churches are going through a 'crisis of leadership' because seminaries as a whole are not preparing a new generation of pastors to work in multi-generational and multicultural settings," the *Los Angeles Times* reported in 2007.[9] This article featured a study by Duke Divinity School (2005) that underscored significant difficulties with generational conflicts and cultural diversity within Asian American communities. Community leaders and pastors struggle with the same difficulties among themselves as well. So what might be an intriguing and growing strength in American society and among American churches—multi-generational and multicultural growth—remains overwhelming to community leaders in both the Asian American churches and the dominating American culture. And American mainline seminaries share in our failed efforts to bridge the gap.[10] We all are struggling to bridge the cultures, the diverse Asian ethnicities, and the generational multicultural formation of our young adults and youth.

With these challenges facing Asian American churches in mind, the questions become: How do ministerial leaders become the conduit for God's loving-kindness embodied in the faith community? How does God's *hesed* to God's people in Asian American churches address the clashes between the generations and cultural differences? If God's *hesed* is manifested in God's justice, then how can Asian American churches demonstrate an expression of God's justice without being forced to give up what might make them distinct? Can Asian American church leaders respond to these questions with a conviction about God's *hesed*, "For your steadfast love is higher than the heavens, and your faithfulness reaches to the clouds" (v. 4)?

8. Abraham Joshua Heschel, *The Insecurity of Freedom: Essays on Human Existence* (1959; repr., New York: Farrar, Straus & Giroux, 1963), 242.

9. K. Connie Kang, "Asian American Churches Face Leadership Gap," *Los Angeles Times*, March 3, 2007; http://articles.latimes.com/2007/mar/03/local/me-beliefs3 (accessed February 29, 2012).

10. Ibid.

Luke 9:49–50

In these verses the Gospel's ecumenical theology comes through clearly. The author pays particular attention to the poor, women, and other disfranchised groups of people. Luke is clearly interested in taking the gospel beyond the original Jewish community to those who do not share the Jewish heritage— that is, to Gentile communities. "Whoever is not against you is for you" (v. 50) is his way of talking about the inclusive character of Christian faith. The faith is grounded in and accountable to both the Jewish community from which it originates and to the wider communities.

One of the critical issues facing Asian American studies, particularly its religious and theological studies, is the role the Asian American communities play in shaping the character and features of Asian American studies as an academic discipline. As in the case of other racial and ethnic communities, Asian American studies emerged as a result of civil rights struggles that called attention to the issues and challenges facing Asian Americans in the racialized society of the United States. Initially, the growth of academic Asian American studies involved community leaders who served as programmatic and curricular advisors. As academic pressures mounted, institutions gradually shunned community involvement. This move made it difficult for cultural formation and interpretation in the intellectual development of the field of studies, especially since the primary objectives of the field were still in debate or formation. Eventually, the field of Asian American studies was cut off from its genesis in the actual community work that exposed the problems of representation in the academy and dominant culture.[11]

Over time, the academy came to acknowledge the "cultural capital" of Asian American studies that resulted from "the conversion of political capital" that emerged in the early period of Asian American communities' civil rights struggles.[12] The Association of Asian American Studies (Triple AS) argues that to sustain this convergence among its purposes is to support these programs to nurture a positive Asian American presence in and "influence upon" American institutions, society, culture, and political life.[13]

In this way, the cultural capital of Asian American studies emerged amid the landscape of political struggle in the academy. These studies, therefore, must remain accountable to the Asian American communities if they are to be credible. At the same time, Asian American studies must continue to demand academic legitimacy as defined by traditional scholarly standards. One of

11. Mark Chiang, *The Cultural Capital of Asian American Studies: Autonomy and Representation in the University* (New York: New York University Press, 2009).
12. Ibid.
13. The Association of Asian American Studies, "Statement," http://aaastudies.org/content/index.php/about-aaas/about-aaas (accessed February 29, 2012).

the critical challenges facing Asian American studies today is to explore a more coherent political and intellectual agenda amid inherently diverse Asian constituencies, ethnically, culturally, and religiously. As with the encounters between the Jewish and Gentile communities shaping the early Christian communities, the legitimacy of Asian American cultural studies within the long-established scholarly criteria of the academy could impede Asian American studies' accountability to its own communities. Asian American studies need to go beyond the foundational academic traditions into the very communities, the "Gentiles," in which its fruits thrive. Preaching from this Luke passage today could help expose these needs between our communities.

Acts 12:1–19

In these parable-like passages Luke skillfully juxtaposes the power of the state and the power of the church; "while Peter was kept in prison, the church prayed fervently to God for him" (v. 5). The narrative of Herod's opposition and demise can help Christians face political opposition with discerning confidence and let *Pax Romana* know that the state cannot stop the church in its mission. What is noteworthy in these passages is Luke's reminder that Jesus warned earlier about the state's power that would be used against his followers (Luke 12:11–12; 21:12–19). A significant question that arises here is this: Will the faithful stand for Jesus as the ultimate Sovereign even when realizing that it is very likely they will pay the price for doing so? Those who have lived in religious freedom for generations have much to learn from these early Christians who just barely emerged from the oppression of a state's power. Dietrich Bonhoeffer calls such a stance "a costly grace."[14]

In the history of the Asian American communities, the price of one's conviction has been costly. Faced with the demand of the U.S. government during World War II for Japanese Americans in internment camp to show their loyalty to the nation, some refused. They were called "No-No Boys." These persons refused to accept the demands of blind loyalty to a culture or nation that imprisoned them for nothing more than their ethnic heritage. They refused to answer questions on their allegiance because they distrusted or feared the integrity and intentions of the questions and the questioners.[15]

John Okada's novel *No-No Boy* (1957) "is an allegory for the postwar experience of Japanese Americans imprisoned in World War II in American concentration camps; [it is] Okada's expression of disillusion and quiet outrage at

---

14. Dietrich Bonhoeffer, *The Cost of Discipleship*, trans. R.H. Fuller (London: SCM Press, 1964), 36.

15. We Be US group, "No-No Boys," http://library.thinkquest.org/trio/TTQ04160/Complete%20Site/loyalty/nonoboy.htm (accessed February 29, 2012).

the forcible eviction and imprisonment of his community and its long-term effects."[16] Oddly enough, Okada and this book faced rejection among Japanese Americans because of his service to the United States during the war. Not until a generation later, after his eventual death, did his work gain the hearing it sought in behalf of the unjust treatment of his community.[17] Although the prayers of the people liberated Peter in the Acts passage today, like Okada we work to give voice to the yet-unanswered prayers of the silenced or the fearful. We preach into the hopes of liberation and a just reconciliation, whether we will live into its celebration or die longing for it!

16. Ti Locke, "In Search of *No-No Boy:* Clasroom Edition Introduction." http://www.resisters .com/nonoboy/teachers/classroom_guide.pdf (accessed February 29, 2012).

17. We Be Us group, "No-No Boy by John Okada," Japanese Internment, http://library.think quest.org/trio/TTQ04160/Complete%20Site/loyalty/Okada.htm (accessed February 29, 2012).

Sixth Sunday after the Epiphany

Charles L. Campbell

JEREMIAH 17:5–10
PSALM 1
1 CORINTHIANS 15:12–20
LUKE 6:17–26

Because Jesus has been raised from the dead, we not only live in hope for the future; we can also live now the new life to which we are called by Jeremiah, the psalmist, and Luke, and trust in the promised resurrection as Paul exhorts us to do.

Jeremiah 17:5–10

Drawing on the wisdom tradition, Jeremiah sets before the people two starkly different options: the way of curse or the way of blessing; the way of barrenness and death or the way of flourishing and life. Unlike the psalmist and Luke, Jeremiah begins with the curses, rather than the blessings. The contrast between the two life options thus builds to a promising image of bearing fruit, rather than concluding on a note of threat. Although verses 9–10 recognize the deviousness of the human heart, Jeremiah's move from the threat of curse to the promise of blessing can be helpful to preachers in shaping the movement of sermons from this text.

Jeremiah's curses and blessings cut to the most basic issue faced by the people of God: trust in the Lord or trust in "mere mortals," the strength of "mere flesh" (v. 5). These options should not be read in terms of merely individual choices, but rather should be set in the political arena of a people and a nation. The call is for the people of God to trust in the Lord for life, rather than in military, economic, and technological powers that promise life but lead instead to idolatry and death.[1] Psalm 146 issues a similar warning:

1. Walter Brueggemann, *A Commentary on Jeremiah: Exile and Homecoming* (Grand Rapids: Eerdmans, 1998), 159.

95

"Do not put your trust in princes, in mortals, in whom there is no help" (Ps. 146:3). The compelling challenge of Jeremiah is captured in an ironic way on U.S. currency. In a context in which Mammon is frequently worshiped, and in which greed has repeatedly led to bursting economic bubbles that have spread suffering and death throughout the land, the currency declares, "In God we trust."[2] The currency of the United States thus becomes an ironic reminder of the stark alternatives posed by Jeremiah.

Jeremiah develops these two alternatives—trust in the Lord, which brings blessing, or trust in human strength, which brings curse—through two powerful images. Those who trust in human strength are like shrubs in the desert, which "live in the parched places of the wilderness, in an uninhabited salt land" (v. 6). It is a bleak image of a barren and hopeless existence. John Calvin has noted that the image suggests vegetation that appears to have life, though the root system is gone. Whereas some saw life in trusting human power, Jeremiah discerned the underlying reality of death.[3] And he revealed this death in the image of the desert. Jeremiah here enacts the fundamental task of prophets, the task of discernment. As William Stringfellow has put it, "Discerning signs . . . has to do with the ability to interpret ordinary events in both apocalyptic and eschatological connotations, to see portents of death where others find progress or success but, simultaneously, to behold tokens of the reality of the Resurrection or hope where others are consigned to confusion or despair."[4]

Jeremiah's alternative image of hope is that of a "tree planted by water, sending out its roots by the stream." And the results highlighted by Jeremiah are striking: freedom from fear and anxiety (v. 8). Trust in military, economic, and technological power, Jeremiah suggests, actually leads to fear and anxiety. Today, his words continue to be borne out in political life. No amount of military or economic power seems to stem anxiety about the future. Politicians regularly play on fears in order to increase military spending, go to war, and push economic agendas. Indeed, since the 9/11 terror attacks, the United States, "the greatest military power on earth," has often been driven (and manipulated) by fear into reactionary responses, which have ironically only increased the cycle of violence and anxiety. And such an anxiety-driven, reactionary fear of the "other" (for example, the immigrant) is likewise inevitable when economic and social privilege become the object of trust and the source of identity. Living in fear and anxiety may be part of the curse that Jeremiah

---

2. See John Kenneth Galbraith, *A Short History of Financial Euphoria* (New York: Whittle Books, 1993).

3. Cited in Brueggemann, *Jeremiah*, 159.

4. William Stringfellow, *An Ethic for Christians and Other Aliens in a Strange Land* (1973; repr., Eugene, OR: Wipf & Stock, 2004), 138–39, 148–49.

pronounces on those who trust in human power. If so, there may be no more important issue that preachers and prophets need to address today than the culture of fear, which holds so many captive. Such anxiety is countered by the great promise of Jeremiah: a people who trust in the Lord no longer need to be driven by the fear that leads to military buildups, warfare, and economic competition—the fear that leads to spiritual, moral, and even physical death. Rather, trust in the Lord bears the fruit of *shalom* beside the life-giving waters.

Nevertheless, Jeremiah concludes, the heart is devious. In our captivity to the powers of death, we often justify the ways of death and discount the way of life; we call death life and life death. As Calvin put it, we settle for the "appearance of life," though the root system is gone. But, Jeremiah reminds us, there is no way to avoid the consequences of our deceptions and illusions. So, with discernment shaped by the vision of God, the preacher/prophet seeks ways to name the powers of death, dispel the illusions, and call the people back to trust in God and the fruits of faithfulness.

Psalm 1

The psalm continues this theme, not only highlighting the alternatives of blessing and judgment, life and death, but even using similar imagery as Jeremiah's. The righteous, again, are like trees planted by streams of water, while the wicked are like chaff that the wind drives away (vv. 3–4). Unlike Jeremiah, however, the psalm reverses the order, beginning with the word of blessing and concluding with a warning to the wicked. A sermon from the psalm would thus have a different movement from the one in Jeremiah.

More importantly, however, the psalm focuses the message around a particular practice. The psalm suggests that Jeremiah's fundamental emphasis on trust in the Lord must be embodied in the practice of delighting and meditating on the law of the Lord. "Law" here should not be understood as a set of rules and regulations, with the negative and burdensome connotations that often has for Christians. Rather, the law is much broader and more positive. It is something to "delight in" (v. 2). It encompasses not only the communal practices called for by God, such as those embodied in the Ten Commandments, but also the larger story that shapes the people of God, a story grounded in the mercy of the God who brought the people "out of the land of Egypt, out of the house of slavery" (Exod. 20:2). The psalmist thus calls for the communal practice of dwelling and delighting in this broadly understood "law," so that it shapes one's life and the life of the community. This practice, the psalmist suggests, nurtures trust in the Lord. In this practice, we not only learn the diverging paths of the blessed and the wicked, but we also receive the power to pursue the ways of life. This practice indeed becomes the stream of water that nourishes a people to live free from fear, in the trust of the Lord. While Jeremiah calls for fundamental trust in the Lord, the psalmist sets forth the central practice that nurtures that trust.

Luke 6:17–26

In this lection, Luke, like Jeremiah and the psalmist, takes up the alternatives of blessings and woes. However, in Luke's hands this wisdom material is transposed into another mode. Through his unsettling blessings and woes, Luke's Jesus stirs the imagination with a vision of the reign of God that is breaking into the world. There are no commands or expectations, but rather simply indicative statements that envision the startling new age that is overturning the old. The language is tensive, virtually at the breaking point. Jesus' words probably even sounded thoroughly paradoxical in their time. The language of "blessing" typically did not apply to the poor, the hungry, the weeping, or the persecuted. And "woes" would not have been associated with the privileges of being wealthy, well fed, happy, and praised. The rationalities and presuppositions of the old age are undone in this radical speech. Everything is thrown off balance. Imaginations are unsettled. New visions are made possible. Jesus creates a space in which people may begin to live into the new reality of God's reign.

In this sense, the words of Jesus flow directly from the actions that precede them. In verses 17–19, Jesus heals people of their diseases and cures those with unclean spirits—all signs of God's inbreaking reign. Jesus' sermon simply brings to speech the new reality that he is already enacting in his ministry. In Jesus, word and deed are one. Through both his life and his speech, Jesus challenges the powers of death in the world and brings the way of life.

The great dangers for preachers with this text are that we turn it into a set of demands or we water down the radical social implications. Jesus' words are not a set of rules, and they are not even a prediction of future judgment. Rather, they are an act of eschatological "prophetic imagination," inviting the church to grieve the old age that is dying and begin living in the new age that is being born.[5] The startling, paradoxical character of the Beatitudes should be enacted rather than explained. The purpose is not simply to bless or condemn individuals, but to expose and overturn the systems and structures that lead to death. The purpose is to expose the powers of death at work in the world and to envision an alternative reality. The words are meant to be redemptive, setting people free from captivity to the old age and creating the space for new and faithful living. They are shocking and startling. But when

---

5. See Walter Brueggemann, *The Prophetic Imagination* (Philadelphia: Fortress Press, 1978).

people live in captivity to the powers of death, we may need to be shocked into freedom and newness.

1 Corinthians 15:12–20

This lection breaks the pattern of the other three, and it may seem a bit out of place. However, Paul's words, like those of the other readings, focus on matters of life and death. Moreover, Jesus' resurrection is the ultimate eschatological reality, the ultimate act in which God's reign overcomes the powers of death and brings life in the midst of the old age. Indeed, there is nothing more threatening to the "powers that be" than resurrection. The powers depend on the threat of death to maintain order and control. They depend on the sanction of death to maintain their authority and privilege.[6] There is no more socially radical and threatening act than resurrection, for death is the ultimate source of the fear and anxiety of which Jeremiah speaks. Breaking the fear of death, resurrection sets us free to trust in the Lord rather than in human power. And resurrection confirms the words of Jesus in Luke—the new age has indeed begun, and resurrection sets us free for life in the reign that Jesus envisions. The threat of death keeps us silent. Trust in resurrection frees us for speech and action. Freed from the fear of death, people may challenge oppressive regimes; speak against racism, sexism, and heterosexism from the pulpit; challenge the growing economic inequalities in the United States; and resist reliance on the deathly way of war. Such are the radical social and political implications of resurrection, which is why it is so threatening to the principalities and powers of this world. Paul is right, at a social as well as a personal level: In the face of the powers that be, we are most to be pitied if there is no resurrection of the dead.

6. See Stringfellow, *Ethic for Christians*, 67–94.

Seventh Sunday after the Epiphany

Stephen G. Ray Jr.

GENESIS 45:3–11, 15
PSALM 37:1–11, 39–40
1 CORINTHIANS 15:35–38, 42–50
LUKE 6:27–38

The term "epiphany" describes an unexpected realization about the truth of a matter. As the Christian tradition has understood the idea, it relates to how in Jesus Christ we see fully the truth about God's love and inclinations toward creation and its future. The texts for the day deal with particular dimensions of both of these truths. In the first instance, they give witness to the conviction that God may bring good out of suffering no matter the intent of any who inflict the suffering and that God places a great power in the hands of those wronged—the power of reconciliation. As well, they point to the idea that in the final analysis God's *shalom* to creation, and the capacity of the oppressed to reflect it into creation, will overrule the workings of evil. God's *shalom* obviates the need for the wronged and oppressed to seek vindication on this side of the Jordan at the expense of becoming that against which they struggle.

Genesis 45:3–11, 15

The story of Joseph's betrayal by his brothers is a tale not only of how sibling jealousy is overcome by love but also of how God uses the least among equals to bring about salvation for all. In a nutshell, the events that lead to today's pericope are Joseph's sale into slavery by his brothers because of their jealousy of both their father's special favor toward him and his penchant to dream. As an aside, their words, "Behold, this dreamer cometh. Come now therefore, and let us slay him" (Gen. 37:19–20 KJV), have significant influence in the Christian lexicon in relating martyrdom to prophetic witness (the exemplary usage being the martyrdom of Martin Luther King Jr.). Through a series of unusual—and, as he comes to understand, divinely directed—events, Joseph

100

is elevated to oversee the Pharaoh's kingdom. In this position he saves not only Egypt but also his own family, who had immigrated to escape a famine that was sweeping across the land (Gen. 39:20–42:6). Our text depicts the moment when Joseph has revealed himself and extended forgiveness to his brothers. In expressing his reasons, Joseph makes clear that it is his belief that God unfolded his life in such a way that not only might they, his family, be saved, but many others also. While perhaps not the original intent, the writers of Scripture and the Christian tradition have appropriated this particular story to exemplify the ways that God unfolds God's *promise* through unusual and seemingly baffling turns of history.

We would do well to notice that God unfolds the continuing *promise* through the heir who is betrayed and cast into slavery by his siblings. Read typologically, this dimension of the story holds significant meaning for the unfolding history of the church. In spite of the brothers' dastardly actions, Joseph is still able to recognize them as his brothers and therefore able to respond with forgiveness and reconciliation; his brothers, however, *because* of their reprehensible deeds are unable to recognize him. Perhaps this is why God places the power of reconciliation into the hands of Joseph and not those of his brothers. These dimensions of the story may be instructive for a perennial problem in the history of the church, wherein one group of heirs to the promise behaves in despicable ways toward another and then experiences problems of reconciliation in facing its actions.

Psalm 37:1–11, 39–40

Where the reading from Genesis might be taken as a cautionary tale of how God overturns our assumptions about into whose hands the continuance of the *promise* and the power of reconciliation are placed, the psalm for today brings a word of hope for those who are experiencing evil while God may be bringing good out of it. More importantly, the psalm counsels a way of being in those moments. The psalmist does this by not only contemplating the allure of power in the face of suffering, but also by being clear that the cost of this seduction is corrosion to the heart. While the psalmist does not deny the seductiveness of power, particularly as a weapon against an oppressor, the writer does point to the final cost of its attainment. In the end, seeking to avenge these maladjusted relations will lead to the one who is wronged becoming precisely that evil enacted in the first place (v. 8). Perhaps the psalmist is saying in a different way what human history has made abundantly clear: namely, the only thing oppression, lethal or otherwise, teaches is how to oppress. Thus it is foolish to believe the objects of lethal oppression will do much more than reenact their own oppression on others, often in more lethal forms. This reality is made abundantly clear in our time by the genocides that unfolded in Bosnia-Herzegovina and Rwanda. In each of these cases the rationale for enacting violent evil was retribution for past wrongs. Thus the psalmist's admonition to readers and hearers to place their final trust in God and not in their power to enact retributive justice is deeply vigilant against becoming precisely the evil for which they seek amends.

Beyond the propensity of retribution to warp the hearts and souls of the oppressed, the clear reality is that those who engage in such a quest lose more often than not. The psalmist would be well aware of this reality as it had unfolded in the history of Israel. We should not, however, read the psalm as an injunction to quietism based in fear. Rather, the psalmist is suggesting that to the extent that the oppressed are able to maintain their sense of themselves, their dignity, and their own value in the eyes of God, the systems that oppress them will not finally succeed and these systems will bear within themselves the seeds of their own destruction. The admonition to trust in God is here an act of revolutionary resistance, because it envisions living and being in ways contrary to the rules of engagement that both engender unrighteousness and further its existence.

1 Corinthians 15:35–38, 42–50

In his ruminations on the spiritual bodies of those resurrected in Christ, Paul makes a significant point. His point is not made by the way that he talks about the resurrected body but, rather, that he talks about it at all. Clearly, his point is that the spiritual bodies of those resurrected in Christ will be every bit as real as the bodies who are hearing or reading this epistle. This point is not surprising to any reader of the text who has a commitment to reading it in its historical setting. My sense is that it is equally important in historical contexts differing from Paul's, such as ours. Maintaining Paul's central conviction, our spiritual bodies as they will be resurrected in Christ are every bit as real as the physical bodies in which we read or hear this epistle.

Two significant reasons undergird Paul's conviction. The first is related to his observation a bit earlier in this epistle that if the resurrection is not real then we, in his words, are to be pitied as fools (15:12–19); pitied not because we have placed our faith in a quaint tale, perhaps inspiring yet finally false, but pitied because we have become a people whose identity and conviction bear false witness against God (15:15). For people who ground their identity in something like faith there can be no greater tragedy than to bear false witness. Correlatively, if the resurrection and our conviction are false, then Paul's counsel in Scripture and the tradition are truly a fool's errand. This is particularly the case for those who bear the burden of oppression and deprivation rooted in unrighteous and evil systems. For, as noted earlier, the central counsel of the Christian faith, which is taken from its Jewish heritage, is to trust God. And to do so is to forgo the satisfaction that comes with retributive justice—the satisfaction that conforms to the logic of the world. Paul's reflections on the spiritual body, as it will be when resurrected in Christ, are not simply conjectures about a possible future for the faithful. Rather, this portion of the epistle may be read as an authorization to live in ways appropriate to the faith now because the future in Christ is assured. It is precisely this authorization that saves the Christian faith from being a ready tool of the unjust and powerful who would otherwise intimidate the weak with the threat that their power in this world is the only *real* power.

Luke 6:27–38

Read in light of the preceding passages, it becomes clear that Jesus is not suggesting simply an ethical system, but rather a way of being in the world which reflects the ways that God is in the world. His portrayal is not grounded in retributive justice or expected reciprocity. The words in which we find the summation of Jesus' direction, "Be merciful, just as your Father is merciful" (v. 36), hearken and draw us to the bedrock conviction of Scripture that humanity is created to reflect the image of God within creation. Put another way, we are to be as God wills to be in the world. More importantly, we are to be this way because it bears witness to the truth of God's inclinations and desires within the act of creation, in the face of the world's logic that knows only power and retribution.

What it means to reflect the *imago Dei* in creation has particular importance for those on the underside of history and their allies. In a world created by the logic of power and retribution, only those who hold power over others reflect the god of that world. The powerful are the only true moral agents in that world, and their enactment of lethal wrath within that world reflects only their own sacred values and righteous actions preserving dominance. One has but to notice that behind every enactment of enslavement, lethal oppression, and genocide is the conviction that the perpetrators are in some way enacting a morality conferred by their god's inclination and desire for the world. Those who are slaughtered and oppressed are reduced to a tableau on which the image of this god is drawn. It is my sense that there is no greater witness to the truth of the Living God's will and desire for creation than for the oppressed to claim their identity as bearers of the image of God—to be in the world in ways that expose lies in the logic of iniquitous power and retribution. On the Christian account of things, it is precisely the reality of resurrection and the guarantee of God's final vindication of the bearers of the image of God that empowers the oppressed, and their allies, to be in the world in ways that continually give witness to this epiphany.

Eighth Sunday after the Epiphany

Seungyoun Jeong

ISAIAH 55:10–13
PSALM 92:1–4, 12–15
1 CORINTHIANS 15:51–58
LUKE 6:39–49

The biblical passages affirm that it is the church's time to participate with confidence and faithfulness in God's redemptive and creative work. Indeed, the church's engagement in God's work is a way to manifest God's presence as a light of epiphany. However, the biblical passages not only command the church's faithful actions but also promise the final victory. Such an eschatological vision of victory and salvation through God's transformative power empowers not only preachers but also the church community. Moreover, the biblical passages indicate that today's divine epiphany in history will occur with the church's proclamation and enactment of justice as God's memorial. Thus this week preachers can describe God's final victory, persuade Christians to righteous actions in faith, and propel the church to become God's memorial and sign in society.

Isaiah 55:10–13

The text is the conclusion of Deutero-Isaiah (chapters 40–55), written by a prophet who was under the Babylonian captivity. In this pericope, the prophet prophesies God's future works: the coming deliverance and the exuberant procession to Zion following God's historical intervention with the collapse of the Babylonian Empire and the victorious career of Cyrus.

By using a parallel between the life-giving rain and God's effective word, the prophet proclaims that God's word will accomplish God's purpose to redeem all people from oppressive structures, traumatic suffering, poverty, and historical misfortune in terms of effectively fulfilling human needs (vv. 10–11). With the images of fertility and abundance, God's promises fill the prophet's confidence in the future triumph of God's righteousness and trustworthiness.

Moreover, the prophet announces an exuberant procession that will bring historical salvation (vv. 12–13). God will overcome historical calamity and bitterness with joy and peace. The prophet metaphorically describes God's visible transformation of all forms of devastation; for example, the transformation of the thorn and brier as a sign of calamity into the cypress and myrtle, which are memorial signs of God's peace and blessing.

Within homiletics, we recognize that God uses a contemporary preacher's revelatory words—in which we believe resides the life-transforming power of God—to further today's liberation and transformation. This text urges contemporary preachers to speak prophetically about restoration and freedom. Like the rain, a word spoken by a prophetic preacher will not return to the heavens until it brings forth life-giving power, giving bread to the poor, creating historical victory for the oppressed, and achieving international peace over the whole world. Indeed, the church's proclamation will not be merely an external sign but a powerful way to bring a miraculous new reality—God's actualized and consummated plan. Finally, as cypress and myrtle serve as a memorial of God's transformative work, so the church today needs a hopeful prophetic vision that liberates people from structural social sin and transforms events for solidarity with justice as God's everlasting sign. The world will absolutely witness a memorial for the Lord unless preachers fall silent, oppressed by the power of social sin.

Psalm 92:1–4, 12–15

Psalm 92, titled "A Song for the Sabbath Day," was sung in a Sabbath temple service during the Second Temple period. First, a psalmist invites the worship community to join in thanksgiving for God's faithfulness by confessing the experience of God's gracious intervention, work for justice, and love (vv. 1–4). The psalmist's testimony revitalizes the community to see anew God's ongoing work for justice in spite of the fact that the prosperity of the wicked and the adversity of the righteous make them distrust God's righteousness and compassion. Next, the psalmist exalts God for the rewards of the righteous (vv. 12–15). With the metaphor of a tree, the psalmist declares that God will bless those who act justly and live faithfully, relying on the impregnable rock of God's righteousness. The psalmist proclaims that the righteous will flourish like trees planted in the sanctuary. For instance, an aged righteous person is like a healthy tree that will still yield righteous fertility because the person's upright life and actions come from dwelling in the uprightness of God.

Psalm 92 reveals the significance of testimony in preaching and worship to God's righteousness and gracious intervention in human history. Giving witness to God's righteousness in our daily lives not only rekindles the faith community's disheartened spirituality but also revitalizes the church's just actions. This is because a lot of people are suppressed by the injustice of the wicked so that it is hard to see God's ongoing righteous deeds. The prophetic hopeful vision for preachers includes the church's communal praise of God's just deeds (vv. 1–4) and the repletion of justice throughout the world under the abundant pursuit of divine righteousness (vv. 12–15).

Luke 6:39–49

This passage consists of Jesus' three teaching metaphors within the Sermon on the Plain, which are intended primarily for his disciples. These three vignettes represent Luke's overall concern with the poor who are on the margins of society.[1] For that reason, we can interpret the expected actions of disciples as charity, love for others, care for the poor, justice for the marginalized, and liberation from oppressive social evil—representations of God's gracious character and Christians' actions serving God's justice.

The first proverbial teaching (vv. 39–42) with two illustrations, one of the blind teacher and the second of the problem of judging a small speck in a neighbor's eye, intends to warn about self-righteous hypocrisy. It implies that people are not disqualified from true discipleship by their flaws, but rather by their unwillingness to see their own weaknesses in the divine light. The first exhortation discloses that God does not request Christians' perfection or some measured excellence of just actions; rather, God wants Christians to examine themselves under a divine light. Even if Christians enact redemptive work for the sake of God's justice, we must do so with humility, since ethical living is not a self-righteous work. We cannot judge our adversaries easily. We preach and enact justice in love and humility.

The second teaching (vv. 43–45) reveals that the external conduct and speech of our daily lives expose whether our souls are faithful and what is in our hearts. Good treasure in the heart will yield loving conduct and speech. Jesus does not simply expose our superficial ethical actions. Instead, Jesus asserts that just action and speech emanate from faith and that there is an inescapable relation between the order of our external lives and our internal faith. Thus, in homiletics, preachers can proclaim that authentic ethical Christian living emerges from a true love toward the poor and from a sincere faith in God. Christians' actions for justice are genuine "good news" to the

---

1. A. R. C. Leaney, *A Commentary on the Gospel according to St. Luke* (London: Adam & Charles Black, 1966), 137.

world when our actions are coherent with our faith and hearts.[2] As A. R. C. Leaney says, "The very purpose of the Gospel of Luke as 'good news' depends on the coherence and integrity of the lives of those who bear its word and [action] of justice and liberation."[3]

In the third teaching (vv. 46–49), Jesus exhorts faithful listening to the message evidenced in obedience by contrasting two kinds of builders. Faithful disciples will put the words of a truthful message into practice, since true hearing inevitably will modify our actions and lives. Practicing God's message, especially concerning the poor and the marginalized in this expanded sermon, is as important as our emotional sincerity in worship, confessing "Lord, Lord!" Believing without action is the lamentable failure of Christian living, since our living is a part of a continuing liturgy. A Christian order for life includes abiding with and for the poor and the marginalized, and it distinguishes obedient Christians from spectators. Christians' just actions, constructed on a solid foundation of the message, will not be shaken or collapse in hard times (v. 48).

1 Corinthians 15:51–58

In 1 Corinthians 15, Paul asserts the resurrection of Jesus, the most fundamental conviction of the Christian faith. Relying on Jesus' resurrection, Paul insists that the dead and the living also will be transformed by God's matchless power and grace. This text is composed of two subunits: instantaneous transformation of both the dead and the living (vv. 51–57) and a call for action because of the prospect of resurrection (v. 58).

Paul declares an ecstatic mystery (v. 51): On the day of the Lord, God's long-promised victory over the powers of sin and death will be fulfilled and God will transform the dead and the living. In declaring the inevitable demise of death, Paul quotes two scriptural texts, Isaiah 25:7–8 and Hosea 13:14. In order to declare an exultant acclamation of eschatological victory over death, Paul asks the rhetorical question "Where, O death, is your victory?" (v. 55). Since the way of transformation in a new embodied resurrection is mysterious, Paul also uses mysterious images of putting a new and glorious cloth between a rhetorical antithesis of immortality and mortality to inspire awe. Paul reveals that God has already actualized the ultimate victory through Jesus, which has implications for Christian hope. Hence, Paul gives thanks for God's redemptive activity in a doxology (v. 57). Our future transformation will totally depend on divine power and grace, as Jesus' resurrection is an inevitable result of divine action.

2. Ibid.
3. Ibid.

Finally, in verse 58b, Paul confidently declares, "In the Lord your labor is not in vain," as the epilogue to the thematic argument of the first unit (vv. 51–57). Paul's imperative words, "Therefore, my beloved, be steadfast, immovable, always excelling in the work of the Lord" (v. 58a), encourage the Corinthians to value their actions within God's ongoing redemptive work. This is because Christians' eschatological hope for God's ultimate victory over the power of death and for our future resurrection under God's pre-ordained plan are the church's communal hope, which evokes more faithful actions as a new way of living.

In this manner, preachers can proclaim that the church's ongoing partici-pation in God's redemptive work and Christians' righteous communal actions are not in vain in the Lord. As Paul is concerned with the significance of Christians' bodily life, so contemporary preachers can proclaim the vitality of the church's historical, social, and political life by reminding Christians that we are living between God's already inaugurated events in Jesus and the longing for fulfillment of eschatological hope.[4] How wonderful truth is! The passage says that our current struggle to realize God's justice and Jesus' love toward all people is not in vain. In this text, God promises that we will take part in God's final victorious festival whether we are among the living or the dead. Now is the time to preach in order to help the contemporary church to be faithful in its actions, and to shout confidently with prophetic exclamation, "'Where, O death, is your victory?' Death, your victory has gone!"

---

4. According to Richard A. Horsley, Paul's formulation includes Christian social, political, and ethical life as an embodied resurrection and a new liberated people from the power of death, since the resurrection body cannot be dichotomized between body and soul. Richard A. Horsley, *1 Corinthians*, Abingdon New Testament Commentaries (Nashville: Abingdon Press, 1998), 217–18.

Ninth Sunday after the Epiphany

Sharon H. Ringe

1 Kings 8:22–23, 41–43
Psalm 96:1–9
Galatians 1:1–12
Luke 7:1–10

Epiphany begins with the visit of the Gentile sages (the magi) to do homage to Jesus. Lest we forget that this story does not belong exclusively to a small people living at the eastern end of the Mediterranean, the readings for this last Sunday of the Epiphany season remind us of both the joys and the responsibilities of that global reach. The readings foreshadow modern struggles between the excitement of living in a multicultural, global world and the abuses of colonialism and imperialism with a religious impetus. These texts invite us to consider the powerful ambivalence of our calling as followers of Jesus Christ.

1 Kings 8:22–23, 41–43

The first reading invites us to fill in the blanks to make a smooth statement. Its syntax is choppy and disjointed, to say the least, with the first section that interrupts a sentence and the long omission between verses 23 and 41. The assigned reading does, however, suggest clear parameters within which to recognize the identity and will of this God whom we worship and who claims our loyalty. At the outset we stand with Israel, hearing Solomon's hymn of praise for God's faithfulness and steadfast love (or "covenant righteousness") that unites God with Israel (vv. 22–23).

With the word "likewise," which begins verse 41, Solomon asks God to extend that same relationship to "foreigners" or outsiders. Their prayers, too, should be granted. God's motive sidesteps an appeal to God's nature and identity in favor of a public relations goal. By such action God's reputation for power and breadth of influence will be known by "all the peoples of the earth" (v. 43).

109

In our time, when global tensions and conflicts seem often to have religious roots, Solomon's prayer would be the equivalent of transposing the prayer "God bless America" into something like "God bless all the peoples of the earth." The prayer is not that God cease to bless us, but rather that God look on everyone with the same generous spirit. Just as the confidence of Solomon's prayer affirms, we can be sure that God is already about that task before we ask.

Psalm 96:1–9

What Solomon believed and trusted about God's inclusive care, the psalmist is celebrating, urging all the peoples of the earth to join in the song. The assigned reading encompasses the first two stanzas of a hymn. Those stanzas invite the whole earth to join in singing to God, praising God above all other gods for marvelous works that encompass creation and that extend to all the nations and peoples (vv. 1–6). The general language of praise becomes more focused and specific in the second stanza (vv. 7–9), as those addressed are told to ascribe glory and strength to the Lord, to bring an offering, and to enter God's presence filled with an awe that takes their breath away.

People committed to the work of justice are often accused of being dour and preoccupied with the seriousness of their ministry. This psalm is a vivid reminder that praising God is always part of the life of faith. "Yes, join God in doing justice, but don't forget to celebrate!" Such is the urging of this reading.

Although the reading stops with verse 10, the psalm could well be read in its entirety (vv. 11–13 as well). These verses add two crucial elements to ground the hymn of praise in the reality of life. Verse 10 reminds us that the God to whom we sing praises is also a God of judgment—equitable judgment, but judgment nonetheless. God's weighing of human actions cannot be dismissed as arbitrary or unfair, but rather it is so appropriate that it demands that we take it seriously. That theme of judgment is continued in verses 11–13, with the heavens, the earth, the fields, and the trees of the forests joining in the hymn of praise, precisely because of God's promise to judge the human inhabitants of the earth with justice and truth. These closing words of the psalm jar us out of our often anthropocentric (human-centered) perspective and remind us of God's commitment—and hence our vocation—to ecological justice as well.

Luke 7:1–10

The story of Jesus and the centurion at Capernaum shatters boundaries and assumptions at every turn. Just when we think we have the story tamed to accord with our own worldview, the story takes another turn and leaves us again scratching our heads.

The first jarring note comes if we read the story from the perspective of Galilee in Jesus' day. A centurion was the incarnation of Roman occupation of the Galileans' homeland. The centurion is not just a Gentile (a non-Jew), but specifically an agent of the Roman military. He also, not surprisingly, is a slave owner, which is an added offense to our modern sensibilities. Instead of coming to Jesus directly for help in healing his valuable human property, the centurion approaches Jesus through some Jewish elders—a "group character" the Gospel writer has prepared us to view with suspicion. They appeal to Jesus on the basis of the centurion's personal generosity in building a synagogue for the Jewish people, as though that monetary gift covered the less desirable dimensions of his life.

Jesus simply does what is requested, but then the plot takes another turn. The centurion, still used to having others do his bidding, sends friends to Jesus with a surprising self-assessment of his own unworthiness (vv. 6–7a) and an even more surprising assessment of Jesus' relatively greater authority (vv. 7b–8). Human subordinates respond with obedience to the centurion's commands, but he is confident that Jesus' word, even at a distance, will be enough to control—even banish—the illness of his servant. The importance of this observation by the centurion is underlined by the fact that it is presented in direct speech. The centurion, like the elders in their appeal to Jesus (vv. 4b–5) and Jesus himself in his conclusion (v. 9b), speaks for himself.

The story ends with word that the slave has indeed been restored to good health (v. 10), but Jesus' words expressing his amazement to the crowd (v. 9b) are even more striking. The centurion, this quintessential outsider, has demonstrated "faith" even greater than can be found among the people of Israel. This explosion of the categories by which we humans attempt to define the boundaries of God's love and saving presence, or others' worth and potential for collaboration in God's project of justice and peace (the *basileia* or kingdom of God), resonates from this story through our own walk of discipleship.

Galatians 1:1–12

Paul's angry letter to the Galatians serves as a warning about the risks of misunderstanding and crossed communication when cultures and traditions are met by the generosity and inclusiveness of God's love. The letter gives testimony to what can go wrong when "the grace of Christ" (v. 6) and the freedom that is our gift from Christ (5:1) encounter human sin. For Paul, we should remember, "sin" is a power that alienates us from God, from our neighbors, and from our deepest selves. It is not a collective term for human naughtiness, but rather a blunt expression that names our insistence that we can get by perfectly well on our own, without grace and without Christ.

Paul begins the letter to the Galatian churches with a detailed self-identification. He writes to them as one sent not by human authorities, but directly by God and Christ (v. 1). In other words, his credentials are the best they can be. He gives them the traditional greeting ("grace and peace") and offers a doxology to God (vv. 3–5). However, the section of thanksgiving for the faith and goodness of the addressees, which was an expected part of a letter in Hellenistic times (see, e.g., Rom. 1:8–15; 1 Cor. 1:4–9; Phil. 1:3–11), is missing. Instead, Paul launches immediately into the issues he wants to raise with them.

His charge against them is that, having heard the Gospel from Paul, they are deserting him and it in favor of a different message being passed off as another gospel. Paul is absolutely clear that proclamation contrary to what he has brought them is, by definition, false (vv. 6–9). His message, like his credentials, is not of human origin, but of divine origin (vv. 11–12).

We are not told at this point the substance of Paul's objection to the direction in which the Galatians are being lured. Later on, however, we learn that after Paul's departure from Galatia, other teachers had arrived with the message that while Paul's message of the grace of Jesus Christ received in faith was the crucial first step for Gentiles to participate in the blessings of Christ, those believers then had to take on observance of Torah to complete their life in faith. Paul's anger comes from his judgment that to require "gospel+anything" is to deny the Gospel.

The problem is not torah itself, for Paul does not forbid Jewish believers to continue to observe it as part of their identity. In fact, to forbid it would be another instance of "gospel+," where what is added is the requirement to give up the Torah. The problem with both a requirement to observe Torah and a prohibition of observing Torah is the claim that justification, which is our gift from God and a function purely of God's grace, is dependent on human achievement. Paul's challenge (and ours as well) is to find ways to communicate the utter simplicity and unfathomable depth of the Gospel in language that takes into account different cultures and contexts of meaning. At stake is pursuing justice in language and thought forms that respect the rich diversity of the human family. The same message—namely, that God's grace is freely given and is sufficient in itself for our salvation—requires different vocabulary and grammar, depending on our human contexts. In a similar way, how that gift translates into a commitment to doing justice is a matter of incarnation in our particularly diverse cultures and historical moments.

Transfiguration Sunday (Last Sunday after the Epiphany)

Ched Myers

EXODUS 34:29–35
PSALM 99
2 CORINTHIANS 3:12–4:2
LUKE 9:28–36 (37–43)

Luke's transfiguration account offers some interesting twists that will guide my reflection here. He reaches far back into Israel's sacred history to identify Jesus' journey to Jerusalem as an "exodus." And he anticipates the cross by framing the episode in a way that prefigures Gethsemane. Even more than Mark, Luke focuses on the failure of the disciples to understand and embrace Jesus' Way, a narrative strategy designed both to sober and to encourage us. The Hebrew Bible and Epistle readings all echo the mountaintop epiphany theme, particularly with their attention to the notion of "glory."

Exodus 34:29–35

Today's Hebrew Bible reading turns to the last of Moses' three great encounters on Mount Sinai in Exodus. Thrice in this vignette we are told that Moses' face was glowing as he came off the mountain (vv. 29, 30, and 35).[1] This emphasizes the transformative effect of having spoken with YHWH, as if the divine glory is contagious. But Exodus is also clear that the holy power of epiphany is dangerous, which is why people are instructed to keep their distance (Exod. 19:12, 21–23), remove their sandals (Exod. 3:5), and hide from YHWH's face (Exod. 33:20–23). These ancient taboos suggest that humans cannot physiologically or psychologically bear the ecstasy of pure encounter

---

1. The Hebrew root *krn*, which means "horn" (so translated in the Latin Vulgate), is also the basis of the verb "to shine"—which is why medieval artists often depicted Moses with horns. Only Matthew's account of the transfiguration alludes to this glow, asserting that Jesus' face "shone like the sun" (Matt. 17:2, cf. Matt. 5:15f); see my comments on Transfiguration Sunday, Year A.

113

with the source of life (we can appreciate this by thinking of our sensate limits around sound, light, or even food or sex). Moses' veil thus symbolizes a protective boundary between YHWH's untamable power and the people, a shroud he dons each time after he delivers the divine message. In Exodus, Israel can *hear* but not *see* YHWH, a conviction that is also expressed in the Ten Commandments' prohibition of images (Exod. 20:4–6).

The notion of divine "glory" sits uneasily with modern rationalism. But to traditional people, this aspect of God was real and could only be perceived somatically. The great mystics, too, have understood glory in sensate terms. We glimpse this in our own encounters with the "glories of nature": beholding the majesty of Niagara Falls or a huge sequoia or a spectacular sunset invigorates not just our souls, but also our bodies. Those who trek deep into the wilderness to commune with rushing streams, mountain peaks, or desert solitude often return with a "glow."[2]

Such sensate experiences of glory are crucial to the spirituality of social justice. We cannot hope to heal our weary world without deeply grasping its beauty and "holiness." We will never understand how *bad* things have become if we have no clue of how *good* the undomesticated, unadulterated creation truly is, mirroring its Creator. Glory fuels righteous indignation.

Psalm 99

Psalm 99 elaborates the theme of YHWH's greatness. The writer seems to search for adequate adjectives, and the refrain (vv. 3, 5, and 9) extolling God's holiness reminds us of Isaiah's temple epiphany (Isa. 6:3; see also Rev. 4:8). As in the other two enthronement liturgies used on Transfiguration Sunday (Ps. 2 in Year A and Ps. 50 in Year B), there is an emphasis here on YHWH as "lover of justice [and] equity" (v. 4).

There are powerful resonances here with the transfiguration story: YHWH speaks to Israel's priests "in the pillar of cloud" (v. 7), and is to be worshiped at the "holy mountain" (v. 9). But there is also a political edge to this psalm that helps us combat our Christian tendency to overspiritualize the "majesty" of God. When the true kingship of YHWH is realized, the "peoples tremble" (vv. 1–2). This psalm directly contests the political empires by which Israel was surrounded.[3] In Hebrew cosmology, YHWH's kingship was exclusive rather than archetypal. That is, it functioned not to *authorize* the rulers of the nations, but to *delegitimate* them (as classically articulated in the prophet Samuel's lament and warning in 1 Sam. 8).

2. See David Abram, *The Spell of the Sensuous* (1996; repr., New York: Vintage Books, 1997).
3. Norman Gottwald, *The Tribes of Yahweh* (Maryknoll, NY: Orbis Books, 1979), 510.

Constantinian Christendom long ago forgot this inconvenient biblical truth. But psalms of enthronement can help us reassert God's exclusive sovereignty, even amid the political terrain of our time. To proclaim, "The LORD is king!" (v. 1) is to relativize all currently reigning presidents and dictators, giving us the political freedom (and responsibility) to boldly pursue the work of social change.

2 Corinthians 3:12–4:2

The epistle backtracks from Year B's reading, picking up Paul's reflection on the metaphorical meaning of Moses' veil. The apostle introduces his approach to this theme in 2 Corinthians 3:3, citing the prophetic notion of a renewed covenant "written . . . on tablets of human hearts" (cf. Jer. 31:31–33; Ezek. 11:19; 36:26; Prov. 3:3). Paul then asserts that Moses' "glory" at Sinai later faded, and has been surpassed by the outpouring of the Spirit (2 Cor. 3:7–8; the Greek noun *doxa* is used no fewer than thirteen times in 2 Cor. 3–4). In a deft and ironic bit of midrash, Paul laments that the understanding of many who "read Moses" has become hardened—the "veil" now lays over their minds, and only through Christ is it lifted (3:14–15; cf. Exod. 34:34).

Christians have traditionally read Paul's argument here through the lens of the doctrine of theological supersessionism, using it to dismiss Judaism and any hermeneutic approach to the Hebrew Bible that is not christocentric. But the long bloody history of anti-Semitism in Christendom should compel us to use a different approach. In fact, Paul is involved in an internecine struggle with his *own* people, and his accusations of blindness are nothing that the Hebrew prophets did not level (e.g., Isa. 6:9–10; Ezek. 12:2; Deut. 29:4). Paul is *not* a Christian categorically delegitimizing Jews!

We should not forget that according to Acts 9:1–8, Paul himself dramatically experienced the transfiguring "light of Christ." The epiphany on the road to Damascus blinded him even as it enabled him to see the searing truth of his work as a leader of the Judean state's internal security apparatus, in which capacity he was notorious for beating, arresting, and jailing fellow Jews who were followers of Christ (see also Gal. 1:12–16). It is not hard to imagine that after his conversion, in his efforts to make lifelong restitution to his victims, Paul was passionate about exposing the "blindness" of those he had formerly worked with and for!

But the apostle is not contending in 2 Corinthians with synagogue leaders. Rather, he is struggling with Jewish Christian teachers who were insisting that Gentile disciples must also follow torah regulations. *They* are the ones who read Torah under a veil because they have not experienced the "freedom" of the Spirit (3:17) and instead "falsify God's word" (4:2). Paul's ultimate desire is that everyone be *transformed* radically into the image of Christ (3:18), which in Romans 12:2–3 he famously contrasts with *conformity* to the deadening and deadly culture of empire.

Luke 9:28–36 (37–43)

Luke's version of the transfiguration reveals that the sort of blindness addressed by Paul certainly pertains to followers of Jesus as well, preventing us from drawing lines too sharply. The Third Gospel sets up the transfiguration scene a little differently than the other two Synoptics: "Eight days after these sayings [Gk. *tous logous*] . . . [they] went up on the mountain to pray. And while he was praying . . ." (vv. 28–29a). The emphasis here is twofold: on Jesus' words concerning the way of the cross just narrated (Luke 9:23–27), and on prayer, a favorite theme of Luke's (e.g., Luke 3:21). The latter is underlined by the fact that Luke inserts into Mark's transfiguration account a note that Jesus' inner circle was "weighed down with sleep" (v. 32). The resonances with Gethsemane are striking and intentional: both episodes concern the struggle between the need to pray for strength in the face of the looming confrontation with the authorities, and the temptation to sleep—which is to say, to live in denial (cf. Luke 22:40–46). On the mountain, the three disciples manage to keep awake to see Christ's conversation with the two men; in the Garden, however, they do not.

Another addition intensifies this theme. Only Luke reports *what* Moses, Elijah, and Jesus discussed: "his departure, which he was to accomplish at Jerusalem" (v. 31). The Greek noun *tēn exodon* (exodus) clearly connects Jesus' fate with the great liberation of Israel from empire. Luke is actually reversing the logic of the old story: whereas Moses led the people away from Pharaoh's slavery system, Jesus is heading into the heart of darkness—the capital city of Roman-occupied Palestine—to speak truth to the powers and to face the consequences. How Jesus' way of the cross—the dreaded symbol of the empire's *defeat* of dissidents—represents *liberation* is, of course, the central challenge of Second Testament faith. It is no wonder, then, that Jesus is consulting with Moses and Elijah concerning this counterintuitive and politically unorthodox strategy—and that the sleepy and fearful disciples would rather build memorial edifices to secure a more conventional religion (v. 33)!

Luke's final change to the synoptic script comes after the voice from heaven has spoken: the disciples voluntarily "keep silent" concerning what they have seen (v. 36). This sets the stage for the epilogue to the transfiguration, which is the extended portion of today's Gospel. It takes place after they had "come down from the mountain" and been met by a "great crowd" (v. 37). The Torah-literate would immediately think of what Moses saw upon his descent from Sinai (see Exod. 32). What ensues is not Israelites dancing around a golden calf, but something perhaps analogous: the disciples' deepening impotence and bafflement.

A man begs Jesus (just named as God's Son, the Chosen) to "look at my son, . . . my only child" (v. 38). Luke several times emphasizes the plight of "only children" of poor (and often single) parents, such as the widow of Nain (7:12) and Jairus's daughter (8:42). He understands the socioeconomic vulnerability of such hard-pressed families, for whom the loss of the last child would mean disaster. The troubling factor here, however, is the revelation that the man "begged [Jesus'] disciples to cast [the demon] out, but they could not" (v. 40).

It is almost as if the silenced disciples are in the same boat as this tortured boy: paralyzed and dumbfounded by the prospect of the cross. This is certainly hinted at by Jesus' weary response (v. 41). His lament regarding this "faithless and perverse generation" (alluding to Deut. 32:5, 20) is surely aimed at the disciples. After all, they have *just been commissioned and empowered* to have "authority over all demons and to cure diseases" at the beginning of this chapter (Luke 9:1)![4] Witnessing the violence of this demon, Jesus restores the boy to his father, which evokes astonishment (v. 43). Jesus will not, however, have as much luck with his own followers, as the following verses suggest (vv. 44–45).

Today's readings challenge the preacher to take on the thankless task of addressing *our* avoidances of and resistances to Jesus' way of servanthood, solidarity, and nonviolence. We are surrounded without and spiritually formed within by a culture of upwardly mobile aspirations, willful neglect of the poor, and social and political violence of all kinds. Yet most middle-class Christians in North America have made a strategic détente with this world; we are simply too content to follow Jesus into conflict with business-as-usual. This makes our churches some of the most difficult places to proclaim the cross—*if* it is desentimentalized and deprivatized, and restored as a metaphor of engaging the powers.

In a culture of self-preservation that primarily sees the "greatness of God" (v. 43) in terms of our own thriving, we fear losing our lives in discipleship because we imagine we are fulfilled and safe under empire. But Luke understands that peaceful coexistence with a world of domination and privilege is an exercise in self-destruction, from which Christ seeks to save us. To confront our personal and public pathologies is as difficult and daunting as Jesus' word of the cross. But that is what discipleship demands of Christians living under empire.

---

4. Luke juxtaposes the commissioning of the disciples much closer to this failure story than either Matthew or Mark. For a detailed, archetypal exploration of Mark's more elaborate version of the boy's possession and its relationship to the disciples, see Ched Myers, *Binding the Strong Man: A Political Reading of Mark's Story of Jesus* (Maryknoll, NY: Orbis Books, 2008), 253–56; and Ched Myers, *Who Will Roll Away the Stone? Discipleship Queries for First World Christians* (Maryknoll, NY: Orbis Books, 1994), chap. 4.

Ash Wednesday

Peter J. Paris

ISAIAH 58:1–12
PSALM 51:1–17
2 CORINTHIANS 5:20B–6:10
MATTHEW 6:1–6, 16–21

From the earliest days of the Christian church, Ash Wednesday has been observed as a time of spiritual preparation for Easter Sunday, which is the most sacred day in the church's calendar, when our Lord Jesus Christ was resurrected from the grave. During that forty-day period (not counting Sundays) churches admonish Christians to repent of their sins and shortcomings through prayer, meditation, fasting, and other acts of spiritual renewal.

Since the biblical writers discerned an integral relationship between the moral life and divine obedience, they viewed immorality as alienation from God's protective care, a circumstance that accounted for the prevalence of suffering and adversity. The worst such time for the people of Israel was the fall of the ancient kingdom of Judah in 586 BCE that was followed by four decades of enslavement in Babylon. During that sorrowful time, Israel witnessed the rise of prophets whose teachings helped renew the nation's moral and spiritual life. Thus, the text from Isaiah 58 is an excellent starting point with which to begin this period of spiritual renewal because it clearly discusses how acts of justice toward the most vulnerable are prerequisites for true worship. Similarly, Psalm 51 constitutes an ancient prayer of confession for one's personal sin against God, whose loving mercy is the source of hope and renewal.

At a later time in biblical history, following the birth, death, and resurrection of Jesus Christ, Paul was called to proclaim the message of redemption to the world at large and his newly founded church in particular. Thus, in 2 Corinthians 5, he proclaims the message of salvation by admonishing its members to be reconciled to God through acts of repentance.

Finally, in Matthew 6, the Gospel teaches that genuine goodness lies not in outward acts alone (e.g., almsgiving, prayer, and fasting) but in the internal motivation for the acts. That is to say, true goodness constitutes the unity of moral actions and spiritual devotion as offerings to God.

Isaiah 58:1–12

In this text the prophet addresses the people who have been in exile for a long while without the necessary resources for a good life. He insists that they learn a primary lesson about the relation of religious devotion and the moral life. First of all, they must publicly acknowledge their wrongdoing in pleading for God's mercy while depriving the weakest members in their community of the necessities of life: food, clothing, and shelter. Most important, the prophet admonishes them to bring their religious devotion into alignment with the demands of social justice toward all of God's people, and especially the least of them.

Reading this text in the aftermath of the 2010 earthquake in Haiti raises many questions about God's justice as well as that of humans. Why should these impoverished people undergo additional suffering? Did God cause the event as a sign of divine wrath, as some heartless people have suggested, or did humans themselves play a major role in its cause? Clearly, even though humans do not know how to predict or prevent earthquakes, they do know where they are likely to occur and how to build defensively to minimize their effect on life and property. The 1989 San Francisco and the 2010 Haiti earthquakes both measured approximately 7.0 on the Richter scale.[1] Yet the former suffered minimal loss of life and property in comparison to Haiti. The difference is due to the defensive construction of buildings, roads, bridges, and so forth. Beyond a doubt, Haiti's impoverishment has been caused by the unjust practices of many corrupt governments in collusion with business enterprises and social agencies, both on the island and beyond. Thus prophetic ministry in Haiti requires Christians to communicate these truths to those who were victimized by the injustices and to do what is necessary to prevent the perpetrators from harming others in the future. Most important, Christians must demonstrate and seek to preserve in their personal and col-

---

1. See U.S. Geological Survey, "October 17, 1989 Loma Prieta Earthquake," http://earthquake.usgs.gov/regional/nca/1989/ (accessed October 20, 2011); Virtual Museum of the City of San Francisco, "San Francisco Earthquake History 1915–1989," http://www.sfmuseum.net/alm/quakes3.html#1989 (accessed October 20, 2011); U.S. Geological Survey, "Magnitude 7.0—Haiti Region," http://earthquake.usgs.gov/earthquakes/recenteqsww/Quakes/us2010rja6.php (accessed October 20, 2011).

lective lives the virtues of justice, mercy, love, and humility to all, and especially to the most vulnerable.

Psalm 51:1–17

This text demonstrates as clearly as any that God's work as creator was not a one-time event. Rather, the penitent voice in this psalm calls for God's power to be manifested in acts of forgiveness and re-creation. These two acts most importantly pertain to a covenantal relationship between the confessor and the God whom he/she trusts. Further, this confession can issue from the mouth of a person or the collective worship of a community. In either case, the aim of the prayer is to manifest a "clean heart" and a "right spirit" in return for a commitment to teach transgressors God's ways so that they might return to a life of faithful obedience. Further still, the psalmist declares God's disinterest in material sacrifices. Rather, "the sacrifice acceptable to God is a broken spirit; a broken and contrite heart" (v. 17). These are the things that unite the religion of Judaism with that of Jesus.

When poor people read this text, they are moved by its emphasis on the inner spirit of the confessor. Even if the one seeking forgiveness should be a king, his words should manifest a humble spirit that is not only genuinely disturbed about his sin against God, but that diligently resolves to live a new life by "teach[ing] transgressors your ways, and sinners will return to you" (v. 13). This prayer of penitence presupposes that the petition can only be granted by the creative power of God, whose divine spirit bonds favorably only with those who remain faithful to the covenantal relationship that God has established with them.

Since God's faithfulness is both abundant and enduring, the truly penitent voice in the psalm clearly knows what God expects—"a broken and contrite heart" (v. 17b). Thus, the confessor promises to sing God's praises in return for deliverance from sin. It has always seemed to me that despite all the many temptations and deprivations around them, the poor and most vulnerable are more apt to demonstrate time and again a profound awareness of their sin and their need for deliverance from its self-destructive consequences. It may be that these are the ones whom God favors.

2 Corinthians 5:20b–6:10

Paul's Second Letter to the Corinthians is one of the most personal letters he ever wrote. It not only displays his own vulnerability, which was certainly not an easy thing for a teacher to do in his day, but most important, it demonstrates a deep and abiding love for the congregation as a whole. Despite the good pastoral advice he offers the congregation, he does not hesitate to condemn the motives and mission of his opponents. Since he, himself, was once a persecutor of Christians, he probably viewed his adversaries in a similar light. Wholly convinced that his message about Christ is clear truth, and knowledgeable of the moral decay in the city of Corinth, Paul confidently advises the church to reconcile itself with God so that it may be transformed to serve rather than obstruct God's calling to be the ambassador of Christ in the city.

Because of their great suffering throughout two and a half centuries of slavery followed by another century of exclusion from civic participation, African Americans have striven to reconcile themselves to the God whom they have trusted throughout their painful history. Because of their relationship with God, they soon discerned that such faith implied reconciliation with all human beings and especially with their enemies. Thus, most of them have striven to reconcile themselves with their oppressors in their desire to help build a common world of justice and civility toward one another. As Paul viewed his suffering in the shadow of Christ's suffering for the redemption of the world, African Americans have also viewed their suffering under a similar light. Hence, the teaching of Martin Luther King Jr. about nonviolent resistance implied the willingness on his part and that of his followers to suffer and even die in their struggle for racial justice. After the mid-1960s this viewpoint was caricatured and rejected by the advocates of black power who, greatly influenced by the teaching of Malcolm X, promoted an aggressive alternative by advocating self-defense by any means necessary. This marked a major divide in black America that continues to exist, though not with the same intensity it once had. Ironically, following the assassination of King, the founding of black studies programs in colleges, universities, and seminaries effected a practical synthesis of these two perspectives in the academic curricula, at least. That divide continues to find unresolved theological expression in the black theologies of James H. Cone, J. Deotis Roberts, and their respective followers.

Matthew 6:1–6, 16–21

One of the major purposes of Matthew's Gospel is to present Jesus as one bent on reforming the notion of discipleship. Previously much emphasis had been placed on the faithfulness reflected in adhering to various religious practices, such as almsgiving, prayer, and fasting, in a regular and precise manner. Instead of such outward expressions of piety, which Jesus condemns as false and hypocritical, he tells his disciples to undertake these practices in private, because God bestows much higher value on the faith in their hearts than on any showcased expression of faith. Most important, Jesus teaches them that the aim of religious practices is to develop a relationship with God. That can be done much more effectively in private than in public. Thus Matthew sets forth a new form of righteousness which exceeds that of the religious leaders of his day. This marks a radically new form of discipleship, which Matthew's Jesus proclaims.

During the days of slavery and subsequent periods of racial oppression, African Americans have recognized the marks of religious hypocrisy. In fact, the hypocrisy of their slave owners' Christianity was the main reason they could not respect either the master or his religion. Thus they sought their own space to worship, to avoid the pollution of such stark hypocrisy. As a result, African Americans viewed their appropriation of the Christian faith as a moral and spiritual alternative to that of their slave owners and oppressors. Jesus' teaching about almsgiving, prayer, and fasting formed the seedbed of African American critique of the slave-owning Christianity that constituted a manipulation of authentic Christianity for selfish gain.

Ironically, the creative imagination of enslaved Africans transformed the slave owners' Christianity in the "hush harbors" on the plantations where they met secretly at night to worship the God who advised followers to pray, fast, and give alms secretly rather than in public. Their constructive utilization of that admonition to undertake secret practices of faith and obedience inspired them to organize their own clandestine meetings, where they discovered the biblical truths pertaining to God's condemnation of oppression and bondage in favor of freedom and deliverance. Their faithful development of this theological orientation provided the foundation for the birth of the historic black church tradition and its unique practices of preaching, testimonies, prayers, and music.

First Sunday in Lent

Nicole L. Johnson

DEUTERONOMY 26:1–11
PSALM 91:1–2, 9–16
ROMANS 10:8B–13
LUKE 4:1–13

On this first Sunday in the Lenten season, these texts call on the faith community to remember its own experience of injustice and oppression as the foundation for its ongoing commitment to seek justice for others. As a reminder that God is with the community in that struggle for justice, the psalmist writes of God's character and promise to rescue and protect those who find themselves in trouble. We also learn that our salvation is bound up in our efforts to do the work of justice and service, and the Gospel lesson reminds us that the way of the cross is not paved with wealth, power, and ease, but with justice, mercy, and kindness.

Deuteronomy 26:1–11

In the Hebrew Scripture reading for this First Sunday in Lent, the passage from Deuteronomy consists of a set of instructions for celebrating the blessings God has granted to the Israelite community. As the foundation for this celebration, the community is asked to remember its previous life of slavery and oppression, "when the Egyptians treated us harshly and afflicted us, by imposing hard labor on us" (v. 6). Such remembrance is precisely the tool for creating an attitude of perpetual thanksgiving. Gratitude prevents the complacency that would allow the community to take credit for its freedom and to say, "Look what we accomplished for ourselves!" The community's very identity is wrapped up in remembering enslavement and liberation. Remembering where we have been and where we might continue to be without God's mercy and justice is an important lesson for the contemporary Christian community.

In their gratitude, the Israelites are to take the firstfruits of their harvest and present them to God (vv. 2 and 10). If we read just a bit further in Deuteronomy, we find that this tithe is the "sacred portion" that goes to provide for the needs of the "resident aliens, the orphans, and the widows" in the land (Deut. 26:13). In asking for these firstfruits, God calls the Israelites—and by extension, contemporary Christians—to ultimate trust. God does not ask us for our leftovers after we have taken care of our own needs or purchased fancy cars, homes, and clothes or have otherwise lived well beyond our needs; God asks us for a sort of "pretax" tithe that directly provides for the needs of those who have little or nothing. In the privilege of serving the poor, we serve God. This calls for a reassessment of how individuals and churches use their financial resources and, indeed, all resources. As Jim Wallis has argued, "Budgets are moral documents. They clearly reveal the priorities of a family, a church, an organization, a city, or a nation. A budget shows what we most care about and how that compares to other things we care about."[1] When church people fight over what color the new carpeting in the sanctuary should be while a local family gets evicted or goes hungry, we have a moral crisis on our hands.

Another social justice issue emerges from this passage that is significant for the twenty-first-century church, particularly in the United States but certainly in other first-world nations as well: the issue of immigration and how the church is called to respond. There is simply no room for exclusion by the church. In calling the Israelite community to remembrance and celebration, God says to the people who have been given this "land flowing with milk and honey" (v. 9): "Then you, together with the Levites and the aliens who reside among you, shall celebrate with all the bounty that the LORD your God has given to you and to your house" (v. 11). As the Exodus story recalled in this passage reveals, God sides with the oppressed, the poor, and the enslaved. In liberating one group and providing freedom and material comfort, God calls that group of people then to embody that liberation for others. The "Levites and the aliens" (v. 11) (and the "orphans and the widows" we read of a few verses later) are included fully: not only are we called to meet their needs, but, moreover, we celebrate God's loving and faithful provision with them. So they are not simply objects of charity; they are integral to the community itself. Therein we recognize that all is God's, not ours, and thus we are called to give from what we have been given.

This passage raises many challenges and implications for social justice for the contemporary church. What is our role in caring for those who have little or nothing? How do we tithe, and how do our financial priorities demonstrate

---

1. Jim Wallis, *God's Politics: Why the Right Gets It Wrong and the Left Doesn't Get It* (New York: HarperCollins, 2005), 241.

our deepest cares and concerns? How might we reassess our family budgets and church budgets in the service of God through service to those in need? How do we welcome and love the immigrant, the orphan, and the widow in our midst? How do we include others so that they are not simply objects of our charitable feelings and duties? How does remembrance of our own suffering and liberation lead us to have compassion for others and to work toward justice for all?

Psalm 91:1–2, 9–16

In these verses from Psalm 91, we find a wonderful picture of God's character. The psalmist uses striking words to describe God, such as "shelter," "shadow," "refuge," "fortress," and "dwelling place" (vv. 1–2, 9). Most of these words conjure images of a *place*. We think of God as many things—creator, parent, and even provider—but here the psalmist gives us an interesting metaphor of God as protective space. The psalmist further emphasizes this concept of God's protection: "I will deliver" and "I will protect"; God also promises, "I will answer them; I will be with them in trouble, I will rescue them and honor them" (vv. 14–15). What wonderful language to describe this dimension of our relationship with the Divine!

The last verse of this lection is particularly significant for the preaching of social justice: "With long life I will satisfy them, and *show them my salvation*" (v. 16; emphasis added). God does not say here, "I will save them later" or "I will grant them eternal life when they die"; there is no indication that salvation is simply a future promise concerned only with eternal life. There is a presentness, a realized eschatological dimension to the idea of God *showing* salvation to those who trust so much that they have made God their "refuge" and "dwelling place" (v. 9).

Therein, the verse raises another question: "What is salvation?" Certainly we do not want to argue for a works-based salvation; as we shall see shortly in the passage from Romans for this First Sunday in Lent, we are indeed justified by faith. However, a problem lies in the fact that in too many evangelical and liberal circles—indeed, in too much of Western Christianity that esteems the individual over the community—salvation is concerned primarily with the "I." If *I* am saved then *I* will go to heaven and *I* will live for eternity with God. However, as the social gospel preacher Walter Rauschenbusch wrote in 1917, eternal life in the future is only one piece of what salvation is about; it is also about the here and now. In his great work *A Theology for the Social Gospel*, Rauschenbusch wrote, "If sin is selfishness, salvation must be a change which turns a man from self to God and humanity"; for Rauschenbusch, authentic salvation involves an "attitude of love" for others and joining "in a divine organism of mutual service" over and above seeking one's own needs and pleasures.[2]

The biblical demand for social justice means that there is a communal dimension to salvation, and that those who live in God as the community of Christ must work to serve God's salvation to others. Our own salvation is bound up in the work of social justice as we struggle to address and correct injustices that we find in the here and now—indeed, as we participate with God in God's work to "rescue" and "protect" those who suffer and who are vulnerable.

Romans 10:8b–13

In his early years as a monk, Martin Luther constantly struggled to feel worthy of his salvation. His belief in a judging God who was primarily to be feared led him to the brink of spiritual and physical breakdown. In Paul's letter to the church in Rome, Luther found his salvation—quite literally! His doctrine of justification by faith is strongly rooted in Romans, and today's lection is one such passage that emphasizes salvation by faith alone.

Of course, centuries of misinterpretation of the doctrine of justification by faith have led to a situation in which pockets of Christians, from time to time, have touted (and lived according to) the idea that salvation is *solely* a profession of faith that need not necessarily result in a changed heart or life. While works of justice and charity are not the prerequisites of salvation, they are the fruits of its authenticity, or, as one pastor puts it, "We do not have to be righteous in order to believe; we believe, in order to be made righteous."[3]

Lest we fall prey to nationalisms, racisms, or other forms of distinction inappropriate for the community called "church," contemporary Christians must heed Paul's injunction not to distinguish between "Jew" and "Greek." We could substitute our own current word pairs to bring Paul's point home to our own contexts: "For there is no distinction between [black and white, male and female, gay and straight, American and immigrant, rich and poor, old and young]; the same Lord is Lord of all and is generous to all who call on him. For, 'Everyone [indeed, EVERYONE!] who calls on the name of the Lord shall be saved'" (vv. 12–13).

Luke 4:1–13

In the narrative of Jesus' temptations in the desert, we meet a hungry Jesus. According to Luke, Jesus had eaten "nothing at all" during his forty days in

---

2. Walter Rauschenbusch, *A Theology for the Social Gospel* (Louisville, KY: Westminster John Knox Press, 1997), 97–98.
3. Karen Pidock-Lester, "Romans 10:5–15," *Interpretation* 50 (1996): 288–92.

the desert. At Jesus' most vulnerable state and, we would imagine, in the midst of great suffering, the devil shows up to offer Jesus food, power, and wealth. In moderation and in the right forms, these things may be blessings from God; but in excess and in the wrong forms, they are a curse.

There are myriad preachable lessons in this passage, yet one clear implication for social justice stands out clearly: the cross is not about excesses of fame, fortune, or power. Too much of Christianity says that if we find ourselves with wealth and power, then this is a sign that we have found favor from God. But when this wealth and power have been achieved on the backs of hurting people, then it is not of God. We are not called to amass money and power—and if Scripture is clear about anything, it is clear about this!

In Luke's rendition of Jesus' temptation in the desert, we learn of all that the cross is *not*. The cross is not the prosperity gospel, and those who preach this distortion of the gospel are tremendously misguided. In the words of Gandhi, who enthusiastically respected the teachings of Jesus Christ but who saw much perversion in the way many so-called Christians live, we are called to "live simply so that others may simply live." If we truly follow Jesus' teachings, then we too must forgo all that the cross *is not* (wealth, power, and the easy path) and must work toward what the cross *is* (justice, mercy, and kindness).

Second Sunday in Lent

Alejandro F. Botta

GENESIS 15:1–12, 17–18
PSALM 27
PHILIPPIANS 3:17–4:1
LUKE 13:31–35

The topic that brings together this week's texts is God's call to remain faithful amid doubt, fear, and temptation. "Do not be afraid, Abram, I am your shield; your reward shall be very great," says God to Abram (Gen. 15:1). "The LORD is my light and my salvation; whom shall I fear? The LORD is the stronghold of my life; of whom shall I be afraid?" proclaims the psalmist (Ps. 27:1). Luke has Jesus quoting Psalm 118, a psalm of assurance and trust in God in the face of enemies. Finally, Philippians 3:17–4:1 exhorts the believers to "stand firm" (4:1) and proclaims the destruction of the "enemies of the cross" (3:18–19) and the salvation of the believers (3:20). The challenges that God's people faced were different in each case: doubts, persecution, death threats, and the temptation of a voluptuary lifestyle.

Genesis 15:1–12, 17–18

This chapter breaks with the previous narrative and has an independent redactional history. Scholars traditionally attribute Genesis 15 to the Yahwist's tradition with a later Elohist expansion (vv. 13–16). The lectionary text focuses on the verses belonging to the Yahwist tradition, that is, the theological tradition within the Hebrew Bible that uses the divine name YHWH to refer to God.

In Genesis 12 we saw Abram leaving his country and family, looking forward to God's promise of becoming a great people and possessing a country; but Genesis 15 finds Abram still without any of those. His fear is understandable. Was God a deceiver? Abram challenges God, "What will you give me, for I continue childless?" (v. 2). When God reiterates the promise of a large

128

progeny and repeats the promise of land (v. 7), Abram is still doubtful and replies, "O Lord GOD, how am I to know that I shall possess it?" (v. 8). *Trust but verify* is always a good policy. God reassures Abram with a solemn covenant, but there is a slight change in the promise. Perhaps God realizes that God will not be able to give the land to Abram and now promises it to Abram's descendants (v. 18). The truth is that God never fulfilled the original promise of the land to Abram, and the only piece of land Abraham owned when he died was Sarah's burial place (the cave of Machpelah, Gen. 23:3–20), where he also was buried (Gen. 25:9–10). The redactors of the Pentateuch noted this problem and added verse 7 in Genesis 12 to harmonize God's promise with what develops later in the story.

In negotiating with God, Abram, although somewhat fearful, remains faithful. He fulfilled his part; he left his family and his country and followed God's call. In this story, it is not Abram who needs to be "justified," but God! Already having left his family and country, Abram is not in a good position to negotiate. He has already done what he was asked to do; now he needs to try to get God to fulfill God's part of the deal. A God that he has just begun to know! Abram's fears are understandable. He has left everything, but to move forward he needs to leave those fears behind. In the same way that Abram's dreams were not wholly fulfilled in his lifetime, our quest for a just society will not likely be entirely fulfilled in ours. Surely Abram thought that he would have many children and own thousands of acres in God's promised land when he left Ur/Haran. But even when he realized that the fulfillment of God's promise would be delayed, he remained faithful. As Martin Luther King Jr. wrote, "Our capacity to deal creatively with shattered dreams is ultimately determined by our faith in God."[1] And after hundreds of years a people came out of Abraham's seed, the Jewish people; and a Jewish nation, Israel, was established in God's promised land. Most of those who have struggled for a just society have not seen their goals fulfilled in their lifetime, but their faithfulness made those goals a reality for later generations.

Psalm 27

In Jewish tradition, this psalm is recited during the Days of Repentance, the first ten days of the Hebrew month of Tishrei, from Rosh HaShanah (the New Year) to Yom Kippur (the Day of Atonement). Although the topic of repentance is absent from this psalm, Jewish traditional interpretation states, "It combats sin by teaching how to prevent it as its source. David declares that the mind which is fully engrossed in single-minded dedication to God's

---

1. Martin Luther King Jr., *Strength to Love* (Minneapolis: Fortress Press, 1965), 95.

service, has no room for sin."[2] Contemporary scholars, however, perceive that the psalm has a different focus and debate its genre and main intention. Is it a declaration of confidence, a complaint of the individual, or a lament of one persecuted?

The first part (vv. 1–6) begins with an exultant declaration of confidence and trust in God, and with certainty that he will overcome seemingly unsurpassable situations. Evildoers, opponents, adversaries, and even an army camping against the speaker are not enough ultimately to challenge the speaker's trust in God. But the fear surrounding this statement is evident in that the psalmist turns to hiding in God's tabernacle and temple for protection. The last sentence of verse 6 states, "I will sing and make melody to the LORD," only to move to an almost desperate cry for God to hear his prayer and a supplication for God not to abandon, hide, or turn away in anger (vv. 7–9).

The NRSV mistranslates verse 10 as "If my father and mother forsake me, the LORD will take me up." The Hebrew, however, reflects a past reality; his mother and father have already abandoned him. The Jewish medieval commentator Ibn Ezra correctly understood this verse as "my parents have left me when they died," and Mesopotamian parallels confirm his interpretation.[3] The author is someone who, after losing his or her parents, has found in God a protective and caring guardian.

It is the assurance of being in God's hand that moves the faithful forward, and a deep faith is what overcomes fear. Martin Luther King Jr. relates, "It was not until I became a part of the leadership of the Montgomery bus protest that I was actually confronted with the trials of life. . . . As the weeks passed, I realized that many of the threats were in earnest. I felt myself faltering and growing in fear."[4] The threats were indeed in earnest, but King reminds us that fear "is mastered through faith."[5] The struggle for social justice requires a leap of faith.

Philippians 3:17–4:1

Paul writes this letter while in prison (Phil. 1:7, 13, 14, 17), perhaps in Rome (1:13; 4:22), in the early 60s. One of his concerns is to warn the community of Philippi against a group (or several groups) that Paul considers to be deviating from his teaching and that could have a pernicious effect on the community. The identity of Paul's opponents in Philippians has been one of the most

---

2. Avrohom Chaim Feuer, *Tehillim 1–72: A New Translation with a Commentary Anthologized from Talmudic, Midrashic, and Rabbinic Sources* (New York: Mesora, 2010), 327.
3. Shalom Paul, "Psalm Xxvii 10 and the Babylonian Theodicy," *Vetus Testamentum* 32 (1982): 489–90.
4. King, *Strength to Love*, 113.
5. Ibid., 122.

debated issues in Philippians scholarship. The main dichotomy that Paul perceives between himself and his opponents is not theological but is based on the different lifestyles that the believers are called to embrace, in contrast to those that Paul deprecates. Not orthodoxy but orthopraxis is the main issue. In order to understand Paul's argument, it is necessary to pay attention to the context of the passage under consideration, where those differences are presented in a more explicit manner.

Paul is here proclaiming the "faith of Christ" (Phil. 3:9; not "in Christ" as NRSV translates)[6] that achieves "righteousness before God." This faith, proclaims Paul, should lead believers to humble themselves and become obedient even to the point of death (Phil. 2:8). The path of humble obedience is the path that Paul calls on the Philippians to follow, as exemplified by Jesus, Timothy, Epaphroditus, and Paul himself, and it implies a very simple lifestyle. Any "confidence in the flesh" (3:3) would turn the community far from this path. The "enemies of the cross," an expression Paul uses always in controversial settings,[7] are precisely those who, instead of the ultimate obedience that might lead to a death by crucifixion, prefer the security of the "flesh." For Paul, the "flesh" denotes everything that is transitory, but also everything that leads away from God's call to humble obedience: "fornication, impurity, licentiousness, idolatry, sorcery, enmities, strife, jealousy, anger, quarrels, dissensions, factions, envy, drunkenness, carousing, and things like these" (Gal. 5:19–21).

Some communities of faith have read this "citizenship of heaven" as an indication that believers should not concern themselves with the problems and crises of our world. But for Paul, a citizen of heaven is not someone who lives in an alternate reality but someone who engages this world with a completely different set of values. Even in regard to what might appear to be mundane eating practices, Paul exhorts believers: "Do not let what you eat cause the ruin of one for whom Christ died" (Rom. 14:15); "For the [reign] of God is not food and drink but righteousness and peace and joy in the Holy Spirit" (Rom. 14:17). With 925 million people suffering from hunger in the world in 2010,[8] one wonders how many millions of lives could be saved by the food that is eaten in excess in the United States every year. Eating less and sharing what we don't need could be one of the simplest ways to save lives in our world.

---

6. See Stanley K. Stowers, *A Rereading of Romans: Justice, Jews, and Gentiles* (New Haven, CT: Yale University Press, 1997), 194–95.

7. Demetrius K. Williams, *Enemies of the Cross of Christ: The Terminology of the Cross and Conflict in Philippians* (London: Sheffield Academic Press, 2002), 30–38.

8. World Hunger Education Service, "2012 World Hunger and Poverty Facts and Statistics," http://www.worldhunger.org/articles/Learn/world%20hunger%20facts%202002.htm#Number _of_hungry_people_in_the_world (accessed Dec. 28, 2010).

This praise of a simple lifestyle is also reflected in the deuteropauline tradition: "but if we have food and clothing, we will be content with these" (1 Tim. 6:8). This is the way of the "citizens of heaven." Those of us who buy wholesale into today's consumerism belong to the category of Paul's opponents: those whose "god is the belly," whose "minds are set on earthly things" (3:19b, 19d), the enemies of the cross who are destined to destruction (3:18–19a). And because it is so easy to fall prey to these temptations, Paul needs to exhort the believers to "stand firm in the Lord in this way, my beloved" (4:1).

Luke 13:31–35

This scene begins with the Pharisees trying to warn Jesus of Herod's intentions to kill him. Jesus gives a defiant response. He calls Herod a fox, and ends his reply by quoting Psalm 118:26. Typically when we find a quotation from the Hebrew Bible in the New Testament, the passage cannot be properly understood unless we look at the whole passage from which the quote comes and not simply the verse that appears in the new text. In this case, Jesus' defiance is made apparent when we consider more of the psalm. "With the LORD on my side I do not fear. What can mortals do to me? The LORD is on my side to help me; I shall look in triumph on those who hate me" (118:6–7); "I shall not die, but I shall live, and recount the deeds of the LORD" (118:17). But even with such strong convictions, Jesus realizes that it is better to follow the advice of the Pharisees, and he leaves the city shortly after. Jerusalem will not see him again until his celebrated entry, narrated in Luke 19:28–40.

One wonders if Jesus was naive enough to expect that supernatural divine intervention would protect him from Herod. His tragic and untimely death should prevent anyone from believing that such an intervention need happen. But, in remaining faithful to God's call to the point of death, he planted a seed that would inspire millions to follow such a faithful journey. His ageless "I have a dream" speech (Luke 4:16–29), rooted in the most pure Jewish traditions of social justice, would remain unfulfilled in his lifetime, as Abraham's dream, as Moses' dream, as Martin Luther King Jr.'s dream; but now it is up to us. Can we fulfill it?

International Women's Day (March 8)

Dawn Ottoni-Wilhelm

JUDGES 19:22–30
PSALM 22:1–11
MARK 14:1–11
PHILIPPIANS 4:2–7

This Holy Day for Justice recognizes the extraordinary acts of courage and determination by ordinary women around the world. In 1908, National Women's Day was established in honor of the garment workers' strike in New York. Thereafter, women in the United States and Europe held rallies to express solidarity with other activists and the Russian women's peace movement during World War I. International Women's Day was first celebrated by the United Nations in 1975 and has continued its global connections. In worship and daily living, Christians are called to greater support of women's rights and their full participation in political and economic arenas of life.

Here's the thing, say Shug. The thing I believe. God is inside you and inside everybody else. You come into the world with God. But only them that search for it inside find it. And sometimes it just manifests itself even if you not looking, or don't know what you looking for . . .

Yeah, It. God ain't a he or a she, but a It.

But what do it look like? . . .

Don't look like nothing, she say. It ain't a picture show. It ain't something you can look at apart from anything else, including yourself.

Alice Walker[1]

Women's bodies call out to us from all four Scripture texts today. Gang rape, torture, and abuse of the unnamed concubine culminate in the dismemberment

---

1. Alice Walker, *The Color Purple* (New York: Harcourt, Inc., 1982), 195.

of her body; the psalmist recites the lament of those who suffer physical illness and abandonment; the woman who anoints Jesus is physically attentive to his impending death; and Euodia and Syntyche are companions of Paul who labor alongside him in the work of the gospel. These and countless other women throughout the world give of themselves, body and soul. Many women are sold as child brides and many are trafficked as sex slaves or forced into horrific working conditions. Still others struggle for freedom and opportunities to improve their lives and those of other women and girls. Often hidden from view, ignored, or silenced, their bodies bespeak both human tragedy and God's life-giving intentions for all people. This International Women's Day, we honor women's bodies as we recall their stories.

Judges 19:22–30

So much rightly disturbs us about the story of the rape and murder of the unnamed concubine that preachers ignore it and hearers resist it. Repulsed by the horrific mix of sexual exploitation and violence, we are tempted to dismiss it as an extreme incident that could take place only in another time, among barbaric people. But many elements of this woman's terrifying ordeal are painfully familiar to women today.

The woman is introduced early in the chapter as the Levite's concubine (*pilegesh*), a "second wife" who is not named or known apart from the man who purchased her. We are not told why she fled to her father's house, but given the Levite's subsequent actions, it is not difficult to imagine that his abusive treatment began well before she left him. Her thoughts and desires are unknown to us; none of her words are recorded. When he finally goes in search of her, the woman's father speaks with him for days on end as they exchange food, drink, and conversation. But we are told nothing of what the woman thinks or feels.

As is true for myriad young women around the world, men controlled the concubine's destiny and decided her fate. According to the United Nations Division for the Advancement of Women, if present trends continue, more than one hundred million girls will be married as children in the next decade, with parents and communities treating them as commodities to be purchased and traded by their prospective (usually much older) husbands.[2] They have no voice in the matter, while their bodies are traded for others' benefit.

---

2. "Elimination of All Forms of Discrimination and Violence against the Girl Child," Report of the Expert Group Meeting (organized by the Division for the Advancement of Women in collaboration with UNICEF), Innocenti Research Center, Florence, Italy (September 25–28, 2006), 14. (See Division for the Advancement of Women, Department of Economic and Social Affairs of the United Nations.)

When the Levite finally leaves the house of his concubine's father with the woman and his servant in tow, they seek a night's rest in Gibeah (Judg. 19:15). He and his host speak at length to one another and then barter with the townsmen who pound on the door, demanding to rape the Levite (v. 22). The host offers to the mob instead both his virgin daughter and the Levite's *pilegesh*; the concubine is soon thrust out the door by the very man responsible for her well-being (v. 25). He gives her to the mob for gang rape to save his own skin.

Even so today, when a Thai girl named Choi was recently sold by her impoverished parents to the owner of a bar in the city of Chiang Mai, it was with the promise that more money would be paid to the family each month in exchange for her services, including enticing men to buy drinks and proposing sex at a price. Although the owner of the brothel often abuses her, Choi has said, "I owe a debt to my parents. If I were to run away, my owner would stop making payments to them."[3]

Although many women have no say in what happens to them, their bodies call out to us. Their feet, like those of the Levite's concubine, carry them far from home as they seek safety elsewhere. Their hands stretch toward thresholds and cling to doorways in desperate search of admittance and aid. Doors are mentioned four times in this passage; the men pound on the door and open it, while the concubine is pushed through and later refused entry according to the decisions of men. Not only her hands and feet but her entire body cries out to us. After she is tortured by the mob, her body is butchered by the Levite, who sends her piece by piece with a message to incite the anger of his kinsmen. All that she has suffered from neglect, torture, and repeated rape is subject to his interpretation, with no word of his complicity in her ordeal. Even the biblical writer uses her body to forward the plot of Israel's escalating cycle of violence that includes the slaughter of Benjaminites (Judg. 20:35–48) and most of the inhabitants of Jabesh-gilead (Judg. 21:8–24).[4]

This is a story told entirely from the vantage point of men who use women's bodies, their lives, and their stories in service to their own ends. What would this story sound like if told from the perspective of the concubine or virgin daughter? If this story and those of countless other women who are traded, abused, and violated teach us anything, it is that we must learn to look and listen where others refuse to see and hear. We must listen to women's bodies, their voices and longings. We must look at their abuse and recognize God's holy desire for life, love, and justice among us.

---

3. David Batstone, *Not for Sale: The Return of the Global Slave Trade—and How We Can Fight It* (New York: HarperCollins, 2007), 55.

4. According to Dana Nolan Fewell, the characterization of women in Judges confirms that "Israel has become a place where women have neither voice nor choice." See Fewell, "Judges," in *The Women's Bible Commentary*, ed. Carol A. Newsom and Sharon H. Ringe (Louisville, KY: Westminster/John Knox Press, 1992), 76–83.

Psalm 22:1–11

When we listen to the opening verses of Psalm 22 alongside Judges 19, we hear something other than the solitary cry of Jesus Christ on the cross. The psalmist's cry echoes in the suffering of women who are scorned, abused, neglected, and ravaged by evildoers, just as Jesus' cry on the cross (echoing Ps. 22) unites him with the multitudinous company of women who are afflicted in body and soul. To recite this psalm is, in the words of James Mays, "to set oneself in its paradigm" and to give permission and encouragement to pray to God for help.[5]

When I served as a psychiatric chaplain at a state mental health hospital, more than half of the long-term women residents had a history of repeated sexual and physical abuse. Usually they suffered at the hands of husbands, boyfriends, fathers, stepfathers, brothers, uncles, and neighbors—male and sometimes female abusers who were not strangers or enemies but allies, care-givers, and partners. In the United States alone, one out of every six women is a victim of rape. And battering is one of the major causes of serious injury and a primary cause of homelessness among women and children.[6] Women who have been raped are often scorned or rejected, as the psalmist decries (v. 6). They know the isolation and abandonment spoken by the psalmist as they cry by day and hear no answer, and call out at night but find no rest (v. 2).

What kind of God does the psalmist turn to in times of crisis and despair? Verses 9 and 10 do not describe a mighty warrior or armed guardian. Instead, images of childbirth and midwifery abound. The psalmist recalls God tak-ing us from our mother's womb and securing our safety and sustenance at her breast. The experience of birth is not easy or painless, and the threshold of new life is both a fearful and a dangerous place. But when others have despised, forsaken, or abandoned us, God is present to deliver us anew. This godly vision of woman's procreative gifts and shared aid is a source of divine power and hope for all people.

Mark 14:1–11

Here is a woman so comfortable in her own body that she is able to reach out physically to Jesus despite the risk of ridicule and reprimand from others. She recognizes what others refuse to see and lovingly prepares Christ for his impending death. Her actions reveal that love is a matter not only of words but of deeds, of hands that bless and resources gladly given. She recognizes

5. James L. Mays, *Psalms*, Interpretation series (Louisville, KY: John Knox Press, 1994), 106.

6. According to the Rape, Abuse and Incest National Network statistics concerning women, http://www.rainn.org/statistics (accessed July 21, 2010).

that Jesus is God's chosen one and anoints him not simply for burial but in a manner that blesses his messianic status—pouring oil on his head (vv. 3, 8). With tender deliberation she lavishes her gift on him. Here is a woman who knows how to love God with heart, soul, mind, and strength.

Her story is worth telling for many reasons, not the least of which is its striking difference from the stories of those surrounding her. The chief priests and scribes feel threatened by Jesus and intend to kill him by stealth (v. 1); she recognizes his divine authority and openly and courageously blesses him. The guests at Simon's house angrily condemn her extravagant action (vv. 4–5); her generous outpouring of love stands in stark contrast to their miserly spirits. It is also obvious that the woman's singular devotion is opposed to Judas's death-dealing duplicity. His actions contribute to Jesus' execution; her actions presage the good news to come (v. 9). She embodies love of God and neighbor as she serves Jesus Christ.

Women have long known the wisdom and necessity of bearing witness with their whole selves, including their bodies. In April 2003, after decades of civil war in Liberia, thousands of Christian and Muslim women formed an unlikely alliance to end the violence.[7] The Women's Peace Building Network arranged peaceful protests and put pressure on President Charles Taylor while drawing the attention of the international community. By June, peace talks had commenced in Accra, Ghana. As the talks dragged on and the war continued to escalate back home, the women were furious that delegates from Taylor's administration and the warlords enjoyed leisurely meetings amid luxurious accommodations. The Liberian women formed a physical circle around the conference center, locked arms, and refused to allow the men's departure until a settlement was reached. The talks soon drew to a close, culminating in removing President Taylor from office. Like the woman who anointed Jesus, these women recognized the death-dealing powers of those around them and were willing to put their lives, resources, and bodies on the line to overcome evil with good, violence with steadfast love.

Philippians 4:2–7

Precious little is known about Euodia and Syntyche, but of two things we can be certain: they labored alongside Paul as leaders in the church at Philippi; and they suffered a disagreement that drew the attention of others. As for the first point, no one doubts that they put their bodies on the line for the work of the gospel. They no doubt gave freely of their time and gifts, risking rejection and enduring hardship. Like Paul, they were missionaries, and he wanted

7. For a full account, see the documentary film *Pray the Devil Back to Hell*, directed by Gini Reticker and produced by Abigail E. Disney (Fork Films, 2008).

their work to continue. Thus Paul accents the importance of their roles in the church by the attention he gives them.

As for the second point, Paul was familiar with congregational discord, including those who disagreed with his leadership (see 2:12). In his Letter to the Philippians he often refers to the importance of seeking the mind of Christ or being of one mind in Christ Jesus (e.g., 1:15–19; 2:1–5; 3:15). The church was experiencing dissension from within and opposition from without, and he called on its leaders, including these two women, to sort through their problems, turn to those who could help mediate their differences, and call on God, who promises peace amid our troubles. However, we must not hastily assume that the discord that concerned Paul was between these two women. There is another possibility; namely, that Euodia and Syntyche were at odds not with one another but with Paul.[8] How often does our current North American culture wrongly imagine and even encourage discord and competition among women when, in fact, many women across cultures have demonstrated tremendous gifts in forming social alliances, forging intimate relationships, and bonding with one another in supportive networks of labor and care? For this we rejoice: that God continues to call forth women to lead the church and proclaim the gospel of Christ's life-giving purposes among us.

8. See Mary Rose D'Angelo, "Euodia," in *Women in Scripture*, ed. Carol Meyers (Grand Rapids: Eerdmans, 2000), 79.

Third Sunday in Lent

Nyasha Junior

ISAIAH 55:1–9
PSALM 63:1–8
1 CORINTHIANS 10:1–13
LUKE 13:1–9

The brown-paper-bag test was a social test among African Americans in the nineteenth and twentieth centuries. Those persons whose skin was darker than a brown paper bag did not pass the test. Not passing the test could result in denied admission to social gatherings or organizations or even a loss of employment opportunities. The roots of this test lie in the preferential treatment extended by some slave owners to slaves with lighter complexions, but regrettably colorism and the brown-paper-bag test have continued among African Americans themselves.

It may surprise non–African Americans that African Americans have discriminated and continue to discriminate against one another in this way. Yet quite similar intragroup conflict and efforts to determine who is one of "us" or one of "them" continue among Christians. For example, some Protestant Christians swear that Roman Catholicism is not a form of Christianity because it allows idol worship. Some Presbyterians think that Pentecostals are one animal sacrifice away from demon possession. Some straight Christians are comfortable with gays and lesbians as closeted ministers of music but not as open ministers of the Word and Sacrament. This week's lectionary texts invite us to consider the ways in which we draw boundaries and define insiders and outsiders. Furthermore, these texts ask us to consider our exclusivity in contrast to the inclusivity offered by God.

Isaiah 55:1–9

The First Testament text for this week comes from what many scholars term Deutero-Isaiah or Second Isaiah. The sixty-six chapters of this book are often divided into First (1–39), Second (40–55), and Third (56–66) Isaiah. Second Isaiah or Isaiah of Babylon was active during the time of the Babylonian exile. Although the exiles have witnessed the fall of Judah, the destruction of Jerusalem, and the collapse of the monarchy, Second Isaiah offers them a message of hope and compassion. Despite all that the exiles have experienced, Second Isaiah offers a new perspective on the covenant between God and the Israelites.

In Isaiah 55:3, Isaiah speaks to the exiles on behalf of God and tells them, "I will make with you an everlasting covenant, my steadfast, sure love for David." This verse recalls the everlasting covenant that God makes with David in 2 Samuel 7. God promises that David's offspring will build a house for God and that God will "establish the throne of his kingdom forever" (7:13). Also, God promises David that David's "throne shall be established forever" (7:16). Isaiah claims that the covenant is not conditional but everlasting. Yet the exiles are probably the last people who want to be reminded of the Davidic dynasty, which was never supposed to fall. The people are in exile away from their homeland and under foreign rule, but the deal is still good.

Isaiah 55 acknowledges that some among them are "wicked" and "unrighteous"; nevertheless, those who return will be pardoned (v. 7). To the exiles, this may seem too good to be true. Isaiah anticipates their objections and skepticism by explaining that God's mercy is beyond human comprehension. This text explains, "For my thoughts are not your thoughts, nor are your ways my ways" (v. 8). Yes, the exiles have been punished. Yes, some of them are wicked and unrighteous. Still, God offers an open invitation to return. Isaiah describes this invitation as a free feast that is open to everyone. While obesity is a public health crisis in much of the developed world, in the ancient Near East food scarcity was a concern. But God provides food and drink to everyone "without price" (v. 1). God welcomes all to the banquet table!

Psalm 63:1–8

The superscription to this psalm includes the notation "a psalm of David, when he was in the wilderness of Judah." The Hebrew versification differs from the English. The Hebrew text treats the superscript as verse 1 and the subsequent verses as verses 2–12. Of course, the superscription was not part of the original Hebrew text, but it offers a glimpse of an early interpretation of this psalm as one seeking comfort. It may refer to David's time in the wilderness of Ziph (1 Sam. 23:14–15), when he was hiding from Saul, who sought to kill him (1 Sam. 20:31). The psalmist is seeking the comfort and intimacy of a relationship with God.

While the lectionary text ends at verse 8, the chapter includes three additional verses. In verses 9–10, the psalmist exclaims, "But those who seek to destroy my life shall go down into the depths of the earth; they shall be given over to the power of the sword; they shall be prey for jackals." After seeking the personal comfort of God, the psalmist wishes for the ruin of his enemies. Those destroyers may be the same as the liars mentioned (v. 11), but the text does not specify who they are or what type of relationship they have with the psalmist. While the lectionary does not include these texts, they can be useful in pointing out the very human desire to exclude one's enemies from the same comfort that the individual seeks. We may not want to admit it, but often our own individual desires include an attendant desire for some measure of payback or revenge against our enemies. The psalmist is "keeping it real" by acknowledging feelings that we may not wish to face. We are human and understandably may have very human feelings toward our enemies. Nevertheless, we can celebrate the God of Isaiah 55, whose thoughts and ways are unlike ours (Isa. 55:8–9); we thereby seek to welcome all.

1 Corinthians 10:1–13

In his First Letter to the Corinthians, Paul includes the Corinthians as descendants of the Israelites by referring to them as "our ancestors" (v. 1). He refers to the exodus, but then he turns immediately to the wilderness experience of the Israelites. He points out that the punishments endured by the Israelites serve as examples to future generations. Paul contends, "[God] will not let you be tested beyond your strength, but with the testing [God] will also provide the way out so that you may be able to endure it" (v. 13). A similar notion is reflected in the popular saying "God won't give you more than you can bear." This saying is often trotted out following the disclosure of a death or loss or even just an admission that things are getting tough. As an African American woman, I am distressed by both this saying and Paul's.

Paul's advice and similar sentiments are often used to support the status quo and to promote the notion that one's burdens are somehow part of God's plan for one's life. In my experience, women especially are made to feel as if they are deserving of their situation and that their suffering is part of God's will. To seek to change one's situation or to combat one's continued oppression may be regarded as a lack of faith in God and in God's plan. Suffering in an abusive relationship is prized more highly than leaving that relationship. Enduring suffering is treated as a sign of strength, but the glorification of suffering has no part in transformative ministry. In this sense, the psalmist's desire to "keep it real" may provide a much-needed corrective to this tendency by validating feelings that Christian women may feel are inappropriate. Paul says, "Keep going." When someone admits flagging strength, other Christians say, "Keep going." In my experience, Christian women say to other Christian women, "Keep going and smile." At least the psalmist is honest about seeking God's comfort as well as revenge against the "destroyers."

Luke 13:1–9

The Gospel text for this week includes a question put to Jesus and his extended response, which includes the parable of the Barren Fig Tree. With a crowd of people gathered, some people relate to him an incident involving "Galileans whose blood Pilate had mingled with their sacrifices" (v. 1). This seems like a perfect time for Jesus to condemn Pilate and the Roman government. Now is the time for unambiguous denunciation. There is no need for ambiguity here. Now is the time for Jesus to be judgmental. He can step up and be on the side of right! Clearly, the Galileans were right and innocent, and the Romans were wrong and guilty. The crowd waits for a great sound bite from Jesus that will sum up their anti-Roman sentiment. And once again, Jesus defies expectations. Instead of saying anything about Pilate or the Romans, he tells the crowd to repent! Unless they repent, they will perish as the Galileans did and as those who died at the tower of Siloam (vv. 3–5). I can imagine the disappointment of those gathered. Jesus has "flipped the script" by telling them to look at their own sinful behavior and to repent.

Jesus continues by relating the parable of the Barren Fig Tree (cf. budding fig tree, Matt. 24:32–35; Mark 13:28–31; Luke 21:29–33). The owner of the vineyard wants to cut his losses and cut down the fig tree that has not produced fruit for three years. The gardener advises patience and greater care. Yet the gardener recommends that if the tree does not become fruitful after another year, then cut it down. There will be a day of reckoning. There are consequences for not being productive. In conjunction with Jesus' earlier comments, this text provides a stern warning regarding the consequences of sin. Despite efforts to point fingers at others, Jesus cautions repentance. Now is the time for digging around more deeply and cultivating fruit of faithfulness (v. 8).

Salt March Day: Marching with the Poor (March 12)

Rebecca Todd Peters

ISAIAH 58:6–12
PSALM 82
ROMANS 12:14–21
LUKE 3:7–14

During their occupation of India, the British had a monopoly on the sale of salt and taxed its purchase. This arrangement burdened the poor. Moreover, Indians viewed the salt tax as a symbol of oppression. On March 12, 1930, Mohandas K. Gandhi (1869–1948) led a march to protest the tax and to call for Indian independence. Such nonviolent resistance in India inspired similar nonviolent civil disobedience in other places (including the Civil Rights Movement in the United States).

> Whatever the ultimate fate of my country, my love for you remains, and will remain, undiminished. My non-violence demands universal love, and you are not a small part of it. It is that love which has prompted my appeal to you.
> *Mahatma Mohandas Karamchand Gandhi*[1]

The life and work of Mahatma Gandhi was devoted to the development of the practice of *satyagraha*. While this term is commonly translated as "nonviolent resistance," Gandhi's philosophy was rooted in a much more transformative understanding of social change that involved conversion of one's opponent toward the goal of justice and peace. The term comes from the Sanskrit words *satya*, meaning "truth," and *agraha*, meaning "holding firmly to." Sometimes Gandhi referred to it as "love-force" or "truth-force." He passionately

---

1. Open letter, "To Every Briton," New Delhi (2 July 2, 1940); published in *Harijan*, (6 July 6, 1940).

believed that the righteousness of social justice was rooted in such a profound truth that it would eventually transform the hearts of the British oppressors (or any oppressors, for that matter) and that the call of justice was to practice *satyagraha* in love even unto death.

For Christians, Gandhi's concept of *satyagraha* sounds similar to the call to follow in the footsteps of Christ as we seek to live into a world of justice and peace. The texts that we turn to today offer deep insights into what a world of social justice ought to look like. At its heart we can see that social justice is rooted in the development of relationships and community that serve as the foundation for embodying and enacting our care and concern for the world. The text from Isaiah offers the prophet's vision of the moral foundations of just communities that call for people to care for the material needs of our neighbors. Psalm 82 offers the insight that divine justice also requires particular attention to those who are the most vulnerable in our communities. The Lukan passage challenges us to think about how we are each called to live out justice in our own setting, and the Romans text offers clear instructions for the norms that should shape community life.

Isaiah 58:6–12

This text is widely regarded by scholars to have been written in the postexilic period after the edict of Cyrus had allowed the Jewish community to return from exile in Babylon to their ancestral lands in Judah. From the books of Ezra and Nehemiah, we know that one of the major initiatives of the returned community was to rebuild the temple in Jerusalem. While the text of Isaiah 58 does not give a clear indication of whether the temple has been completed, the concerns about the proper form and practices of ritual fasting in today's passage indicate that some level of cultic observance is present in the Jewish community in Jerusalem at the time of the authorship of this text by Third Isaiah. The verses that precede today's passage indicate problems with the practices of fasting in the community. While it appears that the people are fasting, their efforts are not bearing fruit; indeed, verse 4 describes the people fasting with quarrels and fighting that "will not make [their] voice heard on high." It seems that despite the cultic observance of fasting, the practice seems to be failing to reach YHWH.

Today's passage, beginning with verse 6, offers an explanation for this failure. While the people appear to be going through the correct motions of the ritual practice, their understanding of the proper attitude and purpose of the fast has fallen short. In this text, the author of Third Isaiah offers not only an exposition on the proper form of fasting, but also a renewed understanding of fasting as a practice intended to strengthen the people's relationship with

God.[2] Fasting as a ritual practice that honors and embodies the covenant relationship between God and the Jewish people is redefined from an abstention from food and drink to a repudiation of the practices of injustice. The fast that the people are to choose moves beyond individual repentance and supplication to emphasize the health and well-being of the community. While the injunctions (share your bread, house the homeless, clothe the naked) are certainly aimed at individual behavior, the collective purpose of these actions is to establish a just community ("repairer of the breach, . . . restorer of streets") within which everyone can thrive. It is only when the people recognize that their health and well-being is tied up with the health and well-being of their neighbors and kin, and they work toward reestablishing communities of justice, that their covenant with God can be renewed as their communities live into blessedness. This blessedness should not be understood as a gift from God for right behavior, but as the fruits of righteousness. The practice of the fast is no easy task: it requires sacrifice and commitment on the part of the people, but the sacrifice required is more than simply abstention from food and drink; it also is an abstention from injustice. With fasting from injustice, the people are called to practice justice as an embodiment of the righteousness that covenant fidelity requires. The covenant relationship that the people share with God is intended to be a model for their own relationships with one another. When the human relationships deteriorate into injustice, their relationship with YHWH, likewise, deteriorates.

Luke 3:7–14

The theme of community relationships and justice as embodying covenant fidelity is echoed in the Lukan passage for today. In this passage we have the most detailed description of John the Baptist's preaching in the Gospels.[3] We know that John was called "the Baptizer" because his ministry was rooted in the ritual practice of "a baptism of repentance for the forgiveness of sins" (Luke 3:3). However, the key to understanding John's use of the Greek term *metanoia* (usually translated as "repentance") comes in today's text. In verse 8, John challenges the crowds who have come out to be baptized that they must "bear fruits worthy of *metanoia*." However, the crowds do not understand what he is calling them to do, and so they ask directly (vv. 10, 12, 14). While *metanoia* is a Greek term meaning "to turn around," it is clear from his response to the crowds that John's baptism of *metanoia* was meant to

2. Mary Chase-Ziolek, "Repairing, Restoring, and Revisioning the Health of Our Communities: The Challenge of Isaiah 58," *Ex Auditu* (2005): 21:153.
3. R. Alan Culpepper, "Luke," in *The New Interpreter's Bible*, ed. Leander Keck et al. (Nashville: Abingdon Press, 1995), 9:83.

signify a transformation in the life of the baptized. In this transformation one experienced a turning toward God that redefined the followers' understanding of the purpose of life. In turn, this *metanoia* would be noticeable in changed behavior (or the "fruits") of the transformed.

John responds to the crowds' queries with very specific instructions—the individuals are called to think about their positions of power and privilege and respond in ways that promote increased justice and solidarity in their community. Those who have more clothes or food than they need are instructed to share out of their abundance (v. 11); those who stand in positions of power (like the tax collectors) or authority (like the soldiers) are called to use their power and authority in ways that embody righteousness or right relation (vv. 13–14). Based on his teachings, we can see that John's teleological vision for the community is a vision of mutuality and justice where those with privilege are called to rethink their understanding of power in ways that promote community solidarity rather than personal aggrandizement. In a world where the benefits and attraction of being a tax collector or a solider lay largely in the possibility that these professions offered for getting rich through greed and exploitation, John's injunction to live righteously, to take no more than one's fair share, and to be satisfied with one's wages was a real call to live against the culture or the status quo.

What is fascinating about John's message is that it was not uniform in the sense that each person must do exactly the same thing to embody this solidarity. Rather, his targeted responses to different groups of people among the crowds demonstrate the ways in which all of us are called to think carefully and critically about our own sources of power and authority to try to determine how God is calling us to use our social position and privilege in ways that promote justice. Just as in the days of Isaiah or John the Baptist, this is no easy task.

Romans 12:14–21

In line with both Isaiah's and John's visions of justice as the fruits of being in right relationship with our neighbors and with God, Romans 12 offers us one more glimpse into God's vision of how the human community should orient our lives toward justice and righteousness. Paul's words in this passage offer an exhortation for how this nascent Christian community should strive to live in harmony and solidarity with the larger Roman community by sharing in both their joys and their pains. Paul challenges this persecuted minority community not to follow their instincts to separate themselves from the people around them, nor to withdraw into the private solace of a community of like-minded people. Rather, Paul calls the Christians to reach out in love to those around them and to try to "live peaceably with all" (v. 18).

In one of the most difficult moral challenges to be found in the Bible, Paul calls the Romans to "overcome evil with good" (v. 21), a message that echoed through the life and teachings of Gandhi as he sought to lead the Indian people in a struggle of *satyagraha* and resistance to colonialism and oppression by embodying such a call. Both Paul and Gandhi believed that kindnesses like hospitality and compassion in the face of evil offered the potential to "heap burning coals" (v. 20) on the heads of one's enemies. Both men were convinced that love, kindness, and compassion had the capacity to shame one's opponents into justice.

It is also important to remember that neither Paul nor Gandhi believed that humans were capable of this kind of supererogatory moral behavior all on their own. While they offered visions of communities rooted in kindness, solidarity, righteousness, and justice, all the prophets in our texts today (Isaiah, John the Baptist, Paul, and Gandhi) recognized that humans need the help and presence of the divine in our lives to support us as we strive toward the ideal of communities of justice.

Too often, like the people fasting in Isaiah or the crowds following John the Baptist, we go through the motions of our ritual practices (prayer, worship, volunteering) without the proper inward motivation and orientation toward God and our task. John's *metanoia* is a fierce moral standard, like Gandhi's *satyagraha* and Isaiah's fasting. Each of these prophets is calling his followers toward an inner transformation of their worldview or their orientation toward the world around them. In covenant relationship with God and with our sisters and brothers, and with the grace of God supporting us, it is possible for us to experience the kind of transformation to which these prophets witness.

Psalm 82

If our first three texts challenge Christians toward a true *metanoia* that embodies *satyagraha* and embraces the biblical notion of social justice, then Psalm 82 offers the reader a glimpse into a divine understanding of what that life of social justice requires. This text, which scholars interpret in the movement toward monotheism from the polytheistic Semitic religious landscape, depicts a divine assembly of gods in which YHWH stands in judgment of the other divine beings for failing to perform their divinely appointed tasks as caretakers and guardians of the people. Because the world, under their care, has become wicked and unjust, they will no longer be allowed to rule (v. 7).

With respect for the rights of the lowly and destitute (v. 3) and care to deliver the needy from the hand of the wicked (v. 4), the psalmist paints a vivid picture of God's intention for justice and right relation in the world. This is no world of charity where people simply feed those who are hungry or clothe

those who are naked. While these actions are valuable expressions of compassion, charity does not adequately reflect the just world that God desires.
Psalm 82 calls for acts of justice that require changes in the social arrangements of the world, changes that empower the poor by creating structures of
justice in our world that ultimately reduce the need for charity. Earnest communities of justice are supported by social, economic, and political structures
that embody and enact justice in the lives of the people. As we consider the
weak, the orphan, the needy, and others in our midst who are destitute, we
must set our communities and ourselves to the task of addressing the root
causes of injustice.

Frankly, our limited imaginations impede our contributions to creating
justice in our communities, but we can begin through work on living-wage
campaigns; housing and educational reform; restorative justice; literacy and
empowerment programs for marginalized communities; and safe, high-
quality child-care programs that support children and working parents. We
are not each called to work on all of these initiatives, but our lives will be
transformed in the work that our communities and we devote to the divine
call to justice represented in today's texts.

Fourth Sunday in Lent

Randall K. Bush

JOSHUA 5:9–12
PSALM 32
2 CORINTHIANS 5:16–21
LUKE 15:1–3, 11B–32

How shall we talk about the boundary experiences of life from a faith perspective? Faith experiences of boundaries are usually liminal in nature. This old-fashioned word relates to places of transition, where an intermediate phase or condition is present as people move between stages in their lives. It is possible to speak about a liminal state between shadows and light or between life and death.

Different perceptions or spaces of liminality offer interpretative insights to these passages for the Fourth Sunday in Lent. The reading from Joshua 5 deals with the liminal place between the end of wilderness wanderings and the beginning of a new life in the land of Canaan. Psalm 32 describes the boundary zone between places of iniquity and places of penitential wisdom. The short passage from 2 Corinthians touches on a type of "double vision," noting the liminality between a human point of view and a Christ-centered point of view. Finally, the parable of the Prodigal Son is full of these transitional moments, such as when the father watches his younger son return or when the father stands outside the "welcome home" celebration, trying to convince the petulant elder son to join in. Since our lives are spent navigating times of liminal transition, and since every movement from injustice to justice involves stepping across barriers and boundaries, there is much contemporary wisdom in the passages for this Sunday in Lent.

Joshua 5:9–12

There are only four readings from the book of Joshua in the Revised Common Lectionary, which makes it all the more unfortunate that the selected

149

passage from Joshua 5 is both too long and too short. It is too long because it begins with a verse that has little to do with the verses immediately following it. It is also too short, because the brevity of verses 10–12 makes it possible to overlook how momentous it was to celebrate Passover in the land of Canaan at long last.

On its surface, verse 9 provides a brief etymology of the place named Gilgal by linking it with the Hebrew verb meaning "rolled away." Yet this rolling away of the "disgrace of Egypt" appears tied to the mass circumcision described in the previous passage (vv. 2–8). Preachers typically neglect the subject of circumcision, although the ritual plays a key role in the Hexateuch (Pentateuch plus the book of Joshua) and casts a thematic shadow reaching into the Second Testament writings of Paul. However, it is also possible to look back a bit further to Joshua 3 and 4, when the Hebrew people crossed the Jordan River as if on dry land. There a different ritual act is cited—this time involving twelve stones carried across the river and then placed as a memorial dedicated to the Lord. In both cases, an act of covenantal commitment takes place. Yet when the stones are in their resting place and while the camps of the twelve tribes are healing from the ritual of circumcision, the Lord reminds the people that the initiative for this entire covenant rested with God and God alone (v. 9).

The significance of this gathering at Gilgal is how a liminal vision unfolded that day. Moses had died; the long years of wandering were over. The people looked back as they retold the story of their exodus in the Passover festival. But on this occasion, they made unleavened cakes from their own grain. The heaven-sent manna no longer needed to come; now "produce of the land" would nourish them (v. 12). A movement from absolute dependence to covenantal independence took place on that day on the plains of Jericho.

A rich and complex drama slowly unfolds. The wandering people have shifted from nomadic dependency to lives of agricultural sufficiency. They had planted crops and were sustained by the harvest, although the land was not fully theirs and many more battles remained ahead. The nature of God's providential care had also shifted. No longer was it confined to literal gifts of daily bread (manna). Now it was present in the growing cycles of annual crops, from which their harvests would then feed them. It was visible in how they put away their tents and could now build homes and communities of faith.

Throughout this passage, many ethical questions remain unspoken: Can God's people lay claim to another people's land? Is God's grace when it provides daily manna different from when it accompanies the farmer during the long season of sowing, weeding, and harvesting the crops of the field? What emerges from this transition time is the assurance that the God who parted the Red Sea and the Jordan River, who is celebrated in memorial stones and

Passover meals, is the same God who provided for the first Passover and continues to supply our needs even today.

Luke 15:1–3, 11b–32

The previous passage described the first Passover in the land of promise, allowing us to glimpse how a time of transition resolved into a new chapter of faith. By contrast, the familiar verses of the parable of the Prodigal Son intentionally conclude with an open ending, forcing us to speculate on whether the liminal transition is faithfully resolved or not.

Luke 15 contains a collection of three parables about a lost sheep, a lost coin, and a lost son. In the preacher's rush to describe the horrors of being lost, it is possible to overlook a key insight, that being lost does not mean one exists in a place outside the potential care and oversight of the rescuer. The sheep lost in the wilderness was still in a place the shepherd could eventually find; the shadowy corner into which the coin had rolled was still within the household of the searching woman. The risk of emphasizing "lostness" as an oppositional category to being "found" is that it can lead to mischaracterizations or dislocation of others as outside of God's grace. Similarly we also risk a false pride that believes some enjoy a place of privilege beneath the wings of the Almighty. All the sheep (in the fold or lost in the wilderness) received the shepherd's initiating care. All the coins (safe in a purse or hidden in a corner) were part of the woman's carefully managed household. And both sons walked paths of "lostness" and "foundness" even as the same father sought to provide them consistent, loving care.

The third parable describes a place of transition in modest detail at least three times. First, a son stands before his father, asking prematurely for his share of the inheritance. The son had stepped away from his family responsibilities and relationships into different choices and potentially calamitous decisions. But even as he turned his back, the father's heart and gaze continued to extend toward the son in a distant land. Second, there is the liminal moment when the son returns to the edge of his father's estate. Earlier the text said that he "came to himself," and his gaze symbolically reconnects with his father's gaze as the prodigal imagines life back at home. His self-discovery and desire for restoration emerged out of a mixture of physical and spiritual motivations; he was hungry and tired, as well as sorrowful about his sins against heaven and home. Yet, as in the earlier two parables, restoration came from the initiative of a searching, loving father, who saw his son "while he was still far off" and offered the fullest of welcomes before the son could utter his well-prepared speech.

Third, the elder son stands in a poignant, unfinished place of transition in the shadows of the family estate but outside his father's joy; so he believes.

Once again, the father took the initiative to remedy the situation and spoke, not in quantifiable categories of privilege and fairness, but rather in qualitative relationship and mutuality. He offers his elder son the vision to see how the one who was dead is now alive, so that the elder son might step away from flawed earthly perspectives fixated on possessions, power, and prestige.

Both sons exhibit personal brokenness in real acts of disrespect and dishonor to their father and toward themselves. Honestly naming how that occurs both inside and outside the father's estate (the church) is crucial. The quality of grace is such that it renders all distorted quantifications of grace as ill timed, ill natured, and ill conceived.

2 Corinthians 5:16–21

The prior readings offer a sweeping vision of the first Passover celebrated after crossing the Jordan River and a depiction of a father's estate celebrating the return of a prodigal son. Paul's exhortation to the church in Corinth embraces these same visions, but describes them in the distinctive categories of human-centered and Christ-centered points of view.

Within a span of three short verses (vv. 18–20), terms for the concept of "reconciliation" appear five times. Paul emphasizes some immediacy to this experience—how in Christ "everything old has passed away [and] everything has become new" (v. 17). As true as that scriptural assertion is, it is hard to imagine how "passing away" and "becoming new" actually occur in acts of reconciliation. Regarding "no one from a human point of view" any longer is difficult when the very means of regarding and relating to one another are so bound up with our essential humanity.

Reconciliation is less a "light switch" and more a "lifestyle" experience. It necessarily combines words and actions, moving away from past prejudices through new patterns of respect, reparations, and shared responsibility. It is seen through how we live together, offer education for our children, provide jobs that have intrinsic worth and future-building potential, how we care for the needy, the lonely, and the stranger in our midst, and by the spirit present in our public worship. That is why Paul names people of faith as "ambassadors for Christ" (v. 20). It is a title of which the primary meaning reflects the active appeal and work to seek healing relationships with God and one another.

Psalm 32

Similar to Paul, the writer of Psalm 32 uses contrasting categories to make clear the movement between sinfulness and happiness, times of torment and times of rejoicing. The vantage point once again looks back in time to a moment when weary groaning marked the day and all strength had dried up as if in the heat of summer (vv. 3–4). It also looks around and ahead, sharing beatitudes of joy for the heaven-sent quality of mercy that forgives sin, preserves from trouble, and surrounds all who trust in the Lord (vv. 1, 2, 7, 10).

Psalm 32 offers a combination of prophetic and penitential outlooks. The "I" language present in several of its verses draws our attention to the personal quality of faith, naming the times of individual struggle and the concrete act of sincere confession and repentance. It is important that efforts to be inclusive in language do not diminish the necessity of allowing the specificity of personal faith to be recognized in words of worship and Scripture.

Yet having said that, it should be noted that the "I" language is always articulated in close proximity to the plural language of the faith community. The same person who confesses transgressions to the Lord (v. 5) then calls all to offer prayer to God (v. 6). The one who announces "happy are those . . . whose sin is covered" (v. 1) goes on to offer public instruction and exhortation to the community of the faithful (vv. 8, 11).

Just as ambassadors must cross boundaries and borders to bring messages of peace, so too must the faithful instructor offer words of correction in both seasons of triumph and times of trouble. This involves personal honesty and vulnerability, lest the analogy of an unruly horse or mule (v. 9) become an appropriate metaphor for our own lives. It involves offering a voice for the voiceless and breaking the silence wherever this reticence has become a means for allowing continued oppression and violence. It is a movement through the liminal spaces of life—celebrating Passovers and other remembrances of the past, being welcomed home and found at last, seeing all of creation from a perspective of grace-full reconciliation, and doing so with a glad heart and shouts of joy. Shaping liminal space is often how Scripture shapes our threshold experiences of life.

Oscar Romero of the Americas Day (March 24)

Ada María Isasi-Díaz

DEUTERONOMY 13:1–5
PSALM 86:1–7
EPHESIANS 6:10–20
MATTHEW 16:24–28

Oscar Romero (1917–1980), Roman Catholic archbishop of El Salvador, was a powerful leader in the struggle for human rights, especially among the poor. Romero opposed military regimes and the brutal methods (including torture and assassination) by which dictators maintained power, and he called for economic, social, and legal justice. On March 24, 1980, Romero was assassinated while lifting the consecrated host during Mass. The preacher could join countries in Central and South America in observing Oscar Romero Day on March 24 (or the Sunday nearest that date) as a sign of respect for this martyr and as an act of commitment to continue the struggle for justice. The fate of Oscar Romero gives haunting testimony to the Lenten theme of taking up the cross.

The present form of the world passes away,
and there remains only the joy of having used this world
to establish God's rule here.
All pomp, all triumphs, all selfish capitalism,
all the false successes of life will pass
with the world's form.
All of that passes away.
What does not pass away is love.
When one has turned money, property, work in one's calling
into service of others,
then the joy of sharing
and the feeling that all are one's family

does not pass away.
In the evening of life you will be judged on love.

Oscar Romero[1]

The readings for this liturgy are a mixture of texts that might well be addressed to Romero and to his enemies. Applying the texts analogically to the life of Oscar Romero, the liturgy serves as a lesson on how to live according to the gospel message of justice and peace.

Deuteronomy 13:1–5

The book of Deuteronomy, part of the legal tradition of Israel, sets forth the commandments of YHWH, making clear that anyone who attempts to lead Israel to a false god will suffer dire consequences. Chapter 13, part of Moses' second address laying out the responsibilities of Israel according to its covenant with YHWH, indicates that obedience is the means through which Israel can assure itself of YHWH's blessings. The tone of this address, as well as of other parts of Deuteronomy, makes clear that Israel saw itself as a prophetic nation with a specific historical role.

In the context of this celebration of Oscar Romero, the text can be read to reflect on the government and armed forces of El Salvador that tried to trick people into obeying them. Romero's mission was to make clear to the government, the people, and the church—including himself—what God was asking of them. Verse 4 is a brief summary of what YHWH expected from the Israelites, and what Romero believed God expected from the church as well as each person: to follow, obey, serve, and hold fast to God. This is the only way evil will be purged!

For Romero, what El Salvador was experiencing had a very specific role within the grand scheme of salvation history: "God and human beings make history. God saves humanity in the history of one's own people. The history of salvation will be El Salvador's history when we Salvadorans seek in our history the presence of God the Savior."[2]

"The prophetic mission is a duty of God's people. So, when I am told in a somewhat mocking tone that I think I am a prophet, I reply: 'God be praised! You ought to be one too.' For every Christian, all God's people, every family

1. Oscar Romero, *The Violence of Love: The Pastoral Wisdom of Archbishop Oscar Romero*, compiled and trans. by James R. Brockman, SJ (San Francisco: Harper & Row, 1988), 145.
2. Ibid., 207.

must develop an awareness, convey an awareness of God's mission in the world, bring it a divine presence that makes demands and rejections."[3]

Psalm 86:1–7

A prayer uttered in the midst of a national crisis, this psalm is an anguished cry to YHWH for help. Most probably written at the time of the Assyrian invasion of the northern kingdom of Israel, the psalm represents the loyal servant who trusts in YHWH asking for his life to be preserved. Israel fell to the Assyrians; Romero was murdered—does YHWH listen to the prayers of those who believe their cry for help will be answered? The situation in El Salvador got worse during the three years Romero was archbishop of San Salvador. But the prayer does not ask YHWH to act as a magician and change the situation. Rather, it asks YHWH to be with the supplicant. The person praying reminds herself or himself that YHWH is gracious and loving. These are the characteristics one needs to find in a friend, particularly in times of trouble. A gracious and loving friend will walk with you, will not let you face needs, difficulties, or dangers alone. That is what one needs in times of trouble! What one hopes for is not to be alone; to be with a friend is an assurance that one will have the strength to face the situation.

Day after day, Romero faced the danger of living in a repressive situation. The kind of prayer in which one attempts to stir up one's own courage and one's hope might have indeed been Romero's prayer. What helped him to keep up his hope, to continue trusting in God, to have courage? Was it the faithfulness of the poor and the oppressed? Was it the commitment of those around him who did not falter in their struggle for justice regardless of the dangers they faced? Was it indeed knowing that a gracious and loving YHWH walked with them?

Ephesians 6:10–20

This passage provides specifics as to what it means to live as a Christian. Taking into account that Paul is in prison when he writes this epistle (v. 13), his perspective on what is required is especially relevant in this liturgy commemorating Oscar Romero, who, though not imprisoned as such, was indeed "chained" by growing threats on his life.

The text opens with a clear statement that we are to rely on the strength and power of God. This is what brings assurance and trust in times of danger and tribulation. Paul uses the metaphor of the body armor used by Roman

3. Ibid., 104.

soldiers to describe what we need in order to be protected by God. The implication here is that the Christian way of life will be a protection in times of distress, in moments when one has to stand up to the devil.

The Greek for "devil" in verse 11 is *diabolos*, the usual rendition of the Hebrew *satanas*, which means "adversary." Paul then identifies those who are the adversaries of God. Among us, on this earth, they are the rulers and authorities. It is not far-fetched to conclude that he was referring to the Roman authorities who had imprisoned him. Then Paul mentions the eschatological enemies, "cosmic powers" and "spiritual forces of evil in the heavenly places," which are linked to the rulers and authorities. The adversary of God, particularly revealed in the temptations of Jesus in the desert (Luke 4:1–13; Matt. 4:1–11) is deceitful, cunningly plotting to make one deviate from what God asks.

Paul urges one to "put on" or to "take up" the armor of God so as to be ready to do battle against God's adversaries (vv. 11, 13). God has fashioned the armor, but each person is responsible for putting it on. Getting ready to do battle against God's adversaries is a joint effort of God and the person. The armor consists of truth, which refers to moral integrity, to the need for honesty about who one is and what one is ready to do.

Truth is linked to "righteousness." The Hebrew concept behind righteousness is that of *tsedaqah*, translated as "justice." This is not justice in the legal sense of keeping the law; it refers to justice in the sense of living a life pleasing to God. Justice is one of the attributes of God, and Christians are called to be holy as God is holy. It is important to notice in the context of Romero's commitment to the poor that victims of oppression were called righteous in the Hebrew Scriptures as early as the prophet Amos (Amos 2:6).

The gospel calls on us to do "whatever will make you ready to proclaim the gospel of peace" (v. 15). Notice that Paul is calling for self-examination. One has to find what one can do worthily to proclaim peace. The Greek *eirene* (meaning peace) is the equivalent of the Hebrew *shalom*. *Shalom* means much more than the absence of war. It means "to be complete, perfect, and full." It refers to a state of wholeness with no deficiency. Here Paul uses *eirene* to characterize the gospel message, and one can read it to mean liberation-salvation.

Verse 16 urges one to "take the shield of faith." For the early Christians, the word "faith"—the word used here in Greek is *pistis*—did not have the sense of intellectual consent that we give it today. The meaning of *pistis* is "'trust,' 'loyalty,' 'engagement,' and 'commitment.'"[4] One can conclude that to have faith means to live according to what one believes. So what are the implications for daily living to those who believe in Jesus?

---

4. Karen Armstrong, *The Case for God* (New York: Alfred A. Knopf, 2009), 74.

Matthew 16:24–28

This scene in Matthew's Gospel actually starts in verse 21, where Jesus tells his disciples he "must go to Jerusalem and undergo great suffering." He explains to them that at the end, he will resurrect. However, faced with the harsh reality of suffering, the disciples try to persuade Jesus to confront the authorities. Jesus rebukes the disciples, calling Peter Satan—an adversary of God—and trying to convince him and all the disciples to set their minds on "divine things," that is, to look at reality from God's perspective. All this happens right before the text we read today. Jesus does not back down, but rather tells the disciples that what is going to happen to him will also happen to them. Just as he finishes talking about his suffering with the announcement of his resurrection, Jesus not only leads the disciples to contemplate the difficulties that await them, but also puts before them the eschatological reward they will receive (v. 21).

Jesus starts by telling the disciples that if they are indeed going to come after him, to follow him, they must "deny themselves." Warren Carter explains what it means to deny oneself. "[It] is to renounce the practice of telling God and God's agent how God's purposes are best accomplished. It is to refuse to place oneself ahead of, or in the place of, the revealer."[5]

In the context of this whole passage, Jesus tells the disciples they cannot fear political and religious authorities. They will be able to stand up to them if they put their trust in God instead of in themselves (vv. 24–25). To take up the cross is not to embrace the violent symbol of subjugation used by the Romans but rather to instill in it new meaning in order to counter oppressive powers. That is precisely what Jesus' resurrection will do, and that is what his disciples will do in remaining open and faithful to the God of Jesus. Verse 25 further explains this reversal of the symbol of the cross: one loses one's life if one tries to save it by giving in to the intimidation of the authorities. However, if one puts on God's mind-set, then one will save one's life even when those with power oppress and kill one. At the heart of this teaching is loyalty to Jesus and to kin-dom, which he is working to establish.

Carter points out that the words "profit," "gain," and "forfeit" place this instruction of Jesus within the realm of the "everyday political, social, economic, and religious life, which though created by God, is claimed by the devil and in need of saving."[6] If the disciples are interested in gaining power, wealth, and status, they are not looking at reality from God's perspective and they will, therefore, not be part of the kin-dom of God now or at the end of times.

---

5. Warren Carter, *Matthew and the Margins: A Sociopolitical and Religious Reading* (Maryknoll, NY: Orbis Books, 2000), 343.
6. Ibid., 345.

Romero, preaching on a text parallel to this one, said the following a year before he was murdered, on April 1, 1979.

> Those who, in the biblical phrase, would save their lives—that is, those who want to get along, who don't want commitments, who don't want to get into problems, who want to stay outside of a situation that demands the involvement of all of us—they will lose their lives.
>
> What a terrible thing to have lived quite comfortably, with no suffering, not getting involved in problems, quite tranquil, quite settled, with good connections politically, economically, socially—lacking nothing, having everything.
>
> To what good?
>
> They will lose their lives.[7]

Verse 27 turns attention to the Parousia, the return of Jesus. On its heels another enigmatic verse anticipates the fullness of the kin-dom of God realized in the present (v. 28). Can we read "the Son of [Humanity] coming in his kingdom" to mean that those who follow Jesus will begin to see a new reality taking shape during their lifetime? Perhaps this realization was the reason why Romero, in the midst of such danger, could say convincingly the day before he was murdered, "Lent is a call to celebrate our redemption in that difficult combination of cross and victory. . . . Our people are well prepared to do so these days; all our environment proclaims the cross. But those who have Christian faith and hope know that behind this Calvary of El Salvador lies our Easter, our resurrection. That is the Christian people's hope."[8]

7. Romero, *Violence of Love*, 154.
8. Ibid., 241.

Fifth Sunday in Lent

Lee H. Butler Jr.

ISAIAH 43:16–21
PSALM 126
PHILIPPIANS 3:4B–14
JOHN 12:1–8

One thread running through each of the texts is God restoring life to the people. Living day-to-day is a series of gains and losses. There will always be an oppressed people, a victimized people, or a poor people, because systemic evil will always seek to dominate this or that group. We must not forget that God is our ever-present help, if we only open our eyes to discern what God is doing. Too often we focus dreadfully on what others have done against us instead of discerning the generative and regenerative power of God. While the road to freedom can be filled with struggle, despair, feelings of aimlessness, and emptiness, God will give us what we need to sustain us through it all.

Be open to know the present activities of the Lord. God declares that our circumstances will be totally transformed. We shall not be isolated nor desolated forever. In the end, God shall restore our losses as a gift from God.

Isaiah 43:16–21

With allusions to events of the past, the prophet describes the Lord God through the actions of God. The prophet describes God as one who makes a way for us when an exit strategy seems impossible. God, who the prophet declares is about to speak, is described as an undefeatable warrior. In an age when we understand warfare to be highly technological and mechanized, when biological manipulations become the next weapons of mass destruction, the description of the prophet continues to define God as greater.

Considering what human ingenuity is capable of producing, it is difficult for many to imagine a God who is capable of doing more than we are in our efforts to overcome the obstacles of nature. We build massive ships that travel on the water. We build powerful submarines that stealthily move underwater. Both ship and submarine carry the most powerful weapons known to human-kind, including armed forces capable of cutting a path of destruction. In spite of our sense of superiority over nature, the levees of New Orleans did break, and other structures designed to withstand great waters do erode. Ships can sink. Submarines can be crushed by water pressure. And no army is invincible.

Hence, God is declared as the one who is able to control the great waters and has power over nature. The prophet's description of God, which is grounded in salvation history, declares that God can control the power of human innovations and the war machine. If we accept the description of the prophet, there is nothing, in all our might, that we can do against God that God will experience as anything more than a minor irritation. Our fires initiated by napalm are as the wick of an oil lamp that God would easily snuff out.

Although the prophet seems to be alluding to things of the past, he declares that God says not to remember the events of the past. Memory can be strength and a resource for survival. Memory can provide a reference point for interpreting events and life circumstances. By remembering the things of the past, one can avoid repeating the mistakes of the past. Remembering one's mistakes can lead to greater successes in one's future. But memory can also be a hindrance. Continuing to hold on to a narrative too tightly can cause one to be stuck in time. Clinging too tightly to a memory can also cause a person to misinterpret life. If you hold too tightly to the former things, you will not be able to embrace new things. This is the critique of many as it relates to the importance of civil rights history and its relevance for today. Is our reference and remembrance of civil rights backward thinking?

The Lord declares, "I am about to do a new thing" (v. 19a). The statement suggests a future action of God. But God goes on to say, "now" (v. 19b). It is not simply a future promise; it is a present and immediate reality. It is the here, but not yet. The Lord cares for and restores the chosen by being present as a sustaining Spirit to encourage their hopeful resistance. Without our memory of the activities of God during the Civil Rights Movement, we have no context for experiencing the new thing that God is doing to advance justice in the here and now. Furthermore, we cannot rest knowing there remains a good that is "yet to come" in the actions of God.

Psalm 126

When God reversed the fortunes of God's people by restoring all that had been lost, their astonishment caused them to experience the moment as a dream. They experienced the moment as a future hope not yet realized. Most people understand dreaming as an act of living into one's deepest hopes and desires in a fanciful way. A dream, therefore, can be the unconscious experience of acting out what one hopes will become one's lived experience. Once their fortunes had been restored, the people thought, "This can't be real!"

America, as the land of dreamers, knows this experience quite well. Many Americans continue to seek the American dream of prosperity. When Senator Barack Obama became the first African American president of the United States, the language of dreams dominated the moment. The deep emotions associated with being African American, coupled with a long struggle for human and civil rights, gave the experience of the moment a surreal quality. This was a dream that was no longer deferred, but the initial experience was astonishment. Many experienced the moment as though God had restored our fortunes. Many identified the moment as a dream come true.

The people, realizing that they were not asleep and were not dreaming something unreal, began to celebrate with laughter and much merrymaking. When people celebrate with good cause, others will look and affirm the importance of the celebration. As was true for the psalmist, nations from around the globe gazed on the United States and declared that a marvelous thing had been done through the election process. World leaders viewed the American people as having taken an important step in their own development as a nation.

It is important that we acknowledge and accept the great gifts given us by God. In our acceptance, we ought also to rejoice and give thanks. Although our labors have been difficult, our hope in God leads us to believe that our harvest will be bountiful. Therefore, we ought to continue laboring and hoping, in spite of the challenges and adversities, knowing that God will bless us bountifully.

Philippians 3:4b–14

Many people govern their lives by the idea that "pride comes before the fall." Viewing pride as a negative attribute moves people to debase beauty as a way of resisting pride. Beautiful attributes of our humanity are regularly degraded. People bear a deep inclination to single out and degrade qualities and attributes thought to be features of otherness. A race can be degraded. Sex and gender can be degraded. Racialized sexuality can be degraded. A social class or community can be degraded. The restoration of any of these degraded attributes requires the reversal of the distortions. Advocating pride becomes an important means of restoration. Pride is identified as one of the seven deadly sins, and few contexts in the Christian heritage acknowledge pride as a good thing. For those people who have experienced extreme oppression, had their identities distorted, and been denied positive self-regard, instilling pride is an important and necessary process. In those instances, pride is far from sin.

The writer declares that he has many reasons to boast. In fact, he says he has more reasons to boast than most. In any category of identification where one might take pride, he says he has more reason to be proud (v. 4b). He goes on, however, to explain how he tempers his pride. He considers all of his achievements to be the direct result of his relationship with Jesus as the Christ (vv. 8–9). He speaks of gains and losses, of grief and rejoicing, as a way of regulating his feelings of pride. Essentially he moves from naming pride as positive to identifying pride as a problem. Yet if we unreflectively adopt this same move, making all pride a problem for everyone, then those whose humanity has been most profoundly degraded will not develop some important pathways of restoration to the glory of God's creation.

Given the cautions against pride that we already live with, where should a person place her or his confidence? I hear the writer suggesting that our confidence should be grounded in our faith and knowledge of the Christ. Whereas pride can sometimes be used to avert suffering and hardship, we must acknowledge that life is a struggle for everyone. Through faith, the powerless become powerful and experience the full meaning of life; yet this experience is not devoid of suffering. Instead of grounding life's purpose in self-worth and pride, the writer suggests we ought to live in hope. While we should never forget the events of the past, we should not allow those events to immobilize us. When we cling to a past as glory achieved, we fail to live into the beauty that God desires for us. Rather than allowing ourselves to be narrowly defined by the events of the past, we must press, struggle, or even strain for the heavenly prize in Christ that calls to us all.

John 12:1–8

Jesus arrives in Bethany six days before the Passover. The identification of six days is possibly a reference to the importance of laboring for six days and resting on the seventh. We must always remember to keep the Sabbath holy. Jesus is once again at the home of Lazarus, Mary, and Martha. Lazarus is at the dinner table with Jesus as a living testimony of the power of life over death. We see in Lazarus that it is possible to be freed from the grip of death. As the narrative develops, Judas and Lazarus's sister Mary of Bethany are introduced to the story. Some persons may associate Mary's costly perfume with Judas, which shifts the attention from Lazarus. If, however, the costly perfume is associated with Lazarus, its beautiful fragrance takes on a different meaning.

Before Jesus raised Lazarus from the dead, the people were hesitant to roll back the stone from the grave, commenting that Lazarus by this time would be stinking from decay. Following the direction of Jesus, they removed the stone, and Jesus restored life to Lazarus's decaying body. As a result, the dinner in honor of Jesus was accompanied by a sweet-smelling fragrance (v. 3). Rather than the house being filled with the stench of death, the perfume filled the house in a celebration of life. Instead of the costly perfume attempting to mask the presence of death, it participated in the celebration of life being restored.

Judas, the conflicted disciple, was also present at the celebration. Although this text presents Judas as a thief (v. 6), there are many different opinions on Judas. There is no clear evidence to indicate that Judas would have been the one to sell the perfume and disburse the proceeds to the poor. Furthermore, the indication that Judas is a thief seems a bit odd here in light of Jesus saying that Mary bought the perfume. Jesus goes on to say that she bought it to keep it for the day of his burial. The fact that she chooses to use it at this dinner celebration suggests that she chose to give Jesus his flowers while he was alive. This dinner and anointing celebrated life in appreciation for the gift of life she received when Jesus raised her brother from the dead.

César Chávez Day (March 31)

Frederick John Dalton

ZECHARIAH 8:9–17
PSALM 73:1–20
2 CORINTHIANS 2:14–17
MATTHEW 20:1–16

César Chávez Day, March 31, commemorates the birthday of César Chávez (1927–1993), a Mexican American who was moved by the poor working conditions, exploitative wages, and other injustices against Latino and Latina farm workers in the United States. Chávez organized the United Farm Workers, which led to upgrading the quality of life for such workers. In addition to honoring Chávez, this day calls attention to the solidarity needed to correct injustice, especially when injustice is inflicted upon workers. César Chávez Day further celebrates the ways in which Hispanic peoples enrich and strengthen the larger life of North America.

It is not good enough to know why we are oppressed and by whom. We must join the struggle for what is right and just! Jesus does not promise it will be an easy way to live and his own life certainly points in a hard direction; but he does promise we will be "satisfied" (not stuffed, but satisfied). He promises that by giving life we will find life—full meaningful life as God meant it to be.

César Chávez[1]

Today's Scripture readings invite us to consider workers, wherever they may labor.[2] Zechariah uses the imagery of field workers possessing the harvest

---

1. Mario T. García, ed., *The Gospel of César Chávez: My Faith in Action* (New York: Sheed & Ward, 2007), 86.
2. In researching the readings of the day, I am indebted to the following scholars: Aelred Cody, "Haggai, Zechariah, Malachi," in *The New Jerome Biblical Commentary*, ed. Raymond E. Brown, Joseph A. Fitzmyer, and Roland E. Murphy (Englewood Cliffs, NJ: Prentice Hall, 1990);

of the land as he promises a future society of peace rooted in truth and justice. The psalmist wrestles with God's presence in a world of prosperity and suffering. Jesus' parable of the Laborers in the Vineyard in Matthew's Gospel reveals God's justice in the kingdom of heaven, a revelation that leaves us astounded and grumbling. Paul warns his readers to beware of false gospels preached by peddlers of death. The gospel of God in Jesus is a gospel of life. In a global economy where so many workers struggle mightily for the bare necessities of life, today's readings have the power to convert our hearts and transform the world.

Zechariah 8:9–17

Today's Scripture reading from the prophet Zechariah speaks to the hearts of farm workers everywhere. Field laborers have strong hands that harvest the fruit of the vine and the produce of the land. Farm workers in this nation and around the world know what it is to toil without adequate wages in harsh and unsafe working conditions. The foes that stalk farm laborers are impoverishment, hunger, unemployment, illiteracy, homelessness, discrimination, and ill health. Against overwhelming obstacles, field workers struggle for a life of dignity, true justice, and blessings of prosperity and peace for their families.

The book of Zechariah is commonly divided into two parts, chapters 1–8 and 9–14, with each part generally considered an independent work. The prophetic oracles, beginning at 7:1 and ending at 8:23, evaluate the past and look to the future. The historical context is the return of the Israelites from exile in Babylon and the rebuilding of the temple at Jerusalem. Zechariah recalls a time of hardships without wages or safety or peace (v. 10). The nation suffered because of evil actions by their ancestors, which provoked the Lord's wrath (v. 14). The text promises that the Lord will treat the surviving remnant in a different manner (v. 11), blessing them with prosperity and safety in the future (vv. 12–13). The Lord comforts the people with the words "do not be afraid" (v. 15) and commands the people to speak the truth to one another, render true justice and make peace, stop scheming against one another, and avoid attachment to lies (vv. 16–17).

César Chávez's life testifies to rendering true justice for the sake of authentic peace. For more than thirty years César Chávez lived as a poor man in solidarity with the poorest workers in the United States. He insisted that the heart and soul of the union community was the willingness to live a simple life

---

Mary Margaret Pazdan, "Zechariah," in *The Collegeville Bible Commentary*, ed. Dianne Bergant and Robert J. Karris (Collegeville, MN: Liturgical Press, 1989); Richard A. Clifford, "Psalms," in *Collegeville Bible Commentary*; Benedict T. Viviano, "The Gospel according to Matthew," in *New Jerome Biblical Commentary*; Daniel J. Harrington, "Matthew," in *Collegeville Bible Commentary*.

characterized by voluntary poverty, sacrificial service of others, and nonviolent activism. While many people admired him, many others reviled Chávez. He was denounced and opposed by growers who saw the farm worker movement as a threat to business as usual. His opponents were correct. César Chávez and the United Farm Workers were trying to end business as usual by establishing another way of doing business, a way in which field laborers could share the fruits of their labor and live in dignity as equal and respected members of society. César Chávez had the audacity to believe that farm workers were important human beings:

> They are important because of the work they do. They are not implements to be used and discarded. They are human beings who sweat and sacrifice to bring food to the tables of millions and millions of people throughout the world. They are important because God made them, gave them life, and cares for them in life and in death.[3]

He imagined a world where every worker benefits from a steady job with good wages and decent conditions and lives in dignity as a child of God. True peace is the fruit of justice, and César's agenda was justice for field laborers.

Psalm 73:1–20

Farm laborers pick the tomatoes, cut the grapevines, gather the olives, dig the potatoes, cut the sugarcane, rake the coffee, reach for the apples, and stoop for the strawberries. They milk the cows, shear the sheep, prune the trees, and bunch the flowers. The products they harvest are transported to markets and tables down the road and around the world. In the global economy agriculture is big business. Transnational corporate conglomerates dominate production, transportation, and marketing of agricultural products. Money flows through the system, leading to expansion, innovation, productivity, and profits. Yet the poor who do the picking, digging, cutting, stooping, and pruning remain poor. They work the land for meager wages season after season with little chance of earning enough money to live in dignity. The plight of farm workers in a global economy of wealth and luxury is not merely poverty; it is destitution. The reality of globalization is that some people prosper while more people suffer. Astonishingly the psalmist links prosperity and wickedness, poverty and righteousness.

Why do some people prosper while others suffer? If God is good to the righteous, why do the wicked prosper? These questions are at the heart of today's psalm. The psalmist presumes that God rewards the righteous and

---

3. Frederick John Dalton, *The Moral Vision of César Chávez* (Maryknoll, NY: Orbis Books, 2003), 9.

punishes the wicked (v. 1). Yet the wicked prosper (v. 3). Many good and decent people live in appalling poverty, suffer cruelly, and die anonymously. Meanwhile, evil and offensive people accumulate astonishing wealth, live by ostentation and pleasure, and die esteemed. Psalm 73 tells us that the righteous strive for purity of heart but are tempted to be envious of the wicked (v. 2). The psalmist presents a detailed description of the wicked in the next nine verses (vv. 4–12). The wicked have healthy bodies that are trim and fit; they exude pride and confidence; they are at ease in life and speak their opinions without hesitation; they are rich and become richer. The wicked are also violent, bloated, stupid, malicious, haughty, oppressive, and boastful rather than faithful. After describing the prosperous wicked, the hymn turns to the righteous. The upright try to understand why the good suffer and the evil prosper, but it makes no sense (v. 16). When the righteous endure physical suffering on a daily basis, it seems that the effort to live a good life is all in vain (vv. 13–14). Yet, according to the psalm, the clean of heart find solace by encountering God in prayer (v. 17). God is united with the poor in a special way. The power of prayer awakens the heart to the only reality, the truth of God. All else is a dream, which will be swept away in a moment. United with God in prayer, the clean of heart experience the sanctuary, which only the faithful know—that God is indeed good to the righteous.

Matthew 20:1–16

Every morning brings uncertainty and hope to workers who must earn their daily bread through physical labor. Workers gather on busy urban avenues and dusty rural roads hoping to be hired so they can eat and have shelter and maybe send some money home to loved ones. Farm workers hope the peaches are ripe or the lettuce needs thinning and the farm labor contractors have room in the vans leaving for the fields. Day laborers seek jobs as gardeners, painters, construction workers, and dishwashers. Many of the day laborers who crowd street corners were once farm workers who toiled in fields and orchards. Steady jobs with good wages and decent conditions are too much to hope for, yet they hope every morning.

In Matthew's Gospel, Jesus' parable of the Laborers in the Vineyard follows the story of the rich young man, and the two stories should be understood in light of each other. The inability of the rich young man to sell his possessions and follow Jesus contrasts with God's generosity in the parable of the Laborers in the Vineyard. The last verse of the section before today's reading establishes the link between the two stories: "But many who are first will be last, and the last will be first" (19:30). Today's parable reveals that God acts generously to include everyone in the kingdom, something that is difficult for us to understand. God has a generous love for all, especially for the poor who otherwise would be excluded and unable to meet their needs. This preferential love for the poor seems unfair to us, but it is just: "Friend, I am doing you no wrong" (v. 13). We grumble about unfairness when others are treated with graciousness: "They didn't work as hard or as long; they didn't earn it; they don't deserve it." Our sense of justice is based on work and merit, and yet here is a story of the justice of generous love. God fulfills the hope of workers with generous love. If the hopes of workers today are not fulfilled, perhaps it is because we are not as loving or generous as the kingdom calls us to be. The kingdom of heaven is difficult for us to grasp. The grumbling laborers parallel the astounded apostles in the preceding story (19:25). The stories of the rich young man and the laborers in the vineyard reveal the eschatological reversal of fortune brought about by God's reign where, as today's reading ends, "the last will be first, and the first will be last" (v. 16). God's love is astounding, so let us respond to that love with generosity toward one another, especially the workers among us.

2 Corinthians 2:14–17

Migrant farm workers have great difficulty finding housing. Often they cannot afford or find decent shelter. Garages are home for some workers. Some laborers live in their cars, others find shelter under bridges or overpasses, and still others live in "camps" of tents or shacks. Some camps appear and disappear in a single season, while other camps remain season after season. Workers live for long periods at a time without access to clean water or sanitary facilities or electricity. The unpleasant odors of pesticides, herbicides, fertilizers, and animal waste fill the air of agricultural areas and permeate clothes and skin. Dust and dirt are everywhere. Farm work is strenuous, and after a day in the hot sun sometimes the only option for bathing is a garden hose or an irrigation canal or a bathroom sink in a gas station along the highway. Poverty does not have pleasant odors; there is a stench to injustice.

In today's reading Paul defends himself to the community at Corinth by telling them that authentic preaching leads to true knowledge of God, which grows within us and leads to life. The wisdom that Paul preaches in Christ is like a delightful fragrance, an image found in Sirach 24:13–17, where wisdom is described in terms of plants with fragrant blossoms that bring forth glorious fruit. Paul writes to the Corinthians that there is a fundamental difference between those who have faith and those who do not. It is the difference between life and death (vv. 15–16). Faith is a gift from God, as is the mission to preach the word of God in Christ. Paul contrasts his own sincerity and the authenticity of his spiritual message with others who preach for money and peddle a phony spiritual vision (v. 17). Every Christian community must recognize spiritual peddlers who sell a spurious gospel—cheap perfume to cover up the stench of injustice, if only we purchase enough of it. The so-called wisdom of the world leads to worn-out and dirty workers who suffer dehumanizing injustice. The wisdom of God in Christ leads to life in glorious fulfillment for all people, for the wisdom of God is justice and righteousness in generous love.

Sixth Sunday in Lent
(Liturgy of the Palms)

Teresa Lockhart Stricklen

PSALM 118:1–2, 19–29
LUKE 19:28–40

Oral cultures, such as those of the ancient world, often used symbols to draw whole worlds of associative meanings together in one word. Modern analysis of a part can often miss the fluidity of the whole. This commentary will focus on tracing the dynamic allusions to past events, people, places, and things, in order to highlight the textural richness of these Scriptures.

Psalm 118:1–2, 19–29

Brent Kinman notes that Jesus' triumphal entry has the same elements as the narratives and psalms surrounding the procession of the ark of the covenant into Jerusalem (see Num. 10:35–36; Josh. 7:6–7; 1 Sam. 4:6–7; 2 Sam. 6).[1] The enthronement psalms, which include Psalm 118, also depict the glory of the Lord's presence coming to rule Israel.

Psalm 118 pictures the Lord coming into the temple like a victorious warrior who has put down the enemy, ushering in a reign of peace for the people. The psalm gives thanks to the Lord, leading the people in a cheering procession (vv. 1–4). The victor testifies as to how God saved him though he was surrounded (vv. 5–18). Then he calls to the people to open the gates of righteousness that he might go into God's house to celebrate the Lord (v. 19) because that which was cast off as nothing has become the principal stone in God's house (v. 22). A call to worship then ensues (v. 24): "This is the day that the LORD has made; let us rejoice and be glad in it!" Then the psalm pleads

---

1. Brent Kinman, *Jesus' Entry into Jerusalem*, Arbeiten zur Geschichte des antiken Judentums und des Urchristentums 28 (Leiden: E. J. Brill, 1995), 59–60.

to God to save the people and give them prosperity (v. 25) before blessing the one who comes in the name of the Lord (v. 26). The subsequent verses lead the people up to the altar of God, where sacrifice is made for the goodness and everlasting mercy of the Lord (vv. 27–29).

Pilgrims in Jesus' day would have sung such enthronement psalms in going up to the temple. In former years, during the Feast of Tabernacles, which celebrated the giving of Torah and God's dwelling with us, the psalm would have been liturgically reenacted as the ark came into the temple with the covenant tablets in it. God's presence would have been celebrated as a returning victor.

The people of Luke's Gospel recite part of this psalm ("Blessed is the king who comes in the name of the Lord!") thereby drawing in all the rich allusions of God's sovereignty, the presence of God, Torah, covenant, and sacrifice that are historically operative in this enthronement psalm. The early church would have seen Jesus as the triumphant victor returning after a battle with evil, going into the temple, making intercession, and offering himself as the sacrifice so that God's mercy could flow to his people.

One of the images of the psalm, that of the stone rejected by the builder becoming the most important stone of the building (v. 22), is especially rich when seen in the light of Luke's mention that should the people keep silent, the very stones would cry out (Luke 19:40). Indeed, the symbol of stones in both Psalm 118 and the whole of Luke can be seen as drawing in a whole world of allusive meaning around the themes of covenant, God's providence, and sacrifice, to which we now turn.

When Jesus set his face to go to Jerusalem, people would have heard echoes of Isaiah's Suffering Servant who "set [his] face like flint" (Isa. 50:7). Flint was used for knives that circumcised Jewish males as a sign of covenant with God. It was also the rock out of which God made water flow in the desert (Deut. 8:15; Ps. 114:8). Interestingly enough, one of the other few times that flint is used in the First Testament is in reference to military horses' hooves (Isa. 5:28), but when seen against Isaiah's mandate to trust not in chariots but only in the Lord (31:1), it becomes clear that God's sovereign way of peace, which is manifest in the weak things of this world, is stronger than the military might of nations.

It is no coincidence that altars are to be made of stone. In Deuteronomy 32:4, God specifies Godself as Israel's rock before going on to point out that the Holy One nursed Israel with the sweetness and light of honey from the rock and oil from flint (Deut. 32:13). Our relationship, our everlasting covenant, with God is rock solid, founded on the goodness and providence of the sovereign Lord.

Stones are also often associated with covenant making, remembering, and renewal in the First Testament. The Torah is written on stone. Covenants and epiphanies are remembered with memorial stones.[2] When Isaiah encourages us to "look to the rock from which you were hewn" (Isa. 51:1–2), he is referring to the Abrahamic covenant, which John the Baptizer plays with when he preaches, "Bear fruits worthy of repentance. Do not begin to say to yourselves, 'We have Abraham as our ancestor'; for I tell you, God is able from these stones to raise up children to Abraham" (Luke 3:8).

Luke 19:28–40

These stony allusions are noteworthy because Jesus is consistently depicted in Luke as someone who breaks Second Temple purity codes to return to the foundation of the Abrahamic covenant whereby all the peoples of the earth, not just those who could keep ritual purity, will be blessed through Israel's covenant. For this theological emphasis on the Abrahamic covenant rather than the temple purity codes, Jesus is constantly harassed by religious leaders who have worked out a careful system whereby they can remain Jewish under imperial occupation. Jesus' emphasis on the divine foundational Abrahamic covenant threatens Israel's peace; hence he is the rejected stone. Yet the godly rock-solid covenant-keeper becomes the keystone of the new temple. The old temple's stones will be cast down (21:6), and a new temple of Christ's resurrected body, the living stones of Christ's disciples (1 Pet. 2:4–10), will be established.

Luke's triumphal entry is full of other allusions to signal that the anticipated Messiah is entering the temple, making claims on prophecies foretold (Zech. 9:9–10), *except* that he does not wield power as we expect. Jesus is no military leader. Instead, our Sovereign comes to us lowly and riding on a colt to usher in God's reign of peace.

This passage also includes other First Testament allusions to assert Jesus' sovereignty. Jesus starts the procession on the Mount of Olives, recalling another passage from Zechariah 14 asserting God's sovereignty. Luke, however, elucidates that the nature of Jesus' sovereignty is one of "peace in heaven, and glory in the highest heaven" (v. 38)—not a peace brokered by military maneuvers, which many triumphal entries in the Roman world celebrated. Luke thus plays with the Zechariah allusions to contrast Jesus' reign of peace with the militaristic apocalyptic expectations of his day.

Other First Testament allusions rattle in the background of this text. First Kings 1 depicts a similar coronation with Solomon riding on King David's mule (1 Kgs. 1:34, 38–40). Another of David's son's, Adonijah, attempted to usurp the kingship earlier and had taken horses and chariots to signify a royal

2. See Gen. 35:14; Josh. 4, for example.

entourage and garner support for his coup d'état. He rode to "the serpent stone" (Zoheleth) to be crowned (1 Kgs. 1:5–9). Solomon, though, is passively placed on King David's mule and rides to Gihon, a pool near Jerusalem whose name recalls one of the rivers of paradise. Luke is clear that Jesus does not get on the donkey; he is set on it (v. 35), like Solomon. Luke's obscure reference to Solomon's royal entry signifies Jesus' entrance to Jerusalem. In being willing to take this mission to its human end, even unto tortuous death, Jesus ascends to the sovereign throne as God's resurrection power vindicates his way of life, thereby restoring the possibility of paradise for all. For Luke, God's reign happens with a divine gift, not the forcefulness of human will.

The people of Luke's Gospel acclaim Jesus as their Sovereign, quoting Psalm 118:26, as noted before. This was blasphemous, not to mention treasonous. Such an action could result in Roman military slaughter of the people, so it is no wonder some Pharisees tell Jesus to rebuke his disciples (v. 39). Jesus refuses, though, telling them that if they were to keep silent, the very stones would cry out (v. 40). Jesus essentially says that he has to do what is in accord with the divine mission. The destructive powers will do what they have to do; God's followers will do what they have to do.

In addition to the other allusive meanings of the stones already discussed, Luke may also be alluding to Habakkuk 2:10–11, where the stones will cry out demanding divine justice when the wicked "have devised shame for [their] house by cutting off many peoples." It is no coincidence that one of the first things Jesus does is cleanse the temple because its economics marginalized the poor (Luke 19:45–46). The reign of Christ requires the inclusion of all people in the economy of God, a commonwealth of the divine inheritance.

Luke's crowd hails Jesus as "king." Jesus conscripts the colt with royal authority (vv. 30–31). His procession is somewhat like Roman triumphal entries. Luke is clear: Jesus is Lord of the universe whose acclamations ring through even stones that will be broken open with resurrection new life. Yet Jesus is a king who executes justice for all, which, as the whole of Luke's Gospel clearly depicts, includes all people marginalized by the Second Temple purity codes—the lame, the blind, the leprous, demoniacs, harlots, tax collectors, Samaritans, Canaanite bitches. Such a list would have been as scandalous as a list of racketeers, sex workers, AIDS patients, addicts, and terrorists is to us. God's sovereignty extends to all of creation, even dumb rocks. Gentiles, children, slaves, and women are exalted as equal to Jewish males. Here is a radical gospel.

In proclaiming Jesus as the sovereign God, we need to be aware of how our depictions of divine power affect those whose access to power has been cut off. If we preach that we are to exercise power like the meek and mild Jesus of our Sunday school days, we are not being altogether biblical. Jesus is not humble in Luke; his face is set like flint to go to Jerusalem to speak to the powers-that-be there, to call out "that old fox" Herod, and to castigate those who oppress the poor, the sick, the marginalized by keeping them from the divine presence—hardly the actions of a meek and mild person who would just as soon avoid the hotbed of political turmoil. Jesus' Way offended many people; otherwise, he would not have been crucified. Luke portrays Jesus with an impudent audacity; Jesus has divine power, which he wields for us and for our salvation through the blood of his sacrifice on the cross of destructive human power.

Only those with power can willingly give it up, however. Asking abused women, children, and the elderly, for example, to trust in God's sovereignty while "bearing their cross" of abuse merits charges of clergy malpractice. The people whom God asks to humble themselves are those who are exalted, arrogant with their power, as the Magnificat proclaims (Luke 1:46–55). Though suffering may result as we, too, confront the powers-that-be with the sovereign Way of God, *everyone* triumphs who follows Christ, for through his ascension, we can all be admitted into the throne room of grace to live within the *shalom* of God's justice, peace, harmony, and wholeness.

Sixth Sunday in Lent
(Liturgy of the Passion)

Teresa Lockhart Stricklen

ISAIAH 50:4–9A
PSALM 31:9–16
PHILIPPIANS 2:5–11
LUKE 22:14–23:56

The passion narrative tells the story of God's passion for us in Jesus Christ, showing us that God will spare nothing to tell us of the divine way of love and justice. Ironically, though, this message occurs in the midst of violence, degradation, and humiliation.

Psalm 31:9–16

A more extensive treatment of this passage occurs in Year A of this series. Couched in a prayer, this passage describes the extreme distress of a victim of torture, abuse, shunning, and/or betrayal. It is easy to see why it was chosen to accompany the passion narrative. Though Jesus heard "terror all around" (v. 13) as people plotted to execute him, he nonetheless trusted in God with the prayer that the Lord's face look upon him with steadfast love (vv. 14, 16). Unlike the author of the psalm, Jesus did not live, but died, though in the end God saved not only him but all of humanity, through the life, death, and resurrection of Christ.

The psalm can be helpful in explicating a Christology that avoids the divine requirement for a victim to appease a wrathful God. With justice in order to follow divine love, Christ can be seen as the one who steps in to take the abuse of sin in our place, similar to someone stepping in front of us to take a bullet or to absorb an abuser's blows so that we might escape. Trusting and drawing strength from the power of resurrection love, we, too, can stand up to the abuse of sin for the sake of God's dominion even in the midst of death-dealing chaos.

Isaiah 50:4–9a

The passage opens with the Suffering Servant declaring that God continually teaches him so that he can be a teacher who knows how to sustain the weary with a timely word (v. 4). He was not rebellious, nor did he turn back from his mission (v. 5). Though he could have run away, he gave his back to the smiters and those who intended to shame him with their abuse, which he looked square in the face (v. 6), trusting the God who is near (vv. 7–8). Here is a picture of trust in the goodness and justice of God in the midst of torture. God helps those whose lives are set like flint against injustice, whereas adversaries to God's way will wear out like a moth-eaten garment, full of exposing holes (v. 9).

The movie *Gandhi* accurately depicts the nonviolent Dharasana Salt Works protest in a way that echoes Isaiah 50. Six abreast, the marchers go forth resolutely to meet soldiers. They do not resist and are beaten until they fall to the ground. Women then drag the men off to minister to their wounds, and the next six protesters step forward to take their beating. This goes on for hours. When exposed by media reports, the British atrocities cause the adversaries to Gandhi's cause to come near to him (v. 8), and British imperialism begins to unravel in India.

It is no wonder that the early church saw Jesus as Isaiah's Suffering Servant. In going forward to the cross, he confronted the abuse of sin and took its blows squarely, without resistance. With Jesus' nonviolent exposure of sin on the cross and his vindicating resurrection, God's truth and justice prevail over death-dealing ways, surely sustaining the weary with this Word.

Luke 22:14–23:56

Luke's passion narrative serves the rhetoric of the Gospel as a whole: it shows the nature of God's sovereign power. Jesus is depicted as a kind of ironic king whose sovereignty outfoxes Herod, Pilate, and the religious leaders.

Like Matthew and Mark, Luke's passion narrative opens with the plot to kill Jesus by the chief priests and scribes. The anointing at Bethany, however, does not follow here. Instead, we see larger forces at work to indicate the cosmic nature of Jesus' apocalyptic battle on the cross. Satan, who had departed from Jesus after the temptation to await "an opportune time" (Luke 4:13), finds Judas open to such opportunity as he strikes a deal to betray Jesus. Perhaps Judas, as a Zealot, desired to force Jesus to take his role as the ruler of the Jews. Jesus' royalty, however, is revealed in ways that differ from the Zealots' expectations.

Indeed, the Passover supper Jesus shares with his disciples announces the nature of Jesus' reign. His new interpretation of the meal indicates that he will not drink wine again until the kingdom of God has come (22:18) and that this reign will happen through the sacrifice of his body and blood (22:19–20). References to the reign of God bookend the whole account, so that the early church would have understood that the odd things Jesus said at this meal pertain to the anticipated sovereign feast with the crucified Jesus as the Passover lamb. Jesus' command for all to share in these elements also indicates the commonwealth ethic whereby all had everything in common and shared with those in need (Acts 2:44–45). Everyone sharing in the prayerful elements of a simple meal—how different from the power grab that constitutes a military coup!

The commonwealth meal leads into teaching on how power is used in God's dominion. Who is the greatest according to God's Way? Those who serve others (22:25–26)! Such service comprises the commonwealth Jesus confers on them (22:29). No keys of power are given with this conferral, as in Matthew 16:19, only the promise that Christ is among us "as one who serves" (22:27). Ironically, Jesus confers the reign of God to "those who have stood by me in my trials" (22:28–29), knowing that, like Peter, they will flee his upcoming trial out of fear (22:31–34). Those who sit on the thrones of God's realm, then, possess none of the world's normal leadership qualities. They are betrayers, cowards, grumblers, dolts—fighting to sit on divine thrones like children during an intense game of musical chairs. Their only qualification, then, is that they are servants of God's commonwealth who are grateful that Christ knows our every weakness (22:31, 34), prays for us (22:32), watches for our turning back (15:20), and forgives us (23:34).

The Lord's reign here does not anticipate an apocalyptic battle on this day, though. Jesus tells them to pack a bag, take a purse, and buy swords—all of which reads like an inventory for battle preparations. If this is preparation for an eschatological military battle, it is downright hilarious: "We have two swords!" the disciples exult (22:38). This apocalyptic spoof may well be Luke's point, for they depart to the Mount of Olives, the place where the anticipated apocalypse was to occur (Zech. 14). Here, Jesus, terrified, prays in the garden while the disciples sleep. So much for the readiness of apocalyptic heroes! The big battle scene comes in the garden when Peter uses one of the two swords to cut off Caiaphas's slave's ear, which Jesus then miraculously reattaches (22:49–51). So much for eschatological battles! "Not with swords' loud clashing," the hymn sings, but "with deeds of love and mercy the heavenly kingdom comes."[1]

---

1. Ernest W. Shurtleff, "Lead On, O King Eternal," in *The Presbyterian Hymnal* (Louisville, KY: Westminster/John Knox Press, 1990), 447.

Luke plays with the anticipated resurrection language associated with the apocalypse. After Jesus responds to their questions, the council rises (from Gk. *anastemi*, the same word used for Jesus' resurrection, which means "stand up"). The upstanding stood up to lead Jesus to Pilate, where we hear additional charges that pique the empire's interest: "He says he's our king who forbids us to pay taxes." Pilate asks if he is the king of the Jews, and again Jesus responds, "You say so," at which point Pilate dismisses the charge as ludicrous (23:1–4). How could such a one possibly lead an insurrection against Rome? Still reluctant to deal with Jesus, Pilate hears that he is a Galilean and sees a way to be rid of him—he can send him to Herod, who has jurisdiction over him. Jesus refuses to answer Herod, so Herod joins the religious leaders and his soldiers in mocking him as a king before sending him back to Pilate. Jesus is thus bandied between all the rulers of Jerusalem as Herod and Pilate become friends over their sport with him. Pilate protests Jesus' innocence not once but three times (23:13–22), providing an ironic parallel to Peter's triple denial. He deems flogging sufficient punishment, but in the end gives in to the crowd's demands to release Barabbas and have Jesus crucified. The anticipated Day of the Lord ends with the Messiah not rising up but cast down, with the ruler of creation caught in the dragnets of political, military, and religious forces. Similarly, the long-awaited, apocalyptic day of judgment against Israel's enemies ends with the Messiah judged guilty by the oppressors and a colluding Israel.

Underneath the mocking royal charge of treason against Rome (23:38), the Son of God is exalted on the degradation of a cross on the outskirts of town over a garbage heap. Only a criminal who admits his own guilt seriously addresses Jesus as Messiah (23:42). According to the expectations of his day, Jesus thus dies as a dud Messiah, an utter apocalyptic failure.

Luke's crucifixion narrative leads us to see that nothing can be more deadly to the oppressed than political, military, and religious powers becoming friends against them. Such alliances create tyrannies throughout the world, as highlighted by the 2011 uprisings in the Middle East and North Africa. The atrocities in Latin America, Rwanda, and Bosnia were whipped into frenzies by the lethal braid of politics, religion, and military power. More subtly, congressional leaders vote raises for themselves and cut social services to the poor because funds are short, while increasing military spending more than 60 percent to fund two wars.[2] At the same time, religious authorities take to the airwaves to support politicians whose policies ensure that little orphan Sally, who has leukemia, will not receive the "experimental" treatment she needs to save her life. Such death-dealing is what Christ died to stop. Divine power

---

2. See "Department of Defense," http://www.gpoaccess.gov/usbudget/fy08/pdf/budget/defense.pdf (accessed October 25, 2011).

does not occur by force or violence, but through kind care and commitment to God's dominion of justice and *shalom* for all of creation.

Philippians 2:5–11

The early hymn used by Paul depicts the power of God. Christ did not consider his divinity something to be clutched tightly. Instead, he let go of his position as God to become truly human. Jesus emptied himself, poured himself out as a slave to serve humanity. This is a shocking statement: Christ, Lord of the universe, becomes the lowest of humanity's low. Jesus humbled himself, serving in obedience to humiliation as a criminal on a cross. For this reason, God "hyper-exalted" him. Here is the reversal of fortune for Jesus and all humanity! Jesus is raised so that all peoples in, under, and above the earth might bow down to him, rather than to empire. Bowing the knee is what one did to the emperor to show subjugation to him; it is not a gesture of worship. Christ's dominion is larger than the domain of the faithful heart. It is cosmic. The languages of all cultures will confess his lordship, which gives glory to God.

Here is the Lord of the apocalypse—one in service to the God of life. To say Jesus is Lord is a cosmic event, acknowledging Christ's rule over all things—creation with its galaxies, air, forests, rivers, and magma; religion with all its rituals, goodness, and failures; politics with all its committee meetings, intrigue, and rhetoric; culture with its discourse, arts, and sciences; family in all its various configurations; and societies' structures and ways of sharing resources, power, and money. It says Christ reigns in heavenly places and prevails over hell.

Following Christ means that we are to serve one another with our God-given power. This does not mean that we are to be doormats for Jesus, humiliating ourselves so that evil can prevail. Christian humiliation exalts God's dominion. Derived from the same word as "humus" (good soil), "humiliation" is being willing to be soil for God's planting of paradise. This means we are to stand up out of the midst of evil against it. Indeed, the two words for resurrection in the Greek mean to wake, rise, or stir up (*egeiro*) and to stand up (*anastemi*). As subjects of Christ, we, too, are an exalted, resurrection people. Waking up to stand up for God's Way in Christ may indeed mean laying our life on the line, as in human rights and environmental protests, but it also means standing up to say Jesus is Lord—not domineering power, not military might, not economic power, not normative systemic usurpation, but Jesus, the One crucified and raised.

Maundy Thursday

Randall C. Bailey

EXODUS 12:1–4 (5–10), 11–14
PSALM 116:1–2, 12–19
1 CORINTHIANS 11:23–26
JOHN 13:1–17, 31B–35

Holy Thursday marks the day in Lent and Holy Week on which we celebrate the Last Supper and the inauguration of the Lord's Supper or Holy Communion, depending on one's denomination. We carry out or reenact these rituals at varying intervals in each denomination. The texts for today bring the rituals and their backgrounds to our consciousness for reflection on their relationship to justice in our own lives.

Exodus 12:1–4 (5–10), 11–14

Exodus 12 contains laws associated with the celebration of the Passover. Its current location in the book interrupts the story of the ten plagues. Chapter 11 announces the tenth plague, the killing of the firstborn Egyptian male children and animals. The ethical challenge of such a story has not been part of black and other liberation theologies.[1] This story line picks up again in 12:21. Interpolated into the story of the preparation for the tenth plague we find the laws for the future holy day of Passover, which effactully slows down and restructures the liberation story.

On the positive side, these laws speak to the need to create rituals to bring to remembrance liberating acts of God. In response to the awareness that not all people in the community could economically afford to meet the requirements, this text encourages others to share resources (v. 4). This is an important lesson for us in the church to learn today. Often we only emphasize the

---

1. Cf. Judy Fentress Williams, "Exodus," in *The Africana Bible: Reading Israel's Scriptures from Africa and the African Diaspora*, ed. Hugh R. Page Jr. et al. (Minneapolis: Fortress, 2010), 84.

importance of the offering to the church but miss out on the offering to less able members.

What is most surprising is the injunction to put blood on the doorposts (vv. 7, 13). Is this a claim by the writer that the notion of a God of omniscience is not fundamental to her or his theology? Otherwise, God would not need blood on the doorpost to identify who might be in the house. In this portrayal of the deity, we can wrestle with how important our notions of God are as they interact with the text.

Psalm 116:1–2, 12–19

This individual thanksgiving psalm presents a liturgy for one who was seriously ill (vv. 3–4) but was healed. The part of the psalm chosen for this day speaks to the fulfillment of vows in the form of bringing sacrifices to the temple in Jerusalem (vv. 17–19). Unlike in the first reading, there is a move from the communal situation to the individual. By the same token, there is no recognition that the individual might not have the financial resources to meet the sacrificial requirement, as is recognized in the first reading.

What is also surprising in having an individual as opposed to a communal thanksgiving psalm chosen for this day is the focus of the first reading. The first reading is about the liberation of the nation and the work of the community to celebrate this liberation. One would have expected a psalm that spoke to communal saving and the communal response to such an act. The main reason for raising this point is that we (U.S. Protestants in particular) emphasize individual salvation and often ignore communal salvation and liberation. Even when texts speak to communal issues, as in the first reading, we often focus on individual issues. This is especially seen in our hymnody, which is exceedingly individual and private and much less communal. We sing "I Am Thine, O Lord," "What Shall I Render," "Jesus Is All the World to Me." While focus on the individual is not inappropriate, the point is that when the text focuses on the communal, we should struggle to see how we demonstrate this dynamic in our own communal lives.

1 Corinthians 11:23–26

Since this day is associated with the etiology of the Eucharist (or Lord's Supper or Communion, depending on one's tradition), it is understandable that this passage from the Pauline corpus is used on this day. Surprisingly, this is one of the few times when Paul deals with the life of Jesus in his writings. For his theology, the life of Jesus is irrelevant. It is the death and resurrection that led Paul in his theologizing. So this is a unique passage coming to us from Paul.

On the other hand, Paul claims that he received this tradition from the Lord. This contradicts his claim in 15:7–9 and in the Lukan account of Paul's Damascus Road experience in Acts 9. When did the Lord talk to Paul about what happened on the night he was betrayed?

Like the first reading for this day, the reading concentrates on rituals and how they should be carried out. Prior to this unit, Paul scolds the Corinthians for the classist and overindulgent practices in which they engage in this ceremony (vv. 20–22). In this unit, Paul relates the tradition of Jesus at a dinner using a loaf of bread as a symbol of his body for those gathered and the cup as a symbol of a new covenant in his blood (vv. 24–25). Paul's focus in this presentation is that the people should remember and therefore proclaim the Lord's death until he comes (v. 26).

While Sanders sees a connection between this tradition and the Exodus of Israel from Egypt,[2] this is hard to substantiate in this Pauline tradition. On the one hand, it is a loaf of bread in verse 23, while the Exodus would have had unleavened bread. Second, in saying "on the night when he was betrayed" (v. 23) and "after supper" (v. 25), Paul never socially locates this event during the Passover. Third, his wording emphasizes Jesus' death and future return, not the liberation of the community. In other words, Paul presents a tradition that is devoid of references to the ritual pointing the community toward doing acts of justice. Indeed, when he scolds the Corinthians for their classist behaviors (vv. 20–22), his solution is not to spread the resources around. Instead he tells them to do their eating and drinking in their own homes (vv. 21–22). Thus, while this reading moves us back to a communal ritual, it does not ground the ritual in the social-justice ethical imperative of the community.

By the same token, the Synoptic Gospels specifically place the events of the Last Supper during the Passover. Just as the writers of the Gospels reject Paul's claim in 2 Corinthians 5:16 that we no longer know Christ "from a human point of view," and therefore decades after his death ground their Gospels in the earthly story of Jesus' life, their situation of the Last Supper during the Passover is a rejection of Paul's depoliticizing of the lynching of Jesus by the Romans. Moreover, by placing this ritual in the context of the Passover they note that the celebration of the liberation from Egyptian slavery has a connection to the actions of Jesus in trying to free his people from Roman occupation and terror. Thus, recording this meal and ritual in the context of the Passover, they depict it as a liberation covenant ceremony to carry on the works of Jesus as the struggle continues. While these Gospel writers also mention the loaf of bread (Matt. 26:26; Mark 14:22; Luke 22:19),

---

2. Boykin Sanders, "1 Corinthians," in *True to Our Native Land: An African American New Testament Commentary*, ed. Brian K. Blount et al. (Minneapolis: Fortress, 2007), 295.

which would not fit the Passover, they make sure the reader knows that this event takes place during this liberation holiday. As we see, this is not how Paul presents the ritual. Rather, he speaks of this as a regular occurrence in the Corinthian church, which does not speak to resistance actions.

John 13:1–17, 31b–35

In the Gospel passage for Holy Thursday we read the story of Jesus washing the feet of the disciples, modeling for them and us how they and we should relate to each other. Omitted from the reading is the discussion of the identity of the person betraying Jesus. Instead the reading jumps to Jesus' instructions to his disciples to love each other on the model that he had demonstrated in his relationships with them. Thus, this passage does not speak to Eucharist, as Callahan correctly notes.[3]

The narrative begins with the narrator telling the reader of Jesus' love for the disciples (v. 1b). The narrator picks up this theme again at the end of the reading (v. 35). While the opening talks about Jesus' relationship with God, the end of the reading refers to the disciples as "little children" (v. 33). Given the age of the disciples, such a designation is surprising to the reader, especially as it is presented as part of a speech from Jesus to his "boys." Verses 3 and 33 speak of Jesus going away. The reader is told in verse 3 that he is going to "the Father." The disciples are told he cannot tell them where he is going and they, like the Jews, cannot go there. This comparison or differentiation between the disciples and the Jews is also strange, since the disciples are Jews themselves, as is Jesus. Given pejorative statements about Jews in the Gospel of John,[4] one could regard such remarks as ethnic slurs, which of course do not exhibit love for all. This demonizing language alongside statements of love placed in the mouth of Jesus by the writer legitimize "insider" vs. "outsider" constructs that become harmful to building healthy, liberating, and just communities.

In washing the disciples' feet Jesus takes the position of a slave, since it was the job of slaves to wash the feet of visitors to the house. This has traditionally been used as the Johannine version of the Synoptic Gospels' emphasis that those who follow Jesus must be servants of others; the first must be the slave to the others (Matt. 20:26–27; Mark 10:43; Luke 22:27a). Peter objects to Jesus washing his feet and then states that Jesus should also wash his face and hands. Jesus responds that his service is a ritual cleansing. This ritual is

---

3. Allen Dwight Callahan, "John," in *True to Our Native Land*, 201.
4. Cf. Robert Carroll, *The Bible as a Problem for Christianity* (Philadelphia: Trinity Press International, 1991), 89–116; and Tina Pippin, "'For Fear of the Jews': Lying and Truth Telling in Translating the Gospel of John," in *Race, Class and the Politics of Bible Translation*, ed. Randall C. Bailey and Tina Pippin, *Semeia* 76 (1996): 81–97.

built into the servanthood/slavocracy model[5] based on the opening and closing statements on loving one another in the community of the disciples. The
troubling part of this portrayal of discipleship is that Jesus does not appear
to liberate slaves, who would otherwise be subjugated to this act. Rather this
portrayal uses the demeaning work of enslavement as the model of discipleship. While Orlando Patterson argues that one should not expect that first-
century CE writers would be opposed to slavery,[6] those of us who have slavery
in our people's background should resist such portrayals. While translators
often try to soften this by using the word "servant," the reality of Roman
culture imposed on the people of the colonies was one of harsh enslavement.
As Jesus is beginning to prepare his disciples for the impending death of the
revolutionary, the lynching/crucifixion (vv. 31–35), the portrayal in this text is
not one of resisting oppression but rather acting like slaves. Preachers are left
then to discern carefully how footwashing rituals might demonstrate justice
for us today.

In all four of these readings there are liberation and justice situations. There
are also rituals associated with them. As we see, while these rituals remind the
people of liberation struggles and events, their explanations within the text
sometimes obscure the justice-and-liberation motif. By the same token, we
have the potential of replacing our own commitments to justice activity with
participating in religious rituals and convincing ourselves that the rituals are
the most important activities in which we participate. One way to preach these
texts is to help congregants recognize the codes in these texts that reduce the
communal justice concerns. Another effort might inject justice language and
commitments into our liturgies around these events and rituals. When we
come to the Table, we should be reminded that we are committing ourselves
to do the types of liberating actions that Jesus might do in our own contexts.

---

5. Cf. Mitzi J. Smith, "Slavery in the Early Church," in *True to Our Native Land*, 11–22.
6. Orlando Patterson, "Paul, Slavery and Freedom: Personal and Socio-Historical
Reflections," in *Slavery in Text and Interpretation*, ed. Allen Dwight Callahan, Richard Horsley,
and Abraham Smith, *Semeia* 83/84 (1998): 263–79.

Good Friday

Rhashell Hunter

ISAIAH 52:13–53:12
PSALM 22
HEBREWS 4:14–16; 5:7–9
JOHN 18:1–19:42

Today is Good Friday. Some say that "good" and "God" have been transposed, and it is really "God's Friday." But, even so, on this day Jesus was crucified. Peter denied him, not once, but three times. The other disciples ran away and hid. Given opportunities to release Jesus, the people instead shouted for his death sentence. This does not appear to be God's day or even a good day for Jesus or for humankind. But, without the tragedy of Good Friday, we would not have the joys of Easter. So while today we experience suffering and pain, we know that soon freedom, victory, and resurrection will come.

The passages for this day all share the theme of redemptive suffering. In the Isaiah passage, we are given a vision of the Suffering Servant who sacrifices for the good of the people. In the Psalter, God hears the plea for deliverance from suffering. In Hebrews 4 and 5, we discover that we will endure no suffering that our Savior has not already experienced. And in John 18 and 19, we experience Jesus' arrest, crucifixion, and burial. Soon resurrection will come and set us free from sin and death, providing us with eternal life. That is what makes this a good Friday.

Isaiah 52:13–53:12

Some, who prefer to forget painful experiences, may be distressed by the image of the Suffering Servant described by Isaiah. Many who are oppressed, however, identify with the redemptive suffering of the servant, for they find in it hope and the opportunity for freedom. In fact, many oppressed people relate

186

strongly to the suffering Christ. African American Christian Womanists,[1] for instance, identify with Jesus because he was persecuted and made to suffer undeservedly, and so are they. Womanists celebrate knowing Jesus as human and divine. Jesus is the One whom they know like a brother, a sister, a mother, or a father.[2] Many Womanists relate to the Suffering Servant because many of them have faced enormous race, gender, and class oppression and are constantly placed in a position where they have to defend their rights to serve, lead, and even preach the gospel of Jesus Christ.

The earliest known African American woman preacher was called Elizabeth. She was a slave, born in Maryland in 1766 and set free in 1796. Her parents were Methodists. She was told that the Scriptures did not sanction women's preaching and that women were not suited to the rigors of travel required of an itinerant minister. Even so, in 1808, at the age of forty-two, she held her first meeting in Baltimore. She traveled in the South and North. When asked by what authority she spoke and if she were ordained, she answered, "Not by the commission of men's hands: if the Lord had ordained me, I needed nothing better." Elizabeth preached almost fifty years before retiring in Philadelphia.[3]

Many African American Womanist preachers continually struggle to be heard. These women, and others who have experienced marginalization, remember the teachings of the Suffering Servant in Isaiah, and the suffering of their own people, and are very aware of what freedom and salvation cost.

Psalm 22

In this psalm, David asks (v. 1), "My God, my God, why have you forsaken me?" Jesus also spoke these words before his death, lifting a plea to God for deliverance from suffering (Matt. 27:46; Mark 15:34). Many persons today have also spoken these words. Those who were financially stable only a few years ago and are now unable to make their mortgage payments or pay their household bills may also ask, "My God, my God, why have you forsaken me?" Many who are unemployed, some of whom lived quite comfortably a few

1. The term "Womanist" was coined by novelist and poet Alice Walker. Many women in church and society have appropriated it as a way of affirming themselves as African American women connected to feminism and to the African American community, male and female.

2. Jacquelyn Grant suggested that Jesus was the central frame of reference for Christian Black women in the past. See Jacquelyn Grant, *White Women's Christ and Black Women's Jesus: Feminist Christology and Womanist Response* (Atlanta: Scholars Press, 1989), 211–12. Also, see Katie Geneva Cannon, *Black Womanist Ethics* (Atlanta: Scholars Press, 1988).

3. See Bettye Collier-Thomas, *Daughters of Thunder: Black Women Preachers and Their Sermons, 1850–1979* (San Francisco: Jossey-Bass, 1997), 41–42.

years ago and are now living lives marked by economic uncertainty, are feeling hopeless and forsaken. These persons in our communities might echo the words lifted up in this psalm, afraid that God might have abandoned them.

The good news is that even when we are despairing, there is hope, for we are never completely alone. God is with us. We are not promised happiness and freedom from human pain. Even Jesus cried out to God to rescue him from suffering. Though this psalm may appear to be one of faithlessness, it also expresses continued faith in God, even in the midst of deep despair. And though it starts out torturous, it ends happily: "From you comes my praise in the great congregation; . . . future generations will be told about [God], and proclaim [God's] deliverance to a people yet unborn" (vv. 25a, 30b–31a). God hears our pleas and offers deliverance. God will not fail us or forsake us (Deut. 31:6d).

Hebrews 4:14–16; 5:7–9

One of the reasons we identify with Jesus is that he endured human suffering and "has been tested as we are, yet without sin" (4:15c). Thus, these passages in Hebrews are inspiring to us, for in them we discover that there is no suffering that we will endure that our Savior has not already experienced.

Hebrews 4 and 5 describe the great high priest, who has endured suffering and empathizes with our weaknesses (4:15; 5:8). We often do not think of great leaders as those who "offered up prayers and supplications, with loud cries and tears, to the one who [is] able to save [them] from death" (5:7). Yet we discover in the pages of Hebrews that the great high priest is not one who seeks power and comfort. Instead, Jesus has compassion for those who are weak, and he died so that we might live.

On Good Friday in 1963, Dr. Martin Luther King Jr. was arrested and jailed in Birmingham, Alabama, for leading a nonviolent protest against racial segregation. While in jail, he read a letter from eight white clergy, published in a local newspaper, calling the demonstrations in Birmingham unwise and untimely. In response, King penned the famous "Letter from Birmingham Jail," in which he wrote that "wait" has almost always meant "never," and that "injustice anywhere is a threat to justice everywhere."[4]

Following the example of Jesus, King's path to leadership was one of suffering, empathizing with the oppressed, and marching for the civil rights of those who were denied dignity and justice. Answering Christ's call to leadership may be uncomfortable and even dangerous, but we are called to

---

4. Martin Luther King, Jr., "Letter from a Birmingham Jail," April 16, 1963, in *I Have a Dream: Writings and Speeches That Changed the World*, ed. James Melvin Washington (New York: HarperCollins, 1986), 85.

undertake the mission of the church even at the risk of losing our lives.[5] As we participate in Christ's realm in the world, we are assured that the One whom we serve continues to be our source of salvation and of life eternal (5:9).

John 18:1–19:42

The readers of John's Gospel find themselves experiencing love and betrayal in the passion narrative of Jesus Christ. Peter has shown great commitment, loyalty, and love for Jesus. When the soldiers came to arrest Jesus, Peter drew his sword and cut off a man's ear. But Jesus ordered Peter to put his sword away, putting an end to violent resistance (18:10–11). In these passages, we see the horrors and the glories of life. Peter, who loves Jesus, is also, paradoxically, the one who denies him three times.

We eventually find ourselves at the foot of the cross, where Jesus' mother, her sister, Mary the wife of Clopas, and Mary Magdalene bear witness to Jesus' crucifixion. Seeing his mother and his beloved disciple standing beside her, Jesus said to Mary, "'Woman, here is your son.' Then he said to the disciple, 'Here is your mother'" (19:26–27). Jesus showed supreme love for his mother and his dear disciple by providing for them, even as he was being crucified. Even in the gloomiest moments, God's love is present.

When Jesus was just a baby, the old prophet Simeon said to Mary, "A sword will pierce your own soul too" (Luke 2:35). After Jesus died, a soldier pierced Jesus' side and Simeon's words seemingly rang true (19:34). Others have had their souls pierced, as they have witnessed their loved ones being killed. Some have stood at the foot of trees after lynch mobs have departed, horrified by the "strange fruit" found hanging there.

Abel Meeropol wrote the poem "Strange Fruit" in the late 1930s after he saw a photograph of the lynching of two African American teenagers.[6] In the poem, Meeropol describes the overwhelming bloodlust betrayal of humanity in the tragically beaten, burnt, and distorted bodies of African Americans hanging as rotting fruit from a tree of hatred. Nineteen-year-old Thomas Shipp and eighteen-year-old Abram Smith were lynched on August 7, 1930, in Marion, Indiana. Studio photographer Lawrence Beitler went to the lynching and set up his camera equipment. Abe Smith tried to free himself from the

---

5. G-3.0400 of the *Book of Order* of the Presbyterian Church (U.S.A.) reads, "The Church is called to undertake this mission even at the risk of losing its life, trusting in God alone as the author and giver of life, sharing the gospel, and doing those deeds in the world that point beyond themselves to the new reality in Christ."

6. Meeropol, a Jewish high school teacher from the Bronx, wrote "Strange Fruit" under the pen name Lewis Allan in 1936. Meeropol set the poem to music, and Billie Holiday recorded the song in 1944. The poem was published in 1937 in both *The New York Teacher* and *The New Masses* journals. See http://educationforum.ipbhost.com/index.php?showtopic=10763 (accessed October 25, 2011).

noose as his body was pulled up by a rope. He was lowered back down, and his arms were broken to prevent him from trying to free himself again. Then he was hoisted back up. In the photo that Beitler took, crowds of people are seen gathered at the foot of a tree. Beitler stayed up all night making thousands of copies of the photo. He sold them the next morning as souvenirs for fifty cents apiece.

But there was a third person, sixteen-year-old James Cameron, who survived the lynching. The mob grabbed Shipp and Smith first and then came back for Cameron. With a noose around his neck, he prayed to God, "Lord, have mercy. Forgive me my sins." Some accounts say that someone stood on a car and yelled, "He's innocent!" No one knows exactly what happened, but at the last minute, the mob decided not to lynch Cameron. Maybe it was because he looked so young or maybe it was because he was the third one and two lynchings had already occurred. At any rate, his life was spared. He served four years in jail and was released. In 1993, the governor of Indiana issued a pardon for Cameron. He later said, "Since Indiana has forgiven me, I, in turn, have forgiven Indiana." He died in 2006 at the age of 92.[7]

I have often wondered if persons in lynch mobs and those in the crowd at Jesus' crucifixion felt remorse or shame. People later recounted that the people in the town square in Marion, Indiana, that day were ordinary, average Americans. Someone said that it was as though they were at a county fair. They were attracted to the spectacle of a lynching. Were people in Jerusalem two thousand years ago attracted to the spectacle of a crucifixion? Were the moods and atmosphere similar?

In John 18 and 19, there is betrayal, but there is also love. And, though violence is prominent, compassion is also present. Just as Jesus ordered Peter to put away his sword when the soldiers came to arrest Jesus, we are commanded to put an end to violence and engage in the world as peacemakers. We are charged to take others into our care as part of the same family and to move beyond tolerance of others to loving and respecting others. This may mean reevaluating policies, reallocating budgets, and challenging the status quo so that we create institutions, businesses, and organizations that are free of prejudice, gender bias, and other practices that deny the humanity of others. The Scripture passages for Good Friday lead us through suffering and pain. Yet, Easter will come, and we will claim the victory, the freedom and the new life that Christ offers us.

---

7. See James H. Madison, *A Lynching in the Heartland: Race and Memory in America* (New York: Palgrave Macmillan, 2003). Also, see James Cameron, *A Time of Terror: A Survivor's Story* (Halethorpe, MD: Black Classic Press, 1993).

Easter Day (Resurrection of Jesus)

Charles G. Adams

Acts 10:34–43
Psalm 118:1–2, 14–24
1 Corinthians 15:19–26
John 20:1–18

Resurrection Sunday springs hope eternal. In preaching the resurrection through Acts, hope transforms life in the face of deathly injustice, empowered by our inward gaze to see instead the face of life in Christ. The psalm finds the source of new life and renewed life in God's enduring love. Tears of death do not wash away Paul's message of life transformed to the Corinthians, nor can darkness in the Gospel eve entomb the struggle for life.

Acts 10:34–43

A tremendous transformation has taken place. Not only has Christ risen from the dead, but Peter has risen from doubt to faith, from fear to love, and most importantly from bigotry to integrity. Prejudice is death. Love is life. The resurrection is not just Jesus' resurrection. It is also your resurrection and my resurrection from anything, anybody, or any ideology that captures us, cramps us, and contains us in a tight and narrow containment of separation, alienation, and isolation from God and from humanity. If we are not risen together in Christ, we will not be available to humankind. If we are not transformed by the resurrection, we will not serve well in community struggle; we cannot effectively reform political life; we will remain bankrupt partners in economic liberation; we will not be joiners of the church, but rather dismembered limbs of the body of Christ if we are not open and available to God. The good news is, however, with Christ's resurrection our own lives are raised from many deaths of mutual destruction; we have been raised together, transformed with Christ, to take a broad view of human community and society.

191

In Acts 10 and 11, there is a wonderful and true story of how the Easter fact and Easter faith gave Peter the power to rise above his pettiness, selfishness, ethnocentrism, and sexism, going high above his separation from Christ and division in the beloved community. The great ideological "isms" in life are like the indelible stains of sin and guilt. They are not easy to overcome. They are not automatically or painlessly thrown off. They touch us deeply. They stain us thoroughly. They become instinctive to individual persons, economic structures, political procedures, and academic preferences. Even our churches are stained with the ideological varnish that we have dragged in from the culture in order to decorate our religions and paint our spiritual institutions. Christianity does not have a good name everywhere. Christianity did not liberate, democratize, or humanize the classes and cultures of many nations, including our own. It practiced the same divisions and disruptions that were destroying human culture. Christianity became an ally to extremist, reactionary, suppressive, nondemocratic, absolutist powers. Christianity is ugly and deadly when it is selfishly and narrowly practiced. It is too powerful to be wastefully applied to a narrow nationalistic purpose.

Christians often stooped into the ideological and maniacal divisions of the cultures where we "practice" our faith. We all want to paint Jesus our color and pin our party label on him. That makes Jesus both partisan and racist. It tells the world that Jesus is not Lord. Only race is Lord. That is why some whites got red-hot mad when a black man was cast to play the part of Jesus Christ in a passion play. They became offended because they worship color and not Christ. This story corrects them. This gospel offends them. Gentiles want to paint him as anti-Semitic. Whites want to paint Jesus as white. Blacks want to paint Jesus as black. Asians want to see Asian features. But the text corrects all of that. Verse 36 says: "preaching peace by Christ—he is Lord of all." All means all! To see ourselves in the face of Christ is liberating and transforming. And to see the face of Christ in the other transforms our gaze still.

Psalm 118:1–2, 14–24

"I shall not die, but I shall live" (v. 17). That is a strange statement, as if one is deciding to live. We always thought that life is not a choice but a gift, unexpected, unexplained, and too often unacknowledged. We always thought that life was not so much a process that we initiate or create, but something that we can only appropriate and perpetuate, because it has been given to us. Life, often even the conditions of the lives we inherit, is a given. So how can Easter challenge us to decide to live? What does our decision have to do with it? Were we not born at a time we did not set? Were we not born to parents we did not choose? Were we not born in a race, a nation, a family, a community, a government, an economy, and a society with preset values? We had nothing to do with our own conception, birth, or earliest infancy, but we were born with the instinct to grow gradually from dependence to self-determination. We were born with a natural inclination to move from being passive to becoming active, to develop from blind trust to active faith and logical thinking, to move from being acted upon to acting upon our own environment, so that even now, in our most passive moments, the environment that we passively inherited at birth has been permanently changed because we are special, we are unique, we are beautiful, and we are here. Your very presence, your very being, your spiritual life, your love, your joy, your zeal, your words, your will, your work, your writing, your voice, your song, your personality all help to reshape and reform, rebuild and redefine, the very social, political, economic, psychological, spiritual, and ethical environment where you happen to be.

When you step into life, when you walk into the workplace, when you come into the church, you cannot help but make it different. Even a passive baby is not totally passive. The minute that baby comes into the world, that baby rearranges the terms and conditions of the whole family and the whole community, and perhaps the whole creation. The furniture of the universe had to be rearranged to make room for you, because you are a unique person who is not predictably and mechanically acting like a thing made by humanity alone. You are a person made by God with God's enduring steadfast love (v. 1).

We love our babies unconditionally, not because of what the baby can do for us, but because of what the baby demands of us. And we know that love makes all the difference, because we reach a joy that we never felt, we never thought, we never imagined, and we take up responsibilities that we never dreamed of having to face. Thus, without knowing it, the baby's struggle "to be" refreshes and renews our own choice to live and to make our environment safe and appropriate for children, and that changes the world, it changes the economy, and it changes all of life.

And even when God decided to come into the world, God did not enter as a fully grown person, but in the mighty power of a helpless baby whose being was a threat to the world as it was. When that baby was born, a dream was born, a dream of a new heaven, a new earth, and a new society. Death could not destroy life ultimately, because God decided to live. When we preach the resurrection to life we preach, "[God's] steadfast love endures forever" (vv. 1, 2).

1 Corinthians 15:19–26

This passage is a brief part of the oldest and longest resurrection argument in the Greek Second Testament. In order to better penetrate the resurrection thinking of the apostle Paul, many scholars suggest we study the entire fifteenth chapter of 1 Corinthians.

This long chapter does not seem long at all. It is lyrical, singing in hearts broken by the radical reality of death. Paul does not euphemize the devastating, tearful, shattering power of death. To those who grieve, death is not a dream; it is an endless nightmare. It is an aching wound that will not heal. It is not a mere transition; it is a long and deep dislocation. Paul, despite his Hellenistic connections, does not minimize or trivialize the power of death.

Paul says to those who deny the resurrection of the dead body of Christ that if Christ has not been raised, all our preaching is in vain. The reality of the bodily resurrection of Jesus is the cornerstone of the Christian gospel, which is the transformative declaration that Christ has been raised from the dead by the ultimate love and power of God. If resurrection is undesirable and impossible, then Christ has not been raised, and if Christ has not been raised, there is no gospel to proclaim, no redemption from sin, no correction for injustice, no love stronger than hate, no faith to drive out fear, no comfort to heal sorrow, no ultimate hope for humanity or history, no future for truth, beauty, and goodness.

Our lesson begins with these words, "If for this life only we have hoped in Christ, we are of all people most to be pitied" (v. 19). Some commentators suggest that the word "only" should be placed very close to the word "hope." The resurrection of Christ dispels the deep darkness of the valley and shadow of death; thereby, our faith is not in vain. We have a faith that affirms eternal life. We have a hope that is fulfilled in a reality of grace that we know and recognize in the transformation of history. We see it every day, when miners emerge from the deep, dark caves where they were trapped for months. Not one of them perished! We saw it when prisoners of war in Iran were rescued, not by guns, but by diplomacy and integrity. We saw it when the Supreme Court voted 9–0 to desegregate public education in America in 1954. We saw it when Martin Luther King declared a dream in 1963 and witnessed the signing of a civil rights bill in 1964 that removed all racial barriers to the use and enjoyment of public accommodations. We saw it when an African American was elected president of the United States. None of these represents a total change or ultimate transformation. We still encounter death and devastation, but they do not define our life; at best they drive us deeper into the hope of resurrection life, and therein transformation seeks new life of justice and healing, until life eternal.

John 20:1–18

It is most significant that Easter did not come at daybreak. The rising of the Son of God was not synchronized with the rising of the astronomical sun of our heliocentric interplanetary system. The light of day did not cause Easter. The light of day only revealed to human sight the Easter event that had already occurred "while it was still dark" (v. 1).

Our greatest blessings come to us when we can barely see them because we have no reasonable right to expect them. Sometimes there is no empirical, political, social, academic, or economic cause for hope, but still we hope. Often no scientifically verifiable argument for faith exists unquestionably; but still we believe. We have not always seen what we believe; still we believe more strongly in what we have not seen than in anything that we have seen. Sometimes we look for love and justice and cannot find them; but we still love and serve people who do not love us or seek justice for any but themselves. Sometimes we have no reason to rejoice; but we still rejoice. All through the night of doubt and sorrow, eternal life is affirmed. Eternal love is demonstrated and justice made possible by the work of God throughout the night.

If we are not careful, we will wait until dawn, when we ought to get started during the night. Too often we wait too late to do what we must do. Do not wait until dawn to do basic things, to learn necessary lessons, to discipline the habits of work. It is never too early to learn linguistic literacy and technological proficiency. Parents must start teaching their children while it is still dark, in the night of their infancy and helplessness. Their intellectual, spiritual, and moral capacity will be determined very early in life. To wait until their day-break years of self-determination will be too late. They need "night school"! They need to be challenged to learn early in the morning of their lives while it is still dark, before television and computers take over, before the mass media take over, before the streets take over! We cannot play suicide roulette with our intellectual and academic destinies, or with death itself. It is never too early to train children to be considerate of others, to value human life, to respect themselves as well as others. Now we give our children toy guns and killer video games. No wonder human life for them is so cheap! We need a resurrection of dead values, principles, and ideals. When we go to the tombs around us in the dark, do we go to gaze at death through our tormented tears? Or will we go to roll away any rock that would hold our loved ones, our neighbors, in tombs not their own?

Second Sunday of Easter

Olive Elaine Hinnant

ACTS 5:27–32
PSALM 150
REVELATION 1:4–8
JOHN 20:19–31

These texts underscore a bold witness to the resurrection in four particular ways: proclamation (Acts 5:27–32), praise or worship (Ps. 150), priestly responsibility (Rev. 1:4–8), and confession or affirmation of faith (John 20:19–31). Each activity is a task of the church, the *ecclesia*—those called out to live *out loud* their encounter with the Risen One and experience of the Holy Spirit. No longer can the apostles of Jesus stay behind locked doors, no longer can they expect Jesus to perform the miracles, no longer can they refuse to stand up for what they believe. Now that they have been given the gift of the Spirit, they must live it out loud. Yes, they are afraid. Yes, they are standing up to higher authority, speaking truth to power. Yes, they are calling everyone and everything to make music—to be fully alive. Yes, they will face trials and persecution, but there is hope.

By preaching these four passages together, we can paint a mural of the early church in action. We can tell their stories of bold acts of confession and proclamation on behalf of Jesus Christ. In addition, we can include stories of other people, such as Dietrich Bonhoeffer, Oscar Romero, Dorothy Day, Nelson Mandela, Mothers of the Plaza de Mayo, Harvey Milk, Martin Luther King Jr., and more recently Bishop Gene Robinson. These people, and many others, moved from the security of locked doors into the world to witness for truth, justice, and peace. They have resisted death and stood for life in the midst of their particular circumstances, refusing to give in to threats and powerful authorities.

Acts 5:27–32

In Acts, as Peter and the apostles continue their work in the name of Jesus, trouble ensues. They attract more and more people through healing and

196

signs, which get the attention of the authorities, and they are arrested again (5:12–18), but set free by divine intervention. This does not hinder their bold proclamation of the resurrected Jesus, nor are the authorities able to stop them. As happened with Jesus and his ministry of miracles and healings, the state (the Roman Empire) and the immediate religious power (Judaism) feel threatened and out of control. They are supposed to be the ones in charge. But Peter proclaims *out loud* a different authority, saying, "We must obey God rather than any human authority" (v. 29). This is "resurrected living." It refuses to be defined by conventional society or established rules. It is also used to justify civil disobedience. But who decides the difference between civil disobedience and witnessing to God? In the Second Testament alone, there are examples of the church and state working together for mutual support (Rom. 13:1–10) and examples of where the church is expected to be counterculture to state authority (Rev. 13:11–18). But it is Gamaliel, one of the Pharisees present at the trial, who states the truth of the matter, "If it is of God, you will not be able to overthrow them" (Acts 5:39). That, then, is the test! Is our proclamation, our living and doing out loud, of God?

Two times in his speech before the council, Peter appeals to their faith in the God of Israel, "the God of our ancestors" and "repentance to Israel" (vv. 30–31), to remind them of the justice-seeking God of the prophets. Especially fitting for testing our witness or social action is the verse from Micah 6:8, "[The Lord] has told you, O mortal, what is good; and what does the LORD require of you but to do justice, and to love kindness, and to walk humbly with your God?" To be challenged by state or religious authority for our beliefs or actions is as difficult today as it was for Peter then. It could well cost us our jobs, homes, families, or our very lives. Our guiding post is the promise of hope and new life in the resurrection.

Psalm 150

This final psalm in the Psalter ends with a twelvefold call to praise the Lord. It calls on every living creature in heaven and on earth to praise God. It calls on every instrument possible to make music, including our own breath and body. It calls us repetitively to live out loud the confidence of God. Praise the Lord!

Within these six verses are instructions about praise: "who is to be praised (v. 1), why God is to be praised (v. 2), how God is to be praised (vv. 3–5), and who is to offer the praise (v. 6)."[1] The opening verses declare God "king" by locating God in the sanctuary, though the Hebrew usage for "king" is not explicit. Because God reigns over the heavens and the earth, all things are

1. James L. Mays, *Psalms*, Interpretation series (Louisville, KY: John Knox Press, 1994), 450.

called to praise this mighty God. Making music for enjoyment is a great act, yet Psalm 150 is about more than making music. It is about bringing the reign of God into being, as Marty Haugen's hymn "You Are Salt for the Earth, O People" suggests. Haugen's hymn insists we are responsible for "bringing forth" the reign of God's compassion, peace, and justice![2]

Urging the president of the United States to bring forth the reign of God is a bold and courageous act not unlike that of Peter. The civil rights elder and retired professor at Iliff School of Theology, Dr. Vincent G. Harding, wrote a letter to President Obama in which he reminds Obama of the impact Billie Holiday's music had on him, as written in Obama's memoir *Dreams from My Father*: "Beneath the layers of hurt, beneath the ragged laughter, I heard a willingness to endure. Endure—and make music that wasn't there before."[3] Harding goes on to press these words back upon Obama's memory in his role as president, urging him to make music that was not there before. Making music that was not there before is equivalent to what Psalm 150 is calling us to do: to praise out loud with what we know and hope for in God.

Revelation 1:4–8

To be faithful to the book of Revelation, we must realize it is a vision and as such defies words of explanation or making sense in a logical way. This collection of writings was meant to persuade by means of symbolic language, images, and emotive means. Revelation 1:4–8 is the confident opening salutation of the apocalyptic visions that John had while on the island of Patmos. Similar to John the Baptist, who precedes Jesus, this John who writes after the resurrection is an outsider, an insignificant person, and writes from a place of no power, authority, or position—that is, until his experience of Jesus. John's knowledge of the Hebrew Scriptures is clear throughout this book as he puts into perspective the bigger picture of Jesus "who is and who was and who is to come" (v. 4), which parallels God's answer in Exodus 3:14, "I AM WHO I AM." This is an example of how the Hebrew Scriptures are employed in Revelation. John uses familiar images or descriptions of the Holy One, applying them to Jesus and expanding on the scope of his ministry, death, and resurrection by including all of the cosmos in the language of a second coming "with the clouds" to "all the tribes of the earth" (v. 7).

Who is speaking to us from marginal "islands"? Whose voice is reminding us of who Jesus is—"the faithful witness, the firstborn of the dead, and the

2. Marty Haugen, "You Are Salt for the Earth, O People (1986)," *The New Century Hymnal* (Cleveland: Pilgrim Press, 1995), 181.

3. Vincent G. Harding, "Our Children Are Waiting for the Music," *Sojourners*, January 2010, 34.

ruler of the kings of the earth" (v. 5)? Whose voice is calling us to our priestly responsibilities to serve those in need, to stand before God on behalf of others, and to stand before the world on behalf of God (v. 6)?

Most recently, the images of suffering and death on our television screens after the earthquake in Haiti spoke to many, many people and mobilized an incredible force for good in response to their devastation. The media coverage also showed the Haitians praising God day and night, acknowledging the Alpha and Omega in their lives. A kingdom of priests rose up with the promise of a new heaven and a new earth, a resurrection from the destruction of life in Haiti. People of all kinds and from all walks of life have committed to rebuilding this poor, often-forgotten country of people who have long suffered from need and neglect. They have chosen to live their priestly duties out loud. When Jesus was alive, his ministry was about the poor and oppressed, with the vision of a transformed world order. His resurrection is no less. John illustrates this in an apocalyptic vision stating clearly that Jesus is the first to be born from the dead—to come to life again.

John 20:19–31

The author of the Fourth Gospel was concerned with making the teachings, death, and resurrection of Jesus accessible to those who had not seen or heard of Jesus before. In this way, it is an excellent choice for our congregations, who are challenged by living two thousand years after the resurrection. The point of the Easter story in its original context was to give hope and empowerment to those surrounding Jesus. It was not about an empty tomb as much as it was about encountering the risen Christ in transforming ways. Jesus' death on the cross was not to save you or me as individuals or to grant a private, personal eternal life. No, Jesus' resurrection is about God's reign in all of creation, with all of creation, as the psalmist sings.

This portion of the Gospel includes one of the most powerful confessions. Thomas confesses, "My Lord and my God!" (v. 28), when he encounters Jesus, who offers himself in fulfillment of Thomas's prescription. This is an affirmation of life. It is about living out loud. So confident of God's presence in his life, Thomas was transformed despite his disbelief. As we, too, are being transformed, we discover many ways we may participate in the reign of God. Homiletician Christine Smith writes about what the reign of God looks like in her book *Risking the Terror: Resurrection in This Life*: "The reign of God . . . looks like fathers throwing parties for sons who were lost and have been found. It looks like laborers working different hours and being paid the same wages. It looks like tax collectors being held accountable and being offered new life. . . . It looks like people placing their lives beside the oppressed and marginalized and resisting violence done to them even if that leads to a murderous cross."[4] These are concrete examples from the gospels of life lived out loud.

How are we living out loud our confessional faith? How are we living as resurrected people who live in a nation with two wars, economic disaster, failed mortgages, and unemployment rates higher than ever? Are we leaving the locked doors of safety to face this despairing world with hope and fullness of life?

Just last week the church sang "Jesus Christ Is Risen Today." From the creation when God first breathed life into the earthling (Gen. 2:7), to when Jesus breathed on the apostles, bringing a new creation that declares a gospel of forgiveness (v. 22), the reign of God's compassion lives in the world. Through our hands, our lives, our faith, and our voices, "Jesus is risen indeed." The mission of the church, as Parker Palmer writes, "is to love the world as Jesus did, not to focus on enlarging membership or bringing outsiders to accept your terms, but simply to love the world in every possible way."[5] The disciples got off to a good start with the offer of peace, the promise of the Holy Spirit, and the message of forgiveness. This is our place to begin anew each day.

4. Christine Smith, *Risking the Terror: Resurrection in This Life* (Cleveland: Pilgrim Press, 2001), 73.

5. Kate Huey, "Reflections and Focus Questions," *Marks of Faith*, April 13–19, 2009; see http://i.ucc.org (accessed January 27, 2010).

Third Sunday of Easter

María Teresa Dávila

ACTS 9:1–6 (7–20)
PSALM 30
REVELATION 5:11–14
JOHN 21:1–19

An immigration raid at a local meat processing plant goes unnoticed, even though a number of families are separated, parents from children, spouses from each other. The oil spill on the Gulf Coast seems too far away and too political to include in a sermon or the prayers of the faithful. A local Islamic cultural center is the target of graffiti, but a neighboring congregation—having a number of sons and daughters fighting the war on terror—prefers to look the other way. The triple denial of Peter immediately after Jesus' arrest comes to light in today's Gospel reading from John. Jesus' interrogatory, "Simon son of John, do you love me?" makes us cringe. We place ourselves in Peter's sandals and wonder if his own denial is going through his mind. With each iteration, we should also be distressed at our own periodic denial and persecution. And yet, like Peter and Paul, God still chooses us to lead a prophetic church.

This Sunday challenges us with the stories of Peter and Paul. The Gospel reading from John 21 presents a personal encounter between Peter and Jesus, their first meeting since Peter's triple denial outside the house of the high priest (John 18). In Acts 9 we encounter the conversion of Saul of Tarsus as he witnesses a vision of Jesus Christ on his way to Damascus. These readings present Peter and Paul encountering Jesus from their injury to the body of Christ—one by his denial and the other by his persecution of followers of the Way. And yet these are the "chosen instrument[s]" (Acts 9:15) through whom Christ will effect the foundation and missionary tasks of the church.

How are we to read these encounters in light of the demands for prophetic leadership today? The drama of the origins of the Christian movement is peppered with real human characters who exhibit the flaws that haunt our

201

commitment to the reign of God. The psalmist certainly understands this convergence of struggle and praise. And this Sunday's reading from the book of Revelation reflects this convergence even within its doxology, "Worthy is the Lamb that was slaughtered" (v. 12). Power and riches, wisdom and strength, honor and glory and blessing are the merits of this Lamb. Yet one of the most glorious eschatological visions witnesses to Jesus' unjust death on the cross. We are left, then, with an understanding that leadership for the reign of God will inevitably confront the powers with the transitory, superficial, and violent nature of their hold on the life of God's people.

John 21:1–19

This last of the resurrection appearances in the Gospel of John finds the disciples engaged in the activities that shaped their daily lives when they first met Jesus. They are fishing, early in the morning before dawn. Jesus appears to them and we witness the miraculous catch of 153 large fish (v. 11). Along with the breakfast scene that follows (vv. 12–19), this encounter reflects the multiplication of the loaves and fish as well as the last supper of Jesus before his death. At the heart of this pericope, Peter's encounter with Jesus and their dialogue both confront Peter with his denial as well as call him forth as the shepherd to the flock that is the nascent church. We are haunted by Jesus' questions (vv. 15–17): "Simon son of John, do you love me more than these? Simon son of John, do you love me? Simon son of John, do you love me?" With Peter we are heavily troubled by the repetition, which transports us back to that shameful moment in the garden of the high priest some days before.

In his questioning, Jesus evokes Peter's denial but also transforms it into a powerful affirmation of mutual love, service, and commitment to leadership. By the end of the interrogation, Peter's affirmation of love for Jesus also grounds his willingness to do exactly what Jesus is asking of him—to tend and feed his sheep, a leadership role that will lead to his martyrdom in Rome. Peter's love for Jesus, a love he professed would include laying down his life (John 13), falters when tested. The moments when faithfulness to the reign of God means a threat against us or those we love—or a threat to the way of life we have already distorted as divine favor, such as access to cheap goods, our addiction to oil, or a readiness for military defense of our nation—we falter in our witness to the truth. Peter's denial is our everyday denial of the many ways in which our lifestyle incriminates us in the work of the "anti-kingdom," practices and customs of consumption and indifference that result in the direct suffering of others and the environment.

Like Peter, our religious leadership needs the direct confrontation with the resurrected Christ, calling our duplicity and hypocrisy to task, in a dialogue that is both incriminating and transforming, recommitting us to the sacrificial love required to tend the flock. Love is, indeed, the prescription to heal our denial of the reign of God, to accept the task of leadership that is handed to us, to guide and teach the faithful in the ways of God's realm. For many, leadership grounded on a witness of love has meant true martyrdom in the name of justice, restoration, reconciliation, and love. For all who choose this path, these "martyrdoms" are personal deaths to the ways of denial and hypocrisy that do violence to others. Aware of the tension between the call to Peter and us, we hear anew Jesus' words, "Follow me" (v. 19b).

Acts 9:1–6 (7–20)

Few scenes in the Christian story evoke as much emotion as this narrative of Paul's conversion experience. We are all familiar with the drama of Saul of Tarsus on his way to Damascus, an agent of the Sanhedrin, rounding up followers of the Way for detention, stoning, or other political and physical torture. Saul experiences a blinding flash of light and the presence of the risen Christ. But he is immediately confronted with the weight of his actions (v. 4b): "Saul, Saul, why do you persecute me?" When Paul asks who speaks, the response comes with an accusation: "I am Jesus, whom you are persecuting" (v. 5b). Jesus' first-person identification with those persecuted by Saul can remind the faithful listener of Jesus' identification with "the least of these" in the Matthean vision of judgment (Matt. 25:35–46). The message here is clear. For Paul, conversion to faith in Jesus as the Son of God demands repentance. He must repent from persecuting the followers of Christ, and he becomes one of the persecuted, set to be "a chosen instrument," who will have to suffer for Jesus' name (vv. 15–16).

Like Peter in the Gospel reading for today, Paul is confronted by the victimized, denied, and persecuted Christ. The call narratives of our two great leaders involve confronting their complicity with the dominant ethos of violence, exclusion, silencing of true witness, and outright persecution taking place in society. Recognizing that authenticity in our lives before the risen Christ is necessary for the foundational and missionary tasks of the church, and it is an essential step in affirming lives dedicated to leadership and service, whether clergy or laity. In turn, the leadership is to lead the community in exercises of renewal that seek similar encounters with those who are victimized. These encounters seek transformed relationships of mutuality and lead to greater authenticity or recommitment to love. In communities of faith today, these exercises take the shape of naming our complicity in real persecutions, the situations where the dominant religious leadership persecutes the image of God among us, in and through society's most vulnerable and excluded.

Most importantly for our task as leadership in communities of faith that seek transformation for justice, Saul's conversion conveys the message of the subversion of fortunes—the persecutor becomes the persecuted because of faithfulness to Christ. In turn, we are to examine closely our positions of power and domination in society, from our local to our global reach, and renounce our duplicity to the best of our abilities and act with repentance integral to following Christ and leading communities faithful to the realm of God. We do this at the same time that we cast our lot with the persecuted of society, those with whom Jesus directly identifies.

Revelation 5:11–14 and Psalm 30

These two readings complete this Sunday's message with words of praise and thanksgiving that still admit to the bittersweet character of serving God. The psalmist recalls how God "restored" life "from among those gone down to the Pit" (v. 3b), and sings about proclaiming faithfulness in good times but being shaken in faith in times of trial. We can certainly look at Peter's experience of denial and restoration as an echo of the psalmist's confession before God, of being shaken in our resolve when our faith is being tested, being shaken to the point of denial. Restoration is at the heart of the psalmist's rejoicing. We understand restoration as a practice and event that first acknowledges the suffering borne by the victim, the downtrodden. True restoration cannot overlook the experiences of injustice and violence that are part of the experience of God's people. The psalmist reminds us of his pain and suffering throughout the psalm. However, though the writer has experienced sorrow and has counted himself with the dead, God works to restore wholeness and joy (v. 11). The psalmist's relationship with God is one grounded on God's intervention on behalf of those suffering and downtrodden, the persecuted and silenced. In this psalm we find an invitation to live into God's restoration. Projects for restorative justice are meant to acknowledge and then remove the sackcloth, and to turn wailing into dancing—to enact God's justice even when we ourselves have wavered in our faithfulness.

In Revelation, all creation gives praise and glory to "the Lamb that was slaughtered" (v. 11). The vision presents total worship to the coeternal Lamb—Jesus Christ—whose life we see laid down for us and whose following means great sacrifice. Glory and power go hand in hand with the sacrifice of a love so great that it leads to laying down one's life for another. Through the example of Jesus' great sacrifice and the service of those who follow, many will recognize the faithfulness that is a mark of the Lamb. We bear the marks of the Lamb when we practice radical hospitality at a personal or communal loss or risk, when we speak up for the voiceless or those whose voices are violently suppressed. We bear the marks of the Lamb when we risk our security in solidarity with those who face vulnerability and risk every day. In the end, the missionary tasks of the church through conversion and transformation are not fulfilled with forced proselytizing and cheap grace. In laying down our lives for service to others, we mirror the Lamb that was slain, and we witness to the uniqueness of Christian love in the world.

Both the personal vision of the psalmist and the cosmic vision of Revelation speak to the parallel suffering of the two great leaders called forth in today's readings. At the heart of leading is "laying down one's life," becoming like "the Lamb that was slaughtered." We cannot allow these to become mere platitudes. We are vulnerable to the threat that denial and persecution can become realities when, as leaders in the church, we cater to the job security of our clergy rather than advocating for food security for all, when we avoid rocking the boat rather than raising uncomfortable truths, when we prefer civil religion rather than risk worshiping the Lamb that was slain, incarnate in those whom we deny and persecute economically, politically, and religiously. In response to this threat, we must engage in and witness to the transforming power of sacrificial love.

This Sunday's readings lift up the weaknesses of Peter and Paul and how their humanity is restored for leadership in the emerging church. Present in each response to leadership is repentance from their victimization of others, of Christ and his followers. Today, we do well in bringing these two moments together, the commitment to leadership with a declaration of our weaknesses, that we may better lead our communities in reestablishing relationships grounded in divine love and justice, made stronger by an honest awareness that the power of our weaknesses has created victims of those who are the face of Christ among us.

Earth Day (April 22)

John Hart

GENESIS 8:20–22
PSALM 104:24–33
REVELATION 22:1–5
MARK 13:24–31

The Revised Common Lectionary does not contain a season or a Sunday that focuses on the natural world. Earth Day (April 22) can help fill this void. Organizers began Earth Day in 1970 to call attention to the growing ecological crisis, focusing on such things as pollution, using up nonrenewable resources, and creating waste that threatens the survival of the environment. Earth Day gives the minister an opportunity to help the congregation think about a theology of the natural world, about how to become better stewards of the Earth, and about honoring the integrity of all created things.[1] Since Earth Day often takes place in the season of Easter, the preacher could argue that from the apocalyptic point of view, the resurrection of Jesus points to the regeneration of the Earth as well as the whole cosmos.

I am the one whose praise,
echoes on high.

I adorn all the earth.

I am the breeze
that nurtures all things
green.
I encourage blossoms to flourish with ripening fruits.

---

1. Contemporary Christian ecotheology/ethics writers often capitalize "Earth" when referring to the planet. This promotes respect for our planet, aligns capitalization with other planets, and distinguishes planet Earth from earth, the soil of Earth.

I am led by the spirit to feed
the purest streams.

I am the rain
Coming from the dew
that causes the grasses to laugh
with the joy of life.

I call forth tears,
the aroma of holy work

I am the yearning for good.

Hildegard of Bingen[2]

Earth Day, throughout the United States and across the planet, has become Creation Day for peoples of faith. What began as an effort to call attention to Earth's plight as a result of human irresponsibility has become a movement to renew and conserve God's creation. People walking and working with their Creator realize that God demands more than religious sacrifices; God requires that people take responsibility for their actions on Earth and renew Earth through projects that undo past transgressions against creation. People recognize, too, that the presence of God Immanent permeates creation. We live and move and have our being in the same God Immanent, and therefore Earth is sacred space. It is, indeed, a sacred commons, or sacramental commons, in which those who are open to divine presence more consciously experience God as ever present. In this sacred space, all people are responsible for ensuring that the commons provides for the common good, which includes the needs of human communities, integrated within a global biotic community—the community of all God's living creatures.

Creation Day readings over the cycle of years reflect periodically on the biblical teaching that the Creator's presence is visible through creation and that people should share creation's gifts, its common goods, so that the needs of all are met. Today's Scripture readings include that perspective, directly or indirectly, and add the dimension of gratitude to God for God's own care of creation.

Genesis 8:20–22

This passage presents a postflood vignette. In the aftermath of the storm's devastation, Noah offers a sacrifice to God, an act of thanksgiving for salvation

---

2. Hildegard of Bingen, twelfth-century Abbess, from *Meditations with Hildegard of Bingen*, quoted in *Cries of the Spirit*, ed. Marilyn Sewell (Boston: Beacon Press, 2000), 252–53.

from Earth's devastation. Noah's sacrifice, which might on the surface appear to be solely that of a human being with his family, actually is on behalf of all life. God's original instructions to Noah were that he should take on board the ark at least one reproducing pair of every form of life. These instructions were, in a certain way, the first "endangered species act." They reiterated a teaching from the first creation story, in Genesis 1:31, that the Creator evaluated *all* creation, not merely its human members, as "very good." Therefore, all "very good" creatures should be saved, at least through representatives of their species, on the ark. God accepts Noah's—and through Noah, all living creatures'—sacrifice and promises never to cause the ground to be unproductive, despite occasions when human evil is particularly manifest, and never to destroy every living creature. The cycles of seasons, climate, and day/night shall not cease and will be an ongoing sign of God's presence and care. Similarly, in chapter 9, immediately after today's reading, God establishes a covenant with Noah, his family, all people, Earth, and all living creatures, domestic and free ("wild"); the rainbow will be a sign of God's presence and care (9:12–17). All of these readings recall the pronouncement of God on the sixth day of creation: *all* creation, not just humankind, is "very good."

Earth Day/Creation Day, when integrated with biblical narratives such as the preceding, should remind Christians daily—in day and night cycles, the changing of seasons, rainbows following a rainstorm, and a special day dedicated to remembering Earth—that every day should be Creation Day, not just the designated April holiday. The secular and sacred converge on this particular day in a special way, but they should remain integrated in Christian thinking and acting all year long.

Today's Genesis text instructs us that after Earth's catastrophic inundation described in the flood narrative, God renewed God's pledge of solicitous care for Earth and all biota, all living beings. It teaches, too, that people should *remember* that creation—Earth and all creatures—are under God's care and will provide for people's needs. We should express prayerful *gratitude* to God for what creation provides—continuing Creation, *in statu viae*.

Psalm 104:24–33

These verses, too, recall the teachings about God's creativity and solicitude that were expressed in the two Genesis creation stories: all creatures are "very good" (Gen. 1), and God creates all biota from the dust of the Earth (Gen. 2). The psalm adds a new twist: God's creativity is ongoing, set in motion to re-create and to renew God's creation. The creative galactic (stellar births and deaths), geologic (Earth's geodynamics, expressed in plate tectonics, earthquakes, and climate and weather variations), and biologic (biotic evolution) processes did not end once and for all after an initial burst of God's creative power, expressed in a mere "six days" of divine creativity. The psalmist declares that we see God's wisdom in ongoing works of God's creativity. Earth is "full" of God's creatures, including in the sea that has "living things both small and great"; God provides for all creatures, and without God's provision for them they would no longer have the breath of life and would return to dust. God's creativity continues in an ongoing way much as when, in Genesis 1, the Spirit of God moves over eternal formless space and creates material forms existing in time: "When you send forth your spirit, they are created; and you renew the face of the ground" (v. 30).

The psalm was written millennia before scientists and laypeople came to understand Earth dynamics and development and the process of the evolution of life on Earth—and perhaps on other planets—over billions of years. The author was unaware, too, of the theological term that would be developed much later in the Christian tradition: creation is *in statu viae*, in an ongoing state of *becoming*, not a static state of *being*. For the psalmist and for contemporary theology, that is, God's work began at a moment in space time, but had inherent in it the fundamental building blocks of macrocosmic creatures—stars, galaxies, black holes, and planets; of living creatures—plants, animals (including humans), and minute microbes. God's creative design also included microcosmic creatures—atoms, electrons, neutrinos, and quarks—all of which would continue to come into being and, over time, develop into the magnificent sacramental universe visible (at times only through the technologies and measurement instruments of quantum physics) to human perception. A thousand years before the Common Era, the psalmist discerned what Copernicus, Galileo, Darwin, Einstein, and others theorized and established as fact much later in human history—the incarnation of the Creator in creation.

Mark 13:24–31

The Gospel text today reflects themes from the Noah story described earlier. Rather than reflect on the past, however, the writer projects into the future: the creating and liberating Word endures. Mark teaches, too, in a way that reflects an idea expressed by the Genesis writer: God's words and promises will endure forever. For Noah and humans thereafter, YHWH's pledge to care for Earth and all creatures would endure (Gen. 8:21–22); for Mark, the words of Jesus—God incarnate in God's creation—will not perish (v. 31).

Mark states that in the end days, the sun and moon no longer will provide light, and stars will fall (vv. 24–25): creation will be darkened, reverting to its chaotic state prior to God's creative activity. But just as God's power overcame space-time chaos with creativity in Genesis 1, so, too, God's coming in the new chaotic period will be visible, this time in the form of the dramatic entrance of the Son of Humanity coming in the clouds with great power, creatively to address social chaos (v. 26). The Son of Humanity (the child of human and divine parentage) will use angels to gather the elect from "the four winds, from the ends of the earth to the ends of heaven" (v. 27), much as Noah had gathered all the animals and his family into the ark. The fig tree provides a lesson (v. 28–29), symbolically, to teach people when this dramatic period will approach: just as the fig tree's budding signifies the coming of its fruit, signs visible in creation (which might be devastating natural occurrences, or disruptive or destructive social events), to discerning eyes, will indicate the coming of the Son of Humanity. An ambiguously named "this generation" (which, like the "days" of creation, could be an extended intergenerational period in human time but not in God's time) will not pass away until these events occur. The heavens and Earth will pass away, but Jesus' words—like YHWH's promises—will remain.

Revelation 22:1–5

The Revelation reading provides a more complete picture of what will happen after the return of the Son of Humanity. A new Jerusalem, which is a renewed Earth (cf. Ps. 104), will be set in place. It will not be an otherworldly paradise, a garden displaced to another "heavenly realm." It will be a place that integrates the best of earthly, urban-rural, town-country characteristics. God will provide for all living creatures, as God did through the garden environment in the second Genesis creation story. In the new Jerusalem, as in Eden, the "water of life" will flow (v. 1). In the new Jerusalem, too, a "tree of life" will provide the necessities of life (v. 2). The tree will have, in today's scientific terminology, "evolved" to be multifunctional in its renewed Earth niche. It will provide not only fruit for food (a different variety each month), as in the Adam and Eve story, but also, through its leaves, medicine for "the healing of the nations." (The water and tree evoke Ezek. 47, too, re-presenting the prophet's vision of the garden restored.)

People will worship God, and God's name will be on their foreheads as a sign of God's blessing; this is a reversal of the "sign of Cain" on his forehead in the Genesis story, which indicated that Cain was cursed by God. Revelation notes further that neither night nor artificial light nor sunlight will be needed in the new Jerusalem: the light of God will illuminate all (v. 5). This, too, is reminiscent of the first creation story: in primordial time, darkness was pervasive, and God created light to overcome the darkness.

diverse as well. Those persons who have not recognized Jesus as the Messiah are present in the heavenly throne room because they did God's will (see Matt. 7:21).

Beyond their diversity, the people of God share some traits in common. They have suffered oppression and persecution, and they have endured the great ordeal or hour of trial (see Rev. 3:10). For their faithfulness, they are clothed in white robes of righteousness (see Rev. 3:4–5), and they hold palm branches as symbols of peace and victory (see 1 Macc. 13:51; John 12:13).

The inclusiveness of the vision remains a stumbling block for the church. We still build walls, even as we tear others down; sometimes we build them to preserve doctrinal purity, sometimes to preserve cultural homogeneity, and sometimes to preserve power. Whatever privileges they safeguard, walls also stifle the good news and divide the church. The good news simply cannot be districted or redlined.[6] Nor can we summarily restrain whole communities of people from doing God's will because we do not accept their claims to discipleship or church leadership.

John 10:22–30

The action in this passage revolves around a straightforward question put to Jesus by the religious authorities and a very interesting response. They ask, "How long will you keep us in suspense? If you are the Messiah [or, the Christ], tell us plainly" (v. 24). Here is the only place in the Gospel where Jesus is asked directly whether he is the Messiah. Jesus answers, "I have told you" (v. 25), though readers are only aware of this proclamation to the Samaritan woman (John 4:26).

More importantly, Jesus continues his response by disclosing his identity as the Messiah in terms of the works that he has done in God's name. The works testify to his identity and therefore answer the question put to him (v. 25).[7] Further, the works disclose his relationship to God. By claiming that he and God are one (v. 30), Jesus reveals that they are united in the work God has given him to do. Jesus also makes this point by saying, "The Father is in me and I am in the Father" (John 10:38).[8] These are characteristic

---

6. These terms illuminate two of the predominant ways that the church resists God's radically inclusive vision. "Districting" refers to the justification of those ecclesial practices that impede inclusion due largely to custom and comfort. "Redlining" refers to a discriminatory practice of bringing a filtered gospel to persons because they occupy certain social and cultural locations (ex-convict, welfare mother, or transgendered person, to name only a few), and because we have a singular interpretation for those locations. Consider that some nineteenth-century slaves in the United States received religious instruction from their masters, excepting release from captivity, which was filtered out of the good news for them.

7. See also John 5:36.

8. See also John 14:10 and 17:21.

expressions in the Gospel of John. Interpreters commonly take these sayings to mean that Jesus and God have one essence, but the centrality of their one work is unmistakable in John and should not be overlooked.

Creating just community is hard work. Creating a community of boundless inclusivity is also hard work. It seems at times that the better we do on one front, the worse we do on the other front. Justice is easier to enact when diversity is at a minimum. Hospitality is easier to give when our guests look and act like us. Inclusivity is easier to champion when power remains consolidated in the hands of a few and is not dispersed to the many. Yet the community that gathers around the throne in Revelation 7 is inclusive and just, diverse and hospitable. One opportunity of Good Shepherd Sunday is to recognize the ways that we testify to or resist the good works by which God assembles a great multitude. What are the social boundaries of our community? Where are the ecclesial retaining walls that thwart inclusion or justice from advancing? What does resurgence look like?

Holocaust Remembrance Day: Yom haShoah (Early April to Early May)

Clark M. Williamson

ISAIAH 65:17–25
PSALM 42:1–6
REVELATION 4:1–11
LUKE 20:9–19

Yom haShoah (Heb. for "Day [*yom*] of Catastrophe [*shoah*]") is sometimes known colloquially as "the Shoah" or as Holocaust Remembrance Day. According to the Jewish calendar, the date is the 27th of Nisan (a date that varies from late April through early May). Holocaust Memorial Day could help congregations mourn the murder of six million Jewish people and repent of anti-Judaism and anti-Semitism. While honoring the particularity of the Holocaust, this remembrance can also encourage synagogue and church to join in mutual resistance to all forms of genocide and racial and ethnic oppression.

> The latest news is that all Jews will be transported out of Holland through Drenthe Province and then to Poland. . . . And yet I don't think life is meaningless. And God is not accountable to us for the senseless harm we cause one another. We are accountable to [God]! I have already died a thousand deaths in a thousand concentration camps. I know about everything and am no longer appalled by the latest reports. In one way or another I know it all. And yet I find life beautiful and meaningful. From minute to minute.
>
> *Etty Hillesum*[1]

We remember the Holocaust in order to celebrate with Isaiah the reestablishment of Jerusalem and the people Israel after devastation and to share the psalmist's confession that our souls are "cast down" and yearning for God.

1. Etty Hillesum, *An Interrupted Life: The Diaries, 1941–1943 and Letters from Westerbork* (New York: Henry Holt and Company, 1996), 150.

217

In turn, we read Luke's vineyard parable from a post-Holocaust perspective as prophetic self-criticism instead of as evidence for God's rejection of the Jewish people, and wrestle with its problematic message. With the author of Revelation we are to delegitimize empire and emperor worship and their analogies in our experience.

Isaiah 65:17–25

Today's reading is a judgment-salvation pronouncement declaring judgment on an unjust people (Isa. 65:1–16) and proclaiming redemption for those within Israel who had been faithful to God and just to their neighbors: "I will indeed repay into their laps their iniquities and their ancestors' iniquities together, says the LORD" (vv. 6–7). But to interpret the Holocaust as God's judgment on the people Israel for their sins is simply obscene. The Nazis were not agents of the Lord meting out God's judgment. Rather, the people Israel by their very existence reminded the Nazis of the God who is God, declaring that to worship race is idolatry. The church as "spiritual Israel" could forsake its faith; physical Israel could not escape its witness to God.

Instead, we interpret today's promise of a new creation as God once again calling all people to practice compassion, justice, and loving-kindness and to commit ourselves once again to a way of life that yields peace and security for all people. God's promise to "create new heavens and a new earth" (v. 17) is a prophetic-apocalyptic herald of a new age for this world in which there will be no more killing. It is not a promise that all things will be put right by God alone and that we need only wait patiently for God to do so. Perhaps God is waiting for us. The rule of God is already "among us" and we have only to act now in the power of the future.

Today's text is about concrete, this-worldly politics; it is not an apocalyptic fantasy. Its focus is on a real, physical city and a particular people, the Jews: "I will rejoice in Jerusalem, and delight in my people" (v. 19a). Jerusalem was indeed restored after the Holocaust. When visitors to Yad Vashem, the Israeli memorial to the Holocaust, walk out of the branch of the museum that commemorates the one and a half million Jewish children killed by the Nazis, they see Jerusalem shining in the sun. The land of Israel and the city of Zion are the storied place where the people Israel were to be God's pilot project in living out God's rule of considerate justice.

Yet the promise of the coming reign of God remains fragmentarily fulfilled. It is not yet the case in the land of Israel that "no more shall the sound of weeping be heard in it, or the cry of distress" (v. 19b). Nor is it true of their Palestinian neighbors. The promise of *shalom*—"they shall not hurt or destroy on all my holy mountain" (v. 25d)—does not allow us to flee from the ambiguities of history. God's promises are incompletely fulfilled; we human beings continue to sin. Instead, it is a bold declaration of trust in God's way of peace and justice. We can hope and work for nothing less than a real time on this real earth when all will be well with all people.

Psalm 42:1–6

Longing and thirsting for God, particularly when circumstances suggest that we are Godforsaken, is profoundly human. Made in God's image, our hearts are impatient for reunion with God, disquieted by doubt and anxiety. A hint to the context of Psalm 42 is the comment in verse 3: "People say to me continually, 'Where is your God?'" In Scripture this question always points to a situation of grave difficulty. It alludes either to the exile or to the calamities in Judea after the return. Herein as with the Holocaust, Israel was at the mercy of other peoples.

Today's psalm remembers God, giving praise and thanks to God in the temple (v. 4) and "from the land of Jordan and of Hermon" (v. 6). Literally this refers to the source of the Jordan River; metaphorically it recalls both the healing waters of the Jordan and the chaos and trouble that water symbolizes.

The psalmist prays to "behold the face of God" (v. 2b) and remembers having kept "festival" with a multitude, indicating that the psalm was to be sung as part of a pilgrimage to the temple on the occasion of a festival. A pilgrimage to the temple was not just to a building; it was a journey to God. The psalmist both remembers having made such a pilgrimage and prays to do so again. Note that although pilgrimages are things that people do, God is also graciously involved in the project. God's welcoming presence makes the journey possible.

How do we recover faith after desolating experiences? The psalmist hints at an answer: "My soul is cast down within me; therefore I remember you" (v. 6). Is the psalmist internally conflicted? Or is the very question of God's absence a way of knowing this is not the whole story? In our longing for those who are absent, they are keenly present to us. Estranged from God, we are nonetheless restless for God. Shortly after the megadeath of the Holocaust, Jews in camps for displaced people met, married, and had children. After experiencing radical evil, that was an incredible act of faith!

Luke 20:9–19

This lection is part of a story of an encounter between Jesus and "the chief priests and the scribes" (vv. 1, 19). The first part purports to describe a verbal contest between Jesus and his opponents over the source of his authority.

They have a debate; he wins it. And the refusal of his opponents to answer a direct question about John the Baptist discloses their duplicity (vv. 4–7). The two-thousand-year legacy of conflict stories in the Gospels has meant ever since that Jews have functioned in Christian rhetoric as the antithesis to whatever Jesus represents.

Disturbingly, the church long interpreted this vineyard parable and its parallels (Mark 12:1–12; Matt. 21:33–46) as supporting the church's claim to have displaced and replaced the Jewish people in the covenant with God. The church construed the parable as proclaiming (a) that "the Jews" crucified Jesus and (b) that God therefore rejected "the Jews" and made a new covenant with the Gentiles who are now God's "new" people. These claims were supposedly backed up by noting (a) that the tenants killed the owner's "beloved son" (v. 15) and (b) that the owner then swore to "give the vineyard to others" (v. 16; another "people" in Matt. 21:43; "others" in Mark 12:9).

This interpretation misreads the parable, which depends on the vineyard of the Lord in Isaiah 5:1–7, which identifies the vineyard with "the house of Israel, and the people of Judah [who] are [God's] pleasant planting" (v. 7). The tenants are not the people Israel, merely the leaders or some of the leaders of Israel. In Luke-Acts they are replaced by a new set of leaders—the twelve apostles. The people are not rejected, but the leaders are. Whether that distinction holds throughout Acts is questionable.[2] Acts does end with Paul's claim that the Jews could not understand his message: "Let it be known to you then that this salvation of God has been sent to the Gentiles; they will listen" (Acts 28:28).

When we look at Paul himself and not at the Paul of Acts, we note that although Paul was deeply grieved that more Jews had not embraced Jesus (Rom. 9:1–3), he adamantly denied that God had rejected the people Israel. "I ask, then, has God rejected [God's] people? By no means!" (Rom. 11:1). He claimed that the covenants belong to them (Rom. 9:4). For Paul the faithfulness of God always trumped the unfaithfulness of human beings, a point that is good news for both Jews and Christians. If God rejects a people because of unfaithfulness, we Christians are surely and justly doomed.

Another problem with the traditional interpretation of the vineyard parable is that while the parable is prophetic criticism, the church directed the criticism at the Jewish "other" and not at itself. In the anti-Jewish literature, the Jews are the target of all prophetic criticism, while we Christians inherit all the prophetic promises. That is quite a good deal for us. But if prophecy is primarily self-criticism, then we need to let the parable criticize us. What kind of tenants did we have, that the vast majority of the killers in the Holocaust were Christians?

2. Jack T. Sanders, *The Jews in Luke-Acts* (London: SCM Press, 1987).

Usually overlooked is the parable's view of the owner of the vineyard, God, who will "come and destroy those tenants" (Luke 20:16). In Luke 19:27 the same verb is translated as "slaughter." What do we make of such a God? Is God a God of steadfast love or does God have fits of temper and violence? The parable depicts Jesus as promising that God will murder the tenants. Is this what Jesus discloses to us? This is the deeper problem of the story. It is impossible to reconcile a God of steadfast love with a God of violence. Hence we cannot dodge the issue: will we preach a God of steadfast love or will we give divine sanction to violence? After the Holocaust, do we need further evidence that the latter option is a death-dealing choice? It is time to reject the notion of the violent God and let the radical love of God defang it.

Revelation 4:1–11

The book of Revelation was written sometime during or after the reign of the Roman emperor Domitian (81–96 CE), who demanded that Christians worship the emperor. Since Augustus, Roman emperors were often proclaimed as divine, with terms such as "lord" and "savior" frequently used. The emperor's "faith" was lauded, his "peace" celebrated, the "good news" of his reign proclaimed.[3] Domitian required people to address him as "our Lord and God" (*dominus et deus noster*). Exiled to Patmos, the author of Revelation was familiar with oppression.

Today's passage describes the "heavenly worship" in symbolic language not easily decipherable. In heaven "a door stood open" (v. 1), a comment reminiscent of Jewish sayings that the gates of the temple, of repentance, are always open. God is accessible. There is "one seated on the throne" (v. 2). John, like pious Jews, does not use the name of God. Verses 3–5 try to describe the glory of God. God looks like jasper, probably a radiant, crystalline kind of jasper, echoing the understanding of God as light. Usually red, carnelian's meaning in relation to God is difficult to determine. Around the throne is an emerald rainbow. The sign of the covenant, the rainbow, points to God's mercy. John's rainbow is green, not a spectrum of colors. Perhaps it is meant to be soothing after God's wrath over sin has abated.[4]

Twenty-four elders wearing white robes and golden crowns surround the throne. Bruce Metzger suggests that they "may represent the twelve patriarchs . . . and the twelve Apostles," symbolizing the two peoples of God. If so, they suggest that God is not yet finished with the church and the synagogue,

---

3. See the discussion of the Priene inscription in John Dominic Crossan and Jonathan L. Reed, *In Search of Paul* (New York: HarperSanFrancisco, 2004), 237–41.

4. Bruce Metzger, *Breaking the Code: Understanding the Book of Revelation* (Nashville: Abingdon Press, 1993), 49.

that our mutual alienation is not God's will. Even though the elders here are males, we need to point out the role of women, and those others marginalized, in the eschatological worship.

There are four strange living creatures "full of eyes all around and inside" (v. 8), eternally watchful. They constitute a choir singing praise to God, whom they refer to as "our Lord and God" (v. 11). They wrest this title from Domitian and restore it to the One to whom it rightly belongs. The Domitians and Hitlers do not have the last word; they are not in control of our ultimate destiny. Next, John will see standing with all these creatures "a Lamb standing as if it had been slaughtered" (5:6). The violence of empire has been replaced by love and tenderness.

Fifth Sunday of Easter

Simone Sunghae Kim

ACTS 11:1–18
PSALM 148
REVELATION 21:1–6
JOHN 13:31–35

This week's lectionary readings invite us to examine and participate in God's creative and redemptive works that encompass all peoples from the time of creation to the coming of the new heaven. The divine intervention and zeal in bringing Cornelius, the Gentile, into the family of God (Acts 10) urges us to be more aggressive in broadening our ministerial scope (Acts 11), especially in this multicultural and global world. The psalmist's vision in Psalm 148 of all creatures praising God, the Creator, presses us to anticipate and hope in the final culmination of the new earth and the new heaven recorded in the book of Revelation. Then, in John 13, God desires us to take part in the "new command" by engaging in self-sacrificing love. This is demonstrated through Jesus' life and death on the cross, and he charges us, his disciples, so to love one another through the Holy Spirit.

Acts 11:1–18

The passage highlights one of the most significant events of God's work during the early church, which involves Cornelius and his household coming to Christ. Peter defends his witness to the Gentiles in response to some zealous accusations over Peter spending time and eating with the uncircumcised. What is significant about this passage is that God is now doing something new and radical that seems to have caught both the disciples and other Jews by surprise.

As seen in the previous chapter (Acts 10), God meticulously and precisely orchestrates the entire event. For instance, the three men whom Cornelius sends to the house where Peter is staying arrive at the very moment when a

223

vision from God puzzles Peter (10:11, 17). In the ensuing narrative, God's reign and divine justice for all is nicely captured in the end of the reading (v. 18), "Then God has given even to the Gentiles the repentance that leads to life." The Greek term used here for "then" (*ara*) signals a solemn and reverent yielding of God's people to the new vision of divine hope. Even so, it is God who initiated this good work through the Holy Spirit who dwells in us.

The passage offers at least two social justice and change-related action plans. First, avoiding dichotomous language patterns can definitely help to reduce schisms and bring people together in harmony. Divisive language patterns as shown in Acts 11—the circumcised versus the uncircumcised, the Jews versus the Gentiles, us versus them—undoubtedly contribute to divisions and discord among individuals, peoples, nations, and even churches. Often the spirit behind these divisions germinates with the feelings of arrogance, pride, and self-love. As the world is becoming ever more diverse and heterogeneous, this type of separatism can cause much disharmony and animosity between people. It clearly goes against God's command for us to pursue peace and live peaceably with all (Heb. 12:14; Rom. 12:18).

Second, today's passage demands from us a paradigm shift in terms of our tradition and nationalism. Peter, too, had to undergo a major transformation in his ways of thinking and understanding who God is and what God is doing. The Lord had to show Peter the same vision three times and correct him three times until he could finally reflect critically on his own religious traditions and go along with God's new ways. Even today we can easily place our tradition and nationalism in equal terms with or above God's transformative challenges. Our retrenchment often blinds us to God's vision or challenges to live joyfully with people from other ethnic, religious, social, and cultural backgrounds.

Psalm 148

Psalm 148 unfolds the psalmist's creative vision of all creatures praising and worshiping God. The catalog of creation is extensive and thorough, including things of the heavens, the earth, the skies, the seas, nature, animals, and finally people. The language used in this text resembles that of the Genesis creation stories (Gen. 1–2). It reminds us, the created, of the importance of being in right relationship with God, the Creator.

A couple of social justice themes surface from the passage. First, the psalmist repeatedly asserts that "all" (Heb. *kol*) creatures must praise God. The word "all" is used ten times in the text as a way of making sure that all in God's creation without exception have been given the privilege and thus entitlement to "praise" (Heb. *halal*) and give highest contemplation to the Lord. This is significant in that praising God does not discriminate among people on the basis of anything internal or external.

For instance, verses 11–12, "Kings of the earth and all peoples, princes and all rulers of the earth! Young men and women alike, old and young together!" inspire everyone to lift up the Lord's name, including people of high social standing as well as those of more common standing, both men and women, and the young and the old. The list concludes with God's saints and Israel. This all-inclusive language of the psalmist humbles us to dialogue with people from different religious backgrounds and sexual orientations, stay open to individuals who come from various social and economic strata, and embrace those with differing political and ideological views.

Second, praising God brings every creation, both the animate and the inanimate alike, before God's presence and thus binds them all together into the universal chorus of the Creator. As diverse and faraway as all creation may be from one another in terms of location, existence, form, and value, Psalm 148 sets forth their common denominator, which is their Creator. They are all made by the same Creator, who causes them to lift up their voices harmoniously as members of the one universal choir. As all parts of creation direct their reverence toward God, they become one family who share the same Lord. This new reality provides us with the courage to reach out to our enemies, may it be between North Koreans and South Koreans, or Iranians and Israelis, to work together as one family in bringing peace and justice for all nations. The south and the north and the east and the west may stand together in preserving the environment and natural resources for future generations.

John 13:31–35

The theme of praising God continues in John 13 as Jesus is having his last supper with his disciples before he is crucified on the cross. Jesus' sacrifice and obedience to God unto death bring about the fullness of God's revelation and thus glorification and praise to Jesus himself and to God (vv. 31–32). The farewell meal is the setting where Jesus washes the disciples' feet and identifies his betrayer. Then comes today's reading of Jesus giving his disciples a new commandment, to love one another (v. 34).

The first social justice and transformation implication raises a practical problem: the love that Jesus commands his disciples to embody is the kind of love only Jesus himself can completely or effectively give. Without doubt, love is the foundation and baseline for all social justice and change. "I give you a new commandment, that you love one another," says Jesus, "just as I have loved you" (v. 34). This echoes one of the First Testament commands to "love your neighbor as yourself" (Lev. 19:18). Yet with this charge Jesus implores us to love as God loves us. Quite frankly, without divine help, we are not able to carry out this love on our own. Our inability to love one another as Jesus mandates should drive us to humbly and thoroughly rely on the indwelling of the Holy Spirit. Any act or employment of Jesus' love we perform is empowered by the Holy Spirit, and thus the Lord alone must be given the credit and be glorified.

Another implication for social transformation acknowledges that the reconciliation of the church itself is possible only through loving each other as Jesus loved. Denominational gulfs, hermeneutical differences, disagreements in worship style, and liturgical variations have caused churches to depart from each other since the early church. It is interesting how Jesus' new command to love came soon after Judas Iscariot, one of his twelve disciples, had departed to betray Jesus (v. 31). Jesus' compassion and affection do not exclude even his worst enemy within his own immediate community. Jesus' unconditional and all-inclusive love on the cross urges us to embrace Christians who appear to fall outside of our own familiar and comfortable boundaries of faith and worship.

Revelation 21:1–6

John's vision of a new heaven and a new earth is the consummation of our ultimate reality upon God's judgment and Satan's final defeat in the previous chapter (Rev. 20).

It is difficult to know whether this new creation refers to a renovation or an entirely new creation.[1] However, we are certain that God is doing something totally new and creative.

This is what all creation, whom the psalmist mandated to worship God (Ps. 148), so eagerly awaits and yearns. The Lord finally is now with humanity as our Sovereign. "It is done" (Gk. *genonan*, v. 6); this almost echoes Jesus' utterance on the cross, "It is finished" (Gk. *tetelestai*, John 19:30). This text envisions the fulfillment of the redemptive work that Jesus accomplished on the cross, and its effect will endure.

The image of water is used in the passage three times. God removes the sea (v. 1), which symbolizes instability and chaos. Then God wipes away every tear (v. 4). And in turn, God offers "the spring of the water of life" (v. 6). God takes away the waters of toxic despair, while promising the quench of a living (John 4:10; 7:38) and everlasting spring (John 4:14).

---

1. See "The Revelation of St. John the Divine," introduction and exegesis by Martin Rist, exposition by Lynn Harold Hough, in *The Interpreter's Bible*, vol. 12 (Nashville: Abingdon Press, 1957), 528.

The creative images of water provoke at least three implications for social justice and transformation. First, we must remember that God holds us accountable for our arrogant atrocities. We often engage in acts of oppression and mistreatment when we forget that God is an active agent judging our injustice. The time is coming when God will dwell among us in God's own reign with a new heaven and a new earth (v. 1). No persons, groups, organizations, or nations will escape God's judgment over injustice.

Second, the oppressed must not lose heart but must hope in the Lord, who will not only wipe away their tears and sorrows but dwell with them forever. God's realm holds the ultimate power, reign, judgment, mercy, and love. We can rule out any threat of discrimination on the basis of age, gender, race, ethnicity, socioeconomic class, and political and educational background. The new world order guarantees no more domestic violence, child abuse, exploitation of labor, genocides, and wars. The only real hope for the oppressed or for anyone else lies in God alone.

Third, until the eschaton, we are to be agents of hope[2] for all, including both the oppressors and the oppressed. The oppressors often turn out to be victims of oppression themselves and thus the unfortunate cycle continues—if not under acts of injustice then by the cooptation of injustice. The final transformation and completion will take place only in the new reality of God's reign. Until then, our job as Christians is to help bring awareness of any wrongdoing on the part of the oppressors along with the forgiveness available to them in Christ Jesus. Likewise, for the oppressed, we ought to offer the hope of God's judgment over oppression, with healing and victory that will surely come in due time. The final reconciliation between the oppressors and the oppressed is something that everyone will witness in the presence of Christ Jesus, the ultimate mediator and reconciler between God and us, as well as all creation.

2. Donald Capps, *Agents of Hope: A Pastoral Psychology* (Eugene, OR: Wipf & Stock, 1995).

Sixth Sunday of Easter

Choi Hee An

ACTS 16:9–15
PSALM 67
REVELATION 21:10, 22–22:5
JOHN 5:1–9

This week's lectionary readings demonstrate how to extend our hospitality to create new life and to envision new relationships with others. These readings rouse us to exercise our hospitality beyond our cultures and traditions. Following Jesus' first steps to bring the good news to the sick, the poor, and the powerless in John, Paul reached out to new neighbors and crossed over boundaries of his own as he followed God's mission to Macedonia in Acts. These inspired movements enrich our imagination to dream a new space and a new hope not only in the holy city in Revelation but also into newly extended relationships here on earth. They urge us to practice Jesus' radical hospitality and extend our horizons beyond our territories and prejudices. The compassion of Jesus and passion of Paul inspire us to follow them in bringing God's healing and abundance into our lives here and beyond.

John 5:1–9

A man has been sick for thirty-eight years. Jesus approaches this person and asks him if he wants to be made well (v. 6). Within the man's response we learn how healing would typically happen in this pool (v. 7). Out of his own experience, he answers Jesus. And Jesus replies with three imperatives: "Stand up, take your mat and walk" (v. 8). These are the same three imperatives found in another healing narrative, in Mark 2:1–12. However, here is a major difference: while the healing story in Mark 2 happens in response to the faith of the man's friends, this healing story in John 5 does not show any sign of

228

requiring faith.[1] Requiring faith is a common condition of other healing stories or miracle stories in the Gospels, but this story does not ask for anything from this person. Jesus simply heals this person and asks him to rise, take up his bed, and walk.

This is a healing story, but also it is a story of Jesus' radical hospitality. Jesus heals a person who does not have faith, who knows deeply suffering and pain. In his condition, he is waiting for healing, but he knows that he cannot reach the pool by himself. This person has lived in his own world, his own prison that no one can reach into except Jesus. He has lived in this place barely surviving and not knowing how to escape. The limitations of his knowledge of healing and access itself obstruct faith. He does not know who Jesus is, nor has he heard of him (v. 13). Unlike other seekers, this man does not seek out Jesus. For thirty-eight years, without any family or friends, he has been alone. His lack of knowledge and his powerlessness prohibit him from looking for Jesus.

However, Jesus comes to this man first. The compassion of Jesus sees the need of this person despite his lack of faith or knowledge about Jesus. Jesus seeks out the sick man and wants to heal him. Jesus' radical hospitality brings healing to the man and makes him well even on the day of Sabbath.

The act of Jesus' hospitality risks flouting his tradition (vv. 9–18). Jesus is accused of violating Sabbath law. However, the attitude of Jesus is, "My Father is still working, and I also am working" (v. 17) to heal the sick, the powerless, the marginalized, the poor, the wounded, and the earth. The compassion of Jesus, his radical hospitality, makes those people well and restores the earth. He does not hesitate to reach out to the people who do not know him.

His hospitality crosses over traditional boundaries and takes risks for people, even risking death. He does not withhold his love from others. He exercises this radical hospitality beyond his death and completes it through his resurrection. He asks his beloved children, his beloved friends, and his beloved community to carry forth this hospitality and keep his commandments.

Acts 16:9–15

The Spirit redirects Paul's mission travel. This story's plot is similar to the one of Peter's mission to Cornelius. Peter resisted God's mission and did not want to share the good news with the Gentiles. However, he had a vision and was challenged by God. In this story, Paul sees a vision and has to follow

---

1. Gail R. O'Day, "The Gospel of John," *New Interpreters' Bible*, ed. Leander Keck et al. (Nashville: Abingdon Press, 1995), 9:579.

what God shows to him. The Spirit guides Paul and his companions to follow God's mission by not allowing them to go as they had planned (v. 7). At the same time, the Holy Spirit gives Paul a vision of a man of Macedonia pleading with him, "Come over to Macedonia and help us" (v. 9). The Holy Spirit guides them by closing one door and opening another. Paul and his companions are sensitive to God's leading. They "immediately tried to cross over" (v. 10). They respond to God's different plan immediately and cross over their limited knowledge and boundaries. They accept God's redirection and believe that God has called them to proclaim the good news to the people in Macedonia. Therefore they cross over without hesitation.

In verses 11–13, Paul and his companions arrive at Philippi, "which is a leading city of the district of Macedonia and a Roman colony." They go "outside the gate by the river" on the Sabbath day. They sit down and speak to *women*. They choose to share the good news with women even though they had seen a vision of a Macedonian man. Paul and his companions cross over their cultural boundaries again and share the good news with a Gentile woman, Lydia.

Lydia is described as a Gentile woman from the city of Thyatira and a businesswoman dealing in purple cloth. Purple cloth is available only for the rich and for royalty in the Roman world. It symbolizes power. Her business draws people from the elite class of Philippi, and the text implies that she is wealthy and influential in her society.[2] She owns her own business and her own home. She is characterized as "a worshiper of God" (v. 14) who can listen to the good news and accept it because the Lord opens her heart. After she accepts the Lord in her heart, she, a Gentile woman, shows her hospitality to Paul and his companions. She invites them to stay at her home, recognizing what they need and wanting to share what she has with them.

When Paul and his companions reach out to the women, the Gentiles, they receive hospitality from these people. When they share their good news, these people open their hearts and share what they have. This is a mutual but radical hospitality to each other.

When we choose to cross over our boundaries, such as race, sex/gender, class, age, national identity, we recognize that we also unexpectedly receive hospitality. When we reach out to others as God reaches out to us, we experience that others also want to listen to us and stay with us. When we share what we have, they also share what they have. As Paul and his companions reach out to Lydia, Lydia also reaches out to them with warm and assured hospitality. She shares what she has: "If you have judged me to be faithful to the Lord, come and stay at my home" (v. 15).

---

2. Gail R. O'Day, "Acts," *Women's Bible Commentary*, exp. ed., ed. Carol A. Newsom and Sharon H. Ringe (Louisville, KY: Westminster John Knox Press, 1998), 400.

Psalm 67

This is a communal song of thanksgiving. It celebrates God's judgment on the people with equity and God's guidance of the nations on earth. Verses 1–3 and verses 6–7 are blessing and praise to God. We find the central message of thanksgiving for God's guidance in verses 4–5.

Verses 1–3 clearly intend for people, Israel in this song, to claim God's blessing on them. God is gracious to them and blesses them. God even makes God's face to shine on them. However, God's way is known not only to them but also to the earth. God saves not only them but also all nations by God's power.

Israel's and all the nations' proper response to God's saving work is joyful thanksgiving (v. 4). All the nations are glad and sing for joy. God's judgment is not in favor of Israel alone, but of all people. God judges all people with equity. Equity is God's justice. God's justice prevails with all the people. God's judgment with equity makes all the people joyful. Not only Israel, but also all nations and the earth praise God because of God's justice.

This psalm celebrates God and God's saving work for all the people and the earth.

God's saving work and blessing do not have limits or boundaries. God reaches out to every one, every living being, every nation, every thing, along with the earth, and blesses them. God reveals God's radical hospitality and care for them every day of their lives and beyond. This radical act of God makes people sing and offer praise. The blessing of God—the love and justice of God—continues on the earth, and the joyous singing from the earth will not stop.

Revelation 21:10, 22–22:5

This passage shows God's perfect reign in God's sovereignty. In 22:1–2, the angel shows John "the river of the water of life" through the very middle of the city. In this new city, the tree of life, which is watered by this river, has the power to heal the nations. It heals people among the nations. It heals the plants, animals, soil, and air throughout the nations. This tree heals the wounded hearts of the nations, their despair and depression. Healing is granted in this new city under God's reign. The tree of life heals every being and every thing.

In 22:3–5, the throne of God and of the Lamb will be in this heaven and people will worship God. They will see God's face and God's name will be inscribed on their foreheads, as they are in the book of life and remain in heaven. Now God's servants will share God's reign.

On the final day, all the nations will be healed and their people will rejoice in God's judgment in equity and be united with God. They will be in God, and God will be in them. Every being and every thing on the earth and in the universe will participate in this ultimate union with God. This union with God will prevail forever and ever.

Jesus' radical hospitality is from his genuine love to us. Jesus invites us to love one another. As he crosses over his boundaries, he asks us to cross over our boundaries, our prejudices, and our injustices. This hospitality requires us to extend our horizons with respect and love for others. It also requires that we need to share what we have first. We know it leads to not only saving others but also saving ourselves in God's ultimate salvation together.

Jesus' radical hospitality comes from love. Because of love, this hospitality brings healing. It starts to heal the oppressed, the marginalized, the powerless, the poor, the sick, and others. It heals nations, the whole creation and the earth. It heals every being and everything in the heaven and the earth. It heals "I" and "us." It heals God and us. In other words, healing starts from our small but radical hospitality. It starts from us through Jesus with the Spirit. Now Jesus dares us to act upon his request, "Love one another."

Peace in the Home: Shalom Bayit
(Second Sunday in May)

Marie M. Fortune

EXODUS 1:15–22
PSALM 84:1–12
1 PETER 3:1–7
MARK 3:31–35

The new Peace in the Home: Shalom Bayit replaces Mother's Day and Father's Day, which often tend to sentimentality, can promote stereotypes of women and men, sometimes idealize family relationships, and exclude persons who are not parents. The purpose of preaching on Peace in the Home is to call the congregation to help all people live in settings of security, love, and justice. It affirms the diversity of family lifestyles common in our churches and cultures, including traditional households, the single life, gay and lesbian families, and biologically unrelated people who live as family. The preacher can make connections to Sexual Assault and Abuse Awareness Month (April) and Domestic Violence Awareness Month (October).

I know many successful adults, like my mother and my husband, who were raised in families that did not fit the conventional mold. Others I know thrived in the care of biological and adoptive surrogates, and even in foster care or institutions. What a family looks like to outsiders is not as important as whether adults know what children [and others] need to develop positively and work to fulfill their responsibilities to each other and to their children.
Hillary Rodham Clinton[1]

In Judaism, "peace in the home" (*shalom bayit*) is a highly valued expectation for every Jewish family. It is the essence of family values—the assumption that family members will live together in peace, respect, and harmony. Peace in the home, rightly understood and practiced, lifts up the essential value of the worth

---

1. Hillary Rodham Clinton, *It Takes a Village* (New York: Simon & Schuster, 1996), 40.

and dignity of each family member. The home should be a place of safety and respect for each one and especially of protection for the most vulnerable.

You are preaching to victims, survivors, and perpetrators of abuse within the family every Sunday. One in three people (at least) sitting in the pews has had personal experience themselves or with someone in their immediate family of physical, verbal, or sexual violence. They are listening very carefully for any word that speaks to them and to their memories or current experiences.

You are also preaching to the bystanders—those who surround victims, survivors, and perpetrators—who see and hear the abuse but do not want to get involved. However, the bystander could be an enormous resource in this situation.

There will be those who are only allowed out of their homes to come to church, who as adults remember clearly the abuse of one parent by the other, who as teens may be in an abusive dating relationship, who as children were sexually abused by an adult or teen. There will also be those who have abused or are currently abusing a family member, some of whom are struggling with guilt and shame but do not know where to turn.

Here we have four passages that speak to family life and relationships. Any one of them can be a roadblock or a resource to healthy family dynamics. Your challenge is to find the resources and preach them.

Do not preach on these passages and focus on peace in the home unless you are ready and willing to have victims, survivors, and perpetrators come to you for help. They will seek you out. They have been waiting for you to bring up sexual or domestic violence.

An Episcopal priest was surprised when three of his parishioners approached him: two were adult survivors of incest and one was a rape survivor. He shared this experience in one of the seminars he was taking on pastoral care and sexual and domestic violence. As we discussed what might have led to this, we found that he had simply said from the pulpit: "I'm taking a seminar on sexual and domestic violence and I'll be out of the office on Wednesday mornings for the next three weeks."

This priest only signaled that he was seeking training and that he was available. That is all he needed to do. We will only hear about sexual and domestic violence when we speak about these issues. The pulpit is the perfect venue to begin opening the door and inviting people to share their experiences and to seek healing.

Exodus 1:15–22

Shiphrah and Puah, two of the named heroines of the Hebrew Scriptures, appear early in the book of Exodus. The context is one of fear. The unnamed

Egyptian Pharaoh is afraid of the Hebrews, afraid of their numbers and their strength as a people. So the Pharaoh intends to exercise some population control. He orders the midwives Shiphrah and Puah to kill the baby boys at birth. This ancient story echoes the femicide of the twenty-first century: the systematic killing of female infants because the male infants are considered more valuable. The killing of children because of their valued or feared gender is an early story of child abuse.

But Shiphrah and Puah refuse to do Pharaoh's bidding because they fear God more than they fear him (v. 17). They know it is wrong to kill the Hebrew babies. Needless to say, Pharaoh is not pleased, and now he commands everyone to throw the baby boys into the Nile. This is the story that sets the context for the birth of Moses in chapter 2. When the Levite woman gives birth to Moses, ironically she does put him in the Nile—in a waterproof basket in order to hide him. Moses becomes the hero who finally leads his people out of slavery and out of Egypt to freedom.

But the subtext in this passage is family. The midwives' refusal to kill the children preserved the Hebrew families. God was pleased and dealt well with the midwives, giving them families also (v. 21). The midwives did the right thing and were rewarded by God. And we remember their names! Walter Brueggemann comments: "Because of their singing the Hebrew barrio became a future-infested place from which has arisen all the later daring dances of freedom, a dance of defiance and gratitude and hope."[2] Children are not expendable. Children are not to be pawns in political or family disputes. Children are not property. Jesus teaches that to children (of both genders) belongs the reign of God.

Psalm 84:1–12

If you are not a survivor of domestic terror, try for a moment to imagine that you are as you read this psalm. As you read these words of joy and praise for the house of God (v. 4) and you ponder your house and your fear in your house for yourself and your children, how can you not wonder about this God?

The psalmist promises that even the sparrow finds a place to lay her young, a safe place to dwell (v. 3). And so you are living in a shelter for battered women; you and your three young children are packed into one room. You share meals with ten other mothers and twenty other children. The advocates promise that you are safe, but your husband has threatened to kill you if you try to leave him.

2. Walter Brueggemann, *Inscribing the Text* (Minneapolis: Fortress Press, 2004), 166.

You know that you have tried to be a good Christian; you have chosen the better part; you have tried to follow Jesus. The psalmist promises, "No good thing does the LORD withhold from those who walk uprightly. O LORD of hosts, happy is everyone who trusts in you" (vv. 11–12). How can you not wonder about this God?

This is the challenge in preaching on Psalm 84. Remember, there is someone in your congregation who is asking these very questions when she or he reads this psalm. How can you help someone struggle with such theodicy? If God is a good and loving God, and I have tried to be faithful to God, why do I suffer?

For the battered woman, these questions flow on two levels. She has tried to do everything she was "supposed" to do for her husband and everything he asks of her, and still why does he abuse her? And she has tried to do everything that God has asked of her, and now when she is in greatest need, where is God? Neither system is working for her. How do you help her go beyond "pie in the sky when we die" theology and begin to see God's hand at work in her life, even in the midst of great trauma, confusion, and fear? God does not promise the absence of pain, but God promises to be present in the pain and that there will be joy in the morning.

Mark 3:31–35

This passage in Mark follows Jesus' appointment of the twelve disciples. He goes home and is surrounded by a crowd who think he is crazy and possessed by Satan. Then his mother and brothers show up and ask him to come outside to see them. So he asks, rhetorically, "Who are my mother and my brothers?" Then as he looks around the group of people sitting with him, he points to them and says that those who do God's will are his mother and brother.

It is beyond imagining that Jesus would disregard his mother in this way. But given his sense of urgency, he may have been saying, "Look, tell them I'm busy and I'll get back to them." It is as if they had called on his cell phone, and he saw who it was and decided not to answer at that moment.

More importantly, Jesus was clearly making a point about family. In the Bible alone we read of multiple variations of families, mostly extended and including various nonbiological members. But Jesus is making a deeper spiritual point: he says his family are those who do God's will. Seems simple enough! He is saying that his people are those who follow God's teaching, which then extends to all his followers.

Why is this passage important in reflecting on the theme of Peace in the Home? Jesus is saying that there is nothing sacred per se about the biological family (particularly the nuclear family in U.S. society). We should choose those who follow God, who live out gospel values of respect, safety, love, and compassion.

"Keeping the family together" is often one of the reasons that a battered woman gives for staying in a situation of domestic terror. It is also one of the reasons she is encouraged to stay in that situation by friends, family, or her pastor. There is no "family" left once violence and abuse are brought into a home. The appearance of mother, father, and children may be maintained in public, but in private, the family has been broken apart. Peace in the home (*shalom bayit*) can only be achieved with those who follow God's will and treat family members with love and respect.

1 Peter 3:1–7

This is a difficult passage, especially as it comes between two passages discussing suffering and its meaning and purpose. First Peter 2:18–25 urges slaves to accept the authority of their masters and 1 Peter 3:8–22 affirms suffering for doing right. A victim of abuse can easily misinterpret either of these passages to justify and accept the abuse itself as God's will. So if you preach on 1 Peter 3:1–7, I encourage you to study also the preceding and following passages and be prepared to address questions about suffering.

Remember that the context here in the early church is a hostile culture. Christians were being persecuted, and at the same time they were trying to understand what it means to have this new life in Christ. The advice given here addresses the social location of citizens of Rome, slaves, wives, and husbands: stay in your place and focus on your inward self rather than on the outward. Perhaps this was practical advice as well: keep your head down and do not rock the boat, in order to survive persecution. This may be sound advice but it should not be understood to accept oppression passively.

The authors of *Study Bible for Women* suggest that the passage on wives refers to Christian women converts in relation to non-Christian husbands.[3] They have asserted themselves by their spiritual conversion and they should now submit to their husbands as a witness to convert them to the new faith. Many Christian battered women have tried this strategy in dealing with an abusive husband. It is seldom successful and should not be recommended.

This passage assumes a relationship that is not abusive but still hierarchical according to the custom of the period. Yet within this discussion, the final verse is critical. The instruction to the husbands (converts) establishes that in God's eyes, women and men are equal heirs to the gift of life. Thus wives are

---

3. Catherine Clark Kroeger, Mary Evans, and Elaine Storkey, eds., *Study Bible for Women: The New Testament* (Grand Rapids: Baker Books, 1995), 508–9.

to be treated with respect. The use of the term "weaker" should not be read as "inferior." Rather it is a recognition that women's social location in that period (and today) means that they have fewer resources and are thus more vulnerable. This passage acknowledges their struggle and husbands' responsibility to watch out for the well-being of their wives.

I recommend using Ephesians 5:22–33, emphasizing the multiple instructions for husbands to treat their wives with respect. The bottom line is that both of these passages have been misused to justify abuse. If we begin with a hermeneutical starting point that Jesus came to bring abundance of life to women and men, then even these passages cannot be used to justify the harm of domestic or sexual violence to one's partner.

Ascension of Jesus

R. Mark Giuliano

ACTS 1:1–11
PSALM 47
EPHESIANS 1:15–23
LUKE 24:44–53

"To God be the glory; great things [God] hath done," says the old hymn.[1] Today's readings, likewise, direct our hearts, voices, bodies, and mission toward the glorification of God. While in many ways the ascension passages are an affront to self-glorification, narcissistic piety, and temptation for personal and corporate power, they help us to discover spiritual empowerment and encouragement in the work of justice in the world through exclusive praise of God; as we lift up Jesus, we ourselves are raised.

Psalm 47

While hierarchical and kingly images of God may be potential stumbling blocks, the inspiring message of Psalm 47 is clear: God is "over all the earth" (v. 2) and all the nations (v. 8); let us respond, says this worshipful psalm, with unconditional praise through orchestrated hand clapping and "loud songs of joy" (v. 1), and an opened floodgate of singing praises to God. Verse 6 alone mentions singing four times.

According to the psalmist, who instructs worship leaders during the time of great kings, Solomon or David, worshipers are to give God praise for who God is (the Lord most high and an awesome king, v. 2), what God has done (formed a people and given them their heritage, vv. 3–4), and where God sits (enthroned over all the nations, v. 8).

Preachers should take note that the spiritual and emotional states of worshipers are not considerations for the psalmist. This is a psalm about God's

---

1. Fanny Jane Crosby, "To God Be the Glory," in *The Presbyterian Hymnal* (Louisville, KY: Westminster/John Knox Press, 1990), 485.

greatness and our call to respond. Sermons should be crafted in such a way that worshipers will sing praises to God not because of temporal or individual successes but simply because God is king. In his hugely famous and beautiful song *Hallelujah*, the Canadian poet and musician Leonard Cohen challenges his listeners to praise God even in a minor key: "There's a blaze of light in every word / It doesn't matter which you heard / The holy or the broken Hallelujah."[2] In other words, the faithful are called to praise God regardless of whether they feel like it or not.

No doubt, as preachers, we can name wonderful occasions when praising in hard times provided strength for the faithful; consider how we begin a funeral service with a hymn of praise, or a justice rally recalling God's faithful acts as part of our story. Still, the psalmist is not writing a prescription to lift us up, but musical instruction to lift God up.

Ephesians 1:15–23

Echoing Psalm 47, Ascension Sunday preachers may choose to explore Jesus' enthronement by the power of God to rouse Jesus from the dead, seat Jesus at God's right hand, and give Jesus authority and power above all worldly powers, other gods, and for all time for the church (vv. 20–23). This final point, Jesus' power and authority, could lend itself easily to a careful but important conversation about the lordship of Jesus in a pluralistic world. While the ascension highlights the name of Jesus above all other names, skillful and responsible preachers will avoid rehearsals of religious triumphalism. It is Jesus who is above all others, not particular congregations, denominations, or even Christianity.

While we may comfortably talk about Jesus above all "worldly powers" (read social, cultural, political, economic) and "for all time for the church" (read "the gathered," Gk. *ekklēsia*), the category "other gods" may prove more of a challenge. Both theological and homiletical care must be taken to ensure that the Christian message of the universal God of love does not denigrate the global diversity of faith. Through God's own Son, God called the church to proclaim a message of repentance and forgiveness of sins to all the nations (Luke 24:7, Gk. *ta ethnē*, those who live under neither the covenant of the law nor the new covenant in Christ).

Ascension Sunday preachers may enjoy liberation from the odd preoccupation with converting newcomers to Christendom, whether they be the Bobo tribespeople of Burkina Faso, the Muslim neighbor who runs the clothing

2. Leonard Cohen, "Hallelujah," from the album *Various Positions* (Columbia Records, 1984).

store down the street, or even the "agnostiterians" who show up to serve meals to the homeless but have not darkened the doors of the sanctuary in years. Ascension Sunday provides the opportunity to point to the revelation of the God of grace, who is above all, and yet has chosen to be with us in our world.

Luke 24:44–53

Look at a Google map of the City of Cleveland; the star that marks the heart of the city is mere steps from the front door of the church I serve. I mention geographic location because I am moved by the fact that numerous times a week a peculiar activity takes place at that heart of our city: a small but diverse group gather in our sanctuary and worship God. Week after week, year after year, blinding lake-effect snow or spring downpour, they gather in faith, as others have for 190 years. Seven days a week mission happens, but at the heart of the faith life and at the heart of the city, there is a worshiping community.

According to Luke, Jesus told the disciples to remain in the city for the fulfillment of God's promise and until they had been "clothed with power from on high" (v. 49). The disciples' waiting was not idle, however. After worshiping Jesus, they "returned to Jerusalem with great joy; and they were continually in the temple blessing God" (vv. 52–53). These are the final words of Luke's Gospel to instruct us in the way of waiting for God.

Those who speak on Ascension Sunday may want to consider the role of worship in the context of urbanization. The Spirit of the risen Christ meets us in the city in work and worship. Some of those who gather in our sanctuary to bless God understand worship on our city's main square as a countercultural act of protest against a city that, like most urban centers, often defines itself solely on economic values. For example, recently one of our city leaders spoke to our congregation about the economic advantages a downtown casino would offer everyone in our city. Asserting an economic belief, he said, "A rising tide will lift all boats." One of the faithful countered, however, with a Christian commentary on the politician's worldly wisdom: "Sir, a rising tide will lift all boats only if all boats are in good repair. How will we care for those for whom a rising tide means drowning?"

Worship in the urban core is itself an act of justice and social transformation, which reverberates out to the city and the region. Once the dominant silhouette on the urban landscape, today's city churches speak from beneath the shadows of towering bank buildings and corporate offices. Yet the worshiping community often acts as the voice of the voiceless, the strength of the powerless, and the presence of hope for a city and its people who often lose hope, yet who seek life and community. Its presence demonstrates the church's refusal to give over the streets to the thugs and the drugs, or the suits and their corporate sprawl, who would otherwise claim the city as their exclusive territory.

Inner-city worship also offers the opportunity for contemplative and restorative peace in a frenetic context where busyness, or the appearance of busyness, is rewarded and stillness is frowned upon as unproductive. The judge who prays in our sanctuary on her lunch hour prior to every new case, or the folks who practice yoga in our chapel at noontime in defiance of the idolatry of work, impress me.

Like many urban congregations throughout America, our faith community lacks the luster of our so-called glory days. Ours is not a particularly popular place except during the big festivals like Christmas and Easter. We do not even have a parking lot, but that makes the choice intentional. We worship not out of convenience, but because we have made the faithful decision to love God and neighbors, and to reclaim our humanity from the unwitting fragmentation, ghettoization, isolation, dislocation, and dehumanization of the city. To some, those who worship among us may seem offensive—the homeless, ex-convicts, and even a few lawyers—but in a place and time where memory is short and history is tailored, uniting as one in worship to bless God in the temple keeps us grounded in a story much older and more defining than even our cities or nations.

Acts 1:1–11

Before ascending, Jesus ordered the disciples to wait in Jerusalem (v. 4). It is in the "city" that the disciples would be "clothed with power from on high" (Luke 24:49). We saw in the Gospel passage that the church's mission is born and empowered in the city, and it is from the city that the witness moves out to the world (Acts 1:8, Luke 24:47).

Practically speaking, however, in many cases the biblical community has long since turned out the lights and fled the city. First, citizens have packed up and moved away from the challenges of city cores—pollution, crime, overcrowding, lack of public space, desegregation, and declining educational opportunities. More recently churches too spiral in the urban drain, with closings imposed by denominational hierarchies surviving on shoestring budgets or by wearied congregations.

While metropolitan areas continue to grow, urban neighborhoods experience decay from a whole host of ailments, such as abandonment, neglect, transiency, and underfunding. My wife and I are often asked why we would want to live in downtown Cleveland. In spite of its great theater district, professional sports, excellent restaurants, and a growing, albeit slowly, population of young professionals and empty nesters, many view the city as dangerous and hostile territory. Ironically, if our cities are unsafe, it is because we tend to use them only as places to fulfill our own private interests, such as attending sporting events or working, as we make haste to the suburbs and exurbs in the off-hours. No one has to care really for the city, let alone invest in it, if "no one" calls it home. No wonder the late Yale scholar Letty Russell compared the city to a battered woman:[3] abused by greed and corruption, neglected and isolated, and then blamed as if the city somehow did this to herself. How easy it is for us to take what we want from our city while disavowing any responsibility for it.

The young prophet Jeremiah (29:7) said that we should work and pray for the welfare of the city, "for in its welfare you will find your welfare." Jesus ordered the disciples to wait in the city for God's promise to be fulfilled (Acts 1:4). It is in Jerusalem, the literal and symbolic seat of political and religious meaning, that God's new Spirit would make itself known, bringing with it a new order.

If we want to see safe and thriving cities in America, then we, too, need to spend time in the city. Shop in it. Participate in its leadership. Invest in it. Worship in it. Dare to call it home. Even those communities nestled safely outside the city must understand that every suburb is a suburb of some city, large or small. The health of the core affects the body as a whole.

While the city often reflects the best of our humanity—music, theater, food, arts, sacred worship—it is also the place where dehumanizing powers and principalities such as domination, self-interest, greed, personal and corporate arrogance, self-righteousness, anxiety, and mental illness flourish. By participating in the life of the city as people of faith, we are hardly immune to those powers. However, as we engage with Jesus as moral agents of healing, transformation, and renewal, we name and confront those powers and principalities with a revolutionary new Word of redemption and a new Spirit of restoration.

---

3. Letty Russell, "The City as Battered Woman," in *Envisioning the New City: A Reader on Urban Ministry*, ed. Eleanor Scott Meyers (Louisville, KY: Westminster/John Knox Press, 1992).

Seventh Sunday of Easter

Luke A. Powery

ACTS 16:16–34
PSALM 97
REVELATION 22:12–14, 16–17, 20–21
JOHN 17:20–26

The readings for this Sunday reveal a form of Christian discipleship that is resistance to the status quo. In Acts, Paul and Silas resist the socioeconomic norm where economy is more important than humanity. Today's Psalms text explores the call to rejoice as resistance to the "gods" of fatalism or despair. The mantra of "come" in Revelation is resistance to isolation and segregation, while John reveals Jesus' resistance to normative divisions through his prayer for unity. These passages reveal resistance as a genuine mode of discipleship in the world.

Acts 16:16–34

In this passage, we meet a "slave-girl" with a special "spirit" who "brought her owners a great deal of money by fortune-telling" (v. 16). A gifted girl is enslaved for the economic gain of the enslaver. Her gifts produce profits. W. E. B. Dubois notes that such profiting stems from the gifts of the vulnerable and powerless, particularly the "gift of sweat and brawn." And he asks the poignant question, "Would America have been America without her Negro people?"[1] What he says of Africans in America is true for all of those oppressed under the mighty hand of pharaohs to build an empire in which they are deemed second-class citizens or perhaps not human at all.

The girl has a "spirit of divination" (v. 16) or literally a "pythonic spirit" (*pneuma pythōna*), not an evil spirit or demon, as some suggest. This "spirit of the Python" does not appear to threaten Paul, but it does annoy him to

---

1. W. E. B. Dubois, *The Souls of Black Folk* (1903; repr., New York: Penguin, 1982), 275, 276.

such an extent that he tells the spirit "to come out of her" (v. 18), which is not the same as a rebuke (cf. Luke 4:35, 41). His different tone could be due to the fact that this inspirited girl does not oppose Paul but actually gets the message straight.[2] The least likely individual, a girl with a different "spirit," tells the gospel truth about Paul and the way of salvation. But Paul soon hears the anger of those who pimp the girl for profits because, for some, nothing is more important than money (v. 19). For them, economy overrides theology and even supersedes humanity.

The owners did not care about the girl, only the money. They retaliate and lie to the magistrates, the chief Roman officials. The owners say nothing about their financial loss and self-interest but rather play on the fear of foreigners, xenophobia, to hype up the crowd. The owners falsely accuse Paul's company and say, "These men are disturbing our city; they are Jews and are advocating customs that are not lawful for us as Romans to adopt or observe" (vv. 20–21). The owners attempt to disgrace Paul and Silas in public by emphasizing their cultural and religious differences. This is the attempt to demonize difference, those who represent the other, just because they are different culturally or religiously. Because they practice their faith differently, think differently about God, and look and talk differently, they must be "disturbing" us. Fear of the unknown and fear of change propels this xenophobic approach. The majority may feel that they will lose their "customs" when other "minorities" migrate into the land and do things differently. It may be the Spanish language or another language that is not English. It may be building a mosque or another religious structure that is not of the Christian faith. But just because people are different, does that mean that one has to fan the fires of fear?

Paul and Silas resist the social status quo due to the "way of salvation" that they are following. Their resistance to the status quo, even unjust economic systems, is not cheap. They engage in costly discipleship.[3] Their discipleship of resistance is serious risky business, a matter of life and death. As a result of the owners' lies and the mob mentality, Paul and Silas are dragged, attacked, stripped, beaten, flogged, imprisoned in the "innermost cell," and have their feet fastened in stocks (vv. 19–24). They are left to die. This is not Starbucks-in-the-sanctuary discipleship.

Their means of strength are to pray and sing hymns to God in nonviolent resistance. They sing hymns, as many have done during times of struggle. Just as the Negro spirituals were songs of resistance, they claim life in the midst of death. The enslaved sang, "Oh freedom, oh freedom, oh freedom over me, and before I'd be a slave, I'll be buried in my grave and go home to my Lord and be free." These spirituals melodiously fought for freedom and liberation

2. John Levison, *Filled with the Spirit* (Grand Rapids: Eerdmans, 2009), 321.
3. See Dietrich Bonhoeffer, *The Cost of Discipleship* (New York: Touchstone, 1995).

of the oppressed as a form of this discipleship of resistance. Not surprising, then, is the notion that music was the heart and soul of the Civil Rights Movement. A melody may be more powerful than any other tool because even singing has the power to change one's condition.[4] We do not know what Paul and Silas sing exactly, but we do know that it leads to liberation, freedom, and salvation. "Everyone's chains were unfastened" (v. 26) and prison doors were opened. Their release leads to the jailer's spiritual freedom and salvation for him and his entire household. A song leads to salvation. A hymn brings healing, not just for Paul and Silas, whose wounds are washed and fellowship nurtured (vv. 33–34), but also for their jailer and his family.

Psalm 97

This psalm begins where the Acts passage ends—with rejoicing (v. 1): "Let the earth rejoice" because "the LORD is king!" Two other times, the psalmist exhorts others to "rejoice" (vv. 8, 12) because of God, "the LORD" (vv. 1, 5, 9, 10, 12). Rejoicing is linked to the Lord's reign. The ritual of rejoicing is countercultural to the prominence of despair over economic forecasts, oil spills, political corruption, insane murders, teenage suicide sparked by bullying, drug and alcohol addiction—the list could go on and on. Today, there does not appear to be much reason to rejoice, because apparently our existential reality does not match with the psalmist's biblical theology, that the Lord "guards the lives of [God's] faithful" and "rescues them from the hand of the wicked" (v. 10). Righteousness and justice may be the "foundation of [God's] throne" (v. 2), indicating that God's reign is rooted in prophetic "qualities of ethical conduct,"[5] but frequently what is right and just are deemed wrong.

There have been cases where the wicked win and the righteous are left in ruin. The innocent have suffered unjustly and the sick have been left to die. The orphan and the widow are overlooked because the social gaze is on the stock market. Thus, discipleship in the shape of rejoicing is a difficult form of resistance to the status quo, since the norm is praise for the mighty dollar and neglect of human needs. Why would one rejoice when life is a wreck for many? The "gods" (of greed, consumerism, racism, sexism, classism) do not appear to "bow down before [God]" (v. 7), despite the declaration. That seems more like a future promise than present condition. Yet the discipleship of rejoicing is a revelation of resistance, which has taken root all over the world despite harsh realities.

4. See Bernice Johnson Reagon, in Bill Moyers and Gail Pellett, *The Songs Are Free: Bernice Johnson Reagon and African American Music*, VHS, directed by Gail Pellett (New York: Films for the Humanities and Sciences, 1991).

5. James L. Mays, *Psalms*, Interpretation series (Atlanta: John Knox Press, 1994), 311.

During apartheid in South Africa, freedom songs could be heard ringing in the streets though it appeared that there was nothing to celebrate. During the aftermath of the 2010 earthquake in Haiti, despite much crying, moaning, and groaning, one could still hear singing in the streets. People rejoiced, not because of their circumstance of rubble. They rejoiced because of the Lord's reign. They sang to resist the other gods that said to just sit, do nothing, and die. They sang because they were still alive. They sang to resist their harsh reality. They sang, just as the enslaved did, as a sign of their dogged faith. They sang as a form of discipleship to resist a wrecked life. Celebration amid earthquake realities has been a lived tradition throughout the African diaspora because celebration is a "nonmaterial African cultural survival."[6] Rejoicing amid ruins does not erase the ruins, but it does recognize the Lord as "most high over all the earth" (v. 9).

Revelation 22:12–14, 16–17, 20–21

Though God is high, God stoops low. God comes near to us and invites us to come: "I am coming soon" (vv. 12, 20), Jesus says. This statement is basically the bookends of this pericope, demonstrating that he makes the first and last move toward us as the "Alpha and the Omega . . . the beginning and the end" (v. 13). "Ultimately, the end is not a place or a time, but a person."[7] And this person comes, but he also invites us to come. "The Spirit and the bride say, 'Come.' And let everyone who hears say, 'Come'" (v. 17). It is a call and response between the speaker and hearer. It is a call to meet each other, to be in each other's presence, not to be separated or segregated from one another. After offering an affirming "Amen" to this testimony from Jesus (v. 20), John then offers a prayer of invocation: "Come, Lord Jesus!"

This warm, hospitable invitation by divinity and humanity to "come" reminds me of the inhospitable legacy of Jim Crow segregation, in which blacks were not allowed to eat in the same restaurant, use the same water fountain, or attend the same school as whites. They were separate and did not have equal resources. There were no invitations, only "for whites only" or "colored" signs. And if one said "come," it was to come and be beaten, battered, and bruised. It was not to come and have life. It was to come (close) to death because of the color of one's skin. But Jesus says "come" to enter a new way of life, even a new city. It is a gift to be received, not a command to obey. Jesus' hospitality is not hostile to others. He shows the way of resistance

6. Olin Moyd, *The Sacred Art: Preaching and Theology in the African American Tradition* (Valley Forge, PA: Judson Press, 1995), 101.

7. Brian Blount, "Revelation," in *True to Our Native Land: An African American New Testament Commentary*, ed. Brian K. Blount et al. (Minneapolis: Fortress Press, 2007), 555.

through how he resists death-wielding inhospitality. He shows the way to live. His invitation is for those in need, the "thirsty," to come and drink this water of life (v. 17). All are welcome, and through his invitation we are wooed to offer a similar hospitality as we say "come," coming out to engage the O/ other, resisting isolation. Anyone who wants to accept this refreshing gift is invited to come. "Come" is a call to discipleship in the manner of Jesus.

John 17:20–26

Jesus prays "that they may all be one" three different times (vv. 21, 22, 23) "so that the world may believe you have sent me" (vv. 21, 23). Jesus links oneness or unity with the world believing that Jesus the Son was sent from God. Oneness is presented as a sign of God's presence in the world and evidence of God's love, as indicated in the words of Jesus, "we are one" (v. 22). Jesus says that God is in him and he is in God, yet he also yearns that the disciples may be in them both (v. 21). Thus, he calls for the disciples to be unified, as God is unified, with the hope that the disciples would be unified (i.e., one) with God.

Jesus prays for the creation and maintenance of unity among the believers. He does this because oneness is a revelation of genuine discipleship in the world. Here, the discipleship of resistance opposes a divisive world. A call to unity resists temptations to divide along racial, educational, socioeconomic, and gender lines. To be divided is easy. To be one is difficult. Even within the church, there are so many divisions across denominational, theological, political, and musical lines. Howard Thurman had good reason to declare that the church has been "divided into dozens of splinters."[8] The daily divisions are perpetuated as the prayer of Jesus appears to have not yet taken root in our hearts and lives: choral anthems or praise and worship music, organs or bands, ordination of women or not, liberal or conservative Christian, suburban or urban congregation, mainline church or charismatic megachurch? Still, the desire for unity as a sign of Christian discipleship rings out from these verses. The pressures to divide are present on many levels, but will we unify for the sake of Christ or die due to destructive divisions? How we answer that question says something about what kind of disciple we are.

8. Howard Thurman, *The Creative Encounter* (Richmond, IN: Friends United Press, 1972), 139.

Day of Pentecost

John S. McClure

Genesis 11:1–9
Psalm 104:24–34, 35b
Acts 2:1–21
John 14:8–17 (25–27)

For Christians, Pentecost celebrates the pouring out of God's Holy Spirit upon the early church. The texts for this day help us answer important questions about what God desires for culture and human community. Genesis 11:1–9 and Acts 2:1–21 help us answer questions such as: What is the nature and purpose of human culture from God's perspective? How is the idea of "unity" sometimes used to destroy God's vision for human flourishing? What does true unity as a diverse people look like, from a Christian perspective? John 14:8–17 (25–27) focuses our attention on another set of crucial questions: What does it mean to be an ethical community? What is our core identity? What help do we have in sustaining that identity? Psalm 104:24–34 suggests the context of environmentalism as one place to think through our social witness. The psalm as a whole asks us to examine our motivations for environmental witness.

Genesis 11:1–9

Many scholars believe that the story of the tower of Babel is designed to explain the origins of ethnic and linguistic diversity. Why are we so diverse and different? Why is there not singularity and unity when it comes to language and culture? Babel is the climax of the primeval history of creation. It tells a tale in which human sin, greed, and idolatry estrange humanity from God and from one another.

From the perspective of social justice, one cannot avoid noticing the role of human technology and achievement in the process of building culture

249

(Babel), especially in a world of diversity. When the people of God entered the land of Shinar, they learned how to make bricks and build houses, places of worship, and cities (vv. 2–3). Initially, this was a good thing. The technology and resources to build a lasting and permanent culture presented a golden opportunity to overcome the pressures of harsh wilderness life that had been so hard on those who were weakest.

One of the key aspects of any culture is that it exists to enable more people to survive the harsh environment of nature and "natural selection." And yet, as culture advances and becomes more complex and self-assured, it can also become a harsh environment, suited only for the "survival of the fittest," who usually are those deemed "normal." The tower of Babel, like many contemporary skyscrapers, is a symbol of the highest achievements of structure and order. As the recent economic crisis and our ongoing ecological crisis remind us, human cultures often adapt to their own inner, predictable, laws of progress, forgetting that it is God who stands behind the laws of culture and nature. Fascinated with their own technological capabilities, the people of Babel said to themselves, "Come, let us build ourselves a city, and a tower with its top in the heavens, and let us make a name for ourselves; otherwise we shall be scattered abroad upon the face of the whole earth" (v. 4).

From this perspective, when God intervened and scattered the people, God was not acting against their building culture. Instead, it was an act against building an oppressive, idolatrous, self-securing culture. From God's perspective, human culture was not to be a place of self-securing idolatry focused on "getting what's mine" at the expense of all others. Rather, human culture was meant to remain open to supporting endless diversity of life and creative expression. God's "culture" is not a closed society, but an environment designed to support more forms of life than could otherwise flourish.

Genesis 11:1–9 became one of the official documents of the Afrikaans Reformed churches during apartheid in South Africa. Apartheid exegetes used this text to prove that God intends for humanity to divide into separate *volke* or ethnic groups in order to fulfill God's plan to "fill the earth" in Genesis 1:28. These exegetes located the sin of the people of God at Babel in the attempt to create a unified culture and language (v. 1). This interpretation, however, misses the fact that the linguistic unity of the human family is a *given* in this story, part of God's original creation, not something they attempt to achieve at this point in history. This reading also denies what the text clearly states: that the sin of the people of God on the plain of Shinar is the attempt to use linguistic unity to achieve cultural and technological independence from God (v. 4).

Acts 2:1–21

The documents of the Afrikaans Reformed churches also used the Pentecost story in Acts 2:1–21 to shore up their argument for separation. They asserted that the great language miracle at Pentecost proves that it is God's will that people should hear God's word in their own native tongue and thus be separated from one another. This interpretation misses the fact that at Pentecost God reverses the dispersion of God's people at Babel by gathering people of all nations and tongues "together in one place" (v. 1), where God speaks to them in the one common language of the Spirit. The unity of the church at Pentecost is further accentuated by Peter preaching to "all" of them in one language after the miracle has occurred (v. 14). Unity, or unity in diversity, is not the issue. What is at issue is the use of exclusionary or divisive forms of unity of any sort to secure oppressive, self-securing claims to power.

Preachers of social justice and transformation, therefore, might focus on the nature and meaning of unity, both Christian and cultural. These stories make it clear that Christian unity is rooted not in exclusivist claims to power (Babel) but in the power of God's Spirit to gather together and foster communication between diverse peoples (Pentecost). Christians should be wary of the all-too-human proclivity to turn any culture or subculture into a self-securing idol, whether it is the culture of the family, race, ethnic group, work, civic club, church, or nation. Unity within God's plans and purposes is always an "open unity"; it reaches out and embraces others, no matter how different, and provides an environment in which they can flourish, nurture uniqueness and difference (even linguistic difference), and yet communicate in and through the Spirit of love and justice.

In today's context, the Genesis and Acts texts together challenge the churches to consider new ways to think about immigration and what it means to live together as an immigrant nation. In a way strikingly similar to the vision imparted in these biblical stories, musician Steve Earle has written a song called "City of Immigrants" that starts from a fundamental premise of the biblical witness: we are all immigrants, exiles, and strangers living together; and attempts to construct walls between ourselves and others can only be motivated by concerns that are, at best, delusional, and at worst, evil.

John 14:8–17 (25–27)

This is one of the great texts of the apostolic tradition. Apostles are those who are "sent," whose primary task is to carry on the work and ministry begun by God in Jesus Christ. This is a very important theme for the church today, especially in a world of almost overwhelming injustice. Those who believe in

Christ "will also do the works that I [Christ] do" and even "greater works than these" (v. 12). John cautions us not to reduce the gospel message to something that might be found in the self-help section of the mall bookstore. There is an epic proportion to gospel ministry. Consider the work still before us: combating the pervasive structural power of evil in the world, reconciling racial and ethnic divisions, healing the deep wounds etched into the body of mother earth, restoring broken and abused lives.

The good news is that we are not alone in this ministry. Unlike the jubilee ethic of Luke, or the legal ethic of Matthew, John's Gospel encourages a communitarian ethic: "I am in the Father and the Father is in me" (v. 11), "I am the vine, you are the branches" (John 15:5). John envisions a community of truth in a hostile world. The Spirit of truth, whom "the world cannot receive" (v. 17), assures the unique witness of this community. Because it is organically connected to Christ, the church is a community of truth that lives in the world in new ways and works within an eschatological vision of love.

But how does this community avoid becoming a narrow, self-securing sect? A key component of this community's life, and one often missed in socially active congregations, is intercessory prayer. Christ encouraged the disciples to "ask in my name" and averred, "If in my name you ask me for anything, I will do it" (vv. 13, 14). Intercession means literally "to go between." The community's "greater works" of love begin in intercession—in becoming a community of people who go between the world and God through prayer.

Intercession is a two-way street. The intercessor goes to the people and discovers their needs, and then takes those needs to God in prayer, asking for divine wisdom, healing, and mercy. The intercessor also goes to God and discovers what God desires for a hurting world, and is empowered by God to do "greater works" that manifest God's desires within families, communities, nations, and globally. At the heart of this prayer is the Holy Spirit, who is the "Advocate" (v. 26). We are intercessory people—a community of go-betweens, fellow-advocates with the Holy Spirit, bringing the suffering of the world to God, and bringing God's healing balm to the world. Both aspects of intercession are crucial to our identity and mission.

Psalm 104:24–34, 35b

This psalm, in its entirety, is one of the great environmentalist psalms. The psalm is a catalog of the wonders of creation, scrolling through the many ways in which every aspect of creation both depends on God and exists in order to glorify God and provide God enjoyment. The first message in this psalm, therefore, is that environmentalism in the biblical context finds its deepest motivation not from our fears and concerns for survival, but from our awareness that all of creation is in covenantal relationship with God and exists for the glory of God. To diminish creation is to diminish one of the primary ways in which God's glory is manifest on earth. To argue for the planet and its health is to argue for that which is most pleasing and important to God.

The second message concerns our place as humans in the ordering of God's creation. Similar to the creation story, Psalm 104 catalogs the ways in which God provides for human beings and their welfare. Our needs are placed into the context of the needs of such luminous creatures as "wild asses" (v. 11), "birds of the air" (v. 12), and "cattle" (v. 14). Here, an important environmentalist principle is reinforced—embedding human life within the larger framework of God's creation. Other creatures on this planet have needs and exist in relationship to God. Human needs are not unimportant, but they are closely related to the needs of other forms of life on the planet.

Verses 24–34 focus on a third important theme: the importance of doxology in the Christian's approach to creation. It is very easy for those of us who are committed to environmentalist efforts to become cynical, angry, frustrated, and strident in our efforts. We see only the ugliness that various forms of human technology have inflicted on the environment, which sometimes clouds our vision, and we lose sight of our overall mission and frame of reference. Verses 24–34 invite us to remember the largest and most important framework for our commitments to healing creation: our absolute dependence on God in all things. The only way to express this dependence is in thankful praise for the great gift of creation itself, seeking to honor God by restoring the beauty of the earth.

First Sunday after Pentecost
(Trinity Sunday)

Kee Boem So

PROVERBS 8:1–4, 22–31
PSALM 8
ROMANS 5:1–5
JOHN 16:12–15

This week's readings invite us to reflect on the mystery of the Trinity. As we reflect on the works of the Trinity in the intimate communion of the three persons of God, we are also invited to participate in the works and the relationship of the Trinity. Christian life is to participate in this life of the Trinity and to actualize its implications for believers to embody in their lives. These implications are related to women, creatures, and Christian life.

Proverbs 8:1–4, 22–31

The first reading presents the first implication of the Trinity as it is related to women. The text introduces a well-known female image of God in the Hebrew Bible, that is, Wisdom. It has been consistently pointed out by feminist, womanist, mujerista, and Asian women theologians that "various understandings of God affect the reality and the spirituality" of women and also men.[1] Therefore these women pay particular attention to this female image of God as a way to speak rightly about God in the midst of our male-centered society and the church. Wisdom here is personified as a female street preacher (v. 1): "Does not wisdom call, and does not understanding raise her voice?" Wisdom raises her voice at every corner of the city, especially about her existence with God in creation.

Wisdom is already introduced with regard to the act of creation in Proverbs: "The LORD by wisdom founded the earth" (3:19). The first reading of this week elaborates further on this point. God creates Wisdom as the first

---

1. Choi Hee An, *Korean Women and God: Experiencing God in a Multi-religious Colonial Context* (Maryknoll, NY: Orbis Books, 2005), 99.

of God's creation: "The LORD created me at the beginning of [God's] work, the first of [God's] acts of long ago. Ages ago I was set up, at the first, before the beginning of the earth" (vv. 22–23). However, Wisdom is not just the result of God's work, but also participates in God's creation: "Then I was beside [God], like a master worker; and I was daily [God's] delight, rejoicing before [God] always, rejoicing in [God's] inhabited world and delighting in the human race" (vv. 30–31). Elizabeth Johnson comments, "Creation is not simply the act of a solitary male deity. . . . [Wisdom] is a beneficent, right-ordering power in whom God delights and by whom God creates."[2] God does not create the world alone but in collaboration with Wisdom. She is the force and joy in creation. She becomes joy for God, for the world, and for humans. This Wisdom is incarnate in the second person of the Trinity (John 1:1–2) and also in the Holy Spirit (John 15:26). This female image of God in Wisdom as God's creative force and joy empowers women living in our male-centered society. This is the social implication of the Trinity for women and therefore transformative for women and men alike. And the theme of collaboration in creation leads us to the second reading of the week: humans as the coworkers of God's creation.

Psalm 8

The second reading of this week provides us with another implication of the Trinity with regard to our creation by calling out humans to be God's coworkers. This psalm begins and ends with praising God the creator in God's sovereignty (vv. 1, 9): "O LORD, our Sovereign, how majestic is your name in all the earth!" Between these two verses praising God as the creator of the universe, the psalm places human beings as God's coworkers who represent God's sovereignty in the continuation of God's creation.

The psalmist speaks of God's caregiving to human beings (v. 4): "What are human beings that you are mindful of them, mortals that you care for them?" Human beings become joy for God in the moment that God creates them and in God's continuing relationship with them. We read here the joy of Wisdom in creation resonating in the joy of human beings.

Human beings become joy for God also as the vessels through which God's joy to other creatures is delivered (v. 6): "You have given them dominion over the works of your hands; you have put all things under their feet." Dominion here means caregiving. As God's joy emerges in care for human beings, God also wants humans to care for other created beings as God's coworkers and so to live in joy with creation. The act of creation in the Trinitarian relationship

2. Elizabeth A. Johnson, *She Who Is: The Mystery of God in Feminist Theological Discourse* (New York: Crossroad, 2002), 88.

is manifested in our acts with God's creation as God's coworkers. Wherever ecological problems such as exploitation of nature, pollution, and global warming persist, this social implication of the Trinity will emerge as God's invitation to active participation in the life of the Trinity through human acts of caring for God's creation.

Romans 5:1–5

A third implication of the Trinity is related to Christian life in general, the character of life in the triune God in particular. Christian life participating in the Trinitarian relationship is formulated in Paul's characterization of Christian life (1) as entering into relationship with God, (2) as being fulfilled through Jesus Christ, and (3) as actualized through the work of the Holy Spirit.

Paul first talks about the place of the second person of the Trinity in Christian life: "We have peace with God through our Lord Jesus Christ, through whom we have obtained access to this grace in which we stand" (5:1b–2a). The relationship of peace with God is possible through Jesus Christ. It is because Jesus is the Word incarnated where God's glory and truth are manifest (John 1:14). Therefore Jesus provides access to this relationship with God.

Then Paul points out an important aspect of Christian life: "We boast in our hope of sharing the glory of God. And not only that, but we also boast in our sufferings" (5:2b–3a). When we as believers enjoy the relationship with God through Jesus Christ, we come to boast about one thing in our life within the Trinitarian relationship, that is, "hope of sharing the glory of God" (5:2b). Paul develops this definite feature of Christian life in the remaining verses. Even if we are suffering, we can still boast about this hope because "suffering produces endurance, and endurance produces character, and character produces hope" (5:3b–4). Our boast in the hope is not dependent on circumstances, but on our character. Christian life as active participation within the Trinitarian relationship produces this hope of sharing in the glory of God.

Paul adds, however, that God does not leave us alone in this process. God provides us with strength and the resource through which we can continue this lifelong journey, that is, God's love brought through the Holy Spirit. Paul says, "God's love has been poured into our hearts through the Holy Spirit that has been given to us" (v. 5b).

Etty Hillesum stands among many who lived such a life that could boast in hope. Hillesum died at Auschwitz in 1943 at the age of twenty-nine. In the midst of the most horrendous experiences in human history, she wrote in her diary: "We may of course be sad and depressed by what has been done to us; that is only human and understandable. However: our greatest injury is one we inflict upon ourselves. I find life beautiful, and I feel free. The sky within me is as wide as the one stretching above my head. I believe in God and I believe in [humanity], and I say so without embarrassment."[3] How could she maintain such an impossible faith in God and other human beings? We cannot but say, with Paul, that she must have built up in the midst of her sufferings a character in which she could boast in hope and that she must have felt God's enormous love poured into her heart through God's Spirit even at Auschwitz. This, too, is the work of the Holy Spirit in the life of the Trinitarian relationship, leading us to the next reading of the week.

John 16:12–15

The last implication of today's texts in the life of the Trinitarian relationship is also about Christian life in general and a life centered on the Holy Spirit in particular. Christian life is walking and living with the Spirit.

As the hour for Jesus to return to God is approaching, the fourth reading of this week starts with the tension between Jesus wanting to say more before he departs and the disciples' inability to understand and live into all the implications of God's revelation in Jesus (v. 12). Reconciliation of this tension only comes from the Spirit, the Paraclete: "When the Spirit of truth comes, [it] will guide you into all the truth" (16:13a). The Spirit will come after Jesus departs to prepare places for the disciples in God's house. The Spirit will then remain with the disciples, leading them in all truth until Jesus returns. The Spirit will stay in relationship with all believers as "the ongoing presence of the revelation of God in the in-between-time."[4]

This relationship with the Spirit that we enjoy now is after all the Trinitarian relationship, "for [the Spirit] will not speak on [its] own, but will speak whatever [it] hears" (16:13b). As Jesus is sent by God (7:29) and speaks and acts according to the will of God as the perfect revelation of God (5:30), the Spirit is also sent by God and declares all that is from Jesus, as Jesus himself says: "[The Spirit] will glorify me, because [it] will take what is mine and declare it to you. All that [God] has is mine" (vv. 14–15a). Therefore the relationship we enjoy in the present time with the Spirit is derived from the Trinitarian relationship. Christian life is all about participating in this life of the Trinitarian relationship and actualizing this life to its fullest potential.

This week's readings invite us to ponder the implications of the Trinity and to live into the Trinitarian relationship. Whether it is the power to name God in the female image of Wisdom on behalf of women living in patriarchal

---

3. Etty Hillesum, *An Interrupted Life: The Diaries, 1941–1943 and Letters from Westerbork* (New York: Henry Holt, 1996), 144–45.
4. Francis J. Moloney, *The Gospel of John*, Sacra pagina (Collegeville, MN: Liturgical Press, 1998), 442.

society, or to act as God's coworkers to continue God's ongoing care for creation and creatures in their suffering, or to build up a character to boast only in the "hope of sharing God's glory" in our lives regardless of our current circumstances, or to live with the Spirit who brings about the Trinitarian relationship within us, it is now the time for us to decide whether we will accept God's palpable invitation into the life of the Trinity.

Proper 3 [8]

Safiyah Fosua

ISAIAH 55:10–13
PSALM 92:1–4, 12–15
1 CORINTHIANS 15:51–58
LUKE 6:39–49

We live in anticipation of the fulfillment of God's promises. Isaiah 55 tells us to expect a time when we will not be captives. First Corinthians 15 describes the coming restoration of our physical bodies. Though we live in the shadow of amazing anticipation and hope, we have many things to learn about life here and now in the realm of God. At times, both the secular culture and the church prefer to think of the teachings of Jesus as lofty ideals, not goals for Christian living. But, as the writers of both Psalm 92 and Luke's Gospel would remind us, righteousness is not just for experts. It is the norm and standard for all who belong to God.

Isaiah 55:10–13

Second Isaiah ends with the same intense hope that characterized its beginning in Isaiah 40. Isaiah 55 reminds the exiles of the sure promises of God as they near the end of their captivity. The entire chapter, with the exception of the prophet's call to repentance (vv. 6–7), is God's speech. The chapter's focus is on God, whose ways are beyond understanding. We are reminded of the sure covenant of David. God's invitation to come and buy food and drink without price, which begins the chapter, goes out to the hungry and the thirsty. Today's verses (vv. 10–13) expand on the reliability of God's promises and paint a joyous picture of Israel's yet-to-be-realized return from exile, similar to that found in Isaiah 49.

In verse 10, God's word is compared to the rain and snow that make the sustaining grains grow for daily bread. This metaphor is one of several used in Second Isaiah to describe the trustworthiness of God's word, with verse 11 echoing a similar promise made in 40:8, "The grass withers, the flower fades; but the word of our God will stand forever." The metaphor suggests mystery. The God who has control over when the rain falls and how much falls at one time knows when and how Israel's captivity shall end. The God who makes the seeds sprout will, through ways beyond human understanding (55:8–9), take care of them.

Look at the promises that God makes about their return (vv. 12–13). They will go out in joy (v. 12). This time they will not be driven out of the country like their ancestors who, after the tenth plague, were expelled from Egypt by a shocked, angry, and vengeful Pharaoh (Exod. 12:31–33). God's promise of a peaceful return suggests that the Israelites, unlike their ancestors in the wilderness centuries before, will not have to war with neighboring peoples as they make their way home. Finally, their restoration will affect more than humankind. Isaiah's oft-repeated image of a rejoicing creation, with this chapter's mountains in song and trees clapping their hands, suggests that the restoration of God's people has implications for the land.

Psalm 92:1–4, 12–15

Psalm 92, which begins with an exhortation to praise God, is one of the few psalms that have explicit suggestions for when or how it is to be used. The inscription says that Psalm 92 is a song for the Sabbath day. The Levites in the temple sang a particular psalm on each day of the week. The weekly list included Psalms 24, 48, 82, 94, 81, 93, and this psalm.[1] The psalmist paints rich pictures of worship in the temple when he or she reminisces about how good it is to give thanks, morning and evening, to the sound of the temple's instruments.

The psalmist cites good reasons for praising God and giving thanks: God's "work" and the "works of [God's] hands" (v. 4), which are references to two different ways that Israel experienced the activity of God. The phrase "works of God's hands" is used to refer to creation (see, for example, Ps. 8:6). Similarly, the phrase "God's works" is usually an indication of "God's saving work on behalf of the people" (see Deut. 32:4; Pss. 44:1; 90:16; 95:9; Isa. 5:12),[2] and the Hebrew word used here, *pō'al*, is frequently translated "deeds" in several modern translations of the Bible. Psalm 92 invites worshipers to praise God for creation *and* for what God has done for them as individuals and as a nation.

---

1. J. Clinton McCann Jr., "The Book of Psalms: Introduction, Commentary, and Reflections," in *The New Interpreter's Bible*, ed. Leander Keck et. al. (Nashville: Abingdon Press, 1996), 4:1050.
2. Ibid., 1051.

In the final four verses of this psalm, the righteous are likened to the familiar palm tree and the cherished cedars of Lebanon that grow and flourish and bear fruit well into old age. Their righteousness points to God, who is an upright and reliable resting place in whom there is no unrighteousness. This description of the righteous functions as a reminder that Israel's worship always had ethical and spiritual implications. The daily and weekly rituals of the temple dramatized processes of inner transformation that made it possible for Israel to keep its side of the two-way covenant with God, "I . . . will be your God and you shall be my people" (Lev. 26:12). Sacrifices offered for sin meant having to wrestle, on some cognitive level, with the personal sin and the corporate sin that stood between them and God. Thank offerings acknowledged God as the source of all good things. These and other rituals of righteousness offered substance and definition to Israel's relationship with God.

Similar things could be said about the twenty-first-century church. Our coming together has ethical and spiritual implications. The rituals used in our gatherings hold both danger and opportunity. They either devolve into something we habitually do together without meaning or they become dynamic, transforming moments in our spiritual lives. Israel lived with the understanding that they were called to be a light to the nations, leading outsiders to faith in God (Isa. 42:6; 49:6). Early Christians saw themselves as living letters, written to be read by observers—even when suffering at the hands of their enemies (1 Cor. 4:9). Just as the Israelites' and the early Christians' quest for righteousness said something to onlookers about the God that they served, the lives of people in the present-day church speak as much to onlookers. How do rituals observed in today's communities of faith affect our ethics and spirituality? Do they cause us to look at ourselves critically or to work for the common good? Do our rituals lead us first to repentance and ultimately to righteousness?

1 Corinthians 15:51–58

Paul calls (v. 51), "Listen, I will tell you a mystery!" These words are from a disturbing conversation between himself and the Corinthians. Believers in Corinth struggled to believe that Jesus literally rose from death. Equally as serious, they struggled to understand how the dead in Christ could live again. It is fortunate that this lengthy chapter from the Corinthian letter was preserved for us, because it has become foundational to our understanding of what the emerging first-century church believed about resurrection. It has also become a primary source for many present-day theological discussions about the resurrection.

The Corinthians were not unique in their struggle to believe in resurrection. Church history points to several recurring controversies over the bodily resurrection of Jesus Christ. Present-day believers continue to have difficulty with both the historicity of Christ's resurrection and the likelihood that believers in Christ will follow suit. God's promise of resurrection from death confronts us with yet another promise that we cannot control, predict, or understand. In spite of our difficulties, this one doctrine continues to be foundational to the Christian faith.

In this summary of Paul's long treatise on resurrection, we observe three things. First, the early church's teachings about resurrection were not new. The promise of resurrection was seen through the lens of an ancient promise from God. "Death has been swallowed up in victory" is a direct reference to Isaiah 25:7–8, which promises that God will swallow up death forever. A second part of this promise, to wipe away the tears from all faces, was repeated by John in Revelation 7:17. Next, the early church believed in a literal resurrection for believers: "this perishable body puts on imperishability" (v. 54). Last, the early church looked forward to the imminent return of Christ and expected that both the dead in Christ and those who were alive at the second coming would receive new bodies.

Paul's reference to imperishability (v. 54), seen apart from its mystery and controversy, frequently triggers responses like "What a relief that we are not stuck with bodies that we have worn out or ruined!" On a deeper level, however, this promised transformation of the physical body offers hope that other transformations are also possible. The belief that flawed circumstances need not be our permanent estate is an extension of resurrection thinking. Belief in the resurrection conditions us to believe that dead marriages have hope, that people once imprisoned by dead works have a future, that imperfect governments and broken economies can be repaired, and that even hurricane-flooded cities or cities buried under the rubble of earthquakes are able to rise again. Much of what we do together in the name of Christ and practically all of our work toward a just and equitable future is influenced by the church's traditional beliefs about resurrection.

The resurrection cannot be observed, counted, tested, or measured in a lab. We are hard-pressed to interview a person who has experienced resurrection about the new imperishable body. The resurrection is a matter of faith. Or as the writer of Hebrews 11:1 says, it is "the assurance of things hoped for, the conviction of things not seen."

Luke 6:39–49

The Gospel lection is taken from a section often called Luke's Sermon on the Mount. This seemingly condensed version, found in vv. 20–49, differs significantly from that found in Matthew 5–7. The content of this sermon in Luke is presented with a Gentile audience in mind—contrasted with Matthew's sermon, which is decidedly more Jewish. A close reading reveals that many of the teachings not included here from Matthew's sermon are sprinkled throughout Luke's Gospel.

Though Luke's sermon appears to be held together loosely, these parables, sayings, and figures of speech work together to teach believers the norms and expectations of Christian discipleship. Early Christians thought of believers as newborn babes (1 Pet. 2:2), as newly adopted children (Gal. 4:5) and heirs of God's promises. Wisdom teachings, like the short sayings found in Luke's sermon, were normal ways that early believers learned Christian discipleship from each other. Today, we use them as ways to orient one another to the life of faith.

Jesus taught in parables and used common speech so that all who had ears to hear would be able to understand him. He used uncomplicated sayings—blind people should not lead one another, lest they fall into a ditch (v. 39); good disciples become like their teacher (v. 40); no one is qualified to judge another, and each of us should instead examine ourselves (vv. 41–42); people, like trees, are known by their fruit (vv. 43–44)—and it does us no good to hear what Jesus is saying and fail to respond. But those who hear and act on Jesus' words are like those who build their houses on a solid foundation (vv. 46–49).

These teachings are not difficult to understand, but they are frequently considered difficult to follow. Though we may consider them difficult, the writings of the early church fathers and mothers reveal that Christians in the early church actually endeavored to live by the teachings of Jesus. It is tragic that secular culture has begun to convince the church that the standard of righteousness represented by Jesus' teachings is unattainable or even unbelievable.

Proper 4 [9]

Diane G. Chen

1 KINGS 18:20–21 (22–29), 30–39   1 KINGS 8:22–23, 41–43
PSALM 96   PSALM 96:1–9
                                                        GALATIANS 1:1–12
                                                        LUKE 7:1–10

The theme "proclaiming God to the nations" permeates the lectionary selections for this week. Beginning with Israel in the First Testament and the early church in the Second Testament, the people of God are to tell the world of God's mighty and salvific works, through which the world experiences God's authority, compassion, and justice. Psalm 96 and the prayer of Solomon in 1 Kings 8 explicitly state that there is no other god besides the God of Israel. The same is implied in the contest between Elijah and the prophets of Baal in 1 Kings 18. Because there is no other god, God is uniquely sovereign over all peoples. God's vision of salvation extends through Israel, the chosen people, to all other nations. Hence Solomon prays that the foreigner who looks to God will receive blessing (1 Kgs. 8); Jesus heals the slave of a Roman centurion (Luke 7); and Paul insists that his commission to preach the gospel to the Gentile churches in Galatia comes only from God and God's Son, the Lord Jesus Christ (Gal. 1).

Psalm 96:1–9 and 1 Kings 8:22–23, 41–43

Using the highest accolades, the psalmist attributes to Israel's God all honor, majesty, strength, beauty, and glory. For the triple imperatives of the opening verse, I prefer the rendition "sing *of* God" to that found in most English translations ("sing *to* God"), because what follows is all about God as creator, savior, king, and judge. All creation—"all the earth" (Ps. 96:1, 9) and "all the peoples" (v. 3, cf. v. 7)—are called to proclaim God and hear God being proclaimed through this new song (v. 1).

This song is new, not because God's greatness is previously unheard of, but because the people's experience of God is constantly renewed. God's mighty works are proclaimed "from day to day" (v. 2), for "[God's mercies] are new every morning" (Lam. 3:22–23). The commands to give due honor to God soon give way to invitations to draw near: "Bring an offering, and come into [God's] courts" (v. 8). Even then, God's power and holiness cause worshipers to tremble (v. 9), not so much in the sense of alienating creator from creature, but of maintaining a respectful and proper distance between the two.

One might object to Israel's monotheistic "imposition" and ask why the Canaanites cannot be left alone to worship their own gods. This question sounds strangely contemporary in today's pluralistic world. The psalmist's answer lies in verse 5: "For all the gods of the peoples are idols; but the LORD made the heavens." That God is Creator is a *truth* claim of the text as well as a *faith* claim. Because God is Creator, unequaled in might and authority, God is fittingly called king and judge. All other deities—or so-called deities—are in reality not gods at all. The Hebrew word *elihim*, translated "idols" in the NRSV, means "rags" or "nonentities." Elsewhere in the First Testament *elihim* connotes something ineffective and futile (Job 13:4; Zech. 11:17). Since *elihim* sounds like *Elohim* ("God"), the play on the word implies that idols are poor imitations of the one true God. They are worthless, like rags, with nothing divine in them whatsoever. Between embracing nothingness and beholding God's holy splendor, the choice is obvious. Only God is deserving of worship. Only God will heed the prayers of the covenantal people.

The setting of 1 Kings 8 is the ceremony at which Solomon's temple is dedicated. The beginning of Solomon's prayer echoes Psalm 96, that "there is no God like [YHWH] in heaven above or on earth beneath" (1 Kgs. 8:23). Furthermore, the almighty God establishes a covenantal relationship with those who respond in trust and fidelity with all their hearts. At first glance, one would expect these to refer to the faithful in Israel, since it is, after all, the Jerusalem temple that is being dedicated. As expected, Solomon prays that God would forgive Israel and answer the prayers of the people in times of personal distress, natural disaster, and national crisis. Yet tucked in the middle of a list of petitions for Israel is a petition on behalf of the foreigner, who is described as one "not of [God's] people Israel," but who "comes from a distant land because of [God's] name" (v. 41). Solomon prays that God would show divine benevolence to those foreigners who, by praying toward God's temple, show that they are already oriented toward the one true God. As they experience the beneficent power of God, they will in turn proclaim God before their own people and spread God's reputation farther afield.

This message of uncompromising monotheism, so central to Psalm 96 and Solomon's prayer, may provoke resistance in today's postmodern society, where political correctness and tolerance are highly valued. Going out into the public arena and pronouncing that "all other gods, except God, are no gods at all" will solicit strong protest and a charge of bigotry. Yet this cardinal conviction of the Judeo-Christian faith cannot be compromised. How, then, can the message of God's sovereignty be effectively delivered and gladly received?

We may begin by examining our own "practical" monotheism, for action sometimes speaks louder than words. If the people of God not only "tell of [God's] salvation from day to day" but also become agents of that salvation in a hurting and unjust world, if they reciprocate God's steadfast love with covenantal faithfulness, then "the foreigners" of 1 Kings 8 and "all the peoples" of Psalm 96 will take notice and be drawn to God because of them.

These two passages are reminders that proclaiming God cannot be done at a safe distance. Christians cannot insulate themselves from the ills of the world and settle for a holy huddle. God's compassion and justice are organic and tactile. They require engagement with the messiness of poverty, marginalization, exploitation, and all other atrocities human beings do to themselves, to one another, and to creation on individual and systemic levels. Is the church willing to enter in and embody its God-talk with concrete and life-giving action?

Psalm 96 and 1 Kings 18:20–21 (22–29), 30–39

The alternate First Testament reading places Psalm 96 in its entirety alongside the story of Elijah and the prophets of Baal in 1 Kings 18. To avoid redundancy, I will refer the reader to the previous discussion on Psalm 96:1–9, bearing in mind that the theme of proclaiming YHWH as the one true God is played out exactly in Elijah's story, where the true (non)identity of Baal is exposed.

The last four verses of Psalm 96 present God as the monarch who judges all peoples with equity, righteousness, and truth (vv. 10, 13). Because God is never unjust, God's judgment anticipates joyous celebration everywhere (vv. 11–12). Those who align themselves with God will enter into God's eternal presence and glory. Yet divine judgment cuts both ways. Those who continue to worship useless idols will reap the consequences of their futile pursuits. Until then, there is still time for course correction.

In this story in 1 Kings, Israel, even as God's elect, must choose between God and Baal. Elijah asks the Israelites, "How long will you go limping with two different opinions? If the LORD is God, follow him; but if Baal, then follow him" (1 Kgs. 18:21). The people do not answer. Their silence speaks volumes about their duplicity. Perhaps they fear Jezebel's reprisal. Perhaps they have lost faith in God after three years of drought. Or perhaps they are unwilling to give up the perverse attractions that come with Baal worship. Whatever the reason, the Israelites limp between two mutually exclusive options, like birds hopping between the branches of a tree. The last part of Psalm 96, which focuses on divine judgment, speaks directly to this situation. God and Baal will not share the same throne. It is time to expose the imposter!

The contest is simple. Sacrifices are to be prepared, one for God and one for Baal. Whoever "answers by fire [to consume the bull on the altar] is indeed God" (v. 24). If Baal is indeed the storm god, he could set the animal ablaze by a lightning bolt. Yet after hours of invocation by his prophets, there is "no voice, no answer, and no response" (vv. 26, 29). Elijah's taunts set off an even more frenetic round of self-flagellation and loud appeal from the Baal prophets, but their repeated attempts to capture the attention of their nonexistent deity result in futility.

Inviting the Israelites to come closer, Elijah first reminds them to whom they belong. Using twelve stones to symbolize the twelve tribes, he builds an altar that evokes the memorial built by Joshua, also with twelve stones, after the Israelites had crossed the Jordan into the promised land (Josh. 4:1–9). God was Israel's God then; God is still Israel's God now. Next, by dousing the altar and the sacrificial animal on it three times with water, so that even the trench around the altar is filled, Elijah makes it impossible for anyone to ignite the sacrifice. It would take heavenly firepower to burn this bull! The point of the contest is the vindication of God's own name by validating that Elijah is God's servant, and by admonishing Israel to "know that [the Lord is] God, and that [God has] turned their hearts back" (v. 37).

Sure enough, God displays approval of Elijah and his prayer in grand fashion. Every single piece of wood and stone, every speck of dust, and every drop of water is engulfed by fire from heaven. The Israelites who were silent earlier now prostrate themselves and confess repeatedly, "The LORD indeed is God; the LORD indeed is God" (v. 39).

This story and Psalm 96 teach us that God will not tolerate dishonor to God's name. The prophets of Baal will be judged. Even God's own people will be judged if they insist on bowing down to worthless entities. Yet, in the end, God's saving agenda is not at odds with divine judgment, whether for Israel or for the nations. Divine justice prevents divine compassion from degenerating into indulgence, and divine compassion mends the broken relationship between the God of creation and the entire universe.

Like Israel, we are recipients of God's compassion and justice. How do we in turn offer them to others within our spheres of influence? When we look at a convicted murderer, a crooked bank executive, or a disgraced politician, it is easy to push for justice and withhold compassion. Elijah's prayer, however, reminds us that even Israel's return to God is dependent on divine grace and not on the people's own volition (1 Kgs. 18:37). In the end, only God is judge. We are called to be instruments of God's compassion and justice to this world, not because we inherently possess these qualities, but because God's grace works in and through us.

Luke 7:1–10

Just as Solomon asks God to listen to the foreigner who prays toward the temple, in our Gospel text we encounter a foreigner seeking help from Jesus, the symbolic "eschatological temple" and embodiment of God's presence. The centurion in Luke 7 is an atypical foreigner. On the one hand, he is Roman, thus presumably an enemy of the Jews. On the other hand, he is a benefactor to the Jews in Capernaum, having built the town's synagogue. He even tries to prevent Jesus from entering his house, so that Jesus will not contract ritual impurity. Yet Jesus is not taken by the centurion's sociopolitical status, his cultural sensitivity, or even his generosity to the Jews. Rather, it is the man's faith that amazes Jesus.

The centurion acknowledges Jesus' authority by believing that all Jesus needs to do is to say the word and his slave will be healed (v. 7). Even though he compares the strength of Jesus' words to his own receiving and giving orders, his insight into Jesus and what he thinks Jesus is able to accomplish go beyond his familiarity with the workings of hierarchical authority. It takes no small amount of trust to believe that Jesus can heal a terminal illness from a distance without even seeing the invalid, as it does to believe that this Jewish rabbi will not be repulsed by the centurion's occupation or ethnicity. Indeed, this foreigner's humility and faith put Jesus' Jewish contemporaries to shame.

By healing the centurion's slave, Jesus demonstrates that God's salvation is for all nations, a note already sounded earlier in Luke's Gospel (2:30–32; 3:6). This story further anticipates the conversion of Cornelius, another Roman centurion and devout God-fearer, in Luke's second volume (Acts 10). The message is clear: God shows no partiality in offering salvation, first to the Jews, then through the Jews to the Gentiles. The echoes of Psalm 96 and Solomon's prayer continue to reverberate.

The fact that the centurion's faith surpasses even that of the Jews should give us pause in making judgments about who is deserving of and capable of appropriating God's grace and salvation. Whereas our issue may not be tensions between Jews and Gentiles, we nonetheless harbor discriminatory attitudes that include and exceed familiar categories of racism, sexism, and ageism. We judge other people's worthiness every time we withhold compassion or refuse to stand up for justice in solidarity with the oppressed, the ostracized, and the underserved. Will we take our cues from Jesus and let God's compassion and justice demolish the dividing lines we draw to protect ourselves? Are we willing to risk the backlash that associating with outcasts and foreigners may bring?

Galatians 1:1–12

Speaking of backlash, we think of Paul, who experiences much opposition, ironically from Jewish *Christians* as he brings the gospel to the Gentiles. Right at the beginning of this letter, Paul insists that he is "sent neither by human commission nor from human authorities"; his gospel is "not of human origin" but "through a revelation of Jesus Christ" (vv. 1, 11–12). Paul's authority comes directly from God, not people. He looks only to God and Jesus for approval. People-pleasing is not his goal, especially in the face of his opponents. With this confidence and conviction, Paul preaches what he considers to be the pure form of the gospel, which he received, not as a tradition passed down by the teachers, but as direct revelation from Jesus Christ. He wastes no time chastising the Galatians for buying into a contrary "nongospel," which demands that Gentile Christians be circumcised and become like Jews before they are acknowledged as full members of God's household. For Paul, this distortion nullifies the all-sufficiency of Jesus' sacrifice and downgrades the true gospel to no gospel at all.

Paul's unyielding loyalty to his divine commission and staunch defense of the purity of the gospel challenge the church today to reexamine its motives and its practices. What gospel are we proclaiming? Are we letting God's name be known to the nations, or are we building empires in the name of church growth and denominational expansion? In our respective contexts and faith communities, who comprise the "nations" where God's unique sovereignty needs acknowledgment and into which God's compassion, justice, and salvation must penetrate? While these "nations" may be faraway places, they may as well be near at hand: unsaved loved ones among family and friends, disenfranchised folks in our neighborhood, and leaders in our governing structures. May this set of lectionary readings bring us back to the basics; that is to say, our task as Christians in this world is to proclaim God to the nations. To do so, we rely not on our own ambitions and efforts but on divine grace and equipping power.

Proper 5 [10]

Song Bok Jon

1 KINGS 17:8–16 (17–24)	1 KINGS 17:17–24
PSALM 146	PSALM 30
	GALATIANS 1:11–24
	LUKE 7:11–17

How can we proclaim life while we also experience death in the world? The texts for this day introduce us to the stories of some biblical characters who struggle with questions of life, death, and praise for the redemption of God liberating them. In 1 Kings 17:8–16, God's abundant grace saves the lives of Elijah, the widow in Zarephath, and her son in a time of scarcity. The psalmist in Psalm 146 praises God, who brings justice for the poor and marginalized. In 1 Kings 17:17–24, God brings the widow's son back to life. Psalm 30 sings of God, who assures the oppressed that God will surely bring joy and dancing to them. In Galatians, Paul argues that when our traditions deny our call to ministry, we must appeal to revelation through our experiences of God as legitimate authority from God. Finally, in Luke 7, Jesus brings a widow's dead son back to life out of mercy, thus proclaiming life for her and for the crowd that was following her.

1 Kings 17:8–16 (17–24)

The writer of 1 Kings records, "Ahab did more to provoke the anger of the LORD, the God of Israel, than had all the kings of Israel who were before him" (16:33). He committed sin against God—that is, after marrying Jezebel (a Sidonian who worshiped Baal), he erected an altar to worship Baal. In this context, God called Elijah to proclaim the message of a drought on the kingdom. Walter Brueggemann argues that drought in the ancient world indicated two things: first, it implied the failure of Baal as a "fertility god," thus acknowledging YHWH as the true God who controlled rain and drought;

270

second, it also meant the failure of Ahab as a king to secure rain for his people.[1] The confrontation of Elijah as the prophet of God against King Ahab led to Elijah fleeing and hiding by the Wadi Cherith (17:3–5) to avoid persecution. Elijah maintained his life by eating bread and meat brought by the ravens and drinking from the wadi.

When the wadi dried up, God commanded Elijah to go to Zarephath, six miles south of Sidon, and live there on the hospitality of a widow. Although God told him that God had already "commanded a widow there to feed you" (v. 9), she certainly showed no such knowledge from God as she responded to Elijah's request by saying that she only had a handful of meal in a jar and a little oil in a jug, which would be used for the last meal for her and her son. However, Elijah was persistent in his request that she feed him first, assuring her that God said that "the jar of meal will not be emptied and the jug of oil will not fail until the day that the LORD sends rain on the earth" (v. 14). Despite her destitute situation, the widow obeyed. A miracle took place; "the jar of meal was not emptied, neither did the jug of oil fail, according to the word of the LORD that [God] spoke by Elijah" (v. 16).

In reading this text, one must not fail to notice that God showed mercy to the widow in the time of destitution. As a widow, her social status was at the bottom of her society. She would more typically receive benevolence from other people. In addition, she was a foreign woman in Sidon who probably worshiped Baal (Jezebel came from the same city). However, despite her socioreligious status, God sent Elijah to redeem her and her son from the time of drought. Richard D. Nelson argues that before Elijah's confrontation with Ahab and Jezebel in chapter 18, chapter 17 describes the change in Elijah as God's prophet moving from "passive to active readiness."[2] Here God uses the widow as God's active agent not only to revive the life of Elijah but also to shape Elijah's vocation as God's prophet.

One great danger of preaching from this text is to ask for monetary sacrifice from those in the margin of society in exchange for prosperity from God. One could easily preach, "If you sow good seeds by sacrificing like the widow did, God would repay you with unceasing meal and oil." Brueggemann argues that this story does not directly indicate the importance of our charity work, but rather God's abundance that overcomes the social inequality that is regarded as natural by the society. Therefore, he says, Elijah's "work is, rather, to enact

---

1. Walter Brueggemann, *1 and 2 Kings*, Smyth & Helwys Bible Commentary (Macon, GA: Smyth & Helwys Publishing, 2000), 209.

2. Richard D. Nelson, *First and Second Kings*, Interpretation series (Atlanta: John Knox Press, 1987), 108.

the *reality of abundance* in a world seemingly *governed by scarcity*."[3] Although our economic system tends to ignore or bypass the economic injustice that produces abundance for the rich at the expense of the poor, God's abundance certainly reaches out to the most marginalized in our society, as God did for Elijah, the widow, and the child.

Psalm 146

The psalmist here praises the Lord who is the Creator of the world, is faithful forever, and executes justice for those on the margin of society. Praising God is inseparable from choosing to give our allegiance only to God, not to mortal leaders. The psalmist regards human leaders' plans as transient and futile. This does not mean that, as Christians, we should not care for politics or support our political leaders. Rather, as James L. Mays writes, it means that we do not trust them for salvation.[4] While the policy and plan of our political leaders often attempt to achieve the greatest good in the society, even sometimes at the expense of the oppressed and marginalized, the reign of God "sets the prisoners free; . . . opens the eyes of the blind . . . lifts up those who are bowed down; . . . watches over the strangers; . . . upholds the orphan and the widow" (vv. 7–9). As the psalmist clearly tells us that the Lord loves the righteous while condemning the wicked, we must answer to God and ourselves, "What would we do when our political leaders follow the way of the wicked?" In his commentary on Psalm 146, Gary W. Charles recalls that in late May 1934, as Lutheran and Reformed and Evangelical Christians produced the Theological Declaration of Barmen to declare their opposition to National Socialism and anti-Semitism, they sang this psalm at their conference.[5] In our struggle with many injustices in our political and economic structures, praise for God calls us to seek salvation in God, whose reign is righteous, liberating, and caring for the oppressed.

1 Kings 17:17–24

In this text, the son of the widow in Zarephath had become ill. There was no breath left in the son (v. 17), which the woman regarded as the sign of his death (v. 18). Frustrated and troubled, she accused Elijah of bringing this calamity to her. Nelson writes, "The presence of this prophet in her house has drawn God's attention to her so that her general sinfulness has registered

---

3. Brueggemann, *Kings*, 214.
4. James Luther Mays, *Psalms*, Interpretation series (Louisville, KY: John Knox Press, 1994), 440.
5. Gary W. Charles, "Hallelujah! Psalm 146," *Journal for Preachers* 31 (2007): 42–43.

on the divine consciousness."[6] She blamed not only Elijah but also herself for this tragedy. The text does not explain why the son became so deathly ill.

According to Elizabeth Kübler-Ross, it is not uncommon for a patient's family members to blame themselves for causing the patient's illness. In the third stage of anguish—bargaining—the family member negotiates with God, offering to act differently if God will intervene and heal the sick. However, in some cultures, such as Korean society, a woman might have been scapegoated and blamed for causing the deaths of her husband or children, especially if the deaths were premature. Her neighbors would point at her, gossiping that her sinfulness or faults contributed to the death in her family. Although she may have had nothing to do with the death, she has to live with the internalized guilt. The accusation of the woman in the text is the cry of a mother who lost her son without knowing what caused his illness.

Without responding to her accusation, Elijah took the son, carried him to the upper chamber, and laid him on his bed. He cried out to the Lord on behalf of the boy, "O LORD my God, let this child's life come into him again" (v. 21). It is said, "The LORD listened to the voice of Elijah" (v. 22). The boy was revived and given back to his mother.

Psalm 30

This psalm extols God, who healed the psalmist from certain illness. According to H. J. Kraus, it could be metaphorically interpreted as the "misfortunes of life."[7] The psalmist is sure that his hardships will not last because he understands that "joy comes with the morning" (v. 5). God turns "mourning into dancing" (v. 11). We must proceed with caution and be aware that Psalm 30 could be easily misunderstood as an admonition for the sufferers to bear with their unfair, unjust, unfortunate situation by merely praying to God and waiting for God's intervention. However, James Cone does not see the coexistence of suffering and hope as internalizing suffering while merely awaiting God's miraculous redemption. Rather, he argues, "The black slaves' response to the experience of suffering corresponded closely to the biblical message and its emphasis that God is the ultimate answer to the question of faith."[8] Their response to their suffering was not focused on rational explanation but on an "encounter with God" that assured them that God was closely walking with them and leading them to redemption.

---

6. Nelson, *Kings*, 111.
7. H. J. Kraus, *Psalms 1–59: A Commentary* (Minneapolis: Augsburg Press, 1988), 355.
8. James H. Cone, *The Spirituals and the Blues: An Interpretation* (New York: Seabury Press, 1972), 62.

Galatians 1:11–24

Through the proclamation of the gospel in Galatia, many Gentiles came to believe in Jesus as their Lord. They welcomed the gospel and were baptized. However, after Paul left Galatia, some people came to the followers of Christ and spoke "a different gospel" (v. 6) to them. These were Jewish Christians who tried to persuade the believers in Galatia that they had to be circumcised to enter into a full covenantal relationship with God. In addition, they attempted to undermine the authority of Paul as a legitimate apostle because he did not have connections with the apostles in Jerusalem. Therefore, in this letter to the churches in Galatia, Paul tries to defend his apostleship by sharing the narrative of his conversion from a persecutor of the church of God (v. 13) to an apostle for the Gentiles and by appealing to the origin of the gospel that he received, not from "a human source," but "through a revelation of Jesus Christ" (v. 12).

Paul's defense of his apostleship raises a critical question regarding the relationship between tradition and revelation: How can one claim one's call to preach as legitimate? In other words, what can one do when one's call is denied by tradition as invalid, illegal, or inauthentic? Reflecting on the struggle of African American Christians whose call and experience often met with disapproval from the dominant society, Brad R. Braxton writes, "Historically, African Americans have believed that the essence and authenticity of one's life and calling neither arise from nor depend ultimately upon the approval of a (white) person or a group of (white) people but on an experience (of God)."[9] As the interpretation of the gospel and religious structure were oppressive to the life, humanity, and faith of African American Christians, they appealed to their experience as God's direct revelation to them that they were unapologetically God's children.

To appeal to revelation as a legitimate approval from God does not mean that one must disregard tradition. Paul attempted to maintain his relationship with other apostles by traveling to Jerusalem, although he could meet only Peter and James, the brother of Jesus (vv. 18–19). Paul did not see tradition and revelation as being in conflict. As Christ promised to be with us as two or three gather in his name, our tradition can work to affirm our call to ministry. However, when tradition is oppressive to certain groups—women, ethnic minorities, or homosexuals, for example—regarding them as inferior, Paul tells us that one must appeal to one's experience of God's revelation as the legitimate affirmation of any call to ministry.

---

9. Brad R. Braxton, *No Longer Slaves: Galatians and African American Experience* (Collegeville, MN: Liturgical Press, 2002), 60.

Luke 7:11–17

Before entering Nain, Jesus healed a centurion's slave and was amazed at the faith the centurion expressed in his request for healing: "I tell you, not even in Israel have I found such faith" (7:9). In this text the widow did not ask for any miracle from him; Jesus "had compassion for her and said to her, 'Do not weep'" (v. 13). Jesus commanded the dead man to rise and he immediately came back to life. The phrase in verse 15, "Jesus gave him to his mother," resonates with 1 Kings 17:23. It must be noticed that the widow's circumstance, not simply the death of the son, moved Jesus to perform the miracle of bringing the dead back to life. Here Robert M. Price argues that this story emphasizes "the 'counter-hegemonic' resistance of Christian widows against the patriarchal hierarchy represented by any who would marginalize her in her loss."[10] Therefore, she represents all women who refuse to be domesticated by patristic hegemony that pushes them to the periphery of the narrative.

While Jesus and the widow are the central figures of the miracle as benefactor and recipient, we must not miss the importance of the crowd that exclaimed praises for God. While the crowd following Jesus was filled with joy and excitement, the crowd accompanying the widow was mourning the death of the young man. In this clash between the realms of life and death, Jesus' miracle transforms the crowd to glorify God, who "looked favorably on [God's] people" (v. 16). This phrase reminds us of the song of Mary, "for [God] has looked with favor on the lowliness of [God's] servant" (Luke 1:48); it also echoes the prophecy of Zechariah, "[God] has looked favorably on [God's] people and redeemed them" (Luke 1:68). God's favor on God's children culminates in the incarnation of God in this world. Therefore, as this text is read or shared, we should be encouraged to look to Christ, who turns our weeping to joy and reverses death to life.

10. Robert M. Price, *The Widow Traditions in Luke-Acts: A Feminist-Critical Scrutiny* (Atlanta: Scholars Press, 1997), 86.

Proper 6 [11]

Carolynne Hitter Brown

1 KINGS 21:1–10 (11–14), 15–21A   2 SAMUEL 11:26–12:10, 13–15
PSALM 5:1–8   PSALM 32
GALATIANS 2:15–21
LUKE 7:36–8:3

Today's Scriptures vividly depict the brokenness of the social world and the depths of its fall from God's covenantal purpose and desire. They tell of sin—sin that is personal as well as systemic. Sin is far reaching, its consequences affecting the innocent and the unborn and eventually extending to an entire nation. The passages from 1 Kings and 2 Samuel illustrate how cultural sin can corrupt an individual (and conversely, how one person's sin can affect a whole nation) and result in terrible outcomes. These stories are helpful to those striving to understand the origin of social injustice in that they explore the progression of sin from the time it takes root in a person's heart to its evil end results. They are both stories of rulers—men who had grown prosperous, self-absorbed, and complacent in their cushy royal lives. Their pride led them to believe that they could do whatever they pleased.

The two psalms for today are attributed to one of those men, King David, after he was transformed through the power of repentance and reconciliation with God. Not only do they address God's stance against evil, but they also speak of forgiveness, a key concept in the work of social justice. The passages from Galatians and Luke elaborate on what forgiveness is and how it produces great love. Because of its healing effect, forgiveness allows for powerful relational changes between people and with God. Humility and the act of asking for forgiveness are also crucial subjects of these texts and prove to be vital to a theology of social justice.

1 Kings 21:1–10 (11–14), 15–21a

The passage in 1 Kings provides a perfect opportunity for preachers to address how structures of power cause and sustain social injustice, often justified in the name of religion. How are structures of power established? How do these forces find the momentum to threaten and overcome the best of intentions? Consider King Ahab, who, in short, does not get what he wants. When he asks Naboth for a vineyard near his house to use as a garden, Naboth refuses to hand it over. As a result, Ahab becomes resentful, sullen, and depressed to the point that he will not eat. It seems a rather childish response for a king.

Ahab's despondency was likely driven by a deep sense of guilt and failure. Naboth's response to Ahab went much deeper than a simple refusal to sell a piece of land. Naboth specifically told Ahab, "The LORD forbid that I should give you my ancestral inheritance" (v. 3). With this response, Naboth stood for righteousness in the face of a powerful and corrupt system. His words pointed straight to the essence of Ahab's and Israel's problem. As a nation, Israel had turned away from God's covenant and was serving foreign idols. In his heart, Ahab knew the truth, but after a lifetime of blasphemy, his conscience was seared. Naboth's words convicted Ahab of deep sin.

There is no excuse for Ahab's behavior—verse 25 says, "There was no one like Ahab, who sold himself to do what was evil in the sight of the LORD"—but he was stuck in the quicksand of systemic evil. Israel's idol worship did not begin with him. Ahab's father, Omri, began building allegiances with surrounding countries, and it was most likely Omri who arranged for Ahab's marriage to the Phoenician princess Jezebel. Omri's introduction of Baal worship was undoubtedly a political gesture. When the prophet Micah asked, "What does the LORD require of you but to do justice, and to love kindness, and to walk humbly with your God?" he specifically accused Israel of failing to follow God's covenant. He said, "You have kept the statutes of Omri and all the works of the house of Ahab, and you have followed their counsels. Therefore I will make you a desolation" (Mic. 6:8, 16). To complicate matters further, Ahab's wife Jezebel was horrifically resolute in her attempts to snuff out the worship of Jehovah. She had the priests of God killed and energetically promoted Baal worship as the national religion. First Kings 18:19 indicates that eight hundred and fifty prophets of Baal and Asherah dined at Jezebel's table. Ahab was hardly alone in his sin.

The magnitude of Israel's religious and political sin makes Naboth's response to Ahab all the more intriguing. First Kings 19:18 states there were only seven thousand people in the entire nation who had not bowed to Baal. Naboth, who was part of a small minority, did not hesitate to tell the king the truth. When presented with the opportunity, he spoke directly to the nation's leader about the nation's problem.

Roger Williams (1603–1683), one of the first Americans to argue for religious tolerance, the separation of church and state, the abolition of slavery, and the rights of Native Americans, formed a colony (later to become Rhode Island) as a refuge for religious dissenters. Williams's most famous work, *The Bloudy Tenent of Persecution, for Cause of Conscience*, uses Naboth's story to argue for liberty of conscience, which he called "soul-liberty," and to discuss what he called a "wall of separation" between church and state. Williams stressed that Ahab and Jezebel's actions against Naboth were deceitfully done in the name of religion. In Williams's thinking, this story is included in Scripture to guide all individuals who are asked to stand against their own conscience to hold fast to their beliefs, even to the point of denying civil authority.[1] Williams likened the "the Church of God" to the nation of Israel, and on that basis claimed "every true Spirituall Naboth hath [his or her] Spirituall inheritance, which [he or she] dares not part with, though it be to [his or her] King of Soveraigne, and though such [his or her] refusall cost [him or her] this present life."[2] Williams reasoned that religious tolerance was the only means for ensuring the liberty of thought necessary for true peace and in keeping with the laws of Christ.

To attack and break down social injustice, one must understand how systems of power develop and gain energy. Often, social injustices stemming from idol worship, such as greed, materialism, pride, and egocentrism, have developed over centuries and have grown increasingly powerful and complex. Naboth's stance against such powers offers a meaningful lesson in how a person or group can begin to address structures of power contrary to God's covenantal plan. In the tradition of Roger Williams, preachers can explain how under the strong arm of social injustice and civil persecution, Naboth held to his "spiritual inheritance." He claimed personal liberty in acting according to God's laws rather than the laws of civil authority.

Psalm 5:1–8

This psalm can be considered a lament, specifically a lament over evil. The psalmist looks confidently toward freedom from enemies. The actual words demonstrate active reliance on God and engaged hopefulness—the writer knows God will hear and answer. When David wrote, "I plead my case to you, and watch" (v. 3), he voiced expectancy. He deeply believed God would bring

---

1. Roger Williams, *The Bloudy Tenent of Persecution*, ed. Samuel L. Caldwell (1644; repr., Providence: Publications of the Narragansett Club, 1867), 3:263.
2. Ibid., 322. Williams was the founder of the first Baptist congregation in America.

about justice. It is no small coincidence that these words are part of a song intended for congregational worship. One can almost hear the flutes accompanying this hymn as God's faithful plead for God to "heed [our] sighing" (v. 1). Liturgy, especially in song, provides congregations with a meaningful way to voice their beliefs corporately. Music unites people and activates memory.

Thematically, the psalm is in ABA format. The A sections (vv. 1–3, 7–8) concern the godly, and section B (vv. 4–6) pertains to the wicked. Such structure allows for comparisons: The godly call on God in humility; the wicked are boastful. The godly receive an abundance of God's love; God abhors the wicked and will destroy them. The godly dwell in God's presence; the wicked will not sojourn with God—they will not stand before God's eyes. The godly petition God in truth; the wicked are full of deceit.

God's nature and stance against the wicked are some of the most powerful expressions of this psalm, particularly considering God's order for the world. God hates, abhors, and destroys evil. Wickedness is attributed to those who are boastful, bloodthirsty, and deceitful. One only needs to open a newspaper or turn on the news to hear how these three evils are at work in the world today. War, genocide, and slavery may feel like far-off problems to some North Americans, but the boasts and deceit of politicians, corporations, and even reality-television stars are ever present. The godly are called to pray and live in utter contrast to the wicked.

2 Samuel 11:26–12:10, 13–15

David's story is not so different from Ahab's. Both men were kings, and both committed murder to get something they wanted. The themes of power and systemic evil apply in both cases, but David's case teaches something different. Although Ahab eventually repented of his actions (1 Kgs. 21:27–29), the passage in 2 Samuel reveals that David's heart was devoted to justice and doing what was right, even in the midst of personal sin. When Nathan told David the story of a rich man who took a poor man's only lamb, David was infuriated and ready to ensure retribution. When his own sin was put in terms of this social injustice, David quickly recognized the evil and selfishness of his actions and admitted he had sinned against the Lord (12:13). Whereas Ahab operated unjustly from the beginning of his rule, David's sin and unjust treatment of Uriah (and Bathsheba) was an exception and not the norm.

Sin is sin regardless of who is performing the evil, and all sin angers God. Nevertheless, this passage reveals God's compassion for those God loves. The abundance of God's steadfast love (Ps. 5:7) is what enables God's people to stand before God even though they sin. When David was grieved by his sin and confessed it, he was told, "Now the LORD has put away your sin; you shall not die" (12:13). Ultimately, God judges a person's inner being, and indeed it was because of David's heart that God chose him as king (1 Sam. 16:7). David's obvious compassion for the poor and vigor for justice, combined with personal repentance, spared his life and allowed him to continue in fellowship with God.

Psalm 32

This psalm follows the story of David and Bathsheba well because it provides a much deeper look at David's innermost feelings of guilt and remorse after committing such unjust acts. His sin took a heavy toll on him. David says, "My body wasted away," God's hand was "heavy upon me," and "my strength was dried up" (vv. 3–4). Confession was the beginning of his restoration. Confession requires honesty, which gives it liberating power. After David confesses to God, his spirit is free from deceit (v. 2) and he no longer needs to work at the exhausting task of hiding his iniquity (v. 5). Psalm 5 explains that God hates deceit, but here David adds that honesty with God restores unity with God (v. 5). God forgives, and the one forgiven gains access to God's power, protection, and guidance (vv. 6–8).

The confession-and-restoration model limned out in Psalm 32 applies to any relationship fractured by sin. The act of confessing wrong allows for communication and initiates the healing process for the one(s) who sinned and the one(s) wronged. It is the first act in restoring broken relationships. Who knows if Southern Baptists will ever wholly sever their moral ties to the slavery stance of their founders? In their 1995 apology for slavery and racism, their claim that they "lament and repudiate historic acts of evil such as slavery from which we continue to reap a bitter harvest" acknowledges that their sin continues to have grave ramifications in the present. Still, their apology to all African Americans for "condoning and/or perpetuating individual and systemic racism in our lifetime" and repentance for "racism of which we have been guilty, whether consciously or unconsciously" is a start.[3] The work of social justice is a long process, as both living into repentance and healing do not take place at once. Unlike God, people cannot see into the heart and judge whether confessions are genuine. David wrote that when he confessed, God "forgave the guilt of my sin" (v. 5). Because he was "upright in heart," God forgave him immediately. People who have oppressed others cannot expect immediate forgiveness. After more than two hundred years of slavery and decades more under systemic oppression who could expect African Americans to trust a publicly spoken word of confession? In cases of structural

---

3. Southern Baptist Convention, "Resolution on Racial Reconciliation on the 150th Anniversary of the Southern Baptist Convention," June 1995, http://www.sbc.net/resolutions/amResolution .asp?ID=899 (accessed May 24, 2011).

and enduring sin, a continual posture of confession and commitment to correct injustice are needed.

Galatians 2:15–21

Here we see that God's covenantal plan with the nation of Israel is now extended to the Gentiles. The former law has passed away, and now all people are welcomed into relationship with God. Restoration of the social world now depends on faith—"A person is justified not by the works of the law but through faith in Jesus Christ" (v. 16). Nonetheless, God's vision for the social world still depends on the inner condition of the heart. Those seeking to commune with God turn from the sinful desires and strivings of the natural body and are "crucified with Christ" so that they may "live to God" (v. 19). Though in a physical body, it is by a transformed spirit that a Christian lives out God's love and social design in the world: "It is no longer I who live, but it is Christ who lives in me" (v. 20).

Ultimately, the Christian believes that true transformation comes through faith in Jesus. If godliness and goodness are obtainable through personal choices or actions, "then Christ died for nothing" (v. 21). All work toward social justice, then, is based on the principle that Christ lives in us. As we strive for reform, we do so in a manner that loves and respects others, believing all people are called to covenant with God through God's grace.

Luke 7:36–8:3

The story of the woman who anointed Jesus keenly demonstrates the transformative power of forgiveness. Although Luke's Gospel does not suggest her identity, Jesus indicates that she had sinned greatly, and he forgave her (7:48). The woman's story and example are so important that they are recounted in all four Gospels (Matt. 26:6–13; Mark 14:3–9; John 12:1–8). Through forgiveness she accessed the type of intimate, loving relationship God intended between God's self and God's people.

Christ's words to the Pharisee may offer the most powerful critique to those pursuing social justice: "the one to whom little is forgiven, loves little" (7:47). Do we have the same compassion for the unjust and the unredeemed as Christ had on this woman? If we could portray the same abundant forgiveness and love to our enemies as Christ showed her, would the transforming work of God be more visible in the social world? Nelson Mandela, perhaps one of the greatest contemporary examples of powerful forgiveness, forgave the very people who harmed and imprisoned him for more than twenty-five years. His uncompromising forgiveness and respect for the humanity of his oppressors—the very respect of humanity denied to him—resulted in the end of apartheid and began the work of social justice in South Africa. Such impulse to forgive and respect another's life could only come from a power greater than ourselves. Such a power always searches for a willing heart— willing to be so transformed. In Luke 7, Jesus models the type of forgiveness needed to disarm sin, even evil and social injustice. The woman who anointed Jesus was a living, breathing example of a willing heart and the freedom that results from the gift of forgiveness.

Juneteenth: Let Freedom Ring (June 19)

James Henry Harris

JEREMIAH 34:8–22
PSALM 66:1–7
EPHESIANS 4:17–24
LUKE 4:31–37

Slavery ended in most of the United States at the conclusion of fighting between the Union and Confederate armies in April and May of 1865. However, slavery continued in Texas until June 19, 1865, when a Union army arrived in Galveston and announced freedom for slaves. That date (Juneteenth) celebrates the actual end of slavery and sometimes includes the reading of the Emancipation Proclamation and an abundant outdoor meal. A Juneteenth sermon might reflect critically on the degree to which people of color in the United States are still in need of emancipation from racism and other systems of injustice.

> The right of citizens of the United States to vote shall not be denied or abridged by the United States or by any State on account of race, color, or previous condition of servitude.
> *Fifteenth Amendment to the U.S. Constitution, 1870*

Juneteenth is African Americans' Independence Day. It celebrates the end of slavery in Texas—a symbol of the South. After the Emancipation Proclamation in 1863, most African Americans remained slaves until 1865. In Galveston, Texas, slaves did not get the word that slavery had ended until June 19, 1865, two and a half years after President Lincoln had freed them.

Jeremiah 34:8–22

The release of slaves (cf. jubilee year in Isaiah 61:1) during the year of jubilee is inherent in the opening words of this pericope: "The word that came to Jeremiah from the LORD, after King Zedekiah had made a covenant with all the people in Jerusalem to make a proclamation of liberty to them, that all should set free their Hebrew slaves, male and female, so that no one should hold another Judean in slavery" (vv. 8–9). Slavery is a cruel violation of the humanity of the other, manifested by domination and oppression. And those who have been enslaved are expected to remember their bondage with the understanding that it will never be repeated. Memory by the oppressed and the oppressor is the key to freedom. John Bracke in his commentary on Jeremiah says, "Jeremiah 34 is rooted in Israel's earliest memory of the Lord who freed slaves from the oppression of Egypt (v. 13). The God of the exodus made a covenant with Israel that provided specific ways for God's commitment to the marginalized and oppressed to be lived out in community."[1]

This text captures a flagrant violation and disregard of the covenant between God and the citizens of Jerusalem. In contravening the covenant, the Judeans know that they are turning their backs on God, thus releasing God from any redemptive responsibility toward them. They have brought upon themselves the wrath of God, seen in a negative quid pro quo. Profaning God's name in violating the covenant made in the house of the Lord causes God to grieve over them and their ancestors before them: "But your ancestors did not listen to me or incline their ear to me" (v. 14). The inability to listen and hear the voice of God emerges from the nature of humanity to rebel against God.

This text reminds me of the American slave experience, in which Southern slave states lost the war but kept the ideology and the practice of interpreting the U.S. Constitution in a manner that maintained slavery and racial segregation before and after the Civil War. Since the Constitution is more sacrosanct than God in a democratic state, Americans have sought wisdom from their forebears. In 1857 the Supreme Court appealed to the Constitution in the *Dred Scott v. Sanford* case, and "led by Chief Justice Roger B. Taney declared that all blacks—slaves as well as free—were not and could never become citizens of the United States."[2]

Six years later, the Emancipation Proclamation by Abraham Lincoln freed the slaves in theory but not in practice. Then the 1896 Supreme Court decision *Plessy v. Ferguson* established "the separate but equal doctrine that pervaded life in the American South for over fifty years."[3] Supreme Court

1. John M. Bracke, *Jeremiah 30–52 and Lamentations*, Westminster Bible Companion (Louisville, KY: Westminster John Knox Press, 2000), 51.
2. See PBS, "Dred Scott Case: The Supreme Court Decision, 1857," Africans in America at http://www.pbs.org/wgbh/aia/part4/4h2933.html (accessed June 10, 2010).
3. Gibbsmagazine.com, http://www.gibbsmagazine.com/Plessy.htm (accessed June 10, 2010).

Justice Henry Brown wrote for the majority ruling against Plessy, claiming that segregation, as in the Separate Car Act, did not violate the Thirteenth or Fourteenth Amendments protecting the citizenship and equality of African Americans.[4]

The use of the law (the U.S. Constitution) to obviate the outcome of the Civil War and the Emancipation Proclamation was a cynical and unethical practice on par with the godless disregard of the covenant by the Israelites when they "broke the legal and solemn oath taken before God by which they had conferred freedom upon their slaves. Jeremiah carefully matched the words of his threat to the baseless disregard of human rights and feelings such actions displayed (v. 17)."[5]

I reside in Richmond, Virginia, the former capital of the Confederacy, where residuals of resistance to the freedom of former slaves still exist. The issue of race in Virginia and the nation has not been resolved by the Civil War or the election of the first black president, who coincidentally has no relationship to American chattel slavery except that his American ancestors were white and potential slave owners. In every sense except skin color, President Obama's racial affinity is as close to whites as to blacks in North America. Even with the advent of a black president, American history and culture, like Israel in Jeremiah, show just how pervasively and dismissively we relegate even our political covenant to a nonbinding status.

For Jeremiah, the Babylonians are now free to plunder and destroy the city because the slaves have been treated unjustly. Injustice toward others is an abomination punishable by "desolation without inhabitant" (v. 22). This text also suggests that the Exodus-Sinai relationship between God and Israel is determinative, such that God is on the side of the oppressed (Israel) and not the oppressors (the Egyptian Pharaohs).[6] And those who have been oppressed slaves should adhere to God's call to free those in bondage of any kind.

These lectionary texts provide a scope into which we can look and glean helpful insights to how we may go about engaging in the task of freeing others, celebrating freedom, being freed from certain circumstances, and being good stewards of freedom. All of these texts are significant reminders that freedom is not free. It carries tremendous responsibility, diligence, determination, and dutifulness.

---

4. Lisa Cozzens, "Plessy v. Ferguson," African American History, http://www.watson.org/~lisa/blackhistory/post-civilwar/plessy.html (accessed June 10, 2010).

5. R. E. Clements, *Jeremiah*, Interpretation series (Louisville, KY: John Knox Press, 1988), 206.

6. See James H. Cone, *God of the Oppressed*, rev. ed. (Maryknoll, NY: Orbis Books, 1997), 57–66.

As we read the story of the fall of Jerusalem, we meet a king and a people who faced an important decision of freeing their slaves. After the Babylonian siege of Jerusalem had begun, the prophet Jeremiah advised King Zedekiah to tell all the people to release their fellow Hebrew slaves in order to gain favor with God. But after some time, the Egyptians sent forces into Judah to help the Hebrews, and then the Babylonians lifted their attack temporarily. As a result, the former Hebrew slave owners, thinking that the danger had passed and they had found favor with God, broke the covenant made with God and bound their slaves once again. Jeremiah was not pleased. Indeed, he rebuked his own people and prophesied that the Babylonians would return and capture their city.

Much like the slaves of the antebellum South, slaves in the days of Jeremiah were victims of the system, and slave owners became slaves to the system because of their dependence on the system working to their advantage. We seal our own fate if we continue to hold others in the proverbial ditch rather than liberating them from the systems that seek to oppress. God desires freedom for all who are in bondage. We can and should be instruments through which freedom is enacted.

Psalm 66:1–7

This text, though totalistic and grand in its tone, grounds this incredible metanarrative in the actions of God as liberator. The beauty of the words of praise is balanced by a reflection on the liberating deeds of God. The psalm pulsates with a language of universalism based on one example of God's salvation of a particular people. The particularity of the reference to the exodus is clear; however, it is not so clear why "all the earth" should sing and say "how awesome are your deeds" (vv. 1–3), especially when slavery, poverty, and evil continue to haunt others who are a part of the world.

These "awesome deeds" are explained as the psalm unfolds (vv. 5–6):

> Come and see what God has done:
>   [God] is awesome in [God's] deeds among mortals.
> [God] turned the sea into dry land;
>   they passed through the river on foot.

This is clearly a reference to the exodus of the Israelites from Egyptian bondage (Exod. 14:21–15:18). They were able to cross the Red Sea as if it were dry land because of the power and presence of the Lord. This act of holding back the sea revealed the glory of the Lord and "is evoked as a defining instance of God's intervention in history on behalf of [God's] people."[7] How awesome!

Psalm 66 invites us not only to remember what God has done through the lives of others but also to celebrate with those people in the blessings of deliverance from bondage that was and is theirs. We should not be so pretentious in thinking that God is our possession. God is not ours; we are God's.

We are called to celebrate when others are freed from the circumstances and predicaments that hold them captive. One of the greatest displays of God's power appears to give sudden advantage to disadvantaged people—the poor, oppressed, disenfranchised, and diseased. Come, share in the celebration of what God has done . . . for you and for someone else!

Luke 4:31–37

As Jesus entered the synagogue on the Sabbath, as was his custom, he began to teach the people who had gathered there to worship. During his didactic enterprise, a man who had been possessed by an evil spirit also entered the synagogue. He cried out to Jesus at the top of his voice, "What have you to do with us, Jesus of Nazareth? Have you come to destroy us? I know who you are, the Holy One of God" (v. 34).

Undoubtedly, a large portion of society is troubled, demon-possessed, bothered, disturbed, and distressed. The questions posed to Jesus by this particular man are interesting and disconcerting: "What have you to do with us? Have you come to destroy us?"

What do people expect when they enter the church or a gathering of a body of believers? It appears this man had grown accustomed to being dejected, alienated, and perhaps harmed at the hands of the faithful. Is this the experience that people take with them as they leave our churches and synagogues, disgruntled at how they were treated because of difference? Whether demon-possessed or not, do people often feel that the establishment—the church—is likely to harm them?

Still, Jesus challenges our understanding and interpretation of his divine authority. He offers the man more than a hard time because of what was within him. Can we, too, speak to the evil within one another without rejecting the other? Can those who are troubled in mind, body, and spirit find something liberating within the community of gathered believers? If one

7. Robert Alter, *The Book of Psalms: A Translation with Commentary* (New York: W. W. Norton, 2009), 224.

believes in the power and possibilities of God, the answer is an emphatic yes. Indeed, we have the power and authority to "bring good news to the poor . . . proclaim release to the captives and recovery of sight to the blind, to let the oppressed go free, to proclaim the year of the Lord's favor" (4:18–19).

Ephesians 4:17–24

Estrangement and alienation have always been a strange reality that has existed between believers and Christ. There is a natural tendency to feel a distance and separation from Christ.

Paul says to the church at Ephesus: "You were taught to put away your former way of life, your old self, corrupt and deluded by its lusts, and to be renewed in the spirit of your minds, and to clothe yourselves with the new self, created according to the likeness of God in true righteousness and holiness" (vv. 22–23). The charge to us is to change our perspective and our purpose. More than a charge, it is a call for us to live into a new understanding of life.

This is a call for transformation and liberation—a radical intellectual and spiritual reformation—that is to embrace the mind of Christ and become a new being, a "new self" (v. 24). What is this new self? This verse raises our understanding of what it should mean to be created in the likeness of God. Christ renews us and teaches us to live into our liberation from our own corruption.

We have the opportunity to lead a transformation of self and world. The corruption from which we are called into transformation also is the corruption that often thrives between us. The church has the responsibility to tear down the walls that divide us and build bridges in order that the alienated and abandoned may also live into their liberation as renewed creations in the likeness of God.

Proper 7 [12]

Edward L. Wheeler

1 KINGS 19:1–4 (5–7), 8–15A
PSALMS 42 AND 43

ISAIAH 65:1–9
PSALM 22:19–28
GALATIANS 3:23–29
LUKE 8:26–39

This week's lectionary readings focus on God's continuous efforts to reconcile the world to God's self in light of the alienation and oppression in
the world. Between fear and faith, between lament and praise, and between
oppression and proclamation, we discover God's faithfulness and call.

1 Kings 19:1–4 (5–7), 8–15a

The passage begins with Ahab informing Jezebel of Elijah's victory on Mount
Carmel and his slaying of the priests of Baal. Jezebel threatens to kill Elijah,
who fears for his life and runs away (v. 3). Entering the desert, the prophet sits
under a juniper tree, and asks "that he might die" (v. 4).

   While the scene may appear to be inconsistent with Elijah's earlier her-
oism, it is consistent with human nature. Even prophets are susceptible to
bouts of depression and self-doubt.

   In verses 5–15, "the angel of the LORD" (v. 7) provides food and water
for Elijah, which sustains him as he journeys to a cave on Mount Horeb,
where the Lord asks what he is doing there (v. 9). Elijah's response identifies his zealousness for the Lord, the unfaithfulness of Israel, his belief
that he is the only prophet left, and the threat on his life (v. 10). Elijah is
then told to stand before God. An earthquake, which is followed by fire,
follows a strong and violent wind, but God is not in any of these powerful
forces. However, "a sound of sheer silence" catches Elijah's attention. God
is in this rather innocent manifestation, and Elijah is asked (v. 13) a second

time, "What are you doing here, Elijah?" He responds as he did in verse 9. This time the Lord tells him to "return on your way to the wilderness of Damascus" (v. 15).

As often happens in the struggle for justice, Elijah feels that he is alone in the struggle and focuses on the faults of the people instead of God's presence, provisions, and power. But Elijah finds God in the most unexpected presence of a gentle, quiet whisper of silence. Sometimes in the struggle for justice it is the quiet resolve of a Rosa Parks that God uses to initiate the movement toward justice and freedom.

God tells Elijah to return to the work by way of the north through the wilderness of Damascus. He is to take a different way home—the way through which God will set in motion a plan for the redemption of God's people.

Isaiah 65:1–9

This pericope opens with God's announcing that God has been available to a people who would not call on or seek God (v. 1). Furthermore, God says, "I held out my hands all day long to a rebellious people, who walk in a way that is not good" (v. 2).

Verses 3–5 describe the pagan cultic practices the people adopted that were abominations to the God of Israel. God says that the people "provoke me to my face continually" (v. 3). Furthermore, they claim that they are holier than those who do not participate in their practices. But God says that these are an offense; "These are a smoke in my nostrils" (v. 5b).

It is tragic that we build systems that oppress the most vulnerable and blame them for their oppression and poverty. We make materialism our god, sanctify it by dubbing it the "prosperity gospel," and ridicule a faith that calls for sacrifice in support of the marginalized. We are then surprised when the God of the oppressed, the God of the marginalized, rejects our worship and our claim to righteousness.

In verses 6 and 7 God announces that the payment is now due for the arrogance and rebelliousness of the nation. God will repay both "their iniquities and their ancestors' iniquities together" (v. 7a). Nevertheless, verses 8 and 9 provide hope for the nation. God proclaims God will act on behalf of God's servants instead of destroying all of them (v. 8b). God will spare a remnant because of their righteousness and "will bring forth descendants from Jacob" (v. 9a). These offspring will inherit the land "and [God's] servants shall settle there" (v. 9b).

God will vindicate those who have done justice and loved mercy. God's justice will not punish the faithful for the sins of the faithless.

Psalms 42 and 43

Psalms 42 and 43 make up a unit, sharing common themes, concepts, and language. While they may at some point have been one psalm, Psalm 42 is a lament and Psalm 43 is a prayer for deliverance.

The opening verse of Psalm 42 compares the longing of a deer for the fresh water of a brook to the soul's longing for God. Verse 2 amplifies the psalmist's longing for God. However, verses 2b–4 articulate the psalmist's anguish that she or he is no longer able to come before God in the temple. The psalmist's agony is magnified by a question (v. 3b) often asked by one's oppressors, "Where is your God?" The psalmist has nothing to hold on to but the memory of a better time when she or he joined in the joyous procession of thanksgiving to the temple (v. 4).

I am sure that there were days while enduring imprisonment on Robben Island when Nelson Mandela had little else to hold on to than the memories of the life he had once enjoyed. The brutality of his incarceration mingled with the inhumanity of the prison guards made it hard to retain hope that the cause for which he was imprisoned would be vindicated.

Verse 5 asks what appears to be a rhetorical question. However, the psalmist claims that hoping in God and praising God is the corrective for a despairing soul. Yet in verse 6 the psalmist again alludes to despair. This vacillation between despair and hope continues in verse 7, where the psalmist declares, "[God's] waves and [God's] billows" roll (v. 7). The psalmist, however, announces her or his trust in God's loving-kindness and declares God's "song" will be ever present, even through distressed nights (v. 8).

The tone changes dramatically with verses 9 and 10, which reveal further the psalmist's pathos. The psalmist is the victim of ridicule. The response in verse 11 returns to the same phrasing found in verse 5; the psalmist affirms that the God of Israel is "my help and my God" (v. 11b).

Psalm 43 continues with the psalmist's plea that God would vindicate and deliver her or him "from those who are deceitful and unjust" (v. 1). The vacillation of the psalmist is again seen in verse 2. On the one hand, God is the source of the psalmist's strength, but on the other hand, the psalmist wonders why God seems so absent or rejecting. Verses 3 opens with the request that God would "send out [God's] light and [God's] truth," and expresses confidence that these will lead the psalmist back to the temple, where the psalmist will again offer praise to God (v. 4). The psalm concludes (v. 5) with the same hopeful statement of God's help as Psalm 42.

There are times when those who love God and are trying to do what is just and good find themselves suffering unjust oppression. Faith in God does not prevent fear and doubt or even despair. However, faith in God does mean that you know God is on the side of the oppressed and that those souls who thirst for God will yet praise God in the sanctuary.

Psalm 22:19–28

Psalm 22 combines a cry for help in the midst of a desperate and life-threatening situation with an exuberant outpouring of praise for God's faithfulness. Verse 19 mirrors the plea of verse 11a and then asks God to "come quickly" with help. The danger the psalmist faces is identified in verses 20–21. The animal imagery is symbolic of the ferocious nature of the attacks the psalmist is facing. However, verse 21 suggests that God has responded to the psalmist's pleas for help. The closing words, "you have rescued me" (v. 21b), indicate that God has come to the aid of the psalmist.

Beginning with verse 22, the psalmist celebrates God's amazing deliverance. The psalmist then invites those "who fear the LORD," the "offspring of Jacob," and the "offspring of Israel" to join in praising God (v. 23). The reason for the praise is identified in verse 24. The psalmist was in a desperate situation. God did not hide from the psalmist in the face of enemies, but God heard the plea for help in the midst of the danger, and God did save!

God does not promise that injustice will not exist, nor does God promise that injustice will not have temporary victories. However, God does promise to hear the cries of those who call. When that occurs, God should be praised and the congregation should offer thanksgiving.

God's faithfulness is the source of the psalmist's praise and empowers the vows made in the face of death (v. 25). Verse 26 affirms God's care for those in need (the poor) and says that they "shall eat and be satisfied." What a vision that is, and what a contrast to the reality of injustice! When the poor can eat until they are satisfied, God's justice will be evident.

The last two verses of our text recognize God's reign in an expanded manner. That expansion will be the result of "the families of the nations" remembering God's faithfulness and turning to God to worship (v. 27). The universal lordship of God is proclaimed by the psalmist in an unmistakable manner: "For dominion belongs to the LORD, and [God] rules over the nations" (v. 28).

Galatians 3:23–29

Continuing Paul's discussion of the relationship between the law and faith, verse 23 opens, "Now before faith came, we were imprisoned and guarded under the law." Several commentators caution the reader not to conclude that faith did not exist prior to the coming of Christ. Rather, this "faith" should be read as referring to "faith in Jesus Christ," which is articulated in verse 22.

In verses 23–25, Paul reveals that the role of the law was to restrain humanity, to discipline and guard humanity until Christ came. Paul does not claim that the law leads one to Christ. Rather, Christ comes to free humanity from the law through one's faith in God's unmerited grace revealed in Christ Jesus. Therefore, the law is no longer needed.

Verse 26 makes a bold statement: "for in Christ Jesus you are all children of God through faith." The radical implication is expanded in the next verse: "As many of you as were baptized into Christ have clothed yourselves with Christ" (v. 27). Being baptized into Christ signifies that the Christian's baptism confirms one's union with Christ and announces that the person has made Christ the lord of his or her life. To have clothed oneself with Christ has moral and ethical consequences. One who is clothed with Christ must emulate Christ and mirror God's justice and love for the world.

A tangible example of what this means is revealed in verse 28, where Paul describes the dissolution of the barriers that separate humanity. The religious and cultural barriers that made Jews feel superior to Gentiles, and Greeks feel superior to others, are not operative anymore in Christ. The class structure that separated slave from free and devalued both in the process was abolished in Christ. The divisions brought about by sexual identity no longer exist in Christ, for all are "one in Christ Jesus." To put on Christ also meant that the injustices perpetuated by those stratifications in society were obliterated in Christ and in Christ's body, the church.

Paul brings the argument begun in verse 6 to a climax in verse 29. Here he emphatically states that those who are in Christ are Abraham's heirs and therefore are heirs to the promises God made.

Luke 8:26–39

This narrative is found in all the Synoptic Gospels, with some important differences.

Verse 27 introduces a man from the city who is possessed by demons, naked, and living among the tombs. Not until verse 29 does Luke give the reader a full description of the extent to which this man has lost his humanity and the measure of control the demons exercise over him.

In verse 28 Luke tells us that upon seeing Jesus the man falls down, identifies him as "Jesus, Son of the Most High God," and begs Jesus not to torment him. The forces of evil recognize the authority that Jesus has over them. However, the pericope also indicates that Jesus sees beyond the demonic possession and recognizes the human being who was created in the image of God.

It is often easier for us to see and focus on the inadequacies and deficiencies of people than to see their possibilities. Consequently, it is easier to treat the other unjustly. For all his shortcomings, the fact that this man had been treated like an animal no doubt contributed to his derangement. The degree to which the man is disconnected from himself is shown when Jesus asks the man his name. His response is "Legion," because so many demons had entered him (v. 30). Verses 31–33 describe how Jesus responds to the demons' request by allowing them to enter a herd of swine. The swine then rush into the lake and are drowned. It is interesting how self-destructive the forces of evil are. Whether in Birmingham or Johannesburg, evil ends up defeating itself because no matter how long it takes, evil cannot stand in the persistent and powerful presence of justice.

The herdsmen who witness the incident report it near and far (v. 34). The people come to see "what had happened " and find the man who had been possessed by the demons, "sitting at the feet of Jesus, clothed and in his right mind" (v. 35). Rather than celebrate the return of a man to himself, their reaction is fear. Furthermore, when they are told how the man had been made well (v. 36), the people ask Jesus to depart (v. 37).

Perhaps the greatest challenge to the effort to create a more just, equitable, and compassionate society is the fear of the unknown and the comfort most people have with the status quo, even if it is oppressive. Harriet Tubman is said to have responded to celebrations of her work as a conductor on the Underground Railroad by saying that she could have freed thousands more if only they had realized they were slaves.

When Jesus returns to the boat, the formerly possessed man begs to go along, but Jesus denies his request (v. 38). Instead Jesus tells him, "Return to your home, and declare how much God has done for you" (v. 39a). Jesus gives credit to God for the man's healing. However, when the man goes away, he proclaims "how much Jesus had done for him" (v. 39b). Luke identifies the work of God and the work of Jesus as interchangeable. That work is reconciling humanity to one another and to God by freeing them from whatever alienates humanity from God and themselves.

Gifts of Sexuality and Gender
(June 29)

Valerie Bridgeman

JOB 17
PSALM 63
JOHN 16:12–15
1 CORINTHIANS 6:12–20

This new feast, Gifts of Sexuality and Gender, envisioned for late June, assumes that sexuality and gender are gifts of God through which people embody covenantal relationship. While the church has often held that relationships between people of different genders are the norm, many people believe that sexuality can be expressed in other modes, including relationships between people of the same gender, as well as those with multiple sexual identities and those who are asexual and questioning. In connection with this feast, the preacher could help the congregation explore ways that it could deepen its understanding of sexual identity and expression.

God didn't tell Noah to pick and choose, including some varieties and excluding others. Therefore, the Ark would have harbored full rainbows of gender expression and sexuality, as well as all other dimensions of biological diversity.

. . . In the story of Noah's ark, the Bible gives a single overarching protection for all biological diversity. The message is comprehensive in its inclusion and without qualification. We should not look to the Bible for affirmation of each new category of diversity that we distinguish. The Ark covers all, now and forever.

Joan Roughgarden[1]

---

1. Joan Roughgarden, *Evolution's Rainbow: Diversity, Gender and Sexuality in Nature and People* (Berkeley: University of California Press, 2004), 398.

As we reflect on gifts of human sexuality, we are forced to admit that for many of us our embodied realities do not seem a gift. And the choices we make growing up about how we will express our lives often are subject to ridicule and rejection. For example, a young girl, self-described as a "geek," decides she loves *Star Wars* and is taunted on the playground. A young boy loves one of the female characters of *Scooby Doo* and decides to dress like her for Halloween and is derided by adults. Neither of these examples is expressly sexual, but in North American contexts, they are codes for gender expressions and treated as such. In the summer and fall of 2010, we experienced a season of suicide among gay teens and gay young adults, or teens and young adults who were considered gay. Many left notes indicating they could no longer bear the burden of living in a society that punished them socially for their sexualities. In this section, I spend time with these texts looking at the ways gender and sexuality intersect with depression, suicide, and a loss of self in culture.

I wonder whether we who name God's name may hold ourselves accountable to build a society where all are safe, where no one is treated as less than human. Gender and sexualities are gifts among all peoples, whether they are bisexual, gay, lesbian, heterosexual, transgender, or questioning/queer. Yet circumstances may arise around the way we live our lives that leave us feeling hopeless and alone. It becomes the communal work of the church and society to make the world safe, an expression of God's love for all. The following texts remind us of the pathos of suffering as well as the passion for justice we all seek.

Job 17

Relief! That is the prayer of Job in this poem. After he has lost all that seems dear to him, he contends with the only relationship that still seems present— that of a God who seems to have abandoned him. Surrounded by accusing friends, he sings a lament regarding his condition. He has become the butt of jokes and the object of gossip. He is, in two words, depressed and suicidal. He is broken in spirit and declares that "the grave is ready" for him (v. 1). Like many who find themselves depressed because of their dire circumstances, Job struggles with a focus on those who mock and provoke him. He blames God for having "closed their minds to understanding" (v. 4). If only they could be open-minded and willing to learn. If only those who consider him a "byword" and a source of gossip would respect and value his life and not assume that his suffering is his judgment as a "sinner." If only he would not be treated with disdain and disregard. We note that derision also leads to disconnection from familial ties. Job embraces Sheol, the place for the dead, as his home; the Pit (also Sheol) as his father; and the worm that consumes the dead as his mother or sister (vv. 13–14). Death and deadly behaviors become parent or sibling, more intimate than close ties. But he embraces them only *if* he can find no hope. And such is the task of the believing, confessing community—to help those who are too close to Sheol in despair to find hope.

I remember a client dying of cancer whose bodily functions had come to a near standstill. He could not perform sexually, and this distressed him. For him, not being able to pleasure his wife became a reason to long for death. He became his own judge and jury, tying his life to the life force of sex. This thought, of course, is not Job's thought. But we depend on a self-perception of usefulness and meaning to hold on to hope.

Psalm 63

How shall we respond to such despair, such fainting of the flesh and thirsting of the soul? According to the psalmist, we turn our face toward God and seek the same God who seems missing in Job's encounter. Here, the psalmist provides an embodied, intimate response to God in lifting hands and singing lips. The body's need is like that of the dry, parched land, making the human connection with creation (v. 1). But in the place of worship, the psalmist finds solace and satisfaction. That satisfaction is "a rich feast" (v. 5) on which the psalmist meditates in the night. These are soulful words, full of bodily pleasure and hope. If Job finds no help, the necessary lament of those who must "ride the dragon down," the psalmist finds God who is at the bottom, in Sheol even, waiting. This God, according to the psalmist, is a help in whom he or she may cling. This hope is not based in fantasy. The psalmist knows that there are those who seek to "destroy my life" (v. 9). This knowledge brings with it an understandable hope for an avenging God. And yet, if Job asks, "Can we go down together?" might we resist the psalmist's avenging inclination and instead ask, "Can we feast together?" In a world where conflict attends relationships precisely around sexuality, a meal prepared might open the door for commonality, for community, for communion. We might see the "enemy" as neighbor, or even friend.

John 16:12–15

Oftentimes my LGBTQA friends wonder out loud about the things Jesus *did not* say to his disciples. For example, there are texts where Jesus speaks about heterosexual marriage and divorce (e.g., Matt. 5:31–32; Mark 10:2–12; Luke 16:18), but there is nothing in the Gospels about same-gender love or relationships. So, my friends tell me, they listen for the Spirit of truth (v. 13) to help them understand both their love of God in Jesus Christ and their love for their partner. How can it be that God would so create me to love someone just like me physically, and condemn me for that same love? they ask. Is this love one of the "many things" Jesus did not say? Sometimes these questions are approached with trepidation and lament and cause deep concern. Sometimes my friends and family members who are gay find reasons to hope.

Of course, people who deny that gay love could possibly be godly love would denounce these questions. But what is clear in this text is that there are many things we do not know. I submit that it takes some humility to listen for a declared truth from God and that we ought to be careful—all of us—about pronouncing with assurance such things of which we know nothing.

1 Corinthians 6:12–20

This passage mixes two topics, food and fornication, in order to address the questions of moderation versus indulgence. Paul, writing for a community that he believes is on the verge of the end of ages, presses them to resist being "mastered" by anything (presumably but the Spirit) (vv. 12–13). The key issue is that the body, the lived reality of all humans, belongs to the Lord; and because we are members of Christ, so are our bodies (v. 15).

But in this text, it all depends on what we understand "sinning against the body" means. Are longtime, committed, and monogamous partners sinning? Are people living in fidelity with one another sinning? And why are we so willing to equate same-gender sex with fornication and prostitution? These questions are essential to nonheterosexual persons, but in a time when many people live as single adults, questions about what is "holy sex" are taken beyond the marriage vows. Is every sexual encounter outside of heteronormative marriage "joining the body of Christ to a prostitute"? The body is not meant for abuse, whether by food or by sexual promiscuity. Whatever does not honor one's humanity and one's commitment to Christ may be allowed, but not "beneficial." How does one tell? What is a Christian ethic of sexuality as it regards this text? How do we answer Paul in an age where we do not hold an antiflesh view of the life of the believer, and where we do not sit on the edge of our seats believing that today might be the very day that Jesus returns? (Even so, come, Lord.)

Harry Knox, then director of the Human Rights Campaign Religion and Faith Program, told a group of students at Lancaster Theological Seminary in November 2010 that LGBTQA peoples have been "clobbered" with this text, along with texts from Leviticus. He notes that heterosexuals often do not hold themselves to abstinence but use this text to forbid sex-positive love among nonheterosexuals. But sex, as a battle zone, is a boundary that people cross because sex is natural. At issue, too, is the fact that the body is the site of this battle zone. Who gets to control what body? How are we to judge the Spirit's work in another's body? I have no answers for the questions I raise. But these are the questions with which I believe we must contend as we wrestle a blessing from these verses in an effort to glorify God in our bodies (v. 20).

All these texts under consideration for this holy day lead us to reflect on how we respond to the embodied realities of ourselves and of others. They push us to think about the pastoral, theological, and biblical mandates we make that sometimes cause great physical and emotional pain, and thereby diminish human life. If Jesus came to give life in abundance, then it seems that learning to live with our full selves in community—celebrated, accepted, and held accountable—is the task before us all. We owe it to those brutalized by our violent words and society to create a safe world that crowds out depression and despair and introduces people to a God who loves the body God made. Then we may all worship with lips and hands, with heart and soul, and glorify God, even in our sexual lives.

Proper 8 [13]

Pablo A. Jiménez

2 KINGS 2:1–2, 6–14   1 KINGS 19:15–16, 19–21
PSALM 77:1–2, 11–20   PSALM 16
GALATIANS 5:1, 13–25
LUKE 9:51–62

The texts for today present several options for the preacher. The readings from 1 and 2 Kings focus on Elijah's ministry. The selections from the Psalter are psalms of lament. Galatians 5 contrasts the works of the flesh with the fruit of the Spirit. And the Gospel reading expounds on the cost of discipleship. Most of these readings suggest a common theme: leadership, particularly the forms, succession, and cost of leadership.

2 Kings 2:1–2, 6–14

The saga of Elijah has a tongue-in-cheek quality that distinguishes it from other biblical stories. This text, which technically concludes Elijah's saga, is not different.

This particular episode cannot be understood unless you read 1 Kings 19, where Elijah flees from Jezebel, has a profound spiritual experience with God at Mount Horeb, and chooses Elisha as his disciple. Here Elijah is ready to ascend to heaven in a "whirlwind," a phenomenon that usually accompanies a theophany (a miraculous appearance of God). Elijah makes up excuses to get away from Elisha and from the fifty men who belong to the company of prophets, but his disciples follow him wherever he goes. This is an amusing or comical detail.

Elijah tells them that God has sent him to Bethel, Jericho, and the Jordan River (vv. 2, 4, 6). At the river, Elijah strikes the water with his mantle, parting the waters and crossing on dry land (v. 8). This extraordinary miracle places Elijah on the same footing as Moses and Joshua, who performed similar miracles (see Exod. 14 and Josh. 3). The miracle evokes Israel's primal story of liberation.

After crossing the river, Elisha asks Elijah for a "double share" of his spirit (v. 9). Elisha takes the role of Elijah's "spiritual firstborn," claiming a double share of the parental inheritance. After Elijah is taken up before Elisha, in confirmation of the inheritance Elisha picks up the mantle and repeats the miracle of parting the waters (vv. 13–14). The fifty prophets, who witness the miracle from afar, affirm that Elisha has indeed inherited Elijah's prophetic authority and recognize him as the new leader of their prophetic school.

A sermon on this text should address issues of spiritual succession and authority. First, we must recognize that most faith communities do not see leadership as a trait to be inherited. Current leadership styles tend to be more democratic. Second, note that verse 14 affirms that Elisha's authority comes from God, not from the mantle. God is the only source of true power and authority. Finally, a narrative treatment of the text can profit from the comical elements of the story.

1 Kings 19:15–16, 19–21

Even extraordinary persons like Elijah have moments of crisis. His crisis occurred after his greatest victories. According to the biblical story, Elijah confronted the false prophets who were urging the people of Israel to worship Baal, the false god of Canaanite fertility (1 Kgs. 18:1–40). The confrontation ended with a big win for Elijah. Elijah also prophesied the end of the punishing drought sent by God (17:1–7; 18:41–46). The rain was swift, once again humiliating King Ahab. But these triumphs would lead to trouble for Elijah.

The victories of the prophet over the infidel king led Jezebel, the queen, to threaten Elijah (19:1–2). Jezebel was born a Phoenician princess and remained devoted to Baal. Under her influence, Ahab had built an altar in honor of Baal in the temple of Samaria (16:32). Stung by the death of the false prophets of the false god, Jezebel threatened to kill Elijah (19:2).

At first glance, Elijah's reaction is incomprehensible. However, people often get depressed after reaching a milestone, a high point in life. We believe that the achievement is unique and that we will live the rest of our lives looking back. One of my old college professors called this phenomenon *kairothanasia*, meaning "death at the opportune time." Novels like André Gide's *The Counterfeiters* present characters who get depressed and even attempt suicide after a moment of triumph or happiness. Therefore, we should not discredit the experience of Elijah, which may be much more common than we think.

The crisis leads to Elijah's flight into the wilderness (19:3–7) and walk to Mount Horeb (19:8). Horeb is one of the two names that the Hebrew Bible uses to refer to the mountain where Moses received the law of God. The other name is Sinai. Once on the mountain, Elijah takes refuge in a cave, where he spends the night (19:9). There the prophet hears the voice of God asking, "What are you doing here, Elijah?" The prophet responds to God with a short speech that appears to be well thought out (19:10). Although Elijah's response seems pious, it is self-interested. Elijah says that he is the only remaining faithful man in Israel.

The divine voice commands Elijah to go outside the cave. Then begins a series of supernatural manifestations of divine power (19:11–12). A strong wind, an earthquake, and a fire break out before the prophet. But God is not in any of these demonstrations.

The presence of God is manifest in the "sound of sheer silence" (19:12). God then repeats the question (v. 13) and Elijah repeats the same little speech (compare 19:14 with 19:10). This only raises the divine wrath. Note that God's response (vv. 15–18) has three important elements. First, God tells the prophet to stand up and return home. Second, God replaces the proud prophet, telling him to anoint Elisha as the new prophet (v. 16). And third, God reminds Elijah that there are seven thousand people who remain faithful to the covenant in Israel. The narrative ends with the account of Elisha's prophetic call (vv. 19–21).

A sermon on this text may address issues of leadership, such as the emotional crises that can affect leaders. Depression and burnout are common among people dedicated to ecclesial, social, or civic service. Religious leaders are not exempt from depression and should not deny it.

Moreover, leaders can delude themselves into thinking that they are irreplaceable divine instruments. This is a common trait among burnt-out ministers, who hide their problems under a mask of triumphalism. The text implies that God has never been without faithful witnesses in the world—thus democratizing our view of religious leadership.

Psalm 77:1–2, 11–20

Psalm 77 begins with a heartbreaking cry, and the poet expresses a number of questions that plague him. The psalmist's stress and anguish are so great that he has lost sleep (v. 4). He remains awake, crying out to God and trying to find an explanation of his problem (vv. 1–3). Verses 5–9 reveal the poet's terrible state of anxiety. After examining his past (vv. 5–6), the question remains (v. 7): "Will the Lord spurn forever, and never again be favorable?"

The psalmist voices a common human experience. At different times, we all doubt God's love and mercy. It is difficult to remain steadfast in times of trial. Sometimes we grow sad thinking that God has stopped hearing our prayer, failed to honor the divine promises. At times, we can even fight with God. How can we survive these times of tribulation?

Verse 10 marks a turning point in the song. After externalizing his doubts and fears, his perspective changes. The psalmist realizes that he has been the victim of his own doubts and despair. God has not failed him. On the contrary, the poet can testify about the mighty acts that God has done in his life (vv. 10–12).

God has also shown his mercy toward Israel (vv. 14–15), especially in the liberation from captivity in Egypt with parting waters (vv. 16–20). The poet who began doubting God's love (v. 8) ends up affirming God's greatness (v. 13). The psalmist has received a new direction in his life, moving from lament to praise.

This psalm raises two important issues related to social justice. The first one is liberation from captivity. Although the psalmist did not experience emancipation personally, he shared in Israel's history of liberation. Past experiences of liberation enthuse the psalmist, encouraging him to endure present trials.

The second issue relates to the emotional consequences of suffering. People who survive critical times can face spiritual and psychological pain. Such grief may push anyone into a deep crisis. As in the psalm, faith can be a divine instrument that can lead us to spiritual and psychological health.

Psalm 16

This is another psalm of individual lament. Here the poet asks for God's protection (v. 1), for God is the only one who has shown him favor (v. 2). The psalmist expresses the conviction that God is the source of everything good. God protects him because the psalmist has publicly worshiped God. This expression of trust is the theological center of the psalm. The rest of the poem simply elaborates the theological implications of this statement.

The Hebrew text of the psalm is not clear, which makes it difficult to translate and, therefore, to understand. In any case, the psalmist contrasts his faith in the God of Israel with the faith of those who worship other divinities (v. 4). In particular, he criticizes their worship, which included offering blood as a libation to their gods. This can point to animal or even human sacrifices.

The psalmist denounces the false gods, affirming faith in the one true God. He confesses that God is his "portion" (v. 5), delighting in his relationship with God (v. 6).

The psalmist also blesses God for the divine wisdom. God is not only his protector, but also his counselor and instructor (v. 7). Such faith is a source of security and stability (v. 8), producing sincere joy (v. 9). The psalm ends by affirming that faith surpasses even death, for God protects the believer from harm and will not allow the believer's soul to decay in Sheol (vv. 10–11).

This psalm suggests several topics for preaching and teaching. God's love, goodness, protection, and wisdom are paramount. However, the topic of spiritual sorrow, developed in verses 4–5, supposes an ideology of conquest. Paired with the condemnation of idolatry, this psalm could be misused as a theological justification for a nationalistic theology. We must beware of all theological readings that foster a manifest-destiny mentality, for they can legitimate repression, oppression, and even genocide. Such reading betrays the real intention of the text.

Galatians 5:1, 13–25

Galatians is a polemical epistle, written by Paul with the intention of defending his theological and pastoral legacy. After Paul planted the church in Galatia, other preachers brought other doctrines to the region. These preachers claimed that Paul's understanding of the gospel was incomplete, for even Gentiles had to observe Jewish ritual law in order to be saved.

Paul criticizes this "Christ + element X = salvation" formula. In this case, X was the law. However, throughout church history, myriad preachers have used a similar formula to expound false heresies. The meaning of "element X" can be constructed as political ideology, racial supremacy, or dreams of financial prosperity.

The problem with this heretical formula is that it relegates faith in Jesus Christ to a second tier. Without element X there is no salvation. Therefore, the new element becomes the deciding factor over faith in Jesus Christ.

This explains why Paul is so adamant in his claims that we are free in Christ and that submitting to the false teachers is tantamount to slavery (v. 1). This statement summarizes the theological content of the letter.

However, freedom can be misused, particularly if someone uses it to legitimate sinful behavior (vv. 13–14). Even if we do not indulge in sinful acts, the heat generated by the controversy can lead us to destroy one another (v. 15). Personal freedom does not justify the oppression of the other, even if the other is a false teacher.

Luke 9:51–62

Verse 51 is the narrative center of Luke's story. It talks about the hardest decision that Jesus ever made. Jesus understood that he had to fulfill a God-given mission, which required traveling to Jerusalem, the capital of Judea, to confront the political and religious authorities. He had to unmask the false leaders who oppressed the people of God. And in that process, Jesus had to sacrifice his life.

Luke employs a literary device to tell us how much Jesus wrestled with this decision. Luke 9:28 says that Jesus retired to a mountain to pray with Peter, John, and James—his inner circle of leaders. We can infer that Jesus withdrew to pray because he was pondering the decision to go to Jerusalem.

Luke 9:51 says that Jesus "set his face to go to Jerusalem." That is a beautiful phrase to describe Jesus' courage. He faces the situation bravely, boldly, and with integrity.

Greek has two words for time: *chronos* and *kairos*. The first one refers to the quantitative and the second one refers to the qualitative aspect of time. Jesus decided to go to Jerusalem in God's *kairos*, at the time appointed by God. Motivated by the certainty of acting according to God's will, Jesus canceled all other engagements and decided to walk to Jerusalem. Like any good leader, Jesus sensed the terrible cost of his trip. Still, he set his face to go to Jerusalem.

A number of people crossed paths with Jesus, some in good faith and others with hidden agendas. They all risked hindering Jesus' mission. Most notorious is the case of John and James, who respond violently to an uncomfortable situation. Residents of some Samaritan villages rejected Jesus and his disciples (vv. 52–53). Insulted, John and James suggest commanding fire to come down from heaven to destroy the villages (v. 54).

Note that the disciples ignore Jesus' character and mission. It is clear that Jesus never would have wanted the death of the Samaritans and it is clear that Jesus never would have used the power of God for revenge. However, John and James appear to ignore Jesus' life-affirming mission.

The text also includes exchanges with three other persons. Each exchange reflects the call and challenges of following Christ (vv. 57, 59, 61). And to each one, Jesus responds with the costs of discipleship in the very real, daily cares of life (vv. 58, 60, 62). The central topic of this text thus is the cost of discipleship. Jesus is willing to pay the high personal cost and warns others of the personal sacrifice involved in Christian discipleship. Jesus remains faithful even when we fail, like James and John, to understand Jesus' character and mission. God calls us to affirm life and to serve life, not to destroy it.

Fourth of July: Seeking Liberty and Justice for All

Ronald J. Allen

JEREMIAH 31:15–26
PSALM 40
REVELATION 12:18–13:10
LUKE 11:33–36

Many churches join the larger culture in the United States by celebrating Fourth of July as Independence Day.[1] However, reflective Christians note that independence from Great Britain in 1776 did not bring freedom to slaves. Moreover, people at Fourth of July events sometimes uncritically wave the flag and celebrate the nation (including national policies that deny God's purposes). However, the preacher can take advantage of the interest in public life generated by the Fourth of July to help the Christian community think critically about the degree to which the United States (or any nation) is truly an environment of liberty and justice for all. What needs to happen for all in this nation to live in liberty and justice?

> Had I the ability, and could reach the nation's ear, I would . . . pour out a fiery stream of biting ridicule, blasting reproach, withering sarcasm, and stern rebuke. For it is not light that is needed but fire; it is not the gentle shower, but thunder. We need the storm, the whirlwind, and the earthquake. The feeling of the nation must be quickened; the conscience of the nation must be roused, the propriety of the nation must be startled, the hypocrisy of the nation must be exposed, and its crime against God and [humanity] must be proclaimed and denounced.
>
> *Frederick Douglass*[2]

1. While these comments focus on the Fourth of July as Independence Day in the United States, they could be adapted for similar days in other nations. Canada, for instance, celebrates July 1 as Canada Day in honor of Canada being officially united as a single country on July 1, 1867.

2. Frederick Douglass first delivered this address in 1852; see, "The Meaning of July Fourth for the Negro," in *The Life and Writings of Frederick Douglas*, ed. Philip S. Foner (New York: International Publishers, 1950), 2:192.

Along with parades, fireworks, picnics, and a long weekend, July 4 celebrations in communities of Eurocentric origin in the United States often generate patriotic rhetoric that celebrates the nation. For Frederick Douglass, a former slave and well-known orator, the Fourth of July is less an occasion to celebrate the achievement of liberty and justice for the middle- and upper-class Euro-American community than a day on which to identify those who are denied liberty and justice and to rouse the conscience of the nation to repent and to rectify the situation. The Scripture passages for today can help the preacher engage Douglass's agenda.

Jeremiah 31:15–26

Jeremiah's ministry began when Judah was an independent nation that had breached the obligations of the covenant through such things as idolatry, injustice, and false alliances. The community did not repent. As punishment, God allowed the Babylonians to overrun Judah and to send its leaders into exile in Babylonia.

Today's reading is from a section of Jeremiah sometimes called the Book of Consolation. The aforementioned punishment was taking place, but the prophet turned the people's vision to the promise that God would restore the community. However, progress toward restoration depended on the community living faithfully according to the covenant.

Today's passage presents a series of oracles organized around family motifs. In verses 15–16, Rachel (an ancestral mother of Judah) weeps because of Judah's disobedience and exile. Thereafter, in verses 18–20, God pays attention to Ephraim (one of Rachel's children, hence, the people of Judah), who deserved punishment but who then insisted, "I took the discipline." Ephraim was ready to resume faithful life. Then God admonishes the community as a daughter ("virgin Israel") to "set up road markers for yourself," that is, to follow the commandments as the route to restoration (vv. 21–22).

As part of the restoration, God created a new thing: "A woman encompasses a man" (v. 22). This statement points to the transformation of the restored community. Old limitations—such as those represented by gender—no longer apply. Indeed, those who were repressed become agents of blessing. Verses 23–26 conclude with a vision of the restored Judah in which the community is animated by authentic worship (v. 23), with people from urban and rural areas living in mutual support (v. 24).

The Fourth of July is an ideal time for the preacher to help the congregation consider the principle dynamics in this text. On the one hand, the United States exhibits many similarities to the unfaithful life of Judah early in Jeremiah's ministry. Many people functionally regard things other than God—such as money, race, social power, military power, or even the nation—as ultimate, and thus fall into idolatry.

The United States has not been overrun, as Judah was by Babylon, but the United States experiences profound social distress in such areas as economic instability, fractiousness among races, shortages of money for social welfare and education contrasted with vast spending for the military, polarization between political parties, and increase in crime with diminishing attention to the underlying causes. While God may not have visited these calamities directly on the United States, if such trends are not reversed, they will undermine the quality of life for all in this country. And still God holds forth a vision of repentance and restoration.

The reading from Jeremiah suggests that the preacher can tell the Rachels of our world that they need not weep disconsolately for their children, for God is already present to lure us toward renewal. Our part is to be like Ephraim: repenting, taking the discipline of our difficult circumstances, and learning from them. We must follow road markers of justice that can guide us toward restored national life. Indeed, we need to be open to "a woman encompassing a man," that is, to transformed ways of reorganizing our national life.

Psalm 40

While this psalm speaks about the experience of an individual, a preacher could use it as a lens for thinking about life in community. This psalm contains two styles of literature not usually found in the same psalm.

The first part of the psalm is a song of thanksgiving (vv. 1–10). The author had been in a desperate situation described only as a "desolate pit" or a "miry bog" (v. 2). God lifted the psalmist and set the psalmist's feet on a rock. Those who trust in false gods should then see what God can do.

The second style in the psalm is a lament in which the psalmist cries out because a new affliction has come upon the community (vv. 11–17). Again, the psalmist is vague about the nature of these difficulties except to imply that they are powerful and that the psalmist had a hand in creating them (v. 12).

From the perspectives of social justice and the Fourth of July, this psalm captures dynamics that are true for many preaching contexts. In connection with the song of thanksgiving, the preacher could recall situations when aspects of the life of the congregation, city, state, nation, or world have been threatened but then something happened to bring about security, peace, and justice. The community gives thanks. Yet, the preacher and congregation could follow the lament part of the psalm to name social issues that continue to leave many people in distress. For example, although the Civil Rights Movement brought about changes to make illegal certain expressions of segregation, racism itself is still virulent in the United States. We can give thanks for Martin Luther King Jr. and for important initiatives for opening the door to a more just and multicultural society while confessing that the Eurocentric community is still racist.

Luke 11:33–36

The Gospel of Luke and the book of Acts presume that history was divided into two eras—the present fractured, unjust world about to end, and the realm of God already coming to expression through the ministry of Jesus but to be completely manifest only at Jesus' second coming. Luke writes to encourage the church to remain faithful while it awaits the final coming of the realm.

Beginning in 11:14, Luke depicts the disciples of Jesus as being in conflict with opponents of the realm of God. In the dimness of the old age, Jesus' followers have received a lamp (v. 33). Jewish writers frequently used the image of "light to the world" to describe the vocation of Israel to be a model (light) for the nations or Gentiles (Isa. 42:6). Luke wants the disciples not to hide their lamp (their witness to the realm) in a cellar but to put it on a lamp stand.

In verses 34–36, the Gospel writer assumes the ancient idea that light is *within* the body and that a human being sees by projecting light out of the body. Thus Luke urges the community to consider whether the body is full of light or dimness, that is, whether the community is living toward the realm of God or is simply continuing the brokenness of the old age. Luke wants the community to make sure that the realm powers the internal light and that the community witnesses through that light to the world, even in the face of opposition.

The Puritans spoke of their initial settlement in New England as a city set on a hill, a light to the world (cf. Matt. 5:14–16).[3] They wanted Puritan community life to model how God wanted people to live together. This way of thinking quickly became commonplace among many people of European origin, and it persists in some corners today.

On the Fourth of July, the preacher could use verses 33–36 as a springboard for reflecting critically on the image of the United States as a lamp on a lamp stand. To what degree does the life of the United States function as a lamp on a lamp stand by embodying values of the realm of God? The preacher can help the congregation identify points at which this country operates within the dimness of fractiousness and injustice in the present age.

---

3. For example, John Winthrop described the new settlement in this language in a sermon in 1630, "A Model of Christian Charity," in *Speeches That Changed the World*, ed. Owen Collins (Louisville, KY: Westminster John Knox Press, 1999), 191–92.

Revelation 12:18–13:10

John wrote the book of Revelation about 90–95 CE, when the churches in Asia Minor (present-day Turkey) were persecuted (or feared persecution) for protesting aspects of Roman rule that affronted God's purposes. In 12:18, John uses the image of a dragon taking a stand on the seashore to symbolize Satan entrenching against the coming realm of God. The dragon presides over the sea, a traditional Jewish symbol of chaos.

A beast rises out of the sea, thus indicating that the beast comes from Satan and brings chaos with it. When John describes the beast as having ten horns and seven heads, the reader immediately recognizes that the beast is Rome. The dragon, Satan, imbues the beast with Satan's own authority (13:1–2). An earlier emperor, Nero, had killed himself, but the dragon sustained the empire and the power of the emperor. People worshiped the emperor, thus becoming idolaters (13:3–4). The blasphemous empire maintained its power through fear and violence (13:5–8). Following a Jewish idea that God sometimes punished sinners with the very means of their sinning, John believed that the Roman Empire, which ruled by violence, would meet a violent end (13:10a-b).

Before setting off the Fourth of July fireworks, the preacher might pause with the congregation to consider the possibility that certain policies and practices of the United States (and related nations) are similar to those of the Roman Empire. For example, some civic ceremonies on the Fourth of July make an idol of this country. We sometimes impose our will on others through arbitrary military action. The world economy, in which the United States is central, effectively enslaves many people in third-world settings. To the degree that governments (and other institutions) maintain power by violence, this nation and others who engage in empire can expect violence in response.

John believed that the time had passed when the Roman Empire could repent. Its doom was certain. However, the United States still has the present moment to repent. In our setting, an enduring and faithful church can alert the nation to these possibilities (v. 10).

Proper 9 [14]

Marjorie Hewitt Suchocki

2 KINGS 5:1–14
PSALM 30

ISAIAH 66:10–14
PSALM 66:1–9
GALATIANS 6:(1–6), 7–16
LUKE 10:1–11, 16–20

The commitment to social justice involves us in a never-ending process of analyzing the conditions that make for ill-being in our society and discerning the most gospel-centered ways of addressing these problems. Because the problems calling for justice are so complex, and because resolving one problem only seems to reveal another, we can become discouraged and "weary in doing what is right." The texts in this lectionary study offer insight, hope, and encouragement for our spirits, and the grace of renewed energy for the work ever before us.

2 Kings 5:1–14

What insight into social justice glimmers from this story, familiar to us even from childhood Sunday school lessons? A captive girl from Israel serves in the household of an Aramean army captain, Naaman, who has leprosy. She tells her mistress, who tells Naaman, that a prophet in Israel can heal his leprosy. So Naaman goes to Israel—not as a conqueror now, but as a supplicant—and asks Elisha to cure him. "Go, wash in the Jordan seven times, and your flesh will be restored" (v. 10) is the answer. Angry at first, Naaman eventually obeys, dips himself seven times in the Jordan, and comes up clean. Just beyond our lectionary reading is the continuation of the tale—in return for the healing, Naaman offers Elisha rich gifts, which Elisha rejects. Elisha's servant, however, reluctant to see such riches go, follows Naaman and tells him Elisha has changed his mind, wanting to give a few things to some mendicants who came his way. Naaman gives him double what he asks, and the servant

311

brings the spoils back to Elisha, who curses him for his action by giving the servant and all his children forever the leprosy that had left Naaman.

The glimmerings of justice are these: kindness and generosity, even to one's captors, as seen first in the girl and then in Elisha's offering of the cure. That Elisha is no respecter of persons is sure, for he heals the foreigner and inflicts illness on his own servant, presumably his countryman. If we focus simply on the cure, then we are impressed by the call to offer healing not only beyond our borders, but even to those who have caused us damage. And the cure is given graciously, without cost. Were it not for the conclusion to the text, where Elisha punishes his servant by making him and his children suffer leprosy, we could read the story of Naaman as a witness to the grace of God, freely offered across all boundaries, and therefore inspiring us to offer what grace and healing we can across whatever boundaries are erected to divide us.

The ending of the tale is also instructive. Perhaps the worth of our actions is to be judged less by how we treat the great and mighty and more by how we treat the least among us, even those we deem unworthy. Our faithfulness in social action is measured not only by how we respond to the great news-worthy disasters, but also by how we respond to the small, daily injustices of a callous society.

Psalm 30

This psalm could well be the kind of praise offered by Naaman following his cleansing in the river Jordan. There is exultation at rescue from a danger not here named—but a danger real enough that the singer was almost dead. "You have brought up my soul from Sheol, restored me to life" (v. 3). Looking back on the danger, the singer proclaims, "Weeping may linger for the night, but joy comes with the morning" (v. 5).

The next verses bring a note of "pride goes before a fall" caution. The singer, during a time of well-being, considered this prosperity the favor of God, and surely a favor that would not fail. "I shall never be moved" (v. 6), he had said. And then the hard times came. "Lord!" he shouts piteously, "What profit is there in my death? . . . Will the dust praise you?" (v. 9). Perhaps we have leave to gawk at the impudence of the man! But even in his impudence, God lifts him up, and the psalm concludes with utter joy: "You have turned my mourning into dancing . . . and clothed me with joy. . . . O LORD my God, I will give thanks to you forever" (vv. 11–12).

The psalm posits a kind of simultaneity of danger and release, mourning and dancing, agony and gladness. To be engaged in the hard work of social justice is to encounter these antinomies daily. It seems that every victory reveals yet another layer of injustice to be addressed; redress in one corner is supplanted by distress in another. We live in the "both/and" world of Psalm 30. Doing so, we claim its joy as our ultimacy, repeating the psalm's amen: O Lord our God, we will give thanks to you forever!

Isaiah 66:10–14

We encounter one of the classic texts bespeaking the gender inclusiveness of God, which is surely a matter of justice, considering the deleterious effects of assuming that male language for God is normative. As Mary Daly so famously said, "If God is male, then the male is God."[1] Of course it is natural to speak of God in human categories—what else do we know so well? We assume that God is like us, only in ways that are far better, far stronger. On the other hand, if God is to communicate with us at all, is it not necessary that God speak to us in languages and forms that we understand? Do not we learn in the doctrine of the incarnation that God bends to us, assuming our form, identifying with us in order to redeem us? And we, because we see God revealed in Jesus, have sometimes assumed that the maleness of Jesus is part of the revelation—God must be male too! Some have even restricted ordination to men on that foolish basis.

This text in Isaiah joins with a few others to disabuse us of divinizing maleness. First the text feminizes the city, Jerusalem, portraying her as a nursing mother. She carries us and dandles us on her knee, while watching the glory of nations pass by, a river of peace. Then the text takes us one further step: it is not Jerusalem that nurses us, carrying us on her hip—it is God. It is God who comforts us as a mother, God who comforts us in the city. The Hebrew Scriptures give us much male imagery of God as warrior and storm God; they also give us female imagery of a healing, comforting, nurturing God.

What do we have, then? A male/female God? Perhaps instead we are given to understand that God, who is more than us—a God of the wondrous and seemingly infinite universe—is more than male or female, but bends to our condition, deigning to use male and female imagery to communicate with us because that is the language that we understand. Saving this: by using male/ female imagery to communicate with us, God transforms male/female imagery, relativizing it rather than divinizing it.

We are men and women together, both offering qualities that can be used by God to image who God is for us. We can call God "mother/father God" as a way of signifying this. But the God who is so revealed to us is a God who ultimately is not captured and contained in any image or figure, but who transcends our humanity.

---

1. Mary Daly, *Beyond God the Father: Toward a Philosophy of Women's Liberation* (Boston: Beacon Press, 1973), 19.

Psalm 66:1–9

We celebrate the works of God, and this psalm focuses on a celebration of God's historic act of salvation history for the Hebrew people when God parted the waters of the sea so that the people could pass over on dry land. But the psalm then treats this historic memory as a metaphor for God's faithfulness to us as well. Our ancestors passed through the river on foot—but *our* feet might slip! The psalm continues beyond the lectionary limitation to speak of times when our feet might well slip. We experience oppressive burdens; we go through fire and water. And then the song of triumph returns. God does not turn us away or withhold God's loving-kindness. God does not allow our feet to slip.

If the ancient Hebrews could take the metaphor of God's parting the sea so that they could pass over dry land, with their feet not slipping, perhaps those of us involved in issues of justice might take the same text as encouragement. Surely the injustices confronting us are monumental. How are we to address conditions caused by the enormity of greed that never seems to have enough wealth garnered to itself, no matter who suffers in the garnering? Are not the greed-filled corporations and their executives our oppressive "burdens" and a river of people who "ride over our heads" (Ps. 66:11–12)? What of the policies that allow this greed to extend itself beyond one nation, pouring the wealth of natural resources from other lands into its giant maw, with no regard for the impoverishment and destruction it leaves in its wake? And what of the corruption of law that such greed purchases, that such devastation and impoverishment should be considered but a natural and lawful consequence of "progress"? Surely in considering such issues we are but tiny things, struggling for safety and justice, dry land in a river of greed.

The psalm says that God will not allow our feet to slip, that God's eye keeps watch on the nations, and that a cleansing happens as we struggle through this fire and water. We shall yet praise God, even while we are in the midst of the waters, seeking God's own dry land.

Galatians 6:(1–6), 7–16

The Galatians passage continues the exhortation of Psalm 66, now in the context of the early church. Paul first speaks of our conduct and attitude toward one another within the family of faith. We are to be patient with one another, forgiving of faults, bearing one another's burdens. We are to be marked by humility and sharing. And then, having described the inner life of the community, Paul tells us not to "grow weary in doing what is right, for we will reap at harvest time, if we do not give up" (v. 9).

We might consider such a description of the early community with a kind of holy envy, knowing that our own communities are subject to controversy and dissension. We are divided into "liberal/progressive" and "conservative/fundamentalist," each sure of our own rightness and the other's waywardness. But if we continue with the text, we find that the same was true of this early ideal community. Their controversy was not homosexuality—although they could well have named their own controversy "scriptural authority," even as some so name the controversy of homosexuality. Paul's communities were struggling over the issue of circumcision. Jesus was a Jew, and the first Christians were Jews, and as such, they had the mark of the covenant with God, which was circumcision. When pagan converts refused circumcision, were they not less Christian than the Jewish Christians? Scriptural authority was an issue, for the Scriptures were the Hebrew Scriptures, and circumcision is certainly enjoined, without qualification. And so the controversy raged—and so have controversies raged, through all the centuries, though the exact nature of the controversies has differed from age to age.

We would do well, in considering the controversies, to consider again the first verses of this sixth chapter of Galatians. We are to bear with one another in humility and gentleness. Learning to live with our diversities, we may yet resolve them in the direction of the love of God, and then we will not "grow weary in doing what is right" (v. 9).

Luke 10:1–11, 16–20

Jesus sends seventy of his followers as a vanguard to cities Jesus himself plans to visit later. They are to heal the sick and announce the reign of God. They are to take no provisions other than the message and healing of Jesus. The text tells us that the seventy went, and then "returned with joy, saying, 'Lord, in your name even the demons submit to us!'" (v. 17).

If we, like the seventy, are to proclaim the reign of God by casting out demonic forces, then we are called to address not only the systems of health care in our country, but the enormous profits and power that lie behind such demons in the addiction industry that makes drugs easily available to our youth and adults. The enormous power of drug addiction sickens not only our own citizens, but also the countries that supply the substances from which these drugs are made.

What if the situation today is analogous to the Prohibition days of the last century? Enormous criminal profits were gained from making alcohol illegal, and the alcohol problem became worse, not better, through unregulated alcoholic content in the bootleg drinks. During Prohibition, crime syndicates became the shadow side of churches in the fight to keep alcohol illegal—for entirely different reasons, of course, and surreptitiously, not overtly. The churches were on the side of morality, and the crime syndicates were on the side of profits. The illegality of alcohol satisfied both.

Are not drug cartels using the same tactic today? By upholding the illegality of drugs, they strengthen their power and ensure continuance of their profitable existence. The horror of violence in Mexico over drug trafficking gives ample witness to the effects of keeping drugs illegal. Legalization of drugs will not eliminate addiction, just as legalization of alcohol has not eliminated alcoholism. But alcohol legalization stopped the violence and subversive activity associated with its illegality. Drugs are not legalized, and both addiction and violence are rampant. Our schoolchildren are coaxed into trying this drug or that. A vast international criminal network has a vested interest in keeping drugs illegal, and just as in the last century when churches were lulled into thinking illegality was the way of morality, even so in this century the church is in unwitting alliance with the drug trade. But drug trafficking is a demon that must be cast out. A sure effect of legalization would be the demise of the drug cartels, just as it was the demise of the bootleggers a century ago. If the churches name trafficking in drugs as well as addiction a demonic evil to be healed, then perhaps the churches will no longer cooperate with drug criminals in keeping drugs illegal. With legality, we might be able to gain a measure of control over the content of drugs and over their use. And we will surely cast out the vicious demon of trafficking.

Shall we address the real demons that wreck lives in other countries as well as ours? Shall we seek the healing that is the mark of the reign of God? We are but seventy, and those who use and profit from drugs are legion. But we, too, might return to our Lord rejoicing, having cast out demons in his name.

Proper 10 [15]

Cláudio Carvalhaes

AMOS 7:7–17
PSALM 82

DEUTERONOMY 30:9–14
PSALM 25:1–10
COLOSSIANS 1:1–14
LUKE 10:25–37

We are living in what the Christian liturgical calendar calls Ordinary Time. What are we to do with these Ordinary Time texts for today? In this week called Proper 10, across the years A, B, and C, I will read these texts with specific places or communities in mind. Based on what liberation theologians in Latin America do with Bible readings in base communities, we will look at the Bible from the *Sitz im Leben*, the social location, of specific communities. This is a different way of reading the Bible. Instead of Bible commentaries near me, I will have the voices of people reading the texts and giving input from their religious, social, political, economic, and historical situations. For some, the result will not be a cohesive reading drenched in many recognizable biblical interpretations or proper citations, but rather an interpretation filled with burning questions, biblical and general commentaries, and theological accounts at the crossroad between a community and a pastor trying to learn how to be part of a community of faith.

Here is how it will happen: At a community's meeting, the pastor outlines what Ordinary Time means in the liturgical calendar and asks the community to read the Scriptures and talk about each text, perhaps drawing connections between them. History and story will be combined in the thick hermeneutical accent of each community.

Any lectionary offers ways of reading the Bible, and this exercise has two goals: first, based on these experiences, you will be able to ask your community what these texts are telling them, and then use that dialogue to prepare your sermon for Sunday; second, seeing how other communities read and talk about these texts in their local context might shed some light into preaching in your own community on this day.

317

For today's lesson, the pastor is living in a small town in the United States in the midst of undocumented people. The pastor begins by saying to the gathering of thirty people: Friends, we are here to read the Bible and figure out what these texts have to do with us and our community in Santa Fe. What is God telling us to consider, to do, to change, to move, to engage, or to transform here today? We are celebrating a liturgical period called Ordinary Time, which in a sense is the daily stuff of life fueled with extraordinary encounters with God. At this crossroads between the ordinary and extraordinary lies what we believe regarding God's presence, God's miraculous works, and our (extra)ordinary lives.

So, what are we to do with these texts in front of us around these times?

The numbers in parentheses below indicate a different statement made by different people in a community attempting to engage critically each text in response to questions raised by their pastor.

Amos 7:7–17

(1) I am a construction worker and a mason; and in my trade a plumb line serves to measure things, walls, and stairs, to determine the center of gravity, or if an irregular angle exists. I think that the Bible is like a plumb line that balances out our lives with God's presence. (2) That's why God is placing a plumb line in the middle of the people here in the text. (3) But God says God will not pass in their midst anymore. (4) Well, that is not good! (5) It seems that the plumb line is showing how off-balance Israel's life is at this point. (6) Things will be destroyed and Israel will go into exile. (7) Once again! (8) Like all of us!

(9) But I always thought that we came to the U.S. because we wanted . . . (10) What? (11) Are you kidding us? Let me ask: who among us are here in the U.S. because you wanted or came to pursue the North American dream? [pause] See, only three people out of, what? Thirty? (12) I came here because I had no choice and I feel I cannot go back because there is no job where I live. Everybody who lives there works for this North American company that owns most of the land around and only a few can get jobs in this oil refinery. (13) People go where the money is. (14) I wish I could live with my family back in my country. (15) Me too! (16) I am here because if I go back, I might be killed in my country. (17) But listen to this: "And Amaziah said to Amos, 'O seer, go, flee away to the land of Judah, earn your bread there, and prophesy there" (v. 12). See! We did fly away from our land. Judah is like the U.S. for us and we earn our bread here! Isn't that wonderful? (18) Yes, but what is this "prophesy there"? (19) Well, I guess it can be the need to tell people here that they have to welcome strangers. (20) Lots of people are against immigration. (21)

There is so much hatred. (22) Sonia had her house invaded by the police, and she was taken to prison. Her daughter was in school. (23) Where is she now? (24) We don't know. (25) Well, never open your door to anybody unless they pass a document signed by the judge and you can confirm it. Lock your doors and call the pastor. (26) But if Immigration knows he is our pastor, they will put him in prison too. (27) No, no, he will have help because he has papers, but we don't. (28) The pastor gave us a number of a lawyer to call in case of an emergency. (29) And a membership ID for our church. (30) When I was stopped by the police, and didn't have a driver's license, I called the pastor and he came to help me, and I was able to go home. (31) So "prophesy" here means to tell people to treat us like human beings! (32) To prophesy for new and consistent immigration reform!

(33) Look, let me read this information from this newspaper I got in the last march for immigration reform: "A new report, 'Raising the Floor for American Workers: The Economic Benefits of Comprehensive Immigration Reform,' by Dr. Raúl Hinojosa-Ojeda, finds that comprehensive immigration reform that includes a legalization program for unauthorized immigrants and enables a future flow of legal workers would result in a large economic benefit—a cumulative $1.5 trillion added to the U.S. gross domestic product over ten years. In stark contrast, a deportation policy would result in a loss of $2.6 trillion in GDP over ten years."[1]

(34) Is that true? (35) Of course it is!! (36) Then, to prophesy is to tell the truth and destroy the myths of immigration, like that we steal people's jobs or bring diseases! (37) We are like Amos—housecleaning people, farm workers, pizza deliverers, dishwashers in restaurants. We pick up trash from the street, we clean movie theaters, and we are babysitters. So we can also prophesy! (38) But we are too vulnerable.

(39) Shouldn't we listen to the text (v. 16) that says, "Do not prophesy against Israel, and do not preach against the house of Isaac"? (40) No way! The United States is not Israel, nor any promised land! (41) Do we prophesy *against* the U.S. or *to* the U.S.?

(42) I don't know if I have the energy to prophesy. (43) I will never do it! (44) Neither will I! (45) I will be quiet and try to survive as long as I can; I am scared to death to go to prison. I am not a bandit! (46) But we shouldn't stop prophesying! (47) We shouldn't, but what else do we have? We have no documents and there are so many people barking like dogs in our ears everywhere. (48) This is what they do to scare us. (49) They cannot win this battle! (50) What should we do?

1. Center for American Progress, "How Immigration Reform Would Help the Economy: Fact Sheet on the Benefits of Legalization," http://www.americanprogress.org/issues/2010/01/immigration_benefits_fact_sheet.html (accessed April 16, 2011).

Deuteronomy 30:9–14

(1) Here is our answer (v. 9); God will prosper us! (2) How? (3) If we turn to God with all our heart and all our soul (v. 10). (4) Perhaps! (5) Hey, where is our faith? (6) I, too, am trying, I am trying, but it is so hard to believe when we are in the eye of the storm. (7) Listen, we are not alone. There are several people out there looking after us, trying to win this battle with us and not for us! We must fight; we have no choice! (8) Listen again to the word of God: "and the LORD your God will make you abundantly prosperous in all your undertakings, in the fruit of your body, in the fruit of your livestock, and in the fruit of your soil" (v. 9). (9) And we don't need to go anywhere to hear the word of God lifting us up; it is right next to us, saying, "This commandment . . . is not too hard for you, nor is it too far away" (v. 11). (10) It feels so hard and far away. (11) It is the work of our community in relation to other communities that will change that! We must connect with other churches and groups of immigrants to engage in this struggle for justice. (12) Because it is better for the United States, even if they don't see it! (13) How do we use facts to turn hatred into welcoming? (14) I don't know, let us keep trying, and we will figure it out along the way. (15) Don't forget, we always have the Holy Spirit with us. Ordinary times do not mean ordinary faith, but daily life lived in the fullness of the Spirit who baptized us all with Jesus Christ! The Spirit will make our ordinary lives into extraordinary events! (16) Alleluia!

Psalm 82 and Psalm 25:1–10

(1) This is our prayer to God day and night (82:2–3): "How long will you judge unjustly and show partiality to the wicked? Give justice to the weak and the orphan; maintain the right of the lowly and the destitute." (2) Yes, this is our prayer every day. (3) We need to tell people "they have neither knowledge nor understanding" regarding immigration facts, and "they walk around in darkness" (82:5). (4) If we believe that immigration has to do with justice issues, then we need to act upon it! (5) And rise up along with God when we pray (82:8): "Rise up, O God, judge the earth; for all the nations belong to you!"

(6) The psalms are our source of strength, and when we don't know what to do, we should always go back to them. We must listen to the psalms and not let ourselves become discouraged. (7) Listen again, then, to this one (25:1–5): "To you, O LORD, I lift up my soul. O my God, in you I trust; do not let me be put to shame; do not let my enemies exult over me. . . . Make me to know your ways, O LORD; teach me your paths. Lead me in your truth, and teach me, for you are the God of my salvation; for you I wait all day long." (8) Wow! Let us read this psalm out loud three times together. . . . (9) Now let us promise each

other that we will read it every morning and every evening before we go to bed. (10) And let us call each other during the week just to read this psalm to each other! (11) Great! (12) That will be nice. (13) A breath of fresh air. (14) The Holy Spirit in an ordinary week. (15) It is hard for us to have an ordinary week. (16) That is so true!

Colossians 1:1–14

(1) Paul is saying that we live together with those who are not here anymore. (2) What do you mean? (3) Well, we have received the gospel of Jesus Christ from people who are not here anymore, but they are still part of us. (4) The huge cloud of witnesses! (5) I understand. (6) And we are to feed each other! That is why we have connections with four other churches in our own countries . . . (7) to hear from them and tell them about the struggles of our lives and mission. (8) Yes! (9) And this is how we survive; we support each other by also repeating to each other the word of God. (10) Like we did with the psalm. (11) So imagine somebody calling us or sending us an e-mail or even a letter that we will read in our worship service next Sunday (vv. 11–14): "May you be made strong with all the strength that comes from [God's] glorious power, and may you be prepared to endure everything with patience, while joyfully giving thanks to [God], who has enabled you to share in the inheritance of the saints in the light. [God] has rescued us from the power of darkness and transferred us into the kingdom of [God's] beloved Son, in whom we have redemption, the forgiveness of sins." (12) Shall we write a letter to send to our sister communities? (13) Yes, let's do it. (14) Shall we read it Sunday? (15) We will; it is part of the lectionary. (16) Oh, I wish we could leave this life of living under the shadows and be able to be in the light of our larger community. (17) But we can. (18) Perhaps, one day! (19) May we never get used to the shadows and darkness of those who don't have documents. (20) God forbid! (21) No, we cannot afford that! (22) Wait, let us not forget that God makes the ordinary extraordinary! Where is our faith?

Luke 10:25–37

(1) Who are we in this text? (2) As a nondocumented immigrant, I feel that we are all like the beaten man; coming from different countries to the United States, as we try to make a living here, our dignity is often stolen, stripped down, and beaten, almost literally. We live half dead and in fear all the time. (3) Oh, come on, it is not that bad. (4) Don't you feel like that? This is how I feel. (5) Still, we must be like the Good Samaritan and help those who are feeling like our brother or sister here. (6) We help our families back in our

countries and we somewhat do like the Good Samaritan. (7) But some of our own people are robbers of our own people. (8) I hate that! (9) But wait, what are we to learn from this passage? (10) To take time and money to care for others. (11) This is almost an illusion. (12) What? (13) Come on, who in our world would stop his or her busy life to help somebody? That is almost impossible. (14) Not really! People do help other people. (15) From a distance! (16) What are you talking about? (17) Remember those who helped you settle here, find a house, a job, and this community. (18) That is true. (19) How fast we forget things! (20) It is so easy to live without solidarity, without living in community. (21) Is it our needs that bring us together, or is it our common love for God? (22) Why don't we help others more often? How does the Holy Spirit work in us? (23) We are both the Good Samaritan and the wounded person on the street. (24) God have mercy on us!

Proper 11 [16]

Joni S. Sancken

AMOS 8:1–12
PSALM 52

GENESIS 18:1–10A
PSALM 15
COLOSSIANS 1:15–28
LUKE 10:38–42

This week's texts speak of the dangers of lives focused on self-sufficiency and self-security. We cannot rely on ourselves in the way that we can rely on God. No matter how well intentioned, human actions often lead to mixed outcomes at best. In Amos, the very earth trembles at the judgments against Israel's abuse of the poor. In Genesis, God fulfills God's promise that Sarah will bear a son despite Abraham and Sarah's disbelief and their attempts to fulfill this promise themselves rather than waiting for God. The psalms speak against trust in material wealth, and in Luke, Jesus lifts up Mary's way of attending to Jesus over Martha's focus on completing tasks. Ultimately, the lection from the Letter to the Colossians points toward the greatest treasure, our source of reconciliation and hope, Jesus Christ.

Amos 8:1–12

This text from near the end of the book of Amos returns to a pattern in Amos, that of God's words of judgment upon Israel, after a departure in 7:10–17 where Amos is interacting (in third person) with Amaziah, a priest of Bethel. Chapter 7 gives us a glimpse into the background of Amos, who was a herdsman and dresser of sycamore trees from the southern kingdom of Judah, called by God to prophesy to the northern kingdom of Israel (7:12–15).

Chapter 8 parallels the pattern of Amos's visions begun in chapter 7. The vision of a basket of summer fruit offers a play on words in the Hebrew text, which suggests that the fruit may signify dead bodies (v. 3).[1] The imagery

---

1. Allen R. Geunther, *Hosea and Amos*, Believers Church Bible Commentary (Scottdale, PA: Herald Press, 1998), 234.

here may seem strange to us, but it bears similarities to earlier images of the Amorites as cedars and oaks (2:9) whom God destroyed and Israel envisioned as grass being devoured by locusts or fire (7:1–6).[2] God threatens to bring destruction on Israel, not "passing them by" (v. 2) as God did in the exodus from Egypt. In this case, Israel will not be spared, temple songs will turn into wailing, and there will be dead bodies everywhere (v. 3). Amos's pronouncements have been aimed at various violations of the covenant; here he turns to those who do not fully keep the Sabbath and instead hurry back to their commerce. Multilayered repercussions of not keeping Sabbath echo in these verses. Both land and people suffer from not taking a break. Land becomes depleted of resources, and people in lower-paying service professions are forced to work when higher-paid executives choose to conduct business outside of office hours. Amos details the shady nature of those who engage in deceitful trade practices that blatantly reveal the theological worldview underlying their practices (vv. 4–6). They do not trust God to provide for their well-being and instead take every opportunity to secure more for themselves, even at the expense of others.

God will direct God's wrath toward those who "trample on the needy" (v. 4), swearing an oath by "the pride of Jacob" which the Lord "abhors" (6:8) as a euphemism for Israel's arrogant pride that relies on its own strongholds and resources to feel secure. God promises to remember unjust deeds and foretells punishment in the form of a mighty earthquake, historically noted throughout the book (1:1; 8:8; 9:5). The event at darkened midday is reminiscent of the plagues of Egypt and the curses for covenant violation in Deuteronomy (Exod. 10:21–23; Deut. 28:29) and further illustrates the power of God, who rules the universe. The devastation will be so severe that the whole land will be cast into mourning (v. 10). As in any situation of extreme devastation, the people will demand an answer, but God will not answer them (vv. 11–12).

Sabbath-keeping is a rare practice in today's world of twenty-four-hour convenience. We wring productivity out of tired people and environmental resources. The devastation wreaked upon Israel in the form of natural disasters is reminiscent of the kinds of disasters, in the form of powerful storms and rising ocean levels, that threaten us due to the effects of global warming. In the case of global warming, the active agents are humans, not God. God's response to covenant violation sometimes comes in the form of active punishment and other times comes in the form of giving us over to the other gods we serve in ways that lead us to experience the painful consequences of our actions. The act of giving us over can be a form of grace, in that it shows us the limitations of our own power and technologies.

2. Ibid., 346.

Genesis 18:1–10a

This text sets up the fulfillment of God's promise to Abraham to provide descendants through Sarah. In chapter 17, God appeared to Abraham to reiterate this covenant, along with the details of circumcision and the promise that Sarah would give birth to a son for Abraham. In chapter 16, Abraham and Sarah had taken the quest for progeny into their own hands by having Abraham father Ishmael through Hagar. This act has painful repercussions, although God steps in, offering safety and blessing to Ishmael (Gen. 16; 21:9–20). Nevertheless, in chapter 17, God insists that the covenant will pass to a yet-unborn son, Isaac, by Sarah. Abraham and Ishmael are both circumcised to signify their covenant with God. Now, at the beginning of chapter 18, we are told that the Lord again appeared to Abraham, but in this case, in the form of three visitors. It is unclear whether something about these strangers set them apart as divine or they appeared to Abraham simply as unknown men. Regardless, Abraham quickly acts to provide for them, running from his tent to bow down before them and offering water and food (vv. 2–5). The visitors agree to receive Abraham's hospitality, and Abraham rushes off again to employ Sarah and another servant to prepare a feast. Sarah "quickly" makes cakes from choice flour, and Abraham runs to the herd to find a tender calf that the servant hurries to prepare (vv. 6–7). Adding curds and milk to the other preparations, Abraham brings the food to the men and stands with them as they eat (v. 8).

In the context of this meal, one of the strangers repeats God's promise that Sarah will have a son. In the verses just after today's section we find that Sarah's response is the same as Abraham's in chapter 17, which is laughter (17:17; 18:11–12). Even though Sarah denies laughing, her response is not lost on God, who asks in 18:14, "Is anything too wonderful for the LORD?" After the three men depart from Abraham, they head toward Sodom, and the Lord announces the fate of Sodom and Gomorrah (18:20–22). Abraham argues for mercy on the cities should the Lord find ten people there who are not wicked. Alas, there are not even ten! Abraham's hospitality is echoed in the hospitality of Lot toward the angels of God who come to destroy Sodom. Lot's goodness, expressed in his hospitality, secures his family's safety.

Christine Pohl explores the practice of hospitality within the Christian tradition, drawing a connection between tending to the physical needs of strangers and acknowledging their "worth and common humanity." Throughout the history of the church, sharing food together has been an important means of "recognizing the equal value and dignity of persons."[3] Pohl suggests that

---

3. Christine D. Pohl, *Making Room: Recovering Hospitality as a Christian Tradition* (Grand Rapids: Eerdmans, 1999), 6.

practicing hospitality today expresses one of the core values of God's reign and connects us with those in the Bible, like Abraham, who took the risk of engaging hospitably with strangers and met the divine.[4]

Psalm 52

This psalm mirrors Amos's concerns about doing whatever it takes to secure wealth and security for self rather than relying on God. The psalmist begins with accusation against one who has acted maliciously through lying and treachery (vv. 1–4). Calling this person "mighty one" has a tone of sarcasm to it, reflecting the person's own puffed-up sense of self (v. 1). The word "but" at the beginning of verse 5 clues us in to a shift in power or tone and begins the next section of the psalm, which speaks of divine judgment against this deceitful person. God will knock those who are puffed-up down to size, so that the righteous laugh at the foolishness of trusting in wealth rather than seeking faithfulness to God (vv. 5–7). Again the word "but" signals a shift. This time the faithfulness of the psalmist contrasts with those who received the divine judgment (v. 8). The deceitful person is uprooted, but the psalmist is "like a green olive tree in the house of God" (v. 8a). The psalm ends with a deep profession of faith, trust, and thanksgiving directed toward God but performed in public, "in the presence of the faithful" (v. 9). This public profession serves as a reminder of the public witness of our own worship. We gather on the Sabbath to bear witness to our trust that God will provide for our needs. We do not need to fill every minute with work to have security. Like the psalmist, our faith and trust are in God.

Psalm 15

Psalm 15 may have a teaching function in helping worshipers learn what is required of the righteous to offer worship to God.[5] The psalm opens with the worshiper's question, what is required to abide or dwell with God? The rest of the psalm provides the answer in the form of ten habits of righteousness expressed in alternating positive and negative form. The positively phrased behaviors are walking blamelessly, doing what is right, speaking the truth from the heart, despising the wicked, honoring the ones who fear the Lord, and standing by one's oath (vv. 2, 4). The negatively phrased behaviors are not engaging in slander, not doing evil to friends, not reproaching neighbors, not lending money at interest, and not taking a bribe against the innocent (vv.

---

4. Ibid., 8, 24.
5. James H. Waltner, *Psalms*, Believers Church Bible Commentary (Scottdale, PA: Herald Press, 2006), 88.

3, 5). The final line of the psalm tells us of God's response to those who live disciplined by faithfulness. "Those who do these things shall never be moved" (v. 5c). They will find steadfast security in God, even if the world around becomes unstable. This psalm speaks of practical life choices rather than ritual behaviors as the measure of righteousness.[6] Jesus ultimately upholds this approach, choosing at times to violate strict Sabbath observance in order to heal the sick and suffering. This psalm can remind us to reflect on our own habits and behaviors as we prepare for worship.

Luke 10:38–42

Just prior to these verses from Luke, Jesus has told the parable of the Good Samaritan, a strong and active image of a divine vision of hospitality (10:25–37). Jesus now has turned toward Jerusalem (Luke 9:51), a journey that will ultimately lead to the cross, but these verses have him stopping to stay in the home of Martha and Mary (v. 38). In this short pericope, Jesus offers a more nuanced view of hospitality. While the Good Samaritan in his parable actively cared for the man in distress, in this case Jesus prefers Mary's attentiveness to the Lord as a means of showing hospitality, rather than Martha's focus on attending to the tasks and chores likely associated with the physical needs of her guests. When Martha complains to Jesus and seeks his support in getting Mary to share in the work, he sides with Mary, and so Martha is left with all the work and a reproach from Jesus (vv. 40–42). While Jesus interacts with more women in Luke than in any other Gospel, the women are not as powerful as those in the other Gospels. Even Martha and Mary are more spirited in John's Gospel (John 11; 12:1–8).[7] This story is disconcerting for a variety of reasons: it pits the sisters against one another, many listeners sympathize with Martha more than with Mary, and it upholds a more passive, "listening" role for women over and against active service directed toward Jesus. While Jesus does not explicitly limit women, his choice of Mary over Martha does send a message.[8] Mary's passive listening does not seem to empower her for an active role as a disciple, and unless carefully framed it might be a harmful role model for women who struggle to find a voice in many settings, including the church. Jane Schaberg offers a redemptive and empowering reading "behind the text" that moves beyond Luke's use of "love patriarchalism" in the voice of Jesus' affectionate chiding of Martha. If women do follow the model of Mary, it can be read as "authorizing women's solid theological education."

6. Ibid., 90.
7. Jane Schaberg, "Luke," in *Women's Bible Commentary*, ed. Carol A. Newsom and Sharon H. Ringe (Louisville, KY: Westminster John Knox Press, 1998), 367–68.
8. Ibid., 376–77 and 377–78.

This kind of education allows women to "see through the text" and Luke's possible motives in order to claim active roles in leadership for the church.[9]

Colossians 1:15–28

This selection from Colossians begins with a hymn (vv. 15–20) about the primacy of Christ, which the letter's author uses to frame and support subsequent comments directed to this Gentile congregation under the leadership of Epaphras (1:7–8; 4:13). The hymn connects the cosmic transcendence of God with Christ's actions on the cross that lead to reconciliation on earth. Establishing and reminding the congregation of Christ's primacy strengthens their need for reconciliation, "you who were once estranged and hostile in mind, doing evil deeds" (v. 21); it also reinforces reliance on reconciliation brought about by God through Christ and the appeal for them to hold steadfastly to their faith and relationship to God (vv. 22–23). The letter addresses controversy and disagreement within the congregation. Some are teaching falsehoods that are mentioned in chapter 2, focusing on a "puffed up . . . human way of thinking." The author appeals to the congregation to hold fast to Christ's lordship over the church (2:18–19); he reminds the Colossians that they only have the life they have because of God in Christ. Paul's testimony (vv. 24–29) highlights highs and lows of faithful service to God's mission. Paul endures suffering (vv. 24, 29), but God empowers him to joyfully bear witness to God's glory among the Gentiles, "which is Christ in you, the hope of glory" (v. 27). Verse 28 shows Paul's approach to ministry: proclamation of Christ, warning or admonishing and teaching "so that we may present everyone mature in Christ." While the word "warning" might strike us as negative, here it has a restorative purpose, to provide discipline that is necessary for discipleship. Paul's proclamation focuses on the person of Christ as the content. The primacy of Christ is upheld throughout this passage and serves as a crucial guide for the church today. Like the congregation at Colossae, we too are tempted to place ourselves at the center of church life when Christ is truly the head of the church. Paul's testimony about ministry puts the focus rightly on Christ and on the helpful potential of discipline within the community of faith as we strive to present an ever more faithful and mature witness to God.

9. Ibid., 378.

Proper 12 [17]

Wilma Ann Bailey

HOSEA 1:2–10
PSALM 85

GENESIS 18:20–32
PSALM 138
COLOSSIANS 2:6–15 (16–19)
LUKE 11:1–13

Like ancient Israel, the church is called to live out its reality conscious of the presence of God and in conformity to the divine will. That is easily said but not easily done. We as individuals and religious communities have differences in how to interpret the divine will and what it means to live faithfully. Clearly, we need to reject that which causes harm to others and particularly to those least able to defend themselves. We try to name and expose wickedness before the people of the world, just as the sins of Sodom were exposed before the world. Prayer is a tool that can help the community to remember to whom it belongs and where its strength lies. The prayer that Jesus taught the disciples recognizes the holiness of God, requests that God's will—not the will of the one praying—be done, and petitions for help every day and in the times of difficulties. The prayer that Jesus taught was not a request for miracles and signs.

Hosea 1:2–10

The Hosea prophecy is set in the eighth century BCE, a century that begins with prosperity for the northern kingdom of Israel and ends with its conquest by the Assyrian Empire. The southern Israelite kingdom of Judah remains intact during this period because of its less useful position in the southern hill country. This description of an unfaithful Israel is told with little reference to pressures from the Mesopotamian and Egyptian superpowers that are vying for control of the ancient Near Eastern military and trade routes. The passage uses the image of an unfaithful spouse as a symbol of Israel's unfaithfulness to God. This is not to be interpreted as Israel's typical behavior, because it is immediately followed by an image wherein the Israelites are called "children of the living God" (v. 10), and another wherein a series of reversals state that those "not pitied" (the symbolic name of a child) will be pitied and those who are "not my people" will be the people of God (2:23). A future restored Israel is envisioned as containing more people than can be counted. The purpose of this passage is to shock Israel with an image of temporary abandonment. It is to call Israel to its best self. The lack of faithfulness to which the passage refers is not a lack of religious devotion. The Israelites faithfully present their offerings and sacrifices to God (6:6). Their lack of attention to justice and neglect of the vulnerable in society demonstrate their lack of faithfulness (4:2). It includes "deceiving, killing, stealing, and committing adultery" (translation mine). Notice that all of these are sins against other people. When people harm other people and undermine the health of the community, they are being unfaithful to God.

Judah, the southern Israelite kingdom, is not yet in the dire straits that the northern one is, but there are hints that the southern kingdom will also suffer. How can a kingdom or community maintain its sense of "called apartness" when the pressures all around (in the contemporary context: pressures from the media, politics, the economy) are trying to force conformity to another standard? The book offers hope in an alternative model—a community living out the love and justice of God.

Genesis 18:20–32

In the Genesis passage, God informs Abraham that God is going to destroy Sodom and Gomorrah. God informs Abraham of the impending doom of the city because, as a leader, Abraham needs to learn about justice. The destruction of the cities, the text explains, is not a capricious act. It is a result of reasoned and rational judgment. The wickedness of the cities calls for this extreme action. Abraham raises an issue. If the entire city is destroyed, the righteous will be destroyed along with the wicked. It would be unjust, he argues before God, to allow the righteous to be punished for the sins of the wicked. The text implies that justice demands fairness and discrimination. Group punishment is inappropriate.

Abraham rhetorically asks God (v. 25; my translation), "Should not the one judging all the earth, do justice?" If God expects humans to do justice, God must also do that which is just. The standard of justice must be the same for divine beings and mortals. God concedes the point. God will not destroy the city if there are fifty, then forty-five, forty, thirty, twenty, and finally ten righteous people in it. It has been suggested in the Jewish tradition that Abraham stops at ten because that is the minimum number of men needed to form a *minyan* (prayer group) and synagogue (when the families of the men are added to the total count). The total populations of Sodom and Gomorrah are not given, so one cannot determine the balance of the righteous to the wicked. It does suggest, however, that a few people doing the right thing can transform a city. In the end, both cities are destroyed, but the relatives of Abraham are removed. It is not clear whether Lot himself is to be considered to be among the righteous. He and members of his family are saved for the sake of Abraham (Gen. 19:29). But justice is carried out. The purpose of this exchange is to illustrate that God should act toward humans according to commonly understood human assumptions about justice.

Psalm 85

Psalm 85 begins with an affirmation that God restored Israel and forgave its people's sins in the past. This knowledge emboldens them to request restoration again. They ask God to dispense with divine anger and deliver them. They ask to be shown divine *hesed* (loving-kindness, faithfulness, graciousness). The Israelites were no different from every other people or group on earth. They were not more rebellious or more stubborn. Each generation had to experience for itself the *hesed* of God in order to affirm with their ancestors the attributes of God and their desire to continue to be in relationship with the Divine.

At verse 8, the tone changes from desperation to hopefulness. We hear a word of *shalom* (peace, wholeness, health) from God. The ones who stand in awe of God will experience good things. *Hesed* and truth will draw near, and justice and peace will kiss (v. 10). These virtues create a surrounding imagery where faithfulness springs up from the earth and justice looks down from the sky (v. 11). The Hebrew word *tsedeq* tends to be translated "justice" when a secular situation is envisioned and "righteousness" when a spiritual situation is envisioned. That distinction does not exist in biblical Hebrew. It refers to that which is right. God determines what is right, and God is concerned about both the spiritual and natural realms. These virtues have a material result: the land will be bountiful. The final lines use anthropomorphic language to describe an immanent God: "Justice will walk before [God] and will set [God's] steps along the way" (v. 13).

Psalm 138

This is a psalm of thanksgiving. The reference to singing before the "gods" (v. 1) suggests that this psalm dates to a premonotheistic theology in Israelite thought, unless the "gods" are a metaphor for something else. The next phrase, referring to bowing "to the temple of your holiness" (v. 2; my translation), appears to be an allusion to the Solomonic prayer in 1 Kings 8 in which the king requests that prayers directed toward the temple be heard and answered. The psalmist continues thanking God not only for divine attributes, such as faithfulness and truth, but also for specific experiences of divine help. God answered when the poet called and strengthened his soul (also "life"; v. 3).

Most of the Psalms probably had their origins in lived experiences, though the specific experiences are only hinted at or muted so that these prayers are suitable for broader use in community worship. In the prose prayers of the Bible, a response to prayer is often described in the text or in dialogue. In the psalmic prayers, a response may be affirmed, though the nature of the response is vague. Here the psalmist affirms that the answer broadened the soul's strength. The affirmation that all of the kings of the earth will have heard reports of divine sayings is reminiscent of Isaiah 2, in which people from everywhere come to learn from the God of Jacob. A difference in this psalm, though, is that the leaders, the kings, are transformed (vv. 4–5).

The contrasting of the humble and the haughty (v. 6) is a technique of wisdom sayings. It is found in Hannah's song in 1 Samuel 2, the Magnificat (Luke 1), and many proverbs. The Psalms frequently refer to trouble in a nonspecific way. Neither the exact problem nor the enemy is named. The Psalms frequently express confidence that God will respond. The merger of thanksgiving and praise with complaint and petition is also characteristic of many psalms. This poem ends on an ominous note, a petition that God would not forsake the one praying (v. 8). It suggests a bit of doubt in the midst of all the affirmation of confidence in God.

Colossians 2:6–15 (16–19)

During the time of the early church, many new religious movements claimed the attention and adherence of people in the Mediterranean world. Christianity itself was a new religious movement. The seekers who found their way to the church could also be seduced by another religion that sounded convincing. One question facing the church was the nature of Christ. The Letter to the Colossians affirms the corporality of Christ, "for in him the whole fullness of deity dwells bodily" (v. 9). This tells us that the issue with which the Colossians were struggling was not the divinity of Christ but the humanity of Christ. Specific doctrines, such as the Trinity, are not explicitly outlined in the Bible and were constructed later in the history of the church.

In this text, baptism is a kind of spiritual circumcision. Circumcision as described in Genesis 17 is a sign of the covenant that God made with Abraham and his descendants. The stipulations of the covenant are that God will be God to Abraham and his descendants and that they will receive a gift of land in Canaan. In Colossians, baptism represents for the individual a radical break with the past. In baptism, the Christian participates in the death and resurrection of Christ (v. 12). This text assures the Colossians that God forgives and erases the failures to live up to the decrees (vv. 13–14). The reference is to *decrees*. The word "dogma" (which meant "opinion" in Greek) enters the church through this word. The problem with the NRSV's translation, "legal demands," is that it reinforces a false view of Judaism as being legalistic. The instruction (which Christians refer to as the law) was a divine gift for the betterment of the Israelite community. It was also received as a gift, not a burden. The text does not indicate which decrees the author has in mind.

The second issue here is that Christians ought to avoid being caught up in things that do not matter. Such things as food and celebrations are not unimportant. Human traditions do have a function in communities. But they are only shadows, not the substance of faith. At that point in history, as now, persons had very different ideas about what it meant to be faithful. That is a good thing. But some people were so obsessed with crafting a correct philosophy and insisting on particular traditions that they were losing sight of what was ultimately important. Certainly this reflection serves the contemporary Christian community well.

Luke 11:1–13

The disciples ask Jesus to teach them to pray. They do not ask this because they have never been exposed to prayer. They are familiar with the long tradition of Jewish prayer, and they have watched Jesus pray many times. They know that John had taught his disciples to pray, and it is safe to assume that they know the content of John's prayer as well. They appear to be asking that Jesus would teach them a prayer that would be special and perhaps unique to those who followed him. The prayer that follows in Luke is similar to the one given in Matthew (6:9–15), but a little simpler. By the time of Jesus, prayers had become ever longer and more complex. Some of them were beautiful, and some served didactic purposes. In this text, Jesus wants the disciples to understand that simple prayers are as efficacious as long, complex ones. It is not the skill and cleverness of the one praying that catches God's ear, but the persistence that will yield a desired response.

Each line of the prayer is distinct. First the prayer recognizes God in familial terms, while affirming God's holiness. Second, there is a wish that God's rule be actualized. Third, Jesus raises a petition that our daily needs be met. The fourth element is a request for forgiveness, with the statement that those who pray will also forgive. Forgiveness, not vengeance or even deserved punishment, must accompany any request for forgiveness. The last element is another petition, to not be brought to a "time of trial." The latter request suggests that Christians had already begun to experience such times. Like any parent, God wants "to give good gifts" (v. 13), and like any parent, God expects that the children will ask, seek, and knock. Parents want children to gain skill in articulating their needs and innermost thoughts, in investigation and in speaking up for themselves and others. These are skills that are developed for prayer and for getting along in the world.

In many congregations, this prayer is said before or after another prayer or in the midst of a longer prayer because we are still not convinced that this is enough, or perhaps we want to be more specific in our requests or cover something that does not appear to be covered by this prayer. The presence of other ancient variants of this prayer suggests that Jesus may have given several forms of the prayer or that the later church adjusted it to its own circumstances. Notwithstanding, Jesus' prayer teaches us that our prayers to God cover not only our deepest concerns for life but include, even require, our attention to how we live with one another.

Proper 13 [18]

Grace Ji-Sun Kim

HOSEA 11:1–11
PSALM 107:1–9, 43

ECCLESIASTES 1:2, 12–14; 2:18–23
PSALM 49:1–12
COLOSSIANS 3:1–11
LUKE 12:13–21

The selection of passages for this week reminds us of our temporality here on earth; all the trappings of our privilege—wealth, status, heritage, and prestige—will pass away. When we leave this earth, we certainly cannot take anything with us, which reminds us that all of humanity, both the poor and the rich, are ultimately the same. We need to be reminded that God's graciousness falls on everyone.

The passages force the rich to give up greed and possess gratitude—to reexamine our lifestyles and change them for the sake of those who are hungry and naked. We are urged to make changes and to share our wealth. God calls for us to repent of the sins committed against our neighbors, even those sins of neglect. These texts warn us not to be so vain, but to serve others and to serve God, to seek heavenly things rather than material wealth. In fact, all the wealth we accumulate could be dangerous if it leads us away from God, but the full life is one that is lived gratefully to God.

Hosea 11:1–11

Hosea lived in troubled and chaotic times. Great political and social instability followed the forty-year reign of Jeroboam II as king of Israel. Hosea found the entire leadership of Israel and the people guilty of both apostasy and spiritual degeneration. However, even in the midst of disobedience, sinfulness, and idolatry, God did not turn away from them and showed the endurance of God's steadfast love.

This passage becomes a magnificent poem of YHWH's dialogue with God's self. The whole passage is about what God has done, Ephraim's response, and

God's unwilling but necessary action. This is followed by God's ultimate restoration of undisciplined Ephraim in the homecoming. It poetically describes
humanity's waywardness and God's faithfulness.

We, like Ephraim, run away from God to faithless idolatry. We disobey
God and create our own idols, such as consumerism, which has become the
new religion. The malls and consumer Web sites have become the temples to
which we faithfully take our offerings. We have sought to proselytize others
not by invitation but by consumption. Most of us know firsthand the temptation to exploit the vulnerability of other people and, even more so, the earth.
Our consumption affects people and nature. The exploited earth cannot speak
to us, but it does confront us with devastating effects. As consumerism continues to be the new religion, we need to take heed of our future as well as the
earth's dire situation. Due to consumerism, globalization, and colonialism,
atrocities continue to occur regularly. The exploited people and the raped
earth speak in painful groans. Injustice exists as long as we ignore the unethical practices of the rich in relationships with the poor.

Even as we live with our idols, God is still near to us and will not abandon
us. Even in our sinfulness, God does not let us go. There will be mercy. For
the Israelites, there is a promise of restoration for the deported and exiled
people, a return to the promised homeland. God's compassion opens the way
to a new start, in rebuilding the land (vv. 10–11). It is only through God's
gracious forgiveness and compassion that we, too, can be restored. Even in
our faithlessness, God remains faithful and never gives up on us. Despite our
destructive actions, the desire God has for us is never destruction, but life.

Ecclesiastes 1:2, 12–14; 2:18–23

These verses are presented as the words of an aged King Solomon, who says
he has tried everything to find lasting pleasure and acknowledges that there
is nothing. Wealth, prestige, sex, and even wisdom are emptiness piled on
emptiness, a striving after wind. One works, scrimps, saves, and then there is
nothing but death. Who knows if one's heirs will use the resources wisely or
foolishly? Money and even life itself are not worth the worry.

This passage is about individual vanity and pride. The West has become
so individualistic that many of us have forgotten about community and have
lost a sense of social responsibility for one another. Instead, we work so diligently to fill the void of our own greed and lust that we fail to understand that
whatever we do will affect others. We quest for money and status, which are
meaningless at the end of life.

This passage calls us to think beyond ourselves and to center ourselves on
God, so that we will be able to open our eyes to see the needs of others. As we

focus on others, we recognize that we are sinning against them. In our own self-absorption, we recognize that in many cases we are robbing others of the basic necessities of life. We are indirectly causing unjust suffering to massive groups of people.

Another "chasing after wind" (1:14, 17; cf. 2:11, 26) can be seen in the disparities related to education. Our society places tremendous emphasis on degrees and credentials, which are typically more readily accessible to those of the privileged classes. In the end, all is in vain. Perhaps the real work is done not in our heads, but with our hands, as we toil and labor under the sun for those in need, for we are all equal in the eyes of God and in the form of our basic necessities—food and water, shelter, and, most of all, love. When we begin to delineate ourselves by education and status, we lose sight of our connectedness to one another and to our home. Disparities cause senseless suffering to others and even to us.

Therefore, we need to reimagine the purpose of our lives. Rather than trying to hoard and gather as much wealth as possible, we can leave behind something valuable, something that will make this world a better place for all. Though the legacy of peace, love, and kindness is not something that we can take with us when we leave this world, it certainly outweighs the pursuit of personal joy, wealth, and prestige.

Psalm 107:1–9, 43

Psalm 107 reads like the description of a great service of thanksgiving after the people's return from exile in Babylon. We have all experienced situations where we have felt devastated by deserts and storms. We know what it is like to feel utterly lost. It is indeed an inexplicable blessing to come home again, to return to God, and to rediscover that God is there to welcome us back.

On the other hand, the affluence we live in sometimes leads us to believe that we have always stayed close to God, that the comfortable life is God's reward for our hard work, and in some ways it strips us of our gratitude. So, we have an inhospitable, often hostile, attitude toward new members who are from Africa, South America, and Asia, in both our communities and our congregations. We tend to think that we are better than they are because somehow we were with God first. This lack of thanks is the opposite of how God desires us to live "faith-fully." Faithfulness entails an embodiment of God's grace, as illustrated in this passage, not only accepting others who may speak another language, eat different foods, express their faith in different ways, but also providing them a safe place in a hostile world, embracing and empowering them.

"Wisdom" grows from the steadfast love of God, who gave food to the hungry and water to the thirsty (vv. 8–9, 43)—the basic human needs by which we are *all* connected, regardless of educational or socioeconomic status. Certainly this is a literal reading of the passage, but in a world where there is so much need, perhaps a literal interpretation of hunger and thirst is appropriate. In many instances, we, the rich, have been the cause of other people's hunger and thirst. We need to make changes socially and politically to eliminate hunger and thirst. One could expand the scope and consider hunger and thirst in other realms of social justice—for example, those who starve in society for acceptance and equality—to which the Lord responds, a lesson for those seeking wisdom in a world in need of redemption.

This is a critically important psalm, because it provides the shape of Jesus' ministry. We take things for granted—everything from running water to the overabundant food choices at the grocery store. The everyday necessities are at our fingertips, yet we forget to give thanks. We forget to pray and to acknowledge that all things are from God. Gratitude runs throughout the psalm. Giving thanks for all God has done is essential for understanding God's grace to us and our corresponding call to bring grace to others.

Psalm 49:1–12

The calling of people is the invitation to all races, ethnicities, and nations to listen to God's message. No matter what our situation, we will all die; no one can avoid death. Life and death are ultimately in the hands of God. The psalm emphasizes that people die; we are temporary, and so is all the "stuff" we accumulate and store away. We all die and cannot take anything with us, and thus we need to reexamine how we are living in the present (vv. 8–11). Are we just accumulating wealth because we have a fancy notion that we will stay forever young? We live with denial; we buy anti-aging creams and have plastic surgery to make ourselves look and feel young. We need to realize that our time on earth is limited.

We can seek out pleasure, wealth, and even wisdom, but as we read in Ecclesiastes, it is all vanity. Wealth can be dangerous, as this psalm warns us, and the wealthy West should take this warning seriously. Wealth cannot redeem someone from death. Material wealth will all come to an end. It is futile.

There is a danger in preaching only about heavenly things to come, because doing so may lead us to forget to work for social justice here on earth. "Let thy kingdom come," as we pray in the Lord's Prayer, really means "Let *my* kingdom go."[1] For God to reign on this earth, we need to let go of our desires

---

1. My seminary professor Ovey Mohammed, SJ, used to repeat this phrase in class.

and our own little kingdoms that we have built for ourselves. We need to let go of our personal pursuit of wealth and power, everything that takes our eyes off of God's will. If God is to reign here and in our lives, then letting go of our kingdom will begin a process of building the just reign of God here on earth. The reign of God then becomes an invitation to everyone to come to the heavenly banquet here on earth.

Colossians 3:1–11

The risk in this passage is to belittle or denigrate the physical world in favor of ethereal spiritual riches. This sounds like a touch of Gnosticism. We need to keep the value of the world as God made it and where Jesus shared in the fleshly parts of life. What Christians are to eliminate are those dispositions that distort our lives and the lives of others. The first list of sins (v. 5) deals with sexual sins, then greed, and then the obsessive love of material things. We, the rich, have bought into gaining worldly fame, wealth, prestige, and honor at great cost. Wealth or the pursuit of wealth can lead to a false sense of security. It may cost us our family, our health, and our friends. It is fitting that the second list of sins focuses on those that damage human relationships (v. 8). We sometimes neglect the foreigner, because we have become xenophobic. We need to be kind and loving to our neighbors.

The old self is the one mired in holding on to what is distorting who we are and God's intention for our lives. To believe in Christ is to put to death all anti-Christlike attitudes and practices in one's life. In itself, Christ's death leaves nothing wanting, but we who claim to be in him need to participate in his death—a death to self, to sin, to our divisive attitudes—so that we can in turn become effective members of Christ's own body. Only then will we be able to help or free others to become members of that same body. To be clothed with the new self may echo the baptismal practice of a new robe signifying a new identity, which in turn makes the Christian community a place where Christ is in all. It is a community, a *basileia* of God, that we need to strive to build with our gifts. It is a place where all peoples, each with a different background, status, or upbringing, can come together as one. For if Christ is in all, then we are all equal.

"There is no longer Greek and Jew, circumcised and uncircumcised, barbarian, Scythian, slave and free; but Christ is all and in all!" (v. 11). The new life and identity has to include caring for the other. Christians often like to put on a new identity, but most of the time, they do not want to do the dirty hands-on work involved in the change. But this is what Christ requires.

Luke 12:13–21

Luke offers what appears to be a bias against the wealthy and powerful. It is somewhat anticlimactic for the man from the crowd to ask Jesus for a rabbinical-style decision concerning family inheritance. Jesus has been teaching on the end of the age, the need for faithful living and witness, and how God provides for all. As usual, Jesus gives a response that the hearer does not want to hear. Jesus talks about the elimination of grubbing for power, prestige, and wealth. Has the man not been listening to him? At verse 15, Jesus addresses the man and then sets up the second stage of his response: the parable of the Rich Fool.

What is missing in this parable is gratitude. The man in the story assumes that he alone has garnered the wealth; it is his alone. *Fool!* He sees the wealth only for himself—not his family, his workers, nor his community. God pushes the mighty from their seats and sends the rich away empty. How should we use wealth? What is the responsibility of the wealthy to the rest of society? Look at Bill and Melinda Gates versus Donald Trump. What about the multimillion-dollar salaries for baseball players while those who hand-stitch the baseballs are paid centavos and their hands are crippled? How about the McMansions for a few while thousands are homeless? How has this man in the text been rich toward God? How has he been in solidarity with the poor and distressed?

The rich man thinks he can control his own life. This is the foolishness of the rich people who do not trust God. Jesus taught that the only source of true security was a relationship with God, the loving Creator who feeds even the sparrows and clothes even the flowers of the field. The man in this story is completely self-centered, separated from God and others by his tie to earthly possessions. Likewise, our greed has made millions go hungry and live without clean water. Our capitalistic hunger has robbed millions of their own dignity and a chance to live a healthy life. This passage requires us to think ethically and justly so that we do not become like the foolish rich man who just feeds his own greed and yields to selfish desires.

This passage highlights our responsibility to the poor of the world. How are we to live so that the wealth can be more evenly distributed? How can the rich live so that the resources are shared with the poor? In giving, one finds satisfaction in seeing others flourish. Indeed, God gave so that we might flourish eternally.

Proper 14 [19]

Arthur Van Seters

ISAIAH 1:1, 10–20
PSALM 50:1–8, 22–23

GENESIS 15:1–6
PSALM 33:12–22
HEBREWS 11:1–3, 8–16
LUKE 12:32–40

The lectionary invites the church to reflect on Abraham's journey of faith as presented in Genesis 15 and Hebrews 11. When these are set alongside Psalm 33 and Luke 12, the nature of God and the compelling challenge of attentiveness to God's future for God's people take on added dimensions. Living in a secular society, the challenge of faith and how it affects our engagement with the future require a careful reading of these lections, including those from Isaiah 1 and Psalm 50, which draw a direct link between our worship and our ethics.

Genesis 15:1–6

Ancient Israel saw the promise of posterity to Abraham (Abram in this passage) as crucially important. Here, in a distinctly theological dialogue, "the word of the LORD" comes to Abram, and he understands God's promise to be his shield and reward (v. 1). The noun "shield" is related to the verb "to deliver" (14:20). The reward is vague and may indicate a sense of being blessed because of his fidelity to God.

Abram then raises the question of posterity (already promised in 12:7 and 13:15–16). Because Sarai has been childless, it appears that Eliezer, the household servant, is to be the heir. But Abram knew that he could not carry on the family name, as only sons have the right of inheritance (Deut. 21:17). Naturally, Abram is puzzled.

God then promises that Abram and Sarai will indeed have a son and heir. God even predicts that the descendants from that son will be incredibly numerous (v. 5)—like the stars in a night sky! In response, the narrator affirms Abram's tenacious faith, and this becomes his distinguishing mark for generations and for the Christian faith even today (Rom. 4:3; Gal. 3:6; Jas. 2:23). The righteousness attributed to Abram includes a commitment to justice and fairness. He has already demonstrated this in offering his nephew Lot the choice of land on which to settle (Gen. 13). Abram has a vivid sense of social justice.

The memory of Abraham (Abram) was incredibly important when Israel experienced two major disruptions. In the eighth century BCE, Assyria made the northern part of Israel a vassal province. Two centuries later, the Babylonians devastated the south and marched its leadership into distant exile. What Israel discovered from Abraham was that faith did not depend on evidence but on the sense that God is the source of promise and hope.

This is Israel's understanding of covenant, and it stands in sharp contrast to our culture's tendency to put all the emphasis on human resourcefulness. In our setting, even faith seems to depend on the person exercising it rather than being a gift from God.

Psalm 33:12–22

Reading Psalm 33 next to Abram's conversation with God is remarkably evocative. This hymn of praise includes directives for the worshiping community about how to live faithfully under God. God drew Abram's attention to the heavens. Here God is Creator of both heaven and earth (vv. 6–9). God is then described as the one who chooses nations (rather than the reverse) and is sovereign over all human history (vv. 12–15). Rulers are cautioned not to take matters into their own hands by waging war, because God is the ultimate ruler and also responds to those who trust God's steadfast love. God is again identified as a "shield" (v. 20; *magen*)—the same word used in Genesis 15. In effect, the worshiping community receives hope and is able to praise Abraham's God.

In our secular society all of this is strange. Everywhere voices spin a web of fear and precariousness, as though God is not related to our world. Countries increase border security and design massive surveillance systems. The world of nature is seen not as God's sacred creation but as land to be claimed and exploited. Disputes between nations suggest that in the end everything depends on exercising power, even though this only leads to greater fear and uncertainty. Real power, however, is not the ability to overpower but is to be empowered by God's steadfast love (v. 22).

Hebrews 11:1–3, 8–16

The preacher might explore the faith of Abraham for the sake of the church facing its own precarious journey. In this exploration, we find that fear often contrasts faith. If fear is all about doubt regarding how the future will unfold, faith is a sense of assurance about what cannot yet be seen. Hebrews 11 makes explicit that, for the church, the source of this confidence is Jesus Christ. Before coming to this climax, the writer goes back to God at the beginning of creation.

Our earthly home is not just something that is here. Through faith (as in Ps. 33) the world is a planet designed with a purpose. This is beyond what we can see but not beyond what we can believe. A God-oriented view of the world and its unfolding history not only gives us a sense of past and present but also disposes us toward a future hope. A scientifically oriented society like ours views the earth as merely a rare planet in our solar system unfolding slowly in the eons of time. A theological perspective, then, appears unconvincing since faith itself is bracketed. Unfortunately, our sophisticated ways cannot create the kind of purpose and hope that come with faith, and so we often treat our earth pragmatically, and with disastrous results.

The writer next turns to the long legacy of faith-keepers, beginning with Abraham. He was sent into an unknown land, but on arriving there he still could not see it as the land of promise. He lived as a sojourner, a foreigner (v. 9). Yet he believed that the promised place for his descendants would be a reality in God's time—a reality that included the social organization represented by referring to a "city" (v. 10). He also could not see how he could be the progenitor of a great nation, but he and Sarah trusted the faithfulness of God. The text of verse 11 chooses an ancient variant that attributes this exercise of faith to Abraham, even though there is stronger manuscript support for the footnoted reading that it was Sarah who by faith received the power to conceive!

In modern times, the United States has applied the notion of a promised land to its conquest of a significant part of North America. Was the European movement from the known to the unknown an act of Abrahamic faith? Is there any real sense in which this land, new to them but already well inhabited, was promised to them by God? That some have claimed this to be so does not make it so. Furthermore, when Abraham entered the land he understood himself as a continuing foreigner, not as a conquering power. The early history of Canada was primarily different in that the English and French immigrants were received for the most part by the aboriginal peoples and worked out a common heritage. That those arrangements were often thwarted and betrayed because of pressures from Europe is a matter for regret and apology. But in the process a new nation came into being that did not create a promised land mythology as justification for its existence.

Luke 12:32–40

This Gospel reading probes the nature of faithful discipleship in relation to the kind of hope that Abraham exercised. The followers of Jesus are addressed as "little flock" (an image of vulnerability) but are assured that they will be recipients of God's new order. It sounds a lot like the conversation between God and Abram in Genesis 15. The Gospel writer, of course, is aware of the flock of likely readers, the church (cf. Acts 20:28–29 and 1 Pet. 5:2–3). The journey ahead would demand considerable trust, since the followers of Jesus would divest themselves of their monetary security by selling their possessions and giving the proceeds to the poor (Acts 4:32–35).

God's new way of living turns everything on its head, because preserving the past or the present does not orient it. The reign of God that will come fully in the future already invades the present. This becomes evident in the parabolic description of how servants are to live, especially as they face the darkness. In the somewhat difficult terms of the text, the master of the house has gone to the home of his bride to be married. The celebrations will go on well into the night, but the master, says Jesus, will return, and his servants need to stay alert to welcome him. The master even promises that if they are faithful, he will treat them like full members of the family. He will be their servant and seat them at his own table to enjoy a banquet! Even if he arrives near dawn, this role reversal will happen (vv. 35–38).

A cautionary element is then added. The reason for alertness is because a thief, assuming that the servants are asleep, might take advantage of the master's absence to rob the house. This unexpected possibility calls for watchfulness, not just waiting, but attentive expectation that something in the future could radically alter the present. At this point Jesus breaks away from his storytelling to enjoin the disciples to be ready for the unpredictable return of the Son of Humanity (v. 40). Suddenly the parable takes on overtones of eschatology. God's ultimate future shapes the journey of life for believers in the present.

Hearing these verses today, the preacher scarcely knows where to begin, because it sounds so utterly foreign. Economic realities are revered so highly as the solution to so many of life's challenges that talk of selling one's possessions and giving massively to the poor is a nonstarter. But perhaps this blunt challenge can alert people to the radical nature of the gospel. The rewarding of faithful servants may be appealing, but reversing social order is another matter. Of course, we may think it is important to secure one's property; some may even want a loaded weapon within reach. But what are we to make of the injunction to be alert for the return of Christ? Now it becomes clear that the Christian vision of life challenges trust in the accumulation of wealth, the ever-widening gap between the wealthy and an increasing underclass, and a view of life that fails to reflect on what the presence of Christ really means. Yet glimpsing this larger reality of God's ultimate restoration of life can free us to live toward God's new order. Then, as Abraham realized, the present does not need to be grasped; one can journey as a stranger no longer bound by society's ways.

Isaiah 1:1, 10–20

The book of Isaiah opens by setting the prophet's preaching in a particular time and place—the latter half of the eighth century BCE. Isaiah begins by impersonating God, so to speak, who stands before the people as a lawyer presenting a case in court. In verses 2–9 God has called creation as witness and described the moral brokenness of the nation and its resulting consequences. Now in verse 10 the accused are addressed as Sodom and Gomorrah, two cities that were notoriously evil and, as a result, had been annihilated (Gen. 19). The sermon, therefore, commences with extraordinarily forceful language. The community needs to listen carefully to what follows!

If modern preachers have a tendency to calculate what they say in their sermons and how they say it, Isaiah moves without any qualifying phrases into what he believes *God* wants to say. God is not impressed with ritual practices and pays no attention to how much people give or how enthusiastically they celebrate. These count for nothing. In fact, God finds them burdensome. Even their prayers are futile. The reason: their hands are dripping in blood. Their relationship with God has been broken by the brokenness of their relationship with their neighbors.

This indictment of religious practices should not be interpreted as a rejection of worship as such. Ethical living is not a substitute for worship but a concomitant. Loving God means loving one's neighbor (including one's enemies), as Jesus makes clear (Matt. 5:44; 22:37–39). Piety and social responsibility belong together.

The sermon now calls for response by spelling out consequences. Confession will lead to forgiveness and blessing. Failure to respond appropriately will mean destruction. In other words, worship should be a transformative act leading people to live their faith in relation to the world around them.

The preacher's task is to present the indelible connection between worship and faithful discipleship. In short, worship is a constitutive act leading people to live God's alternative order in the world around them. This includes seeking just relationships and reaching out to the most vulnerable: the oppressed, orphans, and widows. The movement is imagined as a change of colors—from the scarlet of animal blood sacrifices (v. 11) to the freshness of fallen snow. Refusal to act justly will be a different bloodletting, death that arises from conflict.

More than fifty years ago a preacher filled a large Toronto church, morning and evening, time and again, with sermons that sounded a lot like Isaiah's. He always ended with a blunt benediction: "May God give you restlessness until you find your rest in [God]." He refused to accommodate to an increasingly secular culture. What issues might he address today? Would he denounce the "war on terror" as a bellicose response to 9/11? Would he call attention to the millions of vulnerable people who do not have health care? Would he spell out the effects of human behavior resulting in global warming? Preaching in the tradition of Isaiah means making concrete connections between worshiping God and ethical living.

Psalm 50:1–8, 22–23

Psalm 50 has the sound of Isaianic preaching. God seems again to be in a law court. The psalmist begins by introducing God as the Mighty One who comes in volcanic eruptions and speaks as a judge calling the faithful to account for their behavior as members of the covenant community. Here, as in Isaiah 1, worship appears to fall short. It seems that sacrifices are offered as expressions of merit rather than as thanksgiving, if we include verses 9–14.

Similarly, it is difficult to understand verses 22–23 without going back to verse 16. There the listeners are identified as "the wicked" because their worship runs counter to God's covenant. They have broken covenant commandments, particularly stealing, committing adultery, and speaking against neighbors (vv. 18–20). In effect, this failure reveals that the initial commandments about their relationship to God have also been ignored.

As with the preaching of Isaiah, the negative consequence is announced in strong language: "I will tear you apart" (v. 22). But then the reverse is also stated—salvation for those "who go the right way" (v. 23). When God's covenant requirements are diminished, covenant with God is weakened and results in the impoverishment of human relationships within the community.

These words arise from a theocratic form of government. Translating this into a modern democracy means that the church is called to examine the relationship between its worship of God and its ways of being responsible citizens. Failing to respect property, living promiscuously, slandering, and misrepresenting others all have negative consequences. God's people, however, should realize that their contribution in society is deepest when they see their lives and the life of the world around them in relation to God. Their worship becomes authentic when they make this connection.

Sojourner Truth Day (August 18)

JoAnne Marie Terrell

JOB 23
PSALM 118:1–9, 24–29
COLOSSIANS 3:18–4:4
JOHN 11:7–44

Born into slavery about 1797 in Ulster County, New York, Isabella Baumfree experienced a religious conversion and call to public ministry in 1843.[1] New York, like other northern states, had "gradual" emancipation laws, but Isabella knew in her heart that God had already set her free. So she "told Jesus it would be all right if he changed [her] name" because when she left the state of bondage she wanted "nothin' of Egypt" left on her account. According to her story, the name Sojourner was given to her in a vision, for she understood that she was to walk about the country preaching and doing God's will. To this name she added Truth, becoming a great advocate in the cause of freedom from oppression for African Americans and women.

An extraordinary orator, Sojourner followed her call to lecture and preach for the rights of women and the abolition of slavery. Her work included advocating for black soldiers during the Civil War, opposing the death penalty, and calling for other civic liberties. Her speech "Ain't I a Woman?" addressed to the Ohio Women's Rights Convention in 1851, is among the most persuasive, moving, and timeless testimonies to the God-given rights of women. On this Holy Day for Justice, when we celebrate women's suffrage in the United States, we remember Sojourner Truth's powerful and enduring civil rights ministry on behalf of women, African Americans, and all God's people.

O God, my mother told me if I asked you to make my master and mistress good, you'd do it. And they didn't get good. Why God,

---

1. Since the birth date of Sojourner Truth is not known, we observe Sojourner Truth Day on the anniversary of an event that fulfilled a deep desire of her heart—the ratification of the Nineteenth Amendment in the United States (August 18, 1920) granting women the right to vote.

maybe you can't do it. Kill 'em. I didn't think God could make them good. After . . . my conscience burned me. Then I would say, 'O God, do not be mad . . . if I was you and you were me, and you wanted any help, I'd help you. Why don't you help me?' Well you see I was in want, and felt that there was no help. . . . Truly, I do know God has helped me. But I didn't get a good master until the last time I was sold, and then I found one, and his name was Jesus.

Sojourner Truth[2]

Many influential thinkers have attested to the existence of a "love ethic" in the African American community in and since slavery, an ethic that is not self-serving but is rather *agapē*-like in its capacity to forgive without exacting justice from oppressors.[3] Reinhold Niebuhr wrote that American "Negroes'" capacity to love in the face of oppression was a result of "racial weakness" that prevented the radically disempowered people from mounting armed revolt against their "masters."[4] It is undoubtedly true that some slaves accommodated themselves to the system. Some, without resorting to violence, resisted with well-developed critical voices and some direct agency relative to their plight, which included survival strategies. But contrary to Niebuhr's simplistic claim, there were, in fact, many armed uprisings during slavery that reflected black people's love for themselves as well as their strident demand for unequivocal freedom.[5] For the majority of Africans coming under the influence of Christianity, even as it was preached and practiced in racist perversions, whatever options they chose to negotiate that awful context, nothing could nullify the dictates of conscience toward others—no matter how intractable the slaveholders' penchant for evil—or the persuasive, just, and loving example they found in Jesus. Sojourner Truth's words demonstrate the complexity of the love ethic and the many layers that constitute it: the self-love that lies beneath the existential weight and absurdity of racial and gender oppression; the burning desire for justice, black liberty, and women's equality, and the equally burning desire for personal holiness; the patently irreconcilable nature of oppression with true Christian virtue; the question of theodicy; and, ultimately, the affirmation of (and concession to) the righteousness and sovereignty of God. All of these elements of the love ethic illuminated in Sojourner Truth's dilemma and as practiced among African

    2. Olive Gilbert, *Narrative of Sojourner Truth* (New York: Arno Press, 1968), 214.
    3. Reinhold Niebuhr, *The Nature and Destiny of Man*, vol. 2 (New York: Charles Scribner's Sons, 1943), 88.
    4. Reinhold Niebuhr, *Moral Man and Immoral Society* (New York: Charles Scribner's Sons, 1932), 263–64.
    5. See Herbert Aptheker, *American Negro Slave Revolts* (New York: International Publishers, 1987).

Americans during slavery and the fight for suffrage foreshadowed the nonviolent resistance that Dr. Martin Luther King Jr. crafted from this moral legacy, with which he galvanized the masses for struggle and launched a movement toward an uncompromised liberation.

Although the selected texts depict the existential crises of individuals and the oppression of communities of faith, the sheer, unbounded immensity of God is the dominant theme of each. God the Immensity is spoken *of* and *to*, *honorably* and *appropriately*, which is to say, in ways that honor the character of God, acknowledge the power of God, rely on the wisdom of God, and bespeak unequivocal faith in God's ability and will to redeem those who cry for justice. God's response is given in words and in demonstrations of power, in what happens or is to happen next for the faithful, oppressed signifiers, who yet seek to walk with and to emulate the ways of the One who is always calling us into our own embodied Immensity.

Job 23

The chapter begins the reply of Job to the third discourse of Eliphaz the Temanite, Job's friend and the ardent defender of a conventional theism that attributes to God the perquisites of both a towering transcendence and an irritating immanence. Eliphaz's theology, moreover, punctuates the conventional wisdom of Job's other friends, Bildad the Shuhite and Zophar the Naamathite, disparaging Job's righteousness before the holy God and actually bearing false witness against the suffering, innocent man.

Job, on the other hand, continues to report his embodied experience of oppression (vv. 1–2) and his anguished search for the great, powerful, wise and, above all, *dialogical* presence he has known or wishes to know (vv. 3–7). Like Sojourner Truth's moral dilemma in the expanded canon, his discourse is framed in the language of *theodicy as complaint*; like Truth's questions ("Why God, maybe you can't do it. . . .Why don't you help me?"), his questions assume the Immensity, or "the greatness of [God's] power"(v. 6); like Truth's complaint, his complaint never rises to the level of a slur against the character of God but is rather an inquiry about the hidden face of God (vv. 8–9). Then, what begins as complaint becomes in Job's mouth a song of praise (vv. 10–17) for a God, who, despite being hidden, "knows the way" or road of the oppressed and brings redemption even out of our suffering, whose steps are trustworthy, whose word is to be treasured, who decides our course and brings all things to their just conclusion (vv. 10–14). Such a God, who is at times shrouded in the darkness of our oppressive experiences, is not to be circumscribed by conventional wisdom but utterly revered and anticipated. Thus contemporary preachers may employ this text to demonstrate how to both stand in the truth of one's (individual and collective) oppressive experience and question God in a way that does not vilify but rather adds to the praise of God.

Psalm 118:1–9, 24–29

In the context of corporate temple worship, the psalmist instructs the congregation to give thanks to YHWH (v. 1), who has given to Israel countless military and moral victories on their way from the oppression of slavery to nationhood. Perhaps the most significant cause for thanksgiving is Israel's covenantal relationship with YHWH, one based on *hesed*, or steadfast love, so stated in the antiphonal instructions given to the people collectively and to the priestly Aaronic caste specifically (vv. 2–3). The psalmist then recounts personal victories wrought by God's hand, which clearly indicates Israel's collective belief in a God of radical immanence. The theological or practical reasoning concludes that "it is better to take refuge in YHWH than to put confidence in [humans]" and human rulers (vv. 8–9). Even as the liturgy concludes, the congregational singing persists (v. 24), a prayer of supplication is offered for victories anticipated (vv. 25, 28), and the hymn of praise is taken up again (v. 29).

If the passage from Job attests to the Immensity of God and to human insecurity relative to that very Immensity, this psalm of praise attests to the character of the Immensity as one of a good, loving, absolutely trustworthy Sovereign. As with the psalmist, when we put our faith and trust in YHWH, who alone is God, we will find security (v. 27). This psalm demonstrates for oppressed communities of faith how to speak of God honorably and appropriately, that is, in the language of celebration for victories gained and those anticipated.

John 11:7–44

The raising of Lazarus is described in the *New Oxford Annotated Bible* as the "crowning miracle or *sign*"[6] of Jesus' ministry. The text reflects the audacity of Jesus to speak to death, the ultimate oppression. It first sees him defying the death that surely lay in wait for him while en route to Bethany (vv. 7–8). He speaks obliquely of death, referring to the "sleeping" Lazarus (vv. 11–13); then plainly names the enemy of life without disclosing his intention to restore life (vv. 14–15). When the disciples, including Thomas, Martha, and

---

6. Herbert G. May and Bruce M. Metzger, eds., *The New Oxford Annotated Bible with the Apocrypha* (New York: Oxford University Press), 1303n.

Mary (Lazarus's sisters), and even Jesus' detractors speak of death (vv. 16, 21, 32, 37, respectively), they do so with joyless resignation to its finality. But the text reflects more than Jesus' refusal to succumb to the fear of death—for fear is a kind of death in itself. Jesus bypasses death and speaks to God, whom he addresses with the familial "Father" (v. 41), and thereby asserts his more than passing acquaintance with the power, greatness, wisdom, and will of God.

The lesson for us who are still subject to death in its many forms is this: if a miracle is a sign that points to something greater than itself, then the faithful have to keep looking beyond the miracle for that something greater. As the Scriptures continuously bear out, Jesus, the Son of God, is the Immensity of God incarnate, crucified, buried, risen, and still interceding on our behalf. This same Jesus, who called Lazarus (v. 43) and Sojourner Truth out from the graves of oppression and fear, and into their own embodied Immensity, likewise calls us into a more faithful and just approximation of our God-given character and qualities that make us fit to be called the children of God.

Colossians 3:18–4:4

The epistle is a product of its era: much of the first century was a time of thoroughgoing Advent, during which the early church expected the return of Jesus in fulfillment of their messianic hopes. The unspoken, urgent priority for the saints who were also living in a context of martyrdom and persecution was to be ready for Jesus' return. Implicitly, this immediate expectancy was not preoccupied with subverting the social, economic, and political order. This understanding is a required backdrop for reading practically all of the New Testament. For those of us who have an inherited experience of slavery in relatively recent memory, who continue to experience racism, classism, sexism, heterosexism, ageism, spousal and child abuse, it is very difficult to reconcile the hierarchy affirmed within the epistle with Jesus' clear demand for justice in the Gospels. The writer upholds the existing social order. Yet, perhaps in an abiding concern for justice, the author attempts to provide parity in the balance of contingent earthly powers, between wives and husbands (3:18–19), children and parents (3:20–21), slaves and slaveholders (3:22–4:1), regardless of each one's status. In each of the named relationships, *the authority to which the author concedes is nonetheless authority to be deferred to the coming Lord Jesus, ever loving and ever just.*

Like the epistle writer, Sojourner Truth was a product of her era: her first inclination to "kill 'em"—meaning her oppressors—was overcome by her conscience, and later, by her intimate acquaintance with Jesus. She never lost her capacity for critical thinking throughout her transformation. Likewise, the passage is laced with critical content pertaining to the prevailing social relations (e.g., "Wives, be subject"; "Husbands, love"; "Children, obey"; "Fathers, do not provoke"). If, as we might expect, the early church had an inkling that the Lord Jesus had first come "to let the oppressed go free" (Luke 4:18) and that "where the Spirit of the Lord is, there is freedom" (2 Cor. 3:17), it is not surprising that the passage reserves its most explicit instructions for Christian slaves and its harshest critique for Christian slaveholders. Even though it may not be clear to whom the writer is referring as "wrongdoer" (v. 25), the imprecision is telling. The innocent know who they are, as do the guilty. This insight sheds light on Sojourner Truth's moral dilemma, why she was condemned by what she thought, even though it was she and her people who were obviously wronged. Those who cannot defer to the Immensity cannot experience its liberation. Nor can they ever hope to discern, much less speak, its mysteries.

Proper 15 [20]

Kah-Jin Jeffrey Kuan

ISAIAH 5:1–7
PSALM 80:1–2, 8–19

JEREMIAH 23:23–29
PSALM 82
HEBREWS 11:29–12:2
LUKE 12:49–56

Who among us has not at some point felt the absence and silence of God? This week's lectionary texts provide us with a wealth of material for such times. They are linked by themes and imageries of vine and vineyard, divine council, conflict, family members pitted against each other, the absence and silence of God, justice and righteousness, heroes of faith. In them, we are invited to think critically about our constructions of the divine and models of faith and practices as we engage in the work of doing justice.

Isaiah 5:1–7

This text is generally referred to as "the song of the vineyard," yet it is a juridical parable that ends with an indictment. It begins with the speaker, Isaiah of Jerusalem, stating his intention to sing a song on behalf of his "beloved" concerning the beloved's vineyard, one that is well located on a fertile hill. This beloved friend does everything that is expected of an owner of a vineyard—preparing the plot, planting it with choice vines, and getting things ready for the harvest. But, instead of yielding good grapes, the vineyard produces bad ones (vv. 1–2).

The text now shifts to the owner of the vineyard speaking to the inhabitants of Jerusalem, asking that they "judge between me and my vineyard" (v. 3), to decide who is at fault for the failed crop. The owner assumes that the Jerusalemite audience will rule in the owner's favor and so moves to pronounce a judgment on the vineyard that removes from the vineyard any protective apparatus, which will lead to its devastated state, and forbids clouds from raining on the vineyard (vv. 5–6). The conclusion in verse 7 reveals

353

the identities of the vineyard and the owner, that is, Israel and the Lord of hosts. The indictment is now made explicit: "he expected justice (*mišpāt*), but saw bloodshed (*mišpāḥ*); righteousness (*ṣĕdāqâ*), but heard a cry (*ṣĕ'āqā*)" (v. 7). An obvious play on words occurs here in the Hebrew: *mišpāt* is turned into *mišpāḥ* and *ṣĕdāqâ* into *ṣĕ'āqā*. As in numerous other contexts, we find here the pairing of justice and righteousness. From the root *šāpaṭ*, literally "to judge," *mišpāt* is used either as judgment or justice. It is found often in the legal sense. In prophetic texts, in particular, the word appears frequently in contexts where YHWH litigates against Israel (Isa. 1–2; Jer. 5:20–31; Amos 5:1–17; Mic. 3 and 6). Thus, in calling for justice, YHWH confronts those who exploit others in the society for their own gain, advocating for the integrity of everyone in the society. Righteousness requires that the people of God relate responsibly and ethically with one another in all aspects of life—socially, religiously, and legally.

God expects us to treat and relate to our fellow human beings with justice and righteousness. In the context of the meltdown of the housing market, hundreds of thousands of people have been victimized by the subprime mortgage debacle. There has been no justice and righteousness. Justice preachers need to be cautious to proclaim when our justice causes suffering and our righteousness causes despair.

Jeremiah 23:23–29

Jeremiah here turns his attention to leaders within his own guild, namely, the prophets (23:9–40). Beginning in verse 9, Jeremiah describes the other prophets, both in Samaria and in Jerusalem, as "adulterers" and accuses them of evil, ungodliness, wickedness, and leading the people astray (vv. 9–15). Essentially, Jeremiah dismisses the prophets with whom he is in conflict for lying and misleading people (vv. 16–17). Appealing to the image of a divine council, Jeremiah asserts that he alone has stood in the council of God, that he alone has seen and heard God's word, and that he alone heeds God's word and proclaims it (vv. 18–20). That is Jeremiah's appeal to authenticity.

The lectionary text continues this prophetic conflict. Standing in the divine council, Jeremiah listens in on the conversation. There he hears God ask (v. 23), "Am I a God near by, says the LORD, and not a God far off?" This is a question that gets to the heart of both God's immanence and transcendence. Indeed, this is how most scholars read this text.[1] By insisting on both immanence and transcendence, God asserts that God cannot be domesticated and contained. Therefore, the prophets cannot manipulate God for their own gains and purposes. Not having stood in the divine council, all that the other

---

1. Walter Brueggemann, *A Commentary on Jeremiah: Exile and Homecoming* (Grand Rapids: Eerdmans, 1998), 213.

prophets have are false dreams, lies, and deceit. They even make the people forget God's name. God now affirms that only Jeremiah "has my word" (v. 28).

Justice preachers ought to listen deeply to the rhetoric of this text. We must be careful not to distort Jeremiah to echo some intolerant and hateful rhetoric. For example, people who carry signs reading "No Fags in Heaven" and "God Hates Fags" twist Jeremiah's challenge to his opponents. Denigrating others who do not share the same views and values as evil, ungodly, and wicked finds precedence in Jeremiah.

This text should remind us of the danger of claiming sole access to God and sole possession of the knowledge and wisdom of God. If anything, it should remind us that as much as God is immanent, God is also transcendent, and as humans all we can ever have are glimpses of the mystery of God.

Psalm 80:1–2, 8–19

Psalm 80 is a communal lament that seeks the restoration of the people. Like a number of other psalms (Pss. 23, 28, 68, 77, 78, 79), the psalmist uses a common shepherd/flock imagery to speak about the relationship between God and the people of Israel. The psalm opens with a vocative, "O Shepherd of Israel." The Israelites are here identified as a flock by the names of the more prominent northern tribes of Ephraim, Manasseh (the Joseph tribes), and Benjamin. That this shepherd imagery is used as a royal imagery is made clear with the designation of God as the one who is "enthroned upon the cherubim" (v. 1). As a royal shepherd, God is expected to attend to and care for the flock. Yet the psalmist indicates that the situation is otherwise and addresses God with four imperatives: "give ear," "shine forth," "stir up," and "come" (vv. 1–2). The inattentiveness, hiddenness, absence, and silence of God is made clearer in vv. 4–6, where the psalmist asks how much longer God will be angry with God's people and subject them to eat "bread of tears" and be scorned and laughed at by their enemies.

In verse 8, the psalmist shifts from the imagery of Israel as flock to vine and provides a historical review of Israel's experience of God, beginning with the exodus, moving to the settlement in the land, and concluding seemingly with the monarchical expanse (cf. 1 Kgs. 4:21). Yet after all the careful planting and tending of the vine so that it reaches its full potential, God allows the vineyard to be breached and ravaged. The psalmist asks, "Why?" The language of destruction continues in verse 16.

Strategically situated throughout the psalm is the refrain: "Restore us, O God of hosts; let your face shine, that we may be saved" (vv. 3, 7, 19). In dire straits and confronted with a profound sense of God's silence and absence, the people refuse to let God go.

Verse 14, a variation of the refrain, moves beyond the notion of not let-ting God go. While using a different form of the Hebrew verb for "restore," the psalmist is now asking that the action of the verb be turned on God. The imperative "turn" is the same verb often translated as "repent" (e.g., Ps. 7:12). Thus, the phrase can be read as "Repent, O God of hosts." What audacity, to call God to accountability, to challenge God's inattentiveness, silence, and absence! What boldness, to ask God to turn around and do what a god must do! Could we dare to call upon God so?

Psalm 82

Psalm 82 is a mythological psalm that adapts the concept of the divine council from the ancient Near Eastern worldview to portray the sovereignty of the God of Israel. Such a concept of a divine council appears in 1 Kgs. 22:19–23; Isa. 6:1–13; Jer. 23:18–22; and Job 1:6–12. While in Canaanite religion, El convenes divine council of other gods for the governance of the universe, Israelite writers adapted the image into a monolatrous or monotheistic con-text, making Israel's God, YHWH, the convener of the assembly and reduc-ing other gods to "heavenly beings" (Job 1:6) or "spirits" (1 Kgs. 22:21).

Psalm 82 begins with Israel's God (here referred to as *Elohim*) having dis-placed the Canaanite deity El as the head of the assembly. God convenes the divine council and puts the other gods on trial. Acting as not only a judge but also a prosecutor, God lays out the indictment (v. 2). It is a part of Israel's inher-ited tradition that God expects the people of Israel to be just in judgment and to be impartial (Lev. 19:15). Israel's God expects the same of the divine realm. The indictment continues, but now shifts from a question to a pronouncement with a series of imperatives: "give justice," "maintain the right," "rescue," and "deliver" (vv. 3–4). Such justice needs to be shown particularly to the weaker members of the society—the orphan, the lowly, the destitute, and the needy—to correct the injustice. This requires the people of God to relate ethically with one another in all aspects of life—socially, religiously, and legally.

For the psalmist, failure to treat the weaker members of a society with jus-tice is tantamount to having neither knowledge nor understanding, and walk-ing around in darkness (v. 5). Their failure renders those gods like humans and therefore capable of dying (vv. 6–7). The psalmist concludes with affirm-ing the God of Israel as the only one able to judge the world with justice (v. 8).

Justice-seekers are constantly aware that there is too much disparity in the world. In a time of global economic crisis, the gap between the rich and the poor continues to widen, and the weaker members of society are dispropor-tionately affected. Justice-seekers must continue to speak out against any sys-tem that privileges and supports the wealthy, particularly political structures.

For example, various tax cuts have benefited the very rich far more than any-one else, contributing to the privilege of the wealthy. How does God render judgment on the gods of privilege and power?

Hebrews 11:29–12:2

This lectionary text is a part of a larger unit that begins in 11:1. The length of the unit, however, is debatable. The lectionary includes 12:1–2 as a part of it; indeed, some commentators regard 11:1–12:17 as a unit. Regardless of the unit's boundaries, its focus is clear. It is primarily an exposition of the themes of faith and endurance. Chapter 11 begins with a brief introduction of the meaning of faith. It uses two words to describe faith, "assurance" in reference to God's substance, and "conviction" as proof of the unseen. These themes are oriented toward the future even as the writer provides a historical catalog of exemplars of faith.

With 11:29 the catalog begins to move more rapidly from the events of the exodus and the entry into the land. Drawing from the narratives in the books of Exodus and Joshua, the writer focuses on three episodes: crossing the Red Sea (Exod. 14), the fall of Jericho (Josh. 6), and the sparing of Rahab (Josh. 2; 6:22–25). In each of the episodes, the salvation of the Israelites or Rahab occurs "by faith." This is in contrast to the demise of the Egyptians and the people of Jericho as a result of their "unbelieving" (v. 31; "disobedient").

Indicating to readers that time is running out, the writer mentions six other names from the books of Judges and 1 and 2 Samuel—Gideon, Barak, Samson, Jephthah, David, and Samuel—"and the prophets." Nine actions of faithful courage or profound sacrifice are then listed (vv. 33–34). This list may extend beyond the six named heroes and the prophets. The writer turns atten-tion to unnamed women and other persons who suffered adversity and abuse. Having made this turn to talk about profound suffering in faith, the writer now lifts up Jesus as the prime example of endurance in suffering (12:1–2). Indeed, the writer talks about Jesus enduring the cross.

In preaching justice, we need to be careful not to romanticize these heroes of faith. All of them are humans with virtues as well as flaws. Abraham, Moses, Samson, Jephthah, Rahab, and David are all flawed human beings. Samson's arrogance, Jephthah's rash behavior, David's rape of Bathsheba and his mur-der of Uriah the Hittite brought harm on themselves and their families. Rahab betrayed her own people to secure the safety of her family and the Israelite spies and victory for Joshua and the Israelites. Even in preaching we ought not overlook their shortcomings while affirming their faith.

Equally important is not to glorify suffering. We need to be mindful that there are sufferings that have been caused by structural and systemic sin and evil—racism, sexism, classism, and homophobia. Lifting suffering as a virtue uncritically only perpetuates these structural and systemic social ills. In turn, we would do well to remember the unnamed and the injustice within their lives of faith in our memories and values.

Luke 12:49–56

This passage belongs to the second collection of Jesus' teachings on discipleship within Luke's story of Jesus' journey to Jerusalem. This lectionary pericope comprises two units: division brought about by the coming judgment (vv. 49–53) and the signs of the times (vv. 54–56). Irony abounds in this text. Luke's narrative of Jesus' birth presents him as one who brings peace (1:79; 2:14; cf. 19:38), yet Jesus says here that he has come to bring not peace but division (v. 51).

The text begins in verse 49 with Jesus saying that he will bring fire on the earth. This announcement recalls what John the Baptist said about Jesus baptizing with the Holy Spirit and with fire (3:16). The use of "fire" is certainly apocalyptic and relates to "the eschatological purgation and judgment."[2] Yet the kindling of the fire is not unrelated to the division and strife. In a sense, the "fire" will burn through and sever relationships. Jesus' reference to his baptism may be an allusion to his death (cf. Mark 10:38). It is likely, too, that this may be a reference to the conflict and distress that awaits him at the end of his journey to Jerusalem, a matter that preoccupies him until its completion.

The division that Jesus' ministry brings will tear apart families, setting fathers against sons, daughters against mothers, and mothers-in-law against daughters-in-law. Those who commit themselves to discipleship in Jesus must brace for opposition, even from members of their own families (cf. Mic. 7:6). Such division would have been difficult and devastating in a society that favors community over individuality.

In the second unit, Jesus criticizes those who are skilled in reading weather patterns and can organize their lives appropriately and yet are incapable of reading the signs of the times in relation to Jesus' ministry. Jesus labels them "hypocrites."

While this text reminds us of the cost of discipleship, justice preachers will do well to think carefully and critically about the implications of a Christian message that disrupts and tears apart family units. Such a message in predominantly non-Christian communities has brought harm to families and communities. In the severing of relationships, how are justice and righteousness lived out?

---

2. John Nolland, *Luke 9:21–18:34*, Word Biblical Commentary 35b (Dallas: Word Books, 1993), 708.

Proper 16 [21]

Mary Alice Mulligan

JEREMIAH 1:4–10
PSALM 71:1–6

ISAIAH 58:9B–14
PSALM 103:1–8
HEBREWS 12:18–29
LUKE 13:10–17

This is a great day to reenergize the lengthy season of Pentecost with lections that encourage holy praise and investigate the purposes of the church. These passages guide us in thinking through how God's individual claim on us is properly lived out within communal faith. They remind us that the church's responsibility is to be in service with the world, not as a body somehow separate and superior, but intimately interconnected with all persons throughout God's good creation.

Jeremiah 1:4–10

Although it is not as familiar as Isaiah's call narrative (Isa. 6), congregations may recognize this passage as fitting the model. God taps Jeremiah's shoulder for prophetic employment. Plenty of sermons have been written on his struggle and eventual acceptance of the task. The congregation then dabs its eyes, stands, and incorrectly sings, "Here I Am, Lord" (from Isaiah's call narrative). If listeners are going to get anything other than a sentimental pep talk, we had better dig deeper.

Although God's people needed this specific prophet to interpret their banishment into exile and then the sanction to return, we learn little of the historical Jeremiah from the book bearing his name. Probably an original prophetic writing lies at the book's heart. Disciples or coworkers added stories and sermons attributed to the prophet; material repeats or appears out of chronological order. Themes of destruction and rebuilding introduced in verse 10 foreshadow the odd mixture of ideas, emotions, promises, and warnings that swirl through the chapters. Our focus should be not on poor Jeremiah, but on figuring out what word we need to be hearing through him (and from God) today. Since the book probably came near its current form around the return from exile, we might listen with that community to this "living word . . . to help the people make sense of their tragedy, recover their identity, and move toward the future."[1] This is a fitting word for contemporary congregations, who are frightened that society has so reduced the power of the church that our return from what is "virtual exile" seems impossible. This passage legitimizes prophetic voice, not to spout polemics against society, but to speak a theological word interpreting how we must shape our lives to live in the world God loves.

Just as the prophet needs God to initiate the message, God needs prophets to carry the message. So we need to allow God to fill our mouths with prophetic words for our contemporary situations, not allowing our youth, timidity, disability, gender, or advanced age to deter us. Preachers appropriately move beyond appreciation for ancient Jeremiah to stir a congregation of Jeremiahs to listen to where God is calling them to speak a prophetic word.[2] Listeners should try to discover what word God wants to put into their mouths. What the passage refers to as pulling down, destroying, and blowing up has been happening for years in the surrounding society. So, now could be an important time for congregations to speak the building and planting words, but with divine direction for a just rebuilding, resulting in movement toward the beloved community in which those who have been most neglected are attended to and allowed to flourish.

Psalm 71:1–6

Notice the simplicity of address in this psalm. Whereas other Scriptures offer elaborate titles for the divine, here the psalmist often uses merely "You." Listeners sense the intimate relationship of trust between speaker and the Holy You. Walter Brueggemann reflects: "The psalms are *prayers addressed to a known, named, identifiable You.* This is the most stunning and decisive factor in the prayers of the Psalter. Prayer is direct address to, and conversation and communion with, an agent known from a shared, treasured past."[3] He notes also that the direct address means God is "reachable."[4] Our prayers are not

1. Kathleen M. O'Connor, "Jeremiah," in *Women's Bible Commentary*, exp. ed., ed. Carol Newsom and Sharon Ringe (Louisville, KY: Westminster John Knox Press, 1998), 178.
2. Mary Alice Mulligan and Rufus Burrow Jr., *Daring to Speak in God's Name: Ethical Prophecy in Ministry* (Cleveland: Pilgrim Press, 2002), 35–38. The authors argue that all believers are called to be prophetic.
3. Walter Brueggemann, *The Psalms and the Life of Faith*, ed. Patrick Miller (Minneapolis: Augsburg Fortress, 1995), 34.
4. Ibid., 37.

sent by carrier pigeon, whose safe reception is uncertain. Psalms addressed to the Holy You are heard.

Although it is written in the singular, praying this psalm pulls us beyond individualism when we remember the millions of persons who used the Psalms for millennia before we ever heard them. Marchiene Vroon Rienstra reminds us: "They unite us in prayer with others in all ages and places, whose feelings and circumstances may not always be like ours but who nevertheless are one with us in faith. They create a deep unity of soul and solidarity of spirit as we pray them with the consciousness of the company of these others the world over."[5] Even as we reach for God through these familiar words, we are called to lift our eyes, to see the agonizing situations of others who at this very moment are holding children who will not survive the day, who have no safe place to sleep tonight, who sit on death row, who are contemplating suicide, who just got fired, or who live with suffocating guilt. We can almost hear their voices as we repeat the words. If we are not uttering this psalm from our own situations of fear and pain, we might do well to raise our voices to the Holy You on behalf of others.

Such a poignant and trusting prayer reminds us that all persons are beloved children of the Holy You. Every person is God's child, but this psalm seems to affirm divine compassion as most generously extended to those who are suffering. If we also claim divine parentage, then all persons are our siblings. Thus, those who struggle in life's circumstances should receive the primary and preferential familial assistance. In our praise and thanksgiving of God, we must reclaim our commitment to bring justice to all members of our family.

Isaiah 58:9b–14

Although Isaiah is a collection of writings from different eras and circumstances, Timothy Koch reminds us that tradition received this as a single text, a decision we should honor: "The vision of *each* Isaiah is self-consciously connecting itself to the history, the tradition, the wisdom and teachings of the larger community—as well as to that community's sinfulness and shortcomings. The choice was made deliberately to place each 'Isaiah' into one *incredible* tapestry of the search for righteousness and justice for the world!"[6]

This passage directs our proper fasting away from mortification of the flesh and toward righteousness and generosity. When we "fast" by assisting those struggling for justice, we champion God's purposes. Things change.

---

5. Marchiene Vroon Rienstra, *Swallow's Nest: A Feminist Reading of the Psalms* (Grand Rapids: Eerdmans, 1992), xiv.
6. Timothy Koch, "Isaiah," in *The Queer Bible Commentary*, ed. Deryn Guest et al. (London: SCM Press, 2006), 384.

Notice the setting: Israel has returned from exile, which was expected to be a universe-correcting event. People are stunned that salvation did not break out across the land. Instead, as our twenty-first-century experiences might predict, following social crises and population displacements, society erupts in turmoil. Normalcy refuses to return. Isaiah shows a society where nothing runs smoothly and deprivation prevails. We easily envision the resulting graft, cheating, usury, and power mongering. Scholars point out how these verses target individual behaviors, not directions for Israel. But notice, the individual behaviors make communal differences. Instead of hearing the promise of one's own gloom being lifted by feeding the hungry (v. 10), it makes sense to understand that when one person cares for another, light is lifted in the gloom and both are able to see. When we remove others' yokes, when we offer encouragement instead of barriers to a person's life (or livelihood), all of society is strengthened. When one person becomes "like a watered garden," where food is grown, or "like a spring of water," where thirst is quenched (v. 11), does it not make sense that others can be (figuratively) nourished through that person? In our cities where young people cannot attain employment, where parents are working several jobs in hopes that they will not have to move into their car, where no one feels sure their home is burglarproof, where guns are plentiful and drugs offer relief, where people cannot safely walk outside at night, individuals and congregations who work to remove oppressive restrictions to bring fulfilled lives become literally "repairer[s] of the breach, the restorer[s] of streets to live in" (v. 12). A communal blessing!

The final two verses are helpful reminders that such justice and transformative ministries are overwhelmingly difficult. Our strength comes not from our own efforts alone, trying to "do the righteous thing." God must be the fuel. Keeping the Sabbath keeps us energized with divine power and direction.

Psalm 103:1–8

Psalms, the longest biblical book, bubbles with diverse liturgical poetry, making varying theological claims as well as anthropological statements. Many psalms have been used for centuries in worship for both praising God and educating the congregation. Communal worship helps shape who we are. When psalms are used to praise God as merciful and righteous Creator, our shared worship shapes our identity to assert that the One who called forth the universe created it with an ethical grain. Injustice goes against the grain of the moral universe. Rufus Burrow Jr. describes Martin Luther King Jr.'s "fundamental conviction that no matter how much injustice exists in the world; no matter how badly one group is treated by another, there is a benevolent power that is the beating heart of the universe, one which sides with good, justice, and righteousness . . . the very grain of the universe is on the side of right and justice."[7]

In this psalm we hear God's commitment to even more than justice. The Holy One is merciful and gracious, living out of abundant love (v. 8). As our communal life follows the grain of the universe, our sense of justice will be constantly challenged to be more inclusive, more loving. Of course this challenge is not to ignore (thus allowing) more oppression, but rather to allow God to shape our community of faith after the divine model of rescuing those who are being crushed by injustice.

Each of us has experienced some moment of rescue, as mild as a stranger offering us a dollar when we were 87 cents short in the grocery line or as significant as a helicopter landing on our roof in a flood. One of the gifts of the faith is that the congregation gets to choose where to put its energy in spreading God's justice and mercy. We get to offer the experience of rescue wherever we decide to place our efforts. Individually we may not have many resources, but congregationally we do. We have the freedom to choose to combat neighborhood homelessness, for instance, by organizing low-income rental properties. And psalms tell us that the work of justice blesses God.

Hebrews 12:18–29

Throughout Hebrews, the author contrasts Judaism and Christianity, always finding Judaism lacking (although not criticizing Jewish persons). In the current passage, we are given a contrast between the terrifying, physical experience on Sinai and the transcendent presence of God, accessible through Jesus. Only through Jesus is perfection (sanctification) possible. In preaching from Hebrews, we want to be extremely careful of the anti-Judaism voiced throughout (note the author's frequent comparative uses of "better").[8] Contemporary preachers need to assist congregations in understanding the appropriateness of claiming faith in Jesus Christ, but the inappropriateness of condemning other religious traditions. Occasional preaching on such passages crucially assists the congregation's understanding, but preachers must think through the issues carefully first. This passage has contemporary meaning, but it must be preached in ways that deny supersessionism. Christianity's virulent anti-Judaism did excessive damage through the centuries. It must stop.

Another preaching possibility from this chapter recognizes that in the face of a world full of egocentricity, injustice, and threats of ultimate ecological

7. Rufus Burrow Jr., *God and Human Dignity: The Personalism, Theology, and Ethics of Martin Luther King Jr.* (Notre Dame, IN: University of Notre Dame Press, 2006), 190.

8. See Clark Williamson and Ronald J. Allen, *Interpreting Difficult Texts: Anti-Judaism and Christian Preaching* (Philadelphia: Trinity Press International, 1989), 52–54.

disaster, preachers serve congregations well with a timely word on choosing to live into a sacred reality that cannot be shaken. The apocalyptic prediction in Hebrews needs interpretive assistance if served to the congregation. Eugene Boring notes:

> Apocalyptic thinking . . . provides a framework in which we can affirm (1) the world is the good creation of the good God, (2) the evil in the world is real, but temporary, for (3) at the End, God will destroy evil. Apocalyptic calls us to look for a solution not just upward, to some ideal world, not inward, to find my true self, but forward to God's future.[9]

Many people may fluctuate between sensing the world is never going to change for the better and worrying that the world as we know it even now is deteriorating into chaos. Preaching a theologically meaningful word from Hebrews, calling people forward to righteousness and reverence, may be quite fitting.

Luke 13:10–17

Here is a passage that easily opens to issues of justice and transformation, especially if you want to investigate treatment of persons with disabilities in the church, gender inequality, the need for universal health care, or legalism. However, preachers should beware of treating the passage only literally. After all, Jesus' behavior is said to have fomented a backlash from religious leaders. If this is an enacted parable, we do not want to oversimplify the application. Congregations might benefit from a focus on proper respect for Sabbath, involving suitable rest and worship. Jesus is not implying that we should do whatever we want on the Sabbath. Instead he is advocating what we might call "freeing work." The workaholics among us need to be directed to set aside real time for rest and rejuvenation. Others of us need to be challenged to become more involved in varieties of congregational ministry that seek to liberate neighbors near and distant from the bondages of oppression, prejudice, and poverty. Notice that the responsibility to initiate "freeing work" does not lie with those in need. The woman does not approach Jesus; he reaches out to her.

A thornier interpretation moves us away from identifying with Jesus to considering ways we are unable to stand up straight in the world. How do we resemble the woman? A sermon might look at how white privilege cripples

---

9. M. Eugene Boring, "Everything Is Going to Be All Right," in *Preaching through the Apocalypse: Sermons from Revelation*, ed. Cornish Rogers and Joseph Jeter Jr. (St. Louis: Chalice Press, 1992), 80.

Anglo congregations, for instance, and what healing is needed to free them from it. How can we learn to forgo our privilege in ways that actually free us to stand and praise God?[10]

A faithful sermon on this passage may cause division in the house, for the energy sweeping toward Jerusalem gained strength as Jesus continued to show preference to the "least," pointing out where the "greatest" were wrong. Luke shows, in this final teaching in a synagogue, that the movement toward Jerusalem proceeds through acts of mercy and liberation.

---

10. See Mary Elizabeth Hobgood, *Dismantling Privilege: An Ethics of Accountability* (Cleveland: Pilgrim Press, 2000), and Eduardo Bonilla-Silva, *Racism without Racists: Color-Blind Racism and Racial Inequality in Contemporary America*, 3rd ed. (Lanham, MD: Rowman & Littlefield, 2010).

Proper 17 [22]

David J. Frenchak

JEREMIAH 2:4–13   PROVERBS 25:6–7
PSALM 81:1, 10–16   PSALM 112
                                           HEBREWS 13:1–8, 15–16
                                                  LUKE 14:1, 7–14

Most of us, because of our race, religion, wealth, family status, education, gender, or other social distinction, have been on both sides of the conflict between being privileged and unprivileged. Social privilege exists when one group has something of value that is denied to others simply because of who they are. Privilege then becomes an unjust advantage that gives individuals in that group a competitive edge. For example, such privilege rules our economic system. This privilege frequently results in dehumanizing discrimination that easily leads not only to social conflict but also to violence. Scripture invites us to embrace humility, to set our individual and collective egos aside, to listen to what others have to say, and to engage in critical dialogue to transform privileged inequality.

Luke 14:1, 7–14 and Proverbs 25:6–7

It is the Sabbath, and some of the key religious figures of the synagogue have invited Jesus to dinner after worship. Jesus accepts, even though it is apparent that the invitation is not an act of hospitality but an attempt to snare or entrap him. One immediately senses the tension in the air as a man who has dropsy, a disease incorrectly understood as a sexual disease, lies down near the entrance to the house. Luke says the Pharisees and scribes are watching the scene closely (Luke 14:1). Jesus heals the man, takes on the issue of the legitimacy of healing on the Sabbath, and confronts the Pharisees and scribes with an ethical dilemma for which they have no answer. They are silent, indicating Jesus has removed the snare or trap.

366

Now Jesus continues on the offensive. He addresses the issue of entitlement by reminding the guests of the Wisdom literature's instructions on dinner party etiquette (Prov. 25:6–7). When the guests begin to vie for the seats of honor at the table, he shares a parable: "When you are invited by someone to a wedding banquet, do not sit down at the place of honor, in case someone more distinguished than you has been invited by your host; and the host who invited both of you may come and say to you, 'Give this person your place,' and then in disgrace you would start to take the lowest place. But when you are invited, go and sit down at the lowest place, so that when your host comes, he may say to you, 'Friend, move up higher'; then you will be honored in the presence of all who sit at the table with you. For all who exalt themselves will be humbled, and those who humble themselves will be exalted" (Luke 14:8–11).

Jesus is not telling them something they do not know or have not heard; he is telling them that they are the ones who are not following Scripture. Proverbs 25:6–7 states, "Do not put yourself forward in the king's presence or stand in the place of the great; for it is better to be told, 'Come up here,' than to be put lower in the presence of a noble." If they know the Wisdom literature, and it is safe to assume they do, then they know they again have no argument with Jesus.

In Israel, as elsewhere, the meal table was closely tied to one's social standing. The pecking order reflected the position one held at a table. Places at the table were something like chairs in a band—they all showed rank. The Pharisees who attended this meal (not to mention many others) seemed to think that one's table position not only reflected one's position, but may indeed have created it. Thus, people jockeyed for position at mealtime, so that they could end up in a seat of honor. It is easy to imagine what the scene looked like. Everyone was milling about in a casual manner, in the hope that they just might be standing beside a chair of honor when it was time for dinner. How subtle it was all supposed to be, but Jesus saw it and exposed it.

Jesus did not deal directly with this positioning, but only responded on the basis of it. He told a parable. They all knew, of course, to what he referred. He told them that they should avoid seeking the place of honor, for in so doing they actually set themselves up for humiliation. On the other hand, if one were to take the lowest place, then the only way to move would be up. The host might then come to you and move you up higher, in front of all. What a blessing it would be to be given honor rather than grasping for it!

But it seems that there is more here than feeling good or bad about being moved at the table. Behind all this behavior is the underlying dynamic of privilege or entitlement that comes with power and wealth. We know this because of where Jesus takes the conversation. In Luke 14:11, Jesus moves from the parable to a principle that underlies his teaching throughout the Gospels: "For all who exalt themselves will be humbled, and those who humble themselves will be exalted."

Here indeed is the paradox of the Christian worldview. The ways of our Lord are not human ways. The way up is down. To try to work up is to risk being put down. Those who wish to be honored must be humble and seek the lowly place. Those who strive to attain the place of honor will be humiliated.

Jesus then moves directly to his host and addresses the issue of entitlement directly: "When you give a luncheon or a dinner, do not invite your friends or your brothers or your relatives or your rich neighbors, in case they may invite you in return, and you would be repaid. But when you give a banquet, invite the poor, the crippled, the lame, and the blind. And you will be blessed, because they cannot repay you, for you will be repaid at the resurrection of the righteous" (Luke 14:12–14).

Beyond being a poor dinner guest, Jesus is exposing social decorum as part of the problem with the injustice of society in the distribution of resources. There is evil to be exposed with privilege, and Jesus acts boldly to expose it. It is not just where one sits at the table that gives one status, privilege, and entitlement, but also with whom one is sitting at that table.

We are tempted to give in order to get. Jesus taught that this practice should be not only revised, but reversed. In this world, the socially acceptable thing to do is to invite one's friends and the rich, in order to gain from their reciprocal invitations and hospitality. In God's economy, the value system is different; we are to be gracious to the helpless and to those who cannot pay us back, so that when the kingdom of God is established on the earth (at the resurrection of the righteous), God will reward us with honor. Thus, Jesus advocated inviting as guests at our next banquet the poor, the crippled, the lame, and the blind. Doing so assures us of God's blessing.

Hebrews 13:1–8, 15–16

Often when one hears or considers a presentation about social justice, the focus is on a particular issue or issues. The inherent danger of focusing on issues is that too easily we can fail to appreciate that social justice issues are relational; that is, they are about people. The relationship connection, according to the writer of Hebrews, begins with our relationship with Jesus (vv. 15–16), who sacrificed all so that we should not neglect to do good for others, even though it may be a sacrifice. This is what it means to be the firstfruits.

Based on the assumed relationship with Jesus, the writer of Hebrews concludes his letter with some clear relational advice and ethical exhortations that advance the cause of social justice. The members of the community are

encouraged to exemplify their faith through their relational actions and inter-
actions with one another, the stranger, the persecuted, their marriage partners, and finally their own souls and their material world.

The writer's first exhortation is to remind readers that they are a community of love and that they are to continue loving one another. Brotherly and
sisterly love is the central virtue in the Christian community and is best evidenced in acts of compassion. The writer is letting the community know that
this is what will set them apart from other communities. We who advocate for
social justice do well to remember that justice begins with loving one another.

The second exhortation is to show hospitality toward strangers. Such hospitality often has unexpected rewards, as Abraham and Sarah discovered when
they inadvertently entertained three divine messengers. The writer reminds
readers of their tradition and history and the importance of the stranger in our
midst. The manner in which we position ourselves to the unknown stranger
or unknown culture helps determine, more often than not, whether these
individuals or groups will be treated justly. Certainly this is the case when
looking at the dynamics of racism and immigration.

The third exhortation is to remember those in prison. The prison industry
in the twenty-first century is most certainly a social justice concern. The very
nature of imprisonment and the prison system is to remove individuals from
society so that society can forget them. Here the writer is advocating, in a personal way, that we not only consider those in prison, but imagine we are there
with them. In practical terms, it is about seeing that they do not starve to
death in body or in soul while in prison; we are not to forget or abandon them.

The fourth exhortation focuses on the intimate relationship of marriage
and the importance of faithfulness. The marriage bed should be esteemed,
undefiled by the intrusion of a third person. Scripture is replete with the marriage image symbolizing the relationship between Christ and the church.
Marriage should not be polluted by adultery.

The final exhortation regards how these followers of Christ were to position and see themselves in relationship to their material environment. Contentment is the operative outcome, and love of material things does not
produce contentment. The writer calls for disengagement, stepping back
from a reliance on worldly wealth. A believer should step back from captivity
to materialism because the love of money is the root of all evil. Underneath
most social injustice issues is the love of money.

Jeremiah 2:4–13

Patriotism is a principality and power that all prophets, whether biblical or
contemporary, have to face if they are going to speak truth to power. Prophets

must accept the fact that they will be without honor in their own country. This is not just an axiom but a fact. Anyone who dares to speak a prophetic word that is in any way political, or that can be condemned as unpatriotic, is in trouble.

Chapter 2 of Jeremiah contains some of the harshest words any of the biblical prophets had to say about Israel. The language calls to mind a prosecutor presenting a case before judge, jurors, and a packed courtroom. The phrases "house of Jacob" and "house of Israel" (v. 4) tell us that Jeremiah saw guilt on both sides of Israel's divided kingdom

It was a question of leadership. Jeremiah calls into question the practices of the spiritual and political leaders of the country: the priests who refused to do their job of reminding the people about God and calling them back to serve God; the lawyers who acted as if God did not exist; the rulers who transgressed the law; and the prophets who followed false gods for profit.

Evil frequently is the focus of a prophetic word, and Jeremiah does not shy away from naming evil. Likening God to a fountain of fresh water (v. 13), Jeremiah identifies the evil ways of the people of God. They have forsaken the living fountain and instead dug leaky cisterns to hold and hoard water. The entire text, including the metaphor, refers to the lack of the practice of faith. We see in this text that it is evil to forsake God and it is evil to seek to replace God, whether for reason of insecurity or profit—and Jeremiah makes clear it was for both.

Psalm 81:1, 10–16 and Psalm 112

The psalmist sings the same song as the prophet Jeremiah, only this time the metaphor centers around food (Ps. 81) rather than water. The similarities, however, are remarkable. Like Jeremiah, the psalmist reminds the hearers of their neglected and forgotten history with God, particularly their freedom from slavery in Egypt. The psalm makes clear that God promised to meet all their needs and God invites them to open their mouths widely (81:10). However, the people refused to be fed by God and instead chose to act as if everything depended on them. They were proud and stubborn in their pride, and the psalmist says that God gave them up to their own stubbornness (81:11–12). The psalmist imagines God to be very sorry that the rebellious people of Israel have forsaken their God; and if they were to come to their senses, God would "feed [them] with the finest of wheat, and with honey from the rock [God] would satisfy [them]" (81:16).

Justice and righteousness are repeatedly linked in Scripture. By separating the two and keeping only justice, you have a form of humanism; by keeping only righteousness, you have a form of piety that does not serve the transformation of this earth. While Psalm 81 is a song of lament regarding an unrighteous nation, Psalm 112 is song of praise for righteousness. We have in this song a picture of the character of the righteous.

The righteous are blessed with the promises of God, both because they stand in awe of God and because they are well principled. They are honest and sincere in their professions and intentions; they are upright, good people who deal with others with integrity. They are just and kind and do not do wrong to others, but instead act from the principle of compassion and kindness. The righteous show generosity to those who have less; and the righteous both give away and lend their resources because they operate from the principle of charity and compassion (Ps. 112:4–5).

Such righteousness does not go unrewarded, and this psalm presents a poetic expression of what God wishes for God's people. They will prosper in their hearts and in the world. They will have comfort in affliction. They will manage their affairs wisely and demonstrate good judgment. They will know stability and have a good reputation and a good name with a lasting memory (Ps. 112:6–7). In contrast to the wicked who only think of their immediate glory, the righteous will be known forever because of their liberality and bounty with the poor. The righteous will have a settled spirit and a steady heart that is not easily moved. Their strength will be a source of vexation for the unrighteous who are convinced that the way to get ahead is to be deceitful and exploit their neighbors (Ps. 112:8–10).

While those who champion social justice rightly emphasize that justice is not charity, it is important to remember that righteousness cannot be separated from charity, compassion, and benevolence. If we are to honor the link between justice and righteousness, these three must all be evident and an informing voice in justice.

Proper 18 [23]

Barbara K. Lundblad

JEREMIAH 18:1–11
PSALM 139:1–6, 13–18

DEUTERONOMY 30:15–20
PSALM 1
PHILEMON 1–21
LUKE 14:25–33

Today's texts are as personally assuring as Psalm 139 and as personally upsetting as Jesus' call to hate family and give up possessions. Some will hear dissonance within and between these texts. Deuteronomy holds out a promise of "life and prosperity," which seems far different from Jesus' words about radical downsizing. Making choices and turning from evil are themes that run through Jeremiah, Deuteronomy, both psalms, and Luke. In the midst of these readings, Paul's Letter to Philemon raises questions and challenges assumptions. How can Paul call the slave Onesimus his own dear child and then send him back to his master? Are we even sure that Onesimus is a runaway slave? In all likelihood this Sunday falls on Labor Day weekend. How might this secular theme be in conversation with Deuteronomy's guide for prosperity and blessings or Jesus' call to give up possessions? Perhaps this is a day to preach about slaves who labored without pay and without any day to commemorate their harsh work.

Luke 14:25–33

At first glance this passage seems to need rewriting as Jesus jumps from hating mother and father to bearing the cross to parables about planning ahead, then ends with an abrupt call to give up all possessions. Surely a writing composition teacher would demand that this paragraph be rewritten! Verse 25 marks a transition from the earlier part of chapter 14, which takes place in the home of a leader of the Pharisees. Readers listen along with the guests as Jesus tells two parables about wildly extravagant hospitality. Suddenly the scene changes. Jesus is no longer in anyone's home; rather, he is with the crowds. They are

372

traveling with him, evidently drawn to him by what they have heard and seen. We can assume that the crowds have not heard Jesus talk about going to Jerusalem to suffer and die. Jesus does not ease into his sermon with lovely introductory remarks—"It warms my heart to see all of you here." His tone is urgent. "Whoever comes to me and does not hate father and mother, wife and children, brothers and sisters, yes, and even life itself, cannot be my disciple" (v. 26). That word "hate" is very strong and surely troubling. Fred Craddock reminds us that the word was understood in a different way in Semitic contexts: "To hate is a Semitic expression meaning to turn away from, to detach oneself from. There is nothing of that emotion we experience in the expression 'I hate you.'"[1] Whether that will be helpful to people is debatable, but turning away from whatever keeps us from following fits with the central theme of this passage.

Jesus' sermon is not as jumbled as it seemed at first. The beginning admonitions are tied together with a repeated refrain: "Whoever comes to me and does not . . . cannot be my disciple" (vv. 26–27). That discipleship theme returns in the last verse in a slightly different form. Jesus fleshes out his sermon with two short parables, one about building a tower, the other about planning for war. This tower is not a monument but a tower in a vineyard built to protect against robbers and animals, as in Isaiah 5: "My beloved had a vineyard on a very fertile hill. . . . he built a watchtower in the midst of it" (Isa. 5:1–2). Both parables—one from the country, the other in the courts of the king—press the same urgent question to the crowds: "Have you considered the cost of following Jesus?"

Several years ago, a sermon title was posted on a bulletin board outside a lovely church in New York City: "Following Jesus Is Loving and Practical." Well, not really—loving, yes, but often, not practical! Jesus would not have proposed that title for his sermon. Dietrich Bonhoeffer did not include a chapter with that title in *The Cost of Discipleship*.

Contemporary churches that promise wealth and prosperity seldom quote the conclusion to Jesus' sermon: "So therefore, none of you can become my disciple if you do not give up all your possessions" (v. 33). The word "therefore" signals a kind of summary of what has gone before. Jesus' conclusion is not disconnected from the previous verses, even though it seems abrupt. Choices must be made, and those choices involve our wallets and our bank accounts.

Philemon 1–21

Was Onesimus a runaway slave? That has been the assumption for centuries, but Paul says nothing about Onesimus running away. As Allen Dwight

---

1. Fred Craddock, *Luke*, Interpretation series (Louisville, KY: John Knox Press, 1990), 181.

Callahan points out, "The historical reconstruction of the life situation of Philemon as Paul's appeal on behalf of a fugitive slave can be traced back to the ingenious hypothesis of John Chrysostom. . . . Neither the initial hypothesis nor its later development, however, are rooted in any historical evidence."[2] Interpretation hinges on Paul's appeals to Philemon to receive Onesimus "no longer as a slave [*doulos*] but more than a slave, a beloved brother" (v. 16). Did Paul mean that Onesimus was literally Philemon's slave? Or was "slave" closer to Paul's plea to the Galatians: "Do not use your freedom as an opportunity for self-indulgence, but through love become slaves to one another" (Gal. 5:13)? Surely Paul did not mean that some should literally become enslaved to others.

Pro-slavery advocates were certain that this letter supported both the institution of slavery and the Fugitive Slave Law. After all, Paul was sending this slave back to his master (though the word "master" is not used to describe Philemon). Abolitionists were equally certain that this was not about slavery. One example is set forth in *A Condensed Anti-Slavery Bible Argument* by George Bourne, written in 1845: "A slight examination of the epistle assures us that Philemon was a member of the Christian church, but there is not a particle of evidence in it to prove that he was a slaveholder. . . . Nor is there any evidence that Onesimus was a slave."[3] Bourne's conclusion was that Onesimus was Philemon's natural brother, because of the phrase "in the flesh" in verse 16. African American slaves voiced their own strong critique of the fugitive slave interpretation. Reverend J. Colcock Jones, a white missionary to slaves in Georgia, reported this response to his preaching on Philemon:

> I was preaching to a large congregation on the Epistle to Philemon: and when I insisted on fidelity and obedience as Christian virtues in servants . . . one-half of my audience deliberately rose up and walked off with themselves; and those who remained looked anything but satisfied with the preacher or his doctrine . . . some solemnly declared that there was no such Epistle in the Bible . . . others, that I preached to please the masters; others, that they did not care if they never heard me preach again.[4]

A more recent study by Allen Dwight Callahan comes down on the side of the abolitionists' interpretation: "The problem that Paul engaged in the letter was not that Onesimus was a real slave (for he was not), nor that Onesimus was not a real brother to Philemon (for he was), but that Onesimus was

2. Allen Dwight Callahan, "Paul's Epistle to Philemon: Toward an Alternative Argumentum," *Harvard Theological Review* 86 (1993): 368.

3. George Bourne, *A Condensed Anti-Slavery Argument* (New York: Benedict, 1845), 82; cited in Callahan, "Paul's Epistle," 363.

4. Albert Raboteau, *Slave Religion* (Oxford: Oxford University Press, 1982), 139; cited in Callahan, "Paul's Epistle," 365.

not a *beloved* brother to Philemon."[5] Paul's plea is for reconciliation between these estranged brothers. Perhaps Onesimus was a prodigal who had run away while owing Philemon money. Paul is so intent on their reconciliation that he offers to pay whatever is owed!

Questions remain: is "slave" a metaphor or is "brother" a metaphor? Paul uses familial metaphors throughout this letter. Twice he refers to Philemon as his "brother" (vv. 7, 20), and he calls Onesimus "my child" (v. 10). Yet Paul surely did not mean that Philemon and Onesimus were his blood relatives. Does it matter? It surely mattered to African American slaves when this text was used to defend the Fugitive Slave Law. At its heart this letter is about how Jesus Christ changes everything. A slave is embraced as a beloved brother—surely that would transform master-slave relationships and finally end them. Estranged brothers are reconciled with one another—surely that would transform actual family relationships. Whatever Paul is asking Philemon to do, everything depends on faith in Christ: "I pray that the sharing of your faith may become effective when you perceive all the good that we may do for Christ" (v. 6).

How does faith in Christ change us? If each person is a beloved sister or brother, how will we treat that person? Can faith in Jesus Christ lead to reconciliation within the congregation after a contentious annual meeting? Can Jesus Christ, as center of the church, reconcile people of opposing views within a denomination? Given the long history of interpreting this epistle as a letter about slavery, the preacher has the opportunity to engage the tragedy of slavery and the ongoing price paid by African American people. Whether or not Onesimus was a slave or a brother "in the flesh," he must be accepted and embraced as a partner in the gospel.

Deuteronomy 30:15–20 and Psalm 1

Are we there yet? Surely the children must have been asking that question as they stood on the edge of the promised land listening to Moses' long sermon! These verses are a summary of Deuteronomy, and the book itself is a summary of Torah. Most scholars date the book to around 560 BCE, a time when the people of Israel were not living in the land; "words such as these provided interpretation of the disaster of the exile and guidance for a future return."[6] Jewish people read the five books of the Pentateuch from beginning to end every year. They always end up at the river, hearing once more God's call to renew the covenant before moving on. Moses, too, was addressing a community, including people who had no memory of Egypt. This journey

---

5. Callahan, "Paul's Epistle," 372.
6. Fred B. Craddock, John H. Hayes, Carl R. Holladay, and Gene M. Tucker, *Preaching through the Christian Year: Year C* (Valley Forge, PA: Trinity Press International, 1994), 398.

had shaped former slaves into God's people, but would they remember on the other side of the river? Would they remember in Babylon, with so many options to worship other gods? The choices are set out in pairs: "life and prosperity, death and adversity" (v. 15). Later, the contrast is even starker: "life and death, blessings and curses" (v. 19).

The theology that shapes this passage can be dangerous. Some interpret this text to mean, "If I obey God, I'll be prosperous." That can be as specific as a good job, a bigger house, or a hefty bonus. The downside is that those who do not prosper will feel and be seen as disobedient, and their adversity deserved. How will this be heard by the people on food stamps or the man who lost his job or the woman who has ovarian cancer? Jesus was not afraid to point out the flaws of this theology. While he turned to Deuteronomy to confront the tempter in the wilderness (Luke 4:4, 8, 12), he was not afraid to be critical of prosperity theology. One of his strongest critiques is the parable of the Rich Man and Lazarus. Deuteronomy 28 lays out a long series of blessings and curses, including this picture of someone cursed by God: "The LORD will strike you on the knees and on the legs with grievous boils of which you cannot be healed, from the sole of your foot to the crown of your head" (Deut. 28:35). Jesus purposely mirrors this picture in Luke 16: "And at his gate lay a poor man named Lazarus, covered with sores, . . . even the dogs would come and lick his sores" (Luke 16:20–21). In the parable it was Lazarus who was blessed by God and the rich man who ended up in adversity.

Deuteronomy is God's call to life—"*L'Chaim!*" Woven throughout this book are verses proclaiming that life is more than prosperity. Sabbath means rest for everyone, including male and female slaves, resident aliens, and every animal (5:12–16). Blessings of field and industry are gifts from God: "Do not say to yourself, 'My power and the might of my own hand have gotten me this wealth'" (8:17). Chapter 30 is always in conversation with the great Shema: "Hear, O Israel: The LORD is our God, the LORD alone" (6:4). Loving God above all else brings life in its fullness.

Psalm 1 echoes the contrasts set out in Deuteronomy: those who delight in God's law are like trees planted by the water, but those who are wicked will be blown away like chaff (vv. 2–4). But people may argue with the psalmist. The wicked sometimes make a fortune, and those who are faithful sometimes lose their shirts. While taking that argument into account, the preacher asks the question raised by Deuteronomy: what truly gives life? "God's law!" answers the psalmist. One should not think of a burdensome list of rules, but a life-giving river. Be planted there and your life will never run dry. Enlist artists and altar guild to create a long blue cloth flowing down the aisle of the church and out the door, with the congregation planted by the water. The psalmist's image appears again in Ezekiel 47 and Revelation 22: "Then the angel showed

me the river of the water of life. . . . On either side of the river is the tree of life
. . . and the leaves of the tree are for the healing of the nations" (Rev. 22:1–2).

Jeremiah 18:1–11 and Psalm 139:1–6, 13–18

This is a day to invite a potter into the sanctuary. Of course, the potter in this
text was not in the sanctuary. Jeremiah was called to go to the potter's house.
One thing particularly evident in this book is that Jeremiah was a prophet in
the public square. He did not stay in the sanctuary. He was involved in the
messy business of politics. This is an important reminder that people of faith
are called to be engaged in the public arena. Jeremiah condemns idolatry in
the streets of the city and the courts of the king: "Thus says the LORD: Act
with justice and righteousness . . . and do no wrong or violence to the alien,
the orphan, and the widow, or shed innocent blood in this place" (22:3). At
the potter's house, God's call to turn from evil is not only heard, but seen
and experienced. The vessel is spoiled on the wheel or in the potter's hands.
Then, the potter reworks the spoiled vessel (18:3–4). Can a potter help the
congregation experience this? Like the potter, God's intent is not to destroy
the people but to reshape them in faithfulness and justice. The final words of
this text can then be heard as an invitation: "Turn now, all of you from your
evil way, and amend your ways and your doings."

Psalm 139 is one of the most beloved in the Psalter, assuring the reader
of God's presence in every place and circumstance. But there is more than
gentle assurance here. "Beneath the poetic elegance lies an urgent, if not defiant, juridical appeal that God test the psalmist's moral mettle for the sake
of his acquittal."[7] Evidently, the psalmist has been charged with infidelity
to God. But no matter what others say, their charges are false, because God
has "searched me and known me" (v. 1). The original intent of the psalm has
expanded through time to embrace anyone who feels forsaken or downtrodden. No matter what circumstances I am in, God is with me.

Some years ago at a conference on the church and homosexuality, a young
gay man asked, "How can I believe God loves me when my church says I'm a
pervert?" One of the speakers gave him a Bible. "Turn to Psalm 139," he said
gently, "and read the verses aloud." The young man was nervous but gathered
confidence as he read. "I praise you, for I am fearfully and wonderfully made.
Wonderful are your works; that I know very well" (v. 14). He was overcome
with emotion and could not go on. The speaker did not need to say another
word. He simply embraced the young man.

---

7. William P. Brown, *Seeing the Psalms: A Theology of Metaphor* (Louisville, KY:
Westminster John Knox Press, 2002), 208.

Simchat Torah: Joy of the Torah
(Mid-September to Early October)

Esther J. Hamori

DEUTERONOMY 34:5–12
GENESIS 9:1–17
NEHEMIAH 8:1–12
PSALM 119:89–96

Simchat Torah (pronounced sim-khat tor-ah) is a Jewish holiday celebrating the joy that comes with the gift of the Torah (the five books of Moses). In the synagogue, the Torah scrolls are taken from the ark into the congregation, often accompanied by dancing. Simchat Torah comes after Sukkot in the month of Tishrei (between mid-September and early October). The lectionary readings listed above reflect the practice of reading from Deuteronomy and Genesis in succession, honoring the Jewish practice of turning from the end of the Torah to its beginning. These readings (along with readings from the rabbinic tradition) remind us that interpretation involves ongoing conversation with the fullness of Scripture's many visions.

> Through three things is the world sustained: through Torah, through service, and through deeds of loving-kindness.
>
> *M. Avot 1:2*[1]

Deuteronomy 34:5–12

The story of Moses does not end wholly in glory. Moses dies in Moab, having seen the promised land but unable to enter it. Significantly, the text tells us that Moses was buried somewhere in Moab, but that no one knows his burial place, even to this day. This would be no small thing for an ancient Near Eastern patriarch. Rituals of commemoration at the burial place of a patriarch were an important aspect of ancient Near Eastern religion, a central part

---

1. Author's translation.

of family life, and crucial to the honor and memory of the man himself and his family. To be buried anonymously in a place no one would know about, where one's family could never go to commemorate one's life and pronounce one's name in this now-sacred place, would be among the most terrible fates a man could have. Just as the Year B text, Deuteronomy 34:1–5, can prompt us to consider the excluded in our society, this continuation of the story can lead us to consider all of the anonymous and the disappeared. Who are the people our society does not remember?

The Torah's final words, however, tell a different part of the story of Moses. He may have died and been buried "somewhere" in Moab, but "never since has there arisen a prophet in Israel like Moses, whom the LORD knew face to face." The last verse of the Torah then refers to "all the mighty deeds [lit. "strong hand"] and all the terrifying displays of power that Moses performed in the sight of all Israel."

There is a Talmudic tradition that this final verse of the Torah refers to the smashing of the first set of tablets. Later, the medieval Jewish commentator Rashi suggested that God approved of Moses' actions. He read Exodus 34:1, where God speaks to Moses and refers to the tablets "which you broke," and using a kind of traditional wordplay, he connected the Hebrew relative pronoun *asher*, "which," to the similar word meaning "happy" (as in the name Asher), suggesting that God thought it was good that Moses smashed the tablets.

Rabbi Robert Harris of the Jewish Theological Seminary of America points out that after Moses has broken the tablets and gone back up on the mountain, the new tablets are the ones that *Moses* writes, not God, as in the earlier case (see Exod. 34:4, 27–28). So what have come down to us, all these years later, are the human-produced tablets, not the divine ones. Harris suggests that we could learn from Rashi's interpretation (that God approved of Moses' actions) that "God realizes that what can sustain humankind is *not* the direct address/command/Divine imperative, but a *human* response to what they perceive to be the Divine will." He points out that "as we humans change, of course, so does our notion of what the Divine will is," and that these new tablets are therefore "malleable, and not 'gods of stone,' monolithic, unadaptable . . . This is precisely what God *doesn't* want!"[2]

As we celebrate Simchat Torah, we can continue the ancient tradition of interpreting and reinterpreting biblical texts, according to the life-sustaining practice of remaining open to new understandings of what God might be saying to humankind. Just as Moses was buried anonymously in Moab but left the legacy of the Torah, the instructions in justice, our legacy can be the ongoing effort to understand and enact justice.

---

2. Rabbi Robert Harris of the Jewish Theological Seminary of America; personal communication, February 22, 2010 (used with permission).

Genesis 9:1–17

This is a wonderful example of a text that is commonly read for one message, without regard for its more startling—to some ears, even radical—point. At the beginning of chapter 9, God blesses Noah and his sons: "Be fruitful and multiply, and fill the earth." God tells them that the fear of them shall be upon every animal, bird, fish, and creeping thing; all of these will be food for the people. This text has frequently been used to justify the argument that people have the right to use the earth and its creatures in any way they want.

It should be noted that according to verse 3, until this point in the story human beings were vegetarians. God says, "Every moving thing that lives shall be food for you; and just as I gave you the green plants, I give you everything." It is thought-provoking to see that the view of the biblical author was that eating meat was a concession.

More striking is the way this passage continues to refer to people and animals. The next few verses include the ban on eating blood and also on shedding human blood. Verse 5 says that God will require a reckoning from every animal and human being alike for shedding blood. This already is a startling view of animals and humans together, but we do not stop here.

The rest of the story is commonly referred to as God's covenant with Noah. God does not make the covenant with Noah, however; this covenant is made explicitly and repeatedly with the human beings (every "you" throughout this passage is plural) and the animals, with every living creature together and with the earth itself, over and over and over again. In verses 9–10 God says (emphasis added), "I am establishing my covenant with you and your descendants after you, *and with every living creature* that is with you, the birds, the domestic animals, and every animal of the earth with you, as many as came out of the ark." Note that God does not say "you and your descendants and *your* animals."

This theme carries on. In verse 11, God says again (emphasis added), "never again shall *all flesh* be cut off." This phrase, "all flesh," refers to both humankind and animals, as specified in the next verse: "This is the sign of the covenant that I make between me and you *and every living creature* that is with you." Verse 13 then expands this, as God refers to the covenant "between me and *the earth*." Just in case this was not explicit enough, we get to see several of these phrases emphasized yet again in verse 15, as God promises to remember the covenant "between me and you *and every living creature of all flesh*," and that there will never again be a flood to destroy "*all flesh*." Could the point be hammered home any further? Indeed, God refers again in the following verse to "the everlasting covenant between God *and every living creature of all flesh* that is on the earth." Finally, this passage concludes with God's last words on the subject in verse 17: "This is the sign of the covenant that I have established between me and *all flesh that is on the earth.*"

It would be difficult to exaggerate the place of the animals, of all flesh, in this passage. This is the first covenant we see in the Bible, and it is made with every living creature and with the earth itself. How might we respond to the idea that God's covenant with humankind is equally with all living things, including the earth?

Nehemiah 8:1–12

This is a story of great celebration. The Jews had been living in exile since the Babylonian conquest of Judah in 587/586 BCE, approximately 140 years earlier. Since then, the Persians had taken over, and under the Persian Empire the Jews were finally allowed to return to Israel. The returnees did not come back with great wealth or power. A relatively small group returned to join some other Jews who had been able to stay in Judah, there were tensions between these groups (see, e.g., Ezra 4), and the reconstruction took a long time and was difficult work. Here, in Nehemiah 8, we see the beginning of the celebration of the reconstructed community.

This celebration starts with the reading of the Torah. After being dominated by one empire after another and coming back to Judah only to encounter power struggles with some who had been able to stay there, the people initiate a celebration by telling Ezra the scribe to read to them from "the book of the law of Moses" (v. 1). And in the midst of the power struggles the people had faced, in the previous generations and at that time, Ezra took out the Torah and read to everyone (v. 2), "both men and women and all who could hear with understanding." The next verse repeats this, specifying that Ezra read "in the presence of the men and the women and those who could understand; and the ears of *all* the people were attentive to the book of the law."

This is not the only reference to consideration for all people as equals in this passage. In verse 10, Nehemiah tells the people how to celebrate: they should go their way, eat rich food and drink sweet wine, "and send portions of them to those for whom nothing is prepared." And then we see that this is just what the people do—they go to eat and drink "and to send portions and to make great rejoicing, because they had understood the words that were declared to them" (v. 12).

So we see here consideration of both men and women, of all who could understand, and of people who could not provide food and wine for themselves. In this spirit, in a lot of synagogues, as many men, women, and children as possible are invited to participate in Simchat Torah services by reading, offering blessings over the Torah, and carrying Torah scrolls. Simchat Torah has also become an occasion to celebrate Jewish identity, including in places riddled with anti-Semitism. Soviet Jews celebrated on the streets of Moscow during dangerous times, and on October 14, 1973, a hundred thousand Jews celebrated Simchat Torah in New York by taking to the streets to support Soviet Jewry and the refuseniks. This is a day to celebrate community, equality, and justice.

We may also remember on Simchat Torah how so many people in this text offered their understandings of the book. A long list of people "read from the book, from the law of God, with interpretation." As we see in verse 8, these people "gave the sense" of the reading according to their own new situation. This is the same principle at work in ongoing rabbinic interpretation of texts for new contexts.

Psalm 119:89–96

This stanza of the psalm, like the others, celebrates the Torah and expresses the poet's continued commitment to God's teachings and justice. We also see some ideas here that pick up on themes from the Genesis 9 reading. In the beginning of verse 90 we read, "Your faithfulness endures to all generations." We might initially think this refers to humankind alone, but after reading Genesis 9 we pay more attention to the second half of the verse: "You have established *the earth*, and it stands fast." This does not seem to be a fluke; the psalmist continues, "By your appointment they stand today, for all things are your servants" (v. 91).

Through the rest of the stanza, the poet uses synonym after synonym for God's precepts, decrees, law, commandments, and so on, celebrating that they bring life and delight. Sometimes it seems easiest to combat judgmental religion, the kind that results in real harm—spiritual, emotional, physical, political, economic, and so on—by dismissing all concepts of religious law. But as we see in this psalm again, the Torah should bring delight (v. 92) and give life (v. 93)! Isaiah 51:4 says, "A teaching [*torah*] will go out from me, and my justice for a light to the peoples!" Why is it a matter for celebration when the psalmist ends this stanza by saying that there is no limit to God's commandment? It is because this Torah is God's gift of ethical teaching, of standards of justice, and God forbid we should see a limit to this.

This holiday is called Rejoicing in the Torah, and it is not only a mood, but an action and a choice. We remember the anonymous; we remember the equality of all people and the need for justice for all living creatures and for the earth; we celebrate the opportunity to begin anew every year and to continually reinterpret for our own communities.

Proper 19 [24]

Carlos F. Cardoza-Orlandi

JEREMIAH 4:11–12, 22–28	EXODUS 32:7–14
PSALM 14	PSALM 51:1–10
	1 TIMOTHY 1:12–17
	LUKE 15:1–10

These texts take us through a journey of words overwhelmed with the conse-quences of sin and injustice and the hope of God's grace. These are texts of extremes: divine judgment on human sinfulness is juxtaposed with God's pro-tection of the poor and the possibility of God's grace for restoring humanity's sinful condition. These texts describe the sinful human condition and its con-sequences; they also illustrate God's incredible capacity to change through mercy and graciously transform the human heart for peace and justice.

Jeremiah 4:11–12, 22–28 and Psalm 14

The destruction of Jerusalem is caused by the injustice of the Israelites. The wicked are destructive and foolish. Evil is not metaphysical, ontological, or an esoteric condition of a few. Evil is real, historical, and destructive. Both texts ground evil and its consequences in the experience of the community and the earth. Evil is embodied in the destruction of the earth, the obliteration of the heavens, the trembling of the lands, the devastation of fertile pastures, and the desolation of dwelling places. Evil is not some amusing and old Chris-tian doctrine with implications for the afterlife. Evil is anthropological and cosmological.

Jeremiah, the prophet of God, sees the devastation that comes when peo-ple are foolish and stupid. But for Jeremiah, foolishness and stupidity become skills "in doing evil," absent of any knowledge or action to do good (v. 22). The prophet weaves human characteristics of thoughtlessness with evildoing and the destruction of creation.

Psalm 14:1 suggests a definition for foolishness and stupidity: "Fools say in their hearts, 'There is no God.' They are corrupt, they do abominable deeds; there is no one who does good." Connecting this psalm with the Jeremiah text gives the interpreter an interesting matrix of words and meanings that contest and inform each other. Fools destroy; the wise hope. Fools are corrupted; the wise know that God is active in the world and will restore the faithful.

Fools seek to diffuse the transcendent, and I am not referring to agnostics or atheists as fools. Believers can be fools and wicked. So, how does a believer become a fool or, to keep a Judeo-Christian-Muslim term, an idolater? First, we become fools by diffusing the transcendent, by making the contingent a location of self-interest and self-indulgence and, consequently, of exploitation and destruction. Second, we become fools by elevating our contingent location of self-interest and self-indulgence and our acts of exploitation and destruction to the ultimate—the world becomes flat! Our foolishness carefully masquerades with religious language, mediators, and institutions creating an aura of religious security that defies and denies the uncontainable presence and activity of a God of justice. Foolishness is, as Jeremiah 4:11–12 implicitly suggests, the stupidity of confusing a cleansing wind with the destructive wind of God's judgment. To be foolish and stupid is to live as if our world is flat!

The World Is Flat is the title of Thomas Friedman's best-selling book on globalization and issues of development all over the world. It is a must read. But it needs to be read with other sources, such as Joseph Stiglitz's *Globalization and Its Discontents*.[1] Foolishness comes from elevating a contingent reality to a transcendental reality, eliminating all possibilities of questioning, challenging, and proposing alternative options for life and peace. When a "world is flat" outlook tempts and engulfs believers, it elevates *a* way of being and acting to assume *the* way of being and acting. Believers then deaden our God-given intuition to know good from evil by living as fools—with a complete inability to change and see with new God-given eyes.

Exodus 32:7–14

If God's world is not flat, why should ours be? If Moses' world is not flat, why should ours be? The story in this text has an unexpected ending. God's people "have acted perversely; they have been quick to turn aside from the way that I commanded them," God says (vv. 7–8). The Israelites who were liberated from the hands of the Egyptians, who were liberated from bondage and slavery, have turned to idolatry. As Moses was delayed and as the people

---

1. Thomas L. Friedman, *The World Is Flat: A Brief History of the Twenty-first Century* (New York: Farrar, Straus & Giroux, 2005); and Joseph Stiglitz, *Globalization and Its Discontents* (New York: W. W. Norton, 2002).

ran out of patience, they turned to the ways of fools—they became idolatrous for the sake of a sense of security. The temptation to give ultimate answers in times of uncertainty is idolatry. To make the world flat when the world is round, deeply complicated, extremely asymmetrical, and uncertain is an act of foolishness, although many might call it leadership. God's description of the people's condition is a beautiful metaphor of stubbornness and one-dimensional worldview, the perfect recipe for foolishness: "I have seen this people, how stiff-necked they are" (v. 9).

God's first two commandments are clear: "You shall have no other gods before me. You shall not make for yourself an idol, whether in the form of anything that is in heaven above, or that is on the earth beneath, or that is in the water under the earth" (Exod. 20:3–4). Under these commandments, it seems that God's world is flat: "let me alone, so that my wrath may burn hot against them and I may consume them; and of you I will make a great nation" (32:10).

In God's seemingly flat world, Moses is a beneficiary. Why not let God consume the people? Out of Moses, God will make a great nation. So, why are the people important? Moses stands to benefit from God's momentary loss of perception and history given the immediacy of the foolishness of the people. Even more, it seems that Moses' appeal to God is foolish. Why ask for God's mercy for a disobedient people when one will be the beneficiary of those people's destruction?

Moses reminds God that God's world is not flat but rather a complex history of promises and covenants with this people's ancestors. Moses reminds God that God liberated this people from the power of Egypt. This people are Moses' people. Moses does not play the game of the fool and remains aware of the transcendent character of God while making a plea for mercy, "Turn from your fierce wrath; change your mind and do not bring disaster on *your* people" (v. 12, emphasis added). Moses' conversation with God is an appeal to God's world—not a flat world, but one where God's memory and grace are beyond what is immediate, despite the justification for destruction. Moses knows too well that God's purpose and ways are not fossilized in commandments or in making a time of human foolishness and sinfulness a permanent human condition worthy of destruction. Moses reminds God that this people are God's people. Moses knows that God's purpose and ways are embodied in mercy, compassion, and opportunity for God's creation to be good. Moses appeals to God's justice, to God's graceful cosmology that allows the transcendent to be embodied only by mercy, love, compassion, and justice.

The text challenges the interpreter to see two distinctive characteristics of God's nature. First, God can be persuaded to act in justice because God is connected to the people's story. God is reminded of a history of solidarity. Second, God changes. God is not contained in God's own expectations. The sovereignty of God is demonstrated in God's merciful act, which is a total inversion of what is justified and expected. Wrath is changed to mercy by way of God's solidarity with God's people. Solidarity and change, change and solidarity are the embodiment of God's activity to prevent this world from becoming flat. Change and solidarity should be our embodiment to resist our inclination to be fools and make this world flat.

Psalm 51:1–10 and 1 Timothy 1:12–17

We make the world flat by diffusing the transcendent. When we elevate to transcendence a contingent situation of self-interest and self-indulgence where exploitation and destruction are legitimized, we construct a false ultimate reality. We make our contingent, self-interested, exploitative, and justified flat world our divine order by carefully using deceptive religious language, mediators, and institutions which create an aura of religious security that defies and denies the uncontainable presence and activity of a God of justice. To be foolish and stupid is to live as if our world is flat!

These texts witness to the power found in God's mercy to transform our sinful, foolish condition into one of never-ending desire to follow God's purpose, to be faithful disciples of God. The psalmist does not simplify the struggle of the faithful. The psalmist suggests a constant awareness of our human sinful condition as a key to faithfulness: "For I know my transgressions, and my sin is ever before me" (Ps. 51:3). For the psalmist, God's justice is to be found in God's transformative power to make a sinful person one who has a clean heart, who will teach transgressors God's ways, and who will declare God's praise. The psalmist reminds the reader that a broken spirit, a spirit that resists any claim of making the world flat, a spirit that resists any justifiable ideology that makes our self-interest and self-indulgence the rule of the land, is the acceptable sacrifice to God.

Timothy's verses are a testimony for a trajectory of struggle and change. One of the beautiful things about 1 Timothy is the transformed writer—he was once a flat-world person, a fool, and therefore exploitative and abusive. But through Jesus Christ the writer enters a new journey of faith and being—as a servant. In Jesus Christ the believer receives mercy and is transformed to be an example to others. The text points to the experience of conversion—a process by which Jesus transforms us from fools into faithful disciples and servants of the gospel. Once immersed in a life of sin, a life lived as if the world is flat, a life lived "abundantly in ignorance," we are changed by the grace of Jesus Christ, which patiently transforms us into acceptable disciples.

Conversion is a process totally dependent on the grace of Jesus, yet with concrete and grounded results: we become examples of discipleship. However, becoming disciples who resist any attempt to deform the world as flat requires persistence and tenacity. We cannot do it alone. If it could be done alone, God would not have the glory, ultimately! God's power of transformation operates through communion with Jesus and our communion with the body of Christ. It is a project of Christian discipleship in community.

In Timothy we find a matrix of connections for faithful discipleship: we are connected to Jesus Christ and Jesus Christ connects us with others. Our communities nourish actions of resistance against the forces that justify our foolishness by the examples and support that are shared in our communities. Solidarity and change ground the faithful in the struggle for discipleship that resists any attempt to make this world flat.

Luke 15:1–10

Luke's verses embody resistance to the world becoming flat. The logic of these verses is absurd. Why seek for one when we have many? These texts challenge our assumptions about who is foolish.

The world-is-flat logic claims destructive normative ways of understanding the world: Hindus are polytheistic, Muslims are terrorists, Jews are greedy, the poor are lazy, women are emotional, and children are ignorant. I think you get what I mean. When human constructions are reified, they become normative rule. We elevate our human constructions to the transcendent.

The parables in Luke break any assumption about what is typical and take the reader to an unexpected behavior. The parables reverse the priorities: the shepherd seeks for *one* lost sheep and rejoices and celebrates when the *one* is found. The woman seeks for her *one* coin and celebrates when she finds it. Both parables conclude with heaven's celebration when one fool, one who lives in the world-is-flat logic, discovers God's merciful solidarity. The sinner who repents is the fool who gains new sight and perspective, whose contingent location of self-interest and self-indulgence is recognized not as ultimate but as *contingent*. Consequently, solidarity transforms self-interest and self-indulgence; justice and restoration transform exploitation and destruction. The sinner who repents becomes a wise human being constantly alert to the danger of making the contingent the transcendent and confusing the temporal with the ultimate. The fool becomes wise when discipleship is embodied in solidarity and a prophetic action that seeks justice and peace for all creation, a cosmological vocation to do good. When our sacrifice rejects the one-dimensional claim that the world is flat and embraces God's journey of mercy for all human beings and all creation, then God renews our discipleship day by day and the heavens constantly celebrate our struggle to resist living like fools.

International Day of Prayer and Witness for Peace (September 21)

Willard Swartley

ISAIAH 52:7–10
PSALM 85:1–13
2 CORINTHIANS 5:11–21
LUKE 12:49–53

In 1981, the United Nations established Peace Day for individuals and communities to take practical steps for peace, such as lighting candles, organizing public events, observing a Day of Ceasefire, and making peace in personal and political relationships. In 2002, the UN set September 21 as the permanent Peace Day. In 2004, the World Council of Churches designated September 21 (or the closest Sunday) as International Day of Prayer for Peace. We enlarge the title to International Day of Prayer and Witness for Peace to encourage churches to repent of our complicity in violence, to pray for peace, and to take other actions that witness to God's will for all peoples to live together in *shalom*.

> The basic principles of [Jesus'] way of life cut straight through to the despair of his fellows and found it groundless. By inference he says, "You must abandon your fear for each other and fear only God. You must not indulge in any deception and dishonesty, even to save your lives. Your words must be Yea-Nay; anything else is evil. Hatred is destructive to hated and hater alike. Love your enemy, that you may be children of your Father who is in heaven."
> *Howard Thurman*[1]

The First Testament's prophetic text for today's lectionary is the heart of Israel's messianic vision for peace on earth. In the Psalm reading this peace is coupled with justice. The Epistle presents the Second Testament's golden

---

1. Howard Thurman, *Jesus and the Disinherited* (New York: Abingdon-Cokesbury Press, 1949), 35.

text on reconciliation. Last, scholars sometimes regard today's Gospel passage as a "stopper" to the peace vision of the biblical gospel, but instead see its function within Luke's larger peace (*eirene*) vision, which reminds us of the sober reality that following Jesus is costly. Peace comes at the price of costly discipleship.

Isaiah 52:7–10

The Isaiah text belongs in the catena of First Testament texts that crucially shaped Second Testament theology, even though C. H. Dodd missed it.[2] Its distinctive phrase, "the messenger who announces peace," is parallel to announcing salvation. The one announcing the gospel (*mebasser*) reveals God's reign (v. 7). The Septuagint translation of the Hebrew *mebasser* joins the subject and object into one participle, *euangelizomenos*, from which the words "evangelical" and "evangelize" come. The term means "gospel-announcing," and it needs an object. The object is peace (*shalom*), or in the next line, salvation!

The reason this text belongs among those forming the substructure of Second Testament theology is that it is quoted four times. First, Peter uses it to summarize Jesus' public ministry: He came "preaching peace" (Acts 10:36, which parallels the LXX Isa. 52:7). Second, Paul uses it three times: in Romans 10:15 and twice in Ephesians (2:17; 6:15). *Proclaiming the gospel of peace* is the mission of the church. While *salvation* embraces more than *peace*, peace and salvation complement each other. Salvation is not without peace, peace with God, and peace among humans. The peace of the gospel is religious and social, even sociopolitical. Further, the Christian mission includes peacemaking. If it lacks the message and quest to make peace, even between hostile groups, it is anemic and counterfeit. Paul would call it false gospel (cf. Gal. 1), since peace is at the heart of his gospel version, as Ephesians 2:11–22 indicates.

The *messenger* on the mountain—how beautiful! Why? This messenger comes with good news. In the world of the First Testament and in Jesus' time, the running messenger may be bringing news of victory in war or news that a son is born in the royal household, who shall be heir to the throne. Both of these features are shown in this text. But the good news is not victory in earthly war, but divine victory through God's gift of peace sent from heaven to earth. It is the good news that "a child has been born, . . . and he is named . . . Prince of Peace" (Isa. 9:6; cf. Luke 2:10–12). In Luke, *peace* is the fruit of the newborn Savior, Christ the Lord. All three titles for the newborn were

2. See C. H. Dodd, *According to Scripture: The Sub-Structure of New Testament Theology* (London: Nisbet & Co., 1952).

also titles used by Roman emperors in their claim to divinity. Thus from the outset the entry of Jesus into this world has political consequence: Jesus, not Caesar, is Lord.

That is the point of the last phrase in Isaiah 52:7, "Your God reigns." It is no wonder, then, that Jesus' ministry from start to finish proclaims the advent of the reign of God. Eight times among the Hebrew prophets, and in Isaiah 52:7, such phrases as "Your God reigns" and "Here is your God" (Isa. 40:9), the Aramaic Targum translates "the kingdom of God will be revealed."[3] This contributes to the Synoptic Gospels' central theme, and links the gospel of Jesus Christ directly to God's reign, with Jesus as God's viceroy on earth. In Luke, Jesus begins his ministry by laying out his political platform in the well-known text of Luke 4:16–21.

Verses 8–10 describe God's reign as the restoration "of the LORD to Zion" and the Lord's comfort for Jerusalem, both within the context of singing and praise, that is, celebration. Indeed, the Lord is redeeming Jerusalem. But the vision expands beyond Israel, for the Lord is baring "[God's] holy arm before the eyes of all the nations," not to crush or annihilate them, but so that "all the ends of the earth shall see the salvation of our God." These precisely are the contours of Luke's Gospel narrative in his two-volume work: Jesus proclaims the reign of God, which in Acts is restored not only to Israel but radiates into Judea, Samaria, the Gentile world, and to the ends of the earth. The very phrase "reign of God" occurs in each phase of the gospel's reign expansion. Acts ends with Paul teaching about the "reign of God" in Rome.

Indeed, today's passage, together with the prophetic vision for a (new) "covenant of peace" (Isa. 54:10; Ezek. 34:25; 37:26), shapes Second Testament theology and ethics. Let it also shape the preaching of the church in our time, for peace is not the secular government's concern only, but is first and foremost the gift, concern, and task of those who follow the Prince of Peace, those who run the message of peace across the mountains with a new proclamation, the peace of Jesus Christ. Let this news spread throughout the land, from shore to shore, and make every country of this world beautiful for God!

Psalm 85:1–13

Psalm 85 both celebrates and laments this peace coming to God's people. Fortunes have been restored, but God's anger against the people's disloyalty is not fully abated. Will it ever cease (v. 5)? The people appeal to God, "Will you not revive us again, so that your people may rejoice in you?" This petition

---

3. For fuller discussion see Willard M. Swartley, *Covenant of Peace: The Missing Peace in New Testament Theology and Ethics* (Grand Rapids: Eerdmans, 2006), 15–23.

goes on, "Show us your steadfast love, O LORD, and grant us your salvation" (vv. 6–7). The plea ends, and the people listen for what God will say. The Lord "will speak peace to [God's] people" (v. 8). Faithfulness, repentance, and fear of the Lord are conditions that will bring God's salvation near, into our midst, so that once again "glory may dwell in our land" (v. 9). Yes, it is coming, the world restored to God's *shalom:* "Steadfast love and faithfulness will meet; righteousness and peace will kiss each other" (v. 10).

Does it happen; can it happen? Paul says it did happen, some seven hundred years after Isaiah's vision: "the [reign] of God is . . . righteousness and peace and joy in the Holy Spirit" (Rom. 14:17). Those serving Christ will pursue peace (Rom. 14:19). We may read Paul's peace manifesto as only inner peace (Phil. 4:7), which is indeed important, but it is also at the same time a peace that unites formerly hostile parties. This peace makes one new people, breaking down the class barriers that divide, yet affirming the differences: ethnic identities, gender differences, and social class or status. This is the "kiss"! The bridegroom loves the bride, who with the Spirit says, "Come," consummating what began in Jesus Christ (Rev. 22:17).

Luke 12:49–53

Did Jesus' proclamation of the reign of righteousness, peace, and joy bring a sword? Indeed, it did (Matt. 10:34–36). Where Matthew says "sword," Luke says "division." Luke's version is commentary on Matthew. Both agree that in a specific sense Jesus did not come to bring peace. Did he come, then, to divide, as suggested by the term "sword"? No, Luke cautions, division is the result of the gospel's radical call to discipleship. The two Gospel writers here concur: it sets members of the same household against each other. Some will believe and follow Jesus; others will refuse Jesus and even scoff at his teachings. This is the fallout of the gospel's demand. It does not promise the peace of no conflict, nor does it promise wealth or success. It requires, rather, risking wealth (Luke 12) and success for the sake of the kingdom. But even in the face of opposition, the gospel of peace, in its deeper sense, transcends the *no peace* of this circumstance. Battle imagery occurs often in the Second Testament, describing both the resistance of those who desire to do evil *and* the perseverance of those who follow Jesus, loving the enemy but killing the enmity. War imagery in Scripture does not warrant the warfare of this world that kills and maims people (2 Cor. 10:3–5); rather, the weapons of truth, righteousness/justice, peace-gospel, faith, salvation, and word of God win victory over evil. Believers are to wear this armor of God (Eph. 6:10–20) and thus overcome evil with good. Believers may live with divisions within families and among friends, but never-failing love overcomes, breaking down barriers. In God's time and way such love may win over those who resist. Believers may also be persecuted, but by remaining faithful to the Lamb they will endure in patience to the end. God transforms their blood in behalf of the church.

2 Corinthians 5:11–21

This last text makes clear our calling: seek to persuade others; be urged on by love that empowers us to proclaim the saving gospel; and take up Christ's call and model to be God's reconciliation-ambassadors to the world. The only impetus appropriate for boasting is that we are "beside ourselves . . . for God," not anything about our "outward appearance" (vv. 12–13). The urging-us-on love of Christ is rooted entirely in Christ's death and resurrection: "He died for all, so that . . . [we] might no longer live for [ourselves], but for him who died and was raised for [us]" (v. 15). No longer do we know people from a human point of view, not even Christ (v. 16), for in Christ "there is a new creation: everything old has passed away; see, everything has become new" (v. 17).

What a universal vision, filled with hope, optimism, and courage. The task of believers to be agents of reconciliation is initiated by, grounded in, and empowered by God's own initiative of reconciliation in Christ Jesus. This is highlighted in this chiastic analysis of vv. 17–21:

> a In Christ, *new creation* (old passed away; all become new)
> > b   All this is from God, who reconciled us to himself through Christ,
> > > c   and has given us the ministry of reconciliation;
> > > > d that is, in Christ God was reconciling the world to himself,
> > > > not counting their trespasses against them, and
> > > c' entrusting the message of reconciliation to us.
> > > So we are ambassadors for Christ,
> > > since God is making his appeal through us;
> > b' we entreat you on behalf of Christ, be reconciled to God
> a' that we might become the righteousness of God.[4]

Each unit of the chiasm includes some form of the word "reconcile" (*katallassō*). God initiates reconciliation. God's act in Christ—first, middle, and last emphases—reconciles humans to God (not God to humans by pacifying divine wrath). Humans, reconciled to God, are then enlisted into the ministry of reconciliation. As such, humans are ambassadors *for* or *on behalf of* (*hyper*) Christ's work of reconciliation, and God makes his appeal through

---

4. George Shillington, *2 Corinthians*, Believers Church Bible Commentary (Scottdale, PA: Herald Press, 1999), 127.

us. Again, the appeal, "be reconciled to God," is "on behalf of [*hyper*] Christ" (v. 20). The task is rooted firmly in God's initiative in Christ. All Christian peacemaking efforts must never lose sight of this important feature for their identity and empowerment.

In seminars on my book *Covenant of Peace*, I identify twenty-four Second Testament peace themes, with texts for preaching peace, one for every month for a two-year cycle. I list five here:

- Peace-children of our heavenly Father: Matthew 5:9, 43–45 (*CovPeace*, 56–58); consider also Luke's "love of enemy" parallel [Luke 6:27–36] (*CovPeace*, 130–32; *Send Forth Your Light*,[5] 51–53).
- The Child of Peace is born and inaugurated king: Luke 2:10–14 and 19:38–42 (*CovPeace*, 123–24, 126–28). An upside-down gospel welcomes outsiders to the banquet rather than warring against them (*CovPeace*, 137–38, 148–51).
- Peace with justice: Luke 10–19 and 23:47 with translation: "Truly this was a *just righteous* man" (*CovPeace*, 123–30; 140–44; 170–73 for same emphasis in Acts).
- The "Covenant of Peace" eucharist texts, for Communion Sunday (*CovPeace*, 177–88).
- "The God of Peace": our response—Paul's gift to the church (*CovPeace*, 208–16).
- Peace reconciling us to God and to our enemies: Romans 5:1–11; 2 Corinthians 5:17–20; Ephesians 2:14–18 (*CovPeace*, 197–205).[6]

If Isaiah foresaw, and Luke and Paul testify, that Jesus came *preaching peace*, then Christian preachers today ought to do the same. Preach it, sister; preach it, brother!

---

5. Willard M. Swartley, *Send Forth Your Light: A Vision for Peace, Mission and Worship* (Scottdale, PA: Herald Press, 2007).

6. This is an every-Sunday sermon!

Proper 20 [25]

Catherine Gunsalus González and Justo L. González

JEREMIAH 8:18–9:1
PSALM 79:1–9

AMOS 8:4–7
PSALM 113
1 TIMOTHY 2:1–7
LUKE 16:1–13

The major themes in these passages have to do with discipleship in the use of wealth. Whether we are merchants gaining wealth or we already have some wealth at our disposal, God's justice rather than our own enrichment is to be our guide. A true prophet is one who calls God's people away from sin but who also deeply loves the people and suffers with them in the consequences of sin. Finally, our worship is intended to sharpen our understanding of the will of God and guide us in our lives outside formal worship. Going through the motions of prayer and praise but not being shaped by worship toward increasing justice in our lives is not the worship God deserves or desires.

Jeremiah 8:18–9:1

Who are the poor people? Jeremiah shows us the difficult role of a prophet. He has spent time and energy telling the people that the way they are going is opposed to the will of God. They are breaking the covenant law and can expect serious consequences. He has warned them, and they have not listened. Now he sees the consequences that will come. The land will be destroyed, the people scattered. His reaction? We might think that he is satisfied to be proven right. Now they will see that he was a true prophet! But that is not his response. He loves them. He tried to keep them from this fate precisely because he loved them.

His attitude is God's as well. It is the deep feeling of parents who see the wrong path a child is taking and yet cannot stop the child without destroying his or her freedom. A teenage child cannot be tied down or locked up in order to stop what the parents know is a downward spiral. Loving parents can warn, and yet, when the serious problems come, they are not glad to be proven right. The child they love is in trouble, and the parents suffer as well. We see the same emotion in Jesus' lament over the city of Jerusalem (Matt. 23:37–39).

Jeremiah's pain is real. Though he understands why the people will endure calamities, he will join them in their questions about why God has not ended their suffering. Has God abandoned the holy city? Months go by, and still God seems to have abandoned them. Will there never be healing?

There are some who think they are prophetic when they shout angrily at wrongdoers, but if they do not love the people, they are not of Jeremiah's prophetic tradition. If there is no sorrow for what happens to the people, then the prophetic words may be true, but they lack the character that we see here. Love and justice must go together, and that includes love for those who are unjust as well as for the victims of the injustice. In God, the most perfect justice is combined with the most perfect love.

Psalm 79:1–9

The psalm follows the sense of lament for the punishment the people have endured. There is no question, either in the Jeremiah passage or in this one, that the people had indeed sinned. At least these writers understand that. This is a plea for the punishment to end, for God to forgive the sins of the people and restore their land to them. There has been an invasion, and God's people have been conquered. Many have been killed and have not even been properly buried. Clearly this was done with God's approval, letting the punishment of God's people be carried out by nations that do not know God.

Now Israel asks the question: Will God always be angry? Why does God not punish the nations that have desecrated the holy city and the temple? Time has passed, and there is now another generation that did not commit the sins of their ancestors. Will God punish them for the deeds of the previous generation?

In reading this psalm there can be no doubt that Israel understood that there is forgiveness with God. Some Christians seem to believe that in the First Testament there was no forgiveness, only the requirement that the law be fulfilled, and that only with Jesus did we learn that God was forgiving as well as demanding righteousness. The awareness that God is forgiving fills the prophetic writings and the psalms. Here the psalmist prays for forgiveness for the people's sins and for a restoration of the loving relationship between God and the people. Such a prayer assumes the loving, forgiving character of God, as well as God's demand that justice be carried out in the life of the people.

We need to remember that these psalms were not simply poems written by someone but songs put in the mouths of the people in their worship. The psalm allows the whole community of the faithful to ask for forgiveness. Israel understood what Christians often forget: there is forgiveness with God, but that does not mean God tolerates evil within the people of God. We do not escape responsibility under some manipulation that Jesus paid the price of sin and therefore we do not need to bother about it. That attitude is what Dietrich Bonhoeffer, in *The Cost of Discipleship*, called "cheap grace."[1]

Amos 8:4–7

Amos prophesied in Israel, the northern kingdom, before its destruction. His message was from God, who saw that especially the powerful within the society were constantly flouting the law. The sins that are mentioned here are all economic sins. It is not that the merchants have worshiped false gods, a charge often made in the prophetic literature. Rather, while worshiping the true God of Israel they have lived their lives contrary to what that God demands. They have a "Sabbath only" religion. If they attend worship and carry out the laws for the Sabbath, surely that is enough for God! They even hope the Sabbath will end quickly so they can get back to making money. They take advantage of the poor, perhaps by hiring them for unfair wages or refusing to pay them what is owed or cheating them in what they have to sell. They cheat buyers as much as possible, using false weights and inferior wheat. What is clear from this passage is that the God of Israel, the God of Jesus Christ, is as concerned about our economic life as about our worship. Even beautiful worship, going to church every Sunday, is no substitute for faithfulness in economic activities.

The consequence of these sins will be the destruction of the society. It will be overwhelmed and destroyed, just as the areas around the Nile are destroyed by floods. We may think that it is unfair for the whole society to be destroyed when mostly the merchants are at fault. However, the concern here is the larger society that tolerates injustice and corruption throughout the whole economic life. If those responsible for making sure weights are honest had done their job, there would have been less of a problem. And the social culture helped keep the system functioning disturbingly well. We can hope for ethical individuals, decent employers, merchants who are honest, but individual exceptions do not correct the greater faults throughout society. Truly honest merchants or truly good employers often make the news precisely because they are the exceptions. In our own society, many great injustices

1. Dietrich Bonhoeffer, *The Cost of Discipleship* (New York: Macmillan, 1955), 37–38.

in areas such as lending practices happen because laws are not enforced or because the wider society sees gain for others from the lack of such laws. The God of Israel seeks to make a righteous society, not simply righteous individuals who shine in contrast to the rest of the culture.

Psalm 113

This psalm makes clear that God is on the side of the poor and marginalized. Imagine that in worship those merchants whom Amos attacks are given the words of this psalm to sing! Perhaps even in worship they only go through the motions, singing what is given them without listening to the words. Evidently God should be pleased that they showed up for worship at all. They are simply counting the time till the Sabbath ends and they can return to business. Such an attitude is not unknown among Christians.

This psalm sounds very much like the Magnificat that Mary sings (Luke 1:46–55). The psalm, though, includes the enormous sense of how high God is, how great God's majesty (vv. 4–5). After the description of God's majesty, one might expect that God has more in common with those on earth who, like God, are lifted up above others. Yet that is not the case. God seeks the lowly, not to keep them at the bottom, but to raise them (vv. 7–8). They are to sit with the highest in the land. No wonder the dishonest merchants would prefer to ignore the words of the psalm as well as the prophet!

God's special concern is not only for the poor, but also for those who are powerless for other reasons. In that society, the barren woman was powerless (v. 9). Her husband might well decide to divorce her and take another wife who might give him children. Others in the society considered her cursed by God. In her old age she would have no son to protect her. But God has not cursed her. He will bless the barren woman with a home and children.

The barren-woman imagery can stand for the many in our society who are marginalized for reasons other than poverty: for sexual orientation, for physical disability, for illness. God takes the side of those who are at the bottom of the social ladder, to raise them to the level of those who have a voice. Our concern should parallel God's.

1 Timothy 2:1–7

Paul (or whoever wrote the epistle) is concerned with the content of the people's prayers. The church has the task of being a "priestly people," able to intercede with God for the whole world. This is the same task Israel understood as its own (Exod. 19:6). So often our prayers in church and even privately are focused only on ourselves, members of our congregations, our families, and loved ones. If there is a terrible disaster, then we may include among our concerns those who suffer from the tragedy. For this writer, Christians are able to approach God through Jesus Christ who has come to us, and therefore Christians have the task of praying for the whole world. Proper prayers are acts of justice.

Christians are to pray for all people, especially those whose actions have great effect on others, even kings and other rulers. The reasons for such prayers are twofold. First, we need to pray that those in power will have such wisdom that they will let the society be peaceful (v. 2). Second, we pray because God is working toward the salvation of all (vv. 3–4). Paul was an evangelist to the Gentiles, a highly unlikely group to concern the God of Israel, but Israel's God was the God of the whole creation. Christians in the ancient church prayed for the emperor, even when he was persecuting them. They prayed for all who were sick, dying, in prison, in need, and not only for those who were church members. Our prayers should be as far-reaching. Our prayers should match our intentions for justice in the world. Especially in public prayer—in the Sunday worship of the church—members should be given an example of the breadth of concerns that should inform all of their prayers, public and private alike.

Luke 16:1–13

This is one of the strangest parables of Jesus. The dishonest steward is praised for his wise actions, and that is hard to reconcile. If Amos attacked the unjust merchants, why is this one praised? Jesus says that the steward is wise because he uses what he has at his disposal for a few more hours—until his dismissal takes effect—to improve his future situation. The manager alters the bills of those who owe the master money, thus earning the thanks of the debtors. When he is finally fired, he will have friends who owe him something because of his actions.

The parallel is with all of us. Our hold on this life is temporary. All of us will be forced to leave it at some point. Death is the future of every human being, but right now we have stewardship of some goods. They are not really ours—all belongs to God. But while we have the opportunity to manage these goods that have been given into our stewardship, we should use them to give us a good future in the life that comes after our dismissal from this one. How can we do that? The parable makes it clear: we should use the wealth we have now to make friends among the poor and the marginalized. Then, after this life, those we have helped will welcome us.

The commentary on the parable is the main thrust. If our stewardship of the little we have in this life is not faithful—that is, not used according to God's will—why should we be trusted with the true wealth that is in the life to come? To be honest stewards in this life is to use wealth according to God's will—for the benefit of the lowly. If we prove good stewards here, then in the next life we will be trusted with true, eternal life. If we deal falsely now, using wealth for our own purposes rather than God's, then why should we be trusted with the greater wealth of eternal life? In this life we must serve God's justice rather than seek wealth for ourselves. If we do not do so in this life, why should we be trusted with the greater wealth of God's reign?

The wealth of this world is called "dishonest." For the early church this probably meant that it was part of a fallen world governed by Satan. The wealth we have now is not our own. It is the wealth of another. Our true wealth lies in the future. The dishonest manager of the parable therefore becomes a model for the honest manager that we are to be in this life, but looking forward to the reign of God.

Those who seek justice need to realize the power of wealth. It is not a neutral power. It is used either for God's purposes that are just or for other purposes that are unjust. What we do with the wealth we control—however great or small—is of enormous importance. We either are servants of God or servants of money, ever seeking more.

Eternal life is a great gift. It is the life for which we were created, our own true life. But if our lives are warped, not truly serving God, the gift of eternal life would make us eternal sinners, making the life to come as unjust as this one. Those who become the true servants of God now, using the gifts they have received for God's purposes, are ready to receive the ultimate gift of eternal life with God.

Proper 21 [26]

Noelle Damico

JEREMIAH 32:1–3A, 6–15
PSALM 91:1–6, 14–16

AMOS 6:1A, 4–7
PSALM 146
1 TIMOTHY 6:6–19
LUKE 16:19–31

The readings for Proper 21 explore God's judgment and assurance. The texts speak to different audiences and thus offer different vantage points for witnessing God's redemptive action. Jeremiah and Amos direct their words of judgment to the rich and powerful, while the psalms speak words of assurance to the oppressed. The writers of 1 Timothy and Luke speak to the burgeoning Christian community, the former addressing individuals and the latter challenging the church itself.

Jeremiah 32:1–3a, 6–15 and Amos 6:1a, 4–7

In the eighth century BCE the kingdoms of Israel and Judah began to experience economic desperation and prosperity on a scale they had never seen before. For several hundred years, families had cultivated mixed crops on small plots of land. In good years their subsistence harvest was able to support their families and herds, with a little left over. In lean years, neighbors extended loans to one another that could be paid back in better times. And in dire circumstances, such as insurmountable debt or untimely death, kin could be counted on to redeem (purchase) fields so that land remained in the family.

But this mutual system of support came to a stunning end as the rulers of both Israel and Judah began to consolidate land in order to grow single crops that could be exported and traded for luxury goods and military hardware. Once this land consolidation began under monarchical leadership, the only option for families who fell on hard times was to borrow from moneylenders at exorbitant interest rates. This eventually led to families forfeiting their land to pay their debts. The local courts on which common people depended for justice were powerless, having been suborned on behalf of the king.[1]

Onto this stage of extreme prosperity for the elite and catastrophic ruin for the people stride the prophets Amos and Jeremiah. Amos, who is from Judah, travels north to the kingdom of Israel in the eighth century BCE as this land consolidation begins to pick up speed. His prophetic credentials are surprising. He has not been a prophet nor come from a priestly family. Rather, he was a herdsman, emphasis on *was*.

Perhaps prophecy was the child of necessity for Amos, for herdsmen often grazed their animals on land lying fallow. Had the king or local rulers gobbled up his land and herds in repayment for debt? The text does not tell us. But the fact that his former occupation is prominently noted suggests he may have direct experience in these matters. Amos the herdsman audaciously indicts the rulers of Israel. He promises their flagrant greed and disregard for common people's suffering will bring about their downfall and exile.

In similar fashion, the prophet Jeremiah castigates the kings and rulers of Judah for breaking covenant. "For scoundrels are found among my people; they take over the goods of others" (5:26). "They do not judge with justice the cause of the orphan, to make it prosper, and they do not defend the rights of the needy. Shall I not punish them for these things? says the LORD" (5:28b–29a).

Unlike Amos, Jeremiah is a professional prophet, part of the religious ruling establishment. His prophetic oracles span the time from prior to the first Babylonian siege and deportation through the final downfall of Judah and the exile of the magistrates, priests, and King Zedekiah in 587 BCE. Our text comes from just before Judah's demise, where Jeremiah offers a seditious hope: one day Judah will be restored and land will again be redeemed.

We encounter the prophet under house arrest in the court of the king, as Babylon is invading Jerusalem. Some background is necessary. Prior to his arrest, Jeremiah publicly proclaimed that Jerusalem would fall and King Zedekiah would be taken into exile. However, other court prophets, notably Hananiah, proclaimed that God would ensure Judah's victory over Babylon. The court prophets think Babylon is the problem. The king thinks Babylon is the problem. But Jeremiah vehemently disagrees: Judah's leadership is the problem. He announces that Babylon is God's instrument to correct the rulers who have misused their power for unjust gain. And he advocates they submit to Babylon or be exiled (Jer. 27; 28).

Further, Jeremiah has written a letter to the exiles who had been taken to Babylon during the first siege ten years earlier. He exhorts them to seek the

---

1. For socioeconomic background, see Marvin Chaney, "Bitter Bounty," in *The Bible and Liberation*, ed. Norman K. Gottwald et al. (Maryknoll, NY: Orbis Books, 1989), 250–63.

welfare of Babylon and even intermarry with the people there (29:1–23). The exiles then write to the Jerusalem priests to inquire why this "madman" is not "in the stocks and the collar" (29:26)! Three chapters later, Jeremiah is under house arrest in the palace.

Unfortunately the lectionary reading tells us Jeremiah is imprisoned but then skips to his vision and redemption of the field, obscuring that he is engaged in conversation. Yet if we do not know to whom Jeremiah is speaking and the larger context, preachers and hearers may mistakenly emerge with the triumphant conclusion that the problem is Babylon and that God is always and ever on the side of Judah. To wit, we may speculate on who would buy a field during the time of siege; we may ruminate that the terror of Babylon is fleeting and Judah will endure. In other words, absent the context, we are at risk of preaching the message of Hananiah! *Jeremiah's* message is that things are *not* OK, and it will take more than the absence of the Babylonians to make them OK.

It is critical to know that our text is part of Jeremiah's jailhouse conversation with King Zedekiah, who has asked why Jeremiah is prophesying in this way. The issue is not that the king needs to know the content of Jeremiah's oracle; indeed, he recites it back to Jeremiah (32:3–5). His question is *why*.

At first Jeremiah's response may seem a non sequitur. But if we remember the economic backdrop where Judah's rulers have bilked Hebrew families out of their small farms, it begins to make more sense. The Judah envisioned by God and announced by Jeremiah is one where land will again be bought and sold, where land will again be redeemed by kin according to God's covenant, not taken by greedy rulers. And the rulers will have plenty of time by the rivers of Babylon to reconsider what such a just social relation looks like.

Turning to our passage from the book of Amos, we see a snapshot of Israel's indolent, wealthy leaders "who lie on beds of ivory, . . . sing idle songs, . . . drink wine from bowls, and anoint themselves with the finest oils." Amos insists this "revelry of the loungers" will soon pass away. They will be the first to go into exile because they "are not grieved over the ruin of Joseph" (vv. 4–7). Brazen and self-satisfied, they presume they are entitled to gobble the land and the flocks of the vast majority of the people. Amos would be frustrated if he heard this situation characterized as "the rich getting richer and the poor getting poorer." For the prophet makes absolutely clear that the rich are getting richer *precisely by making* the poor poorer. Their reckless pursuit of luxury and ease is causing ordinary people to suffer tremendously and is a breach of the covenant.

From the sheer amount of resources they control, political influence they wield, and lives they affect, large corporations function as kings and rulers in our day. But operating with the well-accepted aim of maximizing profits comes at a great cost—a human cost. Tomato pickers harvesting in Florida earn poverty wages, about $10,000–$12,000 a year. They have no overtime pay, no sick leave, and no right to organize to improve these conditions. In the most extreme cases, workers have been held against their will and forced to labor in modern slavery. In the United States, fast-food, food service, and grocery corporations contribute to creating conditions of poverty and modern slavery for farm workers by contracting with growers to supply millions of pounds of tomatoes at less than market cost. Squeezed by these enormous buyers, growers pass on the costs and risks imposed on them to those on the lowest rung of the supply chain: the farm workers they employ. When workers first raised issues with wages and treatment, one grower was overheard saying to another, "The tractor doesn't tell the farmer how to run the farm."

But like the prophets before them, farm workers are indicting these "rulers" for helping to create and perpetuate these conditions. Reaching out to consumers, particularly people of faith and students, they created the Campaign for Fair Food to achieve farm worker participation in an industry that has considered them no better than machines.

Through the campaign, some of the largest retailers in the world, like McDonald's and Aramark, have forged agreements with farm workers from the Coalition of Immokalee Workers. These companies are paying an increase to growers to raise farm workers' wages and have committed to purchasing only from growers who comply with the Fair Food Code of Conduct to address human rights violations in the fields.[2] More than ninety percent of Florida growers are in the process of implementing these agreements. This is a growing partnership among farm workers, consumers, corporations, and growers. One grower explained, "In the words of Rabbi Abraham Joshua Heschel, 'Few are guilty, but all are responsible.' . . . For us, you wake up and you realize that maybe this is something we could have done yesterday, but I am certainly not going to wait until tomorrow."[3]

Moving from viewing farm workers as tractors to viewing them as partners is the kind of transformation of social-economic relationships that Amos and Jeremiah demanded. They insisted Israel repair the distorted relationships that produce exploitation. God's judgment is a necessary correction on the path to restoration, for Amos and Jeremiah. And their words echo through the millennia, spurring us to observe covenant ways of life that foster collective well-being and honor both God and neighbor.

Psalm 91:1–6, 14–16 and Psalm 146

Psalm 91 is addressed to those who trust in God for their salvation. The psalm assures them of God's presence in the midst of terror or any form

---

2. For more information on the Campaign for Fair Food, visit www.ciw-online.org.
3. Amy Bennett-Williams, "Tomato Grower, Harvesters Strike Historic Accord," *Fort Myers News-Press*, October 14, 2010, http://www.news-press.com/article/20101014/NEWS01/10140385/1075/Tomato-grower--harvesters-strike-historic-accord (accessed December 1, 2010).

of destruction. This assurance is grounded by God's own promise, spoken directly to the people: "Those who love me, I will deliver" (v. 14). In the ancient world and in our own, too often we blame people for the suffering that they endure; we even call into question the authenticity or strength of their faith. This psalm is a tender address to those who are vulnerable; it is not judgment on them. Deliverance does not guarantee a life free from trouble, but a promise that God will be with those who are terrified. And that promise comes directly from the lips of God.

Psalm 146 extols God as a champion of those who are "bowed down" (v. 8)—prisoners, strangers, orphans, and widows. God executes justice for the oppressed. The psalmist warns not to put trust in princes or mortals, suggesting that God needs to step in because those leaders whom the covenant has tasked with ensuring the welfare of the oppressed often fail to do so. This psalm insists that God takes the side of the oppressed. The idea that God takes sides can feel uncomfortable. At first we might prefer God to be a neutral, disinterested party, treating everyone exactly the same. But such "fairness" would not correct vast inequalities. Instead, God takes the side of the oppressed, lending divine weight to balance the scales of justice and ensure covenant well-being. How might the church do likewise?

1 Timothy 6:6–19

The unknown author of 1 Timothy ascribed this letter to Paul and addressed it to Paul's coworker Timothy. This common ancient practice indicates the author's desire that his words stand in continuity with those of Paul and that these words shape the "right interpretation" of Paul's instructions.

At first glance this passage appears in harmony with the themes of justice lifted up by other scriptural passages for the day, even advocating what we might call "simple living" (vv. 6–9). So preachers may be alarmed to discover that the chapter begins by instructing slaves to honor their masters, "all the more" if their masters are followers of Christ (6:1–2). And while at the end of chapter 6, rich followers of Christ are instructed to "not be haughty" but to be "ready to share" (vv. 17–18), their wealth is never called into question.

Can we imagine the prophets Amos or Jeremiah uttering such words? Contrary to the other biblical passages for Proper 21, the writer of 1 Timothy seems to believe that God blesses the social and economic arrangements of his day (e.g., household codes, cultural-imperial order). For the letter's author, "godliness" is *not* separable from one's situation of wealth or poverty, or one's status of free or slave. Indeed, faith should make one a *better* slave or a *better* person of wealth.

Preachers may want to explore how an emphasis on personal behavior that assumes that "things as they are, are as they should be" can compromise the *shalom* (well-being, justice) God desires for human community, as attested elsewhere in the Bible. How might contemporary appeals for simple living move beyond the exhortation to give up and be paired with action to reshape the very edifices that propel some to wealth or freedom and condemn others to poverty or slavery?

Luke 16:19–31

The author of the Gospel of Luke, writing around 85 CE, positions Jesus in opposition to the Pharisees, the leaders who helped the Jewish community interpret and follow the Torah. Since the destruction of the temple during the Jewish rebellion against Rome fifteen years earlier, Pharisaic influence within Judaism had grown. In the chapters that lead up to this passage, Jesus and the Pharisees square off, as Luke portrays Jesus challenging their teaching, practice, and example. Perhaps Luke viewed the Pharisees as accommodators who had grown in influence during Rome's occupation. He pointedly describes the Pharisees as "lovers of money" (16:14), and it is on the heels of this narrative accusation that Luke has Jesus tell this parable, presumably to an audience including some Pharisees.

A simple reading of the parable is that earthly actions have heavenly consequences. A more nuanced reading is that in this, as in former parables, Jesus challenges his colleagues—the Pharisees—to imagine the world and their actions in it from God's point of view. The parable is an invitation to repentance.

The rich man is wearing purple (v. 19), a color Rome restricted to its people, perhaps indicating that his wealth and influence flowed from his connections with Rome. He has erected a gate to protect himself (and his wealth) from the rabble outside. At this rich man's gate lies Lazarus, a poor man who is starving, ill, and unclean, licked by dogs (v. 21). Lazarus embodies all that is unacceptable. He is the polar opposite of influential. The rich man ignores him at his peril. Let all Pharisees take note.

Now it is tempting to say, "Tut, tut, those Pharisees were just so wrong." But in truth, we enter this parable as the Pharisees—the religious leaders of our day. Further, the parable of the Rich Man and Lazarus is not an indictment simply of personal behavior; it is an indictment of institutional behavior. It asks us, as the church, to look at the gates we have erected and to consider who lies just on the other side, suffering. Have we listened to "Moses and the prophets"? What must we challenge and change within our own church bodies that we may embody in our teaching and conduct the fullness of God's love and justice?

Peoples Native to the Americas Day (Fourth Friday in September)

Martin Brokenleg

JOSHUA 3:7–13
PSALM 3:4–8
HEBREWS 12:14–17
MATTHEW 12:33–36

Native American Day is often observed on the fourth Friday of September in the United States and National Aboriginal Day on June 21 in Canada. Peoples native to North America celebrate their identities, histories, and cultures, and also demonstrate for justice. The preacher could help Eurocentric communities repent of the atrocities they have perpetrated against Native Americans and First Nations or First Peoples (as they are known in Canada) and could also help the congregation become more informed about the culture, practices, and religious beliefs and practices of indigenous communities, especially those shared by original inhabitants and later comers.

> We cannot conclude that other peoples spent centuries in a state of delusion simply because their experiences of God were so different than those of Western peoples. That their experiences could not be either described accurately by Westerners or understood in Western categories of thought does not make them false.
>
> *Vine Deloria*[1]

Joshua 3:7–13

Joshua has a character similar to Moses as he now leads Israel. The Israelites cross into the land promised to them. Representatives of each tribe carry the

---

1. Vine Deloria Jr., *God is Red: A Native View of Religion* (New York: Putnam Publishing, 1973), 293.

ark as Israel drives out many other nations native to that land. This is a glorified history of Israel. The question this raises for today's observance asks us to consider if this is also what has been done in American history related to Native peoples.

Those now in power in the Americas have advanced the imperialistic history that God guided European powers to the new promised land of the Americas. In this version of history, the peoples native to the Americas are the vanquished peoples. God drove out Native people so the "Israelites" could have their homeland. Is this the action of a just and loving God? If so, how is it just and how is it loving? If it is not the action of the God of our understanding, how are we to understand the conquering force? Is this conquest a conqueror's self-delusional justification? Is it a clear and proper understanding of divine action by the God of Jesus? This appropriation of a conqueror's history diminishes Native Americans in history and perpetuates white dominance in the Americas. We now understand the legal concept used throughout history, and which is now enshrined in American court decisions, of *terra nullius*—that a land not owned by Europeans is not really owned by anyone. We also know of the policy that only Christians can discover land, which originated in the Vatican and came to be known in U.S. law as "the doctrine of discovery." How do these legal themes enlighten how we see the glorified history of Israel and of America?

Psalm 3:4–8

The psalmist appeals to God to be a shield against innumerable enemies. God will dramatically vindicate the psalmist and provide deliverance and blessing.

If God protects those who are loved by the Holy One, and since history shows Native peoples dominated by white Americans, does this mean that God does not care about or care for First Nations, or that they did not appeal to the right spiritual powers to merit protection?

Some theologians have stated that God has a preference for the poor. Does it follow that the psalm cries for vindication for Native peoples? Is the vindication against the settlers who came to North America? What could the effect of God's vindication against non-Native people look like? Is there some way a just and loving God would excuse contemporary non-Native peoples from the wrath the psalmist solicits?

Native people understand God to be a help, a support, and a strength. Given what history shows us, is this God actually a protector for Native people of the Americas? Does the force of the psalm even imply that God does not listen to the lament of Native people? If God listens to Native cries, what is the evidence, in light of what has happened to Native peoples' resources, land, population, and socioeconomic status? How does this lament languish, given what we know has happened in our states, in and around our own towns and homes? Perhaps in a lament, the protection of God is only a comforting fantasy. If it is more than that, if God has heard the voices of Native people, where is the evidence? What alternative interpretations validate both the conditions Native people experience even today and the expectation of a just and loving God hearing Native people and vindicating them?

Hebrews 12:14–17

The writer tells the Hebrews to establish positive relationships with others and hold on to God's grace so there will be no bitterness in their relationships. Blessings are a birthright to be held and not traded for even basic necessities. If one trades such a gift, not even repentance will return the blessing. Can repentance be that impotent? When does trade become robbery? To whom does the guilt and repentance belong?

History describes the current success and status of the governments in the Americas. In the past, those governments appropriated Native lands and claimed the resources of Aboriginal peoples. These governments established institutions designed to maintain their dominance and to train First Nations in subservience. This scriptural passage requires deep self-examination of any Christian who profits from living in the Americas. If Christians claim inherited blessings by our faith, what have we traded to rob the sacred blessings of others? What blessings were traded to get those resources?

Perhaps the most difficult lesson from this passage to incorporate in our lives is how to live in peace and holiness in light of blessings traded and blessings robbed. If our inheritance can be traded or stolen, and persons prosper or languish thereby, what will be our chance for repentance that God would acknowledge?

Matthew 12:33–36

Jesus prays for the tree to be either good or bad, since its fruit reveals the nature of the tree. Jesus warns about the power of words. Calling a good thing evil will bring down as much divine judgment as other careless words. Jesus is speaking about the religious leadership of his time and its opposition to him. We easily ignore the negative underside of the history of those nations' past and present treatment of indigenous peoples. This "fruit" has a negative appearance to Native populations who do not share in the wealth of the powerful. If God will judge even what one says, what do the actions and events of the powerful toward Native people portray?

In Native American cultures, the people value knowledge learned from experience. Learning from books, lectures, and study has very low status in the estimation of First Nations. Aboriginal remembering is personal, concrete, and specific in its form. One's own experience is the library of knowledge, and expressions of what is known will be impressionistic and personal rather than linear and didactic. One needs only to listen to a Native elder to hear a distinctive form of knowing, remembering, and telling.

Some experiences generate a lifetime of learning. As a child, my family left our reservation to move to a small city so my father could find work. On one of the first Sundays in that city, my father went to the only Episcopal church in that town for Communion. Arriving early, he sat about halfway up the church, but an usher told him that Lakotas were only allowed to sit in the very back row and he would have to leave. My father left that church and we never attended there. A Roman Catholic priest, who could even speak some of our language, was welcoming and let us sit wherever we wanted. So, for years we attended Mass even though we were not Catholics. Today, in that small city, there is an Episcopalian congregation made up mostly of Lakotas and the priest is a Lakota. That is where I attend when I am in that town on the prairies.

As a psychologist, I know the progression of unresolved frustration and pain. Fundamental emotions of fear, pain, or surprise, if not identified or expressed appropriately, will result in anger and rage. If that anger is not identified and appropriately expressed, it will emerge either inwardly or outwardly. If anger is inappropriately expressed outwardly, it will become violence that will be directed against others, or against property in its more passive-aggressive form. Anger that is either unidentified or unexpressed emerges as self-destructive behavior. In this form, depression or suicidal ideation accompany daily behavior or dramatic actions.

In First Nations today, many social ills are symptoms of the past. Social ills in Native communities are not failings among Native people, nor are they the fault of those who manifest these conditions. These ills are the result of a long history of dominance, imperialistic decisions by the powerful, and enforced colonialism. The social ills are almost identical, no matter which First Nation one investigates. For example, no matter where one finds Native North Americans, similar conditions exist: low educational achievement, high unemployment, poverty, diabetes, alcoholism and other addictions, high suicide rates, posttraumatic stress, and depression. A popular reaction is to blame Native people for these conditions, when they are the result of the policies of colonialism and subservience. Knowing all this mentally does not have the power of knowing these effects personally.

A sense of God's justice should motivate Christians. On a good day, I can at least acknowledge some validity to this hope. I do not see it most days, and

I cannot bear to look too long. I have grown up watching the people I love deeply, and who have cared for me all of my life, suffer beyond what seems endurable. What do I even understand about justice?

Justice is a lofty and abstract ideal that has no reality for my family. They have been diligent and unshakable in their faith in a loving God, although they have precious little evidence of that love. Their lives have been full of suffering. They were ill treated in school. They grew up with little food and no modern conveniences such as running water and central heat. They endured racism in social dynamics and local laws. They were passed over for employment even though all they wanted to do was to live happily ever after. They suffered poor health because of inadequate food. They died young from conditions and illnesses they might not have had if they had decent medical care. Still they said they loved God, and they prayed regularly for God's help and blessing. Where was their shield and blessing? They did not sell their blessing for food; their blessings were taken from them by a social system that devalued them and which also had the complicity of Christians. Is this the "fruit" of which Jesus speaks? If so, the Euro-North American societies have much to contemplate.

A preacher of justice will have to be very convincing to speak to Native North Americans about the history we have experienced. A just God seems far away and not very interested in First Nations. Perhaps the God of the Christians is the God of Israel after all, wiping away all Native peoples so the incoming settler populations can inherit the Americas as their new promised land. If this is so, how should First Nations think of this God?

Proper 22 [27]

William B. McClain

LAMENTATIONS 1:1–6
PSALM 37:1–9

HABAKKUK 1:1–4; 2:1–4
PSALM 137
2 TIMOTHY 1:1–14
LUKE 17:5–10

The readings for this week are rich in profound questions, laments, and cries. But they also offer the possibility that, if God's vision is embraced by faith, even "faith the size of a mustard seed" (Luke 17:6), our lamentations can be transformed into celebration, our sorrow into joy. The "overtaken" and "desolate" (Lam. 1:3–4) of earth can realize God's vision for the city: a place of cooperative community.

But we dare not rush so quickly to offer easy answers to hard questions. This week's texts, especially the Habakkuk and Lamentations passages, provide an opportunity for the preacher to help the congregation wrestle with honest questions on their minds that they might not otherwise speak aloud. And the wise pastor will assure parishioners that such questions do not come from doubt so much as they come from faith. To ask why God does not run the world better means that we are already persuaded that *God runs the world!*

Lamentations 1:1–6

How desolate (lonely) is the city. The city where there once was the beautiful temple where the people gathered to worship has been destroyed by the Babylonians in 586 BCE. Where once psalms of praise could be heard, now laments of sorrow resound. The city is where the best and the worst happen! The city is where the gospel songs and jazz were born. The city is like a widow who has lost her husband; she "weeps bitterly in the night, with tears on her cheeks," and is so very vulnerable because she "has no one to comfort her" (v. 2). Friends (nations) that once were hers (Israel's) have betrayed her and joined with her enemies (Babylonians). And so she weeps.

411

Lamentations is written to mourn for the state of Jerusalem after the exile of the southern kingdom. Nebuchadnezzar has sacked the city and it now lies desolate. Those who are left are unable to function properly, and the community is in chaos. How desolate the city! How desolate are the cities of the United States, of Haiti, of Iraq, of Pakistan! When people are oppressed, desolation comes. Those who should be prospering have been betrayed by corrupt political systems and have become slaves of the very system that should give them hope. But God speaks to us in exile, and God has not abandoned the city. The city is the place where the temple of God has always been—in the center of things, at the heart of the people.

Whether we are conservative, liberal, progressive, or whatever our theological position, we know that sin, individual and corporate, exists in the city aplenty—social, economic, political, and religious. Surely, at times, we are called on to name these sins and call for repentance in the name of the Lord. Or, in our more compassionate moments, we "groan" with Lamentations over such desolation (v. 4), or we weep with Jesus over our city gone awry: "if you . . . had only recognized on this day the things that make for peace" (Luke 19:42).

Walter Brueggemann, in his article "Conversations among Exiles," helps us to see that "Ancient Israel learned [and helps us] to express sadness, rage, anger and loss honestly. . . . [The church] can learn to address these emotions to God, for it is God who is terminating our unjust privilege and deceptive certitude."[1] And yet, we are told through the prophet Jeremiah that even in Babylon we are to marry and have children, build houses, plant gardens and eat what they produce, and "seek the welfare of the city where I have sent you into exile, and pray to the LORD on its behalf, for in its welfare you will find your welfare" (Jer. 29:4–7).

When we begin to understand that our fate is tied to the fate of the cities, we will begin to pray for Jerusalem, for Port-au-Prince, for New Orleans, for Washington, D.C., for Old Mutare, Kabul, and Johannesburg, and all of the cities that have been ravaged and betrayed in whatever form. When we begin to understand that our future is tied to the future of the city, we will welcome the strangers (foreigners, visitors) and invite them to gather with us around a common table, a community bound by a common Creator, Redeemer, and Host! And the table will be the "Welcome Table" that my grandmother believed in and sang about. In these in-between times, it is a table where all of

---

1. Walter Brueggemann, "Conversations among Exiles," *Christian Century*, July 2–9, 1997, 630–32. Brueggemann compares the loss of Jerusalem to "the current loss of old patterns of hegemony that gave privilege to whites and males and their various entourages. . . . The enormous rage that accompanies such a loss shows up in family abuse, in absurd armament programs and budgets, in abusive prison policies, in a passion for capital punishment, and upon the poor in the name of 'reform'" (631).

God's children can gather around in one Communion, at a common earthly meal as a rehearsal for the eschatological banquet.

Habakkuk 1:1–4; 2:1–4

The book of Habakkuk resembles the laments of the Psalms and Lamentations. Writing to returning exiles facing a desolate city, economic shortfalls, and corruption, the prophet laments having no ability to do anything about the violence and injustice that he sees. He asks God for clarification, and he wants God to intervene. God tells him to stay on his watch and to write the vision. Surely, he asks, "What vision?" A vision for God's kingdom, a vision of restored justice and real and lasting peace, a vision of God's people actively working to bring about justice in a weary land.

My teacher in seminary was the late Howard Thurman, a mystic, social philosopher, theologian, great preacher, and the first African American dean of a mainline university chapel, at Boston University. Thurman addressed Habakkuk in a day when racial justice issues crowded the minds of so many thoughtful and faithful people (as they still ought to do): Why does God not hear our plea for racial equality and the end of segregation and discrimination? Why does unearned suffering continue? As Habakkuk asked: "Why is there deliberate injustice?" Or, as Thurman challenged: "Why does the 'evilness' of evil [seem] to be more dynamic and energizing than the 'goodness' of good?"[2]

This is a Sunday for the preacher to help the congregation to face the reality of evil in our world and the grief and suffering—both personal and communal—that come because of it. Any casual observation of the world shows that the wicked do prosper, while "the righteous [are] forsaken" and "their children [beg for] bread" (Ps. 37:25) in the streets. Injustice seemingly thrives in our society around racism, nativism, discrimination because of gender or place of origin or ethnicity, and other indefensible rationales for exclusion or inequality. Immigration and hospitality to those who come from lands beyond our borders are serious issues, and have been for a long time. There is corruption, violence, and desolation in the city and in the countryside as well. The abuses of power, consumerism, and marketplace ethics (and even theologies accompanying them) have devastating results. The poor, the widows, children, those with illness and no health insurance to pay for treatment suffer without relief in sight, mournfully and desperately crying out to God with Habakkuk. Their pains grow out of needs and become so overwhelming that

2. Howard Thurman, "Commentary on Habakkuk," in *The Interpreter's Bible* (Nashville: Abingdon Press, 1955), 6:981.

the anguish and frustration spill over into questions of judgment and startling accusation: "How long shall I cry for help, and you will not listen?" (1:2).

Evil is present, and even though we may feel powerless, it cannot destroy us ultimately if we do not allow it to become the core of our inner life or see it as ultimate. In Thurman's exact and eloquent words: "To say 'Yes' to evil, as if it were ultimate, is to be overcome by evil." He goes on to point out the watchful faith of Habakkuk: "It is the recognition of this fact [that evil is not ultimate] that underwrites the integrity of the prophet's challenge."[3]

The conviction that evil is not ultimate stands throughout the utterances of Habakkuk, behind his outcry against evil and all of his protests. And this conviction is at the heart of preaching and our faith as Christians. It is the door of hope, the audacity to have faith in a God who, as the old Black preacher used to claim: "draws straight with crooked lines." It is the faith that "though the cause of evil prospers, yet 'tis truth alone is strong, truth forever on the scaffold, wrong forever on the throne. Yet that scaffold sways the future, and, behind the dim unknown, God is standing in the shadow keeping watch besides God's own."[4]

The ground rules for evil and goodness are the same. I am a gardener and I love to grow flowers of all kinds. But I know that the same conditions that grow flowers grow poison ivy. Whatever it is that makes wisteria and clematis grow also—and for the same reasons—causes the unwanted weeds of Bermuda and Johnson grass. The difference is that the weeds do not require cultivation and care and attention, but the flowers do. As the famous eighteenth-century saying (attributed to Edmund Burke, with multiple variant phrasings) illumines: "All that is necessary for the triumph of evil is that good men [people] do nothing."

Psalm 37:1–9 and Psalm 137

Psalm 37 warns us to refrain from the evil of wrath even when evil besets us (v. 8). Watching for God, listening for God to reveal and direct (Hab. 2:1–4), trusts that wickedness cannot endure the vision or justice of God (Ps. 37:1–2, 6). Resisting evil, departing from evil, is a way of life, for God loves justice (Ps. 37:27–28) and we may take refuge in God's faithfulness.

Psalm 137 is probably preached from more frequently in the African American church than any other psalm, with the possible exception of Psalm 23. There is clear identification with the Hebrews' captivity and exile to the land between the Euphrates and Tigris Rivers, "by the rivers of Babylon—there

3. Ibid., 987.
4. James Russell Lowell, 1845, adapted by W. Garrett Horder, alt. in *Chalice Hymnal* as "To Us All, Every Nation" (St. Louis: Chalice Press, 1995), 634.

we sat down," and in the posture for mourning, "there we wept" (v. 1). And, indeed, the memory of their once-blessed homeland was cause to weep. Again we hear the laments of Habakkuk and the cries of Lamentations.

It was no accident that I took the title for an African American church song-book I helped to bring into being in 1980, *Songs of Zion*, from this psalm.[5] Then and still now, I have argued that these songs provide vital sources of spiritual strength in harsh realities of oppression, even in captivity and exile. The wonder of the Lord would become that spiritual source in the face of challenge, "How could we sing the LORD's songs [songs of Zion] in a foreign land?" (Ps. 137:4).

African Americans did not "hang their harps on the willow trees" (Ps. 137:2), but instead remembered their Zion's song amid tragic experiences on these foreign shores; they sang and enriched our worship and our culture. They were aware even in diaspora of what Professor Brad Braxton under-scores: "Remembering Jerusalem is painful, but the Psalmist realizes the danger of cultural and religious amnesia."[6] And so they sang their "sorrow songs" that became the songs of the soul and the soil. In spite of the insidious tentacles of racism and oppression, slavery and segregation, they sang. As we gather together for Word and Table, we can sing one of Zion's songs now known around the world: "Let Us Break Bread Together on Our Knees." But only because they sang!

2 Timothy 1:1–14

This is a text about memory. Paul writes to his protégé Timothy, giving some essential instruction on how he should conduct himself in pastoral ministry. Memory, or *anamnesis*, has always been a hallmark of the Christian and Jew-ish faiths, for through memory we recognize who we are in God. The Isra-elites strove to remember that they were once slaves, so that they would not become like those who had enslaved them; they remembered how they had sojourned in a foreign land, so they would treat the resident alien with dignity and respect. Here Paul tells Timothy to remember his faith, and, breaking with Jewish tradition, he tells Timothy to remember the faith of his fore-mothers, not especially his forefathers—that is, the God of Lois and Eunice (v. 5), not the God of Abraham, Isaac, and Jacob! The writer clearly wants Timothy to hold on to what his foremothers have taught him, which was then confirmed by Paul himself by the laying on of hands, teaching Timothy to use

---

5. William B. McClain, ed., *Songs of Zion* (Nashville: Abingdon Press, 1980).
6. Brad R. Braxton, African American Pulpit, African American Lectionary Commentary for Sunday, February 17, 2008; http://www.theafricanamericanlectionary.org (accessed March 30, 2011).

this faith as the basis of a life guided by love, power, and a sound mind, not fear (vv. 6–7).

Paul teaches Timothy to follow this pattern of faith laid down by his foremothers not simply as a matter of doctrinal purity or pedantic sermonizing. His life should reflect what he believes. Taken with the other passages for this week, we can be clear that following Christ involves valuing the other, loving your neighbor and yourself, giving yourself in compassionate service, and acting with humility for the sake of those over whom you have power. It is important that Timothy's examples of faith are female, contrary to many interpretations of the Pauline tradition, which here significantly breaks with traditional notions of women's power to shape the community of faith.

Luke 17:5–10

When the disciples asked Jesus for increased faith, the response they received placed their request back on them. Jesus extols the power of even the smallest faith, the size of a mere seed (vv. 5–6). The ensuing explanation draws heavily from the image of a faith that is humble and small, but also assured. Humility between repentance and forgiveness introduces the question of increased faith (vv. 1–4). And the passage closes with the parabolic humility of a servant (vv. 7–10). Faith requires our humble posture to serve God and to regard each other with that posture of care.

This humility of the faithful servant even echoes from Jesus' earlier regard for the faith of a Gentile, a Roman centurion seeking healing for his own servant (7:1–10). This passage helps us to expand our notions about faith as not simply a declaratory statement about who God is or who Jesus is. Instead it tells us of the humility of faith involving compassion toward the "other" and the trust that flows from living faithfully. The Roman centurion shows remarkable cultural sensitivity to Jewish thought by declaring his unworthiness to have Jesus enter his home. He also shows us how to act toward those over whom we have power. He not only intercedes for his servant; he humbles himself so that his servant can be healed. What a powerful word for the church today! What would it look like if we could humble ourselves in situations where we have power over others, in order to bring health and wholeness to the community? How pleased might God be with us if we would not claim our own rights, but instead stand for the rights of others!

World Communion Sunday
(First Sunday in October)

Joseph R. Jeter Jr.

EXODUS 24:9–11
PSALM 29
REVELATION 19:6–10
LUKE 14:15–24

On World Communion Sunday (the first Sunday in October), congregations across the world partake of Communion. Someone has described the sacred table on this day as 25,000 miles long. In our fragmented world, in which groups often relate with suspicion and violence and even try to destroy one another, the churches of the world coming together to break the loaf and drink the cup is a sign of God's intention for all peoples to live together in love, peace, and justice. The sermon might help the congregation confess ways that it contributes to the fragmentation of the world and to resolve to witness to love, peace, and justice.

Worldwide Communion Sunday begins on the other side of the International Date Line, so that the observance starts first on Sunday morning in the churches of the Tonga Islands, Fiji Islands, New Zealand, Australia, and so on towards the West during the twenty-four hours of the day. This significant observance around the world on the first Sunday of each October has become a day of united witnessing. . . . In a time when there is so much disunity, here is an opportunity to witness in a broken world to an unbroken Christian fellowship.

Jesse M. Bader[1]

---

1. Jesse M. Bader, quoted in: Elmer G. Homrighausen, "Cooperative Christianity in the Local Community," in *Herald of the Evangel*, ed. Edwin T. Dahlberg (St. Louis: Bethany Press, 1965), 118.

In our Communion, we glorify God. How we gather, then, is vitally important to God. We gather to worship God in thanksgiving and to live in God's
reign of love and care for one another.

Exodus 24:9–11

This text is sandwiched between blood and stone. In 24:5–8, oxen were slaughtered and Moses dashed the blood about. In 24:12–18, Moses went up the
fiery mountain of God to receive the tablets of stone. Blood and stone speak
of violence, but verses 9–11 bring pause. They describe a visit with a kind
and tender God. Moses, Aaron, Nadab, and Abihu, along with seventy elders
of Israel, went up the mountain. Nadab and Abihu, sons of Aaron, would be
killed later for offering "unholy fire" before YHWH (Lev. 10:1–2), but in this
encounter there was no hostility. They all "beheld" (gazed intensely at) God,
visually and mentally.

This text has been called a "peculiar and dreadful encounter."[2] Yes, but
those are insufficient adjectives. The seventy-four climbed the mountain and
"they saw God"! That is a stunning statement, for we were all raised to believe
that no one can see God and live (Exod. 33:20). But there was no slinging
blood around in this text. The place was lovely, like heaven itself, and God did
not harm them; God did not "lay [a] hand on [them]" (v. 11).[3]

Then they ate and drank. And that is all the more stunning! Eating and
drinking are the last things that would cross my mind if I were looking straight
at God. There are places where Scripture does not speak particularly well of
food. Jesus said, "Life is more than food" (Luke 12:23), and Paul said, "Food
will not bring us close to God" (1 Cor. 8:8). And yet the confluence of holy
moments and eating shows up time and again in the Bible (Gen. 2:15–16; Isa.
55:1–5; Acts 27:33–38; etc.).

The difference is clear: when people are eating and drinking in holy
moments, the focus is on God and not just on our stomachs. The same goes
for the Eucharist. It is a personal and communal moment with God that can
spread to involve especially those in need. I once shared a chunk of bread
with an old farmer sitting beside a rutty mountain road in Tibet. We could
not communicate with words, but we did communicate simply through eating and smiling. It was a kind of holy moment. When we finished eating, we
bowed to one another and went our separate ways. I was quite sure that he had
never heard of Jesus, and equally sure I did not know what he thought about

---

2. Walter Brueggemann, "The Book of Exodus," in *New Interpreter's Bible*, ed. Leander
Keck et al. (Nashville: Abingdon, 1994), 1:881.
3. There is another unlikely but possible understanding of God not "laying hands" on the
seventy-four Israelites. God was not yet ready to "ordain" them for their mission. See Num.
27:22–23, where Moses appointed Joshua his successor.

our breaking of the bread, but it was a eucharistic event for me. I hoped it was a special time for him. When we gather at the table, we may behold God in the face of one we never imagined.

Psalm 29

Some see this psalm as an ecological text. That argument may be a stretch. It is true that God creates, but this text portrays God with a hostile bent. God "thunders . . . over mighty waters,"[4] "breaks the cedars," "flashes . . . fire," "shakes the wilderness," "causes the oaks to whirl," and "strips the forest bare" (vv. 3, 5, 7–9). There are at least five possibilities for interpretation. First, those in the temple were likely petrified with fear and had gone there in hope of surviving the storm, making all manner of promises if God would spare them. Martin Luther was one of those folk, when caught in a crashing storm: "A bolt of lightning rived the gloom and knocked the man to the ground. Struggling to rise, he cried in terror, 'St. Anne help me! I will become a monk.'"[5] But there is no saint to intervene in this text.

Second are those who love storms and are energized by them. The great nineteenth-century conservationist John Muir was caught in an earthquake in 1872. "He was awakened by a strange rumbling. . . . He ran out into the moonlight meadows [as] the earth twisted and jerked under his feet. He leaped upon [the fallen rocks], shouting: 'A noble earthquake! A noble earthquake!'"[6] Storm chasers and hurricane partiers risk their lives to experience the power of great storms and the possibility of a few moments of exaltation.

Third, and most difficult, is the response vividly demonstrated in the film *Forrest Gump*. In Vietnam, Gump carried his badly wounded lieutenant, Dan Taylor, to safety. But Taylor, having lost both his legs, did not want to be rescued. He wanted to die. He was angry with God and Gump. Much later, Taylor and Gump were shrimp fishing when they wandered into a massive Gulf storm. Taylor climbed the mast and began to rail at God: "Come on! You call this a storm? It's time for a showdown! You and me! I'm right here! Come and get me!"[7] But the storm abated. They made it back to port. And Taylor was changed. God would not grant to him the death he wanted, and

4. J. Clinton McCann suggests that "in the ancient Near East, thunder would be the loudest sound known." See "The Psalms" in *The New Interpreter's Bible*, ed. Leander Keck et al. (Nashville: Abingdon Press, 1995), 4:793.

5. Roland Bainton, *Here I Stand: A Life of Martin Luther* (New York: Mentor, 1955), 15.

6. Linnie Marsh Wolfe, *Son of the Wilderness: The Life of John Muir* (Madison: University of Wisconsin Press, 1978), 157. If Muir had been in Haiti on January 12, 2010, or in Japan on March 11, 2011, I think he would not have seen those earthquakes as noble.

7. *Forrest Gump*, DVD/VHS, directed by Rovert Zemeckis. (Hollywood, CA: Paramount, 1994).

Taylor turned his face to life. You can fight with God, but you will lose . . . and yet win. Ask Moses!

Fourth is the flip side of Taylor's fight with God. When I was a boy I would spend summer weeks on my grandparents' farm. And I remember what happened when a storm descended on the farm. Before we ran to the storm cellar, my grandmother would take me outside. The wind would whip her dress as she looked up into the darkening sky. "What are you doing, Grandma?" I asked. "Checking," she said. "Checking for what?" I asked. "Jesus," she said. My grandmother trusted God and Jesus and the Holy Spirit. She believed Scripture literally and was sure that Jesus would come on a cloud (Matt. 26:64).

The fifth understanding, and I believe the best, comes from Thomas Long:

> We have conceived of God's wrath in ways that are too small, too intrapersonal, and too psychological. We have pictured a wrathful God as a larger version of a wrathful *us*—peeved, petty, and petulant. . . . To the contrary, though, to speak of God's wrath is to speak of God's liberating and redemptive love pitted against all that opposes it, all that would keep humanity captive and in slavery. God's wrath is that expression of God's love that will not allow victims to suffer everlastingly without hope, that will not forever abandon the helpless, that will not allow the forces that destroy and demean human life to speak the last word.[8]

People respond to the power of God primarily with fear, conversion, anger, expectation, or hope. Different people in different places and faiths have different approaches to God. But there is one thing people can say in unison: "To God be the glory." Let it be the last word.

Luke 14:15–24

Rarely do leaders at the table call our attention to the parable of the Great Dinner found here. Jesus was at table in a Pharisee's home with lawyers and Pharisees. Noticing how they scrambled for the best seats, Jesus chastised them. In response, one at table said, "Blessed is anyone who will eat bread in the kingdom of God" (v. 15). He may have wanted simply to break the tension with his affirmation or he may honestly have wanted to multiply the heaven-bound.[9] The parable of the Great Dinner is Jesus' response to him. Someone desired to host a feast and invited many persons. When the time for the dinner had arrived, the host sent out his servant to tell the invitees it was

---

8. Thomas G. Long, "Praying for the Wrath of God," in *Preaching through the Apocalypse*, ed. Cornish R. Rogers and Joseph R. Jeter Jr. (St. Louis: Chalice Press, 1992), 137–38.

9. See R. Alan Culpepper, "The Gospel of John," in *The New Interpreter's Bible*. ed. Leander Keck et al. (Nashville: Abingdon Press, 1995), 9:289.

time. But one after another they made excuses and did not come. The angry host then told the servant to bring the poor, the disabled, and the blind. But the servant had already done that, and the host then said, "Go out into the roads and lanes, and compel people to come in. . . . For I tell you, none of those who were invited will taste my dinner" (vv. 23–24).

The message was clear, and the levity in the room surely subsided. The guests were the invited ones. And so are we. We may have been invited by confession, baptism, and confirmation, but if we make excuses for our heartless faith and our shunning of the church, our invitation may be voided and those who have known nothing about the great dinner in heaven may replace us. This is why the text is rarely used before we gather at the Communion table, because we do not like to hear its implication. But maybe we need to hear it. Maybe we need to come to terms with our excuses about how we have maneuvered God out of our lives. And maybe we need to be God's servants and extend God's invitation to a good dinner now and a great dinner in the future to the poor, the disabled, the blind, and others on the streets.

Revelation 19:6–10

The Revelation to John is like a canvas pinned to the heavens and splattered with multicolored images: images from the Hebrew Bible and other apocalyptic texts, along with the poetic imagination of the author. In our text are several short stories. The apotheosis of verse 6 came neither from a theologian nor from a biblical scholar but rather from the German-born composer George Frideric Handel. Millions of people know the "Hallelujah" chorus in the oratorio *Messiah*, while many others can hum the tune. I seriously doubt that "hallelujah" would be so embedded in praise vocabulary today had not Handel taken a few words from Scripture almost three hundred years ago and set them to a majestic piece of music.

Verses 7–9 urge us to rejoice and give God the glory because Christ is about to marry: "the marriage of the Lamb has come, and his bride has made herself ready." This may sound like a strange image, but we find it throughout the Bible. Here the eschatological marriage and attending feast depict God/Christ as the bridegroom and the people of God, Israel/church, as the bride. Those who have been invited (and indirectly those who have not yet been invited) to the heavenly feast share in the "wedding party at the consummation of the ages."[10] When we lift the bread and cup at tables of remembrance around the world today, we share a foretaste of that great feast in heaven. Three sidebars: Verse 8 describes how she (the church) " 'has been granted to

10. Eugene Boring, *Revelation*, Interpretation series (Louisville, KY: John Knox Press, 1989), 193.

be clothed with fine linen, bright and pure'—for the fine linen is the righteous deeds of the saints." Linen is an ancient material that was and is expensive. Its one great flaw is that it wrinkles as though it were wadded up and stomped on. Dealing with this wrinkle in time might lead us to say that we may likely find the righteous deeds of today's saints in secondhand blue jeans and stained aprons in a soup kitchen.

Verse 9 is an interesting counterpart to Luke 14:15–24. An unnamed angel spoke: "Write this: Blessed are those who are invited to the marriage supper of the Lamb." In Luke those who were invited to the great dinner made excuses and declined. The host was angry and said those who turned down the offer would never eat with him. The angel speaking for God in Revelation said those who were invited to Christ's marriage feast were blessed. No excuses! Blessed!

Verse 10 finds John falling on his knees to worship the angel, but the angel told him not to do that. The angel claimed to be no more than a fellow servant with John and others. Apparently, "in some of the churches of Asia, angelic beings were being exalted, dangerously confused with Christ, and worshipped."[11] John's two-word rebuke was clear: "Worship God!"

There are strong symbols in the text. The voices are thunder. The linen is righteousness. The church is the spouse of Christ. Invitation is blessing. Verses 6–10 give us several perspectives and one overriding theme: Worship God and love one another.

11. Ibid., 194.

Proper 23 [28]

Miguel A. De La Torre

JEREMIAH 29:1, 4–7
PSALM 66:1–12

2 KINGS 5:1–3, 7–15C
PSALM 111
2 TIMOTHY 2:8–15
LUKE 17:11–19

From Tijuana on the Pacific Ocean to Matamoros on the Gulf of Mexico is 1,833 miles of border separating the United States from Latin America. A fifteen-foot-high wall demarcates parts of this line. Landing strips used during the first Iraqi war were recycled in 1994 by the Immigration and Naturalization Service (INS) to construct this wall. The hope of INS was to stem the flow of mainly Mexican immigrants through the San Diego area and Nogales, Arizona. But the flow continues, only now through miles of hazardous desert terrain where many fall victim to the elements. This artificial line is more than just a border between two countries. Some have called it a scar caused by the first and third worlds chafing against each other.

The military might of the United States created the present 1,833-mile-long line at the end of the Mexican-American War (1846–1848). After the creation of this line, Mexicans living north of the line woke up to find themselves in a new country. In effect, it was the border that crossed these Mexicans. The same was true for Puerto Ricans who found their island absorbed into the emerging American empire. Like the Mexicans, they were crossed by U.S. borders with the conclusion of the Spanish-American War (1898).

To live on the borders can literally mean living in the cities that are along this artificial line. But the borderlands are more than a geographical reality; they also symbolize the existential reality of the majority of U.S. Latinas/os. Most Hispanics, regardless of where they are or how they or their ancestors found themselves in the United States, live on the borders. Borders separating Latinas/os from other Americans exist in every state, every city, and almost every community, regardless of how far they may be from the actual 1,833 miles of borders. Borders are as real in Topeka, Kansas; Seattle, Washington;

or Chapel Hill, North Carolina, as they are in Chula Vista, California; Douglas, Arizona; or El Paso, Texas. To be a U.S. Hispanic is to live constantly on the border, that is, the border that separates privilege from disenfranchisement, power from marginalization, and whiteness from "colored." Most U.S. Hispanics, regardless of where they live, exist in the borderlands.

Luke 17:11–19

Therefore, it is good news to find Jesus on the borders, traveling between Samaria and Galilee (v. 11). The disdain some Euro-Americans today hold for their neighbors to the south was shared by the Galileans of Jesus' time toward their southern neighbors, the Samaritans. Nevertheless, Jesus can be found walking in the borderlands, not just the geographical borders, but also those on the edge of disenfranchisement, willing to minister to those perceived to be unclean. On this particular day, Luke tells us of ten lepers who approached Jesus seeking succor for their condition (v. 12). Leprosy is an upper-respiratory-tract infection that primarily manifests itself as skin lesions. A scourge during biblical times, it continues to affect people during modern times. Today the disease does not carry the shame it once did, mainly because it can be prevented, if not cured. But those afflicted with leprosy during Jesus' time had little hope for a healing. Those with the disease were stigmatized by society as unclean, relegated to forced segregation. Hence, when they came to Jesus, they kept a considerable distance, loudly crying out for mercy (v. 13).

Jesus responded by telling the lepers to go and present themselves to their priests. As they made their way to the priests, they discovered a merciful God who healed them of their affliction. One of them, a foreigner, a Samaritan, returned, praising God and thanking Jesus (vv. 14–16). The other nine did not bother to return, but one considered doubly unclean—unclean as a leper and unclean as a foreigner—found both salvation and liberation from his marginalization. He was no longer forced to live in the borderlands. In this passage we discover a Jesus who saves all living on the borders between what is defined as clean and unclean, between native and foreign.

Psalm 66:1–12

It did not matter that the one healed was a foreigner, specifically a Samaritan who was viewed as inferior by the "pure" Jews of the time. God's love or grace is not limited to native Israelites, but is inclusive of all—even those who are unclean as aliens. "Make a joyful noise to God" (v. 1), sings the psalmist. "All the earth worships [God]" (v. 4). It was customary for each nation to fashion its own tribal deities. Gods were only potent among people living within closed communities, but once they crossed borders, their gods became impotent. Gods were confined to geographic locations. To cross borders meant putting away your own gods and accepting the gods of the new land in which you newly dwelled. The psalmist calls for a different approach. Rather than accepting the gods of the new land, whether the gods of capital, the gods of empire, or the gods of ethnic superiority, it is the nations that are called to bless the God of Israel. "Bless our God, O peoples, let the sound of [God's] praise be heard," exclaims the psalmist (v. 8).

But a danger exists when we attempt to force all nations to bless *our* God. A history of violent evangelism has created a conquering Christ that has brought the colonized to despise the good news. The essence of this type of Christ, forged during the centuries of long campaigns against the so-called enemies of the "true" faith, merged avarice and evangelism under the lordship of Christ. The white man's burden of "civilizing" the world became a profitable venture for those missionaries thinking they were saving the world for Jesus. The consequences of the injustices brought forth by the Eurocentric missionary zeal can best be captured by an old African proverb, "At first the Europeans had the Bible and we had the land; now the Europeans have the land and we have the Bible."

The quest for gold in the so-called New World converged with a crusading fervor to rid Europe, specifically Spain, of "infidels," whether they were Jews and Muslims in the homeland, or Native people on the margins of the emerging empires. The Great Commission to baptize all nations so that they can in turn bless *our* God was taken literally, legitimizing European dominance in the world order. In the name of Jesus, women were raped, children were disemboweled, men fell prey to the invaders' swords. Avarice for gold in the Southern Hemisphere and land in the Northern Hemisphere physically, spiritually, and culturally decimated the indigenous population. Can we blame Native American theologian Tink Tinker when he states, "liberation theology for Indian people may require a firm saying 'no' to Jesus and Christianity"?[1]

2 Timothy 2:8–15

The good news that Paul preached—"Jesus Christ, raised from the dead" (v. 8)—was and continues to be lost whenever the missionary venture is transformed into enriching the conquering nations. Evangelism has come to mean converting people into thinking what we think and believing the doctrines

---

1. Tink Tinker, "American Indians Religious Traditions," in *The Hope of Liberation in World Religions*, ed. Miguel A. De La Torre (Waco, TX: Baylor University Press, 2008), 257–73 (quotation, 261).

we believe. Those who refuse to accept our brand of Christianity are branded infidels, enemies of the true faith, thereby justifying their destruction. Yet Paul had a very different understanding of Christianity. To be a Christian is to share the plight of those labeled subversive. Solidarity with the oppressed can lead to being "chained like a criminal"; nevertheless, the acts for justice committed in the name of the good news can never be chained (v. 9). To die with Christ is to live with Christ (v. 11). Those whom society privileges are seldom, if ever, hung (lynched) from trees. Only those living on the borders between power and disenfranchisement can expect to face abuse, persecution, and oppression.

"Rome" continues to execute those who subvert the dominant culture, those who refuse to bow their knees to the Caesars of history, and all they represent. But there is nothing glorious, wonderful, or redemptive about an instrument of death. For God in the flesh to be lynched becomes a scandal because it questions God's omnipotence, signaling the failure of Christ's ministry. In our rush to signify the cross as a sign of hope, a salvific golden symbol to be hung around our necks, we fail to pause on the tragedy, the hopelessness, the failure, the powerlessness of dying with Christ. There is no redemption in Jesus' sufferings or atonement. For those who have suffered marginalization, it is difficult, if not impossible, to claim anything redemptive in suffering.

The good news Paul preached is that salvation does not occur exclusively on the cross. After all, Paul preached Christ risen, not Christ dead on a cross. Salvation is found in Jesus' birth, life, teachings, praxis, resurrection, spirit, and, yes, also death. The importance of Jesus' crucifixion is not atonement; it is solidarity with all who are crucified today so that the few can enjoy their abundant lives of privilege.

To die with Christ so that we can live with him is to die for the same reasons he did, as an act of solidarity with the very least of these. Allowing himself to be hung from a tree was an act undertaken so that divinity could learn, through solidarity with the oppressed, what it means to be among the wretched of the earth. Anselm of Canterbury (1033?–1109) may have us believe that the cross was necessary to satisfy God's anger, that is, to serve as a substitute for us. Sinful humans could not redeem themselves before an angry God who requires a blood atonement. Only a sinless God-as-human-being could complete the process, make restitution, and restore creation. In other words, in order to satisfy God's vanity, God's only begotten son must be humiliated, tortured, and brutally killed, rather than the true object of God's wrath, us humans. Filicide is what placates God. The problem with Anselm's theology of atonement is that it casts God as the ultimate abuser, the ultimate oppressor who finds satisfaction through the domination, humiliation, and pain of God's child. This makes the theology of atonement difficult to reconcile with the concept of a loving Father.

For those from marginalized communities, the importance of the cross is not its redemptive powers, for all aspects of Christ's life, death, and resurrection are redemptive. The importance of Jesus' crucifixion is that this is the point when Christ chose solidarity with the world's marginalized, even unto death. Christ becomes one with the crucified people of his time, as well as with all who are crucified today on the crosses of racism, sexism, classism, and heterosexism. For us to die with Christ so that we can also live with him means that we, too, must find solidarity with the world's crucified people. Today's crosses are places of violence, littered with broken lives and bodies. Jesus' solidarity with the world's so-called failures and powerless leads us to become one with the God of the oppressed. And here is the importance of the cross. The paradox of the cross that Paul preaches is that in spite of what it symbolizes, there is resurrection.

Jeremiah 29:1, 4–7

Rather than preaching Jesus, forcing our doctrines and beliefs on all nations so that they can bless *our* God, we should be Jesus, implementing the radical love shown to all and the deep commitment to justice that Jesus exhibited throughout his ministry. Francis of Assisi has been credited with saying, "Preach the gospel at all times and when necessary use words." Evangelism ceases to be an exercise designed to get the unbeliever to believe the same doctrines as the evangelist, and instead becomes sharing the good news with the nonperson that, because he or she is created in the image of the Creator, he or she possesses worth and dignity. Both the dispossessed who have been stripped of all humanity and those possessed with oppressive power need to hear a word about liberation and salvation, a word that moves them from being the colonized "other" or colonizer toward the discovery of their redemption, even if that faith identity is based on a different religious or spiritual worldview than that of the one bringing the good news. This seems to be the advice Jeremiah sends to those who cross borders and find themselves in a strange and alien land. "But seek the welfare of the city where [God has] sent you into exile; pray to the LORD on its behalf, for in its welfare you will find your welfare" (v. 7).

The foreigners should not be molested nor be taken advantage of by the dominant culture. In return, the foreigners should work for the good of the nation in which the foreigners find themselves. They are to pursue the affairs of life by building houses, planting gardens, marrying off their children, and growing (vv. 5–6). This does not mean forsaking one's identity, one's heritage, or one's God. Jeremiah does not call the exiles to stop being Jewish or worshiping their God. Rather, as foreigners, we are to work for the common good of all who also inhabit the land where we find ourselves. Foreigners should be willing to learn from the land's inhabitants, in the same way that the natives of the land can learn from the stranger in their midst.

2 Kings 5:1–3, 7–15c and Psalm 111

In other words, we should not share the arrogance of Naaman, army commander to the king of Aram. Although the story as found in 2 Kings is problematic—that is, God granting victory to the Arameans (v. 1) or the Arameans carrying a Jewish girl into slavery (v. 2)—still, the mighty was open to learn from the vanquished. Hearing from his slave girl that the cure to his leprosy could be found in Israel, he sends notice to Israel's king asking what he should do. The king, recognizing that as a man of flesh and bones there is not much he could do to produce a cure, tears his garments as a sign of mourning—fearing this is a trap that might endanger Israel's survival (v. 7). But the prophet Elisha sees an opportunity and through his actions, not words, gives witness to God.

When Naaman comes before Elisha, the prophet instructs the army commander to bathe seven times in the river Jordan. But Naaman is put off (v. 12): "Are not Abana and Pharpar, the rivers of Damascus, better than all the waters of Israel? Could I not wash in them, and be clean?" His arrogance in thinking that the rivers back home are superior to those of any foreign land misses the point that God is not restricted by geography. Only by trusting God does Naaman discover the God of all the earth (v. 15).

And hence, the lepers, the borderland inhabitants, and the powerful like Naaman—then and now—learn the same lesson that the psalmist proclaims: "Great are the works of the LORD, studied by all who delight in them" (Ps. 111:2). Of course, this is not an easy task. It is always easy to delight in the hope of the Lord this side of Easter Sunday. It is easy to believe in the shadow of resurrection. But for so many of the dispossessed and the disenfranchised living in the space of Holy Saturday, where all that is known is crucifixion, with all its blood, gore, and torture, hope can become an illusion. From the in-between space of borders, the in-between space of crucifixion and resurrection, sometimes the only thing that we can hold on to is the promise that God's justice endures forever (v. 3).

Night of Power (27th Night of Ramadan)

John Kaltner

LEVITICUS 19:15–18
PSALM 115:1–8
ROMANS 1:19–23
LUKE 6:43–45

The Night of Power (*Laylat-al-Qadr*) is important to the Islamic community because, according to Islamic tradition, that is the night that God revealed the Qur'an in its entirety to the prophet Muhammad through the angel Gabriel (Jibril). The Night of Power is observed on the 27th of Ramadan. Since Islam follows the lunar calendar (which is shorter than the solar calendar), it eventually occurs in all of the months of the solar calendar followed by Christians.[1] Given the tensions between some Christian and Islamic communities, the preacher could use the occasion of the Night of Power to consider relationships between these groups. What do we have in common? Where do we differ? How can Christians encourage respect between the two communities?

> Among [God's] signs are these: That [God] created you from dust; and then, Behold! Ye are [human beings] scattered (far and wide)! And among [God's] signs is this: that [God] created for you mates from among yourselves that ye may dwell in tranquility with them, and [God] has put love and mercy between your (hearts). Verily, in that are signs for those who reflect. And among [God's] signs is the creation of the heavens and the earth and the variations in your languages and your color. Verily, in that are signs for those who know.
>
> *Surah 30:20–22*[2]

---

1. From 2011 through 2020 the date of the Night of Power moves from September to August, July, June, May, and April.
2. Surah 30:20–22 in Abdullah Yusef Ali, *The Meaning of the Holy Qur'an*, 9th ed., Arabic and English Texts (Brentwood, MD: Amana Corporation, 1997), 1012–13.

In our fast-paced, high-tech world, images and signs constantly bombard us. Whether driving in the car, reading a book, or sitting in front of a computer screen, we are interpreting and processing information that comes at us non-stop. Most of the time, we do this without even being aware of it. Today's readings remind us that there is another set of signs that are easy to miss in the midst of our hectic and frenzied lives. They are not of human origin, but come from God, the great sign-maker.

When we slow down and reflect on God's signs, we discover that although the world might appear at times to be divided and chaotic, there is an order and purpose to creation. This is one of the central messages of the Bible and the Qur'an, whose revelation to the Prophet Muhammad, beginning in the year 610 CE, is recalled on this Holy Day for Justice.

Qur'an 30:20–22

This Qur'an passage speaks in "sign language." The Arabic word *ayah*, which means "sign" and can also refer to a verse in the Qur'an, is found five times in it. It is the nature of a sign to point beyond itself to something else that it represents or symbolizes. Islam teaches that creation is full of signs that remind us of God's power and authority over all that exists. In fact, it might be said that the Qur'an considers the world to be one big sign that points to its Creator.

Three different signs are mentioned in these three verses, and each highlights God's role as Creator. The first is the creation of humanity and its dispersal throughout the entire world. The spread of people over the face of the earth is a good thing because it is a sign from God. How different this is from the story of the tower of Babel in Genesis 11, where humanity is scattered across the earth as a punishment for trying to be like God. The second sign is the creation of spouses that enable us to enjoy peace, love, and mercy. Our most intimate personal relationships extend beyond ourselves and are markers of God's concern and desire for us to be happy. The third sign is the linguistic and racial diversity—the Qur'an passage says "your languages and your color"—that exists in creation. The physical differences among us should unite us as living and breathing signs of God's plan rather than divide us into groups and factions.

If our diversity is a sign, why are the differences among us so often an obstacle rather than an opportunity? The answer to that question can be found in the other two uses of the word "sign" in this passage. These things— our creation, our relationships, and our diversity—can be signs only for those who reflect and know. We are all born, relate to others, and live in a diverse world. But the Qur'an explains that only those who reflect on those experiences ever come to know what they really represent. Otherwise we remain ignorant and incapable of embracing the diversity present in the world.

For a sign to have any meaning it has to be interpreted, and the Qur'an refers to that act of interpretation as "reflection." It is not enough just to live in the world. We must ponder it. We have to think about what the world is and who we are in it. Reflection leads to understanding what the signs mean.

Because the word for "sign" and "verse" is the same, we might say that the Qur'an and the Bible are literally filled with signs that point toward God. This Holy Day for Justice commemorates the beginning of the revelation of the Qur'an to the Prophet Muhammad, and the very first words he received bring together the themes of creation and knowledge. "Recite! In the name of your Lord who created humanity from a clotted mass. Recite! Your Lord is the most noble One, who taught by the pen. Taught humanity what it did not know" (96:1–5). We come to know by reading the "sign" language written by God's pen, both in the book of the word and in the book of the world.

Psalm 115:1–8 and Romans 1:19–23

These two readings urge us to be on guard against the temptation to create signs of our own and thereby miss the signs of God that are present in creation. They both speak of this in terms of the idols and images we make that can become the gods we worship. These idols are often created in our own image, and the passages describe them in anthropomorphic terms as having body parts and resembling human beings. But they can take other forms as well, like possessions, attitudes, and unhealthy behavior, which makes them harder to recognize and more difficult to overcome. The Romans text reminds us that there is no excuse for such idol making because, though invisible, God can be known through the works of creation (v. 20).

Psalm 115 expresses very well some of the essential components of Muslim theology and belief. It is so in line with Islamic faith that it is a prayer any Muslim would feel comfortable reciting. The reference to giving glory to God's name in the first verse is reminiscent of what the Qur'an and its readers consistently do. Every chapter in the Qur'an but one begins with the words "In the name of God, the merciful One, the compassionate One." This is a phrase that is often on the lips of Muslims, and they regularly invoke it when they begin everyday activities such as waking up, eating, and praying. Many aspects of Muslim life are undertaken in a way that gives glory to God's name.

Muslims can also identify with the next two verses of the psalm. Islam teaches that God's nature is completely transcendent and beyond the capacity of human comprehension. This sometimes leads non-Muslims to conclude that Muslims worship a distant and inaccessible God, and they might be tempted to echo the question of the nations (v. 2), "Where is their God?" But the Muslim response to such a question would be as immediate and direct as what follows in the psalm—God is in heaven and is free to act in any way (v. 3). This is why the Muslim attitude toward divine will is always one of submission, which is the literal meaning of the Arabic word *islam*.

It can be an interesting and revealing exercise to reflect on how Muslims might read and respond to Christian Scripture, and vice versa. In some cases, such as the nature and role of Jesus, the differences between the two faiths are too profound to lead to fruitful results. But with other texts, like Psalm 115, we are often struck by the similarities in how we each read and interpret God's signs.

Leviticus 19:15–18

It is not enough simply to reflect on God's signs and be able to interpret them. They should also transform one's life and influence how one acts. This passage from Leviticus explains what such a transformation will look like. It is a list of dos and don'ts that describes how to become a living sign. Such a person is the antithesis of those mentioned in the readings from Psalm 115 and Romans who worship idols of their own making.

On one level, it might appear that this reading is speaking about how to treat members of one's own community or group. The references to "your neighbor," "your people," and "your kin" can give the impression that these rules of social interaction apply only to those closest to you. But if we keep in mind the message of the Qur'an text that our presence throughout the earth with all our rich diversity of languages and races is part of the divine plan, then we have to see ourselves as united and connected despite the differences among us. We need to expand our understanding of "neighbor," "people," and "kin" to include every person, regardless of his or her race, gender, sexual orientation, or religion. This attitude of inclusivity is expressed well in the admonition to "not be partial to the poor or defer to the great" (v. 15). All people are equal in God's eyes, and therefore must be treated equally by us.

Twice this string of commands is broken by the statement "I am the LORD" (vv. 16, 18). The phrase is a refrain throughout this chapter of Leviticus, where it or the alternative, "I am the LORD your God," is found fifteen times in its thirty-seven verses. Its frequent repetition is a reminder that when we act with justice and fairness toward all people, we are doing what God wants. Or, as a Muslim would say, we are submitting ourselves to a will greater than our own.

Luke 6:43–45

Jesus often taught through parables that, like signs, point beyond themselves to another reality. In this case, his comments about trees and fruit are really observations on people and their actions. Trees and people are normally a mixture of both good and bad. Even the healthiest tree will sometimes produce a bad piece of fruit, just as the nicest person in the world is capable of being cruel or mean. Consequently, more than the mere presence of goodness or badness, the degree of them matters. Anyone who has ever picked an apple with a wormhole in it knows this to be true. You do not cut down the entire tree because of one piece of rotten fruit.

Yet that is precisely what some of us tend to do when it comes to how we view religions other than our own. The first evidence of something foul afoot within it—be it the behavior of one of its followers, or some belief that strikes us as wrong or dangerous—can cause us to question the validity of an entire faith tradition. Perhaps no religion is more susceptible to such stereotyping and generalizing than Islam. Sometimes we misconstrue the actions or words of one misguided Muslim—one bad apple—as representative of what all Muslims do or say. That is the equivalent of labeling all Christians based on the actions of an abortion-clinic bomber who says he is only following the gospel.

The existence of bad Muslims and bad Christians does not mean the religions to which they belong are bad. Both Islam and Christianity have contributed a great deal to human history and civilization, and many of their followers have given their lives to the cause of peace and justice. In this parable, Jesus points out that good and evil have their origin within the heart of a person. Christianity and Islam both teach that we should always embrace good and reject evil; but they also acknowledge human free will and the capacity to choose. So, when an individual acts wrongly in the name of his or her religion, the blame should rest with that person and not with the faith as a whole.

The various religions of the world are another sign of the diversity that exists within humanity. The Qur'an makes it clear that these various groups are part of God's plan and serve an important purpose. "We have given each of you a law and a way. If God had wanted, [God] could have made you one community. But God wished to test you by what [God] has given you, so outrace one another in doing good. All of you will return to God, and [God] will explain to you the things you disagreed over" (Qur'an 5:48b). If religions are to try to outdo one another through good works, how can any of them be evil?

Proper 24 [29]

Henry H. Mitchell

JEREMIAH 31:27–34
PSALM 119:97–104

GENESIS 32:22–31
PSALM 121
2 TIMOTHY 3:14–4:5
LUKE 18:1–8

One of the most fascinating aspects of human history is its variation. That is no less true of its authors. Although raised in Ohio, I have been a longtime resident of the South. As such, I could almost insist that there were two different Civil Wars, all reported by honest scholars. So, too, is it with readers of the Bible. People see and remember that with which they are most familiar, most identified, and concerned. For purposes of full understanding, one needs to study from all angles of vision. As the victim of unspeakable injustices during my youth in Ohio, I am sensitive even to subtle breaches of justice everywhere. These texts speak candidly to injustice in our midst with reassurance of God's inbreaking, renewal, and care.

Jeremiah 31:27–34

This brief pericope continues a vividly positive flow of God's new promises, followed by what might be called two new major contributions. The first appears to be only a kindly correction for a folk saying, explaining or at least naming the undeserved suffering of the younger set of Hebrew exiles. It leads to individual accountability. The second leads to a completely new approach to relating to God and divine law, and to worship anywhere.

The first contribution grew out of the pain of the younger generation, having to live in exile in Nebuchadnezzar's kingdom. Their suffering was enlarged by the way the elders glibly included the younger generation in accepting guilt. It was bad enough just to be there, but it was unbearable for their folks lightly to say that "the parents have eaten sour grapes, and the

434

children's teeth are set on edge" (v. 29). Add this indignation to their already depressed feelings of undeserved punishment and utter powerlessness.

Jeremiah prophesied that this foolishness had to stop. God declared that there would be punishment only for the persons who did the sin. This was a huge improvement over the prevailing belief that whole communities had to bear the guilt of one person, or else cast him or her out of the family and community. This was a revolutionary venture into the doctrine of individual accountability—justified punishment for the culprit, not the whole extended family.

The awesome significance of this advance may perhaps be best seen in a West African novel in which this earlier rule survived into the twentieth century. An abusive husband was convicted and expelled from the tribe. He was cast loose in the cold, cruel world with no ties. It could be worse than jail or even death, just to avoid the punishment falling on the tribe as a whole.[1] We Americans have taken individualism too far in the opposite direction, but it may be closer to justice than the rule against which Jeremiah (and Ezekiel 18) prophesied.

The second major contribution in this pericope is the "new covenant" in which God writes the law on the inner parts—from the Mosaic tablets of stone, to the fleshy tablets of the human heart (vv. 32–33). This obvious personal growth is only a part of the growth brought on by this new covenant. Hearts are portable, whereas the law on stone was stationary in the ark of the covenant. Psalm 137 manifests the huge significance of this change in locus. Here the exiled Hebrews sit in tears by the rivers of Babylon, as they have been taught that they cannot worship Jehovah anywhere but the temple in Jerusalem.

The Lord could now be worshiped anywhere the human heart could be found beating. Except for this new covenant, the diaspora could have destroyed the faith of the Hebrews, and the Christian faith would never have been born. It is awesome to ponder what could have happened without the word of God through the prophet Jeremiah, in these eight verses.

Psalm 119:97–104

The entirety of Psalm 119 can be seen as a work of religious art, with its acrostic format and choruslike repetitions. Because of its length, of course, it was to be no ordinary service of worship. It is also clear that the law that the psalmist so passionately loved could have been better called "instruction," if not "ode to Jehovah." It certainly was not (codal) legalism, as with

1. See Chinua Achebe, *Things Fall Apart*, 50th anniv. ed. (New York: Anchor Books, 1994).

the Pharisees. It could also be thought of as a prayer. Whatever it was called, this meditating on God's wisdom made the psalmist smarter than elders and teachers, in his opinion. This is hardly a worthy motivation for composing and praying spiritual meditations.

This passage for the day (vv. 97–104) begins with "Oh, how I love your law," a declaration that occurs eight times more in the psalm. This would suggest that this first sentence is representative of the outright romantic mode of the entire psalm, like "How sweet are your words to my taste, sweeter than honey to my mouth" (v. 103). The psalmist especially loves God's judgments, which he lovingly praises seventeen times in the 176 verses of Psalm 119.

He mentions his own judgment and sense of justice only once (v. 121). In similarly brief proportion, he reports his own adherence to God's precepts (v. 100) and his own refrain from evil (v. 101), but does not commit himself to any positive action based on these impressively wise judgments. One gets the impression that his claimed conformity with God's will is focused on God's will as strict personal piety and traditional worship, all of it more abstract than real.

Nevertheless, we learn much about the psalmist's attachment to the Word of God, as written on the heart and etched in memory. When we memorize the Word in joy, whether in childhood or later, it becomes naturally applicable to behavior and influential on values, prophetic as well as priestly.

Supposedly underdeveloped cultures with oral traditions have proven far more successful in planting Scriptures in memory and in everyday behavior than have advanced cultures using the latest theories of education. African Americans in slavery survived and resisted on faith and courage, supported by prodigious biblical memory and insights, without literacy. This form of biblical expertise was an important agent driving the work for liberation and social justice. As late as the 1960s, ex-slave descendents and kindred with this "love of God's instruction" sought justice in the courts of law and their right to vote.

It is high time church education and family devotions return to memorization, as consistently as secular schools teach the alphabet and the multiplication tables. Micah 6:8, the Lord's Prayer, the Beatitudes, and Psalm 23 are at least as essential to an adequate preparation for life. This memorization is not a rigid or simply rote process, but must be learned in a joyful mood somewhat akin to the psalmist, who just plain loved the Word.

Genesis 32:22–31

The story of Jacob's wrestling with God is generally taken to symbolize a struggle with a bad conscience, understanding the nameless blessing as some form of forgiveness. Jacob's actual anxiety, however, was not from conscience, but from fear that his physically superior twin, Esau, would kill him. Jacob's mother, Rebekah, shared his fear and advised him to flee for his life (27:42–45). So the plea for divine blessing in Genesis 32 was more for protection from violence than for forgiveness for sin.

It seems odd that so little is said of the way Esau was cheated of both his birthright to material inheritance (25:29–34) and his paternal blessing bestowing seniority and rule (27:1–40). In the first instance, Esau became a victim of vulnerability to his own hunger. Such exploitation by mother and brother, however, was utterly inexcusable, even though legal. In the second, he was a victim of downright criminal conspiracy. Today, people in some communities feel unprotected by law and obligated to take justice into their own hands like Esau.

When communities seem lawless today, it is strange that nobody considers the facts: in the all-too-frequent conflicts of race and class, public school principals and police officers almost always take the side of the more privileged. Those in authority seek peace, but there can be no peace without justice. People at the bottom feel trapped and defenseless, unable to trust their own government. The best prophetic voices have to be found in the church of Jesus Christ, with an occasional assist from the newspapers and other news sources. Unfortunately, these are slowly but surely dying out as guardians against the tyranny of privileged misinformation—the monitors of justice in more than the abstract.

An important word of good news arises from this famous Bible story in the fact that, whatever the precise identity of the spiritual being with whom Jacob physically wrestled, God is personally interested. The struggle for justice is as important as the generous campaigns to feed the hungry, clothe the naked, and keep peace and love among all members of the human family. It would declare that whenever one works to bring justice and deliver the oppressed, one does so with and through God.

Psalm 121

This psalm remains widely used liturgically, and it is sung at the close of every service at Ebenezer Baptist Church in Atlanta, the home church of Martin Luther King Jr. This psalm is an assurance of God's care given to the faithful. Especially when sung, it communicates a sense of security to match the words. It promises preservation from "all evil" (v. 7).

This promise has sweeping implications. In the first place, Psalm 121 is quite direct in its acknowledgment of the existence of "all evil." The beauty of this First Testament hymn is not bought with blindness, nor does a head in the sand feel the security. Evil thrives in the world all around, as well as inside the person. When the Lord's Prayer asks to be delivered from evil, one should have in mind the evil within as well as the evil without. The preceding petition to be kept away from temptation shows awareness of this universal inner potential for evil.

The protection against the presence of evil reflects the promise and peaceful existence possible precisely where one is at work. Labors like Jesus' commitment to heal the brokenhearted (depressed) or to set at liberty the unjustly captive (Luke 4:18), or Jesus' parable of the Empty House (Matt. 12:43–45), illustrate how full rather than empty the abundant life should be.

We can see the relationship between the life of contentment and security, on the one hand, and the life of fruitful work for the reign of God, on the other, in a corny story told of a missionary who had to cross a jungle area too dense for car or beast. On foot, he had only gone halfway when he was overtaken by dense darkness. He pondered his potential for becoming the breakfast of a wild beast, as he sat sleeplessly and prayed. Suddenly he remembered that our caring God "neither slumbers nor sleeps" (v. 4). Thus assured, he told God, "There is no need for both of us to stay awake." With that, he stretched out and slept the rest of the night in peace, awakening fresh the next morning. Whether as missionaries or advocates for justice or hands for the needy, we can serve best in the empowering certainty that God provides protection for our going out and coming in.

2 Timothy 3:14–4:5

Issues of authorship aside, today's passage offers a very Pauline pastor's manual of practical advice, first as to biblical understanding and lifestyle, and then concerning sermon content. In the former, Paul offers his own life as model for answering any questions Timothy might have had. This is a serious suggestion, based not on false pride, but on a humble objectivity concerning how people learn best.

Many years ago, I heard a great preacher, Howard Thurman, address a great theme, which I have long since forgotten. What I remember is that he first heard this great biblical wisdom from the lips of his ex-slave, illiterate grandmother. This was not his last such reference, nor was he the only sage citing such authority. Indeed, my own humble notes have often included Bible verses introduced: "My Daddy used to say."

In all these cases, it was not a matter of seeking to upstage Bible authority. It was, rather, a way of rendering a truth in memorable as well as concrete, visual imagery, without which authority would have been moot. With the Word served in the context of real life, one had the whole experience as a visual aid to both retention and impact. Paul used his life as an effective teaching tool long before the process had this name. This manifest wisdom shines in primordial cultures and oppressed living conditions.

The advice in 4:1–2 warns that as a preacher, Timothy will be judged if his proclamation of the Word omits even the unpopular judgment of its own people. Today, one seldom if ever hears Paul's rebuke, reproof, or exhortations in pulpits enlightened by contemporary theological wisdom. Predominantly negative preaching took on a bad reputation in many circles, because hellfire and brimstone engendered guilt anxieties, often known to bring on psychoses. At the very least, hellfire did and still does manipulate vast and gullible audiences. This professional criticism is just as legitimate as Paul's advice, so what is one to do?

First of all, since "perfect love casts out fear" (1 John 4:18), sermons must emphasize the positive good news and bring trust, not fear. The awe-type fear that is part of reality must never be more than a third of any sermon, and never in the introduction (to lose the audience), nor in the celebration (one cannot celebrate fear).

The realities of evil and the inevitably hard judgments that God will heap against inhumane cruelty and injustice have to be declared. But they must be declared as the truth in love, not the angry joy so common in some media ministries. And the positive behaviors that must fill the vacuum from which evil departed need more development and warm attention than the evil itself. The overall impact of the sermon, with very rare exceptions, must be a freely chosen and joyous desire to do and to be what the biblical text suggests. The word "celebration" means that one will be glad, not mad, about the will of God, as revealed in the text.

Luke 18:1–8

There are at least three popular options for the interpretation of this parable. Luke said Jesus was teaching persistence in prayer. The narrative taught internally that we should protect the powerless from being cheated and treated unjustly. Jesus concluded with the hope that the exploited would trust God to avenge their unjust treatment. One option not to be found among scholarly writings concerns the class-conscious, unfair, preoccupied judge. He reminds me of some judges and of some red-tape machines called county welfare departments. Some of these, of course, are underfunded and forced to stall. But too often only the persistence of the wrongly treated has been the primary route to justice or just relief for a few people I have known.

Today, too many government officials and agencies have no fear of God or respect for the people they are charged to help. The fear and respect underscored in this text draw on both God and those with the power to enact justice with integrity and humane concerns. Our crying need is for far more such people, agencies, and especially churches.

One of the most publicized of all miscarriages of justice is the number of people convicted of rape or murder now being released after they are proven innocent by DNA tests. It is terrifying to ponder how many other thousands of hurriedly convicted powerless persons lose years of freedom, and even life itself, because someone neglects or denies the full rights of trial. All too often, as the parable laments, justice becomes too bothersome.

It should never be forgotten that the crucifixion of Jesus was an unjust execution, and that the established churches of his day were worse than silent: they urged Pilate's court to "let him be crucified" (Matt. 27:22). Inasmuch as we allow it to be done to them today, we do it unto him.

World Food Day (October 16)

James L. McDonald

2 KINGS 4:38–44
PSALM 42:1–5
1 TIMOTHY 6:6–12
MATTHEW 25:31–46

World Food Day, which was first observed in 1981, takes place on October 16 in recognition of the founding of the United Nations Food and Agriculture Organization. The purpose of World Food Day is to arouse action against world hunger. From the perspective of World Food Day, the preacher can encourage the congregation to engage in comprehensive efforts to end hunger by directly providing food for hungry people, by pressing for patterns of growing and using food that benefit local communities, by taking action designed to change systems of food production and distribution, and by advocating healthy and responsible eating.

No war in all of history has ever killed so many humans and spread so much suffering and disease in any year as world hunger now does annually. So if we cannot solve all of humanity's problems, let us resolve to end at least one by 2030—human hunger. If we fail to do this, we will stand condemned before the bar of history. . . . If there is a scale of divine justice in the universe, we would deserve to choke on our food even as we listen to the cries of the starving.

George McGovern[1]

"God is not an indifferent bystander" (Heb. 12:28–29 *The Message*). The passages for today urge us to look at our lives and our country from the point of

1. George McGovern, *The Third Freedom: Ending Hunger in Our Time* (New York: Simon and & Schuster, 2001), 156.

view of the long sweep of history and then ask ourselves, as George McGovern does, whether there is a "scale of divine justice in the universe." Clearly the biblical answer is yes. The "judge who is God of all" (Heb. 12:23 RSV) cares about the way we live. If we take that answer to heart, then there are clear choices to make—personally and as a nation. At the center of those choices will be our understanding of who Jesus Christ is.

2 Kings 4:38–44

The books of Kings recount the history of Israel (and Judah) from the death of David to the exile of 586 BCE. This period in Israel's history saw both good and evil kings, moral achievements and failures, and religious fidelity and apostasy. Here is where we meet Israel's prophets Elijah and Elisha, who remind the people and their rulers what it means to live faithfully as God's people under God's covenant, and warn of the consequences if they disregard God's commands. Nonetheless, the people and their rulers have drifted away from God, chasing after idols and forsaking their unique identity as God's elect.

In today's reading, Elisha reveals his ability to work miracles and further establishes his credentials as a man of God. In a time of famine Elisha provides food, first by detoxifying a pot of ill-prepared stew, then by multiplying a small gift of grains to feed a hundred people, with some to spare. Elisha's prophetic ministry shows people what they are capable of doing if they stay closely attuned to the Lord.

My colleague David Beckmann, president of Bread for the World, notes that "most spiritually alert people are thoughtful about what God is doing in our individual lives, but often less attentive to God's saving presence in world history."[2] He points out that the world has made remarkable and dramatic progress against hunger over the last three or four decades. Whereas approximately one in three people went to bed hungry in 1970, now it is closer to one in six who struggle with hunger on a daily basis.[3]

This escape from hunger and poverty has been driven in large part by the hard work and faith of poor people themselves. But it is not their efforts alone that have made this possible. Other people and social institutions have contributed. Scientists developed new seeds and boosted the productivity of farmers in poor countries. Agricultural economists, development workers, and extension agents introduced fresh ideas, techniques, and technological

---

2. David Beckmann, *Exodus from Hunger: We Are Called to Change the Politics of Hunger* (Louisville, KY: Westminster John Knox Press, 2010), 9.

3. Ibid., 6.

changes that helped farmers diversify their crops, increase production, and get their products to market in a more timely way. Governments—often at the urging of citizens' groups and farmers themselves—adopted better policies and invested more in agriculture, education, and health to help farmers improve their lives and livelihoods.

This, too, as David Beckmann reminds us, is evidence of God moving in our time and what can happen when people are attentive to that divine movement.

Psalm 42:1–5

Psalm 42 conveys the intense ache of someone searching for a profound experience of the living God, without success. "When shall I come and behold the face of God?" (v. 2) is a cry of anguish. To whom is the question addressed? Verse 1 is addressed to God, but the ensuing question seems addressed to no one in particular. In verse 5 the psalmist addresses his own soul.

The psalmist teeters between hope and despair. The tears, isolation, and emptiness of the present vie with the remembrance of an earlier time when he led a throng with "glad shouts and songs of thanksgiving" (v. 4) into the house of God.

The line between hope and despair is thin indeed; the bigger our hopes, the more profound our despair. If we expect little from life, how much can we be disappointed? But those who have experienced the power and presence of the living God have become filled with hope. Hope lifts our spirits and moves us, body and soul, mind and strength, to imagine a different world. Hope motivates us to risk our lives for the sake of the gospel, to take action for Christ's sake.

But the world does not change on our timetable, and we are tempted to despair. We forget that change is never a straight-line process. Rather, it is two steps forward and one step back, a zig and a zag, an action and a reaction. When someone or some group initiates change, there are forces that resist and push back.

This is something the prophet Elijah did not understand. When he defeated the prophets of Baal (1 Kings 18), he thought that Israel would straighten up and fly right. He had not counted on Jezebel. He had not figured out that change does not come easily or all at once; it takes time and patience, commitment and endurance. So Elijah became depressed and demoralized.

We can feel that way too when confronted with the reality of chronic hunger and poverty and its attendant suffering. This recognition makes the psalmist's anguished cry from three thousand years ago seem very contemporary. We, too, long to see the face of God in a broken world.

Matthew 25:31–46

"Lord, when was it that we saw you . . .?" (vv. 37–39) is the ultimate theological question. Both the sheep and the goats ask it. Neither recognized that Christ was present in "the least of these" (v. 40). The answer depended on where they looked for Christ and what they did in response to what they saw. So, we should analyze where to look for Christ's presence in our world. We also should reexamine how we treat others, what we do when confronted with pain and suffering, and how we react to those whom our society and culture consider "the least." This story is an invitation to reorient our lives.

Someone once told me: "In my experience there is no more difficult group to address about Jesus Christ than a group of Christians." Most Christians see Jesus where they want to see him. Our desire to be stress-free, safe, and secure, our pursuit of happiness and the good life, and our efforts to avoid problems and people who make us uncomfortable blind us to the reality of Christ's presence in our midst and in our world.

Nothing illustrates better our misunderstandings about who Jesus is than his own vision of the last judgment in Matthew 25. It is often called a parable. But most parables begin with something familiar—a woman losing a coin, a boy running away from home, a pearl, a seed—and use it to point to something unfamiliar, such as some quality of the reign of God that would never have occurred to us otherwise. Matthew 25 does the opposite; it begins with the unfamiliar presence of angels and a cosmic tribunal, and moves to the familiar—caring for the sick, visiting the prisoner, feeding the hungry, welcoming the stranger, clothing the naked.

A number of years ago my family and I toured the highlands of Scotland. There were sheep everywhere. And, city slickers that we are, we discovered something that is no doubt obvious to country folk: there are many varieties of sheep and goats. Moreover, some sheep look like goats, and vice versa. In fact, sheep and goats are more alike than different. Both are prized animals. Each is productive and useful; for example, cashmere and mohair sweaters are made from goat wool. There are differences in temperaments but again, the stereotypes do not hold in practice across varieties. So you cannot tell sheep and goats apart by looking at them, by their temperaments, or even by their contributions to the economy. What separates them, Jesus says, is the way they treat "the least"—the poor, the marginal, the dispossessed, the afflicted, the vulnerable. Following such insight, Dietrich Bonhoeffer wrote from his prison cell in Nazi Germany that the challenge for followers of Christ is to see the great events of world history from below, from the perspective of the outcasts, the suspects, the maltreated, the powerless, the oppressed, the reviled—in short, from the perspective of those who suffer.[4]

In this story of the last judgment, those who stand before the throne are nations (v. 32)—not individuals, not churches. This makes the task of those who call themselves Christian even harder. Jesus asks those who follow him to move into the public arena and help shape the policies and priorities of the nations. In the sweep of history, God sent Jesus to save the world—not just some people, or certain types of people, or certain groups, but the world. Nations are judged according to how they care for "the least."

This is an extraordinary claim. When it comes to judging nations, God cares first and foremost about what nations did for those who suffer. God does not judge nations according to their political philosophies, the form of their governments, the power of their economies, or the might of their armies. Not even their creativity, inventiveness, or intellectual sophistication count on the last day. What counts is what they did for those who were hungry, thirsty, naked, or sick, for the prisoner and the stranger in their midst.

1 Timothy 6:6–12

The moral exhortation of Paul's First Letter to Timothy is instructive for us as well. This letter, 2 Timothy, and Titus are called the Pastoral Epistles, and they focus on how the church as an institution should conduct itself. Despite the looming questions of Paul's authorship here, our passage should be read as an instruction from one church leader to another.

Timothy, who is a young man, is now in Ephesus (thirty miles inland from the Mediterranean coast of modern Turkey). Ephesus was one of the great cities of the Middle East during the first centuries after Jesus Christ. It was a vibrant, major trade center, with growing numbers of wealthy people alongside poor people, slaves, and people of modest means. Lots of new ideas swirled around Ephesus; social norms and patterns were changing and challenged. These social and economic forces permeated the church and created conflicts among Christians themselves. Paul and Timothy were friends and coworkers in the faith, and throughout two letters Paul has been worried that Timothy and others might be swayed by false teachers and drawn into the seductive, corrupting influences of the dominant culture in which he lives.

Our verses in the sixth chapter contain a number of well-known sayings. Among them are "we brought nothing into the world, so that we can take

---

4. See Dietrich Bonhoeffer, *Letters and Papers from Prison*, enlarged ed., ed. Eberhard Bethge (New York: Simon & Schuster, 1997).

nothing out of it," "the love of money is a root of all kinds of evil," and "fight the good fight" (vv. 7, 10, and 12). These three sayings become more powerful when they are considered together, as the passage urges.

Paul's plea here is for simplicity and singleness of purpose. The quest to accumulate is corrupting, he says. His words ring true in our time. After two thousand years, we still struggle with our love of money and the urge to hold fast to material goods rather than to "what is good" (Rom. 12:9). Most people will quote Paul's phrase as "money is the root of all evil," but Paul's statement is not so simplistic. Even in Paul's day, money was a necessary ingredient of a well-functioning economy. Moreover, it is not money itself that Paul condemns, but the love of it. Furthermore, the love of money is not *the* root of evil, but one root among many. Finally, evil is not a singular phenomenon, but is manifest in multiple ways.

As George McGovern's words make clear, world hunger in our time easily qualifies as one of the manifestations of evil. And the love of money can clearly be identified as one of the roots of this evil. How is it that we have hungry people in the midst of a global economy that, according to the World Bank, reached $32 trillion in 2007 and may be more than double that by 2030?

Today, we hear the gospel of prosperity—God rewards the faithful with health and wealth—preached in congregations of every stripe across the world. Our difficulty is that we live in the midst of countries and cultures that are thoroughly captured by the love of money. Our own societies and churches are so caught in the web of materialism that we scarcely know the extent of our captivity.

But rather than becoming overwhelmed by the enormity of the problem, we should start with our acknowledgment of the anguish of Psalm 42 and then take the example of Elisha to heart. Elisha was a prophet because he sought to show his own society that small miracles, including feeding hungry people, are possible for those who are closely attuned to God. And then we should appropriate the lessons of Matthew 25 and do the works of justice that will reveal to us the face of God. This is the good fight to which Paul and the gospel call us.

Proper 25 [30]

James Anthony Noel

JOEL 2:23–32
PSALM 65

JEREMIAH 14:7–10, 19–22
PSALM 84:1–7
2 TIMOTHY 4:6–8, 16–18
LUKE 18:9–14

My approach to these texts is literary-critical, since space does not allow for a detailed historical-critical treatment of all that were assigned for today's lectionary reading. The underlying thematic in these texts is judgment/justice/just and righteousness. In Hebrew and Greek the words for "judgment" are *mishpat* and *krisis*, respectively. The words for "righteous" and "just" in Hebrew and Greek are *tsaddiq* and *diakaios*, respectively. Justice, justification, and righteousness are closely related terms. Both the First and Second Testaments conceive justice and righteousness as God's primary attributes. Justice occurs when God delivers the poor and oppressed from their plight and in so doing renders them justified or righteous. The deliverance of the Hebrews from Egyptian bondage is the supreme case in point in the First Testament, and the crucifixion/resurrection event is its supreme instance in the Second Testament.

Psalm 65

This psalm signifies justice when the writer says: "By awesome deeds you answer us with deliverance, O God of our salvation" (v. 5). The awesome deed was the Exodus. The giving of the law subsequent to the Exodus must be placed within this framework. The prophets held Israel accountable to the memory of its deliverance and God's expectation for it to be a just society or nation patterned upon the law. Thus, God's judgment is dual—it destroys oppressors and delivers the oppressed. Being delivered from oppression, practicing justice, and waiting for justice's eschatological fulfillment constitutes being justified, made righteous, or chosen. This entails vigilance over one's status within this divine scheme, lest one fall on the wrong side of the equation. Paul's theology fits within this scheme, as do the Gospels.

That the metaphors of slavery and freedom are particularly prominent in Paul's letters should caution us against downplaying their eschatology in favor of individualistic interpretations and applications. The slave population was as large as 30 to 40 percent of the Roman populace. Paul clearly regards slavery as the most apt metaphor to describe the human condition under the power of sin when he talks about being "bought with a price," "redeemed," "adopted," becoming "citizens," and being "made free from the law" (e.g., 1 Cor. 6:20; 7:23; Gal. 4:5; Rom. 8:15). Therefore, Paul's notions of redemption, salvation, and justification through Christ's crucifixion and resurrection are connected with the exodus event in the First Testament. Both events call for or elicit testimony on the part of those delivered from the power of sin in the form of praise as well as confession—and not necessarily in this order. In Psalm 65, for instance, the psalmist recognizes that God's forgiveness overcomes our iniquities (v. 3). Confession or contrition marks our approach or prayers to God (v. 2); God's response is deliverance, goodness, and plenitude in creation.

Sacvan Bercovitch has shown, in *The Puritan Origins of the American Self*, how the first European settlers in New England imagined themselves as reenacting the Hebrew entry into Canaan. This endowed the Puritans with both a sense of entitlement to the land and a sense of accountability to the God from whom it had been bequeathed. Be that as it may, American culture has been woefully lacking in its ability to be self-critical. It regards itself as representing the ideal of a just society constituted by freedom, democracy, and the rule of law. This was not always the case. During the colonial period, Americans, at least in New England, were accustomed to the genre of preaching termed the "jeremiad" (etymologically related to the prophet Jeremiah), which placed society before the bar of divine justice. Calamity and misfortune indicated God's displeasure over some violation of the covenant that formed the foundation of the New Englanders' self-understanding. This self-understanding is best signified in the phrase "a City upon a Hill," which John Winthrop highlighted in the sermon he preached shortly before the Puritans disembarked from the *Arbella* in 1630.[1] Although the corrupted social structures of Europe precluded sufficient scope for Christians to fashion the kind of society God intended for God's people, here early Americans claimed to be such societies that would be emulated by the entire world. Thus, an ethical standard was posited as the measurement of America's moral health and political future. Both were interrelated. If Americans lived up to this stan-

---

1. See *Collections of the Massachusetts Historical Society*, 3rd ser., 7 (1838): 31–48.

dard, its future was guaranteed. If Americans were derelict, repentance would be required to receive God's forgiveness and continued blessing. Jonathan Edwards's famous sermon "Sinners in the Hands of an Angry God"[2] elaborated on this theological worldview, as did numerous preachers throughout the Great Awakenings.

Some American religious history texts narrate this phenomenon as a movement away from collective self-criticism during the colonial period to individual economic preoccupations during and following the revolutionary period. On closer historical examination, however, we can see that the notion of America as "a City upon a Hill" had reified a sense of entitlement from the very beginning of European settlement—or should we say, conquest—of America. The Native Americans who first encountered Winthrop and the other Pilgrims had, at best, a subjugated space assigned to them in the "City upon a Hill." This was also true for the Africans who would arrive beginning in 1619. European American exceptionalism actually functioned to legitimate Native American genocide and African American slavery as it elaborated itself into such doctrines as Manifest Destiny and racial superiority. Such doctrines absolved the nation from any sense of accountability for the horrors involved in its continued destruction of indigenous peoples during its territorial expansion and the importation and subjugation of enslaved Africans. The American people imagined as "white" people became the object of religious valorization in what sociologist Robert Bellah termed "civil religion."[3] The implicit theology of this religion undergirds America's callous disregard for poverty and racial oppression in the United States and its military interventions abroad designed to protect its oil interests. This implicit theology also undergirds America's judgment on other nations as deficient in freedom and democracy and, thus, requiring tutelage. And our own "deliverance" thereby remains in question!

Jeremiah 14:7–10, 19–22 and Luke 18:9–14

We have such a situation, as described above, in the reading from Jeremiah 14:7–10 and 19–22. Economic distress has forced Judah to a repentance of sorts. The community confesses, "Our iniquities testify against us" (v. 7), and entreats God to act on its behalf. God, however, is not through punishing Judah and says through Jeremiah that the Lord "will remember their iniquity and punish their sins" (v. 10). Jeremiah is even told in verse 11 to

---

2. Jonathan Edwards, *Selected Sermons of Jonathan Edwards* (Memphis, TN: General Books LLC, 2010), 78–97.
3. See Robert N. Bellah, "Civil Religion in America," *Journal of American Academy of Arts and Sciences* 96, no. 1 (Winter 1967): 1–21.

cease praying for the nation; as God expounds, "I do not hear their cry; and although they offer burnt offering and grain offering, I do not accept them; but by the sword, by famine, and by pestilence I consume them" (v. 12). But Judah wants to avoid judgment. They recognize they have no future without God's grace or God's call. In turn, we are left to ask, does America want to avoid judgment? Indeed, does America even feel it has anything to confess? If America confesses, then to what extent does confession bear the work of repentance and transformation? The desire to avoid judgment may not reflect a desire for transformation.

In contrast, the despicable tax-gatherer in the reading from Luke 18:9–14 is willing to accept whatever God intends to do with him for his participation in his people's oppression. A message that calls for national repentance is almost impossible to preach in American churches because it is impossible to imagine ourselves under judgment from God. We suppose judgment belongs more to other nations. We are always somehow exempt from divine judgment and wrath because we are exceptional. Our national piety is more akin to that of the Pharisee in today's reading from Luke 18. If we ever made a national corporate confession, it would contain some form of comparison that would constitute self-justification and self-righteousness. We may not be perfect, but we are not as bad as others. But we cannot have it both ways. Not being as evil as others is not the biblical criteria for being exceptional, or "chosen"— or, let us say, "righteous."

If America persists in regarding itself as exceptional or chosen, it must begin to understand biblically that we do not possess any inherent capacity for doing justice—especially one based on race or nationality—but rather are called to confession and repentance. Simultaneously, we must understand that any blessing we claim requires something of us in terms of the vigilance of our theology and praxis.

2 Timothy 4:6–8, 16–18 and Joel 2:23–32

In 2 Timothy, Paul does not view his justification as something he has earned through his sufferings. He has "kept the faith" (v. 7) in the one who alone can justify or make one righteous. He says: "From now on there is reserved for me the crown of righteousness, which the Lord, the righteous judge, will give me on that day" (v. 8). In essence, as we shall see in Psalm 84, the idea is that one's strength or righteousness lies within God.

We would be misreading Paul if we think during his final days he no longer had a sense of the judgment that would be imposed on earthly structures and systems by the righteous Judge and that he only expected it to apply to individual souls after their departure from the body through death. Nothing could be further from the case. Paul had not abandoned the First Testament notion of God as the judge and ultimate arbiter of human history and its structures. If he had done so, the gospel message would not speak to the oppressed in the way it spoke to African American slaves who, resonating with the revolutionary implications of Paul's message and overhearing the apocalyptic echoes from Joel 2:23–32, sang: "My Lord what a moanin' when de stars begin to fall . . . you'll hear de trumpet sound to wake de nations underground, looking to my God's right hand when de stars begin to fall."[4] Suffering and oppression force one into an apocalyptic mode of imagination and action.

That historic song expresses an apocalyptic and eschatological yearning for deliverance on the part of a community that was enslaved in a nation founded on the principle of freedom. The Declaration of Independence stated: "all men are created equal, . . . endowed by their Creator with certain unalienable rights, . . . among these are life, liberty and the pursuit of happiness." However, the *krisis* structured into American society ensued from some persons being able by law to hold other persons in bondage in this pursuit. In 1857 Chief Justice Taney stated in his opinion on the Supreme Court *Dred Scott v. Sandford* case that "neither the class of persons who had been imported as slaves, nor their descendants, whether they had become free or not, were then acknowledged as part of the people, nor intended to be included in the general words used in that memorial document." Furthermore, since "they had for more than a century before been regarded as beings of an inferior order, and altogether unfit to associate with the white race, either in social or political relations; and so far inferior, that they had no rights which the white man was bound to respect; and that the negro might justly and lawfully be reduced to slavery for his benefit. He was bought and sold, and treated as an ordinary article of merchandise and traffic, whenever a profit could be made by it."[5] In Taney's mind this was ordained by God and, therefore, justified. He legitimated racial oppression through his legal rendering. How often do we continue to distort God's justice, even poison that justice, with our distortions of divine sanction? How will God respond to us, and how shall we respond to God's justice?

Psalm 84:1–7

America's *krisis* is exacerbated by the attitude of many white Americans toward people of color that is identical to Taney's. The only difference is that their language is differently coded. People of color and their allies in the struggle

4. See "My Lord What a Moanin," in *Songs of Zion* (Nashville: Abingdon Press, 1981).
5. See text of "Dred Scott Decision" in *Race, Racism and American Law*, ed. Derrick Bell (Boston: Little, Brown and Co., 1973), 6–9.

for racial equality and justice know what vicious and hateful sentiments lie behind the hysteria around immigration, rallies by Tea Partiers to take their country back, and efforts to repeal the amendments to the Constitution that legally recognized African Americans as citizens. It signifies the continued attempt in America to consign people of color to a subjugated sphere within the "City upon a Hill" now grown into an empire. This means one has to be careful not to individualize and sentimentalize this psalm, in which the writer imagines how wonderful it will be to dwell in God's house (vv. 1–5).

In a society still very much segregated, even among churches, the power issue is who determines those who are welcome into the sacred and coveted space of the social body. That space will be pluralistic only when America engages in a form of confession that circumcises its heart. That means confronting its deep-seated racism head-on. Then what Langston Hughes longed for, even called for, in his 1938 poem "Let America Be America Again" will come to fruition, as the oppressed of this land will be unrelenting to see this country and culture repent and rehabilitate. If this is delayed, the poor and marginalized may begin to see themselves as the agents of the apocalypse as they act on the vision and dreams spoken of by the prophet Joel. Still, Hughes seems to embrace the longing of the psalmist, whose "soul longs, indeed it faints for the courts of the LORD; . . . [to] sing for joy to the living God. Even the sparrow finds a home, and the swallow a nest for herself, where she may lay her young" (vv. 2–3).

Children's Sabbaths
(Third Weekend in October)

Shannon Daley-Harris

DEUTERONOMY 6:20–25
PSALM 128
2 TIMOTHY 1:1–7
JOHN 17:11–16

The National Observance of Children's Sabbaths® weekend was founded by the Children's Defense Fund in 1992 to encourage religious communities to honor children as sacred gifts and to nurture, protect, and advocate on behalf of children. Congregations focus worship, education programs, and activities on the urgent needs of children in our nation and on God's call to respond with justice and compassion. This event is designated for the third weekend of October. The sermon is a vital opportunity to give voice to the crises facing our nation's children—such as poverty, violence, lack of health care, abuse, and neglect—as well as opportunities for us to respond with justice and mercy to improve the quality of life for children in the local community and throughout our nation.

Children come into the world with God's commission to live and learn and sing and dance and grow, then too many are decommissioned by adults who prey on, neglect, abuse, exploit, disrespect, discourage, and mislead them. . . . Children come into the world as God's gifts of life and love yet so many are spurned and not spared the ravages of war and gun violence that murder and maim and corrode their dreams and self-esteem.

Marian Wright Edelman[1]

The texts designated for the Children's Sabbaths Holy Day for Justice affirm the importance of nurturing faith from one generation to the next and remind us that memories of how God has been active in our lives in the past offer

1. Marian Wright Edelman, *Lanterns: A Memoir of Mentors* (Boston: Beacon Press, 1999), 133.

hope and direction for our actions now and in the future. That memory and hope can sustain God's people in difficult times and good ones.

Deuteronomy 6:20–25

The passage from Deuteronomy is part of Moses' exhortations to the community following his announcement of the Ten Commandments. Even at this moment, he not only focuses on the immediate faithfulness of the community but also looks forward to the next and future generations, anticipating the challenges and opportunities for sustaining the unity, integrity, and life of the faith community. How will future generations who do not have firsthand experience of God's deliverance in the exodus be guided? The text anticipates that children will seek answers to understand the basis of their community's faith. Moses charges parents to pass on to their children that God promises well-being and righteousness for those who keep God's commandments.

Moses instructs the community to relate the story of enslavement, exodus, and entry into the promised land as the precursor and foundation for the commandments. Throughout the Hebrew Scriptures, the communal experiences of slavery and exodus are identified as the basis for just, ethical action and treatment of those who are most vulnerable in the community, and the importance of remembering such experience is underscored. "You shall not deprive a resident alien or an orphan of justice; you shall not take a widow's garment in pledge. Remember that you were a slave in Egypt and the LORD your God redeemed you from there; therefore I command you to do this" (Deut. 24:17–18; see also vv. 19–22).

In our own day we know the challenges of communicating past moments of social transformation and liberation—and how we experienced God's hand in them—to generations who were not there to experience them. How do we transmit the meaning of the abolition of slavery? Of the end of child labor in the U.S.? Of women's suffrage? Of the liberation of Auschwitz and Buchenwald and the end of the Holocaust? Of the Civil Rights Movement? Of the women's liberation movement? Of the end of apartheid? Our text invites us to tell our stories, and our ancestors' stories, of distress and deliverance, of captivity and liberation, of the awful and the awesome to our children. We hope that these stories might illuminate and transmit our faith so that children come to know the love, protection, and promises of God, as well as our love for, dependence on, and endeavor to be obedient to God.

Even as we celebrate and learn from those past experiences of deliverance, we are invited to look for the situations today that call us to seek God's liberating action for those yet in bondage who await liberation—from the bondage of poverty, abuse, unsafe communities, epidemic, or other circumstance. We owe the blessings of our lives to God. And we are obligated, as ones whom God has protected and for whom God has provided, to extend the same protection and provision, justice and compassion, to those who are now most vulnerable and in need.

Another insight that this text offers for this Holy Day for Justice is the vision that God "brought us *out* from there in order to bring us *in*." It invites us, on Children's Sabbaths, to consider not only *out* of what bondage we would bring our children—poverty, abuse, neglect, lack of health care, violent schools and neighborhoods, needless suffering, risky behavior—but also to envision *into* what we seek to bring our children—life with sufficient economic resources, loving families, health care, good schools, safe communities, well-being, and positive choices. What is the "promised land" to which every child should be assured safe passage?

Psalm 128

This psalm is understood as a companion to Psalm 127 (see Children's Sabbaths lectionary, Year A). The first four verses are framed as beatitude, beginning with *ashre*, translated "happy" in the NRSV and "blessed" in the NIV. The focus is first on work (v. 2) and then on family life (v. 3). The promise in verse 4 is that one who fears God will be blessed (*yeborak*). Verses 5 and 6 move to benediction, "The LORD bless you . . ." (*yebarekkâ*), a benediction offered not only for the individual but then for the nation with the hope of prosperity, future generations, and peace.

In our world, in which one billion people toil from sunup to sundown yet earn less than a dollar a day, in which each year ten million children under five die, in which millions of children in our rich nation live in poverty,[2] one can hear the words of Psalm 128 only as prayer and not as promise delivered or present reality. (Note that verses 2–4 are all in the future tense in English, not the present tense.) The difficult reality is that faithful people around the world *do not* benefit from their own labor. Life is extraordinarily harsh for a billion people living in extreme poverty. Children, rather than flourishing and sitting at table with their parents, are not thriving—children in our overfed nation suffer hunger, and children in developing countries may be far from home, serving in bonded labor.

This psalm is one of the songs of ascent sung by pilgrims on their way to Jerusalem, striking a chord of hope and expectation even as the pilgrims' feet trudged forward, step by step. The psalm is addressed not to God but to a

---

2. See "Child Research Data and Publications," Children's Defense Fund Research Library, http://www.childrensdefense.org/child-research-data-publications/ (accessed October 22, 2011).

fellow traveler on the way, to encourage, to sustain, to motivate, and to bless. What words will we find to articulate the blessing God intends for us that will encourage, sustain, motivate, and bless another?

As we journey toward justice, the psalm invites us to hold before our eyes this vision of the world God intends. What can we do to realize the promise of a time in which all are nourished and sustained by their work? What change can we create to end economic exploitation, prepare young people for employment, and support parents in securing jobs? How can we transform our society and our communities so that families know happiness, well-being, and a world at peace? What change must we make, what can we put in place, so that all family members flourish and are a blessing to each other? What is needed so that our communities and nations may prosper?

2 Timothy 1:1–7

Paul lifts up in two different ways the faith of several generations. First, he refers to previous generations of his own family and affirms that these Jewish ancestors worshiped with a "clear conscience," just as he does now in his newfound Christianity. Paul shows no need to denigrate or deny the integrity of his Jewish ancestors' faith here. Then Paul affirms the multigenerational faith of Timothy's own family, a faith that was handed from his grandmother to his mother and now to him. On this Children's Sabbaths weekend, we may affirm the ways that each generation can help to nurture faith in the next.

Paul addresses the gift of God in Timothy. Unlike "fruits of the Spirit" (such as patience, love, and humility), which are meant to be the same in every believer, gifts of the Spirit are unique in each person but have the one intended purpose of the common good. On Children's Sabbaths, each of us is called to examine anew what gifts of the Spirit we have received and how we might use them for the common good—especially to improve the lives of children and families. How can we use our voices, the gift of utterance, on behalf of children and justice? What prophetic word might we proclaim? When are we called to identify the "false prophets"—of greed and consumption, of scare tactics, and false advertising that would undermine important change for children? How can we educate others about the needs of children and families and what must be done? Can we decipher policy jargon and make political action accessible to others? What practical ministry can we engage in to make an immediate difference in children's lives?

Paul's letter speaks not just of Timothy's gift, but also of the need to rekindle it. What once burned brightly has died down but not yet gone out. A real fire is rekindled with three things: something that will flare up quickly like tinder or newspaper, fresh wood that will keep the fire going, and oxygen.

To rekindle gifts of the Spirit for the common good, especially of children, we might find that the fresh tinder of a crisis or news item catches attention quickly, but we also need the fresh wood of new partners, ideas, and resources that will keep the fire burning for a long time, as well as the oxygen—*ruach*, breath, fresh wind of the Spirit—to fan us back into flame.

Finally, Paul reminds us that God's gift does not come with a spirit of cowardice, but with power and love and discipline. What fears are holding us back from creating the dramatic change needed to improve the lives of children in our nation and world? How can we remind each other of, and find in ourselves, the spirit of power and love and discipline to build a movement for children that ends child poverty, that assures health care for every child, that redirects young people from prison onto paths of promise, that ensures that every child can live in the fullness of God's intentions for love and justice?

John 17:11–16

Our text is found midway through Jesus' "farewell prayer" following the farewell meal with the disciples and just before his arrest. Having prayed for himself (vv. 1–5), Jesus' prayer has turned to intercessions for his disciples, as he asks God to protect them and sanctify their work (vv. 17–19), and prays for their unity, glory, and success (vv. 20–23). In this pivotal hour, Jesus has turned from addressing his disciples to addressing God on their behalf. His look ahead at life for his followers when he is no longer in the world applies to us as it did to the disciples.

First, we hear Jesus' prayer and expectation that God will protect the faith community so that they may know the intimate spiritual unity reflected by his own oneness with God. In our day, we know how division can damage congregations, denominations, and the work of the church in the world. Justice work, especially as it tackles political and systemic change, can create division and anxiety within a congregation or denomination. How might we fulfill our responsibility to tackle difficult issues of justice and at the same time seek oneness that reflects the very nature of God?

Second, we hear Jesus' words about the relationship of the faith community to the "world." Gail R. O'Day notes that the world (*kosmos*) here does not mean the earth or creation but instead "stands for the sphere of enmity to God."[3] Jesus acknowledges the "hatred" that the world has for his followers who do not belong to it. However, Jesus does not ask God to remove the faith community *from* that realm, but instead prays for God's protection of

---

3. Gail R. O'Day, "John," in *The New Interpreter's Bible*, ed. Leander Keck et al. (Nashville: Abingdon Press, 1995), 9:792.

the faith community *in* the world. The faith community must not be taken out of the world but is sent into it—the world is the realm of our work and witness, that all might know the love and justice of God made visible in the ministry of Jesus.

The call of Children's Sabbaths is not merely to nurture the faith of those children who sit in the pews, who are sheltered in our sanctuary. Children's Sabbaths seeks to discern God's call of justice that sends us out from our sanctuaries to make our nation and world safe for all children. We are sent to transform a world that treats children with cruelty rather than compassion, that benefits businesses more than babies, that generates bursting prisons and sparse high school graduating classes. Our text reminds us that standing up to and against the prevailing standards of the day will not make us popular, but it will make us faithful.

All Saints' Day

Gennifer Benjamin Brooks

DANIEL 7:1–3, 15–18
PSALM 149
EPHESIANS 1:11–23
LUKE 6:20–31

The theme of inheritance runs through the four lectionary texts for All Saints' Day. Luke's rendition of Jesus' teaching on the requirements of discipleship provides a picture of the disciples' inheritance as children of God. It is an apocalyptic vision the likes of which Daniel saw in his dreams, in that it represents the eternal realm where God is sovereign and the blessed, holy ones experience everlasting joy. The everlasting presence and grace of God reveals the glory of God. Paul names it and claims it on behalf of those who are faithful to Christ. It is an inheritance of grace. Yet the idea of the inheritance of the saints raises critical questions about life in the present for those whom society considers of little worth, and who therefore face seemingly insurmountable challenges in the present. The inheritance of the saints of God is realized only by faith in the promise of God.

Daniel 7:1–3, 15–18

Daniel has a nightmare. It depicts a time of war and chaos with turbulent seas and raging beasts. It is no wonder that his spirit is troubled. But Daniel is living in a time of war and chaos under a ruler who wields unimagined power over the populace. The vision is prophetic as Daniel receives the warning about the powers that are about to overwhelm the nation. The warning is clear; more conflict is ahead as pending rulers and new empires will arise and overtake the nations. It is terrifying because it augurs confusion and conflict and oppression that seem unending.

For Daniel and for those who live in this age, the beasts are harbingers of destruction to life. His nightmare of terrors looms on the horizon as he

459

seeks the interpretation of his dreams. For many in this time, the nightmare has already come, and with it the death of their dreams. Many people in our time live under the beasts of militarism, economic meltdown, housing devaluation, and double-digit unemployment that rise up to overwhelm a society already plagued by the ongoing terrors of racism, sexism, classism, and all the attendant ills of poverty. The beasts attack and seek to devour even those who once existed in the safety and security of worldly success. For Daniel the interpretation of his dreams speaks of continuous war as each king rises to overthrow the other, and for us the continuity of conflict is the simultaneous existence of all the ills of society, each seeming to devour as much as it can.

Yet all is not lost. The holy ones will prevail. They will inherit the realm as everlasting because they are the children of the Most High (v. 18). God is sovereign, and the reign of God is the inheritance of the holy ones who walk in righteousness. Daniel's dream offers the possibility of peace and security and the promise of apocalyptic joy. It is the promise of an everlasting realm that calls us to live lives of righteousness and faith. With faith in the divine promise, the nightmare terrors of our world lose their power. God reigns supreme, and the realm of God is assured by faith to all who trust in God.

Psalm 149

This psalm seems a fitting accompaniment for the text from Daniel. If the kings of Daniel's vision bring terror, then it seems right that God's vengeance on behalf of the people should call forth praises (vv. 6–9a). The psalmist calls the faithful to rejoice in anticipation of victory over their enemies. On the one hand, the psalm speaks of what God has done to overthrow the oppression of those who are faithful to God, but on the other hand, it is a call to violence in the name of righteous vengeance on the part of the faithful in order to bring about God's justice. It is at one and the same time a song of thanksgiving and a war cry.

The psalm challenges us to consider carefully the notion of justice as violence. The question of just war leaps to mind, and the issue of divine vengeance wreaked on erstwhile oppressors by human hands is problematic as an act of faithfulness to God. With the dust and the smells of the 9/11 destruction of the World Trade Center towers still in the air, many in the United States consider it their right to wage war in the name of vengeance or even justice. Vengeance belongs to God, and punishment must be left to God, who executes judgment with justice.

Preachers face deep challenges in the uncritical claims our culture or nations make on God in the name of righteousness or even God's faithfulness to respond to our struggles or plight. We sing praises to God as God takes pleasure in humanity and our pursuit of humility (v. 4).

Ephesians 1:11–23

Paul speaks in this text of the promised destiny, the inheritance of the saints. Those who have accepted the redemption and live under the lordship of Jesus Christ live with the promise of an eternal inheritance. Paul's message combines present action with future promise. Those who follow Christ are called to live a life of faith that acknowledges Jesus as the truth of God to the world, the promise of salvation for all people, and the source of wisdom and revelation for their lives. The nonbeliever, of course, may call it the panacea of Christians that enables them to experience the vagaries of life and to remain steadfast in the midst of life's trials. However, it is the hope of their calling in Christ that Christians may have both vision and wisdom to see and understand the presence of God in human endeavors.

Still preachers must respond to the Christian sufferer who hears these words in the midst of what are not uplifting experiences but unending suffering. Paul prays for the Ephesians to experience a wisdom that enables them to see beyond their immediate circumstances in order to know fully the greatness of God's saving, empowering love. But how does one obtain such wisdom? Within both society and the church, people encounter discrimination because of who they are, what they believe, how and where they live, and how much they own. Classism, racism, homophobia, and ageism are only a few of the prejudicial systems that operate in the culture and in persons of authority, and in the way that society's structural power imposes itself over others. Greed and wealth cause some to consider others beneath their feet and do their best to crush them. Confronted by unjust systems and structures of oppression that lead to physical, mental, emotional, and even spiritual suffering, where does one attain such a gift of faith that one can be sustained by it in righteousness and attain the eternal realm of God?

Paul's prayer is itself an act of faith, because it offers thanksgiving for the inherent faith of the church community even as he takes on the role of supplicant on their behalf. Paul speaks from the assurance of his own faith in the divinity of Jesus Christ, who in the very nature of God is imbued with all power and authority over the created order. Yet the powers of the world seem to exert such force that some believe they cannot be overcome. Charles Campbell reminds us that though the powers rebel against God, they are all created by and subject to God.[1] It is an important reminder, because too often we act as though we are subject to the powers of this world. As Christians, we are subject to Christ, who is head of the church and the focus of our faith. The power of Christ enables us to withstand the powers of the world and, by faith, attain the inheritance that Christ has promised all who follow him.

Luke 6:20–31

Jesus is speaking to his disciples, not simply the disciples of first-century Palestine, but to all disciples over time. Luke's rendition of Jesus' sermon, delivered not on the mount but on the plain, figuratively levels the playing field for all his followers. He lays out a standard of living for the community that seems at first glance to upend the norms of society and even to right the wrongs of the unjust and oppressive systems that foster poverty and death. The sermon begins with a word of blessing for those who suffer in the present and a promise of unparalleled reward. It is the inheritance of faith, an eschatological hope of peace and justice.

This lectionary reading seems to lure Christian sufferers into a confrontation between their physical and spiritual conditions. Unlike Matthew (5:1–12), Luke addresses socioeconomic realities of those who live most often on the underside of society. The poor, the hungry, those who are weeping in sorrow, the hated, despised, excluded—in other words, the marginalized "others" of society—are offered the assurance that their physical situation is only for a time. All wrongs will be made right in the coming realm as the poor experience the riches of the realm of God, the hungry are filled, laughter replaces tears, and all are equal and precious in the community as they are in the sight of God. It is the beloved community of the saints of God and a cause for rejoicing.

It is, but not yet, just as the realm of God is now and not yet, and even those who have faith in the promises of Christ are confronted by the reality of a world that is not heaven on earth. Jesus' teaching is a reminder of past sorrow as he recounts the violent end that met the prophets. The oppressed and afflicted who hear it are not assured of their ability to attain the inheritance. How does one live a holy and faithful life in the midst of such trouble and evil? What Luke hopes to offer is the assurance that God is on the side of the other in society. Christ speaks for the other that the world despises or rejects, and justice in the name of Christ calls us to receive the other among us.

The delineations are many and varied, but invariably include the poor, those who have little or nothing of worldly value, who are often despised and

---

1. Charles Campbell, *The Word before the Power* (Louisville, KY: Westminster John Knox Press, 2002), 24.

blamed for their poverty. They are judged negatively because of the mistaken belief that they should be able to pull themselves up by their bootstraps, which denies the reality of systemic oppression. Homelessness, unemployment, ill health, mental and spiritual depression breed hopelessness, and those afflicted are lost to the world. But Jesus turns the table on the world.

Christ's offering routs the belief that those whom the world acclaims will be absolved from their unjust acts; thus hearers of this text may balk at the message and reject the lessons it offers. The reversal of fortune that it represents is so challenging that individual Christians and even the church as a body may tremble at its expression of condemnation. So what does the faithful Christian do? Luke provides a blueprint for helping believers to live faithfully as disciples of Christ. Jesus' teachings, contrary to those found in the Law and in common practice in society, require responses from the faithful. They offer the reward of blessing and make plain the will of Christ for his disciples. Through them, the realm of God takes form and the inhabitants claim their place. They inspire ways of peace and justice in the world and direct us to seek the fullness of life for all people through faith in the promises of Christ.

Proper 26 [31]

Elizabeth J. A. Siwo-Okundi

HABAKKUK 1:1–4; 2:1–4
PSALM 119:137–144

ISAIAH 1:10–18
PSALM 32:1–7
2 THESSALONIANS 1:1–4, 11–12
LUKE 19:1–10

The lectionary readings for this week begin and end with stories of faith, persistence, and conversation. These texts challenge and expand our approaches to social justice, because they offer multiple perspectives and voices. They include the experiences of people who are faithful to God, those who rebel against God, and those who seek simply to be in the presence of God. They also include the experiences of God from God's perspective. These texts expand our images of who should be involved in the work of social justice and how. We often long for concrete examples of how to bring about social justice and have difficulty figuring out where to begin. When we carefully consider these texts, we learn how we may act on God's teachings on social justice.

Habakkuk 1:1–4; 2:1–4 and Psalm 119:137–144

If any prophet understands frustration, Habakkuk is the one. His story is tucked so deeply into the Hebrew Bible that it is often missed. Habakkuk is a prophet who has waited long enough for God. His raw, uncensored emotion is quite telling of the depth of his frustration and could easily be mistaken as whiny, immature, impulsive, and thoughtless. But Habakkuk has long considered his concerns. He boldly goes before God and makes his complaint clear (1:2): "How long shall I cry for help, and you will not listen?" Habakkuk has not yet asked God to do anything. He simply wants God to listen to him. Yet implied in his complaint is his desire for God to *do* something in response to what God has heard!

Habakkuk's question of "how long?" smoothly transitions into "why?" (1:3): "Why do you make me see wrongdoing and look at trouble?" His question reveals that he is not necessarily crying to God because of his own suffering. Rather, he bears witness to the suffering around him. He witnesses destruction, violence, strife, and contention (1:3), each of which perplexes him deeply. Habakkuk is not complaining about the little, everyday annoyances and petty grievances of life. No! He is crying about major issues—the same issues that we encounter in our world today and to which God appears not to respond. Apparently, Habakkuk has already attempted human avenues for change and has been disappointed. The law would normally handle complaints such as his, but the situation makes clear that the law is ineffective. The law "becomes slack and justice never prevails. The wicked surround the righteous—therefore judgment comes forth perverted" (1:4).

It is noteworthy that Habakkuk is not immune to the troubles of his community. He does not resign himself to a "that's just how things are" attitude or become numb to the pain around him. Despite God's seeming lack of response to the prophet's endless list of complaints, Habakkuk continues to take note of the struggles of his community and voice his concerns. Many of us can relate to the prophet's complaints, for we have cried aloud and wondered why God is silent or refuses to answer us in the midst of painful situations that obviously need to be addressed. We are often tempted to give up on our relationship with God or to conclude that God does not exist. Yet the more Habakkuk feels God does not answer and the more evil Habakkuk witnesses, the greater his desire grows for God to address the issues. He is adamant that God address his issues. He firmly announces, "I will stand at my watchpost, and station myself on the rampart; I will keep watch to see what [God] will say to me, and what [God] will answer concerning my complaint" (2:1). Though Habakkuk complains about God's silence, he still wrestles with God. He still has faith! To wrestle with God is to have faith in God, even if that faith is tested or is limited. Faith is a critical part of the lives of those who claim to know and love God.

God finally responds and tells Habakkuk that if he is so concerned about the situations around him and is not satisfied with God's past answers, then he himself ought to "Write the vision; make it plain. . . . For there is still a vision for the appointed time" (2:2–3). God urges Habakkuk and us to think about what God wants for our communities, to write it so that it can be shared with others, and to make it simple enough that everyone can understand it and work toward it. Based on Habakkuk's "how long" question, God is well aware that Habakkuk's patience is running low and he needs a time frame for the vision. Though God does not give specific dates or details, God encourages Habakkuk and us to be patient. God says, "If [the vision] seems to tarry, wait for it; it will surely come, it will not delay" (2:3). Those who are righteous will not be discouraged by the vision; rather they will "live by faith" as the vision carries them forward (2:4).

In the Psalm 119 passage, "the righteous" and "righteousness" appear at least five times in just a few sentences. The psalmist begins by noting that God is righteous. The wicked in Habakkuk's complaints put forth twisted judgments and bring the law to shame. But God's judgments "are right" and God's law "is the truth," according to the psalmist (vv. 137, 142). The psalmist writes while in the midst of trouble and anguish, but with the assurance of God's commandments the psalmist remembers God's teachings even as enemies forget them (vv. 139, 141, 144). The psalmist has complete faith in God. The only request is for God to give the psalmist understanding so that the psalmist may live (v. 144). Just a little bit of understanding can give the psalmist enough encouragement to continue living in the midst of hardship, though feeling "small and despised" (v. 141). The psalmist does not seek answers about "why?" or "how long?" as does Habakkuk. Instead, the psalmist wants to continue to live within the commandments of God.

This approach to adversity differs slightly from that of Habakkuk, who *witnesses* trouble and demands God's attention and response. The psalmist, who *experiences* trouble, asks for understanding. Both of them have faith in God and desire to bring about righteousness despite all that they do not know or understand. The psalmist has found a way to cope with the difficulties of life, while still desiring better circumstances. The psalmist's approach is no less legitimate than the prophet's approach. The gentle and hopeful approach of the psalmist provides a caution for social justice activists who wonder why the "small voices"[1] (my term) are not demanding rights and showing strong energy in changing their conditions. We often approach social justice differently based on our experience of injustice and what resources we may have, find, or need.

Isaiah 1:10–18 and Psalm 32:1–7

God also wants social justice. It is God, not Habakkuk, who now says, "I have had enough" (Isa. 1:11). In this Isaiah text God testifies that humans have become so rebellious and corrupt that their sacrifices, offerings, and festivals to God are worthless. Humans who waste time and money on empty and evil gestures while urgent issues are left unattended do not please God. God is tired to the point that God "will not listen" (v. 15) to empty prayers and gestures. God wants action—action that is just and good. But doing good is not something that comes naturally to all people, especially those of us who

---

1. See Elizabeth J. A. Siwo-Okundi, "Listening to the Small Voice: Toward an Orphan Theology," *Harvard Divinity Bulletin* 37, nos. 2–3 (2009): 33–43.

are accustomed to pleasing God through extravagant gifts, false motives, and filthy hearts. Doing good requires learning a new and pure way of living. Yet learning to do good is not enough. God says, "Learn to do good; seek justice, rescue the oppressed, defend the orphan, plead for the widow" (v. 17). God requires that people learn about doing good and then actually to do it! If Isaiah's people and we are not sure where to begin, God provides examples of how to do good by advocating for the least in society. It is easy to gather information and to learn a wide range of social justice issues, but action—action that is good and just—is required.

God's list of complaints, like Habakkuk's list, is extensive. But at the end, God gives an invitation. God says, "Come now, let us argue it out" (v. 18). Notice that the verse states "us"—God and another or others. Though God has a list of complaints, God does not offer silence or war as solutions; nor does God terminate the relationship. God is willing to try to save the relationship. Trying begins with conversation. Too often, we humans are quick to cut off conversation when we have lodged our complaints against each other or God. We become silent or go to war. But God puts forth a model that requires conversation and reasoning in the midst of disagreements, credible or not. God does not expect for the argument to be one-sided and become a lecture. Arguing and reasoning means that both sides—all sides—participate, and do so in a safe, respectful manner and environment.[2]

What is most incredible about God's offer is that God is the one who has been hurt, yet God also finds the courage to put forth the offer. Starting the conversation ought not always rest on those who have been harmed. However, those who have been harmed are uniquely able to understand the wrong that has been done to them, in ways that others cannot perceive. For example, victims of violence, orphans, widows, abused persons, and those who are enslaved have deep understanding of the violence and neglect against them. They should have the opportunity, however difficult, to lead and invite conversations instead of being the subject of conversations. The conversations of reasoning and arguing should not end with a simple airing of grievances and sharing of perspective, or leave one side more deeply wounded than before the meeting. Rather, the conversation demands a return to God's commandment to do what is good and what is just.

Certainly, the one who has done wrong will have plenty of reasons to not enter into meaningful reasoning and arguing with God and others. In Psalm 32:1–7, the psalmist recalls a time living a life of sin and deceit but keeping

---

2. Some relationships (and ways of relating), particularly abusive and violent ones, require termination. Too many times, preachers have used biblical passages—such as Isa. 1:18—to encourage victims of violence to stay in abusive "relationships" and "work things out." However, arguing, as modeled by God, assumes safety, respect, and honesty.

silent about the deeds and discernment: "While I kept silence, my body wasted away though my groaning all day long" (v. 3). The impact of silence was physically and emotionally evident. We should never believe that those who offer useless and deceitful sacrifices to God while neglecting the pain of others are living lives of happiness and joy. The psalmist, though living a deceitful life, could still feel the strength of God's presence weighing in heavily. The psalmist finally broke the silence: "Then I acknowledged my sin to you, and I did not hide my iniquity . . . and you forgave the guilt of my sin" (v. 5). Acknowledgment of wrongdoing aids in healing and forgiveness.

God forgave the psalmist, and the psalmist was able to declare that those whose sins are forgiven and have clean spirits are indeed happy and have been delivered (vv. 1, 2, 7). The forgiveness, deliverance, and eventual happiness came as a result of conversation, not silence. Like the psalmist, we likely need to seek conversations with those whom we have harmed and try to make those relationships right, just as we do with our relationship with God. If we can reason and argue with God, then we can reason and argue with one another to do what is good and just.

2 Thessalonians 1:1–4, 11–12

The message within this passage is one of encouragement. Though the church of the Thessalonians has struggled in the past—and continues to struggle—they have risen to become a model church. The writers give thanks for the Thessalonians, because their "faith is growing abundantly" and their love "for one another is increasing" (v. 3). Such growth has not been without hardship. The writers continue, "Therefore we ourselves boast of you among the churches of God for your steadfastness and faith during all your persecutions and the afflictions that you are enduring" (v. 4). This community is staying strong and living by faith. The church community probably did not even know that they were doing well. But how wonderful to receive a word of encouragement from their leaders! Their experience reminds us that we should not allow difficult times to weaken our faith and our cooperative spirit.

The work of social justice is often so difficult that we are not able to see any progress. Yet, every once in a while, we ought to reflect positively about the progress that has been made, even if far greater progress requires our endurance. If we continue to encourage each other so that we remember and remind others of our calling, perhaps we might grow more worthy of that calling (v. 11). Though we measure progress by numbers, figures, and facts, there are other indicators, such as increased faith and love, which also show the progress of social justice.

Luke 19:1–10

The righteous are persistent in wanting to be seen and heard, but the not-so-righteous are also persistent. Take the example of Zacchaeus, whose story is mentioned in Luke 19:1–10. "Zacchaeus was a wee little man, and a wee little man was he";[3] such are the lyrics to the children's song that has introduced many a Christian to the character of Zacchaeus. Though the song fails present-day standards of political correctness, it gives a clue to a problem that Zacchaeus faces—his height is an initial limitation for him. Jesus comes to town and Zacchaeus is not able to see Jesus "because [Zacchaeus] was short in stature" (v. 3). His wealth as a tax collector (v. 2) may have afforded him certain luxuries, but when Jesus is coming to town, his limitations prevent him from engaging or seeing Jesus. People may have been blocking his way or even retaliating against him for his unfair tax assessments. Zacchaeus finally decides to climb a tree so that he can see Jesus. With such a large crowd eager to see, Zacchaeus is certainly not the only one in a tree! Jesus is not walking with his head to the sky, looking for people in trees. But Zacchaeus must have been making quite a scene and is able, to the dismay of faithful and righteous ones, to catch the attention of Jesus.

When Jesus comes near Zacchaeus, Jesus sees him and immediately says, "Hurry and come down" (v. 5). Zacchaeus was determined to see Jesus, and he was not going to let his height or his questionable status as a not-so-loved tax collector stop him. Jesus invites himself to Zacchaeus's house. Zacchaeus is "happy to welcome him" but others "began to grumble" about Jesus being a guest in the house of "a sinner" (vv. 6–7). Zacchaeus is probably stunned that Jesus has chosen him among the many in the crowd. He stands before Jesus and says that he will give half of his possessions to the poor and will pay back ("four times as much"!) those whom he has defrauded (v. 8). Zacchaeus acknowledges his sins of fraud and decides to do what is good and just. Jesus, who comes "to seek out and to save the lost" (v. 10), declares that Zacchaeus's change of heart has brought salvation to him and his family (v. 9). Zacchaeus's actions remind us that God's call to do what is good and just is meant for all people. Social justice requires such efforts from everyone. The encounter between Jesus and Zacchaeus reminds us that the power to do justice often comes from the power of seeking reconciliation, responding with repentance when in the wrong, and extending forgiveness.

---

3. See Donna Hanby, *Giving and Receiving Hospitality [Young Children]*, Faith Practices Series (Cleveland: John Hunt Publishing, 2010), 17–18.

Proper 27 [32]

Bob Ekblad

HAGGAI 1:15B–2:9
JOB 19:23–27A

PSALM 145:1–5, 17–21
PSALM 17:1–9
2 THESSALONIANS 2:1–5, 13–17
LUKE 20:27–38

This Sunday's readings invite resurrection hope based on appeal to God's past action, recent testimony, and Scripture. These appeals equip us to resist the powers of death of every sort.

Haggai 1:15b–2:9

In this Sunday's reading, Haggai directly addresses people who are rebuilding their lives in the face of catastrophic loss. The prophet calls for them to put total focus on God's habitation as the basis of fruitfulness.

The exiles have returned home from Babylonian captivity, sent by the Persian monarch to rebuild the temple. After a first attempt in 537 BCE (Ezra 3:7–12), the returnees stopped reconstruction due to poverty and hostility from the Samaritan population, followed by political instability in the Persian Empire. Haggai's prophetic ministry happens at a critical time, between August and December 520 BCE.

Haggai addresses Zerubbabel, the governor of Judah, and Joshua the high priest (1:1–2), urging them to put full effort into rebuilding the temple to host God's presence, so desolation will be replaced with God's glory and abundant provision (1:3–11). Haggai warns that lethargy in temple rebuilding and delay in making God's house the highest priority is directly linked to drought, lack of provision, and ongoing poverty, though these conditions lead the people to hear God's voice and show reverence for God. God's promise, "I am with you," shows that God is with them fully without the building, enabling the people to work in earnest (1:13–14). Rather than minimize the gap between their memory of past glory and their current situation, Haggai here invites

470

accurate memory (2:3): "Who is left among you that saw this house in its former glory? How does it look to you now? Is it not in your sight as nothing?"

People suffering economic downturns, ex-offenders, disaster victims from New Orleans to Port-au-Prince to Pakistan, and anyone living in war-torn places can easily despair when comparing their present toil in rebuilding their lives to an idealized past. God directly addresses the Israelites on the twenty-first day of the month, the last day of the Feast of Booths, as they remember their departure from Egypt and wilderness wandering accompanied by God.

The Lord's assurance of abiding presence before temple completion (2:4) is followed by a stronger promise (v. 5): "According to the promise that I made you when you came out of Egypt. My Spirit abides among you; do not fear!" God promises an impending supernatural shaking that will bring the provisions from wealthy nations into Jerusalem, filling the temple with a greater glory than before, and peace (vv. 6–9).

This reading can help us position ourselves with God's presence and realm as our highest priorities. It encourages both open-eyed realism and a rootedness in our memory of God's presence with us in the midst of past trials.

Job 19:23–27a

This Sunday's reading from Job is filled with extreme hope. Job has just confronted his unhelpful theologian friend Bildad, who explains Job's suffering as God's retribution on the wicked (18:1–21). Bildad's theological defense of God's sovereignty and justice is all too common today, exacerbating oppression and turning people away from God. People racked by poverty, persecution, oppression, and illness experience firsthand that this world is "under the power of the evil one" (1 John 5:19), but are told by too many religious people that God is the author of their merited misery.

Job confronts his "friendly" tormentors, unsure early on about God's place in his misery: "How long will you torment me, and break me in pieces with words? These ten times you have cast reproach upon me" (19:2–3). His laments are raw and uncensored toward God (19:7–20), and he reproaches the theologians who embody abuse, siding with oppressive images of the Divine: "Have pity on me, have pity on me, O you my friends, for the hand of God has touched me! Why do you, like God, pursue me, never satisfied with my flesh?" (19:21–22).

In the midst of torturous trials, Job wants his laments engraved in rock forever (v. 24). I think of the Holocaust museums in Amsterdam and Israel, forensic exhumations of mass graves in Guatemala, and the museum commemorating Pol Pot's killing fields in Cambodia—where the memory of atrocities is kept alive in anticipation of resolution. In the midst of his misery, faith in a redeemer is suddenly unexplainably visible (vv. 25–26): "I know that my Redeemer lives, and that at the last he will stand upon the earth; and after my skin has been thus destroyed, then in my flesh I shall see God."

In Israel the redeemer was the one who advocated for the rights of close relatives who could not defend themselves (Lev. 25:25; Ruth 4:4). It is difficult here to imagine a redeemer who would defend Job from God (or a perception of God). Who could this be? Perhaps the heavenly witness mentioned in Job 16:19, one of the "heavenly beings" of God mentioned in the prologue (1:6; 2:1), or an intercessor angel (33:23–24)?

One thing is certain from the text. Job speaks of his living redeemer as one coming in the future, a human who "at the last . . . will stand upon the earth" (v. 25). Today, there is a critical need for fresh embodiments everywhere of Jesus' disciples ready to advocate for people in misery, showing them God's defending, liberating, comforting Presence, rather than defending the status quo.

Job's embodied resurrection hope comes out of nowhere. He speaks from the context of his devastated flesh. His gaze is fixed on a future redeemer who even after his death he will see, evoking texts like 1 Corinthians 15:25–26, "For he must reign until he has put all his enemies under his feet. The last enemy to be destroyed is death" (see also 1 Cor. 15:55–57; 1 Thess. 4:16–18; Rev. 21:1–4). Jesus is the Redeemer who incarnates a God who has never changed. He embodies life-giving presence, dismissing erroneous images of God that tormented Job and today's excluded ones. Are we living and speaking in full alignment with Jesus' revelation of the death-resisting, victorious God of life?

Psalm 145:1–5, 17–21

This Sunday's first psalm reading goes from high praises directed to God (vv. 1–2) to meditation on God and God's greatness and nearness in the third person (vv. 3–5, 17–21). The psalmist sees himself and this praise as eternal: "My mouth . . . will bless [God's] holy name forever and ever" (v. 21). He addresses God as king, showing conviction that God is above presidents, employers, and all powers.

People who feel powerless (e.g., the returned exiles, Job, prisoners, undocumented immigrants, the mentally ill, slum dwellers, prostitutes) need to be reminded that God is great (v. 3), and especially that God is *kind* (v. 17).

In ways similar to Haggai's call for the people to remember the former glory of the temple, the psalmist exemplifies meditation on God's past works as a recipe for faith and remedy to despair (v. 4). Each generation must pass its testimony of God's mighty deeds to the next. Testimony affirming God as King reminds oppressed people that other competing powers (the United States, law enforcers, abusive partners, mortgage companies, employers, etc.) are not. Everyone needs to remember that God is strong when the powers of darkness threaten. Testimonies of God's past actions make the psalmist's affirmations believable; God is near and saves all people who desire and seek God (vv. 18–19).

The Lord's destroying "all the wicked" (v. 20) inspires hope for anyone oppressed by all-powerful powers. Jesus and Paul's consistent distinction between human enemies, whom they call us to love and bless, and spiritual enemies, whom we are to cast out or subjugate, identifies the wicked as nonhuman powers (legal systems, laws, debts, unjust economic systems, evil spirits, etc.).

Finally, while the psalmist begins with an individual affirmation of endless worship (v. 1), the psalm ends with a surprising declaration of universal eternal worship: "*All* flesh will bless [God's] holy name forever and ever" (v. 21, emphasis added). What would it look like to live out of this radical inclusive word "all," which subverts all us-them distinctions that empower destructive scapegoating?

Psalm 17:1–9

Anyone suffering unjustly could pray this psalm as a cry to the Lord for vindication or relief. The psalmist's appeals to YHWH show that he assumes God is more powerful and just than his adversaries. "Hear a just cause, O Lord, attend to my cry; give ear to my prayer" (v. 1).

Whatever difficulty the psalmist is facing has led him into deep self-examination, the results of which he presents to YHWH. A positive outcome of suffering unjustly or facing any kind of hardship is the occasion for coming into the light of God's presence (1 John 1:7), where clarity, forgiveness, and favor are guaranteed. Are there ways you can identify with the Spirit's help whereby you have opened a door to evil?

The psalmist here has examined himself and finds that there is nothing to confess or change (vv. 3–5), but instead appeals to God in faith: "I call upon you, for you will answer me, O God; incline your ear to me, hear my words. Wondrously show your steadfast love, O savior of those who seek refuge from their adversaries at your right hand" (vv. 6–7). Rather than self-protecting or using preemptive violence, the psalmist here shows how to cry out directly to God for help, security, and protection. The psalmist's assurance of God's favor (v. 8) appears to ground his confidence in the face of enemies (v. 9). Are we willing to open ourselves to living more fully in God's light and trust that God adores us and will protect us?

2 Thessalonians 2:1–5, 13–17

In this Sunday's Epistle reading, the apostle Paul directly confronts false analysis and hope in Jesus' return, informing his addressees of how bad things will get before the Parousia. Those who face poverty, oppression, and hardship of any kind are vulnerable to escapist theories or best-case scenarios promising immediate relief. Paul warns believers of predictions from false prophecies, "by spirit or by word or by letter, as though from us" (v. 2). Paul has already addressed the Thessalonians regarding the possibility of Jesus' immediate return (1 Thess. 2:19; 3:13; 4:15–17; 5:4) and wants them and us alert and ready. But he insists as a protective apostle, "Let no one deceive you in any way" (v. 3). Paul here appears to draw from Jewish eschatological traditions based on Scripture (Ezek. 28:2; Dan. 11:36–38) to argue that an apostasy marked by a man of lawlessness called the son of destruction has not yet come and must show up on earth before the end. One of these texts, Daniel 11:36–37, reads:

> The king shall act as he pleases. He shall exalt himself and consider himself greater than any god, and shall speak horrendous things against the God of gods. He shall prosper until the period of wrath is completed, for what is determined shall be done. He shall pay no respect to the gods of his ancestors, or to the one beloved by women; he shall pay no respect to any other god, for he shall consider himself greater than all.

Paul reminds the Thessalonians that he has already warned them about these things, but he goes into greater detail in 2:6–12. He assumes his readers know what is currently restraining the lawless one, which could be the Roman Empire's maintenance of law and order or Paul's own missionary calling to accomplish proclamation to all the nations before the end (Mark 13:10; Matt. 24:14). He states that the lawless one is already at work, and that God will eventually destroy this one who acts in accord with Satan's activity. Paul warns that those who do not love the truth will be vulnerable to deception by the lawless one's power backed by signs and false wonders.

Paul gives thanks for the Thessalonians and affirms God's choosing them for "salvation through sanctification by the Spirit and through belief in the truth" to "obtain the glory of our Lord Jesus Christ" (vv. 13–14). Paul appeals to his own teachings and writings as authoritative truth for the community, calling them to "stand firm and hold fast to the traditions that you were taught" (v. 15). He calls on Jesus Christ and God to comfort and strengthen the believers, as they will face greater challenges. Careful appeal to Scripture, analysis of our lives and world, and dependence on God for comfort and strength are critical today in order to maintain faith to the end.

Luke 20:27–38

In today's Gospel reading, Jesus is confronted by the Sadducees, who ask him a question regarding an application of Scripture that they assume will expose the implausibility of life after death. The Sadducees, who belonged to the higher, wealthier ranks of the priesthood, were religious conservatives who considered the Torah as inspired Scripture. They did not admit belief in the resurrection of the dead, initiated two centuries earlier in Daniel 12:2–3. What would be the equivalent of the Sadducees today? Unbelief can be cloaked as realism and is certainly conservative. Is resurrection hope being thwarted by a misguided interpretation of Scripture now as it was then?

The Sadducees assume that someone who is married on earth will be married in the afterlife—hence the difficulty in deciding in heaven which brother will get the wife passed on from brother to brother, based on First Testament levirate laws to assure the continuation of the family line (Deut. 25:5–6). Jesus offers an interpretation from the perspective of heaven and the Torah, the latter an uncontested authority for his detractors.

Jesus begins by making a distinction between people in this age and "those who are considered worthy of a place in that age and in the resurrection from the dead" (v. 35), inviting his audience and us as readers not to assume that one's presence in the eternal realm is automatic. He then offers perspectives not directly taught in Scripture until here. Resurrected ones will not be married in the afterlife, Jesus teaches (see 1 Cor. 15:35–50). He goes on to describe in detail the state of resurrected humans in ways that directly challenge the Pharisees' more materialist understanding of the resurrection of the body—inviting the Sadducees and us into a more expansive view. "They cannot even die anymore, because they are like angels and are children of God, being children of the resurrection" (v. 36).

Jesus brilliantly appeals to Moses, the Sadducees' greatest authority, drawing from familiar texts to "prove" the resurrection. Jesus likely gained favor with the Sadducees by attributing God's own words to Moses in Exodus 3 to Moses himself, both affirming Moses' divine inspiration and offering a surprising twist. According to Jesus, since Moses calls the Lord "the God of Abraham, and the God of Isaac, and the God of Jacob," and the Lord cannot be God of the dead but of the living, Abraham, Isaac, and Jacob are therefore *all* alive (vv. 37–38). Hence Jesus seems to suggest that all will be resurrected. Faith in Jesus' victory over death on our behalf and our eternal destiny to live "to him" does not demobilize us, but empowers and emboldens us as agents of liberation here and now.

Proper 28 [33]

L. Susan Bond

ISAIAH 65:17–25   MALACHI 4:1–2A
ISAIAH 12   PSALM 98
                              2 THESSALONIANS 3:6–13
                                  LUKE 21:5–19

New heavens, new earth, new songs! The readings for this Sunday survey the variety of eschatological hopes and eschatological fears that stretch across both testaments. The First Testament texts draw from different stages of exilic and postexilic writings, including visions of the peaceable reign. In Psalm 98, all of creation sings and claps its hands for the coming day of judgment. The Second Testament texts stretch from pragmatic concerns about faithful vocation to rumors of wars and cosmic reversals and to Luke's call for a time of witness and testimony.

Isaiah 65:17–25

Isaiah is one of the most popular books in the Torah, Prophets, and Writings for Christian preaching. In Luke, Jesus reads from the Isaiah scroll to begin his ministry, and the Servant Songs provide theological architecture for the early church to interpret the meaning of the crucifixion. The early church certainly saw itself in the themes of promise and fulfillment that we see in Isaiah, but we should be careful not to preach Christian superiority in contrast to the faith of Israel. For the Gospel writers as well as for contemporary Christians, Isaiah's dominant themes of ingathering, salvation, and restoration offer hope to the world.

    Today's reading comes from the section of Isaiah that scholars call Third Isaiah, probably written by followers of Second Isaiah who were liberated by Cyrus from their Babylonian exile. Chapter 65, addressed to those who have returned to find Jerusalem in shambles, with its agricultural system decimated and its dwellings destroyed, offers reassurance that God has not abandoned

Israel but promises salvation in the form of a redeemed social world. This theme of mercy and forgiveness that echoes through all the First Testament undergirds Second Testament theologies of a redeemed creation, a new heaven and a new earth. The eschatological vision of both testaments is a continuous vision of a just world.

Scholars point out that the primary images of this text relate to planting and building, activities that had been impossible during the exile. The "peaceable reign" images aside, the key claims of this text are about the community's hope to reconstitute its life as self-sufficient and prosperous, reversing a divine curse that hangs over Israel's history.

"You shall build a house, but not live in it. You shall plant a vineyard, but not enjoy its fruit" (Deut. 28:30). At least a dozen references to this curse occur in other books, including Amos, Zephaniah, Jeremiah, and Ezekiel. But it also echoes from Genesis through the Second Testament. In *Christians and the New Creation: Genesis Motifs in the New Testament*, Paul Minear claims that the curse on the land is reversed in the Lukan birth story, where "peace on earth" is a cosmic reversal.

Walter Brueggemann has underscored the importance of access to real estate and the security it provides.[1] The Babylonian exile is a theological problem precisely because the people of Israel have not been in possession of their land; they have been cut off from the possibilities of abundant life that the land represents.

But we should also note the ordinariness and humility of the images of planting and building. Elsewhere in the Scriptures we find glorious utopian visions of Israel's future, but here we find promises of houses and crops, the most basic requirements for any community. This is where the promise for social justice emerges, not in the Technicolor impossibility of the tamed animal kingdom, but in the vision of a new earth that is characterized by the social justice of land-owning, productive farming, housing for each and every one, an end to infant mortality, and longevity for all. The reign of God as a future eschatological hope involves notions of inclusion, belonging, place, security, and abundance.

Isaiah 12

From the portion of Isaiah known as First Isaiah, this song of praise was written during the Babylonian captivity, as a reassurance to Israel that God's promises are to be trusted. Before they had returned to Jerusalem to begin the rebuilding,

---

1. See Walter Brueggemann, *The Land: Place as Gift, Promise, and Challenge in Biblical Theology*, 2nd ed. (Minneapolis: Augsburg Fortress, 2002).

the exiles anticipated "water from the wells of salvation" (v. 3). In its context, this may refer to the Feast of Tabernacles ritual that involved a procession bringing water from the pool of Siloam to the temple. This song may have represented the hope that Israel would soon be able to celebrate its holy festivals.

For Christian communities, as for ancient Israel, the reference to water and salvation serves as a reminder that God's salvation is fundamental to life, as basic to survival as the water that falls from the sky and springs forth from the earth. But the literal sense is also true: water is necessary for life. A social justice approach will allow for reflections on the world's supply of potable water, who controls it, and who suffers from the lack of it. Many of us take water for granted, but access to water is an issue for millions of people. Access to clean, safe, and affordable water is a fundamental human right, essential for a healthy population, environment, and economy. Many low-income communities and communities of color lack access to safe, affordable water for drinking, subsistence, or cultural and recreational uses. Environmental justice is the right of every person to live, work, and play in a safe, healthy, and sustainable environment. Water justice will only be achieved when inclusive, community-based forms of water management are developed and we address the health and environmental burdens that low-income communities and communities of color bear.

Psalm 98

This psalm is part of a series of praise psalms. It is probably included in today's texts for its imagery of a whole creation that rejoices in the coming Day of the Lord. It echoes the Isaiah imagery (peaceable reign), but it also anticipates a day when God's salvation and righteousness and equity will ultimately be revealed. The psalm performs what it anticipates, a complete cosmic reversal where all of creation will rejoice, when all of creation (new heaven and new earth) will offer to God a new song. Again, there are hints of Isaiah, celebrating the accomplishment of what the exilic prophet foretold in Isaiah 42:10. Praise is an expression of shared commitment to the world. We are called on to offer "a new song," not merely in anticipation of the time when God's rule over this world will be fully established, but actually to advance the coming of that judgment.[2] We should be particularly careful, however, when singing praises to God's power and the divine "mighty arm," that we do not perpetuate a theology of coercive action or the idea that "might makes right." From a Christian perspective, we see the power of God always through the lens of the God we know in Christ, a kind of power that is revealed in self-sacrifice,

2. Ellen F. Davis, "Psalm 98," *Interpretation* 46 (1992): 175.

humility, and selfless giving. In Jesus, we see the kind of power that God exercises in taking on the humility and fragility of human flesh and human life and death. Within our American context, we should be particularly cautious about glorifying coercive or military power.

The psalm is also similar to the language of Mary's Magnificat in the Gospel of Luke. After she has been visited by the angel and has visited Elizabeth, Mary bursts into a song that magnifies the Lord's divine strength and restoring character (Luke 1:51–53). Some writers point out that when our lives are devoted to praising God, and to praising this particular kind of divine power and activity, we will ourselves be humbled and turned toward the needs of others. Praise is our best antidote to evil. If our minds are constantly praising God for the kind of divine power that operates on behalf of the poor and the disenfranchised, we will have less time for the temptations of selfishness and power-gathering for ourselves.

When we wonder how praising God will actually perform or advance the work of God's reign, we can consider what happens when we see others pray. Consider the image of Jews at the Wailing Wall, or the sight of Muslims on prayer mats, making a public witness about their praise and devotion. When people pray, they are a living witness, a prompt for us to reorient our thoughts and actions toward God.

Malachi 4:1–2a

This prophetic book also comes from the postexilic period. It is generally more concerned with cultic matters than with visions of a just world or promises of restoration. These apocalyptic verses from the end of the book promise a threatening outcome for Israel if God's mandates are not observed. Preachers should probably read and preach from the full unit of thought, and extend the reading to include verses 2b–6, even if we can understand why a lectionary committee might have felt squeamish about the full reading. The Day of the Lord imagery here includes images of fiery destruction that will reduce evildoers to stubble without a root or a branch left to them. This agricultural reference, although metaphorically used in this passage to discuss the destruction of people, plays in the same image field as the planting and building imagery in Isaiah. The final verses in this chapter complete the allusion: "Lo, I will send you the prophet Elijah before the great and terrible day of the LORD comes. He will turn the hearts of parents to their children, and the hearts of the children to their parents, so that I will not come and strike the land with a curse" (vv. 5–6).

In a brilliant discussion from twenty years ago, Walter Brueggemann called this vision in Malachi "The Terrible Ungluing," with which he finds "end-time" speech unmanageable.[3] Yet, he argues, regardless of how intellectually difficult such notions might be, every generation of believers somehow senses the possibilities of doom and hopelessness just around the corner. Today, American Christians have just recently survived a decade of economic decline reminiscent of the 1930s, we have been scared into believing that terrorists lurk in every shadow, and the rhetoric about climate change is all too often apocalyptic. Preachers who decide to preach from the Malachi text will want to avoid any "us and them" construct, as if danger is only external to Christian faith and the church. We will want to scrutinize our own failures closely and honestly, to be the voice of Elijah who comes to offer a hope of redemption and the opportunity to avoid disaster.

2 Thessalonians 3:6–13

The second letter of Paul to the church at Thessalonica was written within a year or two of the first letter, and it bears many of the same themes and theology. Its authorship, however, is disputed for what is missing in comparison. This letter is heavy on pragmatics and light on theology; there are no brilliant rhetorical arguments for issues such as resurrection, the election of Israel, or the relationship of law and faith.

Where other Pauline writings urge conflict resolution and unity, this text seems to be concerned about public appearances (What will the public think?) and using punitive strategies and exclusion to deal with practical issues. Dealing with the problems of community members who have become idle, the author instructs, "Anyone unwilling to work should not eat" (v. 10). There is no theological argument presented, no appeal to the church as the body of Christ, no appeal to the fruits of the Spirit, nothing beyond an appeal to apostolic tradition, "Because that's what we have done ourselves" (cf. vv. 7, 9).

The danger of taking the letter too literally is that it begins to set up rules for inclusion in the community, leading to a "works righteousness" that is disastrous for communities and very un-Pauline. In a time when our nation has a dangerously high unemployment rate, when theologies of blessing and prosperity are on the rise, and when the Protestant work ethic attributes moral decadence to those who are underemployed or unsuccessful, the chances for abusing this teaching are manifold.

The theological nugget of this text is beyond the practical issue of workers and idlers. The theological crux of the matter is that the idlers have stopped working because they think the end is near, or worse, that the judgment has

---

3. Walter Brueggemann, "The Terrible Ungluing," *Christian Century* 109, no. 30 (October 21, 1992): 931.

already passed and their salvation has exempted them from work. For Paul, the question would have been the more serious question of faith and hope, and how the community was living out its vocation as a community groaning in anticipation of the coming *basileia*.

The social justice prompts in this text are best directed to the eschatological concerns that make work and idling into issues of faith. Those who devote their time to social justice work know that its immediate rewards are few and fleeting, and the temptation to just stop, to weary of well-doing, is always present. If joy and hope and diligent work are signs of God's inbreaking *basileia*, then the lack of these activities would blunt the church's witness to the rest of the world that the work was still incomplete.

Years ago, in Nashville, a particular church van had a slogan painted across the back: "We will work until Jesus comes again." In the broad scheme of the church's witness, idleness is not just an issue of who eats and does not eat. Idleness is not just an issue of church discipline and bearing each other's burdens. Idleness indicates a profound lack of faith and a false witness.

Luke 21:5–19

This pericope about the destruction of the temple shows up in all three of the Synoptic Gospels. Luke's version follows the Markan version fairly closely, with some subtle differences. Two critical distinctions are that Luke is writing for a more generalized Gentile audience than is Mark, and that Luke's Gospel is definitely written after the destruction of the temple. Luke is not as critical of Judaism or of the temple, but takes a history-of-salvation approach to his Gospel, framing the Jesus narrative and the church's narrative within a prophetic fulfillment model. In Luke's Gospel alone, Jesus' ministry begins in the temple, with his public reading of the Isaiah scroll, "Today this scripture has been fulfilled in your hearing" (4:21).

In today's pericope about the destruction of the temple, Jesus does not leave the temple, as he does in Mark. Where Mark's Gospel puts the complimentary comments about the temple in the mouths of his own disciples, Luke's Gospel shifts the burden to anonymous others, perhaps so that his more Gentile audience would locate themselves in the narrative. Where Mark's Gospel was concerned primarily with distinguishing itself from Judaism, by Luke's time (85 CE), Christians and Jews were persecuted indiscriminately. A family crisis between Judaism and Christianity had escalated into a political conflict wherein the young church was persecuted from both sides. No wonder Luke adds to Mark's narrative by discussing arrests and prisons, anticipating the stories in the book of Acts. So Luke's apocalyptic warnings do not stop with wars and insurrections and natural disasters; Luke adds critical conditions of arrest and persecution, which will only further serve their testimony (vv. 12–19).

So, we wade through all the speculation about the destruction of the temple and the wars and famines and we come at last to the realization that the text is not about predicting the end times, but about Christian witness in the interim, that unpredictably long or short time between the crucifixion and the consummation. As Roberta Bondi writes, "Witness, how? Considering the enormity of the world's problems, how can I testify to the Gospel in a massively afflicted world when I am only one person?"[4]

Here, of course, is where the transformative social justice message emerges. We are not one solitary person going off to be a Lone Ranger vigilante for Jesus. As Luke's whole narrative reminds us (through Luke and Acts), the primary activity of the Spirit and the presence of Jesus is to sustain and empower the church for its shared witness.

So, in a time when Christians have aligned themselves with nations and empires, when many believers consider personal safety and personal prosperity to be marks of Christian identity, when we distort visions of the Rapture with such depictions as the Left Behind series, Luke's Gospel offers a dramatically different model of faith. For faithful Christians, there is no escape from the world of suffering and witness.

4. Roberta Bondi, "One Plot at a Time," *Christian Century* 121, no. 22 (2004): 17.

Proper 29 [34] (Reign of Christ)

Jennifer L. Lord

<table>
<tr><td>JEREMIAH 23:1–6</td><td>COLOSSIANS 1:11–20</td></tr>
<tr><td>PSALM 46</td><td>LUKE 1:68–79</td></tr>
<tr><td></td><td>LUKE 23:33–43</td></tr>
</table>

According to Luke, at the time of Jesus' crucifixion three different voices mock Jesus and taunt him to save himself. He is, after all, the Messiah. He is God's anointed ruler. This is the meaning of the inscription hung over him on his cross. But the texts for this Reign of Christ Sunday make it clear that Jesus is not the sort of king who is interested in saving himself and coalescing power and privilege. That is a misunderstanding of what his sovereignty means. Instead the texts for this day give us pictures of alternative understandings of monarchy. Jesus is the type of ruler whose concern is not in saving himself, but in the manifestation of righteousness, justice, and mercy for all.

Luke 23:33–43

In the middle of the Gospel passage for this Reign of Christ Sunday these words loom: "There was also an inscription over him, 'This is the King of the Jews'" (v. 38). Jesus has been put to the cross, crucified along with two criminals—one to his right and one to his left. And Jesus has already been "scoffed at" by the leaders, "mocked" by the soldiers, and he will be "derided" by one of the criminals. As if in response to the inscription, these taunters only recognize kingship in one way: a king should be able to save himself. Such a king would be powerful, and this would be proof of kingship. Yet they mock him because Jesus was never an earthly king. They mock him because they see no evidence of kingship in his person.

These taunts about monarchy stand out starkly against the other criminal's request: "Jesus, remember me when you come into your kingdom" (v. 42). This criminal confesses Jesus to be the Messiah, God's anointed king. Several things coalesce at this moment: Jesus is a king who will not save himself from this cross—death. His death fulfills the Scriptures. His death brings salvation. He is, therefore, a different kind of king. The criminal's voice counters the voices of the taunters. Then the good thief (as this criminal becomes known in history) asks a question about a future kingdom. Jesus' answer complicates even more the understanding of kingship. And the strange character of his kingship continues to reveal itself. It is not just for the afterlife; it is kingship with present implications. Jesus' answer to this good thief becomes one of the last "today" pronouncements of the Gospel (cf. 4:21). Jesus' response means that the kingdom is not a future hope but a present reality. The criminal's confession reminds the reader that throughout this Gospel, Jesus has proclaimed the coming of the kingdom of God.

There are, then, a few themes to highlight for this Reign of Christ Sunday, according to Luke. One theme is that Jesus is a king, but not according to standards of power, influence, and privilege. Instead, Luke's account of Jesus emphasizes his ministry to the marginalized: the poor, the orphans, the women, and even sinners. This includes also his ministry to the rich, and his teaching that there be no chasm between the two. Jesus' ministry is about the reign of God, whose mercy knows no boundaries. We could simply turn our sights to current health care debates and set these alongside Luke's account of Jesus the Messiah. The poor, the developmentally disabled, the physically disabled, these marginalized ones are to receive care and be fed. And woe to the ones who are rich and perpetuate the gap between the needy and the wealthy! This king does not save himself; he is about the salvation of all. While we do not have a king in North America, we do have entities that behave in ways that are critiqued by Jesus' reign, which challenges the validity of any entity that seeks to maintain power, that sustains self-serving interests of money and influence. Insurance and banking industries do not fare well when set alongside an understanding of kingship that is about the safety and prosperity of all members of the kingdom. Money cannot be the goal. The needy and the outcast must profit from this king's system of government.

Another theme is that this salvation for all is not a future hope but a present reality. The today sayings culminate in the "today" said from the cross. And if we are the ones who recognize this king for who he is, then we are to be the ones who participate in and work for this present reality.

Jeremiah 23:1–6 and Psalm 46

The text from Jeremiah is an account of sovereignty. But here the king is portrayed as a shepherd, a common image for rulers in the ancient Near East. There are good shepherds and bad shepherds: in these verses the prophet announces the reprimand of certain shepherds and the restoration of righteous shepherds. The reprimand directed at some shepherds is this: "It is you who have scattered my flock, and have driven them away, and you have not attended to them" (v. 2). The background to these verses is the last years of Judah's existence as a self-governing region as it realizes the impending power of the Babylonian Empire. The leadership is marked by all the descriptors we recognize centuries later: lust for power, greed, and disregard for the needy. The charge is clear: the shepherds have not protected the sheep. They have perpetrated oppression and injustice.

The prophet announces words of hope: there will be other shepherds (v. 4). These shepherds will do away with fear and dismay. These shepherds will gather in and protect the sheep. And, this passage announces, the Lord will raise up a new ruler. This ruler will be of the lineage of David, and he "shall execute justice and righteousness in the land" (v. 5). The primary characteristic of this new king is that he will govern by concern for the care and safety of the people.

This passage can be set alongside Luke's crucifixion scene. There the three forms of mockery derided the so-called king who could not save himself. But in Jeremiah, as in Luke, kingship is not characterized by self-serving power. Kingship, a form of shepherding, is care for all the people.

The psalm appointed for this day is identified as a song praising Zion and the temple. God is extolled as the protector of Jerusalem and the one who establishes peace. God's rule in the particulars of history parallels God's rule over cosmic forces. This psalm, held alongside the prophecy of Jeremiah, speaks to all the ways we can count on God to rule over all the tumultuous waters of our world. It is God's purpose to establish peace, to protect the people, and to put down chaos.

The themes of good shepherding, peace, justice, and safety define kingship on this Sunday. There is a plumb line for our earthly rulers. They are held accountable to these images of kingship. It is within our right and duty to call our local and national and global leaders to accountability. Their charge is the people. And, according to Jeremiah, this responsibility is indivisible from how the weakest members of the polis are treated. It is unacceptable for our rulers to give way to gridlock over policies. History repeats itself, and there are shepherds who misrule.

Luke 1:68–79

This passage from Luke serves as an alternative to Psalm 46 on this day. Instead of a song of praise from the book of Psalms, we have a song of praise, a canticle, from the Gospel according to Luke. This canticle is the Song of

Zechariah or the Benedictus, historically a part of the morning prayer tradition of the church. On this Reign of Christ Sunday, it builds on the images from Jeremiah. A mighty savior is raised up. He is from the lineage of David. Again the promise is for a ruler who will bring salvation to the people. This song assures that the purposes of God are being fulfilled.

This semicontinuous alternative reading echoes the themes of the other texts appointed for the day. This king's rule is not about self-serving authority and power. It is about the safety and prosperity of the kingdom: "to give light to those who sit in darkness and in the shadow of death, to guide our feet into the way of peace" (v. 79). Preachers might choose this alternative text to accompany the Jeremiah reading as a way of heading into the Advent season. In two weeks the lectionary system brings us to John the Baptist again, but as a full-grown prophet. Here he is eight days old, commissioned already in infancy to the role of prophet of the Most High.

All of this underscores the sense of a divine plan. Per Lukan interests, Jesus is the fulfillment of these prophecies. Such a plan is not meant to keep us from active life in Christ. It does not excuse us from participation. Rather, it assures us that life in Christ means life in his reign: "that we, being rescued from the hands of our enemies, might serve him without fear, in holiness and righteousness before him all our days" (vv. 74–75).

If this text is used, the preacher can underscore the coming Advent focus on the promise of God's reign and the ways that we live according to that reign now. There is a connection between this eight-day-old prophet and our life in the reign of Christ: our actions have a proleptic quality to them. This is to say that our actions have meaning now but we also do them in hope that they are signs of the fullness of Christ's reign that is still future. The words about this prophet-child have the same proleptic quality; the fullness of the prophet's impact is not yet known, but it will be.

Colossians 1:11–20

The reading from Colossians underscores the rule or reign of God. The language for kingship is focused on the "kingdom" rather than on the person of king. Or, to use more just wording, it is focused on the kin-dom, or realm, as our way of life in Christ. To understand this focus, it is important to note that this hymn to Christ is set in the context of a prayer for the church.

The hymn itself, thought possibly to be a baptismal hymn, describes Christ as the one for whom and through whom all things in heaven and on earth were created. This includes all heavenly and earthly powers or rulers. The fullness of God is in him and all things are reconciled to God through Christ. Again, these words focus on the work of Christ in that they are ultimately about life in him—the life of the church—the lives of persons dwelling in the realm of God's care. The opening words of this text make this clear: "He has rescued us from the power of darkness and transferred us into the [realm] of his beloved Son, in whom we have redemption, the forgiveness of sins" (vv. 13–14).

This passage speaks of citizenship—our transfer into Christ's realm. This passage continues the theme of the other texts: this reign is present tense and therefore not solely for afterlife. In its context the text functions to give the church strength to live counterculturally. This theme alone serves as a call to action for us. If the reign of God is not for the future but is for now, and if we are claimed in Christ as citizens of this rule, then there is a summons to live from a posture that challenges any aspects of church and state that run counter to this claim—because this reign is about justice and mercy for all!

On this day, then, we claim a ruler who was mocked and crucified but who, even from the cross, announced the presence of his realm. We claim a ruler who surpasses all earthly rulers and judges any evil misrule. This ruler judges the kings of the earth who serve themselves, ignore the needy, and perpetuate any oppression. We praise the One who names us as citizens of a realm of prosperity and safety. And all are to be gathered into this fold.

People of this nation (and around the world) continue to offer assistance and monetary support for nations suffering natural disasters like earthquakes, tsunamis, and floods. This reactive giving is commendable and desirable. But these texts call us to live proactively. They call us to challenge local and global structures that are the outcomes of misrule. The preacher can affirm what congregation members are doing individually or corporately but also call people anew to this work. Perhaps the preacher can identify a few local and global situations that must be challenged. Preaching on this day cannot dwell solely in the images of Christ as the high and lofty One but also must see him as the shepherd, the righteous branch who is jealous about the protection of the fold.

Thanksgiving Day

Traci C. West

DEUTERONOMY 26:1–11
PSALM 100
PHILIPPIANS 4:4–9
JOHN 6:25–35

In spite of recent popular claims that we now live in a postracial society, veiled support for white racism can still be found in varied expressions of thankfulness within Christian worship services throughout the United States. But Christian prayers of thanksgiving should directly undermine racist attitudes and practices. These lectionary passages can help us to recognize how white superiority may be bolstered through praise and thanks to God. These Scripture texts also reveal some possibilities for diminishing the impact of racism by offering countercultural articulations of Christianity.

Deuteronomy 26:1–11

When churchgoers listen to Deuteronomy's description of the "inheritance" (v. 1) given by God, an antiracist analysis is needed. This narrative may comfortably resonate with distorted, popular depictions of U.S. history that celebrate the dominance of pioneering European Americans. A misinterpretation of the "ancestors" (vv. 6–7) in Deuteronomy as analogous to European American "forefathers" can, unfortunately, lend credibility to myths about male and white cultural superiority.

Deuteronomy 26 focuses on rituals of giving thanks for what "the LORD your God is giving you as an inheritance" (v. 1). In contemporary U.S. culture, notions of a unique and overarching cultural "inheritance" from Europe provide some of the most durable foundations for racist arrogance. When Deuteronomic scriptural language about a sacred inheritance for a special people is emphasized in worship, problematic implications for the theology of Euro-American worshipers can emerge. The most commonly taught

488

histories of thought and civilization, as well as the economic development of the Americas, are usually centered on European and European American pioneers. Even the term "classical" in the field of church music identifies composers, instruments, and hymns having origins rooted in European genius. Euro-Americans in our society benefit from the unearned social privileges that this inheritance yields for most of them, such as being seen as innately more capable than others by virtue of racial or ethnic heritage. Without direct theological repudiation, whites frequently have viewed these unearned social privileges as blessings from God. Racist theological assumptions may be unwittingly strengthened by liturgically blurring an emphasis on thankfulness for the unique "inheritance" of God's people brought out of Egypt to the land of milk and honey with gratitude for the legacy of European American forefathers.

The cultural heritage recounted in Deuteronomy 26 concerns the enslavement of a particular Hebrew minority group. The text gives specific guidance about ritual forms of thanksgiving that require the people to recite a unifying narrative that would nurture a *shared* ethnic identity among diverse Hebrew tribes (vv. 4–11). This Scripture should not be taught as a universal reminder to give thanks for "the bounty that the LORD your God has given to you and to your house" (v. 11) without any critical sociopolitical analysis.

Current political rhetoric about preserving the historical legacy of uncritically valorized European American founders exclusively credited with creating the freedoms and wealth of this country can too easily support hateful racial attitudes and discriminatory practices ranging from anti-immigrant policies to hate crimes. There are important truths to be told about stolen Indian tribal lands; kidnapping, rape, and genocidal killing of Native people; enslavement of Africans; exploitation of Chinese laborers; as well as intellectual and political contributions by women and men of color. But these truths are too often considered either irrelevant or peripheral to the moral and cultural inheritance attributed to the European American founders of America. The Deuteronomy passage compels us to analyze the moral values related to racism that are assumed in definitive histories of our national story that we ceremoniously retell. Most importantly, this passage provides an opportunity for worship leaders to reveal the blasphemy of wrapping racist national values in God's sacred blessing.

Psalm 100

A racial justice hermeneutical approach to Psalm 100 also calls attention to some of the ways that hierarchical racial values may have been taught in worship. What does it mean to enter God's "gates" to be in God's presence? If only God's people (v. 3) can enter, who gets to be God's people? While anti-racist preaching on the Deuteronomy Scripture may enable recognition of distorted messages about God that are upheld when white privilege remains unexamined, the psalm creates an opportunity to acknowledge some of the twisted messages about faithful living that can occur.

As antiracist, white feminist Peggy McIntosh has explained, white racism in the United States teaches whites not to notice the privileges of whiteness. She gives examples of white privilege: "I can swear, or dress in second hand clothes, or not answer letters, without having people attribute these choices to the bad morals, the poverty, or the illiteracy of my race. . . . I can speak in public to a powerful male group without putting my race on trial. . . . I can do well in a challenging situation without being called a credit to my race."[1] Since most whites take such privileges of whiteness for granted, that is, come to see them as a normal entitlement, could this sense of entitlement be further reinforced in predominantly white congregations when they corporately read Psalm 100 and thank God that they can enter God's presence because they are God's people? Like whites, but with differing psychosocial consequences, could Christian members of communities of color also align themselves with social hierarchies that are rewarded with everyday privileges based on race, ethnicity, or other categories such as wealth or heterosexuality, blurring these hierarchies with religious criteria for entering the gates of God's favor?[2]

For predominantly white congregations, a critical examination of the religious entitlement gratefully acknowledged in this psalm must be distinguished from white racial entitlement that is usually assumed to be a normal part of our society. The psalm focuses on giving thanks for entrance into the gates (v. 4) and appreciation for being able to occupy a holy place—"[God's] courts" (v. 4)—a place to receive God's favor. This form of thanksgiving, embedded in imperial imagery, can nurture acceptance of hierarchical understandings of and entitlements for certain people. Without proper scrutiny, might the psalmist's approach appear to reinforce the proliferation of indirect articulations of racial animus that remain common in our post–civil rights era?

Sociologist Eduardo Bonilla-Silva has described current problematic racial attacks as color-blind racism. For example, when expressing anti-black racist attitudes, whites tend to avoid blatant assertions about the innate biological inferiority of blacks. Instead, they are more likely to describe deficiencies in black culture that eschew educational achievement or demonstrate a lack of

---

1. Peggy McIntosh, "White Privilege: Unpacking the Invisible Knapsack," excerpt from "White Privilege and Male Privilege: A Personal Account of Coming to See Correspondences through Work in Women's Studies" (working paper, Wellesley College Center for Research on Women, Wellesley, MA, 1988).
2. See a much more detailed discussion in Traci C. West, *Disruptive Christian Ethics: When Racism and Women's Lives Matter* (Louisville, KY: Westminster John Knox Press, 2008).

interest in getting ahead (entering the gates?) with the same degree of ambition that other racial groups exhibit.[3] The new color-blind racism is also characterized by the acceptability of ambiguous racial attitudes. One respondent to Bonilla-Silva's study explained that blacks were often too lazy to study, get a job, and stop complaining and blaming others for their problems, but clarified her statement by adding that she was not referring to "your educated ones, it's not them."[4]

The political nature of Psalm 100 helpfully reminds us of the political nature of worshipful thanksgiving. What does joyous, worshipful thankfulness look like? It entails locating the power of God and placing oneself in direct relationship to it. There are, however, ever-present gods of white racial superiority surreptitiously claiming our allegiance and molding our identities with rewards and penalties that make racial hierarchies seem rational. They erode our clarity that the "Lord is God" (v. 3), which causes us to miss the entire political and theological point of the psalm. Brutal aggression and unyielding competition among racial groups feeds social hierarchies such as white superiority. As Bonilla-Silva explains, ongoing racial hostility is characterized by competing, contested claims among racial groups struggling to change their position in the society. The struggle may be "social (Who can be here? Who belongs here?), political (Who can vote? How much power should they have? Should they be citizens?), economic (Who should work, and what should they do? They are taking our jobs!), or ideological (Black is beautiful!)."[5]

Such racial struggles are further reflected in religious battles over who has sacred worth. This racially competitive ethos requires a continuous state of anxiousness over loss of legitimacy, status, and, of course, the concrete benefits of systemic racism. In the face of this corrosive divisiveness, the psalmist offers a needed reminder of God's universal goodness, faithfulness, and steadfast love that extend "to all generations" (v. 5). Thankfulness to God ought to include mirroring God's loving concern for "all generations," that is, building an equitable social order for *all* who will come after us.

Philippians 4:4–9

The Philippians text also offers a possible antidote to our societal obsession with racial and ethnic competition and domination. In accord with Philippians, Christians might display "gentleness" (v. 5) with everyone, replacing

3. Eduardo Bonilla-Silva, *Racism without Racists: Color-Blind Racism and the Persistence of Racial Inequality in the United States* (Lanham, MD: Rowman & Littlefield, 2003).

4. Eduardo Bonilla-Silva, *White Supremacy and Racism in the Post–Civil Rights Era* (Boulder, CO: Lynne Rienner, 2001), 155.

5. Ibid., 43.

their anxiousness with prayerful thanksgiving (v. 6). Philippians 4 includes an invitation to "rejoice in the Lord always," which is placed side by side with instructions to "let your gentleness be known to everyone" (vv. 4–5). The synergy of this pairing presents a mode of thanksgiving that might at least loosen the sway of white superiority in our culture. The partnership between rejoicing and gentleness offers preachers a way to respond to some of the challenges raised by the Deuteronomy and Psalms passages assigned to this day of thanksgiving.

The Philippians strategy for sustaining nonanxiousness includes placing trust in God to accompany thanksgiving (v. 6), and therefore allowing the peace of God and Jesus Christ to guard "your hearts and your minds" (v. 7). Our God of peace offers an antidote to embattled, anxious jockeying retained in the maintenance of white superiority and the inferiority of peoples of color through various cultural messages and structural inequalities. At the same time, the lure of social status and rewards in the familiar hierarchical, racial pecking order of our society is powerful. We must trust God to guard Christian American hearts and minds against the enticement to become embattled again. However, this strategy also requires actually putting antiracist behavior into practice (v. 9).

John 6:25–35

The Gospel of John passage invites us to pay attention to the crowd. The people in the crowd are not named in John 6. In this lectionary passage, their voices blend into one voice that enters into dialogue with Jesus. They display tremendous neediness through the many questions and demands they make in response to him.

In our own climate of rigid adherence to racial and economic hierarchies, we might recognize the crowd as the nameless group of people who are repeatedly labeled as the lazy ones, such as poor, single black and Latina mothers who need public assistance, those people from whom too many middle-class, educated blacks and Latinos try to distance themselves to establish their respectability in front of whites. Or, the crowd might be made up of the hundreds of thousands of urban gay, lesbian, and transgendered homeless youth, a disproportionate number of whom are black and Latino,[6] from whom too many middle-class married (or desiring to marry) gay and lesbian

---

6. Nicholas Ray et al., *Lesbian, Gay, Bisexual, and Transgender Youth: An Epidemic of Homelessness* (New York: National Gay and Lesbian Task Force Policy Institute and the National Coalition for the Homeless, 2006); Center for American Progress, "Gay and Transgender Youth Homelessness by the Numbers," June 21, 2010.

couples with children want to differentiate themselves to try to establish their worthiness for civil rights equal to those of heterosexuals.

The people in the crowd in the Gospel passage are portrayed as determined seekers of Jesus, insistent in their desire for reliable assurances. Jesus accuses them of only seeking him out because they ate their fill of the bread (v. 26) he had just provided them (6:11–12). They want to know what works to perform (v. 28) for God. It seems a bit harsh when he reprimands them for being concerned about food instead of keeping their focus on believing in the one whom God has sent. In response, the crowd seeks definitive proof "so that we may see it and believe you" (v. 30).

Impoverished peoples, especially those who endure racist and homophobic abuse, are hungry for actual bread as well as for a definitive sign—a great leader or piece of legislation—indicating an end to their marginalization. The people need a reliable signal of societal change that they can trust and believe in. It would seem cruel and uncaring to respond by telling them not to focus on temporary nourishment that feeds their families or their need for community leaders and legislative bodies to address the systemic inequalities that entrap them. Yet the Gospel can be interpreted as pointing to the incompleteness of these necessary remedies. A holistic, radically antiracist Christian response to their longings starts with marginalized people's innate human dignity and moral worth. There is no work that they are to perform or great local community leader who can fully provide what racist and economic dehumanizing practices strip away. There is, however, a restorative confirmation of the sacredness of their lives. The "bread of life" represents a sign affirming the irreducible presence of God that already resides in their ordinary, reviled, human selves.

Contributors

Charles G. Adams, *Hartford Memorial Baptist Church, Detroit, Michigan*

Ronald J. Allen, *Christian Theological Seminary*

Dale P. Andrews, *The Divinity School, Vanderbilt University*

Randall C. Bailey, *Interdenominational Theological Center*

Wilma Ann Bailey, *Christian Theological Seminary*

Dianne Bergant, CSA, *Catholic Theological Union*

L. Susan Bond, *Lane College*

Alejandro F. Botta, *Boston University School of Theology*

Valerie Bridgeman, *Lancaster Theological Seminary*

Martin Brokenleg, *Vancouver School of Theology (Emeritus)*

Gennifer Benjamin Brooks, *Garrett-Evangelical Theological Seminary*

Carolynne Hitter Brown, *Southern Baptist Church, Cambridge, Massachusetts*

John M. Buchanan, *Fourth Presbyterian Church, Chicago, Illinois*

Randall K. Bush, *East Liberty Presbyterian Church, Pittsburgh, Pennsylvania*

Lee H. Butler Jr., *Chicago Theological Seminary*

Terriel R. Byrd, *School of Ministry, Palm Beach Atlantic University*

Charles L. Campbell, *The Divinity School, Duke University*

Carlos F. Cardoza-Orlandi, *Perkins School of Theology, Southern Methodist University*

Cláudio Carvalhaes, *Lutheran Theological Seminary, Philadelphia, Pennsylvania*

Diane G. Chen, *Palmer Theological Seminary, Eastern University*

Choi Hee An, *Boston University School of Theology*

Monica A. Coleman, *Claremont School of Theology*

Elizabeth Conde-Frazier, *Esperanza College, Eastern University*

Shannon Daley-Harris, *Children's Defense Fund, Washington, D.C.*

Frederick John Dalton, *Bellarmine College Preparatory School, San Jose, California*

Noelle Damico, *Presbyterian Hunger Program, Presbyterian Church (U.S.A.)*

María Teresa Dávila, *Andover Newton Theological School*

Miguel A. De La Torre, *Iliff School of Theology*

Bob Ekblad, *Tierra Nueva and The People's Seminary, Burlington, Washington*

Joseph Evans, *Mt. Carmel Baptist Church, Washington, D.C.*

Marie M. Fortune, *FaithTrust Institute, Seattle, Washington*

Safiyah Fosua, *Wesley Seminary, Indiana Wesleyan University*

David J. Frenchak, *Seminary Consortium for Urban Pastoral Education (SCUPE) (Emeritus)*

Lincoln E. Galloway, *Claremont School of Theology*

Kenyatta R. Gilbert, *The Divinity School, Howard University*

R. Mark Giuliano, *Old Stone Church, Cleveland, Ohio*

Chris Glaser, *Metropolitan Community Church, Atlanta, Georgia*

Catherine Gunsalus González, *Columbia Theological Seminary (Emerita)*

Justo L. González, *Asociación para la Educación Teológica Hispana (AETH), United Methodist Church (Retired)*

Esther J. Hamori, *Union Theological Seminary, New York*

James Henry Harris, *Samuel Dewitt Proctor School of Theology, Virginia Union University, and Second Baptist Church, Richmond, Virginia*

John Hart, *Boston University School of Theology*

Olive Elaine Hinnant, *United Church of Christ, Denver, Colorado*

Ruthanna B. Hooke, *Virginia Theological Seminary*

Rhashell Hunter, *Racial Ethnic and Women's Ministries, Presbyterian Church (U.S.A.)*

†Ada María Isasi-Díaz, *The Theological School, Drew University (Emerita)*

Seungyoun Jeong, *Boston University School of Theology*

Joseph R. Jeter Jr., *Brite Divinity School (Emeritus)*

Pablo A. Jiménez, *Espinosa Christian Church, Dorado, Puerto Rico, and Chalice Press*

Nicole L. Johnson, *University of Mount Union*

Song Bok Jon, *Boston University School of Theology*

Nyasha Junior, *The Divinity School, Howard University*

John Kaltner, *Rhodes College*

Grace Ji-Sun Kim, *Moravian Theological Seminary*

Simone Sunghae Kim, *Yonsei University, South Korea*

Kah-Jin Jeffrey Kuan, *The Theological School, Drew University*

Jennifer L. Lord, *Austin Presbyterian Theological Seminary*

Barbara K. Lundblad, *Union Theological Seminary, New York*

Fumitaka Matsuoka, *Pacific School of Religion (Emeritus)*

William B. McClain, *Wesley Theological Seminary*

John S. McClure, *The Divinity School, Vanderbilt University*

James L. McDonald, *San Francisco Theological Seminary*

Alyce M. McKenzie, *Perkins School of Theology, Southern Methodist University*

Marvin A. McMickle, *Colgate Rochester Crozer Divinity School*

Henry H. Mitchell, *Interdenominational Theological Center (Emeritus)*

Mary Alice Mulligan, *Christian Theological Seminary*

Ched Myers, *Bartimaeus Institute, Oak View, California*

James Anthony Noel, *San Francisco Theological Seminary*

Dawn Ottoni-Wilhelm, *Bethany Theological Seminary*

Peter J. Paris, *Princeton Theological Seminary (Emeritus)*

Rebecca Todd Peters, *Elon University*

Luke A. Powery, *Princeton Theological Seminary*

Melinda A. Quivik, *Liturgical Scholar, Houghton, Michigan*

Stephen G. Ray Jr., *Garrett-Evangelical Theological Seminary*

Sharon H. Ringe, *Wesley Theological Seminary*

Joni S. Sancken, *Eastern Mennonite Seminary, Eastern Mennonite University*

Elizabeth J. A. Siwo-Okundi, *Boston University School of Theology*

Chandra Taylor Smith, *The Pell Institute, Washington, D.C.*

Christine Marie Smith, *United Theological Seminary of the Twin Cities*

Kee Boem So, *New York Presbyterian Theological Seminary (Korean Presbyterian Church Abroad)*

Teresa Lockhart Stricklen, *Office of Theology and Worship, Presbyterian Church (U.S.A.)*

Marjorie Hewitt Suchocki, *Claremont School of Theology (Emerita)*

Willard Swartley, *Associated Mennonite Biblical Seminary (Emeritus)*

JoAnne Marie Terrell, *Chicago Theological Seminary*

Leonora Tubbs Tisdale, *The Divinity School, Yale University*

†Arthur Van Seters, *Knox College (Emeritus)*

Traci C. West, *The Theological School, Drew University*

Edward L. Wheeler, *Christian Theological Seminary (Emeritus)*

Clark M. Williamson, *Christian Theological Seminary (Emeritus)*

Scott C. Williamson, *Louisville Presbyterian Theological Seminary*

Scripture Index